THE 1960s

AN EYEWITNESS HISTORY

THE 1960s

Timothy Maga

Foreword by Donald A. Ritchie

☑®

Facts On File, Inc.

9-03
75.00

The 1960s

Copyright © 2003 by Timothy Maga

Foreword copyright © 2003 by Donald A. Ritchie

Maps and graphs copyright © 2003 by Facts On File

Facts On File, Inc.
132 West 31st Street
New York NY 10001

Library of Congress Cataloging-in-Publication Data
Maga, Timothy P., 1952–
    The 1960s / by Timothy Maga.
        p.   cm. — (An eyewitness history)
    Includes bibliographical references and index.
    Contents: To the "new frontier" : January 1960–December 1961—Lost in the Cold War : January 1962–September 1963—Lessons of the Cuban missile crisis : October 1962–December 1963—All the way with LBJ : 1964–1965—Beach Boys America : 1966–1967—The perils of power : 1968—How the "sixties" end : 1969–1970.
    ISBN 0-8160-4809-6 (acid-free paper)
    1. United States—History—1961–1969—Juvenile literature. 2. United States—History—1961–1969—Sources—Juvenile literature. 3. Nineteen sixties—Juvenile literature. [1. United States—History—1961–1969—Sources. 2. Nineteen sixties.]
    I. Title. II. Series.
    E841.M225 2003
    973.923—dc21   2002014119

Facts On File books are available at special discounts when purchased in bulk quantities for businesses, associations, institutions, or sales promotions. Please call our Special Sales Department in New York at (212) 967-8800 or (800) 322-8755.

You can find Facts On File on the World Wide Web at
http://www.factsonfile.com

Text design by Joan M. Toro
Cover design by Cathy Rincon
Maps by Jeremy Eagle and Pat Meschino

Printed in the United States of America

VB JT 10 9 8 7 6 5 4 3 2 1

This book is printed on acid-free paper.

To the love of my life, Patsy Maga,
who made this book "happen"

CONTENTS

Note on Photos viii

Foreword: America in the 1960s ix

Acknowledgments xi

Introduction xiii

1. To the "New Frontier": January 1960–December 1961 1

2. Lost in the Cold War: January 1962–September 1962 38

3. Lessons of the Cuban Missile Crisis: October 1962–December 1963 71

4. "All the Way with LBJ": 1964–1965 113

5. Beach Boys America: 1966–1967 160

6. The Perils of Power: 1968 199

7. How the "Sixties" End: 1969–1970 242

Appendix A: Documents 283

Appendix B: Biographies of Major Personalities 313

Appendix C: Maps and Graphs 337

Notes 345

Bibliography 350

Index 379

NOTE ON PHOTOS

Many of the illustrations and photographs used in this book are old, historical images. The quality of the prints is not always up to current standards, as in many cases the originals are from old or poor quality negatives or are damaged. The content of the illustrations, however, made their inclusion important despite problems in reproduction.

FOREWORD

America in the 1960s

A jumble of exuberance and discontent, idealism and arrogance, freedom and excess, the 1960s were an exciting and confusing time for those who lived through them, and they remain a source of puzzlement and fascination for those born later.

The 1960s opened with the emergence of John F. Kennedy as the symbol of a new generation of leaders, born in the 20th century and forged in World War II and the cold war. Kennedy's generation confidently tackled the problems of the nation and the world, aiming to defeat communism, end racial segregation, abolish poverty, and land a man on the moon before the decade had ended. At the same time, a younger generation was coming of age. Products of the baby boom that had followed World War II, they arrived on campus equally confident and ambitious. At first the two generations shared a relatively common outlook, but the turbulent decade as it progressed confronted them with a nuclear showdown, war, the draft, urban riots, and political assassinations. The two generations drifted apart until their increasingly divergent values and viewpoints polarized into a generation gap.

In America, the decade saw the abolition of racial segregation, the end of discriminatory restrictions on immigration, a new movement toward women's equality, and a vast expansion of voting rights. New public awareness and activism prompted Congress to pass landmark legislation on a remarkable range of issues, from environmental programs to health and consumer product safety. It was a decade of liberalism and New Left politics whose campus protests, antiwar demonstrations, and civil unrest caused political and social scars, law-and-order candidates, and a conservative backlash.

As a college student and a draftee in the 1960s, I have my own share of personal memories. Yet it is startling to realize how many of my generation's most vivid recollections were actually events that we witnessed on television: a president's chilling message on the Cuban Missile Crisis; the shocking report of his death in Dallas, Texas; the shooting of the suspected assassin—televised as it happened; fire hoses and police dogs turned on civil rights demonstrators; the flames of urban riots; the never-ending nightly combat reports and casualty figures from Vietnam; the Chicago police clashing with protesters at the 1968 national Democratic convention; and an astronaut's first step onto the lunar surface. Television shrank our world into a global village, but its images could alternately unite society and drive it apart.

Today, many of the audio and visual images of the 1960s still survive. Remnants of an era that celebrated freedom of expression, they conjure up the counterculture: peace signs, love beads, psychedelic styles, hippies, pop art, the Beatles, Woodstock, *The Graduate, Easy Rider,* and *Hair.* In its own parlance, the decade of the 1960s was a "happening."

Looking back, we can likely agree that the 1960s profoundly reshaped the nation and the world, while disagreeing whether those changes were for good or ill. Its vitality, complexity, and idiosyncrasies make the era as astounding to study now as it was to experience then.

—Donald A. Ritchie

ACKNOWLEDGMENTS

The author hopes that the staffs of the National Archives, the Library of Congress, the U.S. Naval Historical Center, the NASA-Johnson Space Center, King Visual Technology, Bradley University Library, and the Peoria Public Library will accept my general thanks for their assistance in obtaining key documentation, secondary sources, and photos needed for this mammoth effort. Without question, I owe special thanks to the following individuals and their employers: James Hill of the John F. Kennedy Library, Pauline Testerman of the Harry S. Truman Library, Mark Renovitch of the Franklin D. Roosevelt Library, E. Philip Scott of the Lyndon B. Johnson Library, Alice Preston of Camelot Classic Cars, Inc., Fred Gompertz of Mr. Fred's Furs, Kelly Hill and Susan Sherwood of Elvis Presley Enterprises, Marilee Bailey of the Lawrence Berkeley National Laboratory, Chubby Checker and TEEC Recording, Smothers Brothers representative Wendy Blair at Knave Productions, Don Vesey of the Birmingham, Alabama, Public Library, Ken Tilley and Cynthia Luckie of the Alabama Department of Archives and History, Kristen McCormack of the Green Bay Packers, Vickie Ganey of RS Information Systems, Rebecca Karamehmedovic of TimePix, and Dr. Arwin Smallwood of Bradley University's Institute for African-American Studies. An even grander share of thanks goes to my wife, Patsy, for her endless patience and assistance in yet another book project. Another debt of thanks goes to Don and Pat Kline for "always being there" and to the encouragement, advice, and good comradeship of two great teacher/scholars, Dr. Jay D. Dobbin, professor of anthropology/sociology with the University of Maryland-Asian Division, and Emory T. Trosper, Jr., former registrar, University of Maryland-Asian Division and current professor of history and government, Temple University-Japan campus.

INTRODUCTION

"The past is a foreign country. People do things differently there." One of America's favorite poets and philosophers, Ralph Waldo Emerson, made this comment in the 1830s. But he could have said it in the early 21st century as well. In his own way, he was trying to say that the present generation often views the previous generation in one of two ways. They were either "the greatest generation" or far from it. To John Kennedy, Lyndon Johnson, and many of their peers in the 1960s, Franklin Roosevelt and his New Deal movers and shakers of the 1930s were heroes, legends, and mentors. Following in their footsteps was an honor, and expanding upon their political success was good for both career and country. "Getting the country moving again" was the promise of the 1960 Kennedy for President campaign, but it reminded many of Franklin Roosevelt's can-do spirit.

Whether they voted for Kennedy or not, most Americans were ready for a change in 1960. From politics to the entertainment industry, the country's leaders and followers sought new directions, heroes, and missions. The postwar era had to end sometime, and the 1960s represented that transition to greatness. Kennedy served as the first recognized leader of this uncharted path to the "New Frontier," and for a while it seemed as if anything was possible. From the end of racism and poverty to an American on the moon, the 1960s were supposed to make dreams come true. But reality soon suggested something different.

To a large degree, it was the frustration with dreams left unfulfilled that led to the age of protest, student riots, and racial tension. By the late 1960s, the visions of the early 1960s seemed foolish and naive. A country once dedicated to clear-cut goals now doubted its own moral worth. But as the nation moved from great hope to despair, there were plenty of new pop icons to keep people entertained and plenty of consumer society distractions to keep them occupied. As Americans wrestled over the meaning and significance of both the Vietnam War and the Civil Rights movement, popular culture helped define the decade as well.

The 1960s represented a race course of clashing values and concerns, and, at first, John Kennedy promised a thrilling ride to the finish. To Kennedy, history pointed the way to success, and Franklin Roosevelt was one of his favorite historical figures. Roosevelt had been a great visionary, a strong moral leader, and noble champion of the downtrodden. A 1960s version of his New Deal would provide the foundation for the great changes that America seemed ready to embrace. Kennedy's closest colleagues agreed.[1] To Lyndon Johnson, Franklin Roosevelt had been the heart and soul of the Democratic Party. Johnson admired the late president's frenetic legislative efforts, his skillful political

President Franklin Roosevelt's New Deal was the political inspiration behind both John Kennedy's New Frontier and Lyndon Johnson's Great Society. *(Franklin D. Roosevelt Library)*

maneuvering, and endless commitments to doing the right thing. More and not less New Deal activism was needed in the 1960s, both Kennedy and Johnson believed. In their view, President Dwight Eisenhower and the 1950s represented a do-nothing political dark age. The time was right to finish Roosevelt's good work, and a dramatic new agenda was long overdue.

CHANGING TIMES

At first glance, the need for change was not wholly apparent. Since the end of World War II, the country enjoyed a record-setting prosperity. But the 1960s defined change beyond the old Roosevelt notion of New Deal agencies and economic policy making. Change involved social issues, popular culture, and whatever might constitute the American Dream. The successful reformer would have to recognize these facts, and in the 1960s, the champions of change were not necessarily professional politicians.

In 1960, young Americans told the Gallup Poll that rock-and-roll legend Elvis Presley represented American values better than political leaders such as Vice President Richard Nixon and Senate Majority Leader Lyndon Johnson. Even Rod Serling, the popular speaker, screenwriter, and host of the new hit science fiction television series *The Twilight Zone,* insisted that literary figures, filmmakers, and the music industry had a "moral obligation" to champion social change in the fresh new decade. Cynic and critic Gore Vidal agreed, noting that the political community had become "morally bankrupt" and separated from the everyday needs of most Americans. If Washington could not lead, he implied, then the nation would have to find its leadership elsewhere. "Power," said journalist and presidential historian Theodore White, would be "defined differently in the 1960s." That fact, he suggested, meant good news for the country. Diversity encouraged good policy, he concluded, and America deserved the best.

Throughout the 1950s, new words had crept into the American vocabulary that helped describe and characterize an already changing country. Since the mid-1940s, the nation had enjoyed a "baby boom." That meant a record high birthrate averaging 4 million babies per year. The welfare of these children and the type of America that they were to inherit helped explain some of the interest in new approaches to leadership, policy making, and changing American institutions for the better. The parents of the newborns often lived in postwar-built communities outside of the city center. First called Levittowns in the late 1940s, they were "suburbs" by the mid-1950s. The word *suburb* dated back to the era of World War I, but it took on important political and social connotations in the 1950s.

To African Americans, the suburb was the place to which white Americans fled their black neighbors. It encouraged a racial divide, splitting the country and hurting the traditional urban economy at the same time. While the businesses, theaters, and schools of the inner city collapsed, new businesses, theaters, and schools were built for white Americans in the suburbs. Racism, Americans learned in the 1950s and through controversial court cases such as *Brown v. Board of Education of Topeka,* was not only a phenomenon of the Deep South. It was a nationwide dilemma, requiring both citizen and government action to change. America's African-American communities had grown impatient for that change by 1960. There could be, as civil rights leader Martin Luther King, Jr., insisted, no turning back the clock.

In its short history, the United States had not gone through many periods of fast-moving change. Thomas Jefferson had spoken of a "new American Revolution" in 1800 and 1801, but his two-term presidency fell far short of "revolutionary" change. Andrew Jackson's "age of the common man" in the 1830s was also long on rhetoric and short on action, although Lincoln and the period of the Civil War would provide the greatest political and social upheaval the United States would see until the Great Depression and Franklin Roosevelt's New Deal.

Complicating the rush to change in the 1960s was capitalist America's distrust of communist Russia. To those who defeated fascism in the 1940s, there was one leftover "ism" to destroy in the 1960s. Communism had to go. John Kennedy promised not only a man on the Moon by 1970, the end of racism by 1970, and a contented, booming America by 1970, but also total victory in the cold war by 1970. Promising to "pay any price, bear any burden" to defeat communist expansion, Kennedy entered the White House ready to wage nuclear war. He pledged to continue his predecessor's commitment to the besieged government of South Vietnam and lure all the developing nations to America's anticommunist mission. Cold war victory no matter what the cost, a cause once represented by right wing extremists such as Wisconsin's late Senator Joseph McCarthy, now had more respectable champions. Candidate Kennedy's eloquent anticommunist speeches won widespread acclaim, and his commitment to domestic change always fell beneath the priority of cold war victory. Few of the late-1960s hippie or counterculture critics of the Vietnam War criticized Kennedy's early 1960s Vietnam policy, the anticommunist agenda, or general American foreign relations in 1961. The railing against the "Establishment" was yet to come, for U.S. foreign policy had yet to interfere with the domestic scene.[2]

TRUST AND LEADERSHIP

Although some Americans might have recognized Elvis as more influential in their lives than Kennedy and other Washington politicians, they still insisted that their president make things right for them. Early 1960s Americans trusted their political leaders, but that trust would soon be a casualty of the Vietnam War.

Throughout the 1950s, solving great social and political dilemmas was considered a presidential prerogative, and American voters also expected strong moral leadership from their commander-in-chief. As president, Eisenhower had first responded to the concerns of the majority voters, and they were white middle-class males. He had no apologies for this approach, for it was this group that helped define the economic boom. For women, African Americans, ethnic groups, and those concerned about the environment, the 1950s was a time when few were listening to calls for reform. In 1954, a near majority of Americans told the pollsters that poverty, in the land of opportunity, was the fault of the poor themselves.

THE FORGOTTEN MINORITIES

As late as the mid-1950s, one-half of both the nation's African-American and its Native American communities lived below the poverty level. Two-thirds of these communities lived in homes where the chief breadwinner had an eighth-grade education if he was lucky. But an increasing percentage of America's poor were female, and this fact stood in stark contrast to Hollywood and the advertising world's image of the comfortable 1950s housewife. If not in that comfortable position and forced to work, most women's jobs were menial or support staff positions, unprotected by minimum wage legislation and ignored by Social Security. Those same women took home only 60 percent of the earnings of a man working in the same position.

Calls for change could be found on the back shelves of bookstores, but analyses such as Ferdinand Lundberg and Marynia Farnham's *Modern Woman: The Lost Sex* (1947) remained in the best-seller category for years. This book denounced feminism as a "sickness" that encouraged women to abandon their femininity, act like men, confuse the family structure, and offer solace to communists who sought a breakdown of American society. Yet an unusual 1962 Gallup Poll surprised American families. It reported that only 10 percent of American women wanted their daughters to keep silent on the issues of women's rights. The same figure was recorded in reference to women who wanted their daughters to marry early, remain in the home, and avoid a "personally fulfilling life." This type of opinion would serve as the foundation for the later feminist movement.[3] But in the 1950s white male-dominated media, the nation's "moral fiber," it was said, depended upon women and their commitment to home and family. While *Playboy* hit the newsstands for the first time in 1953, celebrating the sexual prowess of men, a sexually active woman was considered a promiscuous threat to both family and country.

In many respects, the discussion over the proper role of women and men in postwar America was a luxurious one, afforded by the prosperous white middle class. While white Americans flocked to the suburbs, African Americans flocked to the cities. Largely unskilled, struggling, and offering little hope to their own children, the new urban poor had few protectors in Washington.[4] Unfortunately, this situation was examined by writers rather than legislators during the 1950s.

Seven years in the making, Michael Harrington's *The Other America* (1962) described an "unprecedented situation in world history." While America's 1950s wealth grew by leaps and bounds for white middle-class suburbanites, both the urban and remaining rural poor were ignored by both government and business. Harrington's "other America" label became a euphemism for uncaring government in the face of obvious poverty. A primary reason, he noted, for Washington's lack of interest in the downtrodden involved its new postwar set of priorities. At the top of the list, he correctly pointed out, was the enthusiastic anticommunist crusade. Given that crusade, the political community had little time for its own people. But, as Harrington noted, communism thrived on poverty. Ignoring America's poor in favor of grand foreign policies could end up being, he warned, Washington's most foolish mistake.

THE KENNEDY SOLUTION

Promising to "take the first steps" to eliminate poverty and injustice in America, John Kennedy seemed the answer to a reformer's prayers. Not too long after his November 1963 assassination, even some of Kennedy's political opponents believed that problems ranging from Vietnam to student unrest might never have taken hold in America had he lived.

In 1960, John Fitzgerald Kennedy looked younger than his 42 years. Born into great wealth, a Harvard graduate, and possessing a gift for political rhetoric, the handsome Kennedy was tailor-made for the new era of television campaign ads, interviews, and debate. Lofty goals and youthful enthusiasm characterized his 1960 campaign for the presidency, but his early career had been much less exciting.

As the senator from Massachusetts, Kennedy held a bad attendance record. Viewing the Senate as marking time to the presidency, Kennedy had been planning a run for the White House since he jumped from his House of Representatives seat to the Senate in the early 1950s. Complex and moody, Kennedy was often misunderstood by the political observers of the day. His father, Joseph P. Kennedy, was also never far behind.

The elder Kennedy had been fired as U.S. ambassador to Great Britain in November 1940. Franklin Roosevelt had concluded that Joseph Kennedy sounded more like an apologist for British appeasement to Hitler than an anti-Nazi representative of U.S. foreign policy. Given Roosevelt's reputation for tolerance in his cabinet, military advisers, and diplomatic corps, the Kennedy firing had been a dramatic exception to his welcoming of different points of view. For a time, the ex-ambassador thought his sons, Joseph, Jr., John, Robert, and Edward, would never have political futures of their own thanks to that firing. He was wrong.

Kennedy family life was often in the school of hard knocks or tough love. Until he arrived in the South Pacific during his World War II naval service and met "regular Americans" for the first time, John Kennedy believed that most families had been brought up the same way. As a youngster, John Kennedy was expected to master the classics, current affairs, and even languages. A nightly dinner with his father and mother at their Hyannis Port estate, John and his brothers later joked, was "worse than Guadalcanal" (a bloody World War II battle). Heavy discussions of politics and history were often the norm, and an unprepared child had to accept certain punishments if he or she could not add to the discussion. This intellectual combat was balanced by the introduction of competitive sports, including football, swimming, and regatta sailing. While playing on the Harvard football team, John Kennedy once finished an entire half of a game with an injured leg. When later asked by the press how he could have endured the pain, Kennedy said that he did not understand the question. "We won," he noted, and that was that.

The children of Joseph P. Kennedy, Sr., took great exception later on when some analysts labeled their family a dysfunctional one. There was love, deep Roman Catholic faith, and the education of a lifetime, Edward "Ted" Kennedy once noted. Public service, they were taught, was a noble calling, and the wealthy had an obligation to assist the downtrodden.

In 1946, a sickly, wounded John Kennedy returned home from the Solomon Islands after World War II to run for Congress in a South Boston working-class district. His father was not optimistic and had always predicted that his firstborn son, Joseph, Jr., enjoyed the family's best political potential. But Joe, Jr., had been killed flying an experimental aircraft in Europe during World War II. John inherited the mantle and won that South Boston district largely because its World War II veterans identified with Kennedy's own wartime misery and heroism.

Helping the downtrodden was not at the top of the new congressman's agenda. He entered an increasingly conservative Congress, and championing New Deal–like reforms could kill his career early. Instead, he wheeled and dealt with the new political right in Congress and did his best to avoid political controversy. Nevertheless, he still made headlines now and then, particularly after his election to the Senate. Kennedy even traveled to Asia, denounced the collapsing French colonial war against the Vietnamese, and complained that America's allies exploited Washington's anticommunist crusade for their own selfish purposes. He was one of the first U.S. politicians to call for Hawaii and Alaska statehood, and he used the unique argument that America must not be a "colonizer" if it hoped to champion liberty in the world. At the same time, he praised Martin Luther King, Jr., for his commitment to nonviolence in his growing Civil Rights movement, proclaiming that positive domestic reform influenced positive views of America abroad. Few politicians were speaking like this at the time, and the headlines came easily. Although Kennedy's statements often stressed intellectual concerns and not the foundations for new policies, he won the attention of the Democratic Party anyway. Being good-looking, witty, and rich did not hurt either.

In 1956, Kennedy's name was entered into the Democratic Party convention as a running mate to Adlai Stevenson. Stevenson, an Illinois governor, had run against Eisenhower in 1952 and lost by a wide margin. Also very bright and funny, Stevenson made no apologies for his vow to continue the work of Franklin Roosevelt's New Deal. He was also no match for war hero Dwight Eisenhower and the voters' desire for a more conservative path in Washington.

In November 1952, President-elect Eisenhower asks for the nation's "trust." *(Abbie, Rowe, National Park Service, Harry S. Truman Library)*

Ideologically, in 1956, the Democrats still favored Stevenson's new New Deal message. Wedding that message to the up-and-coming and more politically cautious John Kennedy seemed to make sense to some delegates to the 1956 Democratic Party convention. But Kennedy failed to win the vice presidential nomination. Stevenson went on to another defeat to Eisenhower, and a 1957 issue of *Life* magazine declared Kennedy the "new moderate hope" of the Democratic Party.

With his younger brother Robert in charge of the campaign, John Kennedy now planned a 1960 run for the White House. The Kennedy family crisscrossed the country seeking political support from Democratic Party activists months before John formally announced that he was "thinking" about the presidency. The 1960 campaign and the resulting Kennedy White House would never be separated from the interests and careers of the Kennedy family.[5]

Only four years his senior, Kennedy's Republican opponent for the presidency, Vice President Richard Nixon, also represented the coming of age of the World War II veteran. Proud of his humble California roots, Nixon touted his foreign policy experience and dodged reporters' questions about shady financial dealings in past campaigns. Although they appeared quite different to voters, Kennedy and Nixon had been acquaintances for years. Both represented youthful enthusiasm in their respective parties, and both suggested that the 1960s presented challenges that only their World War II generation could truly resolve. Their time had come, and America was ready for them.

1

To the "New Frontier"
January 1960–December 1961

Life in the 1960s was not going to be easy, John Kennedy told a Boston Garden crowd in November 1960. His prediction of a struggling, challenging decade ahead had been part of his presidential campaign message for a year. But there was no need to worry. Promising a leadership style of "confidence, hope, knowledge, vitality, and energy," Kennedy suggested that America was destined to do great things before 1970.[1]

MAKING AMERICA GREAT AGAIN

The Kennedy thesis was interesting but flawed. In 1960, America's economy had weathered a recession, yet it still stood at one of its strongest positions in the 20th century. Its military remained unbeaten in war, and its allies rarely challenged Washington's authority in anticommunist leadership. In short, things were going well, and American greatness was not on the ropes. But Kennedy struck a chord in the voting public. Maybe America should reach for the stars, and, to accent the point, the young candidate even promised higher annual expenditures for the country's fledgling space program.

Kennedy's presentation of campaign goals often had a greater impact than the goals themselves. Thirty years after the fact, civil rights leader James Farmer still remembered the words of the first Kennedy speech that he had heard during the early primary season. Skeptical, in the beginning, of a rich white Irish American who claimed an interest in civil rights reform, Farmer was impressed by Kennedy's insistence that the Civil Rights Acts of 1957 and 1960 were inadequate measures. Although Kennedy never offered a complete definition of what an adequate measure might be, Farmer concluded that new, dramatic reforms were in the wings. Eager to "Back Jack" (as one bumper sticker read), Farmer now believed that the 1960s were destined to be the decade of change. He was not alone.

Early in the 1960 campaign, Kennedy had been one of three Democratic candidates considered serious presidential timber by the press. Nicknamed the Holy Trinity, the three were Senator Stuart Symington of Missouri, Senator Hubert Humphrey of Minnesota, and Kennedy. But the 1952 and 1956

Democratic standard-bearer, Adlai Stevenson, continued to have presidential ambitions, as did Senate Majority Leader Lyndon Johnson and Senator Henry "Scoop" Jackson of Washington. The press, on the other hand, found Kennedy most intriguing, and their interests would prove critical to Kennedy's chances throughout the 1960 race.

Kennedy was the first president born in the 20th century and the second youngest (behind Theodore Roosevelt) to enter the Oval Office. As a Catholic, his election vindicated, in a sense, the 1928 landslide loss of the last Catholic Democratic nominee for president, Al Smith, to Herbert Hoover. To his dying day, Smith claimed that much of the opposition against him was due to anti-Catholic bias.

Taking great pains to look centrist and even attack conservatives from conservative positions, Kennedy publicly rejected the label of liberal. Noting in an interview that he was uncomfortable with the liberalism of Humphrey, Stevenson, and other members of his party, Kennedy isolated his Democratic opposition to his left. In spite of the stirring rhetoric in favor of change, Kennedy offered fiscal conservative assurances in favor of a balanced budget. He also rejected federal government intervention in the economy outside of dire emergencies. In foreign affairs, he once complained about President Harry Truman's loss of China to the late 1940s communist revolution there, and he accused the Eisenhower team of a missile gap in America's nuclear defense. The Soviets, he noted, could feel secure behind their nuclear arsenal, for it was larger and deadlier than America's. He had no hard-and-fast data to prove this charge. Given the Republican Party's claim that the Democratic candidates were rank amateurs in foreign policy, Kennedy's effort to put the Eisenhower administration on the defensive was considered a deft political move by his campaign advisers. Privately, the Kennedy campaign remained ill at ease with these off-the-wall accusations, and Kennedy himself was much more complex than his sound-bite charges suggested.

In general terms, Kennedy's charges added up to a promise to win the cold war during his term in office. Although he separated himself from both men, he still endorsed the post–World War II commitment of Presidents Truman and Eisenhower to challenge communism whenever possible. He also reserved the right to advocate new tactics and strategies. According to Kennedy, America's anticommunist mission would never succeed if it stressed raw military matters alone. A number of weapons needed to be employed, he said.[2]

POP CULTURE BECOMES FOREIGN POLICY?

Like many American readers, Kennedy had been quite taken by the thesis of *The Ugly American*. This novel about America's foreign policy troubles in Southeast Asia had been a surprise best-seller throughout the late 1950s. Its authors, William Lederer and Eugene Burdick, became household names as they frequented television talk shows, gave lecture tours, and won accolades from the press for their vision and common sense. Propping up fascist-styled dictatorships in the developing countries alienated the millions who lived in them, Lederer and Burdick insisted. Winning the anticommunist allegiance of those suffering people should be more important to America's cold war victory, they suggested, than assisting corrupt governments. The United States, according to this obvious thesis, was its own worst enemy abroad. Seen as too rich, too arrogant, and too willing to support any government that was not communist, the United States, Lederer and Burdick argued, had pushed the impoverished countries of the world toward communism. Pleasing people, they noted, was more important than pleasing anticommunist dictators, and Washington could lose the cold war if it failed to change its pro-dictatorship policies.

From academe to the dinner table, Americans debated the merits of their "ugly" foreign policy. Kennedy caught on quick. He argued that the United States must be the dear friend of all Asians, Africans, and Latin Americans. His imaginative Peace Corps proposal came out of this point of view, and an unnamed version of it had first appeared in *The Ugly American*.[3] Hooking up to what was essentially a pop culture recommendation for a new foreign policy was a brilliant tactic for its time, especially since the Republican candidate for president, Richard Nixon, said that he was not interested in the opinions of novelists. Turning a novel's thesis into American foreign policy, he implied at the 1960 Republican national convention, would be irresponsible. Naturally, such statements were defensive. As Eisenhower's vice president, Nixon was also being attacked by the Lederer and Burdick thesis.

By the fall of 1960, Kennedy's call for a new spirit of volunteerism on behalf of America's youth, either in reference to Peace Corps work or service in a reformed, highly professional Special Forces of the U.S. Army, always won loud applause. This call for citizen action, combined with a new and expensive economic foreign aid program for developing countries, was meant to suggest that cold war victory was more than possible if vigorous efforts were employed. It also won Kennedy the reputation for thoughtful, innovative programs. Lederer and Burdick sold more books, and Kennedy's image as the new and exciting candidate of 1960 was firmly established. But would it win him the presidency?

To Robert Kennedy, the president's younger brother and campaign manager, the best hope of victory remained the attractiveness of the candidate himself, his gift of oratory, and the continued fascination in the press for the photogenic Kennedy family. The specific campaign issues might be a secondary factor in the long run, but the voter was also supposed to be impressed with Kennedy's mastery of the facts. With these challenges in mind, Robert Kennedy believed in grassroots campaigning. The latter involved flying the candidate in his personal jet to small towns across the country, data-filled stump speeches in unlikely places (such as a pea-packing plant in Beaver Dam, Wisconsin), a massive budget for "visibility" (television ads, billboards, and bumper stickers), and a tireless campaign schedule that took no voter for granted.[4] These were effective tactics, but Richard Nixon had plenty of his own.

NIXON MEANS EXPERIENCE

First winning national attention for his accusations of "traitors in the high councils of our government," Nixon had been friendly with John Kennedy during their early days in Congress together.[5] But the press never warmed to this young Californian, and by 1960 the gloves were off.

Eisenhower had offered only a lukewarm endorsement to the Nixon candidacy, although the president denied that there was friction between himself and the vice president. Since the Eisenhower team took pride in its effort to modernize and streamline Franklin Roosevelt's old New Deal, the Nixon campaign's chief arguments against the Kennedy candidacy remained focused on cold war matters.

Nixon used his many overseas trips on behalf of the Eisenhower administration as an example of his Free World leadership and experience. In general terms, the Nixon campaign portrayed their candidate as a great leader who had been a president-in-waiting for years. Kennedy's credentials, they said, were nonexistent.

Throughout much of the campaign, Nixon assumed that inheriting the record of the Eisenhower administration would be a good thing. The recession and the shooting down of an American U-2 spy plane over Soviet territory reminded him that an administration's record could have its down side, too.[6] Noting that he was too busy leading to be reading, Nixon admitted that he was not that familiar with the precise thesis of *The Ugly American* or of Kennedy's own intellectual appreciation of moral men in American history as portrayed in *Profiles in Courage*. The latter had also been a best-seller, winning Kennedy a Pulitzer Prize for his efforts. The voter surveys suggested that most Americans saw Kennedy as the intellectually gifted candidate in the race. This was a low personal blow to Nixon, who took great pride in his brilliant performance in school. Nevertheless, these same polls did not indicate a solid swing to the Kennedy camp, and Nixon remained on track with his message of leadership and experience.

During the early 1950s, Nixon had pioneered the use of television as a political tool. He had also been a skilled debater during his college days. Those two accomplishments gave him the confidence to face Kennedy in a series of televised debates shortly before the general election. Required to stand at podiums under hot television lights, Kennedy and Nixon were also required to answer difficult questions posed by the press. In written form, their answers would appear nearly identical. But this unprecedented event in campaign history showed something else. Tired from campaigning and not in top form, Nixon appeared agitated, uncomfortable, and struggling to some viewers, especially in the opening debates. Looking his handsome best, Kennedy appeared calm and in command. Follow-up polls gave him a solid win on television, and, to the Kennedy campaign's surprise, large adoring crowds now appeared at their candidate's speeches. Having fought for momentum for months, the last-minute television debates provided Kennedy with the jump start to victory.

However, the Nixon campaign was not down and out. Republican vice presidential candidate Henry Cabot Lodge, Jr., had faced Kennedy in the 1958 Massachusetts Senate race and lost. Lodge now insisted on a stepped-up Nixon campaign against the lackluster Kennedy legislative record, more TV/radio ads, and an appeal for "common sense." The latter was supposed to suggest that Kennedy proposals from the Peace Corps to an expensive space program were dreamy, unrealistic, and dangerous. Nixon, who had played on voter fears in previous elections, suddenly stressed the need for workable government and practical policies. Change was spooky, Nixon reminded the country, and his call for caution had the desired effect on the electorate.

It had been an exciting campaign, and some 63 percent of eligible voters turned out at the polls. This meant the November 1960 election enjoyed the highest voter participation rate in more than 50 years. Yet, Kennedy beat Nixon by only 118,000 votes. His Electoral College success, on the other hand, was much more impressive, giving him a 303 to 219 win. A slight shift of the popular vote in two states, Texas and Illinois, would have made Nixon president. Both states were known for years of voter fraud, and some Nixon supporters urged a recount. But the 118,000 margin was too high of a plurality, and Nixon conceded to Kennedy without a fuss.

Religious bigotry might have had a role in Kennedy's slim margin of victory, but heavy discussions on religious affiliation did not characterize the 1960 election. Nixon remained mum on the matter. Nevertheless, Kennedy was not opposed to raising it now and then during the campaign. He usually said that his religion was not an issue, but that very statement implied that he felt that he was facing, or was soon to face, low-blow attacks from his opposition. It was meant to raise ethical questions about Nixon's tactics, and it often worked. Nixon stuck to his experience and leadership themes in what became one of the toughest and most memorable campaigns of the 20th century.[7]

Despite all the inflammatory rhetoric, great promises, and energetic campaigning, the electorate gave no one a mandate in the 1960 election. In the long run, great change looked attractive to them, but the voters also wanted caution and stability. It was a confusing message for the incoming Kennedy clan, who now had to decide what was campaign rhetoric and what was not. In the meantime, the nation was riveted by what appeared to be their new royal family.

KENNEDY AND COLD WAR VICTORY

At first, most Americans were dazzled by their new president-elect's classy lifestyle. Television viewers saw a handsome, wealthy young man, sipping Dom Perignon with his French-speaking wife, playing touch football with his relatives at their Hyannis Port estate, or sailing with friends near Martha's Vineyard. It was great theater. But would Kennedy be able to deliver on his many promises?

By the time of Kennedy's inaugural address, there was already public concern over whether the new president would be all flash and no substance. News commentators, such as CBS's Walter Cronkite, especially praised Kennedy's choice for vice president, Senate Majority Leader Lyndon Johnson, because the latter had the legislative skills that the chief executive lacked. Yet Kennedy's possible approach to government remained the focus of great speculation. The new president put these concerns to rest in one of the most eloquent inaugural addresses the nation had ever heard.

For the most part, Kennedy's first speech as president was dedicated to cold war challenges, and he merged both foreign and domestic policy-making goals in the name of anticommunist victory. Kennedy asked the country to join him in a great crusade where determination and commitment would always prevail. Nicknamed the New Frontier, the Kennedy administration never saw itself as just another White House team. They represented an important cause, and America's young and talented were attracted to it. The average age of the Kennedy cabinet member and staff official was 44. Nearly all of them held advanced degrees from Harvard University and other Ivy League schools.

Even during his swearing-in
ceremony as president, John
Kennedy wows the nation with his
grace and charm. *(John F. Kennedy
Library)*

Working round the clock was not unusual for them, and they truly enjoyed political debate and policy analysis. Unfortunately, they would soon demonstrate that they loved discussing policy more than making it.[8]

The new defense secretary and former Ford Motor Company chief executive, Robert McNamara, was one of the better examples of a New Frontiersman. Young, ambitious, and a proud workaholic, McNamara would swim numerous laps in the White House pool before attending a midnight cabinet session with the president. He said that it made him fit and mentally prepared for the intellectual jousting that often characterized a Kennedy cabinet meeting. Since the Kennedy team believed that a fast-moving, New Deal–like agenda was essential to success, they were happy to put a youthful, energetic face on the aging New Deal image. All of them were convinced that they possessed the intellectual gifts to accomplish the president's lofty goals of winning the cold war, ending racism, putting an American on the moon, and eliminating poverty.[9]

But the anticommunist cause remained at the root of all policy making in the early Kennedy administration. Founded within the first 100 days of the

New Frontier, Kennedy's innovative Special Protocol Service, for example, proved the point. An arm of both the State Department and the National Security Council, the Special Protocol Service was dedicated to assisting diplomats from developing countries, especially Africa, in Washington, D.C. Dozens of new nations had been born out of the old French and British colonial possessions shortly before the Kennedy administration took office. In segregated Washington, D.C., and its environs, many arriving diplomats were denied housing and even seating in local whites-only restaurants. Because of such policy, several African governments had denounced the hypocrisy of the U.S. democratic cause in the cold war. Democracy, they said, started at home, and American racism had to end. Kennedy took this challenge very seriously, adding that the cold war could be lost at home if local racist laws continued.

One of Kennedy's first political appointments was Pedro Sanjuan, a passionate believer in Kennedy's promise of civil rights reform, to head the Special Protocol Service. Lobbying Congress, which at that time directed the daily administration of Washington, D.C., Sanjuan also argued in front of the Maryland and Virginia legislatures. Insisting that racist ordinances in Washington, D.C., and the neighboring Maryland and Virginia bedroom communities would lead directly to U.S. defeat in the cold war, Sanjuan reminded the legislators that the anticommunist cause was also a battle for "hearts and minds" in the world's developing countries. By the mid-1960s, the term *hearts and minds* would become a common expression of President Lyndon Johnson's while explaining what America was trying to accomplish in Vietnam.

To Sanjuan and his New Frontier colleagues, the cold war had reached a crossroads. Anything could defeat the U.S. cause, and, given the protests of the African governments, domestic racism truly had to go. Years before the passage of civil rights legislation in the Johnson administration, the Special Protocol Service set precedents in civil rights reform in Washington, D.C., Maryland, and Virginia. Legislators did not want to be responsible for any cold war defeat, and even once very staunch supporters of legalized racism voted for civil rights reform on behalf of "people of color" (both foreign and domestic) in their region. The cold war priority prevailed. The African governments and other leaders of developing countries now praised Kennedy for his success. His popularity abroad soon paralleled his high approval ratings at home. But the communist versus anticommunist confrontation continued, and "hearts and minds" policies had little immediate impact on the growing threat of nuclear confrontation between the United States and the Soviet Union.[10]

CAMELOT MANIA

America's fascination with the dazzling style of John Kennedy did not end with his inaugural address. It continued throughout much of his administration, often diverting the country's attention away from threats of World War III, new racial tensions, and a heated-up "brushfire war" in Vietnam. Meanwhile, the presidency did not take Kennedy away from his personal interests, and the country liked to watch. For instance, Kennedy remained a voracious reader, always ready to discuss with the press both the classics and the latest great work in history. The news media had no idea what he was talking about sometimes, such as during a 1961 CBS News interview when the topic turned to

U.S.–USSR tensions. Attempting to describe that tension, Kennedy quoted from memory a number of passages from historian Barbara Tuchman's highly acclaimed book *The Guns of August*. The book analyzed Europe's road to World War I in 1914 and, according to Kennedy, also offered certain implications to readers that the United States was headed in the same foolish direction with the Soviet Union. Kennedy ended up giving a history lesson to both CBS and the country on how wars had begun in the 20th century.

A patron of the arts, Kennedy brought classical musicians to perform at the White House, and he even honored a group of Nobel Prize winners in a special state dinner. The first lady, Jacqueline Kennedy, wore the latest Paris fashions at such occasions, could address a group of visiting European scientists in flawless French, and spoke in a voice that reminded people of Hollywood's hottest sex symbol, Marilyn Monroe.

Kennedy had a gentle sense of humor, a character trait that rejected the Eisenhower administration's conclusion that presidential wit demeaned the office. Most Americans found Kennedy's wit refreshing and not demeaning. When attacked by critics for selecting his younger brother Robert to be the nation's attorney general, Kennedy answered that a budding lawyer should have some on-the-job experience. He promised to keep an eye on him. When asked about an old back injury and whether he was still in pain from it, Kennedy replied that it ached only when the political weather swung too far to the left or right. And when asked why he selected career diplomat Dean Rusk to serve as secretary of state, he said that the new cabinet needed someone who knew where the White House men's room was.

Many members of the press enjoyed Kennedy's wit and charm. Kennedy was the first president to hold regularly scheduled news conferences on television, and all network programs were canceled when the president spoke. On what looked very much like a stage at the local playhouse, Kennedy, some said, arrived at his news conferences to perform in front of the world. Without question, Kennedy controlled much of the agenda, and specific answers to specific questions were never guaranteed. Given the high level of performance, the lack of specifics often did not matter to viewers. Indeed, Kennedy's ability to wow both the press and the voters with his own personality and approach even had a name. Borrowed from a successful Broadway musical about life in King Arthur's court, the Kennedy class and charisma was nicknamed "Camelot." Over the years, the name came to symbolize the entire Kennedy era.

Thanks to his popularity, the president preferred wooing the general public to working the halls of Congress. The former was expected to influence the latter, but that could take years. In the meantime, a coalition of conservative Southern Democrats and a largely united Republican minority in Congress opposed Kennedy's plans for educational reform, urban renewal, better medical care for the country's elderly, and a higher minimum wage. Privately, Kennedy blamed the federal government's slow-moving bureaucracy and a conspiracy of diehard opponents for halting his legislative agenda. Regarding most of his legislation and especially civil rights reform as necessities, he had little interest in detailing his approach to the law. The result was political deadlock, even though Vice President Johnson urged a more wheeling-and-dealing effort on Capitol Hill.

With a pleasant smile, pointing finger, and good humor, John Kennedy was the first and last president of the 1960s to be able to seduce the press. *(John F. Kennedy Library)*

Although John Kennedy greatly respected the political skills of the vice president, this view was not shared by Robert Kennedy and other members of the cabinet. The rough-and-tumble nature of Texas politics and the fact that many in the Texas congressional delegation opposed civil rights legislation made Johnson a suspicious character in the eyes of the New Frontier zealots. Yet Johnson helped build the New Frontier agenda, always reminding his critics how Franklin Roosevelt would have achieved congressional success with it.

To make matters worse in the eyes of the Kennedy team, Johnson had little to say about the moral worth of the administration's reform proposals. He wanted results by any means necessary, and this added to his cabinet-based reputation for uncouth, uninspired behavior. Johnson did not embrace the proper "Camelot" image, but his day was yet to come.[11]

TWISTING THE NIGHT AWAY

Living under the threat of nuclear war had been a fact of life for 1950s Americans, and Kennedy upped the stakes. But escaping the scary politics of the early 1960s was always more than possible. Chubby Checker proved the point. While candidate Kennedy predicted tough times ahead in his summer 1960 nomination speech, "the twist" helped young Americans take their minds off the future.

When "the twist" began its sweep across the country in the late 1950s and early 1960s, it quickly became one of *Billboard* magazine's hottest hits of all time. Twist dance songs remained in the Top Forty charts for two years straight. Americans, young and old, were fascinated with this new way of dancing to rock-and-roll music. Called "dancing apart to the beat," this gyrating, swinging, no-touch dance had its roots in the inner city of Philadelphia. Quite interpretive, requiring no learning curve, the twist lacked any real right or wrong way to be performed. The appearance of song-and-dance man Chubby Checker on the rock-and-roll television shows, *American Bandstand* and its spin-off *The Dick Clark Show,* popularized the dance and made him a star.

Chubby Checker gave rock-and-roll its first great dance, but that was not without controversy. Some parents and music critics regarded the twist as overly provocative, sensual, and, perhaps, even decadent. After all, America's example of classy refinement, the Kennedys, did not twist. At least not right away. When First Lady Jacqueline Kennedy was seen doing the twist at a White House gathering of the rich and famous, even more Americans gave the dance a try. Nevertheless, the controversy continued. Most of the complainers were white, implying a certain racist disgust for the latest influence

The twist was a spontaneous dance craze. Here, students from New York's Riverheart High School are photographed in 1962 while doing the twist in a train baggage car. *(Herman Hiller, Library of Congress)*

of African-American culture on white life. Because of that implication, some of Hollywood's older pop culture symbols and liberals answered the call by being photographed doing the twist. For example, Marlon Brando and Elizabeth Taylor, two hot box office draws of the 1950s and early 1960s, were photographed by *The New York Times* twisting away at a popular Manhattan nightclub, the Peppermint Lounge. The latter with its top performing group, Joey Dee and the Starlighters, decided to play twist music exclusively in an effort to get back at the critics. Press attention led to great success for the Peppermint Lounge and even more visibility for the twist. Meanwhile, Chubby Checker's "Let's Twist Again" won the nation's highest music award, the Grammy. The twist remained in fashion until the next craze, the "British Invasion" music of the mid-1960s.[12]

THE BAY OF PIGS

Americans had plenty of problems to twist away, for the headlines of the early 1960s remained frightening ones. Shortly after taking office, Kennedy authorized the invasion of Cuba. That decision represented the height of anticommunist zeal at the beginning of 1961. It did not, Kennedy learned the hard way, represent good judgment.

Although in power for two years before Kennedy was sworn into office, Fidel Castro's revolutionary government had not forgotten the strong anti-American cause that had united their movement to oust Fulgencio Batista. The latter had been a corrupt dictator who remained in power thanks to American investors and military advisers. His government had even encouraged organized crime to run gambling and prostitution rings in Havana. Since the era of the Spanish-American War more than a half century earlier, the Cuban people had grown to resent all U.S. influence. Batista symbolized everything that was wrong with that influence, and Castro had made good political capital out of it.

From the beginning of his regime, Castro lashed out against the influence of American business in his country. That meant rejecting more than $1 billion in investments and ending U.S.-Cuban trade. Castro's long-winded anti-American speeches had disturbed both American business and the outgoing Eisenhower administration. By glorifying the underdog image of tiny Cuba versus America, the world's most impressive military and capitalist machine, Castro won loud applause from the downtrodden across Latin America. This new appeal worried Washington even more. Yet Castro's political attacks often skirted traditional communist rhetoric and goals. Labeling him a by-the-book communist was not that easy, but it mattered little.

In 1960, following Castro's signing of a trade treaty with Moscow, the Eisenhower administration had had enough. Castro was moving into the Soviet camp, they concluded, and there was no use in trying to win him back to Washington's position. Eisenhower ordered the CIA to begin training for an invasion, and Kennedy continued the effort. It was a strong irony. The young intellectual who warmed to the concerns of developing countries fretted over *Ugly American* policies and could quote popular historian Barbara Tuchman on the folly of war did not give the Cuban invasion decision a second thought. As always, the anticommunist mission took precedence over all.

For a while, Cuba and America waged economic warfare. Eisenhower scaled back on U.S. purchases of Cuban sugar, and Castro retaliated by taking over all U.S. businesses that he had not yet seized. With his country divorcing itself from the U.S.-run capitalist world, Castro turned to the Soviet Union's Nikita Khrushchev for loans and more trade. Khrushchev especially welcomed the propaganda value of a large island, once economically important to the United States and only a short distance from Florida, looking to faraway Moscow for guidance. Khrushchev's public excitement in this matter annoyed the Eisenhower administration, and the United States formally broke all diplomatic ties with Cuba moments before Kennedy took office.

The invasion was slated for mid-April 1961. Pro-Batista or just anti-Castro Cuban refugees were expected to make a beachhead and rally their countrymen to a new government. Although CIA trained and U.S. Navy escorted, the Cuban exiles were supposed to be on their own once they hit the beach at the Bay of Pigs. A special CIA assassination squad was expected to kill Castro before the small invasion force faced any serious counterattack, and the Cuban people were supposed to realize that the Americans would never permit a government like Castro's so close to their shores.

There were too many expectations and suppositions, and everything went wrong. Areas identified as seaweed on CIA-drawn maps were actually coral reefs that sunk or ran aground several landing craft. Aging military equipment failed to work. A Cuban military installation was even located near the Bay of Pigs. Although the invaders were convinced that this base would make it easier for Castro's military establishment to surrender, its location, in fact, made things easier for the defenders to defeat the invasion. Meanwhile, the Cuban people rallied to their government and not to the exiles. With the invasion defeated before it got off the beach, Kennedy refused to order in air support to rescue it.

It took only 48 hours to create this disaster, and Fidel Castro emerged more popular than ever at home and across Latin America. More than 150 Cuban defenders had been killed, along with four Americans, and 114 Cuban exiles. Kennedy told his cabinet that he felt like the ultimate fool, and although some advised against it he made similar comments to the American people in a nationally televised address. The young president took full responsibility for the failure and, in effect, asked for a second chance at anti-communist leadership.

Since his administration was only weeks old, the American people were in a forgiving and tolerant mood. Taking full responsibility, when he could have blamed the Eisenhower planners, was a class act. Kennedy behaved like the "Camelot" gentleman that he appeared to be, and he won high marks in the opinion polls. But the world had just become an even more dangerous place.

In Havana, Castro turned to Khrushchev for more economic aid and for a sophisticated military defense should the Americans try a second invasion. In the White House, Castro was now viewed as the symbol of anti-Americanism throughout the world, and there could be no rest until he was removed from power. Castro's influence, the Kennedy team reasoned, could even have a devastating effect on the president's reelection chances in 1964. With great secrecy, the administration launched Operation MONGOOSE to harass Cuban trade, sponsor commando raids across the island, and enlist organized crime to kill Castro.[13] The resulting tension threatened war between the United States and the Soviet Union, a war caused by a number of Washington versus Moscow confrontations.

THE BERLIN CRISIS

If World War III was not going to begin over Cuba, it certainly could have been sparked by an incident in Berlin. Since the end of World War II, the Soviets had wanted their old wartime allies out of the former Nazi capital. Divided up by the victors over Adolf Hitler's Third Reich, the city symbolized cold war tension at its worst. The noncommunist presence there, Khrushchev complained in January 1961, represented a "dagger near the heart of Soviet Eastern Europe." "Peaceful coexistence" with the United States, he assured the press, was destined to become a happy reality in the 1960s. But the United States and its Western allies would have to leave Berlin first.

If Khrushchev had not made his position clear in early 1961, he tried it again two months after the Bay of Pigs. During June 1961, Kennedy and

In June 1961, an unusually grim President Kennedy meets with Soviet premier Nikita Khrushchev at Vienna. Khrushchev mistakenly found Kennedy to be "maneuverable" and "wobbly" here. *(John F. Kennedy Library)*

Khrushchev met in Vienna. Categorizing a communist takeover of all of Berlin as inevitable, Khrushchev urged Kennedy to support it. If U.S. troops were dispatched to stop him, Khrushchev predicted a nuclear war. Kennedy insisted that American presidents had never appeased aggressors and that there could be no further conversation. But the argument continued.

Khrushchev claimed to be the only real peacemaker in Vienna, while Kennedy made the very same claim. Kennedy saw Khrushchev as a crafty country bumpkin. Khrushchev saw Kennedy as an inexperienced politician and professional-rich-kid-turned-president. Both stereotypes were rooted in fact, and both men were presented with the dilemma of confronting humiliation in the face of allies and domestic critics. To avoid that humiliation, Kennedy and Khrushchev were told by their respective national security advisers that the good world leader must have the courage to accept millions of casualties in a nuclear war.

It was an unhappy state of affairs. The president was convinced the Soviet premier wanted to embarrass and destroy him and that that desire carried equal weight with Khrushchev's other policy concerns. Full military preparedness was essential, Kennedy concluded, but Moscow was also informed that a peace settlement was still possible. In practical terms, this meant a special congressional allocation of more than $3 billion for Berlin defense, Reserve and National Guard unit mobilization, and a new fallout shelter policy for noncombatants in the United States.

Despite the obvious war footing, Kennedy and Khrushchev still told the press that they enjoyed a "readiness to negotiate." Many Germans refused to believe them. Expecting the worst, more than 25,000 East Berliners flocked to the Western zone in July 1961 alone. Politically wounded by the exodus, Khrushchev ordered the erection of a concrete and barbed wire wall to separate East from West Berlin.

Although it did not appear to be the case in public, the crisis ended with Khrushchev's Berlin Wall decision. Anticommunist rhetoric flared from the White House over the wall's construction, and Kennedy's critics urged American action to tear down this new symbol of communist tyranny. Privately, the Kennedy White House breathed a sigh of relief over each brick Khrushchev put into the wall. It meant the Soviet premier accepted the reality of an East and West Berlin. There would be no war. An allied effort to tear down the wall would resurrect the crisis and, most likely, trigger that war. Hence, nothing would be done.

Doing nothing created certain political dangers for a cold warrior. Kennedy dispatched an armored division from West Germany through Red Army territory to Berlin in order to demonstrate U.S. commitment, test Khrushchev, and enlighten domestic critics. Those critics, including Kennedy's possible 1964 election rival, Senator Barry Goldwater, Republican of Arizona, remained skeptical of the president's cold war mettle. In the meantime, the Soviet premier now enjoyed the opportunity to stabilize the East German regime, halt the refugee flow to the West, and improve upon Soviet-Eastern European relations. He had achieved some bottom-line objectives, and a dialogue continued between Washington and Moscow, although it produced little. Kennedy, at the same time, was duty-bound via cold war domestic realities to assail the wall's construction. The rhetoric remained harsh, and political mileage was gained through a later Kennedy visit to the wall; however, the real influence of the Berlin crisis could be seen in Secretary McNamara's efforts to reform allied defense policy in Europe.

Criticized by the Pentagon as a humorless overachiever, too young for his new job, and too much the product of the Harvard Business School and Ford Motor Company management, McNamara ignored the flak and considered the post-Berlin crisis period an excellent opportunity to downplay nuclear options in Europe. By the fall of 1961, McNamara favored heavy stress on conventional forces defense in Europe. Telling the president that America needed a "flexible response" to Soviet threats in Europe, McNamara recommended a build up of North Atlantic Treaty Organization (NATO) forces. NATO had been established after World War II to prevent Berlin-type crises from getting out of hand. It proved useless in 1961, McNamara believed. In keeping with the "new directions" focus of the Kennedy administration, the defense secretary said it was time for innovative strategies to keep the peace.

But McNamara's recommendation equaled something of the cold war heresy. Throughout the 1950s, both American political and military leaders assumed that, given the huge Red Army scattered across Eastern Europe, any war on the European continent would have to be resolved through a nuclear strike by the outnumbered NATO allies. McNamara's proposal did not result in NATO forces matching Red Army forces man-for-man, but it did send a message to Moscow. The United States now favored resolving any armed conflict in Europe via conventional means. Toning down the cold war was the primary objective.

This "new directions" defense policy in Europe disturbed Western European leaders such as France's Charles de Gaulle. The message to Moscow, he said, was a defeatist one. Washington was running away from Europe, de Gaulle complained, and would only use nuclear weapons to defend American soil alone. De Gaulle had been a longtime critic of America's dominant role in NATO and Western European defense matters. His critique was not surprising to the Kennedy team. But his position was not wholly rejected by the other Western European governments either, and his follow-up charge that the Americans were overreacting to the Berlin crisis raised even more controversies.

Kennedy had welcomed his defense secretary's approach, even though a conventional force buildup would certainly cost the taxpayer more money by the time of the 1964 election. In spite of all the tough talk of cold war victory, Kennedy believed that the voters favored fewer and not more nuclear threats. But the young president never had to worry about a post-Berlin crisis debate with the voters. Almost immediately after they were proposed, the Western European governments formally rejected the McNamara-Kennedy defense plan reforms. This angered Kennedy, prompting White House complaints that the Europeans always wanted the Americans to fight their wars for them.

Hoping for a warm, cooperative defense relationship with Western Europe, Kennedy believed that happy allies could achieve great things together. Showing a united front after the Berlin crisis would only assist the anticommunist cause in Asia and even Africa. According to this Kennedy theory, struggling, impoverished communists in developing nations would think twice about their efforts in the face of American-European anticommunist solidarity. As always, the Kennedy team discussed and discussed what that solidarity might bring on the march to cold war victory. And, as always, discussion was not policy. Europe's interests were not the same as Washington's, and Kennedy failed to win this round.[14]

World War III had been averted during the Berlin crisis. Little else resulted from the experience, but keeping the peace during the heyday of cold war confrontation was a remarkable achievement in itself.

THE GEORGE WALLACE FACTOR

To Kennedy, there was "no sense raising hell" if victory could never be achieved. In the cold war, he was convinced that American policy would prevail. On the issue of civil rights, he was not so sure. To a large degree, Kennedy's eloquence on the need for social justice matched his promise of cold war success. Sooner rather than later, some legislative action would be required. Kennedy bided his time.

Throughout 1961, the president's lack of forcefulness on civil rights reform disturbed liberal supporters in Congress. Privately, Kennedy told his brothers that he had no intention of rocking any boat on civil rights until he had a solid mandate for change in the 1964 election. But the civil rights movement was not waiting for the latest Kennedy career move, and the young president was forced to make up his mind. He could live up to the 1960 campaign rhetoric or bend to the racist status quo. If he accepted the latter, that would mean offering tacit support to the Southern resistance to civil rights reform and its emerging leader, Governor George Wallace of Alabama.

For the most part, Wallace won the 1962 governor's race, thanks to racist speeches. Some of his older, more progressive supporters were surprised by the angry tenor and tone of his campaign. Wallace answered them privately, noting that the majority voter did not seem to care about the "old George Wallace" and his causes of educational reform and new roads. Race was everything, he discovered, but he promised to combine "race protection" and "meaningful reform" in due course.

Meanwhile, Governor Ross Barnett in nearby Mississippi made national headlines thanks to his effort to prevent an African-American student, James Meredith, from enrolling at the University of Mississippi. During the fall of 1962, anti-Meredith whites rioted in Oxford, Mississippi, enjoying the encouragement and support of the governor's office. Two people were killed and 375 injured, including 166 federal marshals who had been reluctantly dispatched to calm things down. Barnett reveled in this display of white power but offered little else to his supporters. Wallace remained the man to watch. To Wallace, white rule and beneficial policies for working-class Americans equaled good government for the "average man." More to the point, he meant the working-class white male. Washington-based "dictates," such as civil rights reform, were an interference in the daily life of that "average man," he said. Change, mandated by the federal government, was not good for everybody. The Kennedy administration, Wallace insisted, should be more concerned about the "little guy" than living up to its Harvard-inspired idealism.

During Wallace's rise to power (1960–62), and during his first national spotlight (the 1963 race riots in his state), much of the country remained enthralled by the sophisticated Kennedy and not the country populist Wallace. Like Lyndon Johnson, Wallace's time was coming. A critical turning point in his career took place in 1963.

Quickly living up to his campaign rhetoric to stand tall against integration in the Alabama schools, Wallace, shoulders back and grim-faced, stood in front of the University of Alabama and attempted to prevent any African-American enrollment there. Defiantly stating that segregation must last "forever," Wallace implied that his state was being invaded by a political culture (the federal government in general) that did not understand life and tradition in Alabama or elsewhere. The world press now made George Wallace something of the symbol of racist defiance, and the Kennedy administration took him very seriously.

Martin Luther King, Jr., and other civil rights leaders then targeted Birmingham, Alabama, as a city that had been especially loud in its refusal to comply with civil rights law. Beginning in the spring of 1963, they sponsored a series of sit-ins, pray-ins, and general nonviolent protests across Birmingham. At first, the local white racists exercised restraint. But local leaders, such as Theophilus Eugene "Bull" Connor, soon launched violent police-led assaults (attack dogs, high-pressure hoses, and street beatings). The goal was to break up the demonstrators, drive out the alleged out-of-state invaders, and restore civil peace. Appearing on the nightly television news, the brutal assaults won King a great deal of national sympathy and support. Meanwhile, Wallace's new charge that King's movement was a subversive plot influenced by communist sympathizers gave Kennedy a political hook that he had not yet used.

Indeed, Kennedy had connected civil rights and cold war priorities in the past during memorable public speeches, and the Special Protocol Service had prevailed in the D.C. area, but few in the country had paid attention to it. Now, in a special television address on racial tension in Alabama and elsewhere, Kennedy asked a question: Is America the land of the free "except for the Negro"? If America did not live up to its democratic credo immediately, it would lose the cold war around the world, he warned. The issue of civil rights reform and enforcement was no longer an academic one, he insisted, but a matter of moral obligation. American national security, he said, hung in the balance, and he asked all Americans to evaluate "in their hearts" the issue of civil rights reform.

After months of reluctance, Kennedy realized that he could not lead from behind. He was the first American president since Lincoln to note that the problem facing African Americans was a moral issue involving the entire nation. And he had no intention of permitting George Wallace to control the spotlight any longer. But southern senators were always at the ready to filibuster his new civil rights reform bill, and some were now identifying themselves as Wallace supporters rather than just the Kennedy opposition. His civil rights package would need the legislative skill of Lyndon Johnson to see the light of day.[15]

Kennedy would not live to see Wallace's great takeoff as a national political leader during the late 1960s and early 1970s. But his caution in the civil rights reform effort indicated that he understood the power of Wallace's message, and, for better or worse, he also understood that the Alabama governor could never be ignored.

POP CULTURE STAYS

As always, the twist and rock-and-roll always helped young Americans forget the high tensions of cold war confrontation and race politics. However, the way Americans escaped their troubles was changing faster than the latest Corvette, and the American pop culture scene continued to evolve as well.

In 1961, Americans told the Gallup Poll that the best way to leave all their troubles behind involved a trip to the movies. Yet movie theaters faced stiff competition from television. During the late 1940s and early 1950s, movie attendance averaged 85 to 90 million Americans per week. By the early 1960s, it was less than half that number. With the exception of teenagers attending drive-in movies, few remaining theaters were turning a profit. In fact, at that time more than 70 percent of moviegoers were under the age of 20. Their parents, or the ones truly worried about the problems of the 1960s, were watching television. There was no longer any need to travel and sit in the dark with strangers. One could escape the madness of the world within the comforts of home.

But even the boom in television sales had slowed by the 1960s. As early as 1956, America's major television manufacturers (RCA, Admiral, Zenith, and Sylvania) had foreseen the beginning of the end of endless sales. The cure for a flagging industry, they reasoned, was more technology and better marketing. To the surprise of larger companies such as RCA and Zenith, tiny Admiral corporation's color television division spent the most money on mass marketing and advertising in the early 1960s. But its 21-inch oval screen television cost close to $400 at a time when a decently maintained pre-owned Ford or Studebaker cost the same. Moving the color television set only a few inches from its stationary location in the living room could cause serious color picture distortion requiring expensive repairs. Only major urban areas had the technology to broadcast the color signal, and few programs appeared in color anyway.

In 1961, electronics industry experts predicted that it would take many years for color television to turn a meaningful profit. The press even insisted that the entertainment industry would have to expect more losses as theaters closed and the buying public remained content with their five- or 10-year-old black-and-white televisions. For the consumer, this would mean fewer movies made and poorer television programming produced.

Americans, CBS News predicted in 1961, would soon have to return to the old pastime of reading fiction if they truly wanted to escape daily problems. The intellectual community agreed. Business expert, Harvard University professor, and longtime Kennedy family associate Anthony Solomon especially made headlines with this prediction. Escapism was over, he announced, and it was long overdue. The American people wanted to solve their problems in the 1960s, he explained, not ignore them. A dying movie and television industry meant the triumph of the American intellect, he believed, and that was good news for the country's future.

However, the modern entertainment industry was in transition. It was not dying. In 1963, color television sales began to take off as the television networks promised more color programs and old black-and-white sets broke down. By that same year, the majority of suburban shopping malls had built one- or multiscreen movie theaters in their parking lots, re-creating the full city center/theater experience that had begun to fold in the affluent 1950s. The prediction of the death of the electronic entertainment industry had been premature. Pop culture, which thrived on that industry, was here to stay, and so were America's problems.[16]

CHRONICLE OF EVENTS

1960

January 2: John F. Kennedy announces his candidacy for president at a crowded press conference. After his speech, the questioning centered on whether his youthful candidacy could ever be taken seriously by the voters and if he, in fact, sought the vice presidential nod. Kennedy answered that his candidacy was deadly serious and that he had no interest in the vice presidency.

January 3: In a *Meet the Press* television interview, Kennedy proclaims that his religion will not be an issue in the campaign and that he will not step down if "religious bigotry" insists that he must.

January 4: Ex-president Harry Truman, a Missouri native, tells the press that he favors Missouri senator Stuart Symington for president. Ex–first lady Eleanor Roosevelt says that both Senator Hubert Humphrey and the former 1952 and 1956 Democratic nominee, Adlai Stevenson, are acceptable to her. A poll of Senate Democrats announces that their favorite candidate is Senate Majority Leader Lyndon Johnson, while the majority of newspaper editorials predict another nomination of Adlai Stevenson.

January 6: Senator Humphrey challenges Kennedy to enter the West Virginia primary. Johnson

During the early 1960 presidential campaign, former first lady Eleanor Roosevelt stumps for her candidate Adlai Stevenson *(standing to her right)*. As the Democratic Party standard-bearer in 1952 and 1956, Stevenson had lost both presidential races but remained a popular favorite among many liberals and intellectuals going into the 1960 campaign. *(Franklin D. Roosevelt Library)*

announces that he will stick to his Senate duties, ignore the primaries, and take his chances with the convention delegates in the summer. Symington admits a struggle for funds and endorsements. Only Wisconsin and West Virginia will be "battleground states" in the 1960 primary season, pitting Kennedy against Humphrey in a head-to-head contest.

February: Senator Humphrey announces that a Wisconsin primary win is inevitable, and the Milwaukee press supports his conclusion. Nicknamed "Wisconsin's other Senator" during the heyday of Joe McCarthy's Red-baiting, Minnesota's Humphrey had championed the Wisconsin labor and farm issues that McCarthy ignored.

February 19: Wesley Powell, the Nixon campaign chairman during the New Hampshire primary, denounces Kennedy as "soft on communism." Nixon ran unopposed in the New Hampshire primary, and Kennedy faced a political unknown there. The Kennedy campaign explains Powell's denunciation as a Nixon admission that the Massachusetts senator is the leading candidate on the Democratic side.

February 20: After a year-long analysis of the data, the U.S. Census Bureau predicts the collapse of the family farm in the 1960s.

February 27: Following the example of Greensboro, North Carolina, pro–civil rights sit-ins and demonstrations begin in Nashville, Tennessee.

March: Wisconsin's State Democratic Party Committee director and Kennedy campaign chairman, Patrick Lucey, is defeated in a bid to make the Wisconsin primary a "winner take all" state. The state's delegates were to be apportioned district-by-district, thereby making it possible for Senator Humphrey to take the majority of delegates even if he lost the popular vote. Although months away from the Democratic convention, the Wisconsin primary becomes the most critical test for the nomination. Kennedy tells a group of Wisconsin interviewers that, if president, he would not cancel an overseas summit meeting if ordered to do so by a Catholic bishop.

March 29: An exhausted Kennedy admits to his staff that his presidential aspirations might die in Wisconsin.

April 4: *Ben-Hur* sets the record for winning the most Academy Awards, winning best picture, best actor in a leading role (Charlton Heston), best director (William Wyler), best cinematography (Robert Surtees), and most other categories. Host Bob Hope

jokes that in contrast to the 1960 election, *Ben-Hur's* Roman Empire never looked so good.

April 4: The *Milwaukee Journal* announces an unforeseen Kennedy surge in the polls but predicts a Humphrey victory on the April 5th primary.

April 5: Breaking all Wisconsin voting records for a primary election, Kennedy wins the state with a 56 percent landslide. Elmo Roper of CBS News claims the victory was due to "Catholic Republican crossover voters," and the press, in general, is taken off guard by Kennedy's success. Even Kennedy's most optimistic pre-election polling had predicted a 53 percent win. If key pro-Humphrey congressional districts on the Wisconsin-Minnesota border had shifted only one to three votes to Kennedy, the Massachusetts senator would have swept every district in the state. Kennedy claims the momentum is now with his campaign, and he writes an angry letter to CBS's Roper complaining of anti-Catholic bias.

April 6: Humphrey campaign officials announce that Senator Kennedy's wealthy and Boston Irish-Catholic roots will be his undoing in West Virginia. Despite Kennedy's Wisconsin win, the polls predict a 60 percent to 40 percent Humphrey win in this poor, largely rural, and 95 percent Protestant state.

April: In addition to ceaseless efforts to contact as many voters as possible, the Kennedy and Humphrey campaigns agree to a televised debate. Foreshadowing the later Nixon-Kennedy debates shortly before the general election, Kennedy displays a certain poise and coolness under fire throughout the tough questioning, while Humphrey appears overconfident, agitated, and exhausted. Humphrey loses his lead in the polls.

May: The Newport Folk Festival announces that Pete Seeger and Joan Baez will be their top singers this year.

May: With his new campaign song of "Give Me That Old Time Religion" raising Protestant versus Catholic animosity, Humphrey accuses the Kennedy family of trying to buy votes and exploit the poor. Kennedy staffers respond by attacking Humphrey's lack of World War II heroism, and the campaign turns to mud-slinging.

May 10: Kennedy beats Humphrey in West Virginia by a thundering 61 percent to 39 percent margin, especially taking large United Mine Worker districts and African-American neighborhoods. Kennedy notes that he "sold" himself to the electorate rather than attempting to "buy" them. Richard Nixon announces that his most significant opponent is now John Kennedy, predicting a tough race in the fall.

May 11: The Food and Drug Administration approves the future use of a contraceptive pill.

May 26: An American U-2 spy plane is shot down by the Soviets, and its pilot, Francis Gary Powers, is captured.

July 11: The Democratic convention opens with Eleanor Roosevelt, Hubert Humphrey, and noted columnist Walter Lippmann urging a draft of Adlai Stevenson as the presidential nominee. Lyndon Johnson supporters assail Kennedy's "untested leadership."

July 13: The Wyoming delegation at the Democratic convention puts Kennedy over the top in delegate count (761 required). Seeking legislative experience and a geographically balanced ticket, Kennedy selects Texas's Johnson as running mate. Kennedy delivers one of the more cautious speeches of his campaign at the convention. Although press coverage of his nomination gives Kennedy a boost in the opinion polls, Richard Nixon (nominated during the July 25–28, 1960 Republican convention) is considered the more competent and skilled of the two candidates in those same polls.

July 25: The city fathers of Greensboro, North Carolina, announce that their town will comply with civil rights law.

August: Summer movies predicted to be historic box office successes, John Wayne's *The Alamo* and Frank Sinatra's "rat pack" movie, *Ocean's 11,* fall flat with both audiences and critics. A movie about an employee trying to get ahead at the office by arranging trysts for his boss (*The Apartment*) and the story of a shady traveling preacher (*Elmer Gantry*) attract audiences instead.

August 9: Drug-use advocate Dr. Timothy Leary tries LSD for the first time.

September 11: Held in Rome, the Summer Olympics begins its closing ceremonies. The Soviets had won 43 gold medals and the Americans had won 34.

September 26–October 21: A series of one-on-one television debates, lasting one hour apiece, pit skilled debaters Nixon and Kennedy against each other in a last-ditch effort to win the November election. The first debate, declared a Kennedy success, becomes especially critical to Kennedy chances. Nixon counters with the announcement of "practical" domestic programs and attacks Kennedy's alleged "softness" on communism.

October 1: Overstating his position for an immediate and punishing U.S. military victory in Vietnam, General Lyman Lemnitzer is replaced by the more politically cautious General George Decker as the U.S. Army chief of staff.

October 26: Against campaign advice, Kennedy calls an arrested Martin Luther King, Jr., in Birmingham, Alabama, and expresses his concern. Kennedy wins the African-American vote and the presidency 12 days later.

December: The Motion Picture Association of America reports that *Ben-Hur, Psycho,* and *Operation Petticoat* were the top money-making films of 1960 and that Doris Day, Rock Hudson, and Cary Grant are the top three box office draws.

December: The hottest-selling single records of 1960 were "The Theme from *A Summer Place*" by Percy Faith; "Are You Lonesome Tonight?" by Elvis Presley; and "It's Now or Never" also by Elvis Presley.

December 20: The communist National Liberation Front (or Vietcong) are formally established in Vietnam. More U.S. military advisers are sent to counter their growing influence, and the total number of U.S. troops in South Vietnam nears 1,000.

1961

January: Folk-rock singer Bob Dylan begins his Greenwich Village–based singing career.

January 20: In his inaugural address, Kennedy asks a receptive nation to "ask not what your country can do for you, ask what you can do for your country."

January 21: Prime Minister Hayato Ikeda of Japan and the Harvard-educated Japanese finance minister, Kiichi Miyazawa, become the first foreign dignitaries to visit the New Kennedy White House. Concerned that Japan will turn to communism if the United States does not fully open its trade borders to Japanese electronic and automobile products, Kennedy begins to draft the Trade Expansion Act (TEA).

January 21–24: Avoiding a fight in Congress, Kennedy issues executive orders to increase the quality and quantity of surplus food to unemployed Americans and for an expanded Food for Peace program for struggling Southeast Asians.

January 28: After little cabinet debate, Kennedy approves a counterinsurgency plan to defeat communist inroads in South Vietnam.

January 29: Folk-rock singer Bob Dylan predicts a 1960s revolution in music and a new era of social change. James Garner, the star of TV's offbeat western *Maverick,* also predicts a new era of Hollywood anti-heroes and a growing concern for social justice throughout the artistic community.

January 30: Claiming that America's elderly must not be left behind in his youthful "New Frontier," Kennedy urges Congress to attach health insurance guarantees to its 1960s Social Security legislation.

February 2: Insisting that the economic recession can end quickly, Kennedy asks Congress to increase benefits for the unemployed and include special payments to their children.

March 1: Although he personally doubts that it will do all that much good in the effort to win the cold war, Kennedy establishes the Peace Corps "to carry American skills and idealism" to developing countries.

March 13: Based on the late 1940s Marshall Plan for Europe, the Alliance for Progress is founded to remake the economies of Latin American nations and deaden the anti-American appeal of Fidel Castro. These nations can receive U.S. economic assistance if they renounce communism.

March 23: Believing that a cease-fire in the Laotian civil war could also trigger a regional peace that included Vietnam, Kennedy urges pro-U.S. forces in Laos to lay down their arms. A communist offensive ensues, leading Kennedy to conclude that Southeast Asian problems require military and not diplomatic solutions.

March 28: Doubling the U.S. nuclear missile construction program, creating five new combat-ready divisions as well as new antiguerrilla units, Kennedy begins the most dramatic peacetime military buildup in U.S. history.

April 17–19: America's Bay of Pigs invasion fails.

April 20: Taking full responsibility, Kennedy apologizes to the nation for the disaster at the Bay of Pigs. U.S.-Cuban and U.S.-USSR relations deteriorate.

May 5: Mercury spacecraft astronaut Alan B. Shepard, on his Freedom 7 suborbital flight, becomes the first American in space.

May 9–15: Vice President Johnson visits South Vietnam, concluding that a large U.S. military presence is required for anticommunist success.

May 20: Civil rights advocates known as Freedom Riders are beaten by white racists at the Mont-gomery, Alabama, bus terminal. Attorney General Robert Kennedy dispatches more than 400 federal marshals to the scene. Freedom Rides continue throughout the South, even though Attorney General Kennedy prefers different methods of protest.

May 25: Congress warmly receives the Kennedy space program proposal to put "an American space team on the moon within the decade."

June 9: The struggling dictator of South Vietnam, Ngo Dinh Diem, asks Kennedy for hundreds if not thousands of U.S. military advisers to "modernize" the South Vietnamese military.

July 20: Facing press and congressional reports that predict serious pollution-based diseases by 1970, Kennedy signs a bill that doubles U.S. financial assistance in the fight against water pollution.

August 20: The Soviet construction of the Berlin Wall creates the Berlin Crisis.

September 3: The minimum wage is raised to $1.25. Chevrolet announces that its upcoming 1962 Corvette, the country's top sports car and one of the more expensive automobiles on the market, will cost more than $3,400.

October 1: With baseball fans shouting "61 in '61," New York Yankee Roger Maris hits his 61st home run. This breaks Babe Ruth's single-season record of 60 home runs hit in 1927.

Baseball hero Roger Maris holds up the 61st home run ball and a commemorative shirt representing his 61 home runs, a total he reached during the 1961 World Series. *(Baseball Hall of Fame Library/Cooperstown, N.Y.)*

December: The Motion Picture Association of America reports that *The Guns of Navaronne, The Absent-Minded Professor,* and *The Parent Trap* were the top-grossing films of 1961. The biggest box office draws are declared to be Elizabeth Taylor, Rock Hudson, and Doris Day.

December: The Associated Press announces that the top single records of 1961 were "Tossin' and Turnin'" by Bobby Lewis; "Big John" by Jimmy Dean; and "Runaway" by Del Shannon.

December 11: Two U.S. Army helicopter companies arrive in South Vietnam. Consisting of 33 twin-roter helicopters and 400 men, the two companies constitute the Kennedy administration's first contingent of "direct support" to the South Vietnamese government.

December 14: Eleanor Roosevelt is appointed by President Kennedy to head the President's Committee on the Status of Women, an organization dedicated to gender equity for women in labor, tax, and legal matters.

December 14: Dr. William Anderson, a civil rights activist and president of the Albany Movement, invites Martin Luther King, Jr., to come to Albany, Georgia, and fight for racial justice. King accepts the invitation, bringing national attention to Anderson's desegregation efforts.

December 15: An Israeli court sentences Adolf Eichmann, a former Nazi administrator of the "Final Solution," to be hanged. The sentence is hailed as just by America's Jewish community. Eichmann was heavily responsible for the deaths of 6 million Jews and 5 million "others" in Nazi death camps between 1942 and 1945.

December 15: Kennedy reviews America's Vietnam policy and declares solidarity behind the anticommunist government of South Vietnam. More than 3,200 troops are now in Vietnam.

December 18: Wilma Rudolph, a track star, is named Woman Athlete of the Year by the Associated Press.

December 18: Without consulting the United States, the government of India launches an invasion of lingering Portuguese colonies off the coast of western India. Indian Defense Minister Krishna Menon claims that these small islands had threatened his country.

December 22: Specialist 4 James Davis of Livingston, Tennessee, is killed in action in Vietnam. Some years later, President Lyndon Johnson praises Davis as America's first great hero of the Vietnam War.

December 31: A right-wing coup is thwarted in Lebanon, and President Fuad Chehab's regime lives on. President Kennedy concludes that the Middle East might remain a "powder keg" throughout the 1960s.

EYEWITNESS TESTIMONY

The "Happy Days" End

"Give us this day our daily bread," is still the prayer of human beings in the far corners of the earth. . . . I become more convinced each day that our most powerful material asset in building a world of peace and freedom is our food abundance. The hungry multitudes of Asia, Africa, and the Middle East are far more interested in bread, medical care and schools than in any number of jets and Sputniks. Does anyone wonder what the crafty Khrushchev would do if he had America's surplus food to use in his international operations?

Future Food for Peace director and 1972 Democratic presidential nominee George McGovern claiming, in May 1959, that the cold war could be won without bullets, in The Arthur M. Schlesinger, Jr., Papers, JFK Library.

The Japanese nation can exert little control over the elements which are shackling her foreign trade. These problems—underdeveloped or unavailable nearby supply sources, unstable export markets, inconvertibility of foreign currencies, tariff and export-import quota limitations—are primarily in the field of international relations and their solution is dependent upon the development of goodwill and cooperation between the sovereign nations of the free world. The United States is the greatest economic power in the world today. Actions taken by the U.S. government, which appear to the average American situated in his powerful economy to be minor and unimportant, may have a tremendous effect upon the economies of other, less stable countries. Therefore, the foreign economic policy of the United States is of worldwide significance. . . .

Kiichi Miyazawa of the Japanese government predicting the collapse of his nation's postwar economic recovery if the United States does not accept more Japanese products, late 1950s, in Livingston, Moore, and Oldfather, The Japan Reader: Postwar Japan, 1945 to the Present *(1973), p. 267.*

In my nervousness, I blurted out something about his being a good neighbor and living above me, and did he come down to borrow sugar? The Cuban leader smiled and shrugged as if to say "Crazy Americano."

Later on camera he said, "I am not a Communist." He said that he liked and admired Americans and hoped the United States would understand that he was going to rid his country of the tyranny of the former government. . . . That's about all there was to it, but it certainly was a news maker for the "Tonight" program. I still wish that our country and his could have gotten on as well as we did. I did hope to return one day. I like Cuba and its people very much.

NBC's Tonight Show *host Jack Paar recalling a live September 1960 telecast of his program from Havana during the time of the U.S. presidential election, in Paar's* P.S. Jack Paar *(1983), pp. 128–129.*

I haven't checked these figures, but eighty-seven years ago, I think it was, a number of individuals organized a governmental setup here in this country. I believe it covered eastern areas, with this idea that they were following up based on a sort of national independence arrangement and the program that every individual is just as good as every other individual.

A 1960 Democratic Party brochure poking fun at President Eisenhower's speech-making struggles and how he might have delivered the Gettysburg Address of 1863, in Papers of John F. Kennedy, JFK Library.

Crises there will continue to be. In meeting them, whether foreign or domestic, great or small, there is a recurring temptation to feel that some spectacular and costly action could become the miraculous solution to all current difficulties. A huge increase in the newer elements of our defenses; development of unrealistic programs to cure every ill in agriculture; a dramatic expansion in basic and applied research—these and many other possibilities, each possibly promising in itself, may be suggested as the only way to the road we wish to travel.

But each proposal must be weighed in light of a broader consideration; the need to maintain balance in and among national programs—balance between the private and the public economy, balance between the cost and hoped for advantages—balance between the clearly necessary and the comfortably desirable; balance between our essential requirements as a nation and the duties imposed by the nation upon the individual; balance between the actions of the moment and the national welfare of the future. Good judgment seeks balance and progress; lack of it eventually finds imbalance and frustration.

President Dwight Eisenhower, "Farewell Address," January 17, 1961, John Fitzgerald Kennedy, 35th president of the United States, URL: www.copperas.com/jfk/ikefw.htm.

The colonization of Cuba, he asserted, began with the acquisition of the best land by United States firms, concessions of Cuban natural resources and public services—concessions of all kinds. Cuba eventually had to fight to attain its independence, which was finally achieved after seven bloody years of tyranny "of those in our country who were nothing but the cat's paws of those who dominated the country economically." The Batista Government of Cuba was appropriate for the United States monopolies, but not for the Cuban people. How could any system inimical to the interests of the people stay in power unless by force? These were the governments that the guiding circles of United States policy preferred, he said, and that was why governments of force still ruled Latin America.

Fidel Castro's formal denunciation of the United States is examined in United Nations Review *(November 1960), pp. 63–67.*

If the Soviet Union should continue to gain technologically and acquire preponderant military strength, they would have policy alternatives even more attractive than the initiation of nuclear war. By flaunting presumably invincible strength, the Soviet Union could compel piecemeal capitulation of the democracies. The prospect must indeed seem glittering to the Soviet leaders.

In January 1961, foreign policy analyst Herbert Dinerstein, warning that the Soviet Union could win the Cold War in the 1960s, in Boyer, Promises to Keep *(1995), p. 180.*

Now, look. I happen to know a little about leadership. I've had to work with a lot of nations, for that matter at odds with each other. And I tell you this: you do not lead by hitting people over the head. Any damn fool can do that, but it's usually called assault—not leadership. . . . I'll tell you what leadership is. Its persuasion and conciliation and patience. It's long, slow, tough work. That's the only kind of leadership I know or believe in—or will practice.

In January 1961, Dwight D. Eisenhower responding to critics that his leadership style has been tired and ineffective, in Chafe, The Unfinished Journey *(1999), p. 140.*

The Civil Rights Struggle Continues

Since the close of the civil war the United States has been hesitating between two worlds—one dead, the other powerless to be born. War brought an old order to an end, but . . . proved unequal to founding a new one. Neither north nor south has been willing really to adopt its racial practices to its professions.

Associate Supreme Court Justice Robert Jackson reflecting pessimistically in 1961 on the prospects of meaningful civil rights reform, quoted in Chafe, The Unfinished Journey: America Since World War II *(1999), p. 151.*

The chief emphasis I tried to make was their right to make their own decision. The only reason that I became relevant was because I had lived through certain experiences and had had certain opportunities to gather information and organizational experience. I have always felt that if there is any time in our existence that you have a right to make mistakes it should be when you're young, cause you have some time to live down some of the mistakes, or to offset them. I felt that what they were doing was certainly creative and much more productive than anything that had happened in my life, and it shouldn't be stifled. I must have had sensed also that it was useless to try to put the brakes on, because it was unleashed enthusiasm . . . an overflow of a dam that had been penned up for years, and it had to run its course.

Veteran civil rights activist Ella Baker commenting in early 1961 on the growth of African-American student involvement in the 1960 civil rights cause in Grant, "Political Mama," Ella Baker: Freedom Bound *(1998), Rare Documents File-Civil Rights Movement, Institute for African-American Studies, Bradley University.*

They fired him from the school at which he had taught devotedly for ten years. And they fired his wife and two of his sisters and a niece. And they threatened him with bodily harm. And they sued him on trumped up charges and convicted him in a kangaroo court and left him with a judgment that denied him credit from any bank. And they burned his house to the ground while the fire department stood around watching the flames consume the night. And they stoned the church at which he pastored. And they fired shotguns at him out of the dark . . . all of this . . . because he was black and brave. And because others followed when he had decided the time had come to lead.

Author Richard Kluger admitting that the price of civil rights leadership can be high but arguing in March 1961 that the cause is worth it, in his Simple Justice (1976), *Rare Documents File-Civil Rights Movement, Institute for African-American Studies, Bradley University.*

I will slash my wrists and write an oath in blood that Jack will never run for vice president. We'd let Adlai [Stevenson] go down to defeat alone!

An angry Jacqueline Kennedy responding in January 1960 to reporters who say her husband has the credentials only to be vice president, in Papers of William Attwood, Ambassador to Guinea, JFK Library.

After weeks of muted weekend campaigning, Hubert Humphrey started moving fast in Wisconsin, even crossed paths briefly with rival Kennedy at the Intonville Airport. Shaking hands at a Kenosha factory gate, Humphrey was delighted to discover that more and more people were recognizing him. In the midst of his rising enthusiasm, the buoyant Humphrey still had pensive moments. After an overtime session of handshaking with deaf children at a school in Delavan, he was asked why he spent so much time with nonvoters. Replied Humphrey: "I guess it's because Jack's got a feeling he can win. Me. I'm not so sure, so I'm going to have some fun."

Time magazine staff reporting in March 1960 on the Humphrey versus Kennedy primary contest in Wisconsin, URL: http://www.CNN/All Politics.

Whatever other qualifications I may have had when I became President, one of them at least was that I knew Wisconsin better than any other President. My foot-tracks are in every house in this state. . . . I know the difference between the kind of farms they have in the Seventh District and the First District. . . . I suppose there is no training ground for the Presidency but I don't think it's a bad idea for a President to have

stood outside of Maier's meat factory . . . at 5:30 in the morning with the temperature ten above.

John Kennedy reflecting in January 1961 on the significance of the 1960 Wisconsin primary to his presidency, in The Theodore C. Sorensen Papers, JFK Library.

To the "New Frontier"

Whether we can achieve a world of peace and freedom in place of the fantastically dangerous and expensive arms race. . . .

Whether we can spur the nation's economic growth to provide a more secure life for all Americans, regardless of race, creed or national origin. . . .

Extending America's "New Frontier" into space, John Kennedy promised a man on the moon by the end of the 1960s. On May 5, 1961, astronaut Alan Shepard becomes the first American to fly into space. He and his *Freedom 7 Mercury* capsule are shown here being rescued by helicopter in the Atlantic Ocean. *(NASA/ Johnson Space Center)*

Whether our food surplus can help us build a more stable peace abroad and feed our hungry here at home instead of wasting in warehouses....

Whether the children of this state [named] and nation can obtain safe, decent, adequate public school facilities.

John Kennedy in the opening refrain to a stock stump speech shortly before and after he formally declared his candidacy for the White House. The Papers of Theodore C. Sorensen, JFK Library.

Establish yourselves in the Central Highlands. Like the French before them, the Americans and their puppet Diem will stay in the cities. Then extend your influence into the lowland jungles and the villages of the Mekong Delta. Assault on the cities will be only the last stage of the conflict.

North Vietnamese military leader Vo Nguyen Giap promising his troops on January 1, 1961, that the 1960s will bring victory to their cause, in Olson and Roberts, Where the Domino Fell: America and Vietnam, 1945–1995 *(1996), p. 71.*

We are tired! Tired of being segregated and humiliated! Once again we must hear the words of Jesus: Love your enemies. Bless them that curse you. Pray for them that despitefully use you. If we fail to do this, our protest will end up as a meaningless drama on the stage of history.

If you protest courageously, and yet with dignity and Christian love, future historians will say, There lived a great people—a black people—who injected new meaning and dignity into the veins of civilization. This is our challenge and our overwhelming responsibility.

Martin Luther King, Jr., preaching his most popular 1961 sermon, quoted in Gillon and Kunz, America During the Cold War *(1993), p. 96.*

I am not satisfied as an American with the progress that we are making. This is a great country but I think it could be a greater country.

The reason Franklin Roosevelt was a good neighbor in Latin America was because he was a good neighbor in the United States. I want people in Latin America and Africa and Asia to start to look to America . . . what the President of the United States is doing, not . . . Khrushchev or the Chinese Communists. . . . Can freedom be maintained under the most

severe attack it has ever known? I think it can be and I think in the final analysis it depends upon what we do here. I think it's time America started moving again.

John Kennedy in his opening remarks to moderator Howard K. Smith and the American people during the first Kennedy-Nixon debate of September 26, 1960, in The Kennedy-Nixon Debate Transcript, *Research Room, JFK Library.*

The things that Senator Kennedy has said, many of us can agree with . . . I subscribe to the spirit that Senator Kennedy has expressed tonight. . . . I know Senator Kennedy feels as deeply about these problems as I do, but our disagreement is not about the goals for America but only about the means to reach those goals.

Richard Nixon responding to Kennedy's opening remarks in the first Kennedy-Nixon debate of September 26, 1960, in The Kennedy-Nixon Debate Transcript, Research Room, JFK Library.

An incumbent seldom agrees willingly to debate his challenger, and I knew that the debates would benefit Kennedy more than me by giving his views national exposure, which he needed more than I did. Further, he would have the tactical advantage of being on the offensive. As a member of Eisenhower's administration, I would have to defend the administration's record while trying to move the discussion to my own plans and programs. But there was no way I could refuse to debate without having Kennedy and the media turn my refusal into a central campaign issue. The question we faced was not whether to debate, but how to arrange the debates so as to give Kennedy the least possible advantage.

In December 1960, Richard Nixon examining his decision to debate John Kennedy in The Memoirs of Richard Nixon (1978), p. 217.

I had stood there many times before. It is one of the most magnificent vistas in the world, and it never seemed more beautiful than at this moment. The mall was covered with fresh snow. The Washington Monument stood out stark and clear against the luminous gray sky, and in the distance I could see the Lincoln Memorial. I stood looking at the scene for at least five minutes. I thought about the great experiences of the past fourteen years. Now all that was over, and I would be leaving Washington, which had been my home since I arrived as a young congressman in 1947. As I turned to go inside, I suddenly stopped short, struck by the thought that this was not the end—that someday I would be back here. I walked as fast as I could back to the car.

Richard Nixon remembering his last day as vice president, in The Memoirs of Richard Nixon *(1978), p. 227–228*

I didn't want to be in the White House. I didn't want to do that. If I was going to work in the government at all, I wanted to have a position of my own responsibility, not just taking direct orders from anybody. I didn't want that. If I was going to do it, I had to have a position which had equality of responsibility and prestige, because otherwise I would be resented, and rightfully so, by anybody for whom I would be working or anybody else who had a higher position. So I had to be in the Cabinet if I was going to perform that function. And the only place I could really be in the Cabinet was as Attorney General.

Recalling his first days in the White House in a 1964 interview, Robert Kennedy examines his decision to serve as attorney general in Robert F. Kennedy Oral History Project, JFK Library.

Ethiopians had not been accustomed to 10th grade women teachers who knew anything. In Ethiopia women are good for bearing children and carrying clay jugs on their heads and so we fought that battle when we first got there and eventually proved to them that yes we did know English and we could teach it.

Peace Corps volunteer Ann Martin recalling her 1961 service in Ethiopia, in Paterson, Kennedy's Quest for Victory: American Foreign Policy, 1961–1963 *(1989), p. 297.*

So let us begin anew—remembering on both sides that civility is not a sign of weakness, and sincerity is always subject to proof. Let us never negotiate out of fear. But let us never fear to negotiate. . . .

Let both sides seek to invoke the wonders of science instead of its terrors. Together let us explore the stars, conquer the deserts, eradicate disease, tap the ocean depths, and encourage the arts and commerce. . . .

And if a beachhead of cooperation may push back the jungle of suspicion, let both sides join in creating a new endeavor, not a new balance of power, but a new world of law, where the strong are just and the weak secure and the peace preserved.

All this will not be finished in the first 100 days. Nor will it be finished in the first 1,000 days, nor in the life of this Administration, nor perhaps in our lifetime on this planet. But let us begin.

John Kennedy in his Inaugural Address of January 20, 1961, Research Room, JFK Library.

After observing your car in the Department garage, I would like to thank you for coming to work on February 22nd, a national holiday. . . . The spirit you demonstrated—the spirit of Valley Forge and Monte Cassino—will, we hope, spread through the entire Department of Justice. Keep up the good work.

FBI Director J. Edgar Hoover in a sarcastic note of February 1961, reminding Robert Kennedy, the new attorney general, that the FBI would be watching him, quoted in Turner, Hoover's FBI *(1971) and originated in the Robert F. Kennedy Oral History Project, JFK Library.*

When our young people go to live and work in foreign countries, in villages and schools in the developing world, when they put their hands and their skills to work in the development of this two-thirds of the world which is struggling to advance out of poverty, they are going to make a real contribution, I believe, to world peace. For economic growth in these nations is one of the conditions of peace, and better understanding among people is one of the conditions of peace. And the Peace Corps, we hope, will contribute to both.

Peace Corps director R. Sargent Shriver explaining to the press that after only a few days in the field his organization has been a smashing success, in Shriver Press Briefing, March 6, 1961, The Peace Corps Papers of Gerald Bush, JFK Library.

We thought our standards were just dandy and ought to be met. But we could not fully appreciate what devastation our demands could bring about in their lives. They could. We couldn't. . . . We thought: We certainly can't pass these kids because they don't deserve to pass. We weren't thinking: Gee, if they don't pass this means they're going to have to go back

Peace Corps volunteer Peter Lefcourt offers a helping hand to children in early 1960s Togo. *(Roger Scherman, Peace Corps, John F. Kennedy Library)*

to their villages in failure and disgrace, every avenue of opportunity shut off to them. We weren't thinking along these lines. We mishandled it.

> *Peace Corps volunteer Carol Miller Reynolds remembering that American culture often clashed with East African culture during the opening days (November 1961) of the Peace Corps in Africa, in Paterson,* Kennedy's Quest for Victory: American Foreign Policy, 1961–1963 *(1989), p. 314.*

Pop Culture in the Days of "Camelot"

"What does this thing do?"

> *Soviet Premier Nikita Khrushchev touching the decorative tail fin of a 1960 Cadillac and innocently asking an American diplomat to explain its function, in* "Geneva Briefing Papers, 1961," *WH-6, Papers of Arthur M. Schlesinger, Jr., JFK Library.*

The most potent single influence upon what a child watches on television is what his parents watch.

In homes where parents take the trouble to offer attractive alternatives to TV, the children watch less TV.

A child who watches "too much" television usually is suffering some emotional distress which is causing him to retreat into TV-watching. It's not that he's fascinated with the programs. He's unhappy—consciously or not—with his home life, his school life, or his relations with his friends.

Bright children discover television early, use it heavily, then drift away to other pursuits around age 12, less intelligent children remain enthusiastic viewers for longer.

The quality of most network TV designed specifically for children is limited by the networks' competitive desire to attract maximum audiences for advertisers—usually the makers of toys and breakfast foods.

The conclusion of a 1961 study ("Television in the Lives of Our Children") being reviewed, in Harris, TV Guide: The First 25 Years *(1980), p. 161.*

The hope so fondly held by enthusiasts a few years ago, the hope that television would make certain that the voter would sort out the phony from the statesman, is not proved. I would doubt that under today's system of communication a Lincoln or a Jefferson could be nominated or elected. According to all reports, Jefferson had a most abrasive voice, and did not suffer fools gladly. While being interviewed on some panel program he might have told a particularly obnoxious questioner just what he thought of him, and that, of course, would have been fatal. Mr. Lincoln did not move gracefully, was not a handsome man, had a wife who was no political asset, and he was a solitary man. In our present society, he probably would have been examined at an early age by a psychiatrist, received an unfavorable report, have been told his attitude toward "togetherness" was altogether wrong, and advised to enter a trade school if he could gain admittance.

In November 1961, veteran CBS News correspondent Edward R. Murrow commenting on the negative impact of television on early 1960s politics, in Ambrose and Brinkley, Witness to America *(1999), p. 443.*

Saperstein isn't counting his chickens yet. As he tells it, trying to sell products bearing a name or image follows a pattern. If a fad catches on, sales run up fast when products are introduced. In four or five months, they fall off, after which they either level off or start to dive. "If sales seek a level you know you have a hit," he says.

Saperstein expects the Checker promotion to peak next spring, [and] seek a level in late summer or early fall. "No one," he says now, "would try to predict how far it will go. After all, everyone said Elvis was a flash in the pan."

Business Week *examining the business community's late rush to market Twist-related "teen products" in 1962, in Staff's "'Twist' wiggles into big time,"* Business Week, *December 2, 1961, p. 46.*

It may be the hula hoop, Elvis Presley, or the latest primitive dance—The Twist. It doesn't matter which.

Americans grab at new fads so greedily that promotion-minded companies regularly parlay them into big money. For example, more than $45-million worth of products, including half a million tubes of lipstick bearing the name or image of Elvis Presley, were sold in the past five years.

This season it's The Twist, a violent exercise in hip gyration that already has put many grownups—who have taken to it as avidly as teenagers—to bed with back trouble. Its champion is Chubby Checker, a 20 year-old song-and-dance man from Philadelphia, who is just beginning to cash in on the fad.

Business Week *examining America's latest dance craze in Staff, "'Twist' wiggles into big time,"* Business Week, *December 2, 1961, pp. 44–46.*

Chubby Checker poses for his high school graduation picture in 1960. *(Chubby Checker/TEEC Recording Company)*

There is nothing superhuman, however, about being an astronaut. There is nothing spooky or supernatural about flying in space. I have talked to people, both before and after my orbital flight, who seemed to think that both of these propositions were true and that an astronaut must have to be some sort of Yogi and put himself into a trance of some kind to go through such an experience.

In the summer of 1962, astronaut John Glenn responding to reporters who say that he is America's number-one hero of the early 1960s, in Segel, Men in Space *(1975), p. 15.*

As John Glenn, dressed in a neat dark suit and tan and white tie, stepped out of the Lockheed Jetstar, a great cheer went up. After Glenn hugged and kissed his wife, Annie, long and hard, he hastily wiped his eyes, then grasped David and Lyn and gave his mother a long hug. His father just shook his hand and said, "How're you doing, son?" It was obvious John Glenn was doing all right. His tan face was wreathed in smiles. As the cheering continued someone waved a banner back and forth that read, WELCOME TO EARTH. Another sign read simply, THANKS JOHN GLENN.

Then a parade began that Cocoa Beach residents will long remember. Glenn sat on the back seat of a convertible with one arm firmly around Annie. As he approached, women held up children, babies, even dogs. One woman standing beside the road played a solo on a trumpet. On the lawns of plush motels, steel drum and calypso bands blared out welcoming music. People stood and sat on roofs, on ladders, and, where construction was going on, on tractors and earth movers.

NASA historian William Shelton describing Florida's John Glenn Day in late 1962, in his American Space Exploration: The First Decade *(1967), pp. 209–210.*

Speaking personally, despite the tremendous adventure involved in my relatively simple ballistic flight of *Liberty Bell 7,* I've always felt, as a test pilot, that man should not simply be along for the ride. There are many decisions the little black boxes simply can not make, especially in the gray areas. To the little black boxes it is either *go* or *no-go.* If they're been in complete charge when a signal indicated that the *Friendship 7's* heat shield might be coming loose,

John Glenn's flight might well have ended in disaster. The signal was false. John took charge, and that established man's function in the space once and for all. There was a job for him to do, and only he could do it.

Astronaut Virgil "Gus" Grissom explaining to the press that it is regular Americans, not superheroes or computers, who will determine the success of the country's space program in late 1962 and beyond, in Grissom, Gemini: A Personal Account of Man's Venture into Space *(1968), p. 10.*

In 1962, Paul Goodman remarked that a recent eastern high school poll had found *Mad* a close second to *Life* as the most widely read magazine. ("That is," he added deftly, "the picture magazine that publishes the slick ads, and the cartoon magazine that scoffs at them.")

When Jacqueline Kennedy was pictured in newspapers dancing the Twist, its street credibility dissolved. Dance halls and discotheques—like pop music in general—gain little energy from the patronage of high society but have always relied on the enthusiasm of the young, the working class and the marginalised. Most important dance venues have been away from the mainstream, towards the edge of town.

Pop culture critic Dave Haslam commenting on the "working class" importance of post–World War II music in London's Beat *Magazine in December 1961.* What the Twist Did for the Peppermint Lounge, *p. 4. URL: www.lrb.co.uk/v22/n01/hasl2201.htm.*

What hillbilly music does to the hillbilly music fan is absolutely phenomenal. It transports him into a wild, emotional and audible state of ecstasy. He never sits back sedately patting his palms politely and uttering bravos of music appreciation for the country-style music and nasal-twanged singing he loves by whistling shrilly through teeth, pounding the palms together with the whirling momentum of a souped-up paddle wheel, stomping the floor and ejecting yip-yip noises like the barks of a hound dog when it finally runs down a particularly elusive coon.

In late December 1961 opera critic and Orlando Sentinel *reporter Jean Yothers criticizing rock-and-roll music as a "hillbilly" experience, in Colbert,* Eyewitness to America *(1997), p. 455.*

The Bay of Pigs and Berlin

There will not be, under any conditions, any intervention in Cuba by United States armed forces, and this government will do everything it possibly can—and I think it can meet its responsibilities—to make sure that there are no Americans involved in any actions inside Cuba . . . the basic issue in Cuba is not one between the United States and Cuba; it is between the Cubans themselves. And I intend to see that we adhere to that principle . . . this administration's attitude is so understood and shared by the anti-Castro exiles from Cuba in this country.

President Kennedy denying that the United States will be invading Cuba, five days before the Bay of Pigs invasion, and at an April 12, 1961 news conference, Research Room, JFK Library.

I asked about the Cubans' morale. He said, "Last night they were really mad at us. But today they have calmed down a lot and, believe it or not, they are ready to go out and fight again if we will give them the word and the support."

With that he jumped up from his chair and began pacing back and forth in front of his desk. His anger and frustration poured out in a profane barrage. Over and over he cursed everyone who had advised him: the CIA, the Chairman of the Joint Chiefs of Staff, members of his White House staff. "I was assured by every son of a bitch I checked with—all the military experts and the CIA—that the plan would succeed," he said.

Richard Nixon recalling an April 1961 meeting with John Kennedy during the Bay of Pigs invasion, in The Memoirs of Richard Nixon *(1978), p. 234.*

Bob Kennedy's reaction to the news of the Bay of Pigs fiasco was emotional and belligerent. During a series of National Security Council meetings following the invasion by the Cuban expatriates, he was one of many who felt that we must do something—anything—to somehow regain the ground that we had lost. The Kennedy Administration had suffered acute embarrassment, and neither Jack nor Bob Kennedy was accustomed to setbacks. For years they moved from success to success, and here, for perhaps the first time in their political careers, was evidence of a gross misjudgment.

Chester Bowles, the U.S. ambassador to India and Kennedy family friend, recalling the April 1961 Bay of Pigs, crisis in Robert F. Kennedy Oral History Project, JFK Library.

Was it true, he asked, that people in Communist countries couldn't get out? And wasn't an American who went to Russia accused of being a Communist when he came home? When I told him the Russians were in effect prisoners in their own land and that fifteen thousand American tourists would be going to the Soviet Union in 1959, he seemed genuinely surprised. "This is very interesting," he said. "I should have more time to talk with people who travel and who know about these things."

Foreign affairs reporter William Attwood interviewing Fidel Castro, 1961, in Attwood, The Twilight Struggle: Tales of the Cold War *(1987), The Papers of William Attwood, Ambassador to Guinea, JFK Library.*

I think jet fighter bombers and missiles in Cuba could impose a degree of blackmail upon the United States in our dealing with our problems in all parts of the world, which would be extremely serious for us.

Secretary of State Dean Rusk, one month after the Bay of Pigs in May 1961 predicting to Congress what might happen next, in Cuban Crises File, Research Room, JFK Library.

His beautiful wife of French descent made such a sensational hit with Parisian masses that the President quipped, "I am the man who accompanied Jacqueline Kennedy to Paris." The exquisitely gowned First Lady traveled with forty pieces of luggage, and while in Paris, she purchased a French gown to wear at the glittering dinner-ballet at Versailles Palace. Her personal maid took care of the wardrobe, and Jackie devoted long hours each day to French, Australian, and English hairdressers, who tried to outdo one another with elaborate coiffures for the photogenic First Lady.

White House reporter Ruth Montgomery remembering the Kennedys' triumphant May 1961 visit to Paris in her Hail to the Chiefs: My Life and Times with Six Presidents *(1970, p. 240.*

The Alliance for Progress represents the response of free peoples to the problems of our times. Like Tiradentes and Jefferson, who helped forge the political philosophy of the New World, we are given the opportunity to set economic and social goals whereby the age-old specters of fear, want, disease, and ignorance can be overcome. Together then, let us press for-

First Lady Jacqueline Kennedy poses for her first official portrait.
(Mark Shaw, Library of Congress)

ward under this Alliance and meet these challenges so that our peoples can enjoy that full incasure of Order and Progress for which Brazil and the United States are so well known and for which we both can be justly proud.

President Kennedy, summer 1961, urging the Brazilian government to welcome his new Alliance for Progress organization, in Formulation of the Alliance for Progress, a July 1961 memo in the Theodore C. Sorensen Papers, JFK Library.

If we were expelled from that area and if we accepted the loss of our rights no one would have any confidence in US commitments and pledges. . . . If we were to accept the Soviet proposal US commitments would be regarded as a mere scrap of paper. West

Europe is vital to our national security and we have supported it in two wars. If we were to leave West Berlin, Europe would be abandoned as well. So when we are talking about West Berlin we are also talking about Western Europe.

John Kennedy stating his position in 1961 on the future of Berlin, in Berlin Crisis, White House Central File, JFK Library.

(1) A clear demonstration of Western determination to defend the Allied position in Berlin, at the risk of war if necessary.

(2) An active diplomat program, including negotiations with the Soviet Union, designed to provide the Soviet leadership with an alternative course of action which does not endanger vital Western interests in Berlin.

The State Department recommending in July 1961 that President Kennedy take two approaches to resolve the Berlin crisis, in White, Kennedy: The New Frontier Revisited *(1998), pp. 110–111.*

We are committed to no rigid formulas. We seek no perfect solution. We recognize that troops and tanks can, for a time, keep a nation divided against its will, however unwise that policy may seem to us. But we believe a peaceful agreement is possible which protects the freedom of West Berlin and allied presence and access, while recognizing the historic and legitimate interests of others in assuring European security.

Kennedy assuring a peaceful, diplomatic solution to the Berlin crisis during a full 1961 speech before the United Nations General Assembly, quoted in the United States Department of State's Documents on Germany, 1944–1985 *(1986), p. 796.*

New Frontier Diplomacy

The United States has a powerful capacity to destroy, in all practical respects, the Soviet Union, either before or after a first strike. I might indicate, without being able to follow too far down the track, that a considerable increase in the certainty of certain kinds of technical information about Soviet capabilities and installation has greatly increased the nuclear power of the United States, because its targeting has been so more efficient. This has been one of the major changes in the last 2 years in that respect.

> *Secretary of State Dean Rusk assessing the spring 1961 impact of the Bay of Pigs invasion and the Berlin crisis on U.S. nuclear defense during a closed congressional hearing, in the U.S. Congress's* Executive Sessions of the Senate Foreign Relations Committee, Vol. XIV *1986, pp. 73–74.*

There are times when a Secretary of State must learn to say nothing at considerable length.

> *Secretary of State Dean Rusk stating a favorite May 1961 expression, quoted in the Robert F. Kennedy Oral History Project, JFK Library.*

We consider that we must recognize the dangers of exclusive reliance on general nuclear war as an instrument of policy and make the effort required to build a strong non-nuclear capability as well. We believe that the United States and the NATO Alliance must, in the worlds of President Kennedy, "have a wider choice than humiliation or all-out nuclear action."

> *In May 1961, Secretary of Defense Robert McNamara assuring Congress that the White House will always attempt to negotiate with the Soviets. Quoted in the* U.S. Congress's Executive Sessions of the Senate Foreign Relations Committee, *Vol. XIV (1986), p. 151.*

In 1961, an employee with the Federal Emergency Management Agency displays "survival supplies" for the proper family fallout shelter. *(National Archives)*

I suppose that all of us feel the same about December 7, 1941. However, we are now trying to IMPROVE Japanese-American relationships, and I doubt that calling the Japanese names each year is calculated to achieve that purpose.

President Kennedy responding to a bill proposed by Massachusetts Congressman Leo O'Brien to make Pearl Harbor Day (December 7) a national holiday, in Kennedy to O'Brien, May 4, 1961, in Box 62 of the White House Central File, JFK Library.

I would appreciate receiving a weekly report on what progress we are making on Civil Defense. Do you think it would be useful for me to write a letter to every home owner in the United States giving them instructions as to what can be done on their own to provide greater security for their family, or should we look into this at a later date after your organization has been completed.

President John Kennedy to Secretary of Defense Robert McNamara, August 10, 1961. "Civil Defense." URL: www.NAIL.org/civildefense

Laos and Vietnam

Our government forces are better armed. But officers admit the Communists have them running in circles. Maj. Nguyen Bang, the 34-year old chief of Darlac Province, points wearily at his maps and says: "Not even half the trails are shown. We almost never know where the Viet Cong are until they strike. By the time we get our forces there they are gone."

Robert P. Martin reporting that Vietnam will be a difficult war to win in "Jungle War from the Inside: An Eyewitness Report," U.S. News and World Report *(October 30, 1961), p. 10.*

I am shocked at the report on the spread of polio in the Trust Territory. It seems to me that this is inexcusable. How much would it have cost to have taken precautionary steps? Is there a difference in treatment for United States citizens in this country and the people for whom the United States is responsible in the Trust Territory? In short, I would like a complete investigation into the reason why the

United States government did not meet its responsibility in this area.

President Kennedy arguing that the "whole Cold War is at stake" and complaining to Secretary of the Interior Stewart Udall that America needs to take care of its "wards" in the U.S.-administered Trust Territory of the Pacific Islands, in a Kennedy memo to Udall, November 4, 1961, Box 940 of the White House Central File, JFK Library.

When the Prime Minister replied proudly that there were no Communists in his country, his high American official host said in embarrassment, "Then we can't help you. Congress would never vote you aid unless there is a Communist threat." On the Prime Minister's way home, he stopped in Paris and asked his friend the French Foreign Minister for a favor: "Lend us some of your Communists, to start a riot or two and get on American television." The Frenchman replied, "I'm sorry, we want U.S. aid too. We need every Communist we've got."

White House aide Harris Wofford remembering a popular late 1961 joke in the early Kennedy administration, in Papers of Harris Llewellyn Wofford, JFK Library.

Ending Racism

Everything happened so quick. There was a standstill for the first two or three minutes. . . . They were closin' in on us, and we were standin' still tryin' to decide what should we do in order to protect the whites we had with us. But then you had a middle-aged white female hollerin,' "Git them niggers, git them niggers . . .," and that urged the crowd on. From then on, they was constantly movin' in. I don't think she ever hit anybody or threw anything whatsoever. Just the idea she started, just kept pushin' and pushin' and pushin'. . . . It started just like that.

Freedom Rider William Harbour remembering a race riot in 1961 Alabama, in Raines, My Soul Is Rested: Movement Days in the Deep South Remembered *(1977), Rare Documents File-Civil Rights Movement, Institute for African-American Studies, Bradley University.*

The issue before the world today is whether democracy works better than tyranny or tyranny better than democracy. Your aid and support in passing the Public Accommodations Bill will eliminate a source of embarrassment that greatly damages our relations with not only the neutral nations of the world, but many nations which are stoutly with us in the fight for freedom. This Bill if passed will prove that democracy does work, that in a democracy the rights and privileges of the individual are protected in accordance with the will of the people. . . . The Department of State comes to you now with a request. GIVE US THE WEAPONS TO CONDUCT THIS WAR OF HUMAN DIGNITY. The fight for decency against Communism is everyone's war in America.

Pedro Sanjuan, the director of the Special Protocol Service, urging the state governments of Maryland and Virginia to end racist legislation. Address by Pedro Sanjuan, September 13, 1961, Box MS78-21/Campaign in Maryland in the Papers of Pedro Sanjuan, JFK Library.

From the Montgomery bus boycott to the confrontations of the sit-ins, then on to the Rock Hill jail-in and now to the mass assault on the Mississippi prisons, there was a "movement" in both senses of the word—a moving spiritual experience, and a steady expansion of scope. The theater was spreading through the entire South. One isolated battle had given way to many scattered ones, and now in the Mississippi jails they were moving from similar experiences to a common experience.

In October 1961, civil rights activist Taylor Branch explaining how protests against racism became a "movement," in D'Angelo, The American Civil Rights Movement: Readings and Interpretations *(2001), p. 281.*

Adding the new dimension of civil disobedience to the popular struggle and bringing the other two branches of the federal government into action made major progress toward racial integration possible—and necessary. . . . The government of the United States is pro-

pelled by three engines—the legislative, executive, and judicial—but before John Kennedy became president, it was operating, in civil rights, on only one engine, the judiciary. The issue did not fully engage Kennedy either, until the movement for civil rights and the violence used in combating it brought the matter to a head so forcefully that he could not put it aside.

Harris Wofford, John Kennedy's civil rights adviser, assessing the late 1961 transition of the civil rights cause in Papers of Harris Llewellyn Wofford, JFK Library.

I thought a good deal more needed to be done. I felt that of course this was the area in which we had the greatest authority; and if we were going to do anything on civil rights, we should do it in that field where we had the authority. And number two: I felt strongly that this was where the most good could be accomplished. I suppose that's coming out of a political background, but I felt that the vote really makes a major difference. From the vote, from participation in the elections, flow all other rights far, far more easily. A great deal could be accomplished internally within a state if the Negroes participated in elections and voted.

Attorney General Robert Kennedy explaining his 1961–62 priorities in civil rights reform, in Robert F. Kennedy Oral History Project, JFK Library.

A lot of troops were used to get me in the University of Mississippi. Really a lot of troops. . . . I mean I don't think the Russians sent that many into Czechoslovakia. It seemed to me very clear that Bobby Kennedy was the main man in determining that these steps be taken. Had they not made the decisions they made, the course of my life would have been different. Bobby sent the marshals. He could have sent just two. His decisions kept me alive. I'm still here.

James Meredith recalling his 1962 effort to attend the University of Mississippi, in Robert F. Kennedy Oral History Project, JFK Library.

2

Lost in the Cold War
January 1962–September 1962

The threat of nuclear war "haunted him," Kennedy press secretary Pierre Salinger remembered of his boss. According to Salinger, Kennedy worried about the impact of his own rhetoric on the escalation of the cold war, and he shared these same worries with his brothers and family friends. In his inaugural address, Kennedy had noted that the United States must never negotiate out of fear, but it must "never fear to negotiate." In those strident days of the cold war, engaging in nuclear diplomacy with the Soviets was easier said than done.

LAWRENCE OF ARABIA MEETS THE NEW FRONTIER

"Here, let me take your bloody rotten picture for the bloody rotten newspaper." With these words, a veteran newspaper reporter denounced, in his view, the hypocrisy of an alleged hero, the hero's country, and his country's foreign policy. In reality, the reporter misjudged his subject. He was also actor Arthur Kennedy, and the hero was another actor, Peter O'Toole. Both stars appeared in 1962's biggest blockbuster film, *Lawrence of Arabia,* and it won the Academy Award for best picture that year. The movie was about the fascinating life of British adventurer and intellectual T. E. Lawrence, his love for the Middle East, and his disgust for colonization. The movie implied that long before there were "ugly Americans" in the 1960s, there were "ugly Englishmen" during the era of World War I. Although a troubled soul and an unusual hero, T. E. Lawrence, the film suggested, was one Englishman who was a notable exception to the colonial status quo of the day.

President Kennedy, a fan of the film, said that the United States had much to learn from men like Lawrence. The president implied that Lawrence, or at least O'Toole's masterly portrayal of him, constituted another one of those "profiles in courage." Lawrence's view that an ethical foreign policy should include the needs and wants of developing nations (such as those residents in Saudi Arabia) bolstered the anti-"ugly" foreign policy message that the Kennedy team also supported. As always, the Kennedys were good at connecting policy to a phenomenon in popular culture like *Lawrence of Arabia.* But talking about ethics in foreign policy and making ethical foreign policy were two different matters. It was also unlikely that the real Lawrence, who died in the mid-1930s, would have remained silent on the issue of American arrogance in developing nations of the world. In practice, the Kennedy administration escalated the nuclear arms race and lost little sleep over the possibility that Lawrence's beloved Middle East might be blown up in the process.[1]

Throughout much of 1962, Kennedy's so-called buzz words in anticommunist speeches continued to suggest a horrible confrontation to come. The 1960 campaign talk of a "missile gap" was soon replaced by "massive retaliation," "flexible response," and "doomsday" strategies. *Massive retaliation* was a term often used by Secretary of State John Foster Dulles in the 1950s to describe America's nuclear solution to communist expansionism in Europe and the developing nations. Kennedy not only expanded the definition to include both nuclear and conventional forces, but he also insisted that the commander-in-chief alone reserves the right to respond to communist pressures as he sees fit. Labeled *flexible response,* this Kennedy policy represented the triumph of executive privilege at the time and placed a certain life-and-death power in the hands of the Oval Office that rejected congressional interference. Since President Harry Truman had announced that the cold war was equivalent to a national emergency, the presidency enjoyed the benefit of the doubt in most defense matters. Hence, Kennedy's concern that he now controlled the very future of the planet.

An obvious example of the translation of cold war victory rhetoric into policy was the Defense Department's answer to any possible Soviet expansion into Western Europe. It involved a certain doomsday strategy of firing off nearly all U.S. nuclear missiles at the Soviet Union. By 1962, 82 percent of America's nuclear missiles were pointed at Soviet targets alone. The anticipated casualty figure was conservatively pegged at 300 million dead. Although his own speeches had always implied such a response, Kennedy was shocked and angered to learn in 1962 that this was the only contingency supported by his military.

Some of the reasons behind the doomsday approach involved simple matters of expense. In the early 1950s, some 400,000 U.S. troops stood at the ready in Europe, an equal number of dependents often lived with them, and another 100,000 U.S. government workers added to the mission. America's huge trade surplus helped pay for their bases, salaries, and material. By 1960, the rising European economies, changing trade policies, and the opening of U.S. corporations in Europe ended those heady days of surplus payments. Good financial management of the U.S. military infrastructure in Europe became part of the Kennedy administration's effort to end the economic recession at home, although little was said about it in public. As the Eisenhower White House had long suggested, it was cheaper to rely on a nuclear arsenal than maintain huge overseas bases. Kennedy continued this approach in spite of his speeches in favor of the large combination of conventional and nuclear forces. It also put the world in great jeopardy. Meanwhile, the Western European governments were supposed to endorse America's every move, and Kennedy assumed that they stood in complete solidarity with his defense plans. He was wrong.

Announcing that the U.S.–Western Europe defense arrangement was equivalent to a "Grand Design," Kennedy touted American-European cooperation as unified, cooperative, and happy. But the European governments worried that Kennedy saw their home as a nuclear battlefield, that their booming economies were irrelevant to the United States, and that America's congressmen, businessmen, and average citizens had no say in the matter thanks to executive privilege. As in the case of the doomsday strategy, Kennedy was shocked to learn that the European governments had minds of their own, even favoring more attempts at negotiations with Moscow than were politically acceptable to U.S. voters.

The Grand Design was symptomatic of a certain policy approach in the Kennedy administration that was as flawed as it was unfortunate. Like many Americans, Kennedy had assumed that the anticommunist allies recognized U.S. cold war leadership without dissent. This allowed the young president to speak of the allies in very general, regional terms. As the anti-"Ugly American" policymaker, Kennedy was supposed to recognize that regions were made up of individual countries and governments with their own ambitions and agendas. But he drew the line on nuclear defense issues. Meanwhile, challenges to America's nuclear authority did not have to come from Europe.[2] The Japanese were the first to lodge an official complaint, although it took some time for Kennedy to accept their point of view.

Responding to a series of public demonstrations against American nuclear-powered submarines and aircraft carriers making port in Japan, Prime Minister Hayato Ikeda pointed out to Kennedy that his country remained extremely sensitive to nuclear matters. He worried about American nuclear accidents in Japanese ports, and he also worried that the American bases in Japan would be an early target of Soviet nuclear missiles during any war between the United States and the Soviet Union. Instead of evaluating the prime minister's concerns, Kennedy ordered Dr. Edwin Reischauer, the U.S. ambassador to Japan, to lecture Ikeda on the need for allied solidarity. Admired in Japan for his flashy Kennedyesque lifestyle and mastery of the Japanese language, Reischauer had given public lectures on the need for Japanese solidarity in the past. Since the Japanese always sought a greater share of the American market for their developing export economy, Reischauer warned them that their dream of full penetration of the U.S. market could remain quite elusive if they did not fully welcome U.S. defense policies.[3]

To Kennedy and his New Frontiersmen, individual policies in the allied ranks equaled confusion behind the lines. A united front was necessary for cold war victory. Reischauer and other Kennedy men in the field were expected to succeed with their lecturing efforts, and that was that. In official cabinet discussions about Japan and the European allies, fellow anticommunist nations were referred to as "lieutenants" as opposed to partners. "Lieutenants," Secretary McNamara noted in the summer of 1962, do not consult with generals. They follow orders.[4] Nevertheless, McNamara agreed with national security advisor Walt Rostow that the military terminology might be demeaning to some allies. Nations such as Japan or Great Britain would now be asked to "coordinate" their defense policies with the United States, thereby avoiding abrasive terms such as *ordered to comply with Washington*.

The key to successful "coordination" involved allied acceptance of what the Defense Department called Mutual Assured Destruction (MAD). Two points were critical here. First, Kennedy insisted that only the United States could launch an assault against the Soviets. The allies were to remain in a supportive role and avoid any nationalist sword rattling of their own. Second, a potential nuclear attack on the Soviet Union did nothing to halt the growing appeal of communism in former European colonies. Promising some financial assistance, Kennedy urged the Europeans to build up their conventional forces. This could only be interpreted by communists in developing nations as an expanding potential force against them. But the Kennedy cabinet was divided on what that might mean for America's anticommunist allies in developing nations. The specter of a returning European army, whether under U.S. command or not, would not win the United States many friends in these former European possessions. It was also unlikely that the Europeans would support such a return themselves, for their top defense priority in the 1960s was self-preservation in the face of the huge Red Army to the east.

The Kennedy administration had no problem analyzing this dilemma. Finding a workable policy was another matter. In June 1962, just four months before the Cuban Missile Crisis, Secretary of State Dean Rusk admitted that it was just a matter of time before the United States truly faced the threat of World War III. It was "anybody's guess," he noted privately, how that crisis might be handled and where the allies would stand.[5] A lone-wolf character such as T. E. Lawrence, who jousted against the status quo policies of the hour, would have had little chance of success in the Kennedy cabinet of 1962. Any Kennedy cabinet member who suggested a retreat from cold war confrontation ran the risk of being labeled soft on communism. That remained the political kiss of death at the time. Although Kennedy's public image suggested that he welcomed T. E. Lawrence–like dissenters in his own policy-making efforts, that was not an accurate picture of the Kennedy team.

FAILURE ON CAPITOL HILL

Demanding solidarity from Capitol Hill was as difficult for the Kennedy team as nuclear diplomacy with the allies. Shortly after taking office, Kennedy and his supporters in Congress successfully reformed the House Rules Committee to benefit White House legislation. Since the Rules Committee remains the first, and some say, most important stop for legislation en route to becoming law, the press touted Kennedy's success as a brilliant political move. But this did not guarantee an easy time for the Kennedy domestic agenda. The Rules Committee would never be receptive to legislation it deemed overly ambitious, and Kennedy lacked the progressive, New Deal–like coalition in Congress to win quick passage for his proposals.

Kennedy's 1960 campaign and especially his inaugural address suggested that his administration would have a certain Olympian reach. From eradicating disease to ending racism, Kennedy promised to take bold "first steps." The enthralled public met this commitment with resounding approval ratings, and the pressure was on the Kennedy White House to make good on it all.

Through his own lofty rhetoric, Kennedy had built a legislative agenda that required Herculean efforts to create, argue, and pass. Because of the heady ambition of the New Frontier, Kennedy's legislative record would always look weak to those who expected great drama and excitement in every Kennedy measure. Much of what Kennedy passed into law did not fulfill those

Sophisticated and elegant, First Lady Jacqueline Kennedy contributed to the aura and mystique of the New Frontier. Here, Kennedy displays a beautiful silver pitcher that was donated to the White House collection. *(John F. Kennedy Library)*

expectations, leading many to conclude that the Kennedy domestic record was hollow. However, this was not the case.

Although it might have been nuts-and-bolts to some, Kennedy's legislative successes were obvious. The minimum wage increased. A special fund was created for manpower training and area redevelopment. His "first step" to fully opening the United States to products from Japan and elsewhere (the Trade Expansion Act or TEA) was hailed overseas as a great example of American generosity. More Americans rose above the poverty line in the early 1960s than at any time since the Korean War, and the Commerce Department credited Kennedy for creating a new era of uninterrupted growth.

Declaring himself a believer in more conservative than liberal fiscal policies in 1962, Kennedy even decided that a tax cut that risked budget deficits would, at the same time, build upon the consumer power of the American voter. This fiscal approach, nicknamed "New Economics," meant that the president was not a slave to New Deal solutions. Helping industry could also mean helping workers. Most U.S. industrialists welcomed this point of view, although the tax cut was not finalized and passed until after the Kennedy assassination. U.S. business particularly welcomed Kennedy's insistence that a balanced budget was important for the country's future. At the same time, Kennedy's defense spending increase and the space program brought more billions into the economy. In fact, by the time an American did indeed reach the moon (July 1969), more than $25 billion was spent on space exploration projects alone.

Kennedy's success with bread-and-butter economic issues won few accolades in their day. Especially for his diehard supporters, the real test of Kennedy effectiveness involved the passing of education, transportation, civil rights, and medical care reform bills. In the education bill, Kennedy's reputation as the Harvard man and *Profiles in Courage* scholar was supposed to play a pivotal role. Or so said the press. But the pivotal role was played by Republican Adam Clayton Powell from New York City's Harlem district. During the educational reform fights of the 1950s, Powell had always added an integration rider to any legislation. The latter always resulted in tough Southern-led opposition and defeat. This time, Kennedy convinced Powell to cease his efforts, for a specific, sweeping civil rights bill was also on the agenda. It worked, but the opposition to the Education Bill came from an unexpected quarter.

As a Catholic, Kennedy could have included aid to private schools in his general education package, but he refused to do so. There was to be no special treatment or provisions for Catholic schools; however, Catholic educators assumed there would be. These Catholic educators fought the Kennedy bill because of this exclusion and played a leading role in the bill's defeat. The threat of a Constitutional challenge, based on the separation of church and state axiom, complicated matters as well.

In the transportation bill, Kennedy, like Eisenhower before him, was ready to finance new highways projects, bridge construction, and almost anything that benefited America's car culture. On the other hand, Kennedy spoke at length about his travels overseas, his observation of elaborate public transportation systems in the major European capitals, and how similar or improved-upon systems in the United States could ease gridlock, move urbanites more efficiently, and save cities money. Having truly benefited from the transportation legislation of the 1950s, the American automobile industry was shocked. Kennedy could not be serious. Meanwhile, conservatives attacked the transportation bill as foolish urban planning based on "European ideas." Although the public transportation section of the bill was not a priority part of the legislation, the resulting debate led to its defeat. Kennedy said that the American people expected innovative legislation in the 1960s, but Congress simply was not in an innovative mood.

Compromising on the legal language of these measures would have gone a long way to deaden some of the opposition. But Kennedy, enthusiastically supported by most of his cabinet, often saw his efforts in a strong moral light. Instead of cutting, changing, or softening aspects of his own legislation in Congress, Kennedy brought his case to the American people. His oratory and general popularity were always powerful strengths, and he won loud applause for his commitment to "new directions without compromise." In 1962, at Milwaukee's Serb Hall, a popular gathering spot for union activists and Democratic Party supporters, Kennedy, paraphrasing Woodrow Wilson, assaulted the "small minds" in Congress who did not understand the necessity for change. To fight for the integrity of all the details in his legislation, Kennedy insisted, was what any good president must do. It was a matter of leadership as well as decent law. He urged his listeners to support him, lobby their congressmen, and continue the march to the New Frontier. It was classic Kennedy, and the speech was repeated elsewhere. But it had little impact on Congress. The transportation bill was defeated, as was the president's effort to provide government-led health care protection to America's elderly.

Vice President Lyndon Johnson had a simple solution to all of Kennedy's legislative problems. Urging moderation and Franklin Roosevelt–style wheeling and dealing, Johnson had little use for cross-country speaking tours when serious legislation faced a tough fight on Capitol Hill. The gracious president always thanked Johnson for his advice, but Attorney General Robert Kennedy wondered if the vice president was truly a good New Frontier supporter. Robert Kennedy believed in the high moral worth of White House legislation, and congressional deals compromised that worth.

The tenor of the times also rendered President Kennedy's frenetic national tours useless. Since much of Kennedy's administration was marked by its serious foreign affairs crises, the press thought that the president's speeches on behalf of domestic legislation efforts, such as transportation and education, lacked significance, passion, or even interest. In the face of the endless threats of World War III, heavy discussions about subways, schools, or elder care seemed quite irrelevant to America's so-called newspapers of record, the *Washington Post* and the *New York Times*.

It was much more difficult for the press and the voters to disregard the civil rights fight. In spite of Kennedy's eloquent calls for social justice, his administration kept civil rights reform on the back burner for more than 18 months. During this period, Kennedy appointed five federal judges in the South who strongly supported the segregationist tradition. Meanwhile, Kennedy's civil rights bill was carefully crafted only after civil rights demonstrations increased and federal marshals had been dispatched.

Taking a high moral tone, this legislation was challenged by the very Rules Committee that the Kennedy team had rebuilt to fit the White House agenda. Lacking precise references to legal jurisdiction and desegregation expenses, the original Kennedy civil rights bill resembled more the stock speech than enforceable law. Courting accusations of racism, the Rules Committee asked the White House for a more specific piece of legislation. John and Robert Kennedy responded in the same way as they had with the transportation, education, and health care reform bills. A public speaking offensive was launched, but the law was not changed. The result was an awkward limbo for one of the more important examples of 20th-century social legislation. Its passage would require the legislative skill of Lyndon Johnson, and a later day.[6]

The great arguments over social reform and race relations were also yet to come. In 1962, most white Americans had more questions than answers about social change. Most of the warning signs of changing America were symbolic ones and sometimes more obvious in popular culture than in popular politics. For instance, a great symbol of 1950s materialism, sexism, and escapism, actress

Marilyn Monroe, died in early August 1962. Born Norma Jeane Mortenson in 1926, Norma Jeane (later Jean) became Marilyn 20 years later. This model-turned-actress was usually described as a "blonde bombshell," "bubble head," or, according to author Norman Mailer, "the Stradivarius of sex."[7] Always stylish and alluring, she represented the good life of the 1950s, and she had no apologies for it. But behind the glitter were years of personal torment as well as drug and alcohol abuse. Her career and, some say, her good looks were fading in the early 1960s. Marilyn Monroe's death, thanks to an overdose of 47 Nembutal and chloral hydrate pills, represented the end of a Hollywood era.

While Marilyn faded, a new pop icon emerged. Bob Dylan could not have been more opposite of Hollywood glitter and escapism. In fact, wedding Woody Guthrie–like protest messages to his folk-rock music, Dylan represented a new type of 1960s superstar. Released in 1962, *The Freewheelin' Bob Dylan* was his second album, but it was his first moneymaker. Once describing himself as a simple country boy living the simple life in New York City, Dylan praised the politically active poor, rejected materialism, and saw youth protest as pure and heroic. Without question, 1962 was a transitional year for this young Minnesota transplant, but, as he predicted in his music, times were changing for the whole country as well.[8]

SUKARNO AND DE GAULLE

Time and experience taught the Kennedy White House that compromise just might be the art of politics as well as foreign policy. Dealing with Indonesia's Achmed Sukarno and France's Charles de Gaulle especially proved the point. Even more than Cuba's Castro, Sukarno touted himself as the new 1960s leader of the nonaligned developing nations, urging other Asian, African, and Latin American nations to follow his lead. Although he never considered his beloved France part of the developing nations, the leader of that country's Fifth Republic, Charles de Gaulle, had as much use for the cold war as Sukarno. He was particularly proud of his "all-azimuth defense." That meant his nuclear missiles were pointed both at Moscow and Washington, D.C.

To the Kennedy team, Sukarno was the most dangerous man in the Asian/Pacific world, and de Gaulle held a similar title for Europe. In 1958, the Eisenhower administration had even dispatched a Central Intelligence Agency (CIA) hit squad against Sukarno. Led by veteran covert operations specialist Alan Pope, the CIA mission failed. Pope was captured, put on trial, and jailed for life. The entire matter proved to be a grand embarrassment to Eisenhower, but he won the follow-up public relations war. An angry Eisenhower publicly denied that his administration would ever attempt to kill a foreign leader, and the American people believed him.

As a major oil-producing nation, Indonesia had great economic worth to the United States, and Sukarno enjoyed a considerable degree of respect across the Asian/Pacific region. As a resistance leader against both the early 1940s Japanese occupation and then against the Dutch who attempted to reestablish their colonial regime there, Sukarno also had a reputation for invincibility. If anyone could survive on the outskirts of the cold war, it would be he.

To President Kennedy, Sukarno was an itch he could not scratch. Thumbing his nose at allied solidarity in the cold war, the Indonesian leader made political capital at home and elsewhere with his anti-American speeches and calls for "Guided Democracy" (a compromise of capitalism, communism, and traditional village rule in Indonesia). From a second assassination effort to outright invasion, the Kennedy administration weighed their options for months.

In 1962, the Indonesian–U.S. relationship worsened when Sukarno threatened to invade West Irian in New Guinea. Controlled by a lingering Dutch government, West Irian was one of the last examples of Asian/Pacific colonialism. Sukarno vowed to destroy it. The Dutch government, a close American ally in Europe, insisted that the United States was sworn to its defense anywhere, anyplace, anytime. A Dutch-Indonesian war could provide the Kennedy administration with the needed excuse for armed intervention and the end of Sukarno. Yet the Kennedy cabinet debated and debated the matter.

With Vietnam slowly becoming the symbol of American anticommunist efforts in Southeast Asia, could the United States afford two wars in that region? Could the United States live with Sukarno's disparaging speeches? Prominent economist and Kennedy security policy adviser Walt Rostow believed that Sukarno was doomed because of his country's own poverty and misery. "You can't eat 'Guided Democracy,'" he liked to say. Sooner rather than later, Rostow predicted, the Indonesian leader's own people would rise up against him. But the Communist Party was strong there. Sukarno could be replaced by someone even more opposed to the American cause. It was a tenuous situation, making 1962 a decisive year.

Once it was concluded that continuing to deal with Sukarno made better sense than trying to displace him, President Kennedy dispatched his brother Robert to a private summit with the Indonesian leader. Sukarno agreed to release Alan Pope from prison, and the Kennedy administration promised never to launch new assassination squads and never to assist the Dutch. A modest U.S. aid program was arranged, and Sukarno hinted that he would downplay all future nonalignment/pro-"Guided Democracy" efforts. The peace was then assured, but this type of diplomacy failed to spread to nearby Vietnam.[9] At the same time, the Kennedy team desperately sought some sort of arrangement with de Gaulle. It was not easy.

Although the French leader's policies never had the White House contemplating a war, de Gaulle did prove most annoying and frustrating to the Kennedy team. Without question, he was a maverick, a loner, and a champion of France's lost honor and glory.

De Gaulle's Fifth Republic was the product of a military coup staged on his behalf only three years before Kennedy was inaugurated. Coming to power to rescue France from its disastrous war in Algeria, de Gaulle established all the trappings of democracy. But there was no doubt who truly was in charge. Like Sukarno, de Gaulle had been a World War II leader of Free French forces in exile and enjoyed a heroic reputation at home. Like both Sukarno and Kennedy, he was also a charismatic president with a flair for the dramatic.

Some of the friction between the United States and France was of Kennedy's own making. De Gaulle had removed NATO headquarters from French soil before Kennedy was elected, forcing the new president to inherit an already struggling Franco-American relationship. Kennedy's cabinet spoke openly about the European nations most important to American policy, namely West Germany and Great Britain. To de Gaulle, this admission symbolized

America's cold war arrogance, as well as the immaturity and tactlessness of the young Kennedy team. To Kennedy, it was policy.

Defeated and broke after its colonial wars in Vietnam and Algeria, France, the Kennedy administration concluded, was no longer a major player on the world stage. This did not mean that the U.S. government was now anti-French or had no use for France in its cold war victory plans. The Kennedy administration still wanted the French to be good "lieutenants." To do so, they were expected to take a closer look at their economy, welcome efforts to connect the currencies and trade policies of neighboring European countries, and stand ready to assist nearby West Germany should World War III result.

To de Gaulle, Kennedy was asking his country to play second fiddle to their historic enemy, the Germans. He was asking it to redesign its currency, one of the last remaining symbols of French pride and independence. He was asking a once great nation to do nothing as the two dominant English-speaking powers, the United States and Great Britain, drew even closer together. In short, Kennedy was asking too much in de Gaulle's view, and, to Washington's annoyance, the French leader spoke his mind accordingly. Because of his nuclear arsenal, de Gaulle's critical comments had to be answered, the Kennedy administration reasoned. How he should be answered was a matter of great debate until Kennedy himself ended the matter. "We must never give up on de Gaulle," he told the cabinet in 1962.

Kennedy and de Gaulle met only once. Along with the first lady, Jacqueline Kennedy, the American president made his official visit to Paris in May 1961. Politically, Kennedy won nothing from de Gaulle. He urged the French president to recognize American leadership in the cold war and surrender all nuclear decisions to U.S. military guidance. De Gaulle refused.

Publicly, the Kennedy trip was a success, forcing many Frenchmen to question the anti-Kennedy conclusions of their president. With great pomp and circumstance, the Kennedys dazzled the French press and public with a display of Camelot charisma and charm. Thanks to this public relations coup and his own dogged determination, Kennedy believed that de Gaulle would eventually see things the American way. However, this would never be the case.

As always, unity and solidarity were viewed as essential foundations for cold war victory throughout the Kennedy era. Sukarno and de Gaulle pointed out that the world was not necessarily either pro-American or pro-Soviet. To Kennedy, that was always an interesting suggestion, but just another obstacle to overcome on the way to U.S.-led success.[10] Laos provided even more obstacles.

THE LAOS CRISIS

If a great Southeast Asian war was not to take place in Vietnam or Indonesia, the next candidate was Laos. In fact, at times throughout Kennedy's first months on the job, it was anybody's guess which country would carry the brunt of the U.S.-led anticommunist effort. Of these three nations, Laos presented the most staggering complications to the Kennedy team. Even the names of the Laotian politicians were confusing.

In the late 1950s, right-wing forces within Laos's new postcolonial coalition government seized control with CIA support. Prime Minister Souvanna Phouma, a prince in the Lao royal family, had tried to keep pro- and anticommunist forces in the coalition together, but his ouster ended the truce. Phouma's own half brother, Souphanouvong, was in charge of the Pathet Lao procommunist forces, and the latter led a violent crusade against the right-wing coup leader, Phoumi. Considered weak even by the CIA, Phoumi was eliminated in a second coup shortly before Kennedy took office. He was replaced by a right-wing activist named Phoui. Former Prime Minister Phouma then joined up with his half brother Souphanouvong, strengthening the Pathet Lao opposition to the right-wing regime. It was an incredible mess, but the U.S. government paid close attention.

In one of his last speeches on foreign affairs as president, Dwight Eisenhower had urged the incoming Kennedy administration to strengthen anticommunist forces in Laos. The future of Southeast Asia depended on it, he said. Kennedy welcomed the challenge, especially after both Vietnam's Ho Chi Minh and Premier Khrushchev complained that the violence in Laos was the fault of the CIA and general U.S. policy.

Although his own National Security Council described the crisis in Laos as a dynastic one whereby one royal family member competed against another, Kennedy also worried about the communist versus anticommunist dynamics of the contest. The communists, he believed, were about to win. Given the Bay of Pigs, it would be another cold war embarrassment that he could not afford.

Kennedy kept the American people informed about the problem, always stopping short when asked by the press if a large U.S. military expedition would soon be heading to Laos. Given this poor nation's remoteness from American life, the press seemed more interested in how Kennedy pronounced Laos with his Harvard/Cape Cod accent. Kennedy referred to it as "Layous."

While the press joked and Kennedy smiled, the CIA recommended an immediate U.S. military rescue of anticommunist forces in "Layous." Kennedy weighed his options. If U.S. respect was to be maintained in the region, Kennedy concluded, something had to be done soon. Inaction could trigger the feared domino effect noted in many 1950s political speeches, including his own. The domino effect was defined as the collapse of one anticommunist nation leading to the collapse of its anticommunist neighbors and so on. At home, as his administration inched closer to the 1962 congressional elections, the last thing Kennedy and his Democratic Party needed were Republican accusations of being soft on communism. Finally, if Laos went communist, the Pentagon predicted that the nation would be used as an arsenal for communist North Vietnam to supply arms to their supporters in South Vietnam.

Given the twists and turns of Laotian politics and the larger regional interests of Southeast Asian anticommunism, Kennedy hoped that whatever he did in Laos would have a positive impact on nearby Vietnam. Hence, his decision to sponsor a cease-fire. The British prime minister Harold Macmillan had especially championed this approach, and Kennedy welcomed the advice. To work, America's allies in Laos would have to lay down their arms first. Once the guns were silent throughout the country, a regional peace plan including Vietnam might be the next step. Kennedy ordered the cease-fire, and it failed. The Pathet Lao interpreted it as American weakness and attacked progovernment positions.

Although the general military situation remained in stalemate for some time, Kennedy felt foolish. Vowing never to let his guard down in Vietnam, he moved away from cease-fires or other diplomatic arrangements there. It was time to hold the line against communist expansionism in Southeast Asia, he reasoned.[11]

THE QUIET AMERICAN GETS LOUDER

Ironically, few Americans knew much about Southeast Asia, or Vietnam in particular. For those who were not regular readers of the *Washington Post* or the *New York Times,* the details of America's complex Vietnam policy remained quite elusive. If there was anything akin to public knowledge about Vietnam and its troubles, it came through the back door of popular culture. In late 1958, noted filmmaker Joseph Mankiewicz brought British author Graham Greene's novel *The Quiet American* to the screen. The film continued to make the rounds in neighborhood showings for the next two and a half years. Starring Audie Murphy and Michael Redgrave, the film represented a dark, brooding view of everyday life in Vietnam. Given Murphy's real-life background as one of America's most-decorated war heroes, he was an excellent choice to play the American espionage agent in the film. Murphy had played himself a few years before in his own personal tale of World War II heroism, *To Hell and Back.* The film was a great success, offering the young veteran a lucrative new career. Unfortunately, the film critics were rarely kind to Murphy, and film audiences found Mankiewicz's *Quiet American* to be a disturbing film that was unfit for the straight arrow Murphy.

The plot involved a cynical British journalist and drug addict (Redgrave) who resented the growing presence of American power in 1950s Vietnam. Murphy's espionage agent symbolized that power, and Redgrave's aging character also resented the young U.S. agent's success in winning the affections of the same Vietnamese girl that he pursued. The film depicted Vietnam as a place that was as sleazy as its main characters. Its viewers probably wondered why any Westerner would have a political interest in such a horrible place. Years after the Vietnam War, they would still be wondering the same thing.

In 1961, the key to winning the American public's support for a Kennedy administration rescue of South Vietnam involved heavy public relations. The sleazy image had to go. Convincing Americans that South Vietnam's problems were due to the larger international communist conspiracy was essential. But the ins and outs of Vietnamese politics confused the White House. Kennedy needed facts.

In early 1961, Kennedy dispatched a fact-finding mission to South Vietnam that included General Maxwell Taylor and Walt Rostow. They returned to the White House with a dismal report about communist inroads there. But they also predicted that President Ngo Dinh Diem could hang on with more U.S. military support. Kennedy had to make a decision, and his answer represented one of the defining moments of the 1960s. The days of America's quiet influence in Vietnamese affairs were over.

Kennedy entered the White House with fewer than 1,000 U.S. military advisers attached to Diem's struggling Army of the Republic of Vietnam (ARVN). The once united nation of Vietnam had been divided at the 17th parallel into the anticommunist South and procommunist North at the Geneva Conference on Asia during the spring of 1954. Based on the decision that had divided Korea at the 38th parallel, the Geneva Accords confirmed the French military defeat of their 70-year-old colonial government in Vietnam, called for free elections to unite the two Vietnams within a couple of years, and, in the meantime, recognized Diem in charge of the South and the mysterious communist and nationalist, Ho Chi Minh, in charge of the North. Within months, it was apparent to the Eisenhower administration that Ho, also the former anti-French resistance leader, would win the unification elections. Consequently, these elections were never held, and Ho began a campaign of terror to win control of the South.

Although Eisenhower publicly praised him as the "Churchill of Asia," Diem was his own worst enemy. A French-speaking Catholic, businessman, and dictator, Diem dreamed of a Western-style urban-based economy furthered by his American protectors. The U.S. government could identify with those

Rarely photographed outside of a propaganda setting, Ho Chi Minh is seen here in 1948 during the early days of the Vietnamese struggle against the French. *(National Archives)*

dreams, but the South Vietnamese people could not. The real South Vietnam was more than 90 percent Buddhist and agrarian. The average family viewed the French language and Western ideas as anti-Vietnamese, and they had little use for Diem's dictatorship. Diem was in serious trouble, and Kennedy had inherited another mess.

Specifically, the Taylor-Rostow mission recommended an immediate dispatch of 8,000 troops and a huge economic assistance package. Although aware of Diem's liabilities, and hoping that he would reform his family-run dictatorship before it was too late, Kennedy welcomed the Taylor-Rostow recommendations. Under Secretary of State George Ball did not, but he was the only obvious and vocal naysayer in the Kennedy cabinet. According to Ball, South Vietnam was going through a social revolution, and there was no democratic infrastructure to support. If the United States dispatched an army, he predicted that the locals would consider it an invasion. The original expedition of 8,000 would eventually need 300,000 to rescue it. This slow pattern of escalation would be a rerun of the French experience from 1947 to 1954. The Kennedy administration, Ball quipped, was supposed to be "smarter than the French."

In his own way, Ball attempted to remind the president of his Senate days when he waxed poetic on the need to view developing nations with humanity and concern versus raw anticommunist goals. Kennedy informed him that he was all wrong about Vietnam, and that the U.S. mission was much more noble than the selfish colonial policies of the French. Ball did not relent. He asked whatever happened to the young man who had asked his country to reject the "ugly American" and recognize the dreams and aspirations of developing nations' residents. Kennedy responded by ordering U.S. troops to Vietnam.[12] The president later told his brother Robert that Ball's comments had disturbed him. But what could he do? Cold war reality suggested a military response.

THE NEW PACIFIC COMMUNITY

Kennedy idealism might have waned in the face of numerous cold war crises, but that did not mean his New Frontier was over. Using their Latin American–based Alliance for Progress as an example, the Kennedy administration favored a massive "economic offensive" in the Asian/Pacific region. Involving more money and more participant nations than Kennedy's Latin American effort, this economic offensive was formally named the New Pacific Community (NPC). It soon symbolized the Kennedy determination to kill the appeal of communism in impoverished Asian/Pacific countries, and it represented one of the young president's strongest weapons in the effort to win the cold war by the end of the decade.

Between April and November 1961, Secretary of State Dean Rusk honed his plan to replace United Nations assistance efforts in the Far East with American ones. According to Rusk, the United Nations was ineffective in that region, and he agreed with Kennedy that the cold war would be won or lost in the Pacific. To counter the creation of an Asian/Pacific communist sphere of influence, Rusk proposed the most costly organization ever devised by an American government. Although rooted in U.S. national self-interest and various campaign pledges, Rusk's New Pacific Community organization was described to the press as an example of American generosity and commitment.

On paper, Rusk's plan looked like a winner. A new United Nations–like organization for the Asian/Pacific region would be established. It would be headquartered in Australia, a postwar symbol of capitalist and democratic success in the Pacific. Building that headquarters on U.S. soil, Rusk argued, would raise too many questions about the United States's own selfish goals and interests. The American taxpayer would be asked to pump roughly $50 billion into the organization, and Rusk predicted that the required raise in taxes would not be opposed by the voters. No thinking American, he said, wanted another Korean War or any other Asian conflict. A booming economy in the Asian/Pacific region would end that possibility.

The real key to voter approval, Rusk believed, was the participation of burgeoning economies and pro-U.S. governments in the region. Japan, New Zealand, Taiwan, and even Britain's Hong Kong colony would be asked to raise money for the new organization's many upcoming relief and assistance projects. This would constitute a united front of capitalist involvement, Rusk said, and it would bring quick results.

Some Asia/Pacific nations, of course, would not be invited to join. North Korea, North Vietnam, and China were labeled the enemy in Rusk's grand design. Their divorce from the NPC, Rusk predicted, would leave them in poverty and struggle. Their own people would observe the capitalist success in nearby NPC member nations and want the same thing for themselves. The result would be pro-capitalist, pro-U.S. revolutions across the Asian/Pacific communist world. The United States might never have to dispatch one division of troops to influence these events. The capitalist appeal would win the cold war every time.

The Kennedy team applauded the Rusk plan; there was no dissent. In fact, Kennedy hoped the New Pacific Community would eventually become the centerpiece of his foreign policy. The press always hailed his abilities as a foreign policy crisis manager, but the New Frontier was about setting new goals and achieving them. This could be the Kennedy legacy that historians wrote about for years. Or so the Kennedy cabinet concluded.

Indeed, the true key to success remained capitalist participation in this expensive plan and the downplaying of the United States's real monetary contributions to the effort. Winning early support from Prime Minister Ikeda of Japan and especially veteran Prime Minister Robert Menzies of Australia was critical to the final victory. In late 1961, no one in the Kennedy administration thought that there would ever be a problem with their grand scheme.

Although he was a conservative, a businessman, and a longtime strong supporter of U.S. foreign policy goals, Prime Minister Menzies had his doubts about the New Pacific Community. Politically, Menzies was hurting in the polls. A display of Australian nationalism might go a long way in winning wavering voters and embracing an anti-American stance was the best tactic. But Menzies's opposition to the NPC went beyond domestic political concerns. He firmly believed that a major Australian role in the new organization would make his country something of America's "51st state." In other words, Australia's future would be determined by U.S. foreign policy interests. His country's economy was booming, and it had had little assistance from the United States. Now, the Australian government was expected to tax its people heavily in a go-for-broke effort, Menzies complained, to throw money at poverty. It was unrealistic, he told the White House, and it was his final word.

Kennedy was shocked and angered, but he took no action to topple Menzies. In the long run, Kennedy concluded that his own pressure and persuasion would win over the Australians. Time, he thought, was on his side. But Menzies was only one worry. Ikeda was especially vocal in his opposition to the NPC. According to him and his Harvard-trained finance minister, Kiichi Miyazawa, the Japanese export economy would be destroyed under the Kennedy plan. All Japan wants, Ikeda argued, was a decent slice of the U.S. consumer market and similar advantages elsewhere. Contributing to cold war victory schemes was too expensive, too distracting, and not in Japan's interest.

Kennedy could not believe what he was hearing. Again, he concluded that his own charm, backed up by the power and determination of his government, would sway the opposition before long. But Lyndon Johnson saw things differently. Bolting from his support of the NPC plan in 1962, Johnson urged the president to give it up. The plan was dead in the water, he said. It was time to stress traditional cold war tactics, such as escalating the U.S. military presence in South Vietnam. But abandoning the New Pacific Community in favor of Johnson's hard-nosed tactics alone also meant abandoning New Frontier idealism.

Perhaps remembering his father's advice, John Kennedy did not want to "shrink in the face of adversity." As late as November 1963, and only days before his assassination, Kennedy had not given up on the NPC.[13] He planned to visit Japan and Australia in early 1964 and return home with Japanese and Australian commitments to Rusk's innovative organization. It was not to be, and Johnson quickly shelved the entire project soon after he became president.

KENNEDY, KING, AND REFOCUSING THE AMERICAN AGENDA

To John Lewis, a Martin Luther King adviser and future congressman, both Kennedy foreign and domestic policy making was about new directions and goals. Giving up on any aspect of this approach was impossible for the Kennedy team, Lewis once wrote, because policy making remained part of a higher cause for them. Hence, they could never abandon their foreign policy dreams, and they could never abandon their belief that civil rights must be legislated in strong moral terms.

Although many might disagree with Lewis's conclusions, there was little doubt that the Kennedy administration struggled with the significance of the Civil Rights movement. According to Lewis, civil rights street tactics in 1962 and 1963 pushed the administration into active policy-making reform. That in itself, Lewis believed, was an amazing accomplishment.

Perhaps more accurately described as a Southern-based phenomenon than a national movement before the early 1960s, Martin Luther King and his supporters represented a powerful new force for change while Kennedy sat in the White House. King also had to deal with his standing as a national figure with great influence. Picking and choosing the right place and moment for protest was more important than ever, and the whole world was watching. Yet King often moved from one protest event to another without much planning. For example, in December 1961, he was asked by Dr. William Anderson, a black osteopath, to help rally the civil rights cause in Albany, Georgia. King went to Albany expecting to make a speech. Instead, he organized a march, got arrested, and became intimately involved in what was known as the Albany Movement.

The Albany Movement had been jump-started by two young black activists, Cordell Reagon and Charles Sherrod. Together with a handful of supporters, they attempted to shut down the segregated transportation system of their town. At first, they were regarded by their African-American elders as too young and too wild to follow or support. But their brutal arrest and jailing united the black community, protest marchers grew into the hundreds, and King said that he would be happy to spend Christmas in jail with them if necessary.

King believed that his own arrest would lead to more protest and victory in Albany. But Albany frustrated his movement as much as Congress frustrated Kennedy's civil rights reform bill. By August 1962, King had been arrested three times in Albany, more protests did indeed result, and the local police chief, Laurie G. Prichett, remained committed to law and order. Although he physically resembled the stereotypical white Southern lawman, Prichett exercised great caution, rejected brutality, and hoped to keep the national public eye off his city. Prichett even read civil rights demonstration literature in order to better understand his opponent's mission as well as avoid the dispatching of federal marshals to Albany. Meanwhile, the Albany Movement disagreed on tactics.

Some Albany activists favored more examples of nonviolent street demonstrations. Others favored a more angry approach, and still others wanted civil rights supporters everywhere to join them in an Albany show of force. With King in and out of jail, questions of leadership and direction were obvious; King, however, still wondered why he had not quickly succeeded in Albany. When King opted for nearly two months in jail rather than pay a token fine, the mayor of Albany (under Prichett's advice) paid the fee. An astonished King went free, and the protests went nowhere.

King took full responsibility for the confusion of the Albany demonstrations, and the matter represented a turning point for him. He then recognized that better organization was needed, but, in many ways, the emotional people power aspect of his movement was its greatest strength. It was an unfortunate dilemma but one that showed that the civil rights cause truly had a national constituency.

King's organizational problems were not easy to resolve. In the long run, he clung to the belief that it was up to the Kennedy administration to act in a disciplined, coordinated way, and pass civil rights legislation. They had been little help in Albany. Seeing a no-win situation for King, the Kennedy White House had avoided any involvement in the Albany matter. That troubled King, but it was time to move on. The Kennedy administration responded to acts of brutality against blacks, such as in Alabama, but kept its distance if whites, such as in Georgia, kept their cool. In the meantime, the nation's African-American community had come to adore King, and the civil rights leader finally realized that this was a powerful message to the segregationists as well.

King's discovery of his own importance and the realization that better organization made good sense was demonstrated in his efforts to discredit "Bull" Connor, the commissioner of public safety in Birmingham, Alabama.

King was on familiar turf there, and white moderates were attempting to oust Conner as a leftover ultra-segregationist and brute who brought shame to the city. Helping this cause, side by side with his own desegregation effort in Birmingham, required a delicate touch. Connor had broken up previous civil rights demonstrations with shocking displays of brutality. King had to denounce him without alienating white reformists and without encouraging the usual bloodshed. By praising the reasonable majority of whites and blacks in Birmingham, King emerged a statesman and won a considerable degree of national sympathy in 1963. That sympathy, he believed, would force white leaders to begin desegregating Birmingham. But there was a price to pay for focusing national attention on Birmingham's troubles. It stimulated another arrest and jailing, including solitary confinement.

In October 1962, "Bull" Connor campaigns to keep his Birmingham, Alabama, Commission of Public Safety free of "outside influences" and political change. *(Birmingham Public Library Department of Archives and Manuscripts)*

Concerned about more racial violence and matters of jurisdiction, the Kennedy administration expressed its sympathies to the King family, had the FBI check on King's condition in jail, but did nothing to win his release. Eventually, as black-versus-white tension mounted in Birmingham and rumors spread that Connor was trying to break King, the Justice Department dispatched Burke Marshall, the Kennedy administration's best civil rights mediator, to negotiate a peace there. Actor/singer Harry Belafonte raised King's $50,000 in bail money, but a number of mostly white Southern religious leaders denounced King as guilty as Connor for inciting violence. The accusation angered King, resulting in a passionate defense of civil disobedience and the just cause of racial harmony.

King emerged from the Albany and Birmingham experiences a tired but truly powerful national leader. He had won a full endorsement from the nationwide African-American community for his commitment and courage. Many days of struggle lay ahead, but a certain optimism was associated with the civil rights cause of 1963 that had not been there before.[14] To both King and the Kennedy administration, certain lessons had been learned. Perhaps most important was that there was still a place for idealism, commitment, and the premise that one must "never shrink in the face of adversity."

CHRONICLE OF EVENTS

1962

January 1: In a New Year's Day military parade, Fidel Castro displays a number of Soviet-made MIG fighters. Months before the Cuban Missile Crisis, CIA observers of the parade theorize that Castro is receiving all types of military hardware from the Soviet Union.

January 3: Secretary of State Dean Rusk reports to the Organization of American States that Cuba represents a Soviet "colony" in the Western Hemisphere. He notes that more than $100 million in Soviet military assistance has been shipped to Havana, and he predicts that Castro will soon transform his country into a base of "agitation and subversion" on behalf of his Soviet benefactors.

January 4: The pro-French colonial and banned Secret Army Organization announces a new campaign of terror in Algeria and elsewhere. Some 600 people are murdered shortly after the announcement. Paris also becomes the target of terrorist bombings, and President Charles de Gaulle implies that the United States should be concerned. President Kennedy states that his administration has no interest in French colonial matters.

January 19: CIA analyst George McManus reports to Attorney General Robert Kennedy that the destruction of the Castro regime is a "top priority" for U.S. national security in 1962.

January 22: At its annual meeting in Punta del Este, Uruguay, the Organization of American States denounces Cuba as a radical communist state, urging member nations to avoid any contact with its "ruthless dictatorship."

January 29: After more than three years of unsuccessful negotiations, the American, British, and Soviet governments announce that an agreement to end nuclear weapons testing cannot be reached. They had met in 353 separate sessions. The American and British delegations claim that, from the beginning, the Soviets never took the discussions seriously.

February 1: The Joint Chiefs of Staff promise President John Kennedy that all contingency plans for the invasion of Cuba will be completed shortly.

February 3: President Kennedy declares Cuba an outlaw state, authorizing a full embargo on all U.S.-Cuban trade. Castro claims that the United States is waging war against innocent men, women, and children in Cuba.

February 8: Secretary of Defense Robert McNamara announces the creation of a new military command in South Vietnam. This Military Assistance Command, Vietnam (MACV) is put under the direction of General Paul Harkins, a strong supporter of Kennedy's New Frontier policies.

February 10: The Kennedy administration releases convicted Soviet spy Colonel Rudolf Abel in exchange for Soviet-captured U-2 pilot Francis Gary Powers. Shot down over Soviet airspace during the 1960 campaign, Powers's spy mission was denounced in Soviet propaganda for months.

February 14: America's first lady Jacqueline Kennedy takes the nation on a televised "Tour of the White House."

February 20: Piloting *Friendship 7,* John Glenn becomes the first astronaut to orbit the Earth. This historic mission is considered a dramatic step in the NASA effort to put an American on the moon.

February 20: The CIA presents a six-phase schedule for Operation MONGOOSE to President Kennedy. MONGOOSE involves the overthrow of the Castro regime, and the target date for full success was expected to be October 1962.

February 20: Averell Harriman, the assistant secretary of state for Far Eastern affairs, testifies before a closed hearing of the Senate Foreign Relations Committee that dealing with the Diem regime is "difficult" but that all is well with America's Vietnam policy.

February 26: The palace of South Vietnam's President Diem is attacked by two American-trained pilots flying American-made jets. The palace compound is bombed and strafed, but Diem survives this coup uninjured.

March: In San Francisco, trailblazing comedian Lenny Bruce is charged with violating the city's obscenity laws.

March: President Kennedy tells an interviewer for *The Saturday Evening Post* that the U.S. "will never strike first" against the Soviet Union.

March: The Department of Justice sends a bill to Congress that would make "certain forms of police brutality" (such as breaking up civil rights demonstrations) a federal crime. It receives little congressional support.

March 1: For the time being, President Kennedy orders MONGOOSE planning to stress intelligence

Astronaut John Glenn climbs into his *Friendship 7 Mercury* capsule for his famous triple orbit of Earth. *(NASA)*

gathering efforts alone. Meanwhile, the White House continues its policy of isolating Castro from the rest of Latin America.

March 2: Wilt Chamberlain of the Philadelphia Warriors scores a record-setting 100 points in a single basketball game against the New York Knicks.

March 6: Despite questions of Francis Gary Powers's patriotism for being captured alive, the Defense Department announces that the downed pilot will not be disciplined or charged with any crime.

March 9: First led by students, a violent protest movement begins against the Guatemalan government of Miguel Ydigoras Fuente and the corrupt 1961 election that confirmed his presidency. Ydigoras claims that Cuban spies have stimulated the protest and asks for U.S. support.

March 14: An international summit begins in Geneva to win the total disarmament of nuclear weapons. The French government refuses to participate, and Premier Khrushchev announces that any weapons inspection team that includes Americans will be refused entry into the Soviet Union.

March 14–16: General Maxwell Taylor argues with President Kennedy that MONGOOSE cannot work without a direct U.S. military role and invasion.

March 19: Soon considered the musical champion of social change in the 1960s, Bob Dylan releases his first record album. Simply titled *Bob Dylan,* the record includes tunes such as "House of the Rising Sun," "Talkin' New York," "Song to Woody," "See That My Grave Is Kept Clean," "Highway 51," and "Man of Constant Sorrow."

March 22: America's MACV launches its Strategic Hamlet program across South Vietnam. This rural pacification campaign is expected to safeguard entire areas from enemy infiltration and influence.

April–June: When America's Jupiter missiles become operational in Turkey, Premier Nikita Khrushchev considers sending a Soviet delegation to Cuba to discuss Soviet missile deployment there. Facing opposition in his own government, Khrushchev must persuade his detractors that the Americans will not discover the missiles or do anything about them if they do. Following the conclusion of the Soviet-Cuban missile deployment agreement, Khrushchev permits his generals to decide on how many Soviet missiles would be emplaced.

April 7: Once the second most powerful bureaucrat in the Yugoslavian communist government, Milovan Djilas is arrested for having exposed military secrets in his book *Conversations with Stalin.* Now doubting that communism can work in his country or anywhere else, Djilas advocates a compromise between communism and capitalism that wins the attention of American intellectuals.

April 9: Producer Robert Wise accepts the Academy Award for best picture of the year for his musical/social commentary *West Side Story.* Maximilian Schell wins best actor honors for *Judgment at Nuremberg,* Sophia Loren wins the best actress nod for *Two Women,* and both Robert Wise and Jerome Robbins win the best director Oscar for *West Side Story.*

April 10: At the age of 21, Stu Sutcliffe dies of a brain hemorrhage in Hamburg, West Germany. Sutcliffe is credited with coming up with the name "Beatles" for his favorite Liverpool rock band, as well

One year after releasing his first album, Bob Dylan performs with another folk singer, Joan Baez, during the 1963 civil rights demonstrations in Washington, D.C. *(National Archives)*

as persuading that band to adopt his unique mop-head hair style.

April 20: Responding to the growing success of the prointegration Freedom Rider movement in the U.S. South, a prosegregationist group in New Orleans offers free one-way tickets plus expenses to African Americans who want to leave the South for northern locations.

April 25: In spite of ongoing nuclear disarmament talks, the U.S. Defense Department conducts an atomic bomb test near Christmas Island in the Pacific.

April: America's Jupiter missiles become operational in Turkey. Premier Khrushchev, while vacationing near the Turkish border, allegedly decides to place missiles in Cuba in retaliation for Kennedy's Jupiter decision.

April: Switching government steel orders to companies that hold down prices, President Kennedy puts heavy pressure on small steel companies to resist the 6 percent rise in prices advocated by U.S. Steel. Kennedy claims victory in the government versus steel industry crisis.

May 8–18: Operation WHIP LASH is conducted in the Caribbean. This U.S. military war game is meant to test American readiness in the coming fight against Castro. The massive size of this effort persuades Soviet policy makers that a U.S. invasion of Cuba is inevitable.

May 12: After months of quiet, the procommunist Pathet Lao launch an offensive against progovernment positions in northern Laos. The attack moves President Kennedy to rely on more military solutions for Southeast Asia than negotiated settlements.

May 17: Although President Kennedy urges America's allies to be generous to all those "fleeing communist tyranny," the British colonial government in Hong Kong constructs a large barbed wire fence on its Chinese border to halt refugee movement into the colony.

May 30: After meeting with visiting Soviet diplomats, the Cuban regime decides to accept Soviet nuclear missiles for its new defense system.

June 1: The United Nations announces that the world's largest city is now Tokyo, Japan, with a population of more than 10 million. The global population is estimated to be 3,100,000,000, and 44 percent of all adults are still believed to be illiterate.

June: During the Albany Movement protests, Martin Luther King urges the Kennedy administration to issue a "Second Emancipation Proclamation." King believed that the proclamation would symbolize the White House's full solidarity behind the civil rights movement; however, the Kennedy administration disagrees with King's timing.

June 11: The feuding princes in Laos agree to form a coalition government and recognize neutralist Souvanna Phouma as its leader. President Kennedy has little hope that it will contain the growth of communism there or halt North Vietnamese penetration.

June 14: A top secret test of America's Thor nuclear missile fails. The missile's nuclear power source falls into the Pacific Ocean, and President Kennedy authorizes a massive and successful search effort for it.

June 15: Several dozen student activists and members of the Students for a Democratic Society (SDS) meet at a United Auto Workers educational camp in Port Huron, Michigan. Largely authored by Tom Hayden, the Port Huron Statement results from this gathering. Generally regarded as something of a constitution for the American New Left of the 1960s, the Port Huron Statement resurrects 1930s slogans of American leftists, calls for more social programs and civil rights legislation, denounces the excesses of the cold war, and touts the value of "human independence, self-cultivation, and creativity."

June 17: At the U.S. Open, 22-year-old Jack Nicklaus defeats Arnold Palmer in an 18-hole play-off to win his first major professional golf championship.

June 18: Disliked in Washington due to his sometimes outrageous anti-American statements, Canadian Prime Minister John Diefenbaker is defeated in his country's national elections. Refusing to step down from his post, Diefenbaker forms a minority government with a promise of economic reform.

June 20: For the second time within a three-week period, a top secret test of an American Thor nuclear missile fails. Another search effort must be launched to find its nuclear power source at the bottom of the Pacific Ocean.

June 25: In a 6-1 decision based on First Amendment interpretations, the U.S. Supreme Court in *Engel v. Vitale* agrees that reciting prayers in the New York state public school system is unconstitutional.

July 2: A Cuban-Soviet summit in Moscow arranges the precise schedule of nuclear missile deployment in Cuba. A renewable five-year accord is signed whereby the Soviet Union maintains full jurisdiction over all missile defense matters throughout the island nation.

July 15: Carrying nuclear weapons, Soviet cargo ships begin their journey to Cuba. U.S. spy planes report that the ships are sailing high in the water, a sign that little cargo outside of a specific military shipment might be on board.

July 18: America's Telstar satellite begins transmitting the first television signals from space.

July 22: Hailed as another grand step in the race to the moon, the *Mariner* spacecraft is launched.

July 25: The CIA reports to President Kennedy that 11 CIA guerrilla teams are already in Cuba, laying the groundwork for a U.S. invasion. Nevertheless, the CIA also warns that time is running out for U.S. action.

July 26: While celebrating the ninth anniversary of the beginning of his revolutionary movement, Castro announces to his supporters that another Bay of Pigs–like invasion of Cuban exiles is unlikely. If the U.S. military invaded, he promises to defeat the landings with recently acquired "new arms." He offers no specifics.

August 4: Marilyn Monroe, America's hottest sex symbol of the 1950s and early 1960s, is found dead from an alleged overdose of sleeping pills.

August 6: Admitting that the Caribbean is now part of the "U.S. hemisphere," the British government folds its 307-year-old colonial rule over Jamaica. Trinidad and Tobago become independent from Britain days later.

August 13: Castro amends the Soviet-Cuban military assistance agreement, insisting that his own forces must play a leading role should Cuba be attacked.

August 15: An agreement temporarily transferring the authority of West Irian in New Guinea to United Nations rule prevents a war that might have included the United States. With reluctant U.S. approval, the United Nations surrenders its West Irian administration to Indonesia the following year.

August 17: Weighing new intelligence information, CIA Director John McCone still believes that the Soviets are setting up offensive missiles in Cuba. Secretary of State Rusk and Secretary of Defense McNamara disagree, noting that the missiles must be defensive.

August 20: General Maxwell Taylor informs President Kennedy that only a U.S. invasion can overthrow the Castro regime and, therefore, recommends a new, more militant version of Operation MONGOOSE. Kennedy agrees that a stronger MONGOOSE is needed but continues to reject a direct U.S. invasion.

August 23: Upon President Kennedy's urging, the National Security Council (NSC) meets to discuss CIA Director McCone's worries. McNamara and Rusk continue to argue against McCone's views, but Kennedy asks the NSC to plan for the possibility of offensive nuclear weapons in Cuba. That plan, National Security Memorandum 181, is completed by the end of the day. It includes U.S. military options and analyzes the psychological and political impact of offensive weapons in Cuba.

August 26–September 6: A Cuban delegation arrives in the Soviet Union to win Premier Khrushchev's signature to the revised Cuban-Soviet military cooperation agreement. Khrushchev rejects their plan to announce the missile deployment to the world. He also refuses to sign any formal agreement.

August 29: An American U-2 reconnaissance flight photographs Soviet missile sites in eight separate locations throughout Cuba. Claiming that there is no evidence of a Soviet military presence in Cuba, President Kennedy informs a news conference that the United States will not be invading Cuba anytime soon.

August 31: President Kennedy is informed that the U.S. Air Force has confirmed the existence of Soviet missiles in Cuba.

September 3: Security adviser Walt Rostow advises President Kennedy that the Soviet SAM missiles discovered in Cuba do not pose a direct threat to the United States; however, he recommends that anti-Castro activists overthrow the Cuban dictator as soon as possible.

September 4: Attorney General Kennedy meets with the Soviet ambassador, Anatoly Dobrynin, to explain U.S. policy. Dobrynin insists that there will never be offensive nuclear weapons deployed in Cuba. After being informed of this conversation, President Kennedy supports the drafting of a statement that accents the point that the United States "will never tolerate" offensive weapons in Cuba.

September 10–19: Representatives from Great Britain's 15 Commonwealth nations and nine colonial possessions meet in London to discuss Prime Minister Harold MacMillan's plan to join the European Common Market. Although the British dominions worry about the success of their own exports to the Common Market, they agree that the British must make up their own minds on the issue. MacMillan predicts that the Common Market will become the third-largest world economic force behind the United States and the Soviet Union.

September 13: A series of Ku Klux Klan–supported burnings of African-American churches in Georgia prompts a public denunciation by President Kennedy. He also promises federal protection for voter registration drives in black communities across Georgia.

September 13: Once again, President Kennedy assures the press that the United States is not planning an invasion of Cuba. In a stern official statement, he warns Premier Khrushchev that the United States will "do whatever must be done" to protect its interests if Cuba becomes a significant Soviet military base.

September 20: With only one dissenting vote, the U.S. Senate passes a resolution authorizing the president to use force, if necessary, to halt Cuban aggression and all Soviet assistance that makes it possible.

September 21: Soviet Foreign Minister Andrei Gromyko accuses the United States of fomenting "war hysteria," but at the same time, he warns that any U.S. assault on Cuba or Soviet ships heading to Cuba will mean war.

September 25: In a devastating first-round pummeling, Sonny Liston knocks out Floyd Patterson to become the heavyweight boxing champion of the world.

September 26: The new president of independent Algeria, Mohammed Ben Bella, announces that his country will be following the example of Indonesia's Achmed Sukarno and declaring its "nonalignment" to Moscow or Washington in the cold war.

September 27: The U.S. Air Force sets the date of October 20, 1962, as the earliest possible time a tactical air strike on Cuba (in support of a massive U.S. airborne and amphibious assault) can successfully take place.

September 30: With several hundred federal marshals at his side, James Meredith becomes the first African American to enroll at the University of Mississippi in Oxford, Mississippi. Riots result across the town of Oxford, and more than 3,000 federalized National Guardsmen and other soldiers reestablish the civil peace.

EYEWITNESS TESTIMONY

Cold War Realities

I spoke a year ago today, to take the Inaugural, and I would like to paraphrase a couple statements I made that day by saying that we observe tonight not a celebration of freedom but a victory of party, for we have sworn to pay off the same party debt our forebears ran up nearly a year and three months ago.

Our deficit will not be paid off in the next hundred days, nor will it be paid off in the first one thousand days, nor in the life of this administration. Nor perhaps even in our lifetime on this planet, but let us begin—remembering that generosity is not a sign of weakness and that Ambassadors are always subject to Senate confirmation, for if the Democratic Party cannot be helped by the many who are poor, it cannot be saved by the few who are rich. So let us begin.

President Kennedy at a January 1962 Democratic Party fund raiser, celebrating one year in office by poking fun at his January 1961 inaugural address, in Selected Speeches, Research Room, JFK Library.

We talk about the reduction of U.S. and U.S.S.R. armed forces to 2.1 million by the end of the first stage. We talk about a cutoff of the production of fissionable materials during the course of the first stage; we talk about a curb on the transfer of nuclear materials and nuclear know-how to nations not having it; we talk about outer space with no bombs in orbit, and with peaceful cooperation and notification; all of these things could be done, in the opinion of the Defense Department, and, of course, all of these things are being coordinated within the executive branch as policies which would be followed.

William Foster, director of the Arms Control and Disarmament Agency, explaining to Congress in April 1962 that nuclear disarmament can be accomplished, in the U.S. Congress's Executive Sessions of the Senate Foreign Relations Committee, Vol. XIV (1986), p. 388.

The President was completely overwhelmed by the ruthlessness and barbarity of the Russian Chairman. It reminded me in a way of Lord Halifax or Neville Chamberlain trying to hold a conversation with Herr Hitler.

Britain's Prime Minister Harold Macmillan discussing in April 1962 President Kennedy's view of Nikita Khrushchev since he took office. Quoted in Fursenko and Naftali, "One Hell of a Gamble:" Khrushchev, Castro, and Kennedy (1997), p. 66.

If at any time the Communist buildup in Cuba were to endanger or interfere with our security in any way, including our base at Guantanamo, our passage to the Panama Canal, our missile and space activities at Cape Canaveral, or the lives of American citizens in this country, or if Cuba should ever attempt to export its aggressive purposes by forces or the threat of force against any nation in this hemisphere, or become an offensive military base of significant capacity for the Soviet Union, then this country will do whatever must be done to protect its own security and that of its allies.

President Kennedy answering a question about Cuba and U.S. security at a September 13, 1962, news conference. His statement constitutes fundamental American policy concerns during the entire Cuban Missile Crisis period, in Public Papers of President John F. Kennedy, 1962, Speeches, JFK Library.

I can well understand why our people are impatient, a great many of them, and fed up with the sort of thing they have been asked to put up with in recent years. On the other hand, I hope they will be patient just a little longer. I think that things are much worse in Mr. Khrushchev's camp than is generally understood here. It would be tragic, in my opinion, if we were to permit ourselves to provoke a general showdown with the Communist world that would be damaging to both of us at a time when what was needed was only another year or two of patience, and we would find our problem much easier.

George Kennan, veteran cold war policy maker and U.S. ambassador to Yugoslavia testifying before Congress in late 1962 and urging patience and caution from the Kennedy administration, in the U.S. Congress's Executive Sessions of the Senate Foreign Relations Committee, Vol. XIV, (1986), p. 29.

Living and Coping with the New Frontier

In defense to the charge that the Twist is lewd and "dirty," I can only say that any movement can be made to appear suggestive, depending on the dancer himself. I have often watched couples waltzing or doing a fox trot and have been more embarrassed than when viewing the most uninhibited Twisters. Because Twist music has a strong beat and an exciting rhythm it can be distorted into a suggestive dance—if the dancer wishes to make it so. Due to the fact that a great deal of freedom and self-expression enter into the dance no two people will do the Twist in the same manner. Thus one dancer may appear suggestive on the dance floor while all the rest will just be termed "uninhibited" and "graceful." Generally the eye of the critic will be drawn to the exhibitionist and the Twist is immediately condemned.

Chubby Checker defending the Twist, in Checker and Holder, "To Twist or Not to Twist," Ebony, February 1962, p. 106.

The Twist? I'm sitting this one out. It's dishonest. It's not a dance and it has become dirty. Not because it has to do with sex. Everything does. But it's not what it's packaged. It's synthetic sex turned into a sick spectator sport. Not because it's vulgar. Real vulgarity is divine. But when people break their backs to act vulgar, it's embarrassing.

Social dancing was never meant to supply vicarious kicks for spectators. When it does, watch it! The oldest hootchy kootchy in the books has become the latest thing. Who would believe it? From the dawn of time, the classic way of showing male potency has been the same pelvic movement. In African fertility dances, you always find it naked, honest.

Trinidad-born dancer, actor, and artist Geoffrey Holder declaring the Twist "lewd and uncreative," in Checker and Holder, "To Twist or Not to Twist," Ebony, February 1962, pp. 107–110.

Tricia and Julie at fifteen and thirteen were still too young to exert a major influence on my decision, but I wanted to hear their views. When Julie saw that Pat and I had such a strong difference of opinion, she said that she would approve whatever I decided. Tricia was the only one who took a positive line: "I am not sure whether you should run," she said, "but I kind of have the feeling that you should just to show them you

aren't finished because of the election that was stolen from us in 1960!"

Richard Nixon asking his family in late February 1962 if they will support his 1962 campaign for governor of California, in Nixon's The Memoirs of Richard Nixon (1978), p. 240.

He had been on the "Tonight" program with me, and against his own judgment and that of his many advisers, I got him to play the piano. It was an unusual moment, with Richard Nixon playing a ricky-ticky tune that he had composed. Marshall McLuhan, the media analyst, had written in his first book that if Nixon had played the piano on the "Tonight" program in the 1960 campaign, he would have won the election.

Jack Paar, the host of NBC's Tonight talk show, recalling a March 1962 guest appearance by Richard Nixon, in Paar's P.S. Jack Paar (1983), p. 135.

The Republicans taunted Kennedy for his inability to cash in on his Democratic majorities, but the president made no bones about the fact that Southern Democratic defections made every vote a cliff-hanger. "You can water bills down and get them by," he said, "or you can have bills which have no particular controversy to them. . . . But . . . we have a very difficult time, on a controversial piece of legislation, securing a working majority." Yet, as Theodore White has pointed out, "More . . . new legislation was actually approved and passed into law . . . than at any other time since the 1930s."

Kennedy staffer and friend Theodore Sorensen countering March 1962 accusations that the Kennedy White House could not work with Congress, in Papers of Theodore C. Sorensen, JFK Library.

"Some of them have been hard to believe. Today Barnett said to me, 'Why can't you persuade Meredith to go to another college? I could get some money together and we could give him a fellowship to any university he wanted outside the state. Wouldn't that be the best way to solve the problem?'" Bobby couldn't believe it.

Former Kennedy White House staffer Arthur Schlesinger, Jr., remembering Attorney General Kennedy telling him in March 1962 about Mississippi Governor Ross Barnett's approach to avoiding violence over the enrollment of James Meredith at the University of Mississippi, in Papers of Arthur M. Schlesinger, Jr., JFK Library.

In matters of the spirit, I am sure young Americans would learn a good deal in this country and it could be an important experience for them. The government of the Punjab and the Minister for Community Development apparently want some of your Volunteers, and we will be happy to receive a few of them—perhaps twenty to twenty-five. But I hope you and they will not be too disappointed if the Punjab, when they leave, is more or less the same as it was before they came.

India's Prime Minister Jawaharlal Nehru explaining his reluctance to accept American Peace Corps volunteers, in an April 1962 letter to Peace Corps Director Sargent Shriver, in Wofford, Of Kennedys and Kings: Making Sense of the Sixties *(1980), Research Room, JFK Library.*

Kennedy was ambivalent about what we should do to help Diem. Like many of us, his judgment was clouded by three assumptions—first, that Chinese expansionism was the driving force behind Communist aggression from the North (in October 1962, after seizing Tibet, the Chinese killed six thousand Indian troops in Himalayan border fighting, and an invasion seemed imminent); second, that the domino theory, to which Kennedy subscribed as much as had Eisenhower, meant that all of South Asia was in jeopardy if South Vietnam were overrun ("If we permitted Laos to fall," said Ike as he left office, "then we would have to write off the whole area"); and third, that the partition line drawn across Vietnam at the 17th parallel was in fact an international boundary, and the southern part of the country consequently a sovereign state.

Reporter and diplomat William Attwood recalling President Kennedy's April 1962 view of Asian affairs in his The Twilight Struggle: Tales of the Cold War *(1987), The Papers of William Attwood, Ambassador to Guinea, JFK Library.*

The critics . . . told us that the economy would reach full employment . . . without government stimulus, indeed that such stimulus would simply run off in inflation. It didn't. Late in 1962 they told us that a $2 1/2 billion tax cut was all the economy could stand, that a tax cut of several times that amount was not

only unorthodox but bizarre, and would generate "simply enormous deficits." It didn't.

In 1965, former Kennedy administration economic adviser Walter Heller recalling the 1962 critics of New Frontier fiscal policies in Morris, A Time of Passion: America 1960–1980 *(1984), Excerpts included in the Robert F. Kennedy Oral History Project, JFK Library.*

And how would we do on something that was far more controversial, where we didn't have a Sam Rayburn, couldn't bring along a lot of these southerners that he could in this kind of fight? How much more difficult it was doing that. And I think it's a good lesson. *The New York Times* used to write editorials all the time that the President should use his art of persuasion and get these bills through the House, little knowing or realizing or bothering to realize that this was, then, far more

During ceremonies at Saigon, South Vietnam, the Vietnamese Air Force pledges its support for President Ngo Dinh Diem after an October 1962 political uprising there. *(National Archives)*

difficult. We could point to this, where we won this fight—but only after much bitterness and only with that much strength. How much more difficult it was when the odds were much higher against us!

> *Robert Kennedy during a 1964 interview with John Bartlow Martin, recalling the spring and summer 1962 battles with Congress, in The Robert F. Kennedy Oral History Project, JFK Library.*

At a press conference on April 2, 1962, I asked him, "If you had it to do over again, would you work for the Presidency? And can you recommend the job to others?" JFK flashed a broad grin, and his blue eyes twinkled as he replied, "The answer to the first is yes, and to the second is no."

> *White House reporter Ruth Montgomery recalling an April 1962 question-and-answer session with President Kennedy in her Hail to the Chiefs: My Life and Times With Six Presidents (1970), p. 247.*

The point is continuously raised that President Kennedy only realized that there was a civil rights crisis the night after Birmingham in 1963, or otherwise he would have tried to obtain the passage of legislation in '61 or '62 or '63. That's ludicrous, really, on the basis of the facts. Number one: Nobody would have paid the slightest attention to him. If he had sent up a more comprehensive bill, it would never have gone very far in any case—as seen by the civil rights bill that we did send up, where nobody rose to great support. When the filibuster took place, we didn't even get fifty percent of the vote.

> *Robert Kennedy during a December 1964 interview with Anthony Lewis, defending his older brother's approach to civil rights going into 1963, in Robert F. Kennedy Oral History Project, JFK Library.*

Sukarno, de Gaulle, and Challenges to New Frontier Diplomacy

The Soviet Union has always lent and intends to continue lending friendly and disinterested assistance and support to all countries in their struggle for freedom and independence and in their efforts to overcome their age-long economic backwardness.

> *In August 1962 Premier Khrushchev answering U.S. charges of undue Soviet influence in Indonesian politics, in Maga, John F. Kennedy and the New Pacific Community, 1961–63 (1990), p. 59.*

This legislation makes it possible for the United States to fulfill the obligations voluntarily undertaken by us at the close of World War II in recognition of the common sacrifices made by the Philippine and American people. The war causes enormous damage to the Philippine Islands. The payments under this bill, together with the $400 million already appropriated, will help repair that damage. I am particularly gratified that the legislation provides that the amounts paid will, to a large extent, be reinvested in the Philippines economy.

> *President Kennedy responding to congressional critics who say that his $73 million aid bill for the Philippines is an attempt to "buy their loyalty" in the cold war, in Kennedy message to Congress, August 30, 1962, POF/Box 39, JFK Library.*

The present power situation in Indonesia certainly has advantages for them [Soviets], not least in the flow of friendly words from President Sukarno. By providing their aid, economic as well as military, the Soviet leaders presumably hope to forestall a major crackdown on the Indonesian Communists.

> *The State Department Strategic Planning Division warning President Kennedy in its summary of U.S. 1962 troubles with Indonesia, that the Soviets will soon be making inroads in Indonesia. Quoted in Feith, "Soviet Aid to Indonesia," Nation (November 3, 1962), p. 11.*

We have no illusions that amelioration of this problem will resolve all questions concerning Indonesia. We are aware that Indonesia will continue to pose problems that will require our best efforts to meet. However, we believe that Indonesians, especially the large and potentially influential moderate group, will be better able to withstand the pressures of Communism and to move more rapidly to normal developments only when they no longer are distracted by this dispute.

> *President Kennedy suggesting to Australian prime minister Robert Menzies that Sukarno's Indonesia is a frustrating problem that distracts the United States from larger cold war concerns of summer 1962, in the State Department's memo "Status and Atmosphere of U.S.-Australian Relations," 1962, POF/Box 111, JFK Library.*

Our commitments on the Indo-China peninsula could be lost if the bottom of Southeast Asia fell out to Communism. It therefore remains our objective (1) to keep Indonesia independent and out of the Sino-Soviet camp, (2) to help Indonesia become a politically and economically viable nation, and (3) to help solve Indonesia's stabilization and recovery problems and eventually launch a national development plan.

Based on the tension and threats of the U.S.-Indonesia crisis in the summer of 1962, Secretary of State Dean Rusk urging President Kennedy to get tough with Sukarno. Quoted in the memo of Rusk to Kennedy, October 2, 1962, NSF/Box 338, JFK Library.

Asia lit all kinds of candles in his mind. This was especially true because rural, impoverished Asia, in contrast to industrialized, prospering Europe, evoked memories of his native central Texas.

Eric Goldman, a special assistant to Lyndon Johnson, recalling Vice President Johnson's trip to Southeast Asia during the Indonesia crisis, in his The Tragedy of Lyndon Johnson *(1969), p. 386.*

The day was long past when—traditional friendship aside—Washington insisted on regarding Paris as just another of its proteges to be dealt with like everyone else, in the context of the various collective organizations: NATO, SEATO, UNO, OECD, IMF, etc. Now the Americans acknowledged our independence and dealt with us directly and specially. But for all that, they could not conceive of their policy ceasing to be predominant or of ours diverging from it. Basically, what Kennedy offered me in every case was a share in his projects. What he heard from me in reply was that Paris was by all means disposed to collaborate closely with Washington, but that whatever France did she did of her own accord.

Eight years after the fact, French president Charles de Gualle recalls his 1962 fight with President Kennedy over French independence from U.S. foreign policy goals, in de Gaulle, Memoirs of Hope: Renewal and Endeavor *(1971), p. 255.*

In these conditions no one in the world, and especially in America, could say if, where, when, how and in what measure, American nuclear weapons would be used to defend Europe.

During a January 14, 1963, press conference, President de Gualle claims that the United States has little interest in defending its European allies, in Mates, Nanalignment: Theory and Current Policy *(1972), p. 332.*

We must face up to the chance of war, if we are to maintain the peace. . . . Diplomacy and defense are not substitutes for one another. . . . A willingness to resist force, unaccompanied by a willingness to talk, could provoke belligerence—while a willingness to talk, unaccompanied by a willingness to resist force, could invite disaster. . . . While we shall negotiate freely, we shall not negotiate freedom. . . . In short, we are neither "warmongers" nor "appeasers," neither "hard" nor "soft." We are Americans.

President Kennedy, during a mid-January 1962 visit to the University of Washington, trying to sum up general U.S. policy goals during the complicated Laos crisis, in The Public Papers of President John F. Kennedy, 1962, Speeches, *JFK Library.*

In order to agree upon measures which should be taken for the common defense, and there possibly the rule of unanimity might apply. Therefore, this indication—there would be no commitment, but it was contemplated that this communique would purely carry an inference that since the United States had taken action to be of assistance to the Government of the Republic of Vietnam to meet this type of aggression, it could be considered a reassurance as to the attitude of the United States and other countries in this area.

Averell Harriman, the assistant secretary of state for Far Eastern affairs, testifying before congress in February 1962 and avoiding a direct answer on whether U.S. forces will be dispatched to Laos, in the U.S. Congress's Executive Sessions of the Senate Foreign Relations Committee, Vol. XIV, *(1986), p. 220.*

At the Honolulu conference in July 1962 Defense Secretary McNamara once again asked MACV [Military Assistance Command, Vietnam] commander General Paul Harkins how long it would take before the Viet Cong could be expected to be eliminated as a significant force. In reply [the MACV commander] estimated about one year from the time Republic of Vietnam Armed Forces and other forces became fully operational and began to press the VC in all areas. . . . The Secretary said that a conservative view had to be taken and to assume it would take three years instead of one, that is, by the latter part of 1965.

One of the Vietnam War's key decisions of the summer of 1962 is quickly summarized in the 1962 MACV report of the Department of Defense's United States–Vietnam Relations, 1945–1967, Book 3 *(1971), Research Room, JFK Library.*

From my earliest associations with Vietnam (1951) I have been concerned about US handling of information from that area. . . . This included deliberate and reflexive manipulation of information, restrictions on the collection and censorship of reporting. The net result was that decision makers were denied the opportunity to get a complete form of information, determine its validity for themselves, and make decisions.

Lt. Col. Henry A. Shockley from the Defense Attache's Office in South Vietnam, recalling in 1975 the "information problem" in summer/fall 1962 Vietnam War policy making, in Ford's CIA and the Vietnam Policy Makers: Three Episodes 1962–1968 *(1998), p. 8.*

Eisenhower did not know what to do in Southeast Asia and was glad to leave it to the Democrats. Still I cannot fault him for handing us a problem with no solution. The Indochina problem was intractable, the way both Eisenhower and we defined it. Just how intractable, our nation would learn painfully over the next fourteen years. . . . Would Eisenhower ultimately have gone to war in Vietnam as we did? I do not know. . . . We were left only with the ominous prediction that if Laos were lost, all of Southeast Asia would fall. By implication, the West would have to do whatever was necessary to prevent that outcome.

Secretary of Defense Robert McNamara recalling the impact that ex-President Eisenhower still had on the new Kennedy administration's Southeast Asian policies during mid- and late-1962, in his In Retrospect: The Tragedy and Lessons of Vietnam *(1995), pp. 29–50.*

It is abundantly clear that statistics received over the past year or more from the GVN officials and reported by the US mission on which we gauged the trend of the war were grossly in error.

CIA Director John McCone assessing the relevance of Vietnam battlefield reports for 1961 and 1962, in Memorandum of Conversations Held in Saigon, 18–20 December 1963, December 21, 1963, *CIA Reports Files, JFK Library.*

It must be recognized that the fall of South Vietnam to Communist control would mean the eventual Communist domination of all of the Southeast Asian mainland. . . . Of equal importance to the immediate losses are the eventualities which could follow the loss of the Southeast Asian mainland. All of the Indonesian archipelago could come under the domination and control of the USSR and would become a Communist base posing a threat against Australia and New Zealand. The Sino-Soviet Bloc would have control of the eastern access to the Indian Ocean. The Philippines and Japan could be pressured to assume, at best, a neutralist role, thus eliminating two of our major bases of defense in the Western Pacific. . . . It is, in fact, a planned phase in the Communist timetable for world domination.

General Lyman Lemnitzer, chairman of the Joint Chiefs of Staff, urging President Kennedy to recognize "domino theory" concerns in his mid-1962 Vietnam policy, in Department of Defense, United States–Vietnam Relations, 1945–1967, Book 3 *(1971), Research Room, JFK Library.*

We never saw much of the enemy. We saw his handiwork—the ravaged outposts, the defenders with their heads blown off, their women lying dead beside them—but more often than not, the enemy only showed himself when he had superior strength. The first lesson that an American advisor in Vietnam learned was that the enemy was good; then if he stayed on a little longer, he learned that this was wrong; the enemy was very good. He learned that the Vietcong did very few things, but that they did them all well; they made few mistakes, and in sharp contrast to the government forces, they rarely repeated their mistakes. The American officers also learned that the enemy had a reason—political, psychological, or military—for almost everything he did. Even when he appeared to be doing nothing, we learned belatedly and bitterly that this did not mean that he was inactive, only that he was content to *appear* inactive.

New York Times *reporter David Halberstam remembering February–September 1962 Vietnam, in his "The Face of the Enemy in Vietnam,"* Harper's Magazine *(February 1965), p. 10.*

One day I received a call from an old associate, Rod Markley, Ford Motor Company's vice president in charge of government affairs, who said he had learned something he thought I would wish to know. He said that Red Duffy, Ford's vice president in charge of the company's East Coast plants selling to the Defense Department, had been told that unless his division made a financial contribution to the Democratic Party, the contracts would be canceled. I had worked with

Duffy for years while at Ford. When I angrily asked Rod why Duffy had not reported what was clearly a grossly illegal act directly to me, Rod said Duffy feared that those in the Defense Department to whom I would refer the matter would retaliate against Ford.

Former Ford CEO and Kennedy's secretary of defense Robert McNamara remembering defense contract corruption shortly before the October 1962 Cuban Missile Crisis, in his In Retrospect: The Tragedy and Lessons of Vietnam *(1995), p. 92.*

The Indochina crisis, unlike the others Kennedy inherited, was entirely of our own making, did not directly affect our national interest and got worse instead of better during his presidency—though not as bad as it would get after his death.

Veteran political correspondent, Vietnam reporter, and diplomat William Attwood summarizing Kennedy's role in Southeast Asia policy making before the Cuban Missile Crisis, Papers of William Attwood, Ambassador to Guinea, JFK Library.

The advantage of the Communist system over our system is the fact that they don't have to pay attention to your allies. They don't have newspapers that leak, to whom things are leaked—and only things that they want appear in papers.

Robert Kennedy discussing the Kennedy administration's South Vietnamese and French allies and during the Indochina crisis of 1962 implying that few of them are trustworthy, in Robert F. Kennedy Oral History Project, JFK Library.

The New Pacific Community (NPC) Proposal

Much has been discussed about some of us Americans who are "ugly." Our next job, Mr. President, yours and mine, is to invite our fellow Americans out there and implore them to open their eyes and not be "ugly," because we Guamanians are proud that we now may be permitted to show what we have to offer. I am confident that, of those who find their way out there, none will be disappointed.

Pacific policy specialist Arthur Dellinger praising, in his own way, President Kennedy for including the U.S. Territory of Guam in his New Pacific Community organization proposal, in Dellinger memo to Kennedy, August 1962, Guam Files/Box 101, JFK Library.

The "new wave" of international communism is advancing to the Pacific, as far as the Fiji Islands. To cope with this situation, I feel that it is necessary for the free nations on the Pacific to initiate and develop more effective systems of cooperation and friendship, including, perhaps, the New Pacific Community.

Prime Minister Eisaku Sato of Japan suggesting to President Kennedy on September 19, 1962, that the Japanese government might someday be receptive to the founding of a New Pacific Community organization, in Sato to Kennedy, September 19, 1962, White House Central File/Box 62, file document without page number, JFK Library.

Castro, King, and Doing the Right Thing

I am amazed that, in the West, where you suppose that there are cultured societies and that people think, there's such a strong tendency to associate historical events with individuals and to magnify the role of the individual. I can see it myself: Castro's Cuba, Castro did this, Castro undid that. Almost everything in this country is attributed to Castro, Castro's doing, Castro's perversities. That type of mentality abounds in the West; unfortunately, it's quite widespread. It seems to me to be an erroneous approach to historical and political events.

Fidel Castro, after nearly a quarter century of refusing interviews with American reporters or officials, discussing leadership and economic issues with historian Jeffrey Elliot and California Congressman Mervyn Dymally, in Elliot and Dymally, Fidel Castro: Nothing Can Stop the Course of History *(1985), p. 51.*

There are three things which are real: God, human folly, and laughter. The first two are beyond our comprehension. So we must do what we can with the third.

An inscription on a mug given by President Kennedy to aide Dave Powers in either 1962 or 1963, Display item, Museum wing of the JFK Library.

I think that we had done a great deal, made a major effort on voting. I felt strongly about the fact that voting was at the heart of the problem. If enough Negroes registered, they could obtain redress of their grievances internally, without the federal government being involved in it at all. We had found inadequacies in the law in areas where we felt that the law could be improved. Perhaps—because it was voting, and it was such an elementary, basic right—we could obtain acceptance by Congress.

Attorney General Robert Kennedy, in a 1964 interview with Anthony Lewis, discussing his office's civil rights approach and strategies during the 1962 voter registration drives of his brother's presidential administration, quoted in Robert F. Kennedy Oral History Project, JFK Library.

King tried to keep himself and his colleagues from catching the paranoia of which they were targets. As they began to assume that the FBI was bugging just about every place King went, he would joke about it, according to Andrew Young, and "when somebody would say something a little fresh or flip, Martin would say, 'Ol' Hoover's gonna have you in the Golden Record Club if you're not careful.'" But there was a chilling effect in the knowledge that the strategies they talked about in their meetings or on the telephone were known to the government with whom they were dealing—that such inside information would probably be in the hands of the President himself.

Harris Wofford, President Kennedy's special assistant for civil rights and future U.S. senator, assessing the impact of FBI harassment of Martin Luther King's inner circle during 1962, in Papers of Harris Llewellyn Wofford, JFK Library.

I thought that the Justice Department did a tremendous behind-the-scenes job of pulling the Birmingham community together. The country, I think, could have gone either way. Either there could have been a response to nonviolence in the creative, nonviolent manner that Martin had designed and the Kennedy Administration supported. Or there could have been a rejection and frustration. Birmingham was in such a state, then, that either the black or the white community could have gotten out of hand any minute.

Andrew Young, the former executive vice president of the Southern Christian Leadership Conference and a future U.S. ambassador to the United Nations, noting that 1962 Birmingham and related Alabama challenges represented a critical transition point for the civil rights movement, in Robert F. Kennedy Oral History Project, JFK Library.

3

Lessons of the Cuban Missile Crisis
October 1962–December 1963

During early 1962, a majority of Americans admitted to the Gallup Poll that World War III was inevitable. Heavy casualties were to be expected, they said, but the American way of life would somehow prevail. If they had had any knowledge of U.S. top secret defense policy and the number of nuclear weapons involved, their latter conclusion might have been different. It took the events of October 1962 to change their minds.

While Americans expressed their World War III concerns to the Gallup Poll, the Soviets quietly began to supply the Castro regime with an astonishing number of offensive nuclear weapons. According to their original plan, the Soviets intended to give the Cuban government a total of 42 medium-range missiles by 1963. With a range of more than 1,100 miles, those missiles could easily reach America's heartland. An additional 24 intermediate-range missiles

At the beginning of the Cuban Missile Crisis, John and Robert Kennedy (left) meet in what will be a number of personal conferences about U.S. policy options. *(John F. Kennedy Library/Cecil Stoughton)*

71

were offered but never arrived. Their range doubled that of the medium-range missiles. Forty-eight outdated Soviet bombers were also promised, and more than 40,000 Red Army advisers were assigned to Cuban duty.[1] It was difficult for the Soviets to hide a military assistance program of this magnitude, and its discovery by the United States triggered the World War III–threatening Cuban Missile Crisis.

THIRTEEN DAYS IN OCTOBER

To the outside world, it was business as usual at the Kennedy White House in early October 1962. A visiting girls choir from Arkansas sang for the president on the White House back lawn. Kennedy joked with the press about his inability to carry a tune and offered wisecracks about certain personalities running in the upcoming congressional elections. No one knew that the president had already been informed by U.S. Air Force intelligence about the Soviet missile program in Cuba. Yet rumors of a strong Soviet military presence there had already made page one of both the *New York Times* and the *Washington Post*. These press accounts fueled attacks by Republicans against Kennedy's "weak hemispheric policy." In fact, shortly before Congress recessed for the 1962 congressional elections, Senate Democrats had countered Republican charges by writing and passing a resolution in favor of using "massive retaliation" against Cuba if the Soviets continued their military role there. The vote was 86–1, although no one in Congress knew about the Soviet buildup in Cuba.

The charge of being soft on communism, and in America's own backyard, continued to be politically devastating in fall 1962. Kennedy especially worried about the fate of his Alliance for Progress and whether Congress would continue to fund a program championed by an allegedly weak president. Up-and-running for more than a year, the alliance had already made significant contributions to infrastructure development in Latin America. But nobody seemed to notice. It was the continued existence of Castro's blatantly anti-American regime that dominated all hemispheric concerns.

Both Kennedy supporters and detractors did not need the knowledge of missiles in Cuba to demand a militant anti-Castro stance. Even New York's senator Jacob Javits, an avowed liberal Republican who had supported the Kennedy administration in most matters of legislation, announced that if there ever was a war-threatening crisis involving Castro he doubted that the White House had the "courage" to wage a limited nuclear war. Senator Homer Capehart, a proud Republican conservative from Indiana, insisted that the president must announce a 1963 timetable for a Cuban invasion, and popular columnist James Reston, a Kennedy supporter, urged the White House to demonstrate its leadership and expose Soviet-inspired tyranny in Cuba. The political pressure was intense, and, combined with Kennedy's own eloquent promises to defeat communism as soon as possible, the existence of the missiles in Cuba only hastened the march to war.

Kennedy answered his critics in public at the same time that his administration debated a response to the Soviet missile program in private. The president particularly disliked *Newsweek*'s pun and accusation that he was a "Profile in Indecision" when it came to Cuba. Offering a vague response, Kennedy announced that his administration would do whatever must be done to protect

U.S. security. Now, still in top secrecy, his administration began to debate just what that might entail.

For what is officially regarded as 13 days (often labeled from the late afternoon of October 14 to the early morning of October 28, 1962), the world teetered on the brink of nuclear war. Should the United States attack, the Defense Department estimate for Eastern European region casualty figures ranged from 70 million to 300 million dead depending upon the target priorities. After the crisis, and when further in-depth studies were accomplished, those estimates were found to be low ones.

In general terms, the Joint Chiefs of Staff favored an immediate air strike against the Soviet missile emplacements in Cuba. They could not guarantee 100 percent accuracy, and they admitted that as many as three or possibly more nuclear missiles might still be fired at the United States. In the meantime, if the Soviets retaliated against U.S. bases in Turkey, seized Berlin, or both, the most effective American response was the nuclear obliteration of most Soviet cities. Kennedy and his cabinet debated whether this threat of nuclear destruction should be announced to the American people. Brushing aside concerns from his closest aides that this announcement might cause a panic or stimulate reckless demands for an American first strike, on October 22, 1962, Kennedy went on television and explained the peril facing humankind.

To ordinary Americans, the announcement that their country might soon face a nuclear attack came as quite a shock. Although they had been voting against candidates who were "soft on communism" for years, it had been a political matter and nothing more. Suddenly, anticommunism meant a life-and-death struggle here at home, and the tension took its toll. Most Americans, the Kennedy White House soon discovered, wanted peace and security for their families.

Entire regions of the country now faced nuclear obliteration, and their residents prayed for peace. For Americans living in the northern sections of the country or in areas that Castro's missiles could never reach, their fear was focused on radiation sickness and not on obliteration. From Seattle to Boston, northerners flocked to the grocery stores, buying out every possible necessity to survive a long period of locked-up seclusion in their homes. Most civil defense authorities agreed that if the wind blew north from the nuclear-destroyed south, the radiation poisoning that came with it would remain intact for at least two months. The governors of northern states even stationed National Guardsmen at certain grocery stores in order to protect food supplies, prevent total buy-outs by only a handful of people, and provide a sense of order and discipline. America's churches were open on weeknights so that the concerned faithful could make their peace with God. The once vigilant anticommunist America had become America the scared.

This fear and nervousness took the political community by surprise. The U.S. electorate was supposed to consist of iron-willed anticommunists who were always ready to go the distance against tyranny and evil. Obviously, the anticommunist cause had its limits, and many Americans were now concerned about survival and not cold war victory. The Kennedy administration had to deal with this unexpected reaction. Their own belligerent speeches had played a role in the escalation of the cold war, and a basic question needed to be answered soon. Was American security truly at stake in the Cuban Missile

Crisis or was it a matter of making good on campaign promises? If it was the latter, then there was no good reason for World War III. Over the 13-day period of the Cuban Missile Crisis, the Kennedy administration concluded that diplomacy and not war was the best solution. The trick was convincing the Soviets that peace was in their interest as well—without making Premier

President Kennedy officially authorizes the U.S. "quarantine" during the Cuban Missile Crisis. *(John F. Kennedy Library)*

Khrushchev lose face in the eyes of his volatile generals should he agree to remove the missiles from Cuba.[2]

As early as 1961, Khrushchev had concluded that Kennedy was young, inexperienced, and wobbly on important issues both at home and abroad. In the matter of Cuba, he had assured the Kremlin that Kennedy could be easily maneuvered. The nuclear missiles would be hated in Washington, but little would come of it. After all, he argued, the forced removal of the missiles would trigger World War III. Unless Kennedy went mad, Khrushchev said, the young president did not have the stamina for a horrible war. In the meantime, the Soviets would tip the balance of power in the Western Hemisphere, adding clout to the message that capitalism was waning and communism was the future. According to his memoirs, Khrushchev was questioned by his own government for tempting world war over a propaganda stunt, but the Soviet dictator insisted that all would be well.[3] He was mistaken.

Since the term *blockade* was unacceptable in international law, Kennedy imposed a "quarantine" against Soviet ships carrying military hardware to Cuba. In the 20th century, the term *quarantine* dated back to the Franklin Roosevelt administration's cautious response to the Japanese invasion of China. The term *blockade* was associated with an act of war. In the 1962 quarantine, the U.S. Navy was ordered to halt, board, and inspect, if necessary, suspected Soviet vessels. Any ship could be turned back into international waters or seized, but the Kennedy administration hoped the Soviets would never let the situation get that far. The decision for war would rest with the Soviet government and not Washington. That was the point. Ideally, the quarantine was supposed to convince Khrushchev that the best policy involved an end to supplying Castro and the beginning of negotiations with the White House.

At first, Khrushchev denounced the U.S. quarantine but also kept Soviet ships away from the U.S. Navy. This did not mean the tension was over. On October 26, the U.S. Navy stopped and boarded a Soviet-charted Panamanian vessel, *Marcula,* to verify it was not carrying nuclear weapons bound for Cuba. In response, Khrushchev sent a letter to Kennedy, noting that he was ready to remove the missiles if the U.S. military did not invade Cuba. The following morning the White House received another official letter from Khrushchev insisting that the missiles would be taken out of Cuba only if the United States did the same with its missiles in Turkey. Deciding that a power struggle must be going on in the Kremlin, the Kennedy cabinet wrestled over the meaning of these contradictory letters. The first letter, they concluded, sounded more like Khrushchev and the second more like his generals. Answering only the first, the White House accepted Khrushchev's proposal.

Attorney General Robert Kennedy personally conveyed the U.S. decision to the Soviet ambassador, Anatoly Dobrynin. Dobrynin's colleague, V. I. Zorin, the Soviet ambassador to the United Nations, had already embarrassed his country by refusing to admit in public that there were missiles in Cuba. This was in the face of photographic evidence presented to the United Nations and the world by U.S. Ambassador Adlai Stevenson. Urging Dobrynin to state the obvious and discuss the World War III threat, Stevenson exclaimed that he was prepared to wait "until hell freezes over" in the interest of keeping the peace. Stevenson's candor won international acclaim and also erased certain doubts in the White House that he was too much of the humanitarian to represent tough U.S. security interests.

On October 28, Khrushchev agreed that the missiles would be dismantled as long as Kennedy left Cuba alone. The tension and the threats subsided, and the 13-day threat of nuclear war was over. As the world breathed a sigh of relief, the Kennedy administration turned to verification matters during the next several weeks. They wanted United Nations inspection teams to verify the missile dismantling work, but Castro refused. The dismantling moved slowly. On November 20, 1962, Kennedy ended the U.S. Navy quarantine with his announcement that all known missile sites had been shut down. Finally, in January 1963 at the United Nations, both the U.S. and Soviet governments formally declared an end to the Cuban Missile Crisis.[4] Most Americans thought it had been over for weeks but welcomed the officially declared truce.

POP CULTURE SOLDIERS ON

Threats of nuclear war or not, the movie and music business continued to make a great deal of difference in the everyday lives of America's youth. In the summer of 1962, the Motion Picture Association of America announced that youth-oriented films had made the most money in the opening months of the 1960s. One of the biggest hits of 1962 was *Blue Hawaii*. First released in time for the student vacations of the Christmas 1961 holiday, *Blue Hawaii* continued to win box office records in its neighborhood theater runs throughout 1962 and early 1963. Its star, Elvis Presley, said this musical represented the peak of his career, and the film's signature song, "Can't Help Falling in Love," became something of a theme song at Presley concerts for the rest of the superstar's career.

While Elvis remained the King in both the movies and on the radio, the general entertainment industry attempted to adjust. Veteran film director John Ford, whose favorite star, John Wayne, still rivaled Presley for box office sales, insisted that both young and old movie watchers still liked to see great examples of traditional American heroism and values on the screen. Elvis, he implied, did not embody those values. Ford's *The Man Who Shot Liberty Valance,* a western starring Wayne, James Stewart, and Lee Marvin, was supposed to prove the point. During the Cuban Missile Crisis, Ford and his long-standing Hollywood colleagues said that the heroes of *Liberty Valance* represented justice, commitment, and the best in American life. Wayne played an old-fashioned, eye-for-an-eye hero in the small frontier town of Shinbone. Stewart played the upstart Shinbone lawyer who favored peace and reason. Marvin, who played the film's villain, Liberty Valance, was supposed to represent, according to the critics, both the dark side of Americana and even the Soviets during the ongoing Cuban Missile Crisis. Despite a great deal of promotion, star power, and critical attention, the film was not a great success for Ford. Hollywood wondered why.

Once the mainstay of Hollywood productions, the western was losing out to Elvis and a hip, young audience that preferred modern settings to horses and six-guns. The western formula plot had remained largely unchanged since the early days of film. *Liberty Valance* was an adequate example of the genre, but it was time for a new genre.

Hollywood needed a replacement for the tired western hero. Ironically, he came from Britain, preferred an Aston Martin to horses, ordered his drinks

In the early 1960s on the eve of the "British Invasion," Elvis Presley remains the rock-and-roll "King" both on the radio and at the box office. *(Used by permission, Elvis Presley Enterprises, Inc.)*

"shaken not stirred," and represented a new breed of high-tech hero. Ian Fleming's cold war superspy, James Bond, leaped from book to film in the early 1960s with *Dr. No* and *From Russia With Love*. But it would take months before the handsome young star of these adventure films, Sean Connery, became a household name in America.

Part of what would be known by the mid-1960s as the "British Invasion," the early Bond films were not quite right for the Cuban Missile Crisis–frightened Americans of late 1962. The films had their cult following in the few East

Coast cities where they were first shown, but it would be their second or road-show release, after the high tension of the cold war simmered down, that finally won the attention of America's youth. To some, Bond's quick wit, playboy antics, reliance on high-tech killing machines, and attraction to the comfortable life represented the ideal male of the 1960s. More to the point, his flashy, contemporary heroism matched Elvis's flashy, contemporary music.[5] He was overdue.

A NEW CONGRESS

After the Cuban Missile Crisis, U.S. voters were in the mood to reward all those who had kept them alive. When Khrushchev proclaimed that he accepted Kennedy's no-invasion guarantee, the U.S. congressional elections had been just days away. Years later, some historians would argue that Kennedy worsened U.S.-Soviet relations and threatened war only to win more Democratic seats in Congress. Indeed, the post–Cuban Missile Crisis Congress would be much more to Kennedy's liking. Liberal New Frontiersmen from Wisconsin to California entered Congress as freshmen. But this would not guarantee easy passage of such controversial legislation as civil rights. In the meantime, American voters did not have to wait 20 years to read a revisionist historian's account of Kennedy's so-called real intentions. Shortly before voting day in November 1962, former president Eisenhower even claimed that Kennedy had manufactured the entire Cuban matter. But few voters agreed. Kennedy won the hearts of even some of his critics by noting that there were no victors in the Cuban Missile Crisis, "only survivors." It was a modest statement, and the American public approved.[6]

Where one stood on the Cuban Missile Crisis and when became a litmus test in some 1962 races and again in 1964. Governor Gaylord Nelson of Wisconsin, who mobilized the National Guard in his state early in the crisis, won reelection easily because of that quick decision. Two years later, he was sent to the Senate in a landslide election, largely thanks to his success in reminding the voters that he had cared about their security sooner and faster than most American politicians of the day. Like many Democrats who benefited from the Cuban Missile Crisis, Nelson interpreted the entire matter as a lesson in peacemaking. Later, he became one of the first elected officials to challenge the constitutionality of America's unilateral role in Vietnam.

One of the biggest losers of November 1962 was Kennedy's rival of two years earlier, Richard Nixon. Seeking California's governorship and not a return to Congress, Nixon had decided to run against the incumbent governor, Pat Brown. At first, the polls ran 5 to 3 in the former vice president's favor. But Eisenhower's attack on Kennedy after the Cuban Missile Crisis also had a negative impact on Nixon's campaign. Making matters worse, the ex-president told the press that Nixon had done little to qualify himself for state government service. It was a bizarre turn of events. Privately, Eisenhower, along with the Federal Bureau of Investigation's (FBI's) J. Edgar Hoover, had urged Nixon to run, establish a reputable political base, and challenge Kennedy again in 1964. Going back to Congress as a freshman would be demeaning, they all agreed.

The nation watched the California race closely. From fashion to politics, it seemed to many that California represented all the latest trends of the new decade. To some, this California election was a referendum on the status of Kennedy's influence, the impact of the Cuban Missile Crisis, and the future of Richard Nixon. Consequently, to the grand annoyance of congressional candidates who sought more press attention, the California election took on a degree of drama usually reserved for presidential contests.

At first, Nixon was overly optimistic. His opponent in the Republican primary elections was Joe Shell, the leader of the California State Assembly. A strong critic of his own party, Shell courted endorsements from the right-wing John Birch Society and other diehard conservatives. Thinking it would be easy to isolate Shell as a right-wing extremist, Nixon anticipated a great landslide victory. He continued to work on his new book, *Six Crises,* avoided specific issues in his speeches and made TV appearances that emphasized his human side. Nixon's campaign critics in 1960 had complained that he always looked wooden or distant on television. In 1962, he was seen joking and carrying on with his family or playing dance hall tunes on his piano for TV talk shows. But few in his family wanted him to run again. Nixon won his party's nod in the primary, but Joe Shell took over one-third of the vote.[7] The time for optimism was over.

Nixon's race against Governor Brown was not easy. Dodging charges that he sought a second chance at Kennedy only from a position of power, Nixon was pressured by Brown to "make a commitment to California." The former vice president vowed to serve a full four-year term if he won the election. That meant he would not be able to run for president in 1964. Kennedy would have to face other opponents, such as New York's Nelson Rockefeller or Arizona's Barry Goldwater. The future of the Republican party would, most likely in Nixon's view, be determined by them.

Things went from bad to worse for Nixon. The Brown campaign claimed that while serving as vice president Nixon had used his position to win a defense contract for his brother's business in California. Nixon denied the charge, and he even claimed that Kennedy could have used this particular accusation against him but was too "gracious" to try. That comment implied that Nixon had little regard for Brown, and the election suddenly became a debate over Nixon's choice of words, ethics, and tactics. With his campaign receiving little or no coverage during the 13 days of the Cuban Missile Crisis, Nixon tried to separate himself from Eisenhower and the Kennedy critics by endorsing the president's general handling of U.S. foreign policy. Brown charged that the former vice president's word choice, once again, was in poor taste. According to Brown, Nixon's vague endorsement of New Frontier diplomacy, and not the specific matter of Cuban policy, was a backhanded insult of the White House. The Nixon comeback was doomed. He lost to Brown by 297,000 out of nearly 6 million votes cast.

Herbert Klein, Nixon's close associate and adviser, read the concession statement to the press, and Klein found that most unusual. Throughout the nation's long political tradition, the defeated candidate met the press personally. With reporters yelling "Where's the vice president?" an angry Nixon finally took the stage. Noting that the press was "delighted" to hear that he had lost, Nixon claimed that many reporters had been "after" him since his days on the House Un-American Affairs Committee. He was tired of "getting the shaft," he said, and added, "You won't have 'Dick' Nixon to kick around anymore."[8]

To some, Nixon's bizarre exit from politics symbolized the ultimate victory of Kennedy's New Frontier and the beginning of a new era of bipartisan cooperation. In any event, it was time to move on. To Robert Kennedy, the period following the November elections and the Cuban Missile Crisis truly encouraged reflection and reconsideration. The flaming win-the-cold-war rhetoric had been as much a casualty of late 1962 as Nixon had. Talk of cold war victory now seemed callous and reckless. The moment was right to take another one of the New Frontier's "first steps," and this time in the direction of both foreign and domestic peace.

NEW DEAL REVISITED?

One important example of Kennedy's post–Cuban Missile Crisis experimentalism involved economic policy. In 1963, Kennedy decided to make an economic attack on U.S. poverty the centerpiece of his reelection campaign. His rhetoric was clear. All the energies once used to win a cold war on the battlefield, he said, should now be translated into winning "the war against poverty" at home. In fact, the proposed "war" was not as expensive as it sounded. The budget would remain well

Participants of the March on Washington await a speech by Martin Luther King, Jr. *(National Archives)*

below $1 billion, and precise target areas would be stressed. The primary target was the U.S. South, and Kennedy expected to win the quick support of his largest cadre of conservative critics (southern congressmen) because of it.

Lyndon Johnson especially found merit in the southern target, for it would win strategic political support for other New Frontier bills such as civil rights. But the Kennedy team was divided on the effort's ideological worth. Secretary of State Dean Rusk thought it might win the attention of the world, offering further demonstrations of democratic generosity versus communist platitudes. But even some of Rusk's own men, such as Soviet affairs specialist George Kennan, insisted that poverty was a fact of life. No one policy would ever eliminate it, he said. Robert Kennedy strongly disagreed, urging that his brother make a swing tour through impoverished Appalachia with the press in tow. On November 20, 1963, just two days before his assassination, the president decided that the "war on poverty" must be an irreversible commitment for his administration; however, he wanted a balanced policy of generosity for middle-class Americans as well. Kennedy was killed before he could define what that balanced policy might be, although he had offered hints throughout 1963.

Kennedy's balancing of antipoverty programs with a middle-class tax cut was unique for its day. Offering a little something to everyone was in keeping with New Deal efforts, but the tactics and methods were classic 1960s New Frontier. Socialist writer, politician, and economist Michael Harrington even claimed that Kennedy's plan put an end to New Deal procedures. To Harrington, Kennedy's economic musings helped Wall Street first and Main Street last, but he admired the president's commitment to action. As always, Kennedy had his share of critics, and his agenda truly needed help by fall 1963.

Kennedy's treasury secretary, C. Douglas Dillon, tried his best to rescue it all. The son of a millionaire banker, Dillon suggested that there should be no special sector of the economy that benefits more from Kennedy's economic policies than others. No poor, middle-class, or wealthy neighborhood should be singled out. Let the money flow, he argued, and good investments would result. Scared to death that their special interests might be harmed by an open tax cut decision, Capitol Hill lobbyists succeeded in delaying the president's 1964 economic plans. It would take Kennedy's assassination and Johnson's skillful maneuvering to see a socially balanced economic package of tax cuts and antipoverty measures pass through Congress.

Some special interests (particularly liberal ones) won out in the Johnson-negotiated final bill, but the bottom line was a grab bag of budgetary proposals for the general economy. This was Johnson's biggest pitch, learning quickly from the no-win debate over who deserved more money and who did not. By November 1964 and Johnson's own formal election to the presidency, the gross national product had moved steadily upward and unemployment had been cut down to 4.1 percent. But Kennedy had laid the groundwork.[9]

THE NUCLEAR TEST BAN TREATY

Given the Cuban Missile Crisis revelation that most Americans wanted peace and not "massive retaliation," Kennedy saw an opportunity for new directions in foreign policy as well. Years later, Robert McNamara remembered that the

Kennedy cabinet feared that nuclear war was inevitable during much of the Cuban Missile Crisis. They felt lucky to be alive, he noted, and no one wanted to live through another October 1962.

Although he had been chosen largely because of his managerial skills, McNamara learned the hard way that America's defense apparatus was frighteningly difficult to manage. It was also geared for global destruction. To McNamara, the potential for nuclear holocaust remained too high, and the Kennedy administration had a moral obligation to lessen it. His point of view always implied that the Kennedy team was partially responsible for bringing on the Cuban Missile Crisis, and this remained a controversial point in cabinet discussions. In spite of the Defense Department's recognition of the nuclear danger, Kennedy still headed a government that maintained the most destructive arsenal in U.S. peacetime history. He agreed with McNamara's call for serious disarmament discussions with the Soviets, but there were political dangers to consider as well.

For a time, the Kennedy team debated whether or not to launch a disarmament drive after the 1964 election. Over the months, the voters would be educated about the need for less and not more confrontation with the Soviets. Vice President Johnson pointed out that liberals and even moderates might support nuclear disarmament no matter what. On the other hand, as memories faded of the Cuban Missile Crisis, Johnson warned that conservative political activists might resurrect loud public support for massive retaliation. Timing was everything in politics, Johnson reminded the cabinet, and something had to be done sooner rather than later.

The machinery for doing something was already in place. Founded in 1958, the United Nations Disarmament Commission had been mandated with the task of slowing the East-West arms race. Particularly between 1958 and 1961, the U.S. and Soviet delegations at the commission could agree that radiation posed a danger to the entire world, that nuclear testing must halt someday, and that nuclear arsenals outside of existing ones must be discouraged in other countries. Considering the U.S. versus Soviet tension, these were interesting agreements. They had had no impact on Washington and Moscow's defense policies, and their disagreements were bitter ones.

The commission's membership argued over their mission and purpose. The Americans favored a general arms control pact. The Soviets favored a nuclear test ban treaty first, and then arms control talks would follow. Compromise was difficult, although both the Americans and British had agreed to support a Soviet-sponsored nuclear testing moratorium. This support remained voluntary, and the Cuban Missile Crisis had exposed the folly of the commission's endless discussions. The volatile debate over verification procedures should a test ban schedule be arranged had ended the commission's work. Kennedy had to decide if this debate should be resumed and under what circumstances.

As he had demonstrated during the Cuban Missile Crisis, Kennedy preferred full disclosure to the American people. Whereas National Security Adviser Walt Rostow advocated a cautious and secret approach to the disarmament cause for years to come, the president decided to test the political waters. In a Harvard University speech, Kennedy eloquently condemned those who had learned nothing from the Cuban Missile Crisis. The Americans who favored the "peace of the grave," he said, were not assisting U.S. security. Implying that a ban on nuclear testing might be the "first step" to a meaningful disarmament pact, Kennedy suggested that containing the nuclear threat was not being "soft on communism." There were other means outside of nuclear destruction to demonstrate the anticommunist commitment.

For its time, Kennedy's marching away from "massive retaliation" promises was a daring move. It was also well received in the polls. Kennedy's public gamble worked, providing him with the new image of nuclear disarmament leader. Of course, a specific U.S.-Soviet agreement was now required, and that was the real test of this gamble.

Between July 15 and August 5, 1963, the Americans and the Soviets resumed their nuclear arms discussions. This was possible thanks to a groundbreaking agreement to focus on explosions that could be verified by remote detection systems only. Khrushchev's caution during these talks was difficult for the Kennedy administration to analyze. Both McNamara and Rostow believed that Khrushchev was under heavy pressure from Stalinist opponents to demonstrate his competence as a national leader. To his critics in the Kremlin, Khrushchev had misjudged the American reaction over Cuba and had threatened his nation's destruction because of it. To others, Khrushchev was the man who surrendered too quickly to Kennedy's pressures when he could have attacked the United States and won. The White House was not sure which critics were the most troubling to the Soviet premier, but there was a general consensus that Khrushchev's days as the unassailable leader of his country were quickly coming to an end. Time was running out for an agreement in 1963.

In August 1963, the elusive accord was finally reached. Formally called the Treaty Banning Nuclear Weapons Tests in the Atmosphere, in Outer Space, and Under Water, it was also known as the Partial Test Ban Treaty to diplomats or the Nuclear Test Ban Treaty to the media. This unprecedented U.S.-Soviet arrangement prohibited all but underground nuclear tests. The latter was exempt from the ban because, at the time, remote underground sensing gear was unavailable. An underground test was also impossible to detect by other National Technical Means (NTM). NTM referred to intelligence collecting systems used to monitor nuclear tests, including spy satellites and electronic monitoring devices.

During the summer 1963 negotiations, both the Americans and the Soviets were reluctant to discuss their respective reconnaissance operations and capabilities. It became quite the sticking point, and Kennedy was easily frustrated by the slow-moving nature of the new talks. The negotiations developed the "National Technical Means" euphemism to avoid arguments over specific intelligence efforts. This decision over semantics led directly to the signing of the agreement. The careful avoidance of divisive arguments over intelligence operations would become a characteristic of arms reduction talks for the remaining years of the cold war.

Also forbidding explosions that would spread radioactive debris beyond the testing country's own territorial limits, the Nuclear Test Ban Treaty was a large, complex document. But the signing ceremony was short and even fun. Khrushchev was in top form there, joking, laughing, and obviously suggesting that the Soviets welcomed peace, too. At long last, he said on a more serious note, the Americans welcomed his aging 1950s call for "peaceful coexistence" between communism and capitalism. But the American president was the scene stealer here.

In the press, Kennedy was now hailed as a great peacemaker. He even won warm endorsements from some of the United States's critics in the allied camp (such as Japan).[10] Ahead lay the 1964 campaign, the hint of easy victory, and the promise of more diplomatic innovations. But the reelection would also be a referendum on civil rights and increasing racial tensions. More work needed to be done.

NONVIOLENCE AND ATTORNEY GENERAL KENNEDY

In 1963, Martin Luther King, Jr., described the goals of nonviolent civil disobedience in his "Letter from Birmingham Jail." This detailed document offered examples of successful nonviolence use in the past and connected his methods to religious and philosophical principles that deserved respect and recognition.

Perhaps the most memorable passage of the "Letter" involved his description of anger. He said that he saw it in the eyes of his own young daughter who could not enter the amusement park she had dreamed of enjoying. He could see her disappointment turning to rage against the white community, and her bitterness might last a lifetime. He railed against the poverty that condemned the black community, and he warned that fellow civil rights activists were on the edge of "violent expression."

With the use of fire hoses and attack dogs, the Birmingham police had broken up civil rights demonstrations and jailed as many as possible. Bull Con-

Determined to end all civil rights "threats" to what he calls "his city," Birmingham's "Bull" Connor confronts nonviolence demonstrators. Connor's efforts began to lose him support from Alabama moderates and some conservatives. *(Birmingham Public Library, Department of Archives and Manuscripts)*

nor continued to proclaim that his segregated city would never "give an inch." Angry young blacks retaliated by assaulting police and burning down white-owned stores in the town's most struggling neighborhoods. King's pleas for calm helped ease the tension, but some 1,300 remained in jail while the White House concentrated on its Nuclear Test Ban negotiations.

As the Kennedy administration contemplated the best course of action, events were moving too fast for the racist tradition in Birmingham. For the first time, every national television news program put the civil rights issue at the top of its coverage. White extremism was condemned in that coverage, and the Birmingham city fathers began to worry about the future of their home. Meanwhile, King's "Letter" was already touted as an example of great American political literature, and the majority of white business and political leaders began to lobby for calm. A biracial council was established to police racial desegregation in Birmingham, and social peace was restored.

Behind the last-minute scenes of this sea change in Birmingham had been Robert Kennedy's Justice Department. Tired of the charges of leading from behind on the issue of racial violence, the Kennedy administration finally intervened in Birmingham. To many African Americans, it was better late than never. Boldly disagreeing with FBI conclusions that King's movement was either influenced or infiltrated by communists, Attorney General Kennedy urged Alabama authorities to accept federal law. He was not beneath using anger and threats of his own, and he was never in a compromising mood. This did not mean that his office fully endorsed King's efforts. Robert Kennedy disagreed with the civil rights leader on tactics, strategy, and even his choice of words with the press. In spite of these differences, King recognized the larger issues at hand. The Kennedys and their federal government were his allies, and city- or state-based ordinances that championed discrimination were destined to fall because of it.

John Kennedy became especially visible during the 1963 civil rights battles, clearly supporting Justice Department efforts. As always, the president connected Birmingham's problems to America's greater effort to champion democratic values in the world. Is America, he asked his viewers in a nationally televised address, the land of the free "except for the Negro"? This address constituted Kennedy's strongest civil rights statement of his presidency, confirming King's belief that "victory for justice" was at hand.

One of the major lessons of Birmingham for King was the significance of social status in the civil rights struggle. Most of the civil rights leaders and early activists could claim some sort of middle-class background. Yet much of the effort in Birmingham had been carried by the urban poor. The latter were eager for change, and King addressed the matter squarely. Ending black poverty, he proclaimed after the crisis, must be the new central goal of the Civil Rights movement. Attorney General Kennedy offered his support for this decision, noting that his brother's administration shared similar goals.[11] But there was another voice in this matter, and, in his own way, he had championed the concerns of impoverished African Americans long before King and the Kennedys. His name was Malcolm X.

Born Malcolm Little in 1925, Little abandoned his slave name in favor of X (which was supposed to symbolize his unknown African name) when he joined the Nation of Islam or Black Muslims in the late 1940s. His father had

Proud and defiant, Malcolm X
challenges his critics. *(Herman Heller,
Library of Congress)*

been a Baptist minister and an admirer of black nationalist Marcus Garvey, but
Malcolm, at first, followed a life of crime and not his father's example. Jailed for
robbery in 1946, Malcolm spent six years in prison. Following his release, he
became a Nation of Islam minister, championing black pride, opposing integration, and castigating whites as the enemy. Concentrating his message in the
black ghettos of northern cities, Malcolm X urged his listeners to strike out
against their white oppressors. Eloquent, dedicated, and usually in the company
of numerous body guards, Malcolm X represented the opposite of King's message of nonviolence. He also scared white America.

When challenged by King's supporters over what his specific goals might
be, Malcolm X rarely had an answer. He talked vaguely about a new black

homeland and the end of poverty, but the bottom line to the Malcolm X appeal was his message of impatience, desperation, and violence. Ironically, as he became a national figure, Malcolm X began to recognize that he might be able to attract a number of followers outside of his traditional power base. At the same time Martin Luther King recognized the significance of poverty and impatience in the civil rights struggle.

In the spring of 1963, Robert Kennedy's office sponsored a conference with urban black leaders, scholars, and writers. Most of them hurled accusations at Kennedy and white America in general. The attorney general was shocked at this expression of hatred, commenting to his staff that he could reason with King but not with the emerging new leadership of the civil rights cause.

At the very moment the Kennedy administration began to worry about the level of anger in the black community, their civil rights bill was sent to Congress. In its support, King led the largest protest march to that date in Washington, D.C. He also delivered his most eloquent speech ("I Have a Dream") on behalf of racial justice. Concerned about the negative impact on white America of a massive demonstration that doubled the population of Washington, D.C., the Kennedy administration maintained a low profile. Eventually, they helped in the march's organization after it was apparent that King was determined to lead it.

King's March on Washington was an amazing achievement, but it had little or no immediate impact on improving race relations. The civil rights bill lingered in Congress, and a church bombing in Birmingham killed four black girls two weeks after King left the nation's capital. In August 1963, Malcolm X even denounced King's March on Washington as a Kennedy-orchestrated "farce."[12] Without question, the Civil Rights movement had come a long way during the New Frontier, but its future seemed quite uncertain at the time of John Kennedy's assassination.

ENDLESS PROSPERITY?

In September 1963, the U.S. Commerce Department issued a report that confirmed the issue of economic disparity. According to this data-filled study, the buying power of America's white middle-class suburban neighborhoods had increased by 43 percent during the first two years of the 1960s. In contrast, the buying power of urban blacks had decreased at a similar rate. Venturing into social analysis, the report predicted an "explosion of racial tension" by the late 1960s unless government increased its efforts to remake America's city centers. Both King and Malcolm X used the report to highlight their own concerns about the economics of racism. In November 1963, John Kennedy commented privately to his brother Robert that the already ambitious "war on poverty" might have to be revised and upgraded before it was too late.

In one of his last news conferences, Kennedy offered an optimistic economic analysis. American industry was riding the wave of a new economic boom, families were spending more than ever, and government coffers were full and soon to be as generous as possible to the nation's underprivileged. In short, the New Frontier message of vigor and commitment continued, and it had the ring of a revised 1960 campaign speech.[13] But in terms of the civil rights struggle, 1960 was a long, long time ago.

Hidden beneath the Civil Rights movement and New Frontier planning was another matter of growing social concern. Its headline-making potential was yet to come, but as early as November 1961, 50,000 American housewives had left their homes to support a massive demonstration called the "Women Strike for Peace." Moved by Kennedy's call for change, the strike's organizers were white middle-class women who had supported feminist issues most of their lives. But the size and mission of the strike suggested that women's issues were no longer reserved to a handful of activists. The news media was especially taken by the fact that strike participants were women not normally associated with political causes. Arguing that America's defense policy was reckless, dangerous, and, therefore, antimotherhood and antifamily, the strike women added a new twist to the cold war debate. Adding that cold war solidarity also kept women confined to the home or shunned from leadership roles in business, the strike asked the Kennedy administration to consider "equity" for women, too.

Kennedy's Commission on the Status of Women was supposed to investigate these concerns, but Congress also investigated the political motivations of the strike leaders for more than two years. The House Un-American Affairs Committee considered strike participants communist sympathizers who attacked family traditions. The women countered that their only political allegiance was to family survival in the nuclear age and equal opportunity in the workplace. Throughout 1962 and 1963, both the investigators and the investigated claimed that they were the ones who represented true Americanism.

At first, civil rights leaders found the debate amusing. Comfortable white housewives, Malcolm X quipped, were arguing for a bigger piece of the pie. But a soon-to-be feminist leader, Betty Friedan, considered the early 1960s a test of fire for feminist issues. For the first time in 50 years since the debate over women's right to vote, the issue of a struggling underclass based on gender was a matter of government and public discussion. Prosperity and its benefits, Friedan said, were determined by white males.[14] The issue of civil rights was more all-encompassing than most of these men believed. Getting this message across would take years. Like Kennedy's New Frontier, Friedan and her women's rights colleagues took a "first step" of their own in the early 1960s.

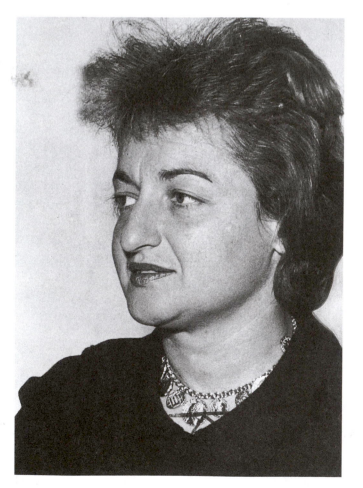

Peoria, Illinois-born Betty Friedan is photographed near the time of the publishing of her landmark book, *The Feminine Mystique. (Fred Palumbo, Library of Congress)*

DEATH IN DALLAS

To continue the New Frontier mission into the mid- and late-1960s, John Kennedy needed a decisive reelection victory. Barely beating Richard Nixon in 1960 had been a source of embarrassment for both the Kennedy family and the Democratic Party. A solid Kennedy win in 1964 would give him better political clout with Congress.

Although it was not unusual, the Texas Democratic Party was squabbling over the president's policies and the role of their favorite son, Lyndon Johnson. Success in Texas was essential to the Kennedy reelection, and on November 21, 1963, Kennedy arrived to shore things up. The first lady accompanied him, though she still disliked political junkets. Meanwhile, Kennedy enunciated the usual New Frontier themes but with more jokes than normally delivered. Being charming and funny could only help.

During the early afternoon of Friday, November 22, John and Jacqueline Kennedy arrived in Dallas. Sitting in the back of a black Lincoln convertible, Kennedy and his wife waved to a crowd that lined the length of his route to a lunchtime speech. The state's conservative governor, John Connally, and his wife sat in the front seat. As they passed a book depository, three shots were fired. One hit the president's neck and the second tore apart the top of his head. Connally was wounded as well, and Kennedy was officially pronounced dead at Dallas's Parkland Hospital a half hour later.

Whether a fifth grader at Holy Cross elementary school in Milwaukee, a leading businessman, or housewife, many Americans found the Kennedy assassination to be a defining moment in their lives. As December 7 (Pearl Harbor) was a day to remember for an older generation or September 11 (terrorist attacks) for a generation to come, November 22 would be a day of reflection for survivors of the 1960s. The news media covered the follow-up events of Kennedy's funeral with reverence, and an official period of mourning governed the nation's daily life for the next three days.

Lyndon Johnson took the oath of office aboard Air Force One during the trip that brought Kennedy's body back to Washington, D.C. Jackie Kennedy, her clothes still soaked in her husband's blood, looked on during the ceremony. While the new president's plane made its journey home, Dallas police arrested Lee Harvey Oswald. A 24-year-old ex-Marine, Oswald was also wanted for the killing of a policeman earlier that same day. A member of a pro-Castro lobby group, Oswald had lived in the Soviet Union and had a Russian wife. He claimed to be innocent of the charges against him. Two days after his arrest, while being transferred to a different jail, Oswald was shot by Jack Ruby, a nightclub owner well known to the police, at point-black range with a pistol. The murder was caught live by network television news.

Given the bizarre circumstances of Oswald's murder and lingering questions about the young man's mysterious past, Johnson ordered an immediate investigation of the Kennedy assassination. Supreme Court Chief Justice Earl Warren headed a commission of seven men, including congressman and future president Gerald Ford. Interviewing more than 500 witnesses and employing teams of forensics specialists, the Warren Commission compiled a lengthy report. Announced from its National Archives-housed headquarters in September 1964, the Warren Commission found Oswald solely guilty for the president's murder. There was no conspiracy, they insisted, but doubts remained in the public mind.[15] From Mark Lane's popular book *Rush to Judgment*, published only two years after the Warren Commission disbanded, to Oliver Stone's blockbuster film *JFK* in the early 1990s, Americans demonstrated their continuing fascination with the possibility of conspiracy.

The conspiracy advocates rarely agreed on one scenario, but they did agree that the Warren Commission was an example of weak research and hasty conclusions. To the commission's critics, Chief Justice Warren had been more interested in calming the nation's fears and protecting President Johnson than in finding the truth. The CIA alone, the Mafia alone, a CIA-Mafia connection, the FBI, Lyndon Johnson, right-wing Defense Department extremists, mysterious Cubans, or at least some sort of large hit squad that included or framed Oswald were, at one time or another, exposed as the "real" killers in the vast literature of conspiracy books, articles, and films.

In the Capitol rotunda, President John Kennedy's body lies in state for the nation's mourners to pay their respects. *(Abbie Rowe, National Park Service, Harry S. Truman Library)*

To some Americans, the White House lies and cover-ups during the dark days of the Vietnam War and the Watergate scandal added credibility to the work of the assassination conspiracy advocates. Thanks to this doubt and concern, public pressure was strong enough to force Congress's hand. In the late 1970s, a special investigative subcommittee was founded in Congress to investigate the Kennedy assassination. Once again, no evidence of a conspiracy was discovered, although some congressmen made headlines by concluding that their own investigation might not have been good enough.[16]

Without question, Camelot and its dramatic "first step" policies ended too abruptly for most Americans. Kennedy's flash, eloquence, and endless commitment was missed immediately and bemoaned for years. This helped explain some of the attraction to bizarre conspiracy theories and to later politicians from Gary Hart to Bill Clinton who promised anything reminiscent of the New Frontier. Meanwhile, Americans wrestled with the significance of Kennedy's senseless death and what his administration had achieved for the country. The conclusions varied as much as the conspiracy accounts. Perhaps the best epitaph for Kennedy's New Frontier came from French writer and philosopher André Malraux. Kennedy, he said, was a "brilliant maybe," destined to do great things but given little time to try.

CHRONICLE OF EVENTS

1962

October 1: Admiral Robert Dennison, the commander-in-chief of the U.S. Atlantic Command, is ordered to "be prepared" to begin a naval blockade (or "quarantine") against Cuba.

October 2: Secretary of Defense Robert McNamara names six instances whereby U.S. military action must be taken against Cuba. They include Soviet assaults on West Berlin, Soviet positioning of offensive nuclear weapons on Cuban soil, a Cuban attack on America's Guantanamo Naval Base in Cuba, a popular uprising in Cuba requiring U.S. aid, a Cuban assault on its Caribbean neighbors, or the president's decision that U.S. security interests are in peril.

October 6: U.S. troops are ordered to increase readiness in anticipation of an imminent attack on Cuba.

October 11: Calling for reform and Christian unity, Pope John XXIII opens the 21st Ecumenical Council or Vatican II. It is the largest gathering of Catholic church leaders in history, and delegates from Protestant denominations are invited to attend.

October 14: Another U-2 mission over Cuba confirms the existence of medium range ballistic missiles (MRBM).

October 16: Once informed of the solid evidence of Soviet MRBMs in Cuba, President Kennedy orders the creation of the Executive Committee of the National Security Council (ExComm) to study the appropriate course of action.

October 18: During an ExComm debate, Attorney General Robert Kennedy asks what the moral consequences might be of an American first strike against Cuba. He worries that it would constitute a "Pearl Harbor in reverse."

October 19: Under President Kennedy's orders, new ExComm working groups begin to plan for both an air strike and a naval blockade of Cuba.

October 20–November 21: Chinese Communist border troops cross into Indian territory and the China-India border war begins. The government of India requests U.S. military aid on two occasions while Chinese forces continue to advance. To the world's surprise, the Chinese government announces a cease-fire and withdraws its troops.

October 20: Claiming that a surgical air strike over Cuba would not work and that a full-scale invasion would lead to many casualties on both sides, President Kennedy opts for the naval blockade contingency. Formal approval is offered 24 hours later, and Kennedy also agrees to address the nation about the crisis within the next 48 hours.

October 22: Seventeen congressional leaders are briefed about the Cuban Missile Crisis by President Kennedy himself. The majority support the blockade plan, although several, led by Senators J. William Fulbright and Richard Russell, insist that the blockade will not remove the missiles. They urge an immediate air strike or invasion.

October 23: President Kennedy signs the proclamation to "quarantine" Cuba.

October 24: William Knox, a U.S. businessman, spends more than three hours talking with Premier Khrushchev. The latter promises to give attack orders to any Soviet vessel stopped by the U.S. Navy. In any event, Kennedy activates the naval blockade or "quarantine" (The Interdiction of the Delivery of Offensive Weapons to Cuba). The president comments to his brother Robert that he might be impeached if he takes no action at all. Preliminary reports from the Caribbean note that Soviet ships have stopped in front of the U.S. Navy blockade line.

October 26: The Brazilian ambassador in Havana, Luis Batian Pinto, delivers a message to Castro on behalf of the U.S. government. The message assures the Cuban leader that the United States will not invade his country if the nuclear missiles are removed. In a long, personally authored message to the Kennedy administration, Premier Khrushchev calls for a settlement. He promises no action against the United States if the United States takes no action against Cuba. A second message confuses the Kennedy team, and it suggests continued confrontation. Hence, Kennedy ignores the second and responds affirmatively to the first within 48 hours.

November 2: President Kennedy announces that the Soviets are dismantling their missile bases. He also declares that there have been no "victors" in the World War III–threatening Cuban Missile Crisis, only "survivors."

December: Spartacus, West Side Story, and *Lover Come Back* are declared the top box office draws of 1962 by the Motion Picture Association of America, and for the second time in the young decade, Doris

MRBM LAUNCH SITE 3
SAN CRISTOBAL, CUBA
27 OCTOBER 1962

LAUNCH AREA

NUCLEAR WARHEAD BUNKER U/C

PERMANENT BLDGS

OPEN STORAGE

TRENCH

This photograph of an MRBM launch site helped build the tension of the Cuban Missile Crisis. *(John F. Kennedy Library)*

Day, Rock Hudson, and Cary Grant are named the top three movie stars of the year.

December: The Associated Press names the top three hit record singles of 1962 as "The Twist" by Chubby Checker, "I Can't Stop Loving You" by Ray Charles, and "Big Girls Don't Cry" by the Four Seasons.

December 23–24: The 1,113 prisoners of the 1961 Bay of Pigs invasion are released. This was contingent upon a deal that required the United States to deliver more than $50 million in medical aid and food to the Cuban government.

1963

January 1: In his New Year's message, President Chiang Kai-shek of Taiwan predicts that with U.S. help the communist regime in China will fall in 1963.

January 2: Five U.S. helicopters are shot down by the Vietcong in the Mekong Delta of South Vietnam.

January 14: Rejecting President Kennedy's call for nuclear peace and cooperation, French president Charles de Gaulle announces that his country will be determining nuclear policy on its own.

January 15–21: In a meeting of the international communist parties in East Berlin, Premier Khrushchev denounces those fellow communists who criticize his decision to withdraw Soviet missiles from Cuba.

March 19: President Kennedy pledges $6 million to create a Common Market for Central American countries.

April 2: Led by Martin Luther King, Jr., a major civil rights demonstration begins in Birmingham, Alabama.

April 10: With its crew of 129, the U.S. nuclear submarine *Thresher* mysteriously sinks.

May 2–7: Using attack dogs and fire hoses, the police in Birmingham, Alabama, break up pro-civil rights demonstrations. More than 2,500 are arrested, including dozens of children.

May 4: Kennedy family friend and Justice Department official Burke Marshall heads to Birmingham, Alabama, to negotiate an agreement that might calm both sides of the increasingly volatile civil rights crisis there.

May 6: Historian Barbara Tuchman wins the Pulitzer Prize for her best-selling investigation into the origins of World War I (*The Guns of August*).

May 9: Upon U.S. urging, President Diem of South Vietnam begins the Strategic Hamlet program. In the effort to isolate certain rural villages from Vietcong penetration, the residents of those villages are resettled in government-controlled internment camps.

May 11: The bombings of a civil rights leader's home and an integrated motel lead President Kennedy to send federal troops to bases near Birmingham, Alabama.

May 23: Fidel Castro receives the Soviet government's highest honor, the Hero of the Soviet Union Award, during a special ceremony in Moscow.

June 3: Hailed as a champion of world peace, Christian unity, and Roman Catholic Church reform, Pope John XXIII dies at the age of 81 following a brief 4 1/2-year reign.

June 10: Especially hailed by women's groups, the Equal Pay Act passes Congress with its promise of "equal pay for equal work."

June 10: In Saigon, Ngo Quang Duc, a Buddhist priest, becomes the first in a long line of suicides by self-immolation in protest of the corrupt regime of South Vietnam's President Diem.

June 11: Governor George Wallace of Alabama refuses to permit the registration of two black students at the University of Alabama. President Kennedy federalizes the Alabama National Guard, and Wallace reluctantly permits the registration to take place.

June 12: Medgar Evers, civil rights leader and field secretary for the NAACP, is killed by a sniper in Jackson, Mississippi.

June 23: Golfing favorite Arnold Palmer is defeated by Julius Boros, who goes on to win the U.S. Open.

June 26: During a special trip to Western Europe, President Kennedy visits and condemns the Berlin Wall.

August: A critique of gender roles, marriage, and housewives, *The Feminine Mystique* by Betty Friedan, reaches best-seller status.

August 5: Representatives of the U.S., Soviet, and British governments sign the Nuclear Test Ban Treaty. A direct and positive result of the Cuban Missile Crisis, the treaty outlaws nuclear tests underwater, in the atmosphere, and in outer space.

August 21: In a desperate effort to demonstrate the power and privilege of the Saigon regime, South Vietnamese troops assault a number of Buddhist temples.

August 22: Former Kennedy rival for the Massachusetts Senate, Henry Cabot Lodge, becomes the U.S. ambassador to South Vietnam.

August 28: Martin Luther King, Jr., delivers his "I Have a Dream" speech to thousands of civil rights supporters during the March on Washington.

On April 10, 1963, the U.S. nuclear submarine *Thresher* sinks, shocking a nation that had great faith in the superior technology of its navy. *(U.S. Naval Historical Center)*

With thousands of supporters gathered to hear him speak, Martin Luther King, Jr., delivers the most famous speech of his career, "I Have a Dream." *(National Archives)*

August 30: The "hot line" telephone link is established between the White House and the Kremlin. Its purpose is to provide instant communication between the two major world powers in the effort to prevent a possible nuclear confrontation between them.

September 2: Alabama governor George Wallace attempts to block the integration of Tuskegee High School and a number of grade schools. Once again, President Kennedy federalizes the Alabama National Guard, and the Wallace defiance ends.

September 15: A Birmingham, Alabama, church used as a gathering location for civil rights marchers is bombed. Four little girls are killed, and 20 others are wounded. The National Guard and state troopers are required to put down the follow-up rioting.

November 1–2: Hoping that a coup will lead to successful democratic reform, President Kennedy sup-

ports the overthrow of the Diem regime in South Vietnam. Diem and his brother, Secret Police Chief Ngo Dinh Nhu, are murdered.

November 22: President Kennedy is assassinated while riding in an open car in downtown Dallas, Texas. Lyndon Johnson is sworn in as president later in the day. Lee Harvey Oswald is arrested for Kennedy's murder but is killed during a jail transfer 48 hours later.

December: The Motion Picture Association of America announces that the top-grossing movies of 1963 are *Cleopatra, The Longest Day, and Irma La Douce.* Doris Day and Rock Hudson remain top box office draws, along with veteran actor John Wayne.

December: The Associated Press names "Sugar Shack" by Jimmy Gilmer and the Fireballs, "He's So

With heads of state and others looking on, John Kennedy's burial service comes to an end at Arlington National Cemetery. *(Abbie Rowe, National Park Service, Harry S. Truman Library)*

Fine" by the Chiffons, and "Dominique" by the Singing Nun as the top three single records of 1963.

December 18: Claiming that Moscow is as racist as Birmingham, Alabama, nearly 600 African stu-dents in Moscow protest Soviet racism and the mys-terious death of a black student from Ghana.

December 29: The Pentagon reports that U.S. troop strength in South Vietnam now numbers more than 16,300 men.

EYEWITNESS TESTIMONY

The Cuban Missile Crisis and the Nuclear Test Ban Treaty

We nuclear scientists felt free to have broad political discussions on international and domestic issues. These discussions occurred spontaneously at the workplace in the course of working on a production problem, or were sparked by political events. Andrei Sakharov frequently took part in these debates, and his participation gave greater significance to the conversation. . . . We discussed everything: our history, with its drama and absurdities; the politics of the day; and the changes in the world that were wrought by the creation of nuclear weapons. It was difficult to have a complete understanding of this last issue. Many of us had taken part in nuclear experiments and seen nuclear explosions with our own eyes. On the one hand, we—better than anyone else—understood that for the first time in human history a weapon had been created that could destroy all humanity. On the other hand, the possibility of total annihilation that these weapons carried dictated restraint in the relationship between the superpowers.

Vicktor Adamskii, a former theoretical physicist at Arzamas-16, a key Soviet nuclear weapons laboratory, explaining in a 1995 interview that on the eve of the Cuban Missile Crisis in early October 1962 he and his fellow nuclear scientists admired the United States, opposed nuclear war, and had little use for the Soviet Premier, Nikita Khrushchev, quoted in Victor Adamskii, The Bulletin of Atomic Scientists *(1995), p. 1. Available online. URL: www. thebulletin.org/issues.*

It is clear that this Nation, in concert with all the free nations of this hemisphere, must take an ever closer and more realistic look at the menace of external Communist intervention and domination in Cuba. The American people are not complacent about Iron Curtain tanks and planes less than 90 miles from their shore. But a nation of Cuba's size is less a threat to our survival than it is a base for subverting the survival of other free nations throughout the hemisphere. It is not primarily our interest or our security but theirs which is now, today, in the

greater peril. It is for their sake as well as our own that we must show our will.

President Kennedy informing the nation in October 1962 that he has learned from the Bay of Pigs disaster and that America's anti-Castro policy remains firm, in Public Papers of President John F. Kennedy, 1962, Speeches, *JFK Library.*

There's a medium-range ballistic missile launch site and two new military encampments on the southern edge of Sierra del Rosario in west central Cuba. . . . On site of one of the encampments contains a total of at least fourteen canvas-covered missile trailers measuring 67 feet in length, 9 feet in width. The overall length of the trailers plus tow-bars is approximately 80 feet. The other encampment contains vehicles and tents but with no missile trailers. . . . We can find nothing that would spell nuclear warhead in term (*sic*) of any isolated area or unique security in this particular area. The mating of the nuclear warhead to the missile from some of the other short range missiles there would take about, uh, a couple of hours to do this.

Art Lundahl, from the National Photographic Interpretation Center, briefing President Kennedy and his advisers on October 16, 1962, on the photographic evidence of Soviet missiles in Cuba, i n Box 52/Classified Subjects, Papers of Theodore C. Sorensen, JFK Library.

Well, I don't myself think that there is any present—I know there is no present evidence, and I think there is no present likelihood that the Cubans and the Cuban Government and the Soviet Government would, in combination, attempt to install a major offensive capability. Now, it is true that these words "offensive" and "defensive," if you try to apply them precisely to every single item, mislead you. Whether a gun is offensive or defensive depends a little bit on which end you are on. It is also true that the MIG fighters which have been put into Cuba for more than a year now, and any possible additions in the form of aircraft, might have a certain marginal capability for moving against the United States. But I think we have to bear in mind the relative magnitudes here. The United States is not going to be placed in any position of major danger to its own security in

Cuba, and we are not going to permit that situation to develop.

McGeorge Bundy, a former Harvard University dean turned White House assistant for national security affairs during an ABC News television interview of mid-October 1962, explaining to reporter Elie Abel that rumors of a developing crisis over Cuba are false, in Box 49/Classified Subjects, Papers of Theodore C. Sorensen, JFK Library.

Well, it's a goddamn mystery to me. I don't know enough about the Soviet Union, but if anybody can tell me any other time since the Berlin blockade where the Russians have given us so clear provocation, I don't know when it's been, because they've been awfully cautious really. The Russians, I never. . . . Now, maybe our mistake was in not saying some time *before* summer that if they do this we're [word unintelligible] to act. . . .

President Kennedy on the evening of October 16, 1962, closing a top secret White House meeting on the developing Cuban Missile Crisis, in Box 52/Classified Subjects, Papers of Theodore C. Sorensen, JFK Library.

I think that we ought to consider getting some word to Castro, perhaps through the Canadian ambassador in Havana or through his representative at the U.N. I think perhaps the Canadian ambassador would be the best, the better channel to get to Castro, get him apart privately and tell him that this is no longer support for Cuba, that Cuba is being victimized here, and the Soviets are preparing Cuba for destruction, or betrayal. You saw the [*New York*] *Times* story yesterday morning that high Soviet officials were saying: "We'll trade Cuba for Berlin." This ought to be brought to Castro's attention. It ought to be said to Castro that this kind of base is intolerable and not acceptable. The time has come when he must, in the interests of the Cuban people, must now break clearly with the Soviet Union and prevent this missile base from becoming operational.

Secretary of State Dean Rusk, in an October 16, 1962, meeting with President Kennedy, arguing that there is always room for diplomacy and reacting to the top secret reports that there are Soviet missiles in Cuba, in Box 49/Classified Subjects, Papers of Theodore C. Sorensen, JFK Library.

There are two propositions I would suggest that we ought to accept as foundations for our further thinking. My first is that if we are to conduct an air strike against these installations, or against any part of Cuba, we must agree now that we will schedule that prior to the time these missile sites become operational. I'm not prepared to say when that will be. But I think it is extremely important that our talk and our discussion be founded on this premise: that any air strike will be planned to take place prior to the time they become operational. Because, *if* they become operational *before* the air strike, I do not believe we can state we can knock them out before they can be launched. And if they're launched there is almost certain to be chaos in part of the East Coast or the area in the radius of 600 to 1,000 miles from Cuba.

Secretary of Defense Robert McNamara, at the beginning of the Cuban Missile Crisis, arguing that a total military victory in Cuba might be impossible, in NSC Executive Committee Record of Action, October 1962, Box 52/Classified Subjects, Papers of Theodore C. Sorensen, JFK Library.

He was a contemporary man. His basic sensibility was not shaped by the Depression, World War II, or McCarthyism. It was shaped by modern traumas like the Cuban Missile Crisis. He quoted Bob Dylan, Erik Erikson, and Marshall McLuhan in his speeches. He spent time talking to Tom Hayden and Allen Ginsberg. He read Camus and Voznesensky. When he visited new cities, he saw the black nationalists before he saw the mayor. He was, like very few men who seek worldly power, an alienated man. He was shy, and so were some of his closest friends, like Burke Marshall and Robert Morgenthau. He stammered and his hands trembled. He walked in a slouch like a man who did not want to be noticed. His handwriting was small and squiggly. I once asked him what he might have become if he had not been born a Kennedy, and he answered, "Perhaps a juvenile delinquent or a revolutionary."

Jack Newfield, a reporter and former charter member of the Students for a Democratic Society (SDS), describing Robert Kennedy at the time of the Cuban Missile Crisis in his Robert Kennedy: A Memoir *(1969), pp. 18–19.*

The people the CIA had originally were not very good. Then they put this fellow Fitzgerald on, Des

Fitzgerald, who I thought was much better. We had a terrible experience with the ones who were handling it at the time of the missile crisis. They were going to send sixty people into Cuba right during the missile crisis. Nobody knew what they were doing. They never told or explained. I just heard about it because one of the fellows who was going to go wrote me, or got in touch with me, and said, "We don't mind going, but we want to make sure we're going because *you* think it's worthwhile." I checked into it. And nobody knew about it. The CIA didn't. The top officials didn't. We pinned it down to the fellow who was supposed to be in charge [William K. Harvey]. He said we planned it because the military wanted it done. I asked the military, and they never heard of it.

Robert Kennedy, during a 1964 interview, recalling the mid-October 1962 confusion of a covert operation against Castro during the Cuban Missile Crisis, in The Robert F. Kennedy Oral History Project, JFK Library.

I have enjoyed that warm reception I've gotten from my fellow Elis as I drove into the city. But they will learn, as this country has learned, that the Democratic Party is best for them as it is for the country.

President Kennedy campaigning for Democratic congressional candidates in New Haven, Connecticut, October 17, 1962, in The Public Papers of President John F. Kennedy, 1962, Speeches, JFK Library.

This is the week when I had better earn my salary.

President Kennedy discussing the Cuban Missile Crisis with former Secretary of State Dean Acheson, October 18, 1962, in Box 49/Classified Subjects, Papers of Theodore C. Sorensen, JFK Library.

Within the past week, unmistakable evidence has established the fact that a series of offensive missile sites is now in preparation on that imprisoned island. The purpose of these bases can be none other than to provide a nuclear strike capability against the Western Hemisphere. . . . This secret, swift and extraordinary build-up of Communist missiles—in an area well known to have a special and historical relationship to the United States and the nations of the Western Hemisphere, in violation of Soviet assurances, and in defiance of American and hemispheric policy—this sudden, clandestine decision to station strategic weapons for the first time outside of Soviet soil—is a deliberately provocative and unjustified change in the status quo which cannot be accepted by this country, if our courage and our commitments are ever to be trusted again by either friend or foe.

President Kennedy, during a live television broadcast of October 22, 1962, informing the nation about the Cuban Missile Crisis, in The Public Papers, President John F. Kennedy, 1962, Speeches, JFK Library.

On October 22, the day when Kennedy spoke on the radio and on television, we already had 42,000 troops in Cuba and three missile regiments (one division). The sites were ready for two regiments (not yet for the third). None of the missiles was placed in combat readiness. They had not yet been fueled, nor supplied with oxidating agents. The warheads were some 250 or 300 kilometers from the launch sites, and had not yet been released for use. . . . We were all ready and willing to fight to the very last man. We didn't just plan an initial resistance. We even decided that if it proved necessary—if large tracts of the island were occupied—we would form guerrilla units in order to continue defending the interests of revolutionary Cuba. I'm using the very words that we used in 1962. That's the way we were then. We did not have anywhere to withdraw to.

In 1992, Soviet General Anatoly I. Gribkov discussing his October 22, 1962, role in preparing Cuba's defense in Blight, Allyn, and Welch's Cuba on the Brink: Castro, the Missile Crisis, and the Soviet Collapse (1993), p. 238.

This matter did come up in connection with our thinking in the Cuban matter early in October in a wholly different context. We were considering, as you know, the necessity of a strike against these missiles in Cuba. The most immediate and, shall we say, relevant retaliation by the other side might have been conventional strikes against these missiles in Turkey.

Now, had we struck the missiles in Cuba this would have, except for this capability, thrown the nuclear decision to the Soviet Union. In other words, these vulnerable first strike type weapons accessible to Soviet conventional capability proved to be a drag on us at the time of the Cuban decision because we just did not know what way this thing would escalate, given an opportunity for an immediate and similar retaliation.

Secretary of State Dean Rusk, at a February 1963 top secret closed hearing of the U.S. Senate Foreign Relations Committee, testifying about U.S. policy during the height of the Cuban Missile Crisis, in the U.S. Congress's Executive Sessions of the Senate Foreign Relations Committee, *Vol. XV (1986), p. 104.*

So why did Khrushchev risk so much for so little? There were a number of plausible reasons which together may have driven him to do it: he needed a foreign policy success after a year of reverses in Africa and Latin America and even Berlin, where the Wall was hardly a monument to the glories of communism; he may have been trying to bring the wayward Chinese leaders back into his fold with a display of toughness; perhaps he hoped to break the deadlock on disarmament and Berlin by an action that would shock but not provoke Kennedy as it did, and he was persuaded by Castro early in 1962 that the Americans were planning to avenge their defeat at the Bay of Pigs.

Ambassador William Attwood, from his 1962 diplomatic post in Africa, contemplating Khrushchev's reasoning during the Cuban Missile Crisis, in Papers of William Attwood, Ambassador to Guinea, JFK Library.

Bob McNamara was very good. Tommy Thompson [then Special Advisor on Soviet Affairs to the Secretary of State] was tremendously helpful, much better, in my judgment, than Chip Bohlen [Thompson's predecessor at State, recently named Ambassador to France]. Chip Bohlen ran out on us—which always shocked me. He was there for the first day, and then he went on a boat and went to France. That wasn't necessary; he could always have postponed it. We said he could fly over, but he decided to leave this country in a crisis such as that when he had been working with all of us for such a long period of time. We didn't know Tommy Thompson, and this put Tommy Thompson in the middle of it. But Tommy Thompson was terrific—very tough—always made a good deal of sense and, really, was sort of the motivating force behind the idea of giving the Russians an opportunity to back away, giving them some out. Ted Sorensen [Special Counsel to the President] was very helpful. He made some sense: Although he wasn't as vocal as some of the others, his position was the right position. Ed Martin [Assistant Secretary of State for Inter-American Affairs] was very helpful. And Douglas Dillon [Secretary of the Treasury], although he took a different position [he favored an air strike against Cuba] you know, always made sense.

Robert Kennedy, remembering the White House personnel involved in the Cuban Missile Crisis decision making of mid-late October 1962, in The Robert F. Kennedy Oral History Project, JFK Library.

I think the reasons why we have to do something are quite clear. I don't think there was anybody ever who didn't think we shouldn't respond. But why the different actions? At least I've attempted to communicate why we took the course we did, even though, as I've said from the beginning, the idea of a quick strike was very tempting, and I really didn't give up on that until yesterday morning. So I may. . . . After talking to General Sweeney and then after talking to others, it looked like we would have all of the difficulties of Pearl Harbor and not have finished the job. The job can only be finished by invasion.

President Kennedy, during a top-secret October 22, 1962 cabinet discussion on Cuban Missile Crisis options, wondering how history will view his decision making, in Box 49/Classified Subjects, Papers of Theodore C. Sorensen, JFK Library.

Further U-2 flights are ordered, and six U-2 reconnaissance missions are flown during the day. In the freewheeling discussion, participants cover a number of different options for dealing with the Cuban situation. The principal options discussed are: (1) a single, surgical air strike on the missile bases; (2) an attack on various Cuban facilities; (3) a comprehensive series of attacks and invasion; or (4) a blockade of Cuba. Preliminary discussions lean toward taking some form of military action. As discussions continue on proposals to destroy the missiles by air strike, Robert Kennedy passes a note to the president: "I now know how Tojo felt when he was planning Pearl Harbor."

A White House "ExComm" transcript of October 27, 1962, summarizing a mid-October 1962 Cuban Missile Crisis cabinet meeting, in GWU Net. "ExComm." URL: http://www.gwu.edu/ nsarchiv/nsa/cuba

While the explanation of our action may be clear to us, it won't be clear to many others. Moreover, if war is the consequence, the Latin American republics may well divide and some say that the U.S. is not acting with their approval and consent. Likewise unless the issue is very clear there may be sharp differences with our Western Allies who have lived so long under the same threat of Soviet attack from bases in the satellite countries by the same IRBMs. . . . I confess I have many misgivings about the proposed course of action, but to discuss them further would add little to what you already have in mind. So I will only repeat that it should be clear as a pikestaff that the U.S. was, is and will be ready to negotiate the elimination of bases and anything else; that it is they who have upset the precarious balance in the world in arrogant disregard of your warnings—by threats against Berlin and now from Cuba—and that we have no choice except to restore that balance, i.e. blackmail and intimidation *never*, negotiation and sanity *always*.

Adlai Stevenson, U.S. ambassador to the United Nations, urging President Kennedy in mid-October 1962 to seek a negotiated settlement in the Cuban Missile Crisis, in GWU Net. "Cuban Missile Crisis," URL: http://www.gwu.edu/ nsarchiv/nsa/cuba

What will the Soviets do in response? I know the Soviets pretty well. I think they'll knock out our missile bases in Turkey. What do we do then? Under our NATO Treaty, we'd be obligated to knock out a base inside the Soviet Union. What will they do then? Why, then we hope everyone will cool down and want to talk!

President Kennedy pondering the possible late October 1962 Soviet response to an American air assault on Cuba, in Box 49/Classified Subjects, Papers of Theodore C. Sorensen, JFK Library.

These new weapons arriving in Cuba are not only directed against the United States. Let there be no misunderstanding. There are other strategic targets in this hemisphere—in your countries—which they can devastate with their lethal loads. . . . In the face of this rapid build-up, no country of this hemisphere can feel secure either from direct attack or from persistent blackmail.

Secretary of State Dean Rusk addressing the Organization of American States (OAS) and trying to convince the Latin American governments that the Cuban Missile Crisis is their crisis too, in late October 1962, in The Public Papers of President John F. Kennedy, 1962, Speeches, JFK Library.

It seemed clear on that fateful Saturday afternoon, October 20, when he made his decision for the quarantine, that an air strike would be a swifter and more popular means of removing the missiles before Election Day, and that a quarantine would encourage a prolonged UN debate and Republican charges of weakness in the face of peril. Yet he never contemplated changing that course for political reasons. Others have since accused him of overreacting for reasons of personal and national prestige to a move that did not really alter the strategic balance of power or pose an actual threat to our own security. But Kennedy recognized that appearance and reality often merge in world affairs; and if all Latin America had thought that the U.S. had passively permitted what was apparently a new threat to their existence, and if all our Western allies had thought we would not respond to a sudden, secret deployment of missiles in our own hemisphere, then a whole wave of reactions contrary to our interests and security might well have followed.

Former White House aid Theodore Sorensen based on his experience as one of President Kennedy's top advisers in October 1962, attacking the critics of Kennedy's handling of the Cuban Missile Crisis, Theodore C. Sorensen, JFK Library.

I welcome Chairman Khrushchev's statesmanlike decision to stop building bases in Cuba, dismantling offensive weapons and returning them to the Soviet Union under United Nations verification. This is an important and constructive contribution to peace.

President Kennedy, in a public statement of October 28, 1962, announcing the end of the Cuban Missile Crisis, in The Public Papers of President John F. Kennedy, 1962, Speeches, JFK Library.

I agree with you that we must devote urgent attention to the problem of disarmament, as it relates to the whole world and also to critical areas. Perhaps now, as we step back from danger, we can together make real progress in this vital field. I think we should give priority to questions relating to the proliferation of nuclear weapons, on earth and in outer space, and to the great effort for a nuclear test ban.

President Kennedy, in a private statement of October 28, 1962, to Premier Khrushchev, declaring nuclear disarmament the best legacy of just ended Cuban Missile Crisis, in Box 52/Classified Subjects, Papers of Theodore C. Sorensen, JFK Library.

When you look at all those misjudgments which brought on war, and then you see the Soviet Union and the United States, so far separated in their beliefs . . . and you put the nuclear equation into that struggle; that is what makes this . . . such a dangerous time. . . . One mistake can make this whole thing blow up.

President Kennedy, during a December 17, 1962, television interview, carefully testing the political waters in favor of a nuclear test ban treaty, in NSC Memorandum on Cuba Talking Points, March 4, 1963, Box 37A-38, NSF-Cuba, JFK Library.

The thought of spending two weeks with two children in a close dark hole [family bomb shelter] was too horrible to think of and we knew we had to do something. Now that we women have started we will no longer be content to be dull uninformed housewives.

A future participant in the 1963 "Women Strike for Peace" protest in Washington, D.C., connecting women's issues and nuclear policy, in May, Homeward Bound: American Families in the Cold War Era *(1988), p. 88.*

Enmities between nations, as between individuals, do not last forever. . . . And if we cannot now end our differences, at least we can help make the world safe for diversity. For in the final analysis our most basic common link is that we all inhabit this planet. We all breathe the same air. We all cherish our children's future. And we are all mortal.

President Kennedy, during a June 10, 1963, speech at American University, clearing the way for a nuclear test ban treaty with the Soviets, in The Public Papers of President John F. Kennedy, 1963, *Speeches, JFK Library.*

I feel myself it is a good treaty. It is largely based on the treaty that was tabled in Geneva by our representatives in August last year. It goes back to conceptions which President Eisenhower and his advisors had several years before that, and I think it carries forward certain principles which are very much to the interest of the United States. It is the beginning of an agreement with the Soviet Union on checking the tempo of the arms race. There are many things that it does not do, which I think per-

haps are clear to you, but it doesn't reduce in any way the number of nuclear missiles and nuclear weapons that exist in the world. It doesn't reduce in any way the hazards of war, but it is a first step in the direction of getting nuclear weapons under some sort of control.

Undersecretary of State Averell Harriman, the chief negotiator of the Nuclear Test Ban Treaty, explaining the treaty to the Senate Foreign Relations Committee, during a closed hearing of July 29, 1963, in the U.S. Congress's Executive Sessions of the Senate Foreign Relations Committee, *Vol. XV, (1986), p. 446.*

Pop Culture in Transition

It was inevitable that someone would think of it, and now it is here. A paperback book vending machine has just been introduced, and it has exciting possibilities for libraries. The U.S. in 1962 is an affluent society where very few of the adults using a library cannot afford the price of a paperback—often less than the cost of a hamburger and coffee.

Library Journal predicting that "Book-O-Mat" dispensing machines will dot the American landscape by the mid-1960s, in Staff's "Book-O-Mat," Library Journal, December 1, 1962, p. 1.

The thumping success of *The Beverly Hillbillies* has already sent some serious thinkers to the wailing wall, and when you tune the program in, you are supposed to ask yourself, "What is America coming to?" As I am still laughing, I think back to the days when custard pies and Keystone Cops were flying through the air and a lot of people were convinced America was a cultural "desert"—the 1920 word for "wasteland." (A question I asked then has never been answered: What can you do with a custard pie except throw it?)

Veteran film critic Gilbert Seldes criticizing the critics of "escapist television," December 1962, in Harris, TV Guide: The First 25 Years *(1980), p. 65.*

There are plenty of great ballads (the title track, a brilliant, deceptively topical love song; "In My Room," Brian's wrenching ode to childhood), surfing songs (the exciting "Catch a Wave;" "Hawaii," a virtual radio ad for the tourist industry), and another great doo-wopping Roger Christian car song ("Little Deuce Coupe"). But the rest is once again mostly filler, including a couple of surf-rock instrumentals and a couple more odes to surfing that are marred by terrible lyrics.

The critics tearing apart Surfer Girl, *the third-released album by the Beach Boys, 1963, in "Surfer Girl,"* Wilson & Alroy's Record Reviews: The Beach Boys, p. 2. *URL: www.war.org/brian.html.*

The new Corvette Sting Ray has won the coveted CAR LIFE AWARD FOR ENGINEERING EXCEL-LENCE. Forgive our lack of modesty here, but we agree on hundred per cent with the editors of CAR LIFE. They think the new three-link independent rear suspension gives the car handling that's far and away the best thing ever to come from Detroit. So do we. They think the performance is on a par with any production sports car ever built. So do we and, we might add, so will you. Unfortunately, not everyone has had a chance to drive one of the new ones yet, because demand has exceeded production, but when your chance comes, you won't believe it! You've never driven a sports car that rides so well, yet handles so beautifully in the bargain. You never sat in a car that'll turn so many heads and cause so much comment among the less fortunate drivers you pass. This car is a winner! And you'll share CAR LIFE's enthusiasm by the time you've hit forty miles per hour and second gear!

Chevrolet advertising its successful premiere of the wholly redesigned Corvette for 1963, in the back cover advertisement of the Chicago Auto Dealer Association's Program of the 55th Annual Chicago Auto Show, *February 1963.*

Women are beginning to look like men. . . . Although the trousers suit for women was launched at absolute summit of the fashion world, I suspect that the inspiration came from farther down the slope. One influence has been the enormous (and, I do think, justified) success of the Beatles. Their hairdos and even their clothes have been copied by young people of both sexes, not only in England but all over Europe, to such an extent that an American news weekly ran a photograph of an English boy and a girl, similarly coiffed and clad, with the caption, "Which is which?", while Mollie Panter-

Downes, the British correspondent for the *New Yorker,* wrote of the "identical, sexless uniform of pants, leather jackets, and long hair." Cilla Black, the girl rock-and-roll singer who also comes from Liverpool and has the same manager as the Beatles (her first American appearance is scheduled for March), has her blue jeans custom-tailored, and Rita Pavone, the Italian teen-age singing idol of Europe, wears a boy's haircut and clothes.

If this theory is true, then it is pretty much of a joke on women, because it means that the duchesses, baronesses, countesses and other high muckamucks are paying upward of $1,000 apiece for outfits inspired by rock-and-roll teenagers (and proletarian ones at that, tsk-tsk) and that these clothes will eventually be copied by other women everywhere with

In contrast to the "perky girls" image and lifestyle, some women choose political activism. Here, participants in the "Women Strike for Peace" are photographed on 47th Street in New York. More than 800 women took part in this demonstration, serving as a foundation for later actions taken by women's rights and antiwar activists. *(Phil Stanziola, Library of Congress)*

the happily snob thought that they are wearing something sanctioned by the nobility.

Fashion critic Helen Lawrenson complaining that British influences in American fashion are leading to the "masculation of American womanhood," in her "Androgyne, You're a Funny Valentine," Esquire, March 1963, pp. 80–83.

"She's a pixie, a Peter Pan type with a day breaking smile and mischief in her eyes, and she's finding it hard to believe that she's living in a real world, what with one fabulous thing after another happening to her!"

The enchanted pixie described by *Teen* in May 1963 was Cindy Carol, who was walking on air because she had just been chosen to play "the most enviable role in cinema history"—Gidget in *Gidget Goes to Rome.* Teen showed pictures of Cindy in New York on her way to fabulous Rome—jumping for joy in Times Square, craning her neck to look at tall buildings, and peering through "the magic heart-shaped window" display at Tiffany's. . . . She embodied all the qualities of an all-new, up tempo, happy-go-lucky sixties person who peppermint-twisted her way onto center stage as the curtain rose on a decade that promised to be fun. When asked to describe herself, Cindy said, "I'm hysterically happy." The perky girl was a living exclamation point.

Ex-"perky girl" Jane Stern describing her May 1963 colleague Cindy Carol, in her Sixties People *(1990), p. 7.*

For the first time in its 10-year history, the Corvette Sting Ray is in such demand that the factory has had to put on a second shift and still can't begin to supply cars fast enough. The waiting period is at least 60 days, and dealers won't "deal" a bit on either coupes or roadsters. Both are going for full sticker price, with absolutely no discount and very little (if any) overallowance on trade-ins.

Technical Editor Jim Wright expressing amazement over the public frenzy to buy the new 1963 Corvette, in his "Corvette Sting Ray," Motor Trend, May 1963, pp. 18–23.

Mary Quant and her husband Alexander Plunket Greene, a young thin pair of English adventurers in London, discovered what no one in England knew—there was a whole new "want" among bright young English girls for new, young, skinny clothes that sometimes have the look of fancy dress. Right for them. In their adventuring, Mary Quant and Plunket Greene, going against everything expected of them, are so close now to fantasy success that they seem to be one melon-cut grin. Mary, as she is known, looks like one of those wispy child heroines—leggy, skinny, with soup-bowl bangs, very pale painted mouth, heavy black liner on upper and lower lashes; Plunket Greene is tall, fair, easy, not quite the man one would pick for big cigars. Together they are a matched team.

In the beginning, they opened a shop for a bouillabaisse of clothes—sweaters, sleeveless shifts, peculiar odds and ends which soon led Mary to designing (at first, more thought-up clothes than designed clothes) things bought out as fast as they arrived at the shop. The risk: little. The adventure: big. The prognosis: increasing success, including having her clothes at Lord & Taylor. The pair now have the Quant line plus two London shops called Bazaar, in addition to a huddle of sports clothes, called, "The Ginger Group." They have pepped up a Scottish sweater company with pants and long sweaters and knickerbockers. (Mary will soon do a shoe collection.) The Rolls-Royce people have asked her to do a coverall for them. No matter what she does, she is direct; calls raincoats by no esoteric name, just says made of "oil cloth," calls a country suit "Basset Hound," and a pinafore dress, "Cad."

The staff of Vogue *magazine nominating the fashion-setting Mary Quant and her husband as among the most influential people in early 1960s American life, included within a list of notable politicians, scientists, and astronauts, in their "The Adventurous Ones," Vogue, August 1, 1963, pp. 74–75.*

"In the fifties young people had a rebellion without a cause. In the sixties we have so many causes we don't know what to sing, write, or just do something about first," explained Phil Ochs, another outstanding and prolific writer in the protests-set-to-music-movement. "There's been a real switch from [James] Dean to Dylan," he continued. "Dean had no message, y'see, but Dylan—Dylan doesn't give answers outright, but he's asking questions all the time—and they're good questions—and nobody says, 'What does he mean by that?' His images are clear."

Reporter Betty Rollin recalling a June 3, 1963 interview with the innovative folk music artist Phil Ochs, in her "A New Beat: Topical Folk Singers, Their Songs," Vogue, *September 1, 1964, p. 83.*

He returned to Hollywood with an entourage of 10 in a private railroad car. But despite this initial ostentation, he began to lead a relatively quiet personal life. His dress became less jazzy; his cars were fewer in number and more conservative. He collected books on medicine ("I always wanted to be a doctor") and classical records by Caruso and Kirsten Flagstad. He seldom went out. Gradually the glittering people have stopped inviting him places. He could not be happier. . . .

On the surface Elvis remains unruffled. "I always wanted to be somebody, and feel like somebody," he explains, "but I never expected to be anybody *important*. I figure if these things bother me too much, though, I could always go back to driving a truck."

C. Robert Jennings explaining that Elvis Presley shed his rebellious past in the summer of 1963 and became a "quiet," isolated man on the eve of the "British Invasion," in his "There'll Always Be an Elvis," Saturday Evening Post, *September 1, 1965, p. 79.*

In "the provincial cities" (Liverpool, Birmingham, Manchester, Cardiff, Belfast, Newcastle and all) the seeds were being sewn for a worldwide musical and cultural revolution. In ports such as Liverpool, there had developed a music "culture" fiercely independent of London and which was influenced by the availability of rare imported American music at the point-of-entry to the U.K. London might as well have been 3,000 miles away—these kids loved Rhythm 'N Blues and Rock 'N Roll, not the saccharin substitute.

By the early '60s in these cities a large and highly competitive band scene emerged in which hundreds of 'local' bands vied to find and perform the latest imported songs and to get the attention of the discerning young audiences, hungry for anything authentic and new. In Liverpool, the music they played was an amalgam of American product performed with a touch of the famous Mersey humour and individualism.

Veteran music critic Dave "Digger" Barnes examining and recalling the pop music scene of the summer of 1963, in his "1960s British Pop Culture: Where is Liverpool Anyway?", pp. 2–3. URL: http://www.home.clara.net/ digger/sixties/info3.htm.

Stoddard is your typical "trickster" like Brer Rabbit or Tom Sawyer, amoralists who enjoy playing with the truth. Maybe Ranse didn't kill Liberty Valance the man, but Valance was more than just a man, he was the symbol of a whole social structure. In this sense, by bringing law, democracy (and the railroad) to Shinbone, Ransom Stoddard very much is the man who shot (and killed) Liberty Valance. . . .

Lawyers are the appointed agents of change in American society; they perform this necessary social function because they have the imagination to see a possible future and the skill and tenacity to make that vision a reality. And even the lawyer's loose way with the "truth" is necessary if he or she is going to help society rethink its conventional wisdom in the process of creating new social values. And sometimes the lawyer even gets the girl.

Constitutional law professor John Denvir criticizing movie director John Ford's depiction of the "trickster" lawyer (Ransom Stoddard, played by actor James Stewart) in the controversial 1962 western The Man Who Shot Liberty Valance, *in his October 1962 review and complaint "The Lawyer Gets the Girl— And Creates the Future," p. 2. URL: http://www.usfca.edu/pj/ articles/liberty.htm.*

And no matter how tired he gets, when he hears that laughter and applause . . . well, it rejuvenates him. In 1963, for example, an old eye ailment put Hope in a San Francisco hospital. His doctors warned him that his vision could be impaired seriously if he didn't rest, and told him to cancel his scheduled tour of U.S. bases in Africa and the Middle East. Eventually, Hope's troupe of entertainers left without him. But the thought of remaining home in bed gnawed at his pride. Thirty-six hours later he caught a commercial flight and joined the cast in Turkey. "The moment I saw those boys' faces," he says, "something snapped within me and I got well."

Military reporter Trevor Armbrister remembering a 1963 Christmas show by comedian Bob Hope, in his "The GI's Best Friend," Saturday Evening Post, March 12, 1966, p. 94.

The Civil Rights Struggle Continues

We never wanted to get very close to him just because of these contacts and connections that he had, which we felt were damaging to the civil rights movement. And because we were so intimately involved in the struggle for civil rights, it also damaged us. It damaged what we were trying to do. There was more than one individual who was involved. That was what was of such concern to us. When we were sending the legislation up or when we were so involved in the struggles of Birmingham, Alabama, if it also came out what he was doing, not only would it damage him but it would also damage all of our efforts and damage any possible chance of the passage of legislation.

Robert Kennedy, during a December 1964 interview, remembering that late 1962 and early 1963 FBI accusations of communists on Martin Luther King's staff had a serious impact on civil rights measures, in The Robert F. Kennedy Oral History Project, JFK Library.

Dammit, send the Justice Department word, I ain't compromising with anybody. I'm gonna *make 'em* bring troops into this state.

Alabama governor George Wallace daring the Kennedy administration to intervene in the Birmingham civil rights protest, late 1962, in The Papers of Burke Marshall, Box 17/Wallace, JFK Library.

The reason we sent the marshals in—it was to avoid the idea of sending troops. Now, we thought that marshals would be much more accepted in the South, and that you could get away from the idea of military occupation—and we had to do something.

Attorney General Robert Kennedy explaining to White House chief of staff Kenneth O'Donnell why federal marshals were needed during the 1963 Alabama race riots, in The Robert F. Kennedy Oral History Project, JFK Library.

The Freedom Riders do not seem to have hurt President Kennedy much. It is brother Bobby in the Attorney General's office, rather than President Jack, who has been blamed.

Samuel Lubell, a Southern political strategist, assessing the impact of Kennedy administration civil rights policy on early 1963 Democratic Party fortunes in the South, in The Robert F. Kennedy Oral History Project, JFK Library.

Kennedy has too many brothers.

A white middle-aged Mississippi housewife summing up early 1963 civil rights policy, in The Robert F. Kennedy Oral History Project, JFK Library.

We were looking for solutions. We abandoned the solution, really, of trying to give people protection. We ran through that a dozen times over the period of a thousand days because there were always things arising where people would say, "Why don't you furnish protection? Why don't you send in marshals? Why don't you send the troops in?" We were resisting that all the time, except when we had some legal basis for it or felt that we had some legal basis and the situation warranted it. We were always struggling with that. Now, we had to do something to deal with this kind of a problem. The country wanted something done and would support action being taken. That's why we moved in the direction that we did.

Robert Kennedy, one year after his brother's assassination, reflecting on the New Frontier approach to civil rights policy after the spring 1963 Birmingham crisis in The Robert F. Kennedy Oral History Project, JFK Library.

We're not goin' to have white folks and nigras segregatin' together in this man's town.

Birmingham's Eugene "Bull" Connor challenging in the spring of 1963 the Kennedy administration, in Morgan, A Time to Speak (1964), p. 87.

I grew up in the South and never thought about it. We never talked about that thing. We used to play ball on Saturday against the black team from across the streetcar tracks. It never lasted past two innings because it always ended up in a rock battle. Nobody ever got hurt. And we both used the old swimming hole. Blacks would come down there and catch us in the creek and take our clothes and run with them. Or we'd go there when they were there, and we'd take their clothes and run

Only three months before John Kennedy's assassination, the three Kennedy brothers pose outside of the Oval Office at the White House. *From left to right:* Robert, Ted, John. *(John F. Kennedy Library)*

down to the creek, tie knots in them, and put rocks in them, and throw them back in the creek. This was just a way of life. Nobody ever thought much about it. . . .

Arthur Hanes, the mayor of Birmingham, Alabama, denying in April 1963 that white supremacy is an important cause in his life, in Powledge, Free at Last? The Civil Rights Movement and the People Who Made It *(1991), p. 200.*

The Kennedy Assassination

Welcome Mr. Kennedy to Dallas: A City so disgraced by a recent Liberal smear attempt that its citizens have just elected two more Conservative Americans to public office. A City that is an economic "boom town," not because of Federal handouts, but through conservative economic and business practices. A City that will continue to grow and prosper despite efforts by you and your administration to penalize it for its non-conformity to "New Frontierism." A City that rejected your philosophy and policies in 1960 and will do so again in 1964—even more emphatically than before.

Mr. Kennedy, despite contentions on the part of your administration, the State Department, the Mayor of Dallas, the Dallas City Council, and members of your party, we free-thinking and America-thinking citizens of Dallas still have, through a Constitution largely ignored by you, the right to address our grievances, to question you, to disagree with you, and to criticize you.

With a full page ad in the Dallas Morning News *of November 22, 1963 (the day of the Kennedy assassination), Bernard Weisman, chairman of the so-called American Fact-Finding Committee, warning President Kennedy of a hostile reception during his Dallas visit, in his "Welcome Mr. Kennedy,"* Dallas Morning News, *November 22, 1963, Section 1, p. 14.*

After consulting with Mrs. Connally and others on the scene, the consensus is that the governor was quite fortunate that he turned to see what happened to the President. If he had not turned to his right, there is a good chance he probably would have been shot through the heart—as it was, the bullet caused a tangential wound.

Dr. Tom Shires, chief of surgeons at Texas Southwestern Medical School, telling the Dallas Morning News *that Texas governor John Connally, shot with John Kennedy in Dallas, was a lucky man, in Quinn, "Governor Connally Resting Well,"* Dallas Morning News, *November 23, 1963, Section 1, p. 1.*

This still should not reflect on the image or character of Dallas. There were too many sincere people extending Mr. Kennedy a warm greeting, filling the streets, standing along the roadways.

I challenge anybody who says this reflects the character of the people of Dallas. This was the horrible action of a mentally deranged person. I just cannot conceive yet that it happened here.

Mayor pro tem of Dallas Carrie Welch telling the Dallas Morning News *that Dallas is not to blame for the Kennedy assassination, in Raffeto, "Act of Maniac,"* Dallas Morning News, *November 23, 1963, Section 1, p. 15.*

When Mrs. Kennedy came into the hospital, she walked immediately behind the President's stretcher crying. Her clothes were spattered with blood. It was all over her front and her hands and legs. They took the President into an emergency room and when I came in a few minutes later, the last rites had already been given. I saw the President lying on a stretcher, blood still dripping profusely from the body.

As we waited, Mrs. Kennedy came in. She was sobbing quietly. She walked slowly to the stretcher, looked down at the President's face. The she took her marriage ring from her left hand and reached down and picked up the President's left hand and slipped the ring on his ring finger. Then she leaned over and kissed the hand she'd put the ring on. Then she straightened up and backed away and left the room.

Dallas ambulance driver Aubrey Rike telling the San Diego Evening Tribune *what he witnessed in the Parkland Hospital emergency room, in Manning, "Jackie Leaves Ring with Her Husband,"* San Diego Evening Tribune, *November 23, 1963, Section A, p. 4.*

Basically, the case is closed. We had a good case this morning, and we have a better case tonight.

Just hours before the murder of accused assassin Lee Harvey Oswald, Dallas police chief Jesse Curry explaining to Dallas Times Herald *reporter George Carter that all evidence points to Oswald, in Carter, "Similarity to Death Gun Tightens Murder Case,"* Dallas Times Herald, *November 24, 1963, p. 1.*

Just as he came into an area which gave me an unobstructed view from my higher position, I saw a rather sudden movement below me and to my right. My eyes was glued to the viewfinder. My impulsive first thought was that it was a cameraman moving out into a position which might obstruct my view. He was probably six feet away, to my right and below me. The man ran across an area that was open along the railing where two television cameras were taking pictures through the railing. Just in that fraction of a second, the second I had observed the man's movement, I tripped the shutter of my camera. I had started to take a picture an instant before that, but the distraction of the man's movements caused me to delay a fraction of a second. In that same second a man's falsetto voice screamed, "You son of a bitch!"

Following his return to Washington only hours after the Kennedy assassination, President Johnson addresses the nation from Andrews Air Force Base. "I ask for your help and God's," he pleads. *(John F. Kennedy Library)*

I made the picture, with the thought foremost in my mind to get my picture before my view was obstructed. I had no idea the man was going to shoot Oswald. I was still looking into the viewfinder when the curse ended and the shot rang out, like putting a period quickly at the end of the sentence. It was now obvious to me that this man was firing a pistol. The man had moved quickly and almost ran down Oswald. His face and hat were right in Oswald's face when he fired.

Veteran Dallas Morning News *staff photographer Jack Beers describing Jack Ruby's killing of Lee Harvey Oswald, in his "Front Page Photo Tells Grim Story,"* Dallas Morning News, *November 25, 1963, Section 1, p. 1.*

This is a sad time for all people. We have suffered a loss that cannot be weighed. For me it is a deep personal tragedy. I know the world shares the sorrow that Mrs. Kennedy and her family bear. I will do my best. That is all I can do. I ask for your help—and God's.

Lyndon Johnson making his first official statement as president to the American people following the Kennedy assassination, in Staff, "The Government Still Lives," Time, *November 29, 1963, p. 26.*

Now on one of the last nights I will spend in the White House, in one of the last letters I will write on this White House stationary, I would like to write my message to you. I am sending it only because I know how much my husband was concerned about peace and how important the relations between you and him were to him in this concern. He often cited your words in his speeches: "In the next war, the survivors will envy the dead."

You and he were adversaries, but you were also allies in your determination not to let the world be blown up. You respected each other and could have dealings with each other. I know that President Johnson will make every effort to establish the same relations with you. The danger troubling my husband was that war could be started not so much by major figures, as by minor ones.

Only nine days after the assassination of her husband, former first lady Jacqueline Kennedy writing Soviet premier Nikita Khrushchev, in Jacqueline Kennedy to Khrushchev, *December 1, 1963, URL: jfk-info. com/rus-jackie.htm.*

The Kennedy-Johnson Transition and the "Great Society"

One of the major advantages that President Johnson will enjoy is that his potential opposition is almost hopelessly divided. When the political harmony of Washington's present crisis mood has faded, the President can expect to face two major groups of detractors within his own party: those liberals who find him too conservative and those Southerners who feel he has deserted their cause. Both of these groups may feel next August that they might prefer one of their own as a nominee. But the possibility of their agreeing on a candidate seems dim.

The New York Times *accurately predicting only one day after the Kennedy assassination that Johnson's first year in office will be successful and end with his election to the presidency, in Warren Weaver, Jr.'s "The Johnson Presidency" editorial for the* New York Times, *November 23, 1963, p. 1.*

We have talked long enough in this country about equal rights. We have talked for a hundred years or more. It is time now to write the next chapter, and to write it in the books of law. I urge you again, as I did in 1957 and again in 1960, to enact a civil rights law so that we can move forward to eliminate from this nation every trace of discrimination and oppression that is based upon race or color. There could be no greater source of strength to this nation both at home and abroad.

President Johnson informing the House of Representatives where he stands on Kennedy's lingering civil rights reform bill, on November 27, 1963, only five days after the assassination of John Kennedy, in The Public Papers of President Lyndon B. Johnson, *1963, Speeches, Lyndon Johnson Library.*

Johnson lies all the time. He lies even when he doesn't have to lie.

Recalling his December 1963–January 1964 view of Lyndon Johnson in a later 1964 interview, Attorney General Robert Kennedy deciding to run for a New York Senate seat, in The Robert F. Kennedy Oral History Project, *JFK Library.*

Bobby, you don't like me. Your brother likes me. Your sister-in-law likes me. Your daddy likes me. But you don't like me. Now, why? Why don't you like me?

In January 1964, Lyndon Johnson asking Attorney General Kennedy about their personal differences, in The Robert F. Kennedy Oral History Project, *JFK Library.*

Bobby Kennedy's just another lawyer now.

In January 1964, Teamster boss and Robert Kennedy nemesis Jimmy Hoffa describing Attorney General Kennedy's position in the Johnson administration following the assassination of President Kennedy, in The Robert F. Kennedy Oral History Project, *JFK Library.*

John Kennedy could speak of death like all other subjects, candidly, objectively and at times humorously. The possibility of his own assassination he regarded as simply one more way in which his plans for the future might be thwarted. Yet he rarely mentioned death in a personal way and, to my knowledge, never spoke seriously about his own, once he recovered his health. He looked forward to a long life, never talking, for example, about arrangements for his burial or a memorial. He had a will drawn up, to be sure, but that was an act of prudence, not premonition; and asking Ted Reardon and me to witness it on June 18, 1954, he made it the occasion

Famous for his photographic memory and passionate commitment to liberal causes, Vice President Humphrey pleads for greater cooperation on civil rights reform from the 1965 Congress. *(Yoichi Okamoto, Lyndon B. Johnson Library)*

for a joke: "It's legal for you to do this—because I can assure you there's nothing in here for either of you." Two years later, driving me home one evening at high speed, he humorously speculated on whom the Nebraska headlines would feature if we were killed together in a crash. . . .

Personally I accept the conclusion that no plot or political motive was involved, despite the fact that this makes the deed all the more difficult to accept. For a man as controversial yet beloved as John Kennedy to be killed for no real reason or cause denies us even the slight satisfaction of drawing some meaning or moral from his death. We can say only that he died as he would have wanted to die—

at the center of action, being applauded by his friends and assaulted by his foes, carrying his message of reason and progress to the enemy and fulfilling his duty as party leader.

Theodore Sorensen reflecting on the assassination of his close firend and boss John Kennedy just weeks after the event, in Sorensen, Kennedy (1965), pp. 841, 844

President Truman gave me many good suggestions and wise counsel from his own experience of being suddenly thrust into the Presidency. He pledged his support for our efforts in Vietnam. He told me he had faced the same problems of aggression—in Greece and Turkey and Korea. He said that if we didn't stand up to aggression when it occurred, it would multiply the costs many times later. He said that his confrontation of those international challenges—particularly in Korea—had been horrors for him politically, bringing his popularity down from a high of 87 per cent to a low of 23 per cent. But he said they represented his proudest achievements in office.

Lyndon Johnson reflecting in the spring of 1964 on the difficulty of making U.S. foreign policy, in his The Vantage Point: Perspectives of the Presidency, 1963–1969 *(1971), Research Room, Lyndon Johnson Library.*

4

"All the Way with LBJ"
1964–1965

Respect, it is said, must be earned. For Lyndon Johnson, it was an uphill fight. Following the Kennedy assassination, the press was most unkind to the new president. From the eastern establishment newspapers, such as the *New York Times* and the *Washington Post,* to the *CBS Evening News,* the American people were reminded that Johnson lacked the style and polish of Camelot. He was, they suggested, something of the country bumpkin and consummate deal maker. If John Kennedy was Dom Perignon, tuxedos, and Harvard, Lyndon Johnson was Budweiser, a hunting shirt, and a Texas community college. The American people had grown used to Kennedy's flamboyant style, magnificent oratory, and dramatic "first step" politics. The drab, uneasy Johnson seemed a stark contrast to the Kennedy excitement, and the future was more uncertain than ever. Even those who voted against Kennedy in 1960 now told pollsters that they missed his "leadership" just days after Johnson took office. One poll noted that 65 percent of American voters claimed to have voted for Kennedy. The real figure was 49.7 percent. Now compared to Abraham Lincoln in terms of his "greatness," Kennedy was transformed from politician to superhero overnight.[1]

KENNEDY PROMISE BECOMES JOHNSON RECORD

Politically, Johnson inherited a great deal of excess baggage. Most of Kennedy's original proposals lingered in congressional committees, and much of the country doubted the new president's intentions. The most unkind in the press found significance in Johnson's Texas roots, the state where his beloved predecessor was murdered and the home of Lee Harvey Oswald as well. Some who questioned the conclusions of the Warren Report and worried about an assassination conspiracy wondered if Johnson might have been involved. Shortly before he died a decade later, Johnson told an interviewer that he knew some Americans saw him in a conspiratorial light. It troubled him. Most Americans, however, would see Johnson as the "Vietnam president" who built upon Kennedy's New Frontier.

Moving beyond the New Frontier agenda was a great challenge, and America's political divisions became particularly apparent at end of 1963.

Kennedy's old East Coast liberal power base doubted Johnson's credentials to lead the civil rights fight. Once again, his Texas roots made him suspect. The political right, on the other hand, worried about Johnson's loyalty to southern racist traditions, his commitment to anticommunism in light of Kennedy's Nuclear Test Ban Treaty, and his general association with the visionary New Frontier. To Johnson, the most obvious danger to passing Kennedy's proposals into law was found on the right and not the left. Whether they admired him or not, the Left, Johnson believed, would help him in civil rights matters and all reform legislation; the Right would not. Johnson had to convince concerned conservatives that reform was in their interest, and this required a certain Olympian reach. Meanwhile, if he could not win the respect of the American people in matters of style, he would win it on points of law. Americans love a winner, and Johnson hoped to succeed where the Kennedy White House had failed.

He wasted little time. Significantly, Johnson's first legislative announcements to the nation were broadcast from Congress and not from the Oval Office. He was always at home at Congress, and he hoped to make a point. Important legislation was stalled, the country was watching, and he demanded new law immediately. Specifically, Johnson spoke of the need to pass the tax cut bill and all civil rights legislation. In terms of the latter, Johnson reminded his audience that African Americans had waited 100 years for significant reform. They should not have to wait another day.

The new president's impatience symbolized his brand of politics. Still considering Franklin Roosevelt his "political papa," Johnson transformed the New Deal into the same type of myth and legend that the American people were applying to the New Frontier. To Johnson, Roosevelt's politics of action needed an immediate resurrection, and he planned his administration to be a virtual rerun of FDR's commitment, dedication, and legislative success. Whether that could be truly accomplished was uncertain at the end of 1963, but Johnson drew the battle lines.

Claiming that "our dead president" would appreciate it, Johnson told Congress to pass the lingering legislation as soon as possible. For a time, this would be Johnson's best lever on his former congressional colleagues. Who among them would dare vote against the wishes of the martyred superhero, Kennedy? It might mean the end of their careers, Johnson implied, making the tax and civil rights bills a matter of personal survival for many members of Congress.

Most of Kennedy's proposals became law by the end of February 1964, but Johnson realized that his hold on Congress might be short-lived. Using the "our dead president" argument was never good enough. He brought his own skills to the legislative fight. Working what he called the "two-shift day," Johnson kept in close contact with individual congressmen for the first several hours of a given day, napped and swam after lunch, and worked his "second" day until one or two in the morning. In constant contact by phone with legislative aides both in the White House and Congress, Johnson remained in the political fray. And he enjoyed it. His official White House sculpture even depicted him talking on the phone. But it also might have shown him giving "the treatment." Whether dealing with congressional leaders or foreign dignitaries, Johnson could be most demanding. Using strong language and keeping

President Johnson is photographed in his most frequent pose, phone in hand. *(Yoichi Okamoto, Lyndon B. Johnson Library)*

his face only inches away from his subject, the 6'4" Johnson took the politics of persuasion to high extremes.[2] Nicknamed "the treatment" by his staff, Johnson's efforts at personal persuasion rarely failed.

THE "GREAT SOCIETY" MISSION

Transforming New Frontier vision into the Johnson record required a plan. Once the nation had grown used to its new president, Johnson intended to define his own administration in his own terms. Yet continuity with the popular New Frontier was also essential to success, and Kennedy had amassed what Franklin Roosevelt would have called a "brain trust" staff. Most of those brilliant men were asked to stay on with the new Johnson White House, and the president had his favorites. He admired Robert McNamara for his hard-nosed, no-nonsense approach to management. He also liked Dean Rusk, for he had been a successful outsider to Kennedy's Harvard team. Johnson saw himself in the same light. At first, Robert Kennedy stayed on as attorney general; however, his differences with Johnson over issues ranging from legislative tactics to personality kept the two men permanently at odds. More to the point, Johnson did not want to be known as the president who was "sandwiched between Kennedys." He suspected Robert Kennedy had presidential ambitions of his own, and he was right. Johnson rejected loud Democratic Party appeals to make the slain president's younger brother the new vice president. There could never be an independent Johnson administration if Robert Kennedy remained a heartbeat away from the Oval Office. Or so Johnson concluded.

The bottom line for the new president was marrying Kennedy's "first step" politics and memory to a respected Johnson-defined cause that continued to win results in Congress. In spite of growing debates over the level of U.S. troop strength in Vietnam, whether nuclear disarmament could ever work, and the ever-increasing foreign aid bill, Johnson kept nearly all his public comments focused on domestic affairs. It was the first time since the early New Deal that the emphasis of the U.S. national government did not remain on foreign policy.

In order to announce his own direction and purpose, Johnson also needed a great, headline-making success. John Kennedy's antipoverty policy was perfect for the task. Its mission had been deemed overly ambitious by government analysts, and its press critics were many. The white middle class complained that the "war on poverty" ignored them and promised higher taxes. Civil rights advocates complained that it sidestepped the race issue. And conservatives everywhere complained that the federal government did not have the authority to remake the social map of the United States with the taxpayers' money. In 1963, few would have predicted a war-on-poverty success in Congress, but Johnson passed his Economic Opportunity Act in the spring of 1964. By promising more tax cuts, along with new jobs in the defense industry, construction, and education, Johnson argued that the war on poverty benefited all Americans and not just one sector of the economy. Claiming to have been born and raised in poverty (although his own mother disputed it), Johnson's off-the-cuff comments on the misery of America's underclass had been more emotional and effective than the carefully crafted speeches of his wealthy predecessor.

Johnson's success failed to provide his desired independence from the Kennedy era. Because America's minorities constituted the bulk of the impoverished, the Equal Opportunity Act also redirected the nation's attentions to the fate of civil rights legislation. To the press, enacted civil rights legislation would equal the true beginning of a new presidential administration. Johnson welcomed the challenge.

Although known for making deals with congressional opponents to assure success, Johnson this time stressed the undecided and swing voters in the Senate. The goal was to win 67 of the 100 senators to support civil rights legislation, for that was the magic number (according to Senate rules) to prevent a legislative block by one member (filibustering). Cutting off a filibuster attempt (or cloture) meant the difference between success and failure in this debate. One senator, reading into the official record for hours, could kill the legislation.

Johnson concentrated his efforts on the Republican minority leader, Senator Everett Dirksen. Like most of his fellow Republicans, Dirksen had no complaint against the civil rights cause. On the other hand, he believed that it gave the federal government too much authority over the states and local communities. He also worried that the legislation would lead to hiring quotas in private business. Johnson convinced Dirksen that he had no grievance against the private sector and had little use for quotas. This argument was accompanied by dozens of government contracts for Illinois, Dirksen's home state, along with federal judgeships for Dirksen loyalists. At the same time, Johnson went out of his way to demonstrate the White House's friendship toward Senate Republicans, posing for cozy pictures next to Dirksen and his family. The campaign worked. On June 10, 1964, a coalition of Democrats and Republicans passed the Civil Rights Act (which prohibited discrimination in public accommodations). A southern-born president had put an important nail in the coffin of legalized discrimination in the South and elsewhere. The nation then focused on the Johnson steamroller, and the mourning for Kennedy began to fade. Although months in coming, the moment had finally arrived for Johnson to declare his own administration, agenda, and mission.

FDR might have been the new president's mentor, but Johnson had no intention of bringing America back to strict 1930s solutions. Times had changed, he said, and even his own staff wondered what this old New Dealer had up his sleeve. The basic motivation in government service, Johnson once noted, should be to "help people." With that in mind, he once thought that the catchy logo for his administration must be the "Better Deal." The expression had become a mantra in his early 1964 speeches. Whereby FDR had offered a New Deal and Truman a Fair Deal, Johnson insisted that he had learned from the mistakes of both. He would offer a Better Deal. Assisting those who did not benefit from the postwar economic boom would be one of the program's primary characteristics. To Johnson, this commitment did not pit the interests of the middle class against the poor or alienate industrialists for the sake of class warfare. Instead, he talked in terms of unity, claiming that there was enough wealth for all classes to enjoy.

If American capitalism could truly demonstrate its equality and openness, that success would also be a powerful message to the communists. In the face of U.S. determination, communism did not have a chance. Both liberals and conservatives, Johnson believed, desired cold war victory and a government that was efficient and helpful to all its people. Stating that this approach would bring about a "Great Society," the term expressed Johnson's ambitions more aptly than Better Deal. It stuck, even though he was later accused of taking the name from a socialist economic reform package.[3] Johnson claimed to have never read anything penned by socialist reformers. The Great Society continued.

BARRY GOLDWATER'S MESSAGE

Johnson's observation that his administration was threatened by the right more than the left rang true in late 1964. Ironically, it coincided with his election to the presidency and the utter defeat of his major Republican opponent, Senator Barry Goldwater of Arizona. As early as the summer of 1963, the Kennedy camp had already assumed that the Republican nominee would be Goldwater, the former air force career officer. That appeared to be good news from the start. Goldwater was supported by the energetic ideological right of his party, but that was the extent of his popular support at the time. Since they voted in a bloc, this conservative support group was powerful enough to win Goldwater the nomination, but the presidency remained far from his grasp.

To Goldwater, the federal government had been moving in the wrong direction since the days of Franklin Roosevelt. New Deal involvement in the economy, he said, had been meant to be temporary. Later presidents and congressmen never understood that fact, he complained, and created an era of "creeping socialism." From education to highway construction and even race relations, Goldwater argued that local communities needed the final say in their destiny. Although he had little use for racism, his words were comforting to southern whites who believed that Washington had interfered with their segregationist way of life. In fact, when Johnson's Civil Rights Act was passed, the president's first reaction was that Goldwater, who voted against the act, must now have the support of thousands of Southern white racists.

In foreign affairs, Goldwater called for unspecified "militant actions" to win the cold war. He denounced the United Nations as an international collective that preached policy to the United States. Kennedy's call for cold war victory by 1970 was not being met, he implied, although he dodged questions from the press that suggested he favored World War III to meet the deadline. "Extremism in the defense of liberty is no vice," he announced at the 1964 Republican convention. Later claiming that he meant only to express his patriotism, Goldwater encouraged a mountain of criticism with this one sentence alone. The Democrats used it against him for the remaining days of the campaign.[4]

Budding national figures, such as Ronald Reagan, flocked to Goldwater's conservative cause, but it was not yet the nation's cause. Whereas the Goldwater campaign eventually favored a major U.S. military effort in Vietnam, Johnson announced that Vietnam was a war for "Asian boys" and not Americans. Little did the electorate know that U.S. involvement in Vietnam was growing well beyond what was reported to the press. But it might have been irrelevant had they known. To many electoral experts, supporting the Johnson campaign was a way for the voters to express their support for the Camelot legacy and the new president's achievements on its behalf. Johnson won election by 61.1 percent of the vote, beating Franklin Roosevelt's landslide record over Alf Landon in 1936. Great Society liberalism, some believed, had won its ultimate endorsement.[5] It was also a last hurrah.

To both Goldwater's and Johnson's right had been Governor George Wallace of Alabama. Enjoying little chance of wresting the Democratic nomination from Johnson, Wallace, a fellow Democrat, ran against Johnson in several state primaries anyway. Insisting that blue-collar whites were being ignored by

Washington, that "do-gooding" liberals did not understand the needs of the common man, and that Johnson had no right to preach morality to Southerners, Wallace openly courted the racist vote in his own folksy, populist style. Taken together, Goldwater and Wallace had a devastating impact on the once solid Democratic South. Their success there marked the end of the New Deal coalition in that entire region and made race the most divisive campaign issue in years. But the numbers were unmistakable. Johnson's victory was so complete, veteran ABC newsman Howard K. Smith predicted that the Republican Party would never recover from its defeat. Johnson knew better, and it was time to get on with the Great Society.

CIVIL RIGHTS SUCCESS

Johnson began his own first term with a powerful pro–Great Society majority in the 89th Congress, including nearly 300 of the 435 members in the House of Representatives. Always the realist, Johnson was more than aware of the warning signs in the South. The civil rights cause was dividing the country, and much of his native South was against him. Thanks to this problem, he planned to slow down the reform effort for more than a year. The nation, he believed, needed to accept the new era of the Civil Rights Act. But the next step was expected to be another dramatic undertaking.

During the 1964 Democratic national convention, the country had watched the all-white Democratic delegation from Mississippi denounce the civil rights agenda. Since most African-American communities in that state were denied the right to vote, it was easy to see why the Mississippi delegation had such strong opinions. There could be no further advancement of African-American issues, Johnson concluded, unless the right to vote was guaranteed in every community across the nation. The impact of this reform would be obvious. Given the demographic strength of African Americans across the U.S. South, the makeup of entire congressional delegations and statehouses could be changed forever if that right to vote was established and enforced.

Privately, Johnson predicted an ugly fight over the issue unless he won more legislative successes in other areas. Passing health care reform measures, such as Medicare, in addition to new infrastructure bills ranging from transportation to education, could only elevate his reputation as a winner whom anyone would be foolish to oppose. At the same time, Johnson spent weeks courting a concerned business community. In one special White House conference after another, Johnson urged business leaders to support the continuing war on poverty and related civil rights measures. Great results, he promised, would be apparent within the next decade. Well-trained, well-educated employees who welcomed a chance in the capitalist system were better than angry demonstrators in crime-ridden neighborhoods, Johnson told them.

Supporting the Great Society, the president said, was good for business. But this was an uneasy courtship and a very trying effort. Even the new vice president, former Minnesota senator and early civil rights advocate Hubert Humphrey, thought the White House was doing more to enlist the support of business than most Republican presidents of the 20th century. He also predicted that most of Johnson's enlistment efforts would fail, and he was right.

Maintaining a low profile on civil rights in 1965 was also easier said than done. Martin Luther King's movement had grown more impatient, and supporters of civil rights reform everywhere thought an offensive and not a slowdown was necessary. Once again, the liberal charge was heard that John Kennedy would have done better, acted quicker, and won results. It was a low blow for Johnson. Years later, the impatient civil rights reformers of 1965 claimed that it was during this period that the New Left was truly born in America. The New Left complained that the Great Society was well intentioned but too slow, too cozy with business, and more interested in deal making than in morality and justice.

Since the president's infrastructure bills during his so-called interregnum on civil rights also elevated the employment rate in both the white- and blue-collar sectors of the economy, Johnson expected his Democratic Party coalition to win elections for many years. That fact, he hoped, would also prevail over the civil rights concerns of whites working in these newly created jobs. But this hope was dependent upon years of continuing government incentives and economic growth.

Johnson waged two wars at once, and this was his biggest problem. The war on poverty and the war in Vietnam drained the treasury. Even in 1965, Johnson already faced a financial nightmare because of them. While the White House dreamed of a quick victory in Vietnam, Great Society programs were underfunded shortly after they began. This brought about yet another debate over American racism.

Most of the young men sent to Vietnam were African Americans, and the majority casualty figure was a 19-year-old black man who did not even have the right to vote. To early African-American critics of Johnson's Southeast Asia policy, such as Malcolm X, Vietnam was always a racist war whereby a white president dispatched potential undesirables to fight struggling people in a developing nation. Johnson was shocked by the accusation, but the civil rights cause was forever taking on a new shape.[6] The president was sometimes the last to know. Without question, Johnson liked the cute nickname "legislator in chief"; however, he learned the hard way that leading the civil rights reform effort took more than a success or two in Congress.

THE TONKIN GULF RESOLUTION

Since his vice presidential tour of Southeast Asia in the spring of 1961, Johnson had favored more and not less military action in that region. For a time, the November 1963 assassination of President Diem had given hope to the U.S. government that political reform was possible in South Vietnam. But Diem was succeeded by a revolving door of political personalities in Saigon, antigovernment protests continued, pro-Ho Chi Minh communists grew in strength, and South Vietnam remained one of the world's poorest countries. To Johnson, demonstrating America's anticommunist commitment was essential to U.S. foreign policy. That was especially important because World War III, or nuclear confrontation with the Soviets, was considered taboo. Only a show of U.S. military strength in the hot spots of Southeast Asia, and presumably where America might easily win, could keep the nation's anticommunist credentials intact. Such was the reasoning of 1964 and for the next several years.

Propping up an anticommunist regime in Saigon had been a dilemma for both Presidents Eisenhower and Kennedy. At the heart of the dilemma was the lack of public support for a dictatorship that often ruled with an iron fist. Beating back its own homegrown opponents, along with North Vietnamese infiltrators and troops, was more of an American concern than a South Vietnamese one. But in those days of can-do politics and Great Society ambitions, few in the White House doubted that full success was in reach. Yet South Vietnam remained an alien, faraway place to most Americans. They would need justification for any U.S. escalation of the war, and that war would have to be won quickly if the expensive Great Society programs were to continue.

An "incident" in the Gulf of Tonkin near North Vietnam provided that justification. To this day, historians disagree over what exactly took place there. Still others disagree on the meaning and significance of the Tonkin Gulf Resolution that followed it. From the beginning, Vietnam would be America's most controversial war.

It is generally known that on August 2, 1964, the U.S. destroyer *Maddox* was on an "eavesdropping" mission off the coast of North Vietnam. Just to its south, U.S.-backed South Vietnamese commandos were launching a surprise assault on the enemy island of Hon Me. U.S.-backed or not, the commandos found the resistance overwhelming, and they were forced to retreat. North

The U.S. destroyer *Maddox* and its crew remained at the heart of the controversy surrounding the Tonkin Gulf Incident and the follow-up Tonkin Gulf Resolution. Photographed on *Maddox* on August 13, 1964, are Captain John J. Herrick, USN, commander Destroyer Division 192 (*at left*), and Commander Herbert L. Ogier, USN (*right*). (*U.S. Naval Historical Center*)

Vietnamese patrol boats pursued them into the Tonkin Gulf and apparently concluded that the *Maddox* was part of the commando mission. This was not the case. President Johnson preferred to keep U.S. military operations in the Tonkin Gulf separate from South Vietnamese activity. An exchange of fire between the *Maddox* and the patrol boats took place. Several of the North Vietnamese vessels were damaged or destroyed. The *Maddox* was later joined by *C. Turner Joy,* and another North Vietnamese attack was reported. Again, several North Vietnamese vessels were said to have been sunk in the follow-up U.S. Navy report. That report remains a controversial one, for some claim that a second attack never took place. Indeed, no visual sightings of enemy craft could ever be confirmed.

Knowing that the details were sketchy, Johnson still regarded the basic fact of an attack on the U.S. Navy as the only matter of concern. This was good enough, many historians believe, for Johnson to announce a new, more dramatic role for the U.S. military in Vietnam. Like President Truman in the Korean War, Johnson moved cautiously. He authorized a reprisal bombing raid over North Vietnam, but the larger decision making centered on what the Kremlin might or might not do. Any quick escalation of U.S. firepower in South Vietnam could be perceived in Moscow as a general assault against the communist world. The dreaded World War III might be the result. Johnson telephoned Premier Khrushchev, assuring him that the U.S. military escalation in Vietnam did not mean an affront to the Soviet Union. He also cabled North Vietnam's Ho Chi Minh, warning him of dark days ahead if he refused to halt all military action against South Vietnam.

Through it all, Johnson implied that the U.S. Navy was an innocent victim of a Pearl Harbor–like sneak attack in international waters and that North Vietnam had forced his hand. But this was a most interpretative matter. The United Nations, North Vietnam, South Vietnam, and the United States could not agree on a definition of international waters. Three, seven, and even 12 miles from the North Vietnamese coastline were declared international boundaries, and U.S. Navy spy missions were not innocent affairs. Even the U.S. aircraft carrier *Ticonderoga* was in the Tonkin Gulf on the night of August 4, 1964, and its Crusader jets were also involved in the incident.

On August 5, 1964, a somber President Johnson asked Congress for special powers to conduct the Vietnam War. There would no longer be any effort to disguise American troops as "advisers." Johnson's new special powers elevated the executive privilege of the presidency, granting him the right to dispatch troops and finance any military action without Congress's approval. A quick response was essential to victory, Johnson told the nation, and the country supported him. Only two senators dared to question the president's reasoning. Senator Wayne Morse (Republican of Oregon) and Senator Ernest Gruening (Democrat of Alaska) both had constitutional objections. Pointing out that the presidency never enjoyed sweeping powers during America's other wars, Morse and Gruening asked Johnson why he needed special executive privilege to wage what was described as an easy war.

Viewed as over-the-hill outsiders to the anticommunist cause, these two elderly men were shouted down by their younger colleagues as fools who should have retired long before. Within three years, they would be trumpeted as unsung heros by the burgeoning antiwar movement. Never recognizing their

The U.S. aircraft carrier *Ticonderoga* played a covering role in what the press soon called the Tonkin Gulf Incident. *(U.S. Naval Historical Center)*

later hero worship by young radicals, Gruening and Morse always insisted that they were motivated by constitutional concerns alone. Meanwhile, Johnson privately hailed the Tonkin Gulf Resolution as a great triumph for the presidency. "It was like grandma's nightshirt," he said. "It covered everything."[7]

"GUNS AND BUTTER"

In an effort to put many minds at ease, Johnson told the country not to worry about finances. Vietnam would be over soon, and the Great Society would remain on track. In short, America was rich enough to wage war against Ho Chi Minh and domestic poverty at the same time. It would continue to enjoy, he insisted, both "guns and butter."

Freshman Democratic Senator Gaylord Nelson of Wisconsin disagreed. As the governor of Wisconsin during the Cuban Missile Crisis, Nelson had won a considerable degree of respect for his tireless effort to prepare Wisconsin for the worst. His ultimate reward was a victorious run for the Senate in 1964, and few voters doubted his commitment to anticommunism. On the other hand,

Nelson doubted the "guns and butter" thesis. Tonkin Gulf Resolution or not, he urged Congress to keep a close watch on Vietnam expenses. He also thought Gruening and Morse had been dismissed too quickly by his new colleagues, and he worried about the legal implications of the resolution. Johnson was on the verge of becoming "King Lyndon I," he said, and it was the Senate's fault. He proposed an amendment to restore Congress's role in defense policy, but the chairman of the Senate Foreign Relations Committee, Senator J. William Fulbright, killed the proposal when it reached his desk. On behalf of the president, Fulbright questioned Nelson's loyalty as a Democrat during a time of war and reminded Nelson that he was a freshman member of the Senate. Ironically, Fulbright had been a longtime watchdog of potential presidential abuses, but, once again, anticommunist concerns took precedence. Fulbright later regretted his action, noting that at a critical time before heavy U.S. casualties were inflicted in Vietnam, a meaningful discussion about Vietnam policy goals and objectives was rejected.

In February 1965, Johnson's "guns and butter" thesis endured its first great test. At Camp Holloway near Pleiku in the Central Highlands of South Vietnam, some 180 U.S. soldiers along with several hundred Army of the Republic of Vietnam (ARVN) personnel were attacked by the Vietcong. The area had been an important observation post for the French during their version of the Vietnam War, and the United States resumed the same mission. In a well-planned assault, the Vietcong rushed through the camp shooting at everything in sight. In only 15 minutes, more than 100 Americans were wounded and eight killed. The U.S. military was both shocked and embarrassed. A terrorist assault on a U.S. military hotel at Qui Nhon on the coast of South Vietnam added more insult to the injury.

Concluding that joint South Vietnamese and American pacification programs were not working in Vietnam, Johnson decided that swift Tonkin Gulf Resolution action was required. First, he ordered all U.S. military dependents out of Vietnam. Second, he announced a series of air strikes on North Vietnam. One of the more ambitious strikes, a B-52 mission code-named ROLLING THUNDER, would continue for three years. On March 8, 1965, more than 3,500 U.S. Marines arrived in Vietnam via a ceremonial amphibious landing that was supposed to remind Americans of World War II victories in the Pacific. Twenty thousand additional troops soon followed.

Secretary of Defense Robert McNamara admitted privately that he had no idea how much the spring 1965 escalations might cost the economy or the Great Society in general or what the casualty figures might be. He assured both the troops and the American people that as many comforts of home as possible would be sent to Vietnam. The new troops were needed to guard existing bases and help the South Vietnamese hold the line, he said. In keeping with the Tonkin Gulf Resolution, Congress was not consulted.

During their top secret cabinet meetings, both Johnson and McNamara worried about a military collapse in Vietnam. Money remained a constant problem, too. As early as 1965, air war costs in sorties against secondary targets in South Vietnam reached the total cost of all air operations in the Pacific during World War II. National Security Council adviser Walt Rostow admitted that he had no idea how much had been spent on the primary targets in North Vietnam. Johnson's usual answer to these problems was a historical one. He

reminded his cabinet that Congress tried to investigate the White House's handling of the Spanish-American War in 1898. The war's great monetary expense
had not been anticipated, but who remembered that fact? Johnson asked.
America beat the Spanish hands down and entered the world stage because of
it. People remembered the victory, he said, and Congress's investigation was
viewed as an insult to wartime heroes such as Teddy Roosevelt. Johnson predicted similar good fortunes for the presidency after the Vietnam victory.

Of course, a quickly negotiated settlement with the North Vietnamese
would always be welcome, and Johnson gave it a good Texas try. Ho Chi Minh
remained unreceptive, and it was most frustrating to the president. Johnson had
wheeled and dealed throughout his political life, but Ho rebuffed every deal.
Later historians would criticize Johnson for applying domestic, back-slapping
political strategies to foreign policy making. However, Johnson's approach to
Vietnam was much more complicated. Short of total war, the president was
ready to use any tactic to win in Vietnam. Sadly for Johnson, a depressed
Robert McNamara, fresh from another trip to South Vietnam, told him in the
spring of 1965 that a World War II–like commitment might be the only way to
succeed there.

To the North Vietnamese, Johnson's lobbying for some sort of peace deal
meant that the Americans must be losing on the battlefield. It was in their
interest to stay away from deals. In April 1965, Prime Minister Pham Van Dong
of North Vietnam insisted that peace was possible only after Johnson withdrew
his troops and welcomed a coalition government of communists and anticommunists in Saigon. The North Vietnamese were not optimistic over this matter,
but they gave it a try. In Washington, this solution was seen as an easy means for
communist coalition members to seize the entire government. Hence, Johnson
regarded it as a nonnegotiable issue. There would never be a coalition government in South Vietnam, and Johnson's successor, Richard Nixon, maintained
this stance as well.[8]

THE TELEVISION WAR

Vietnam was the hottest news issue of the 1960s, and the American people had
their favorite sources of information. Television was that number-one source,
and CBS News was their favorite.

Since its election coverage of 1956, the *CBS Evening News* began to win
the lion's share of news watchers. Its commitment to investigative journalism,
combined with in-depth interviews and no-nonsense commentary, vowed
audiences in a time long before flashy cable news networks and the Internet.
CBS chief executive Fred Friendly predicted that by 1970, most Americans
would get their news from his network. He was not too far off the mark.

The newspaper was not dead, but it was fading. During the 1960s, the
Columbia University School of Journalism claimed at the end of the decade
that the nation's newspapers went out of business at the rate of 16 per month.
To many Americans, all the relevant news was now offered in a quick half-hour
format, and they had no apologies for watching it. Veteran journalists and edu-
cators, from Benjamin Bradlee at The *Washington Post* to Harvard's Edwin
Reischauer, criticized the trend, forecasting a new "cult of ignorance."
Unscrupulous politicians and businessmen would soon exploit this coming

epidemic of American ignorance, American historian Arthur Schlesinger, Jr., once said, and British historian Hugh Trevor Roper even warned that an American version of an Adolf Hitler–like government was possible because of it. Ironically, most of these complaints and predictions were printed in newspaper "op-ed" pieces, and most Americans ignored them.

Upset by the recession of the late 1950s, both middle- and working-class Americans were laboring longer hours to continue the benefits of prosperity. Coming home to hours of newspaper reading was not in their interest. NBC's trailblazing *Huntley-Brinkley Report* won numerous awards and endless praise for its cerebral treatment of "hard news," but millions of TV viewers preferred a straightforward presentation of the days happenings—without 24-letter words. CBS's Walter Cronkite fit the bill perfectly.

Inheriting the format of the baritone-voiced, chain-smoking Edward R. Murrow, Cronkite gave the news in an objective, stone-faced fashion, introduced investigative reports with the air of a grand presidential announcement, and looked like a favorite uncle or grandfather. He cried when announcing the death of President Kennedy, and that unprecedented display of emotion in the face of a hard news story underscored the tragedy of the event to many Americans. By 1965, he was considered one of the most trusted men in the world, a symbol of the new influential leader in the electronic age. Thousands of viewers watched him during controversial reports to see if his famous stone face might crack. His raising of the left eyebrow, for instance, while reporting on Martin Luther King's March on Washington was interpreted as a personal endorsement of the Civil Rights movement by some critical viewers. He had few comments when taken to task for this alleged example of television news bias, noting matter-of-factly that all he had done was raise an eyebrow.

Like most Americans during the early months of the Johnson administration, Cronkite had no doubt America would prevail in the Vietnam War. As a former World War II correspondent, he had seen the horror of war, but Vietnam was different. President Johnson touted America's technological superiority over an outgunned enemy, and early CBS News reports from Vietnam stressed the same point. Visiting South Vietnam in 1964, Cronkite went along on a low-flying bombing mission over a Vietcong stronghold. Thoroughly enjoying himself, Cronkite reported the mission the way one would describe a thrill ride at an amusement park. Concluding that the struggling and impoverished enemy did not have a chance against such high-tech machines as the F-4 fighter, Cronkite noted that all was well with the American cause in Vietnam. Within one year, this tenor and tone changed dramatically.

To its credit, in 1965, CBS decided to take a closer look at the everyday life of the American foot soldier in Vietnam. The reports from both government and military spokesmen in Saigon always differed from the accounts of the men in the field. Hence, this closer look. CBS reporter Charles Kuralt shocked America with his reports of Charlie Company and their on-patrol duties near a rubber plantation outside Saigon. Day after day, for two weeks straight, Americans got to know the young men of Charlie Company. They watched some of them die, learned that the enemy was determined to win, too, and, for the first time, wondered what it all meant. To the annoyance of officials in Washington

and Saigon, Kuralt's folksy, personal, and award-winning journalism stimulated similar reports from the entire news media. The American tradition of muckraking, investigative journalism had finally come to Vietnam, and the myth began to grow in certain U.S. military circles that the press was responsible for an atmosphere of defeatism in the United States.

Vietnam would be America's last war where reporters like Kuralt had free rein to film and report as they saw fit. By late 1965, the relationship between

Like the men of Charlie Company made famous by CBS's Charles Kuralt, the men of H Company, 2nd Battalion, 7th Marines try to survive the hell of Vietnam in 1965. *(National Archives)*

the Vietnam press corps, the U.S. military, and the U.S. embassy were permanently strained. The grunts (American infantrymen), Kuralt had reported, always understood the folly of the Vietnam War, but officialdom never listened. To Kuralt and his colleagues, the U.S. embassy and military press releases in Vietnam, always delivered to reporters at 5:00 P.M., were "The 5 O-Clock Follies." In those releases, the enemy was forever "on the ropes." America's involvement in Vietnam would be over soon, they announced, for there was "light at the end of the tunnel" (inevitable military victory).[9] None of this was apparent in the field, but the U.S. military commitment continued.

THE BRITISH INVASION

To the white middle-class American youth of 1964 and early 1965, the invasion that interested them most had nothing to do with Vietnam. In February 1964, the Beatles came to the United States for a concert tour and, to many, their arrival signified the success of British culture within American consumerism. The Beatles (John Lennon, Paul McCartney, George Harrison, and Ringo Starr in their final format) remained the well-dressed quartet from Liverpool who, thanks to experimentalism, catchy harmony, and unique haircuts, changed the direction of pop music. After years of Elvis, Chubby Checker, and other homegrown rock-and-roll pioneers, American music fans were ready for innovation and change. The Beatles filled the gap at a critical time, and their wildly enthusiastic young fans proved it.

Appearing on CBS television's popular variety program *The Ed Sullivan Show*, the Beatles won an even greater national audience than they thought was possible. Early Beatles hits such as "I Want to Hold Your Hand" and "She Loves You" were romantic songs that especially appealed to teen life and concerns. The screaming adulation or "Beatlemania" for this mop-haired group confounded and even worried parents. But American music adjusted to the Beatles' sound and not the other way around. The Beatles led the way to American pop chart success for their own British-based competition—from the irreverent blues-based rock group the Rolling Stones to vocalist Petula Clark. But the Beatles had staying power and were often hailed as Elvis's replacement in true rock-and-roll leadership.

Less than two years after their American tour, the Beatles abandoned the road. Wealthy beyond their dreams, the group turned to Indian philosophy and drugs for solace. Although they preferred to do their work in a studio, their dominance of the American rock music industry remained assured. But music was not the only indication of the British presence. Fashion was another obvious example.

Working out of a small dress shop in London's Chelsea district, young designer Mary Quant changed the look of American women. Her brightly colored short skirt design, usually with stripes and a broad belt, was nicknamed the "miniskirt." Largely designed for very thin models also wearing high boots, the miniskirt was not for everybody. The nationwide department store chain of J. C. Penney first marketed the dress in the United States, causing an immediate sensation as a "sexual revolution" item. America's young women tried their best to fit into one of Quant's designs, annoying feminists who pointed out the unrealistic goals being set by the fashion industry.

During a Boston-based "Twiggy" look-alike contest in 1967, a local young woman models Mary Quant fashions. *(Ted Polumbaum/TimePix)*

Quant's clothes, also called the "Mod" or "Chelsea" look, were especially well displayed by British fashion model Leslie Hornby. Professionally known as "Twiggy," Hornby was a short and skinny working-class girl from London who adorned most of America's fashion and even news magazines throughout the mid-1960s. "Thin is in," she said, but, once again, this set difficult, unhealthy standards for many American women.

Although there were arguments over whether the British invasion was started by James Bond or the Beatles, it was obvious that American life was fast becoming globalized in ways it had not experienced before. From Beatles haircuts to women's fashion, there were more opportunities for Americans to dress in their own way. America was not alone in trying to set certain standards, and the British influence was usually seen as a positive one as long as it did not disturb American politics or the leading domestic industries. In short, the invasion had little impact on the big-picture issues of the day, although the new songs and fashions always encouraged listeners and buyers to "do their own thing."[10] That advice was as American as apple pie.

SAIGON U.S.A.

While the American people remained fascinated by the British invasion, their government continued to move into South Vietnam. Given the good life at home, the war abroad did not have to be one of scarcity and deprivation for America's military personnel. Some of those domestic comforts even accompanied American troops to the battlefield. For lucky American businesses, winning a Vietnam defense contract was a ticket to success and even a saving grace. The troubled Schlitz company, for instance, and its "Beer That Made Milwaukee Famous," enjoyed a temporary monopoly on beer sales to American troops throughout Southeast Asia. This economic boon prompted the company to change its logo for a while to "Schlitz, Milwaukee and the World." Television news reports showing Schlitz beer being parachuted to grunts in the field annoyed some World War II veterans who had never enjoyed such luxuries, but these reports offered a false image of Vietnam combat duty. By late 1965, most Americans were well aware of what Johnson privately called "that bitch of a war."

As CBS's Bruce Morton reported in fall 1965, a consumer could buy anything in South Vietnam "except peace, justice, and democracy."[11] From cigarettes laced with opium to the large population of prostitutes, Saigon was, General William Westmoreland once quipped, a "buyer's market." Many of the American consumer items that were intended for U.S. troops or targeted South Vietnamese civilians ended up on the Saigon black market. The number-one black market item in the mid-1960s was U.S. powdered milk. CBS even did a special report on the "milk issue," using it as a symbol of U.S.–South Vietnamese corruption. American officials admitted on camera that they made money on the black market and saw no harm if a Vietcong family bought U.S. milk as well. That the Vietcong had U.S. consumer items in their possession, these officials reasoned, was a good thing. It might woo them to the capitalist side, they said. Corruption had been elevated to a noble, patriotic mission, and CBS's Morton asked his viewers to consider the ethics and meaning behind American objectives in Vietnam.[12]

President Johnson found the press interest in Saigon corruption more annoying than their combat coverage. However, he took no action to leash CBS or the other media giants. Some 80 percent of the American people were still telling the Gallup Poll that a pull out of U.S. troops from Vietnam would lead to the communist takeover of all of Southeast Asia. America's mid-1960s concern over Vietnam was not yet significant opposition. Meanwhile, Johnson temporarily halted Operation ROLLING THUNDER in the undying hope of bringing Ho Chi Minh to the negotiation table. For some months in 1965, the battlefields were quieter than usual, and Johnson saw this as the right moment to bargain with Ho. Johnson's staff could not agree on what the quiet meant. General Maxwell Taylor of the Joint Chiefs of Staff and Undersecretary of State George Ball believed that the enemy was lulling the United States into a false sense of security. Johnson said that the enemy had been humbled by his post–Tonkin Gulf escalation of the war, and he told Taylor and Ball that they must be more optimistic. But Ho had sent four brigades south to the Saigon area and put other troops on a heavy training schedule. He answered Johnson's call for talks by launching an offensive.[13]

Ho's primary target was the South Vietnamese military, and in May and June of 1965 it looked as if America's ally was ready to fold. The CIA even informed the president that more U.S. troops might not save them. Secretary of Defense McNamara joined Johnson in mulling over the possibility of a total war commitment of tens of thousands of fresh U.S. troops in the field. There was, however, the obvious problem of U.S. public support in the face of the new and negative press reports. It would help if there was a new leader in Saigon whom the American people could respect and support.

Johnson favored Nguyen Cao Ky, a former daredevil pilot and up-and-coming young South Vietnamese military officer, to serve as the new leader. Handsome, eloquent, and convincing when he called for great reforms, Ky reminded Johnson of a Vietnamese version of John Kennedy. And that was exactly the type of image that Johnson wanted to present to the American people. Preferring stylish and brightly colored clothes, Foster Grant sunglasses, and fine champagne, Ky, as Johnson hoped, did become the focus of press attention. *Life* magazine even declared Ky's wife the most beautiful first lady since Jacqueline Kennedy.

However, Ky did nothing to halt Saigon corruption, failed to offer promised reforms, and championed a military solution that was not supported by Johnson.[14] Ky favored an invasion of North Vietnam led by South Vietnamese troops and heavily supported by the U.S. military. Johnson considered this an invitation to Soviet involvement and World War III; however, he had no objection to Ky talking about it in public. He drew large crowds in Saigon when he did, and, for the moment, that display of popular appeal was what Johnson wanted to see in the new leadership.

Ky remained an enigma. He could denounce the United States as an interfering giant in his country and then ask how he might better help the anticommunist cause at the same time. The American press did not know what to make of these contradictions and found his frequent discussions about the rebuilding of postwar Saigon overly optimistic, odd, and out of place. Johnson had not found the John Kennedy of South Vietnam.

Things could have been worse. In Johnson's eyes, Ky was always a better American ally than his predecessors, Phan Khac Suu and Tran Van Huong. These two leaders admitted that they had no plan to defeat the communists. South Vietnam's future, they had concluded, remained in God's hands alone. But they were wrong. The future remained in Lyndon Johnson's hands.

Deciding whether that future depended upon American unilateral efforts was Johnson's call. The lack of American allies in the Vietnam effort was obvious from the beginning. Not even the Korean War had been a strictly unilateral effort. The United States might have carried the brunt of that war, but that meant it did so with allies at its side. In the effort to avoid the charge that Vietnam was "Lyndon's War," Johnson launched his "Many Flags" campaign in the mid-1960s. This was an attempt to win volunteer troops from the Asian/Pacific world to assist U.S. and ARVN troops in Vietnam. It was a controversial plan from the beginning. Japan, for example, would have to change its constitution to dispatch troops overseas, and Prime Minister Eisaku Sato, although a passionate anticommunist, had no intention of doing so. Furthermore, other Asian nations would probably reject a role in Vietnam simply because Japan, their hated World War II occupier, was involved.

New Zealand and Australia sent some troops, but the most controversial arrangement was made with President Park Chung Hee of South Korea. The latter was as much of the wheeler-dealer as Johnson, and he agreed to send troops in exchange for a large U.S. aid package. Some 300,000 South Koreans served in South Vietnam. Rejecting any watchful press, the South Korean Marines won a quick reputation for ruthlessness. All atrocity reports were denied personally by President Park. Johnson had no opinion on the matter; Vietnam was already a "filthy war."

But it was a "filthy war" with a good side, the president still insisted. From new harbor facilities for Saigon to decent-paying U.S. military base jobs for South Vietnamese civilians, Johnson also saw the Great Society in action over there.[15] Consequently, the U.S. influence was supposed to be more positive than negative, and the war would not last forever. However, by the mid-1960s, it had already gone on longer than most Americans thought it would. For Johnson, the question remained whether the Great Society could continue at home, much less overseas. A rough road lay ahead.

President Johnson addresses a pro–Vietnam War rally in 1966. This photograph is later used as a public relations poster by the White House to promote the president's Vietnam policies. *(Yoichi Okamoto, Lyndon B. Johnson Library)*

ESCALATION

As early as 1965, Johnson later told his biographer Doris Kearns Godwin that the Vietnam War had ruined his chances for reelection and ended the forward momentum of his Great Society. The liberal wing of his Democratic Party was needed for a successful war on poverty, but these were the very people who were beginning to question their nation's role in Vietnam. For Johnson, 1965 and 1966 would be pivotal years. Secretary of Defense McNamara promised him a turnabout of the Vietnam situation before it was too late, but there was little evidence to suggest that could happen. Vietnam became McNamara's home away from home, and, thanks to yet another fact-finding mission, he managed to win 40,000 more fresh troops for General Westmoreland in the late spring of 1965.

By the summer of 1965, the White House no longer asked how many U.S. troops were necessary in Vietnam. The question was how to deploy them. General James Gavin especially added to the controversy. Gavin had been World War II's youngest general, Kennedy's ambassador to France, and in the mid-1960s he was the country's chief public advocate of an "enclave strategy." Something of the expert on France's mistakes in Vietnam, Gavin warned that the United States was headed in the same awful direction as the French. Large numbers of troops, distributed across Vietnam, Gavin warned, did not work for them and would not work for the United States. The Vietcong would simply kill large numbers of Americans, and this misery would be covered daily by network TV. Gavin's public relations campaign resounded in the Oval Office. Claiming that he admired Gavin's analysis, Johnson announced that South Vietnamese troops would be fighting across their country by themselves. America's forces would defend American bases and established positions. It was time for the ARVN, he said, to shoulder more burdens.

General William Westmoreland opposed this decision. Arguing that the South Vietnamese military would be destroyed while American troops relaxed on comfortable military bases, Westmoreland insisted that the primary mission of the war involved the rescue of the Saigon government's armed forces in the field. An additional 150,000 U.S. troops, he insisted, could accomplish the task. Johnson hesitated, but eventually compromised Westmoreland's request by dispatching 95,000 troops.

Ironically, Westmoreland could not guarantee military victory even with his original request of 150,000. But America always had more than troops to throw into the fight, and Johnson underscored the point. The president believed that American technology would fill in the gap and help the newly arrived U.S. forces win the war in 1966 at the earliest or 1967 at the latest. From cluster bombs dropped just above the enemy's heads to electronic spy gear planted near North Vietnamese infiltration routes to the walleye guided missile, Johnson had great faith in the amazing array of high-tech gear that was available to the military in the mid-1960s.

CIA Director John McCone bolstered the president's thesis. To McCone, all comparisons to the French military strategies of the early 1950s were foolish, due to the technological developments of the 1960s. The National Security Council's Walt Rostow agreed, but Undersecretary of State Ball, as always, urged Johnson to withdraw before the United States was forced to face defeat.

Explaining a retreat to the American people after the many promises of victory, Johnson told Ball, would be tantamount to political suicide for himself, all White House officials, and much of the Democratic Party. The North Vietnamese were not supermen, Johnson argued, and by 1967 they would be begging for peace. Again, as always, there were no facts to back up this position, but wishful thinking continued to rule the day.

Accompanying the decision to stand firm in Vietnam were hundreds of new bombing missions ordered over North Vietnam. More than 5,000 sorties were flown in the summer of 1965 alone, and that doubled the raids of the previous year. Secretary McNamara was largely responsible for the effort. Wiping out the enemy's ability to wage war was essential to victory, he noted. In addition to the usual munitions factories, all bridges, railways, and power stations were added to the bombing targets. Short of nuclear war, McNamara believed North Vietnam had to be humbled. Yet Johnson worried about what he called the Defense Department's "bombs away" approach. The potential for killing Soviet or Chinese visitors in Hanoi or Haiphong, the two major North Vietnamese targets, had now escalated with the war. A threat of World War III, he feared, always loomed because of it.

Bringing together a brain trust of "wise men" helped Johnson deal with the new pressures of Vietnam decision making. The "wise men" were supposed to include America's finest and most experienced defense policy experts. In reality, they included aging architects of cold war confrontation, such as former Secretary of State Dean Acheson. They told Johnson what he wanted to hear, and "stay the course" remained the usual message. In fact, their larger worry was that the president might appear soft on communism if he stuck to "enclave strategies" or hinted at retreat. Victory, they agreed, was only months away.

Adding to the confusion was the communist position in the mid-1960s. Ho Chi Minh preferred a low-key approach on the battlefield until the new arrivals of American troops were in position. He concentrated on supplying his far-flung units in South Vietnam, creating an entire division (the 70th Transportation Group) for this task. Time, as he always said, was on his side. Meanwhile, in Beijing, the Chinese government offered mixed signals to Washington. At first, they insisted that their involvement in a Vietnam War was contingent only upon an American advance into Chinese territory. Then a group of Western journalists learned that China was preparing a significant aid plan for North Vietnam. The Chinese denied these reports, even though high-ranking government officials were quoted in them.

Even more confusion reigned in Moscow. Brezhnev and Kosygin sought a Soviet-Chinese accord on Vietnam whereby some sort of "united front" on assistance to Ho would be established. Yet the Chinese government issued a specific policy paper denouncing this type of arrangement. Declaring that the North Vietnamese should follow the example of the Chinese Communist Party of the 1930s and 1940s, Beijing told Hanoi to win its battles on its own.

To Johnson, the communist confusion was more evidence that the United States was destined to win the war. But even if it meant heavy casualties for the U.S. Air Force over North Vietnam, Johnson continued to insist on careful, strategic assaults on selected targets. A widespread bombing campaign, Johnson

concluded, would end the communist confusion and unite North Vietnam, China, and the Soviet Union against the United States. Almost as one voice, the Pentagon disagreed. General Westmoreland was especially vocal on this point, noting that the president's growing fears of World War III were exaggerated and harmful to military strategy. The accidental deaths of Chinese or Soviet citizens in North Vietnam would lead to no military action against America, he predicted, but Johnson continued to ignore him. Years later, McNamara described the mid-1960s years of the Vietnam War as a period divorced from reason and common sense. America's can-do spirit overrode the facts, logic, and critical decision making.[16]

While America's mission in Vietnam escalated into a full-scale war, the American mission in space continued to escalate as well. The "prime crew" of the *Apollo 1* space mission (*from left to right*) Edward White, Virgil "Gus" Grissom, and Roger Chaffee pose for their NASA publicity shot shortly before their death by fire during a launching pad accident. (*NASA/Johnson Space Center*)

SENATOR ROBERT KENNEDY OF NEW YORK

The mid-1960s were also years of decision for Robert Kennedy. At the Democratic convention of 1964, Kennedy had received a longer, louder standing ovation than President Johnson. Kennedy's appearance at the convention offered a means for John Kennedy admirers to voice their approval for the Camelot legacy, and the convention was filled with Democratic stalwarts who bemoaned the passing of the New Frontier. To the Johnson family, this was "Bobby's convention," an embarrassing reality for an accidental president. The first lady, Lady Bird Johnson, thought that Robert Kennedy deliberately sought the limelight to accent a future run for the White House. Maybe, she worried, that race would be against her own husband. The worries were misplaced. At least in 1964, Robert Kennedy had sought a spotlight on his upcoming race against Senator Kenneth Keating of New York.

Since his younger brother, Teddy, was already in the Senate, a Robert Kennedy win in New York would create the first older-younger brother team in the Senate since Dwight and Theodore Foster in 1803. At first, it looked like a tough uphill fight. Keating was a moderate Republican who had denounced Barry Goldwater as an extremist. A staunch anticommunist who had little use for civil rights, Keating could still make a liberal-sounding speech to the proper New York City audience. Meanwhile, Kennedy's Massachusetts credentials won him the charge that he was a "carpetbagger," a non–New York resident and shameless opportunist who planned to use the Senate as a stepping-stone to the presidency. In reality, John Kennedy had spent more time in New York before running for Congress in Massachusetts than Robert Kennedy had spent in Massachusetts before running in New York.

Senator Keating claimed that he had no White House ambitions whatsoever. All he wanted to do, he insisted, was represent New York. He urged the nation to support him in the battle against the arrogant Kennedy "incursion." Former John Kennedy backers, such as author Gore Vidal, actor Paul Newman, and historian Barbara Tuchman, flocked to Keating's campaign, offering him a high profile in the media. The once pro–New Frontier *New York Times* even attacked Kennedy's "invasion of the state," and former Vice President Nixon said he found the Kennedy campaign "sad and unethical."

Running far behind in the polls during the opening weeks of the campaign, Kennedy stressed New Frontier and Great Society issues while promising a vague new Bobby Kennedy agenda at the same time. It worked. Isolating Keating as an overly cautious politician who refused to recognize the paramount issues of the day, Kennedy appealed to a coalition of liberals and minorities to sweep him into office. Much of his landslide over Keating was due to the "coat-tail effect" of Lyndon Johnson's success in New York, but Kennedy still considered his hard-fought Senate seat a "decent divorce" from the Johnson White House. Establishing the promised new agenda, unique from his older brother's or Johnson's, would be the hard part. To President Johnson's annoyance, Kennedy made no mention of the White House or the Great Society on the night of his campaign victory.

Quoting Emerson and Lincoln, Kennedy's first Senate speech was masterly oratory, reminding many of the glory days of the New Frontier. But within weeks, Kennedy broke with the administration on a key issue. He was extremely critical of the Dominican Republic invasion. Although noting that he had little use for communists, he also announced that he had little use for right-wing juntas. America's record of intervention in the Caribbean was a mistake, he said. On the other hand, he did not make similar comparisons to the American effort in Vietnam. Insisting that the president's new Vietnam escalation policies needed careful study, Kennedy always troubled the Johnson White House. But he was not an early antiwar leader.

The debate over proper civil rights reform, on the other hand, led Kennedy to take an in-depth look at Great Society efforts. As attorney general, he had set much of those reforms in motion, but he had been a distant Washington bureaucrat during much of that early fight. As senator, he toured big-city ghettos and visited impoverished African-American communities in the rural South. The latter particularly shocked him. Born and raised in great wealth, Kennedy had never been that close to horrible poverty before. It added a sense of urgency for him, and he found Great Society programs lacking in most areas. The press followed this transformation closely. The *New York Times* began referring to Kennedy, once considered "callous and ruthless," as a "new man" who was "thoughtful and caring."[17] Kennedy was now considered a presidential hopeful of the far future. However, as always in the 1960s, events moved quickly.

CHRONICLE OF EVENTS

1964

January 1: President Johnson sends a message to Premier Khrushchev urging improvements in Soviet-American relations and a resulting new era of peace. He also sends a message to the South Vietnamese government pledging full U.S. military support throughout 1964.

January 4: Mickey Wright, a golfer, is honored as Female Athlete of the Year by the Associated Press.

January 9–10: Thanks to a dispute over the flying of the American flag over the Panama Canal Zone, two days of anti-American rioting leads to the deaths of 21 Panamanian demonstrators and four U.S. soldiers. Panama temporarily cuts off diplomatic ties with the United States after President Johnson refuses to amend the U.S.–Panama Canal Treaty.

January 11: In a hail of controversy, the surgeon general's office of the Johnson administration announces that cigarette smoking can lead to cancer.

January 11: Young Peggy Fleming becomes America's top figure-skating champion.

January 15: President Johnson asks Congress for a $5.3 billion budget to win the "space race" against the Soviet space program. Special Counsel to the President Theodore Sorensen resigns to write a book about John Kennedy.

January 20: Los Angeles Dodgers pitcher Sandy Koufax is named by the Associated Press the all-around Athlete of the Year.

January 23: Thanks to a congressional resolution, the new National Cultural Center in Washington, D.C., is renamed the John F. Kennedy Center for the Performing Arts.

January 25: France's Charles de Gaulle announces that his country will be opening an embassy in communist China. President Johnson denounces the decision, and the government of Taiwan breaks off all ties with France.

January 30: Major General Nguyen Khanh proclaims himself chief of state in South Vietnam following a bloodless coup. Khanh pledges victory over the communist opposition, but his government will be short-lived.

February 4: President Johnson witnesses the signing of the Twenty-fourth Amendment to the Constitution. The amendment eliminates the poll tax as a condition to voting. This was the first time that a constitutional amendment was certified in the presence of an American president.

February 6: In reprisal for the U.S. Coast Guard's seizure of four Cuban fishing boats in Florida waters, Fidel Castro cuts off the water supply to America's Guantánamo naval base in Cuba. President Johnson orders an emergency water shuttle service from nearby Jamaica and authorizes the building of a $5 million salt water conversion plant at Guantanamo.

February 7: British rock sensation the Beatles begin their first American tour.

February 9: The Beatles appear on America's highly rated *Ed Sullivan Show.*

February 9: The Winter Olympic Games are concluded in Innsbruck, Austria. The Americans win only six gold medals to the Soviet Union's 25.

February 10: President Johnson asks the Congress for a revolution in health care, calling for new hospitals, insurance protection programs, and elder care. The House of Representatives passes the most comprehensive civil rights reform legislation in the nation's history.

February 18: In a deliberate effort to punish wayward allies, President Johnson halts all U.S. military assistance to Britain, France, Morocco, Spain, and Yugoslavia until they stop their trade negotiations with the Castro government.

February 25: Sonny Liston is knocked out by young boxing sensation Cassius Clay in the fight that determines the heavyweight champion of the world.

February 29: Marking the end of 100 days in office, President Johnson holds his first live television news conference. He announces the development of the A-11 aircraft, claiming that this type of American technology will defeat communist threats.

March 8: Stating that Martin Luther King's message of nonviolence is not working, Malcolm X announces in New York that he is forming a new black nationalist party that will stress self-defense against white racists.

March 16: Announcing that his primary goal is to rescue American youth from a life of misery, President Johnson submits his "war on poverty" legislation to Congress. Its budget is more than $962 million in its first year alone, and a new Office of Economic Opportunity is required to administer its programs.

March 25: In a dramatic Senate speech, J. William Fulbright, the chairman of the Senate Foreign Relations Committee, announces that America should learn to coexist with Castro's Cuba and that the Panama Canal Treaty should be revised according to the wishes of the Panamanian people. President Johnson publicly condemns the speech.

March 27: A devastating earthquake of over 8.4 on the Richter scale destroys much of Anchorage, Alaska, and neighboring communities.

May 28–29: In a Jordanian suburb of Jerusalem, the Palestine National Congress meets for the first time since 1948. At the meeting, the Palestine Liberation Organization (PLO) is born. Sworn to return Palestine to the Palestinian people, the new organization denounces the friendly ties between the United States and Israel.

June 3: Led by student activists, more than 10,000 demonstrators take over downtown Seoul, South Korea. Demanding an end to the corrupt regime of President Park and all U.S. assistance to his government, the demonstrators are attacked by South Korean troops. Park issues a martial law decree that remains in effect for the next several weeks.

June 22: Three civil rights activists are first recorded missing in Mississippi. The bodies of Michael Schwerner, Andrew Goodman, and James Chaney are found in early August, and 21 white men, including the sheriff of Nashoba County, are arrested. The charges against 19 of them are dismissed, and, in December, the federal government drops the last two charges as well.

Surrounded by cabinet officials and key members of Congress, President Johnson signs the Tonkin Gulf Resolution. *(Cecil Stoughton, Lyndon B. Johnson Library)*

July 2: Announcing that she has been a CIA informant for four years, Juana Castro Ruz, Fidel Castro's sister, defects to Mexico.

July 2: Banning religious and racial discrimination in America, President Johnson signs the Civil Rights Act into law.

July 18: Stimulated by high racial tensions, looting and rioting begins in New York's African-American neighborhoods of Harlem. The rioting spreads to Brooklyn's Bedford-Stuyvesant district, and within the next month similar riots occur in Chicago, Philadelphia, and New Jersey.

August 2–7: The *Maddox* and *C. Turner Joy,* two U.S. destroyers in the Tonkin Gulf, report attacks by North Vietnamese patrol boats. In response, President Johnson wins the Tonkin Gulf Resolution from Congress. The latter grants the commander-in-chief "special executive privilege" to conduct the war in Vietnam.

September 22: Soon considered James Bond's rival on the small screen, the hour-long adventure-drama *The Man from U.N.C.L.E.* premieres on NBC television.

September 27: The Warren Commission releases its 888-page conclusions on the assassination of President Kennedy. Lee Harvey Oswald, they proclaim, acted alone.

October 14–15: Replaced by hard-line Stalinists Aleksei Kosygin and Leonid Brezhnev, Nikita

One month after the November 1964 Vietcong attack at Bien Hoa, another Vietcong attack kills two Americans and injures 107 at the Brinks Hotel officers' quarters in Saigon. *(National Archives)*

Khrushchev falls from power after a 10-year reign as the boss of the Soviet Union.

October 16: Claiming that it is truly now a world power, China announces its first successful nuclear test. The Chinese leadership also calls for a world summit on nuclear disarmament, but their request is ignored by the West.

October 24: Having symbolized the new, modern, postwar Japan, the Summer Olympic Games conclude in Tokyo. America's athletes win 90 gold medals to the Soviet Union's 96.

November 1: Vietcong mortar fire on the U.S. air base at Bien Hoa kills four Americans and wounds 72 more. Five American jet bombers are destroyed and 15 others damaged. President Johnson regards the attack as an embarrassing setback for U.S. forces in South Vietnam.

November 3: With a record-breaking landslide total, President Johnson wins his own term in office after defeating Senator Barry Goldwater of Arizona. Former Attorney General Robert Kennedy is elected to represent New York in the U.S. Senate.

December: The Motion Picture Association of America announces that *The Carpetbaggers, It's a Mad, Mad, Mad, Mad World,* and *The Unsinkable Molly Brown* are the top three box office successes of 1964. Once again, Doris Day and Rock Hudson are the top box office draws (along with Jack Lemmon).

December: The Associated Press announces that the top three single records of 1964 are "I Want to Hold Your Hand" by the Beatles, "Hello, Dolly!" by Louis Armstrong, and "She Loves You" by the Beatles.

December 10: Martin Luther King, Jr., wins the Nobel Peace Prize.

1965

January 2: Representatives John Bell Williams (Democrat of Mississippi) and Albert Watson (Democrat of South Carolina) are stripped of their seniority by the Democratic majority for having supported the presidential campaign of Republican Barry Goldwater.

January 4: President Johnson outlines his Great Society plans during his State of the Union address, asking for Congress's approval of new programs in education, health care, urban renewal, and environmentalism.

January 18: Martin Luther King, Jr., is punched and kicked by a white racist while attempting to reg-

ister at a hotel in Selma, Alabama. He was the hotel's first black guest.

February 1: Demonstrating against racism in voter registration procedures, Martin Luther King and more than 700 supporters are arrested in Selma, Alabama. He spends the next four days in jail, and President Johnson promises swift action on new voter rights legislation.

February 3: The U.S. Air Force Academy announces that 105 cadets will be expelled due to a cheating scandal.

February 6: The U.S. military base at Pleiku in the Central Highlands of South Vietnam is successfully attacked by the Vietcong. In response, President Johnson orders a series of bombing campaigns against North Vietnam.

February 10: After a Vietcong assault on Americans in Quinhon, U.S. and South Vietnamese planes launch the largest single air assault against North Vietnam to date in the Vietnam War.

February 16: Together with Canada's Royal Canadian Mounted Police (RCMP), the FBI and New York police foil a plot by an extremist group to destroy the Statue of Liberty, the Liberty Bell, and the Washington Monument.

February 21: Shortly before he was to address a rally in New York City, Malcolm X, the former Black Muslim leader and founder of the Black Nationalist movement, is murdered. Three men associated with the Black Muslims are arrested.

February 26: Jimmie Lee Jackson, who was shot earlier in the month while marching in a civil rights demonstration, dies in Marion, Alabama.

March 8–9: No longer called "advisers," the first "combat troops" (3,500 U.S. Marines) arrive to protect America's Danang air base in South Vietnam.

March 11: Civil rights advocate Rev. James J. Reeb of Boston dies in Selma, Alabama, from a beating received three days earlier by three white racists.

March 19: After years of threats, the Indonesian government finally seizes three American companies operating within its country. President Johnson hints that the United States might take "swift action" against this move.

March 23: *Gemini 3* is launched with the first U.S. two-man crew, Virgil I. "Gus" Grissom and John W. Young.

March 24: America's *Ranger 9* spacecraft transmits photographs of the moon's surface for a live television broadcast in the United States.

March 20–25: Martin Luther King, Jr., begins a 54-mile voting rights march from Selma to Montgomery, Alabama. President Johnson federalizes the Alabama National Guard to protect the marchers and orders in additional forces. Some 25,000 demonstrators deliver a voting rights petition to Alabama governor George Wallace at the end of the march.

April 9: Dubbed the "largest controlled sports environment in the world," the Astrodome, a domed stadium, is officially opened in Houston, Texas.

April 11: In what is called "the night of the twisters," a series of tornados sweeps throughout the American Midwest killing 253 people and causing more than $235 million in damages.

April 28–May 5: To halt the possible spread of Castro-influenced communism and to protect U.S. citizens, President Johnson orders the U.S. military to intervene in the politically volatile Dominican Republic. U.S. troop strength reaches a maximum of 20,000 there, and fighting continues even after a May 5 truce is signed between the warring factions. U.S. forces are soon replaced by troops from the Organization of American States (OAS).

April 29: After talks with President Johnson, Prime Minister Robert Menzies of Australia dispatches 800 troops to assist the South Vietnamese military. His decision is politically unpopular throughout Australia.

May 5: Governor Paul Johnson of Mississippi and former Governor Ross Barnett are acquitted of criminal contempt charges stemming from their effort to prevent the admittance of James Meredith to the University of Mississippi in 1962.

May 24: The Supreme court nullifies a law that permitted post offices to intercept and read mail from communist countries.

May 26: Dedicated to banning billboards and even junk yards from any close proximity to an important road, President Johnson sends his highway beautification bill to Congress.

June 3–7: Gemini 4, carrying astronauts Edward White and James McDivitt, is launched on a four-day mission. Part of the mission requires a spacewalk by White, a first-time experience for any American astronaut.

June 8: The Pentagon announces that the overall commander of U.S. forces in South Vietnam, General William Westmoreland, will be ordering his troops to engage in direct combat with the Vietcong enemy.

June 19: Air Vice Marshal Nguyen Cao Ky, at the age of 34, becomes the leader of South Vietnam. The Ky government is the eighth to take power since the assassination of President Diem in November 1963.

July 28: Announcing that the United States "will never retreat" from the anticommunist mission, President Johnson doubles the American draft from 17,000 to 35,000 per month to assist the war effort in South Vietnam. Total U.S. troop strength is increased from 75,000 to 125,000 men.

July 30: Medicare assistance for the elderly becomes law.

August 6: President Johnson signs the Voting Rights Act.

August 11–16: What was a protest against brutality and racism in the Los Angeles police department becomes a race riot of major proportions in the impoverished African-American neighborhoods of Watts. Thirty-five people are killed and $200 million in property damage results.

August 21–29: During their *Gemini 3* mission, astronauts Charles Conrad, Jr., and L. Gordon Cooper set the record (eight days) for the longest manned spaceflight.

September 2: Chinese Defense Minister Lin Piao calls for a great new revolution that will lead to final victory over Western influence at home and American imperialism abroad. Characterized by its political turmoil and brutality, this marks the beginning of the "Cultural Revolution."

September 15: Featuring the first African American, Bill Cosby, ever to co-star in an hour-long action-adventure series, *I Spy* premieres on NBC television.

September 28: Fidel Castro announces that antigovernment Cubans can leave the country in small boats if they wish. The announcement leads to a five-year-long exodus of nearly 1 million Cubans to south Florida and elsewhere.

October 4: The new pope, Paul VI, visits New York in order to deliver a prayer for peace in front of the United Nations General Assembly.

October 15–16: Beginning with a march through Berkeley, California, and ending at the Oakland army base, several thousand antiwar demonstrators kick off a national protest campaign that includes specific marches in Boston, Philadelphia, New York, and Ann Arbor, Michigan.

October 18: In Manchester, New Hampshire, David Miller, age 22, becomes the first person arrested under a new federal law that bans draft card burning.

October 22: Having been personally championed by the first lady, Lady Bird Johnson, the Highway Beautification Act is signed into law.

November 2: Norman Morrison, a 31-year-old Quaker from Baltimore, burns himself to death in front of the Pentagon during a protest against the Vietnam War.

November 9: The biggest electrical power failure in U.S. history paralyzes New York and neighboring states. Adequate power is not restored until 48 hours later.

November 13: The luxury cruise ship *Yarmouth Castle* burns and sinks en route from Miami to Nassau in the Bahamas. Eighty-nine vacationers are drowned.

November 17: Retired air force general and passionate anticommunist William Eckert becomes the new commissioner of baseball.

November 27: Pegged at $100 billion, a federal government record is set for spending in given fiscal year.

December: The Motion Picture Association of America announces that *Mary Poppins, The Sound of Music,* and *Goldfinger* are the top box office successes of 1965. The top box office draws are Sean Connery, John Wayne, and, for the sixth year in a row, Doris Day.

December: The Associated Press announces that "(I Can't Get No) Satisfaction" by the Rolling Stones, "You've Lost That Lovin' Feelin'" by the Righteous Brothers, and "Wooly Bully" by Sam the Sham and the Pharaohs are 1965's top-selling single records.

December 15: Previously spared due to President Johnson's concerns that an accidental bombing of Soviet ships could spark World War III, North Vietnam's chief port of Haiphong is bombed by the U.S. Air Force.

December 17: Soon hailed as the "John Kennedy of the Philippines" by the U.S. State Department, Ferdinand Marcos becomes president of the Philippines following an election campaign marked by widespread violence and corruption. Promising a variety of reforms, Marcos also vows to maintain U.S. military presence in his country.

December 24: Suspending U.S. bombing of North Vietnam, President Johnson declares a Christmas truce in the hopes of opening peace negotiations with Ho Chi Minh. Ho rejects all negotiations unless the United States permanently halts all bombing and removes its troops from South Vietnam.

EYEWITNESS TESTIMONY

Civil Rights Achievement and the "War on Poverty"

There were many who felt . . . that the torchbearer for a whole generation was gone; that an era was over before its time. . . . But I have come to understand that the hope President Kennedy kindled isn't dead, but alive. . . . The torch still burns, and because it does, there remains for all of us a chance to light up the tomorrows and brighten the future. For me, this is the challenge that makes life worthwhile.

Robert Kennedy speaking in 1964 to 3,000 students at the Free University of West Berlin, in Speeches: Sen. Robert F. Kennedy, Research Room, John F. Kennedy Library.

One of the tragedies of today's situation is that the motives of the white liberal community, even the meaning of the Judaeo-Christian tradition, are being seriously questioned by some Negroes. The Black Muslims are perhaps the most dramatic example of various extremist Negro movements that have arisen in reaction to the cruel past. Their appeal is tragically racist; they deny that all men are brothers. If white Northerners feel at all smug about their treatment of Negroes, let them be reminded: The Black Muslim movement is essentially a phenomenon of the urban North, of the Negro ghettos, of poverty, of inadequate education, and—again—of broken promises.

Senator Hubert Humphrey reflecting on the state of the Civil Rights movement, summer 1964, in Public Statements, Research Room, Lyndon Johnson Library.

It was done . . . by bribery, by payments to informers, by whatever eavesdropping was then permitted under the bureau's rules, by the sowing of suspicion among Klan members so that none knew who was an informer and who not, by infiltrating and deception, and in at least one incident by the participation of a bureau informer in the planning and attempted execution of a murder.

It did not appear to those involved at the time, and it does not appear to me now, that the criminal conspiracy of violence that existed in the State of Mississippi then could have been handled by less drastic measures.

Ten years after the fact, Justice Department official Burke Marshall praising the FBI for its role in diminishing the effectiveness of the Ku Klux Klan during the civil rights debates of summer of 1964, in The Robert F. Kennedy Oral History Project, JFK Library.

If he did what the Department of Justice did, said, recommended, suggested—and particularly me—then he could always say that he did what we suggested. . . . He had a particular problem being a southerner. . . . So I think that for political reasons it made a good deal of sense. Secondly, our relationship was so sensitive at the time that I think that he probably did it to pacify me.

Robert Kennedy claiming that President Johnson might have blamed him if the summer 1964 civil rights legislation failed, in The Robert F. Kennedy Oral History Project, JFK Library.

People are just not going to stand and see their children starve and be driven out of school and be eaten up with disease in the twentieth century. They will forgo stealing and they will forgo fighting, and they will forgo doing a lot of violent things and improper things as long as they possibly can, but they are going to eat, and they are going to learn, and they are going to grow. The quicker you find it out, the better.

President Johnson discussing his summer 1964 objectives behind the "war on poverty" legislation to a chamber of commerce delegation visiting the White House, in Lyndon B. Johnson Research Room, Lyndon Johnson Library.

It is essential that we guarantee the constitutional rights of every American. But what good are those rights without the guarantee that all Americans be provided an education that will enable them to participate fully and creatively in American life? We may meet the challenge of school desegregation, but that isn't the whole story. We have a long way to go to overcome the tragic results of segregated education and the fact that we have, for so long, denied Negroes the opportunity for higher education.

Hubert Humphrey in 1964 linking education reform to civil rights and the war on poverty, in Public Statements, Research Room, Lyndon Johnson Library.

Recently a judge told me of an incident in his court. A fairly young woman with six children, pregnant with her seventh, came to him for a divorce. Under his questioning it became apparent her husband did not share this desire. Then the whole story came out. Her husband was a laborer earning $250 a month. By divorcing him she could get an $80 raise. She was eligible for $350 a month from the Aid to Dependent Children Program. She had been talked into the divorce by two friends who had already done this very thing. But any time we question the schemes of the do-gooders, we are denounced as being opposed to their humanitarian goal. It seems impossible to legitimately debate their solutions with the assumption that all of us share the desire to help those less fortunate. They tell us we are always against, never for anything. Well, it isn't so much that liberals are ignorant. It's just that they know so much that isn't so.

Actor and political hopeful Ronald Reagan denouncing the war on poverty efforts of the Johnson administration, in 1964, in The Public Papers of President Ronald Reagan, Pre-Presidential Collection, Speeches, Research Room, Ronald Reagan Library.

I promise to break the tragic pattern of decayed neighborhoods, slums, and poverty, and to provide decent housing and expanded opportunities for stable jobs for those discarded in the wake of technology.

New York Senate candidate Robert Kennedy promising more ambitious domestic reforms than President Johnson's Great Society, in "Kennedy Proposes Legislation," New York Times, October 7, 1964, p. 37.

The many brutalities of the North [he said in 1965] receive no such attention [as in the South]. I have been in tenements in Harlem in the past several weeks where the smell of rats was so strong that it was difficult to stay there for five minutes, and where children slept with lights turned on their feet to discourage attacks.

In central Harlem, over 50 percent of all housing units are seriously deteriorating or dilapidated, as opposed to about 10 percent of housing units in this condition occupied by whites. Thousands do not flock to Harlem to protest these conditions—much less to change them.

Senator Robert Kennedy, during a 1965 speech in New York City, calling for a new, extensive urban renewal program, in Speeches: Sen. Robert F. Kennedy, Research Room, John F. Kennedy Library.

In most jurisdictions, from one-third to one-half or more of those accused of crime will be acquitted or have their charges dismissed. Many more will have their sentences suspended, or be allowed to pay a fine. In fact, less than 10 percent of those arrested in New York City can expect to be sentenced to prison terms. But for thousands of these, . . . poverty will rule that the mere act of arrest will result in imprisonment—and the loss of job, self-respect, separation from family, and possible ruin. This is not the law of reason.

Senator Robert Kennedy, at the 1965 U.S. Governors' Conference, charging that racism continues to influence and pollute the justice system, in Speeches: Sen. Robert F. Kennedy, Research Room, John F. Kennedy Library.

I have always felt it was a handicap for oppressed people to depend so largley on a leader, because unfortunately in our culture, the charismatic leader usually becomes a leader because he has found a spot in the public limelight. It usually means that the media made him, and the media might undo him. There is also the danger in our culture that, because a person is called upon to give public statements and is acclaimed by the establishment, such a person gets to the point of believing that he is the movement. Such people get so involved with playing the game of being important that they exhaust themselves and their time and they don't do the work of actually organizing people.

Without mentioning Martin Luther King, Jr., by name, civil rights leader Ella Jo Baker complaining about King's "centralized leadership" approach near the time of his assassination, in D'Angelo, The American Civil Rights Movement (2001), p. 212.

The 1964 Election

I won't change my beliefs to win votes. I will offer a choice, not an echo. This will not be an engagement of personalities. It will be an engagement of principles. I've always stood for government that is limited and balanced and against ever increasing concentrations of authority in Washington. I've always stood for individual responsibility and against regimentation. I believe we must now make a choice in this land and not continue drifting endlessly down toward a time when all of us, our lives, our property, our hopes and even our prayers will become just cogs in a vast Government machine. . . . My candidacy is pledged to a victory for principle and to presenting an opportunity for the American people to choose.

Republican Senator Barry Goldwater, on the patio of his Arizona home, declaring his candidacy for president in early 1964, in Public Statements, Research Room, LBJ Library.

You are as brave a man as Harry Truman—or FDR—or Lincoln. You can go on to find some peace, some achievement amidst all the pain. You have been strong, patient, determined beyond any words of mine to express. I honor you for it. So does most of the country.

To step out now would be *wrong* for your country, and I can see nothing but a lonely wasteland for your future. Your friends would be frozen in embarrassed silence and your enemies jeering.

I am not afraid of *Time* or lies or losing money or defeat.

In the final analysis I can't carry any of the burdens you talked of—so I know it's only *your* choice. But I know you are as brave as any of the thirty-five.

I love you always.

Lady Bird Johnson persuading her husband to run for president in early 1964, in White House Diary, Research Room, Lyndon Johnson Library.

To me the high point of the whole primary campaign remains the frosty night in New Hampshire when we were informed that Goldwater would participate in a torchlight parade. And here he came, sitting with an embarrassed and foolish grin in a pony cart pulled by a grotesquely small horse. Ahead of him was a high school drum and bugle corps dressed in Indian feather bonnets, playing "Blue Moon." And ahead of them was a pudgy high school girl, with blue and frozen knees, carrying, of all things, a United Nations flag.

Reporter Charles Mohr remembering the bizarre 1964 Republican primary in New Hampshire and the irony of Barry Goldwater, a staunch opponent to U.S. participation in the United Nations, led through the streets of Manchester by a U.N. flag bearer, in his "Times Talk," the New York Times, March 10, 1964, p. 1.

Discerning the outlines of the primary scuffle is a little like watching an angry hippopotamus battle a swarm of bees. . . . In sum, to a neutral observer on the scene, through a characteristically Californian confluence of typical circumstances, the primary has the dream-like aspect of a pillow-fight underwater, with neither contender landing any telling blows, yet with either, or both, liable to sudden blackout—while galleries at the pool side shout encouragement only dimly linked with action below.

Reporter Gladwin Hill criticizing the primary system, in what is soon regarded as an excellent example of 1960s American political literature, his memorable "Pillow-Fight Underwater," the New York Times, May 18, 1964, p. 1.

Many concerned people have urged me to indicate my preference among the possible Republican candidates or to try to dictate the Republican party's choice of a Presidential nominee. I do not intend to attempt this. It is not my proper role. I do fervently hope, however, that the person selected will be a man who will uphold, earnestly, with dedication and conviction, the principles and traditions of our party. . . . As the party of Lincoln, we Republicans have a particular obligation to be vigorous in the furtherance of civil rights. . . . It requires loyal support for the United Nations in its peacekeeping efforts. It requires calm, painstaking study of all the infinitely complex situations that confront us. . . . followed by firm decision and prompt but carefully conceived action.

Former president Dwight Eisenhower, in his own cautious way, expressing a concern that Barry Goldwater might be the wrong nominee for his party, in his "Statement of Principles," the Herald-Tribune (New York), May 18, 1964, p. 1.

So long as he [Goldwater] was merely a symbol of conservatism in the Senate, talking primarily to partisan audiences, his views were not minutely studied, but in the primary campaigns they were. For the first time, his policies had to be considered seriously in Presidential terms, as the policies he would actually adopt if nominated and elected.

Veteran political columnist James Reston arguing that Barry Goldwater was an odd candidate to be taken "seriously," in his "Goldwater," the New York Times, June 2, 1964, p. 1.

Meanwhile, the Johnson television spots were exploiting the fears and ignorance of the voters. . . . Shortly before eleven Saturday night a little girl licking an ice cream cone appeared on millions of television screens all over America. While the little girl concentrated on ice cream, a woman's voice—tender and provocative—told her that people used to explode atomic bombs in the air, but the radioactive fallout made children die. The voice then told of the treaty preventing all but underground nuclear tests . . . now a man who wants to be President of the United States voted against it . . . his name is Barry Goldwater, so if he's elected, they might start testing all over again . . . a crescendo of Geiger counter clicks almost drowns out the last words, then came the announcer's tag line: "Vote for President Johnson on November 3rd . . . the stakes are too high for you to stay home."

The West Coast regional director of the Goldwater for president campaign, Stephen Shadegg, charging that Johnson election officials used dirty and unethical tactics against his candidate, in his What Happened to Goldwater?: The Inside Story of the 1964 Republican Campaign *(1965), p. 80.*

A great strength of the two-party system is that basically we have been in general agreement on many things and neither party has been the party of extremes or radicals, but temporarily some extreme elements have come into one of the parties and have driven out or locked out or booed out or heckled out the moderates. . . . I think an overwhelming defeat for them will be the best thing that could happen to the Republican party in this country in the eyes of all the people. Because then you would restore moderation to that once great party of Abraham Lincoln and the leadership could unite and present a solid front to the world.

President Johnson during a television broadcast of October 24, 1964, urging Republicans to reject Barry Goldwater and vote Democratic, in Speeches: Lyndon Johnson, Research Room, Lyndon Johnson Library.

Whatever your views are, we have a Constitution and we have a Bill of Rights, and we have the law of the land, and two-thirds of the Democrats in the Senate voted for it and three-fourths of the Republicans. I signed it, I am going to enforce it, and I am going to

While the 1964 election captured the attention of America's voters, the arrival of the Beatles in the United States captured the attention of young teens. *(Billy Ray/TimePix)*

observe it, and I think that any man that is worthy of the high office of President is going to do the same thing.

President Johnson ignoring campaign advice to say nothing about the divisive civil rights issue while delivering an election-eve speech, and urging "fellow Southerners" to support his civil rights reforms and his election, in The Public Papers of President Lyndon B. Johnson, 1964, *Speeches, Lyndon Johnson Library.*

I am a man who enjoys life. There are far, far more things that I should like to do, to experience, to accomplish, than I shall ever have time for. Public service—to which I am devoted—denies a man as much, certainly, as it gives to him. The demands of this life are insatiable: There are never enough hours in the day, days in the week. Children grow up before one realizes how time has flown by. Often one feels frustrated by the sheer impossibility of leading a normal family life.

> *Democratic vice presidential candidate Hubert Humphrey, in a rare candid statement for its time, reflecting on the strains of public life and campaigning, in his* The Cause Is Mankind: A Liberal Program For Modern America (1964), *The Cause Is Mankind, Research Room, Lyndon Johnson Library.*

Voting Rights and Racial Tension

The majority of men only dream their nightmares. The inescapable monsters, the searing thirsts, the surreal horrors and tortures, the soul-killing crimes and guilt—these disappear upon waking. But in the ghettos of this world, waking does not change a thing; the frustration and absurdity and madness continue. The real life of the ghetto inhabitant is inseparable from nightmare. It is as if nature, or society—that is, all of us—had played a cruel joke and denied the victims a basic "out." No wonder millions upon millions of the denied think that Mother Nature is a maniac.

> Look *magazine senior editor Chandler Brossard investigating black ghetto life, following the urban race riots of 1965, in his* "A Cry from Harlem," Look, *December 15, 1965, pp. 125–129.*

Worse than the bigot, in God's eye, is the fanatic. Bigots are often peaceful churchgoers who sing a nifty psalm; fanatics don't have that much sense of humor. Bigots are despicable, but fanatics are dangerous. A bigot's mind is shut—but so, mercifully, may be his mouth. A fanatic can't shut up. Bigotry is a disease of the soul; fanaticism is lunacy with a program. Scratch a bigot, and you uncover fear; scratch a fanatic, and you uncover rage.

> *Veteran columnist Leo Rosten berating politicians and fellow journalists for misusing the terms* bigot *and* fanatic *during the 1965 race riots, in his* "How to Hate in One Easy Lesson," Look, *December 15, 1965, p. 26.*

The time has come for equality in sharing in government, in education, and in employment. It will not be stayed or denied. It is here. . . . America grows. America changes. And on the civil rights issue we must rise

with the occasion. That calls for cloture and for the enactment of a civil rights bill.

> *Everett Dirksen, the Republican minority leader of the Senate shifting his position in late 1965 against the growth of federal government influence, and urging fellow Republicans to support President Johnson's civil and voting rights legislation, in* Public Statements File: The 1964 Election, *Research Room, Lyndon Johnson Library.*

You do not wipe away the scars of centuries by saying: Now you are free to go where you want and do as you desire and choose the leaders you please. You do not take a person who, for years, has been hobbled by chains and liberate him, bring him to the starting line of a race, and then say you are free to compete with all the others, and still just believe that you have been completely fair. Thus it is not good enough just to open the gates of opportunity. All our citizens must have the ability to walk through those gates. This is the next and the more profound stage of the battle for civil rights. We seek not just freedom but opportunity. We seek not just legal equity but human ability, not just equality as a right and a theory but equality as a fact and equality as a result.

> *President Johnson seeing success ahead for his 1966 civil rights legislation and announcing the next phase of his reform effort at the end of 1965 in* The Public Papers of President Lyndon B. Johnson, 1965, *Speeches, Lyndon Johnson Library.*

The liberal-left-wingers have passed it. Now let them employ some "pinknik" social engineers in Washington to figure out what to do with it. We must destroy the power to dictate, to forbid, to require, to demand, to distribute, to edict. . . . We must revitalize a government founded in this nation on faith in God.

> *Alabama governor George Wallace, during a Christmas 1965 speech to his closest supporters, attacking President Johnson's civil rights achievements in 1964 and 1965, in Greenhaw,* Watch Out for George Wallace *(1976), p. 72.*

The Vietnam Escalation

It is within our ability and unquestionably our interest, to cut loose from established myths and to start thinking some "unthinkable thoughts" about the cold war and East-West relations, about the under-developed countries and particularly those in Latin America, about the changing nature of the Chinese communist threat in Asia and about the festering war in Vietnam. . . . No nation can achieve by diplomacy objectives which it has conspicuously failed to win by warfare [and] our bargaining position is a weak one.

J. William Fulbright, chairman of the Senate Foreign Relations Committee, during a landmark speech in 1964 before the U.S. Senate, cautiously suggesting that the Vietnam War might be already lost, in Margolis, The Last Innocent Year: America in 1964, The Beginning of the "Sixties" *(1999), p. 101.*

Early this morning the USS Maddox was attacked by three DRV PT boats while on patrol approximately 30 miles off the North Vietnamese coast in the Gulf of Tonkin. The Captain of the Maddox returned the fire with 5-inch guns and requested air support from the carrier Ticonderoga on station nearby in connection with reconnaissance flights in that area. Ticonderoga jets arrived shortly and made strafing attacks on the PT boats resulting in one enemy boat dead in the water, two others damaged and turned tail for home. The Maddox reports no personnel or material damages.

The U.S. Navy, in what later becomes a most controversial report, informing President Johnson of an "incident" in the Tonkin Gulf on August 2, 1964, in Vietnam Country, Research Room, *Lyndon Johnson Library.*

The challenge that we face in Southeast Asia today is the same challenge that we have faced with courage and that we have met with strength in Greece and Turkey, in Berlin and Korea, in Lebanon and in Cuba. And to any who may be tempted to support or to widen the present aggression I say this: There is no threat to any peaceful power from the United States of America. But there can be no peace by aggression and no immunity from reply. That is what is meant by the actions that we took yesterday.

President Johnson asking Congress on August 4, 1964, for special executive privilege to conduct the Vietnam War and informing them of an enemy attack on the U.S. Navy in the Tonkin Gulf, in The Public Papers of President Lyndon B. Johnson, 1964, *Speeches, Lyndon Johnson Library.*

I am unalterably opposed to this course of action which, in my judgment, is an aggressive course of action on the part of the United States. I think we are kidding the world if you try to give the impression that when the South Vietnamese naval boats bombarded two islands a short distance off the coast of North Vietnam we were not implicated. . . . I think what happened is that [Nguyen] Khanh got us to backstop him in open aggression against the territorial integrity of North Vietnam. I have listened to briefing after briefing and there isn't a scintilla of evidence in any briefing yet that North Vietnam engaged in any military aggression against South Vietnam either with its ground troops or its navy.

Senator Wayne Morse as one of two dissenting voices, challenging President Johnson's version of the Tonkin Gulf Incident and voting against the Tonkin Gulf Resolution, quoted in the U.S. Senate's Joint Hearing on Southeast Asia Resolution before the Senate Foreign Relations and Armed Services Committees, 88th Congress, Second Session, *August 6, 1964 (1966), p. 1.*

Now, therefore, be it Resolved by the Senate and House of Representatives of the United States of America in Congress assembled, That the Congress approves and supports the determination of the President, as Commander in Chief, to take all necessary measures to repel any armed attack against the forces of the United States and to prevent further aggression.

Congress formally granting President Johnson's request for special powers to conduct the Vietnam War with its August 1964 Tonkin Gulf Resolution, quoted in the U.S. Department of State's Bulletin, *Vol. 51, No. 1313, August 24, 1964, p. 268.*

The Vietnamese know just as we do that the Viet Cong are gaining in the countryside. Meanwhile, they see the enormous power of the United States withheld, and they get little sense of firm and active U.S. policy. They feel that we are unwilling to take serious risks. In one sense, all of this is outrageous, in the light of all that we have done and all that we are ready to do if they will only pull up their socks.

But it is a fact—or at least so McNamara and I now think.

White House aide McGeorge Bundy informing President Johnson in January 1965 that both U.S. policy and prestige requires a strong U.S. military response in South Vietnam, in William Bundy's Vietnam Manuscript, Papers of William Bundy, Lyndon Johnson Library.

As practical men, they cannot wish to see the fruits of ten years labor destroyed by slowly escalating air attacks (which they cannot prevent) without trying to find some accommodation which will exercise (*sic*) the threat. It would be to our interest to regulate our attacks not for the purpose of doing maximum physical destruction but for producing maximum stresses in Hanoi minds.

General Maxwell Taylor telling President Johnson in January 1965 that an escalation of the Vietnam War will lead North Vietnam to the peace table, quoted in Gardner, Pay Any Price: Lyndon Johnson and the Wars for Vietnam *(1995), Research Room, Lyndon Johnson Library.*

It's a mistake to negotiate when losing.

Senator William Proxmire (Democrat of Wisconsin) reacting to President Johnson's announcement that the White House will be launching a "peace offensive" against North Vietnam, January 1965, in Papers of Sen. Gaylord Nelson, State Historical Society of Wisconsin.

In Viet-Nam a Communist government has set out deliberately to conquer a sovereign people in a neighboring state. And to achieve its end, it has used every resource of its own government to carry out its carefully planned program of concealed aggression. North Viet-Nam's commitment to seize control of the South is no less total than was the commitment of the regime in North Korea in 1950. But knowing the consequences of the latter's undisguised attack, the planners in Hanoi have tried desperately to conceal their hand. They have failed and their aggression is as real as that of an invading army.

The State Department issuing a press release explaining America's position in South Vietnam, quoted in the U.S. Department of State's Bulletin, Vol. 52. No. 1343, March 22, 1965, pp. 404–427.

There may be many ways to this kind of peace: in discussion or negotiation with the governments concerned; in large groups or in small ones; in the reaffirmation of old agreements or their strengthening with new ones. We have stated this position over and over again, fifty times and more, to friend and foe alike. And we remain ready, with this purpose, for unconditional discussions. . . . These countries of Southeast Asia are homes for millions of impoverished people. Each day these people rise at dawn and struggle through until the night to wrest existence from the soil. They are often wracked by disease, plagued by hunger, and death comes at the early age of forty. . . . We would hope that North Vietnam would take its place in the common effort just as soon as peaceful cooperation is possible. . . . For our part, I will ask the Congress to join in a billion dollar American investment in this effort as soon as it is under way. And I would hope that all other industrialized countries, including the Soviet Union, will join in this effort to replace despair with hope, and terror with progress.

President Johnson, in an April 1965 speech at Johns Hopkins University, calling for peace with North Vietnam and promising to extend his Great Society economic reforms to Southeast Asia, in Vietnam Manuscript, Papers of William Bundy, LBJ Library.

A major task for President Johnson is to explain to the American people and to the world the basic American contention that Vietnam is crucial to American security, to the freedom of all Southeast Asia, to small nations everywhere, and to the hopes of containing Communism in Asia and the Far East. It is important that he explain that the methods the United States is employing to defend South Vietnam are the wisest and most effective.

The New York Times *advising President Johnson in a 1965 editorial on how to make a speech about his Vietnam policy, in "Vietnam's 'Wider War,'"* New York Times, *April 6, 1965, Section A, p. 38.*

I was a real reporter once, but I was not suited for it by physique or temperament. Real reporters have to stick their noses in where they're not wanted, ask embarrassing questions, dodge bullets, contend with

During August 1965 in Vietnam, General William Westmoreland (*right*) introduces the visiting secretary of defense Robert McNamara (*center*) to a group of senior South Vietnamese military officers in Danang. *(National Archives)*

deadlines, and worry about the competition. In my youth, I did all these things, while trying to figure out an easier line of work.

CBS News reporter Charles Kuralt reflecting on his decision to leave Southeast Asia in the summer of 1965 following his trailblazing work on Vietnam's "Charlie Company," in his On the Road With Charles Kuralt *(1985), p. 1.*

Between 1963 and 1965, for example, when political chaos gripped South Vietnam and the lack of cohesiveness in the nation's heterogeneous society became clearly evident, the United States could have severed its commitment with justification and honor, though not without strong political reaction at home. . . . Even after the introduction of American combat troops into South Vietnam in 1965, the war still might have ended within a few years, except for the ill-considered policy of graduated response against North Vietnam.

> *General William Westmoreland, the overall commander of U.S. troops in South Vietnam during much of the war, claiming in his postwar memoirs that either a U.S. withdrawal or military victory could have been achieved in summer 1965, quoted in his* A Soldier Reports *(1976), p. 99.*

Many of the people who were associated with the war . . . were looking for any excuse to initiate bombing. . . . The DESOTO patrol was primarily for provocation. . . . There was a feeling that if the destroyer got into some trouble that would provide the provocation we needed.

> *Former Undersecretary of State George Ball charging in 1977 that the Johnson White House deliberately provoked the mid-1965 events that led to the escalation of the Vietnam War, quoted in Charlton and Montcrieff,* Many Reasons Why: The American Involvement in Vietnam *(1978), Research Room, Lyndon Johnson Library.*

We are confronted with a dilemma, unquestionably, that is difficult to face up to, as a result of the extremes of McCarthyism and the extremes of Goldwaterism. The people have more or less put the Communist menace on the back burner. You immediately become a dangerous character or suspect if you express strong feelings about the system and some question about the activities of Communists as a result of these other two extremes.

I don't want us to get into that dangerous position. I love this system, and I don't want us to either be addicts of some other system or tools of some other system. The thing that troubles me more about our government than nearly anything else is that they will see a line from Peking, Hanoi and Moscow about a month ahead of the time I see it there. I see it being openly espoused by so-called devotees of our system. It is almost taken in text.

> *President Johnson, during a summer 1965 cabinet meeting, expressing his concern that the growing U.S. antiwar movement is offering encouragement to the communist enemy, in Box 3 of the Lyndon B. Johnson Cabinet Papers, Meeting of June 18, 1965, Lyndon Johnson Library.*

You know it is a view which I have long held that there are no significant American interests which dictate an essentially massive, unilateral American military effort to control the events in Vietnam or even on the Southeast Asian mainland as a whole. . . . In what direction are we going in Vietnam? The absence of a clear answer to that question seems to me to be the crux of the difficulty which has confronted us all along.

> *Senate Majority Leader Mike Mansfield expressing his Vietnam concerns to President Johnson, in McGeorge Bundy (with Mansfield correspondence attached) to Mansfield, June 29, 1965, Box 5 of the National Security File, Lyndon Johnson Library.*

Our economy has lots of room to absorb a defense step-up. Nobody can seriously expect that the kind of program you outlined is going to overheat the economy, strain industrial capacity, or generate a consumer buying boom. . . . The overall effects are most likely to be favorable to our prosperity.

> *Gardner Ackley, the chairman of the Council of Economic Advisors, assuring President Johnson that the Vietnam War will be good for the economy, in Ackley to Johnson, Memo on Vietnam, July 30, 1965, CEA Administrative History Correspondence, Vol. 2, Part 1, Lyndon Johnson Library.*

The stakes in Vietnam are extremely high. The American investment is very large and American responsibility is a fact of life which is palpable in the atmosphere of Asia and even elsewhere. The international prestige of the United States and a substantial part of our influence are directly at risk in Vietnam. There is no way of unloading the burden on the Vietnamese themselves and there is no way of negotiating ourselves out of Vietnam which offers any serious promise at present.

There is one grave weakness in our posture on Vietnam which is within our power to fix—and this is widespread belief that we do not have the will and force and patience and determination to take the necessary action and stay the course. This is the overriding reason for our present recommendation of a policy of sustained reprisal.

> *The National Security Council informing President Johnson in 1965 that he has no choice but to escalate the war in Vietnam, quoted in Sheehan,* The Pentagon Papers; As Published by the New York Times; Based on Investigative Reporting by Neil Sheehan *(1971), pp. 227–233.*

Miscalculation by both the U.S. and North Vietnam is, in the end, at the root of the best hindsight hypothesis of Hanoi's behavior. In simple terms, it was a mistake for an Administration sincerely resolved to keep its risks low, to have the 34A operations and the destroyer patrol take place even in the same time period. Rational minds could not readily have foreseen that Hanoi might confuse them . . . but rational calculations should have taken account of the irrational. . . . Washington did not want an incident, and it seems doubtful that Hanoi did either. Yet each misread each other, and the incidents did happen.

Former Johnson White House aide William Bundy rejecting the late 1965 argument that the United States sought a war with the North Vietnamese, in his Vietnam Manuscript, Papers of William Bundy, LBJ Library.

If the objectives of our policy remain the same, the war in Vietnam is just beginning for the United States. Worse, all the choices open to us are bad choices. . . . America stood to lose far more at home and throughout the world by the more extensive military pursuit of an elusive objective in Vietnam.

Senate Majority Leader Mansfield urging President Johnson to review 1966 policy objectives for Vietnam before it is too late, in Mansfield to Johnson, December 18, 1965, Box 30 of the National Security File, Lyndon Johnson Library.

People will really be startled!

Congressman Wilbur Mills, chairman of the House Ways and Means Committee, urging President Johnson not to disclose the full 1966 budget for the Vietnam War, in Larry Levinson (with Mills recommendations) to Johnson, December 29, 1965, Box 4/FI, Lyndon Johnson Library.

The Dominican Republic Intervention

Santo Domingo is rife with rumors of a coup, promoted by announcements over two radio stations that a number of army officers, including Army Chief of Staff Rivera Cuesta, had been arrested. Word of the overthrow of the government spread like wildfire and brought crowds into the street, much horn-blowing,

and a concentration of some 1,000 persons at the palace who were dispersed by a water truck.

Tom Mann, the undersecretary of state for economic affairs, reporting to President Johnson in an April 1965 report about the growing chaos and confusion in the Dominican Republic, in White House File: The Dominican Republic, Research Room, Lyndon Johnson Library.

All indications point to the fact that if present efforts of forces loyal to the government fail, power will be assumed by groups clearly identified with the Communist Party. If the situation described above comes to pass, my own recommendation and that of the Country Team is that we should intervene to prevent another Cuba from arising out of the ashes of this uncontrollable situation.

U.S. Ambassador W. Tapley Bennett urging President Johnson in April 1965 to order American troops into the Dominican Republic, in White House File: The Dominican Republic, Research Room, Lyndon Johnson Library.

I have ordered the Secretary of Defense to put the necessary American troops ashore in order to give protection to hundreds of Americans who are still in the Dominican Republic and to escort them safely back to this country. This same assistance will be available to the nationals of other countries, some of whom have already asked for our help.

President Johnson, during a special television address to the nation on April 28, 1965, announcing his decision to send U.S. military forces into the Dominican Republic, in White House File: The Dominican Republic, Research Room, Lyndon Johnson Library.

It's a tragedy that has been sold to the country by a lack of candor and by misinformation.

In late April 1965, Senator William Fulbright denouncing President Johnson's decision to intervene in the Dominican Republic, in Public Statements File: The Dominican Republic, Research Room, Lyndon Johnson Library.

Men were running up and down the corridors of the Ambassador Hotel with tommyguns, shooting out windows, and through the roof and through the closets. Our citizens were under the beds and in the closets and trying to dodge this gunfire. Our Ambassador, as he was talking to us, was under the desk. We didn't think we had much time to consult in any great detail more than we had talked about up to that time, but we did make the announcement about 8 o'clock and immediately asked the

Trapped in a firefight in Santo Domingo during the Dominican Republic intervention, U.S. troops protect a local boy from snipers. *(National Archives)*

OAS [Organization of American States] for an urgent meeting the next morning.

President Johnson, during a June 1965 press conference, recalling a report from Santo Domingo on the night of his decision to intervene in the Dominican Republic, in The Public Papers of President Lyndon B. Johnson, 1965, Speeches, Lyndon Johnson Library.

I had 237 individual conversations during that period and about 35 meetings with various people. Finally, on Wednesday afternoon at 4-something, we got another warning that we should have a contingent plan ready immediately, and a little before 6 o'clock we got a plea, a unanimous plea from the entire country team, made up of the Ambassador, the AID [Agency for International Development] Director, CIA and the USIA [United States Information Agency], and the Army, Navy, and the Air Force, to land troops immediately to save American lives. Now, of course, we knew of the forces at work in the Dominican Republic. We were not unaware that there were Communists that were active in this effort, but 99 percent of our reason for going in there was to try to provide protection for these American lives and for the lives of other nationals. . . .

So having gone in and secured the place, . . . we now think that there are two essential things that are left to be done: One is to find a broadly based government under the leadership of the OAS that will be acceptable and approved by the Dominican people; and second, to engage in the comprehensive task of reconstruction of that nation, in trying to make it possible for 3 and 1/2 million to have an economic comeback.

President Johnson, during a June 1965 press conference, reviewing his Dominican Republic intervention policy, in The Public Papers of President Lyndon B. Johnson, 1965, Speeches, Lyndon Johnson Library.

The integrity of the U.S. commitment is the principal pillar of peace throughout the world. If that commitment becomes unreliable, the communist world would draw conclusions that would lead to our ruin and almost certainly to a catastrophic war.

Secretary of State Dean Rusk telling President Johnson that the intervention policies for South Vietnam and the Dominican Republic share similar objectives, in Rusk to Johnson, July 1, 1965, Box 43 of the National Security File, Lyndon Johnson Library.

I'm more aware of the problems of more people than before. I am more sensitive to the injustices we have put on the Negro, for instance, because I see and talk to him more now. I'm a little less selfish, a little more selfless. . . . In this place, you can't get any higher and the only thing you want to do is what's right.

President Johnson telling reporters James Cannon and Charles Roberts that his Great Society, Vietnam, and Dominican Republic policies are just, fair, and overdue, in "Interview with the President," Newsweek, August 2, 1965, pp. 20–21.

British Invasion and Pop Culture Issues

What really got them were the American teenage car sorties. The Beatles left the airport in four Cadillac limousines, one Beatle to a limousine, heading for the Plaza Hotel in Manhattan. The first sortie came almost immediately. Five kids in a powder blue Ford overtook the caravan on the expressway, and as they passed each Beatle, one guy hung out the back window and waved a red blanket.

A white convertible came up second, with the word BEETLES scratched on both sides in the dust. A police car was close behind that one with the siren going and the alarm light rolling, but the kids, a girl at the wheel and two guys in the back seat, waved at each Beatle before pulling over to the exit with the cops gesturing at them.

In the second limousine, Brian Sommerville, the Beatles' press agent, said to one of the Beatles, George Harrison: "Did you see that, George?"

Harrison looked at the convertible with its emblem in the dust and said, "They misspelled Beatles."

Reporters William Whitworth and Tom Wolfe describing the arrival of the Beatles in New York in February 1964, in their "How does one go about meeting a Beatle?: The Beatles Arrive," New York Herald Tribune, February 7, 1964, p. 1.

What causes an international craze like the current Beatlemania?

First the Beatles needed a symbol that would make them stand out in people's minds, a symbol such as the coonskin cap that Walt Disney gave his Davy Crockett creation. For a symbol it was decided to exploit their already overlong hair. The Beatles let it grow longer and bushier, combed it forward—and then had it immaculately trimmed. The result was not only eye catching but evocative. Such hairdos were common in the Middle Ages, and the new coiffure suggested the ancient roots of England. . . .

Frankly, if I were in the business of manufacturing mophead Beatle wigs, I would worry. Crazes tend to die a horribly abrupt death. It was not so long ago, after all, that a good many unwary businessmen got caught with warehouses full of coonskin caps when the Crockett craze stopped almost without warning.

Historian and Saturday Evening Post *writer Vance Packard adding some historical analysis to Beatlemania, in his "Building the Beatle Image,"* Saturday Evening Post, *March 21, 1964, p. 36.*

They can't read music, their beat is corny and their voices are faint, but England's shaggy-maned exports manage to flip wigs on two continents. . . .

The fans call Paul the handsome one, and he knows it. The others in the group call Paul "The Star." He does most of the singing and most of the wiggling, trying to swing his hips after the fashion of Elvis Presley, one of his boyhood idols. In the British equivalent of high school, Paul was mostly in the upper ranks scholastically, unlike the other Beatles. "He was like, you know, a goody-goody in school," remembers one of Paul's boyhood friends. He also, as another former classmate remembers him, was a "tubby little kid" who avoided girlish rejections by avoiding girls.

With a certain gusto, critic Alfred Aronowitz attacking The Beatles, *Beatlemania, and lead singer Paul McCartney, in his "Yeah! Yeah! Yeah!",* Saturday Evening Post, *March 21, 1964, p. 31.*

Iacocca has produced more than just another new car. With its long hood and short rear deck, its Ferrari flair and openmouthed air scoop, the Mustang resembles the European racing cars that American sports-car buffs find so appealing. Yet Iacocca has made the Mustang's design so flexible, its price so reasonable, and its options so numerous that its potential appeal reaches towards two-thirds of all U.S. car buyers. Priced as low as $2,368 and able to accommodate a small family in its four seats, the Mustang seems des-

tined to be a sort of Model A of sports-cars—for the masses as well as buffs.

In a mid-April 1964 cover story, Time *magazine praising the new Ford Mustang "pony car," in Iacocca,* Iacocca: An Autobiography *(1986), p. 77.*

Britain's hero is America's hero. . . . There is a ritual truth in the battle between loner Bond, operating with his wits and his license to kill, and SPECTRE, the organized, calculating embodiment of evil. We are prepared to grant the reality of a fight between the one and the many, the individual and the group, the virtuoso of virtue and the chorus of catastrophe, and having granted this reality, we can then afford to allow even the most extravagant daydream particulars, as lively embellishments.

Newsweek *magazine, with a certain poetic flair, examining why two James Bond movies (Dr. No and From Russia With Love) have become hits in America, in Staff's "From 'No' to Yes,"* Newsweek, *April 13, 1964, pp. 93–94.*

Why do you listen to folk music? "Because it is honest," answers a young devotee on the Harvard campus. "Because a folk song tells the truth, it tells real stories about real life and it doesn't mince words. Commercial songs, pop music can't be honest—they're censored by the people who control society and make the rules." Valid or not, this is a good explanation as any why young people in increasing numbers are embracing folk music. The phenomenon is a strange one. It consists of a rediscovery by city youth of what is essentially country idiom, an urban folk revival that feeds upon songs of love, hate, birth, death, and work that were born in the fields and on the prairies.

Saturday Evening Post *investigating the early 1960s appeal of folk music to middle-class urban youth, in Staff's "Just Playin' Folks,"* Saturday Evening Post, *May 30, 1964, p. 25.*

"We don't prostitute ourselves, we don't compromise. We say what we've got to say. We're not afraid to tell people the emperor isn't wearing clothes." According to John Court, one of their two personal managers, the group has turned down guest appearances on 12 network programs. "Important shows like Perry Como, Bob Hope, Andy Williams, Garry Moore, Danny Kaye," he says. But they all wanted Peter, Paul and Mary to change themselves. This ranged anywhere from a physical change, like shaving off the beards, to a figurative change—playing beatniks in a coffee cellar or some other far-out characters."

John Court, one of the managers for the folk singing group Peter, Paul and Mary, telling the Saturday Evening Post *that mainstream television continued to reject or misunderstand the folk artist throughout the early 1960s, in Aronowitz and Blonsky, "Three's Company: Peter, Paul and Mary,"* Saturday Evening Post, *May 30, 1964, p. 30.*

It began in London. The whole fad seemed to provoke just that kind of vaudeville-*is*-dead response. The newspapers trotted out such reliables as "the naked truth" and "my bare lady." Debbie Reynolds snapped through a press agent that toplessness "is a bust." Kim Novak came out for "All or nothing at all." Bob Hope, in a scatter-shot of gags hit the mark twice. "Instead of *Playboy,* the guys will be buying *Ladies' Home Journal,*" he said. "It leaves nothing to my imagination, and at my age it's good to have an imagination."

But this was only the beginning. Art Buchwald spoke of 1964 as "the year the bottom fell out of the top." The *Washington Post* editorialized, mindful of Adam's fall: "In a world resolved to remain wicked, beauty is seen in the brassiere, not in the bosom." In London, "Shock Frocks," topless evening gowns, were on sale, and publicity stunts involving bare-chested models and "starlets" burst out all over.

Newsweek magazine poking fun at the summer 1964 "topless bathing suit" craze in America and elsewhere, in Staff's "Can You Top This?", Newsweek, *July 6, 1964, pp. 72–73.*

"I was just in Lexington, Kentucky," she drawled into the microphone, tuning her guitar. "I thought you went to Kentucky to watch the races, but they tell you to bet. . . . Bet on a horse, any horse, they say. And somebody from *Sports Illustrated* asks you what horse. I bet on a horse, a nice shiny horse. He came in seven steps behind." She leaned forward with a half-smile. "But I didn't tell the guy from *Sports Illustrated.*" Plink. Another song: "Stewball"—about a horse.

The audience was warm. This was the Joan Baez they knew. Blue jeans, torn turtleneck T-shirt, gently snide, gently knocking the outside world, gently singing her gentle songs. . . .

Bob Dylan, one of the greatest and most prolific folk song writers of the era, is scruffy, blond, unshaven, skinny, and at first glance, as appealing as pot cheese. He is from Hibbing, Minnesota, where, according to a self-portrait in verse, he "ran away from home at 10, 13, 15, 15 and 1/2, 17, and 18," and was "caught an' brought back all but once." Although Dylan with his puny voice and plain-talk poetry, is indisputably unique ("I'm not a folk singer, man—I jes' write conversations with myself—an' I never think, I never think, I never think") he rides highest of all on the new wave of writer-performers of topical songs.

Reporter Betty Rollin examining the style and approach of folk singers Joan Baez and Bob Dylan during a 1962 concert, in her "A New Beat: Topical Folk Singers, Their Songs," Vogue, *September 1, 1964, pp. 60, 82–83, 130.*

Can you spot the changes in this different breed of cat? Probably not. For the 1965 Jaguar XK-E has the same sleek silhouette that has made this the most dynamic and best-looking car on the road today.

Under the hood, it's another story. The 1965 XK-E is equipped with a new, more powerful version of the race-proven XK engine, for even quicker response and acceleration. It features four-wheel disc brakes (driver-proven for hundreds of millions of miles) for safe stops at high speeds; four-speed synchromesh gearbox that handles as smooth as a friendly kitten; all-around independent suspension to iron out roads and flatten corners; newly designed, more comfortable bucket seats; monocoque body construction (like the airframe of a jet) for added strength without extra weight; fully instrumented dash panel, with aviation-type toggle switches. In short, the new XK-E is a driver's car.

Britain's Jaguar Motor Company answering American charges that its top import, the XK-E, lacks in both quality and reliability and insisting that all previous problems have been remedied in its new 1965 model, within a full page ad in Road & Track, *December 1964, p. 18.*

Race will be of no importance, just as in Cosby's comedy act. He is a stand-up satirist who happens to be colored. In "I Spy" he wants to be treated like any other spy. In one scene, filmed in Hong Kong, "This little Chinese kid rubs my face, and it doesn't rub off. I don't want to be typecast having my face rubbed. If anyone else rubs my face, I'm going to rub back."

Newsweek interviewing African-American comedian turned TV spy Bill Cosby, in Staff, "The Spy," Newsweek, December 14, 1964, p. 51.

The idea that the Queen would bestow titles upon the quartet of mopheaded pop singers stirred emotions of anger, amusement, approval, and apathy. . . . Some Beatle fans were aghast: "They've gone respectable," wailed one teenager; "the damn Establishment's got 'em," moaned another. . . . The Beatles? After the first glow of pride, they had second thoughts. "It almost makes us wish we'd never got it," said Lennon. "The whole affair is getting to be a drag," added Ringo.

An Associated Press reporter in June 1965 examining the reaction to Queen Elizabeth awarding the Beatles with the Most Excellent Order of the British Empire (M.B.E.) title, in the Associated Press's The World in 1965: History As We Lived It *(1966), p. 114.*

For every girl who enters the villa, a dozen may linger outside, pining for an invitation. "Sometimes he'll let me in," says an impressive blonde in a leopard-skin coat. "It depends on his mood. Other times I wait for three or four hours before I drift off. Just to tease him, we'll sing, 'We love you, Beatles; oh, yes we do-hoo,' before we go though."

An Elvis Presley fan near Elvis's private estate poking fun at her idol being "in the shadow of the Beatles," in Jennings, "There'll Always Be An Elvis," Saturday Evening Post, September 11, 1965, p. 78.

"Elvis has sort of a dread fascination for lonely women," explains Dr. Harold Greenwald, a prominent author and psychologist. "He seems to be uninhibited and wild. And there is a hint of cruelty to him. When he sings, he is like a method actor: He is in some fantasy of his own which coincides with the fantasies of his listeners.

Paradoxically, other observers feel that Elvis is successful because he projects purity. "He's a clean-cut, clean-living man," says Sam Katzman, producer of two Presley pictures. "There's not a blemish." Adds an M-G-M spokesman, "They never go to bed in a Pres-

ley picture. Otherwise, mammas wouldn't let their kids come."

Saturday Evening Post reporter C. Robert Jennings examining the early appeal of Elvis Presley, in his "There'll Always Be an Elvis," Saturday Evening Post, September 11, 1965, pp. 76–79.

Until now, Negro performers have sung, danced, juggled or, like Jack Benny's man, Rochester, played foxy family retainers, But in *I Spy*, a sweatshirt-and-dagger vehicle about a pair of U.S. undercover operatives masquerading as traveling tennis bums, Cosby launches a racial revolution. For the first time a Negro will be featured on television as the star of a dramatic series—breaking a barrier that not even Nat King Cole, Sammy Davis or Lena Horne could overcome. As *Variety* put it, Bill Cosby is TV's Jackie Robinson.

More significantly, Cosby's role is not fashioned to fit a Negro. Teamed with white actor Robert Culp, Cosby wrestles with villains and ogles pretty girls, just like any upstanding TV hero. At times his fresh charm and casual humor so overshadow Culp that the show commits the heresy of subordinating the white man to the Negro.

The abrupt change of roles could well provoke angry protests from TV audiences, particularly in the South. Yet show-business executives are keenly aware that the surge for civil rights throughout the U.S. has endowed the Negro with a new image and thereby new box-office appeal. Executive producer Sheldon Leonard, one of TV's most skilled entrepreneurs (Danny Thomas Show, Andy Griffith Show, Gomer Pyle), packaged *I Spy* with very practical goals in mind. "We'll get adverse mail, but we'll also get support," he insists. "There are more men of goodwill than men of ill will, more guys in white hats than in black hats—and you can translate that into dollars and cents."

Veteran foreign correspondent and Vietnam expert Stanley Karnow examining the significance of I Spy *while visiting the show's on location film crew in Hong Kong, in his "Bill Cosby: Variety Is the Life of Spies," Saturday Evening Post, September 25, 1965, pp. 86–87.*

After executive-producer Sheldon Leonard decided he wanted Cosby as a regular on *I Spy*, he expected much more trouble than he actually got. Since Cosby was hired before co-star Culp, Leonard anticipated difficulty along that line, but Culp was happy to work with Cosby once he saw Cosby's acting in the pilot film.

"Then everybody told us we were going to have trouble with sponsors," recalls Leonard, "but none of the boggie men we had foreseen ever materialized. We have more sponsors than we need."

Cosby avoids racial material in *I Spy* because he has built a non-racial image through his particular style of comedy. Yet, he freely admits that his job is a by-product of the "revolution." "Negroes like Martin Luther King and Dick Gregory; Negro groups like the Deacons and the Muslims—all are dedicated to the cause of civil rights," notes Cosby, "but they do their jobs in their own way. My way is to show white people that Negroes are human beings with the same aspirations and abilities that whites have." It looks as if Cosby's own aspirations and abilities are quite clear. "After eight shows," says Leonard, "Bill was as advanced as many actors are after eight years."

Ebony *magazine assessing the significance of Bill Cosby's role on* I Spy, *in Staff, "I Spy: Comedian Bill Cosby is first Negro co-star in TV network series,"* Ebony, *September 1965, p. 66.*

The muu muu has gone mod and turned into a granny. It happened in Los Angeles, and within a month grannies had shown up on Wilshire Boulevard in broad daylight, at the Beatles concert in the Hollywood Bowl, at Disneyland and U.C.L.A.

A granny is not a grandmother but a garment: a dress that covers the wearer from neck to ankle, a kind of nipped-in Mother Hubbard gussied up with Victorian furbelows and bows. Real-life grannies would not be caught dead in one: grannies are only for girls.

In Los Angeles, grannies have become *de rigueur* for dates and general after-school wear. "They are a good change from Capris and a top for parties," says 20-year-old Gail Eckles. "They make you feel so dressed up," added 14-year-old Cathy Milligan, who owns three of them. "It's a study in contrast," explained one designer. "The kids go from the wild, wild short dresses to the neat little granny." Another observer has a better theory: "The kids want it because it is something mother won"t copy."

Newsweek *examining the "granny" dress and, describing the latest fashion craze as "something of the anti-British response," in Staff, "Going to Great Lengths,"* Newsweek, *October 8, 1965, p. 81.*

5

Beach Boys America
1966–1967

"Make no mistake about it," President Johnson told the doubters of his Vietnam policy. "We are going to win." In 1966, those few who questioned the president's promises made sensational headlines. Meanwhile, the rest of the nation watched and waited. It also had other interests. Years later, CBS newsman Walter Cronkite noted that in the mid-1960s more people were concerned about what the latest Top Forty hit from the Beach Boys might be than about the news from Vietnam. An American homegrown answer to the leading British bands of the day, the Beach Boys sang about a quiet after-school or after-work youth culture that sought the perfect wave and not the perfect politics. They represented an America, troubled or not, still at peace with itself. That peace shattered quickly, and the Beach Boys soon symbolized a gentle, naive America before the height of radical protest, more political assassinations, economic worries, and the always bad news from Southeast Asia.

SOLIDARITY

In 1966, Representative Clement Zablocki (Democrat of Wisconsin) informed President Johnson that his support for the Vietnam War was waning. Predicting that the war's expense could bankrupt the U.S. Treasury, Zablocki suggested that the war would soon have a wider impact on American life than the White House dared to admit.

Standing at 5' 3", "Little Clement," as Johnson called him, was the chairman of the House of Representatives Foreign Affairs Committee, a moderate, and a supporter of the Great Society. Losing a man like Zablocki could mean losing the support of the entire House of Representatives, and Johnson was concerned. But a curious thing happened. Zablocki admitted that he had little use for South Vietnam and America's mission there, but his heavily working-class district had volunteered hundreds of young men for the fight. Many had died, and an immediate pull-out of Vietnam would be tantamount, Zablocki said, to stepping on their graves. They would have died for nothing. The real guilt in this mess, Zablocki believed, belonged to Congress. It was he and his colleagues who once praised the Tonkin Gulf Resolution and now had little authority to curb presidential power or end the war. The presidency had become too powerful and too divorced from the people, Zablocki insisted, and he vowed to end the Tonkin Gulf Resolution presidency as soon as the war was over.

This was both good and bad news for Johnson. On the one hand, Zablocki's comments meant that Congress had given the White House a green light to continue its Vietnam policies without a legal counterattack by a winning majority of its members. On the other hand, the presidency would never be the same after the war. Johnson would not live to see the 1973 War Powers Act and its denunciation of the 1960s approach to war. But he learned early in the debate with Zablocki that Vietnam transcended discussions about troop strength and military strategy. By the mid-1960s, it now involved the future of the presidency, the economy, and legislative-executive relations.

Congressional relations used to be Johnson's forte. It, too, was becoming a casualty of the Vietnam escalation. Democratic Party solidarity behind the Vietnam War was now impossible to find. Embarrassingly for Johnson, some of the loudest pro-Vietnam statements came from Republicans. In 1966, Senator Dirksen, long hailed as the Republican Party's most eloquent speaker, claimed in a dramatic address that if Ho Chi Minh won his war in Vietnam, Americans would soon be fighting a communist invasion "in the streets of San Francisco."

In 1966, a tired and worried President Johnson shakes hands with U.S. troops during his swing tour of South Vietnam. *(National Archives)*

Vice President Humphrey countered that Dirksen might have exaggerated the situation, but he also believed that Ho Chi Minh was doomed to fail.[1]

Ironically, Humphrey had little use for the war, told Johnson so, and had been left out of National Security Council discussions because of it. Being on the outskirts of power was a frustrating experience for the frenetic vice president. He concluded that a prowar speech or two just might win him back the good graces of the president. He was mistaken.

By the mid-1960s, the Vietnam debate raged in both the halls of Congress and in the streets. Although the original antiwar demonstrators always claimed that their efforts were characterized by spontaneity and moral outrage, there was organization to much of what they did. That organization came under the umbrella of the difficult to define American New Left. Traditional socialist and communist parties in the United States had a hard time figuring out the youthful Students for a Democratic Society (SDS), the Weathermen, the Spartacist League, and even the so-called counterculture or hippies. But they represented the new 1960s trend in leftist thought.

To Gus Hall, the longtime chairman of the struggling Communist Party–USA, the antiwar activists were on the outskirts of both socialist and communist ideology. Hall had run for president many times and never won more than 1 percent of the vote. To what the U.S. press nicknamed the New Left, Hall was a tool of the Soviet government and as divorced from humanitarianism and morality as the White House.

According to student protest organizer and SDS founder Tom Hayden, there was never supposed to be a hard-and-fast ideology for the American New Left. He and his colleagues carefully selected certain points of view from a number of leftist philosophers and prided themselves on the evolutionary nature of their movement. For instance, they admired France's Jean-Paul Sartre for his existentialism. The latter was a philosophy that embraced a number of the concerns of international communism but rejected government tyranny. Instead, existentialism stressed the commitment of the individual, and his or her own talents, to make a better world. They admired Germany's Herbert Marcuse and his complaints about "one-dimensional man." To Marcuse, humankind lived under an unnecessary threat of endless capitalist versus communist wars, whereby only political systems benefited and not the common person. Meanwhile, the New Leftists made up their history as they went along. Hayden believed that John Kennedy would have never escalated the Vietnam War and that Ho Chi Minh was the "George Washington of Vietnam."

Distrusting all those "over 30," Hayden's SDS promised a reformed university system that stressed the liberal arts and peace studies alongside an America that spent more time on civil rights reform, environmentalism, and disarmament. Whereas conservatives used to be associated with isolationist, take-care-of-America-first causes, this position shifted to the left in the mid-1960s. The political spectrum was becoming difficult to figure out.

To the SDS, which slowly became the dominant political force on university campuses in the mid-1960s, the Vietnam War was the product of an "evil foreign policy," and there could be no rest until Vietnam was united under Ho Chi Minh's rule. All of this was absolutely outrageous for its day, especially to the parents and grandparents of the SDS protesters. The press spent a considerable amount of time trying to determine how this "generation gap" had been born, and the usual answer involved the growing revulsion over the war in Vietnam. Most journalists predicted that both street demonstrations and the SDS would grow if the Pentagon was forced to draft young men out of the universities. They were right.

Much of the antiwar movement consisted of middle- to upper-middle-class white males of university age. In the mid-1960s, any male student in an institution of higher learning could apply for "student deferment status." If a B or B− grade average was maintained in his studies during a given year, the student was spared from a draft system that would most likely send him to Vietnam. General Lewis Hershey, Johnson's elderly director of the selective service system, targeted the downtrodden, suggesting that the military gave them an opportunity to leave the northern urban ghetto or the impoverished Southern countryside. Sadly, that also continued to assure that the average Vietnam veteran remained a 19-year-old African American. This gave credence to the growing black radical complaints that Vietnam was a "racist war." Indeed, the protest movement would grow in 1968 when the draft system reached into the largely untapped white middle class.[2]

THE DOMINICAN REPUBLIC DIVERSION

Vietnam was not the only war involving Americans in the 1960s, and Johnson had evidence that his military could prevail in a small tropical country. In the last years of his presidency, Johnson would hold up this other war as an example of American military prowess, and he always hoped that Ho Chi Minh would get the message. The issues were complicated and far removed from Southeast Asia, but the Dominican Republic intervention became Johnson's case study for success in developing nations.

In 1962, Juan Bosch had won the presidency of the Dominican Republic. A leftist in charge of an impoverished, struggling Caribbean island nation, Bosch faced a host of obstacles. Poverty was on a rapid rise, the United States was suspicious of a leftist government so close to Castro's Cuba, and there had not been a freely elected government in the Dominican Republic since the 1920s. A right-wing coup quickly ended Bosch's dreams of fast-moving reform, but pro-Bosch supporters decided not to give up the fight. By the spring of 1965, the resulting violence had ended what was left of law and order in the Dominican Republic.

In Washington, President Johnson received a clouded picture about what was truly going on. For instance, W. Tapley Bennett, the U.S. ambassador to the Dominican Republic, insisted that thousands had been massacred across the country by pro-Bosch leftists. Bennett favored the right-wing government, and he had no idea who had been killed by leftists. Confusion or not, Johnson decided to act. He told his cabinet that he had no intention of letting "another Castro" take power in the Caribbean. It would mean the end of his administration, he said, if he did and the end of respect for America in the noncommunist world.

Throughout his decision making on the Dominican Republic invasion, Johnson made comparisons and not contrasts to Vietnam. A massive display of U.S. firepower, followed by the destruction of Bosch's so-called constitutionalist rebellion, was supposed to echo across Hanoi. The United States would prevail, and, like Juan Bosch, Ho Chi Minh was expected to accept the fact that his days were numbered. Since most of Bosch's armed supporters in Santo Domingo, the nation's largest city, were presumed to be communists, taking this metropolitan area would symbolize that American victory.

At the same time Johnson was dispatching thousands to Vietnam, he sent some 33,000 troops (mostly marines) to the Dominican Republic. Luckily for the White House, the marines advanced quickly, and the April–May 1965 intervention was successful. These troops were soon assisted by 2,000 soldiers from the Organization of American States (OAS), largely because Johnson insisted on a "More Flags" effort. That insistence won him a great deal of animosity from the Latin American governments for the remainder of his term, while much of the Latin American press criticized Washington's first military intervention in the region in 30 years.

To blunt the growing criticism, Johnson urged the OAS to form an Inter-American Peace Force to keep order and reestablish the political system throughout the Dominican Republic. The peacekeeping mission worked, and in the resulting 1966 election, Joaquín Balaguer became the first postrebellion president. Neither the constitutionalists nor the former junta leaders were welcome in the new government. This did not stop Balaguer from attempting to kill or jail all his real and imagined opponents. But the existence of an up-and-running Dominican government did allow the United States to easily withdraw the last of its troops in September 1966.[3]

From the invasion to "More Flags" to the creation of a new, working regime, Johnson reveled in the victory. Vietnam was next, but there was still pressing domestic concerns to consider.

THE BEACH BOYS IMPACT

Lyndon Johnson might have had a pressing political agenda, but America's white middle-class youth were more interested in rock-and-roll than in politics. Although the Beatles and other foreign bands displaced the country's rock-and-roll favorites of the late 1950s and early 1960s, there was one California-based band that thrived in the midst of the British Invasion. Carl, Dennis, and Brian Wilson's creation, the Beach Boys, challenged the British-led status quo and won.

The Wilson brothers, along with cousin Mike Love and family friend Al Jardine, had been trying to find a unique sound since their high school performing days early in the 1960s. Murry Wilson, the hard-driving father of the Wilson boys, was a songwriter who believed his talented sons might have a chance in the recording business if they could only create a distinctive, recognizable sound. That sound became a combination of Chuck Berry–influenced guitar playing and George Gershwin–influenced harmony. Their lyrics stressed their own southern California interests, namely pretty girls, surfing, and fast cars. Although the Beach Boys became a fascination on regional southern California radio as early as 1962, few station managers elsewhere believed that they had national appeal. Within three years, however, those managers were proven wrong, and Beach Boys tunes challenged the Beatles at the top of the charts.

On the edge of fame, the Beach Boys pose for a 1962 publicity shot. *Clockwise from top:* Brian Wilson, Carl Wilson, Mike Love, Al Jardine, and Dennis Wilson. *(Hulton Archive/TimePix)*

In spite of the ugly news from both Vietnam and America's urban ghettos, the Beach Boys sang about a contented white middle-class youth concerned about dating, driving, and surfing. Their 1966 album *Pet Sounds* later influenced the work of the Beatles on their highly successful album, *Sgt. Pepper's Lonely Hearts Club Band*. But quick fame and riches led Beach Boy member Brian Wilson to a world of alcohol and drugs, arguments broke out within the group over new directions and sounds, and the Wilsons became forever linked to the nation's quiet, innocent days before the madness of Vietnam and racial violence dominated American life. They represented the heart and soul of mid–1960s America. Beatle Paul McCartney claimed years later that the Beach Boys added to the legend of innocence lost during a difficult time.

The struggling B-movie-making studio of American-International Pictures (AIP) had even translated the Beach Boys's youth culture message into film. Starring former child star Annette Funicello and early 1960s singing sensation Frankie Avalon, the so-called Beach Party movies of AIP dominated the Saturday afternoon matinee slots at America's local theaters. Simple boy meets girl scripts, augmented by southern California-based tunes as well as slapstick comedy, made films such as *How to Stuff a Wild Bikini* (1965) and *Beach Blanket Bingo* (1965) teenage hits. Like Beach Boys music, these films glamorized California and white middle-class American life and, again, soon represented something of the calm before the storm. By the end of the 1960s, the Beach Party movie was already long out of vogue, and the Beach Boys jumped on the bandwagon of the socially relevant music suddenly spearheaded by the Beatles and American folk-rock artists. Forever stereotyped, the Beach Boys struggled with the changing times of the late 1960s. Their new sound of protest and criticism was complimented by some critics but rejected by longtime fans.

At a Florida drive-in theater, teenagers view Annette Funicello and Frankie Avalon in AIP's hit escapist "youth culture film" *Beach Blanket Bingo*. (Henry Groskinsky/TimePix)

To the dedicated and consistent protest singer, the mid 1960s represented an opportunity to gain recognition and respect in the music industry. Joan Baez had been singing protest songs since her debut album, *Joan Baez,* in 1960. Her expressive, wide-ranging voice, folk guitar specialty, and association with Bob Dylan always won the attention of civil rights workers and early antiwar activists, but she often received more press attention for her political views and actions (like not paying her taxes in protest of the Defense Department) than for her music. That would change as the country entered its new age of protest in the late 1960s, and Baez was already in position to claim a leading role in the transition. Although he insisted that his music simply flowed and spoke to a receptive audience, Bob Dylan noted that performers like himself and Baez were the new poets of a new generation. Indeed, the folk-rock artists of the day won more fans than ever before, and their songs of peace and social justice became anthems to the antiwar movement as much as the "Star-Spangled Banner" and "God Bless America" remained significant to supporters of the Vietnam War and the White House.

On the big and small screens of the mid-1960s, America remained fascinated by the antics of James Bond–like superspies. They did not have to be British. American television led the way, and, like the Beach Boys, TV's heros were homegrown. For instance, on *I Spy,* young comedian Bill Cosby became the first African American to star in an hour-long adventure series. *I Spy* also featured Cosby with a white co-star and partner, Robert Culp, the former lead of a TV western (*Trackdown*). The new series profiled the missions of two hip, wise-cracking young American spies in the Far East and elsewhere. Shot on location by award-winning cinematographer Faoud Said, *I Spy* was an expensive production with a unique big-screen look.

Although it did not break any viewing records, the show was still a decent success for NBC television. Together, Cosby's Rhodes scholar character (Alexander Scott) and Culp's more street-wise, karate-chopping character (Kelly Robinson) made the cold war look cool. In fact, Culp and Cosby's characters were two 30-something Beach Boys or tennis bums living the good life overseas. They just happened to be spies.[4] NBC producer Sheldon Leonard fought hard to include Cosby in this show, for network executives worried that racist Southern affiliate stations might refuse to broadcast *I Spy* or that sponsors would refuse to advertise during the program for fear of white consumer backlash. All of these fears proved groundless. The show's fans loved the hip banter between Cosby and Culp, and *I Spy* demonstrated that a black man could be portrayed in both everyday and extraordinary circumstances on prime-time TV.

Blacks had starred in small screen variety shows, but *I Spy* finally opened television to greater opportunities for African-American performers. Nevertheless, Cosby offered a low-key performance, keeping his on-screen character away from political commentaries. He fought scripts that accentuated the racial issue, preferring to stress the genuine on-screen friendship with Culp and leave it at that. Cosby won both critical acclaim and Emmy awards for his efforts.

I Spy stood in contrast to other trendy spy shows. For instance, *The Man from U.N.C.L.E.* was a flashy daring-do Bond-like feature geared to a Friday night crowd of preteens with nothing much else to do. Although only a half

In a photo meant to promote the 1965 premier episode of NBC television's *I Spy,* actors Robert Culp (*kneeling*) and Bill Cosby pose for entertainment photographer Allan Grant. Cosby becomes TV's first African-American star of an hour-long adventure/drama series. Culp plays "tennis bum"/spy Kelly Robinson, and Cosby plays tennis coach/spy Alexander Scott. *(Allan Grant/TimePix)*

hour long, *Get Smart,* starring comedian Don Adams, poked fun at the entire spy film genre and appealed to a Saturday night stay-at-home older crowd who thought the Bond craze was silly. Meanwhile, *I Spy* relied on crisp dialogue, fancy camera work, and character development.

The communists never had a chance on *I Spy,* and, in the mid-1960s, most Americans believed that cold war victory in the real world was just as inevitable. But U.S. cold war optimism faded quickly. By the late 1960s, the confident, upbeat spies of *I Spy* looked tired and out of place. The cold war was no longer cool, and many of Culp and Cosby's young, original fans were protesting in the streets and not sitting in front of a television set. The show was canceled after only a three-year run. *The Man from U.N.C.L.E.* and *Get Smart* met a similar fate as the nation lost its faith even in TV's fantasy world of suave as well as funny good guys with high-tech killing gear.

Even more escapist TV programs suffered from U.S. changing tastes. A later and rare example of both small and big screen success, the original *Star Trek* episodes also enjoyed less than a three-year run straddling the challenging years of the mid- and late 1960s. Both cautiously and overtly attempting to analyze 1960s social and political problems within a science-fiction format, *Star Trek* like *I Spy* was an NBC gamble. Even though the program enjoyed a strong and vocal cult following, it was not enough to sustain high ratings and significant advertising sponsorship. The U.S. entertainment industry was in transition, but in what direction remained to be seen.

THE VOTING RIGHTS ACT SUCCESS

Although America's attentions turned more and more to Southeast Asia, the Civil Rights movement continued its struggle for racial justice. When Martin Luther King, Jr., learned of President Johnson's signing of the Voting Rights Act, he cried. Noting that he had never seen a white politician so in line with the Civil Rights movement, King believed that Johnson would go down in history as one of America's finest leaders. Johnson surprised white politicians, too. His public announcement of the Voting Rights Act included a rare display of charisma and genuine emotion. Although jovial, back-slapping, and folksy in private, the public Johnson was wooden, distant, and slow-talking. But the Voting Rights Act success had energized him. Throwing his arms in the air, he concluded his speech about a "new era of justice in America" by shouting the civil rights slogan: "We Shall Overcome." Vice President Humphrey commented that Johnson should have combined this type of public passion with private legislative skills years before. Johnson, however, was trying to make a once-in-a-lifetime point. Civil rights reform was not going away, and white politicians everywhere would have to adjust accordingly.

But adjust to what? Harvard intellectual and Assistant Secretary of Labor Daniel Patrick Moynihan surveyed the plight of mid-1960s African Americans and made recommendations to Johnson for further civil rights legislation. His post–Voting Rights Act report was more of an essay than a legislative proposal, but that underscored the latest problem for the Great Society. To Moynihan, the greatest challenge to black America did not involve George Wallace or the Ku Klux Klan. It was the collapse of the average African-American family, the growing urban crime rate, and the continuing cycle of poverty. To Moynihan, the big city riots of the mid-1960s had nothing to do with race. This was an issue of "lawlessness," he said, and he told Johnson to enact tough anticrime measures to counter future riots. Johnson responded with a television address on that point alone, promising swift action against looters and arsonists during any upcoming disturbance in America's large cities.

Much of Moynihan's effort simply bolstered the established direction of the war on poverty. He also denounced the spokespersons for violent expression in the black community as thugs masquerading as political prophets. The president welcomed this tough assessment and realized a hard-nosed approach to civil disruptions could win him needed conservative support. As always, Johnson feared political backlashes from the Right more than from the Left. By 1967, public opinion polls were suggesting that Johnson was soft on crime. In other words, according to conservative whites, the Great Society programs were somehow responsible for racial tension and violence. Hence, Johnson's new "tough on crime" stance in 1967, although Republicans and southern Democrats like Wallace charged that the president was a latecomer to the cause of law and order. The law-and-order concern in urban white communities was fast becoming a synonym for anti–civil rights opinions and positions; however, most whites denied that was the case when asked by pollsters, academics, and journalists.

To the New Left, which continued to win more and more visibility in the press, Johnson's post–Voting Rights Act approach was symbolic of liberal failure. The urban riots, they said, were not about crime. They were about a racist political system that had dehumanized blacks since the days of slavery. Consequently, black rage and crimes against whites were long overdue and even justified. The liberal wing of the Democratic Party was beginning to agree with them, complaining that expensive social programs were not going to solve race issues overnight. Vocal liberals, such as former journalist and New York congressman Allard Lowenstein, compared Johnson's "racist war in Vietnam" to his social blindness at home.

To Johnson's amazement, the Right took the liberal complaint a step further, pointing out that the federal government blundered and stumbled with white middle-class tax dollars over a no-win war in Vietnam and a social experiment at home. Barry Goldwater, whose career and political philosophy had been deemed out of step with the 1960s only months before, quickly became an icon to conservatives who believed that Johnson had lied and schemed to protect his domestic and foreign policies.

Was America coming apart at the seams? Was Johnson to blame? Popular news and feature magazines, such as *Look* and the *Saturday Evening Post,* dedicated special issues to these questions in 1967. Both magazines claimed that the White House's obsession with the Great Society and Vietnam represented a certain political and social collapse. These were strong words for so-called middle-of-the-road journals. But Johnson paid little notice, and his agenda remained on track.

The new Civil Rights Bills of 1966 and 1967 called for an end to discrimination in the housing and rental industries. More apparent in the big northern cities than in the smaller southern ones, black families were often denied the right to move into the neighborhood of their choice. The denial was especially apparent in the new white suburbs of Chicago, Detroit, and New York, for "white flight" from the crime-ridden city centers was often protected by local ordinances.

Johnson's fair housing legislation alienated his core supporters of northern middle-class whites. Like Kennedy before him, Johnson had concentrated his civil rights efforts in the South. But racism was a national problem, and Johnson's new reform effort stressed that point. The legislation's loudest critics, a coalition of conservative Republicans and northern Democrats in Congress, insisted that whites would now be forced to sell their homes to angry black radicals. These were fright tactics—but effective ones. Any legislation that furthered the cause of radicalism was anti-American, the coalition leaders believed, and Johnson's once friendly Congress turned hostile.

Johnson's new Equal Employment Opportunity Commission (EEOC) tried to accomplish the same antidiscrimination agenda as the fair housing legislation. But its larger mission involved a dramatic initiative for full and open on-the-job opportunities or "affirmative action." Although the EEOC was supposed to help enforce existing civil rights legislation, it spent most of its time answering employment complaints. Its larger goal of ending racism in the workplace was difficult to define and implement. More to the point, Johnson was not sure where the nation stood in this effort and how fast the EEOC should move. As far as the White House was concerned, at least the agency was up and running. The specifics could be worked out later. Johnson expected better results and easy passage for fair housing, but it remained a tough sell.

Making fair housing the centerpiece of his post–Voting Rights Act effort in civil rights reform, Johnson struggled to win the nation's support. It took the assassination of Martin Luther King, Jr., in 1968 to see it pass into law. Using tactics reminiscent of his post-Kennedy assassination dealings with Congress, Johnson insisted that the martyred civil rights leader would have wanted new laws. It worked, but it was a last hurrah. The Open Housing Act marked the end of Johnson's civil rights crusade.[5] The crusade in Vietnam and the 1968 election would take over from there.

THE END OF INNOCENCE

In 1966 and 1967, the typical antiwar and antidraft demonstrator was described as a 19-year-old white male student, born and raised in a middle- to upper-middle-class suburb, who enjoyed rock music, alcohol, and might have experimented with illegal drugs. During the first organized antiwar demonstrations in Washington, D.C., more news reporters gathered at the Pentagon and Washington Monument than demonstrators. From the beginning of the protest era, questions of effectiveness and impact were raised. Could one protester or one protest influence events? While the growing antiwar movement wrestled with that dilemma, Congress offered hope to the antiwar cause. A congressional break with Johnson over the war could mean the difference between success or failure for the entire peace effort.

During early 1966, Senator J. William Fulbright concluded that Congress had a moral obligation to answer the concerns of the American people. America's Vietnam mission was fast becoming the dominant political issue of the day, and he found it amazing that the White House continued to ignore millions of voters. In legal terms, the Vietnam War raised an age-old problem for Fulbright and his congressional supporters. What was more important in American life: the president's executive privilege or the peoples' First Amendment right to know? As the senior author of the 1944 Fulbright-Connally Resolution, Fulbright had moved a powerful president, Franklin Roosevelt, to cooperate with Congress on security matters during the middle of a war. It was time, Fulbright believed, to compel one of Roosevelt's biggest fans, Lyndon Johnson, to follow suit and answer the tough questions about Vietnam. This endeavor, he concluded, would be much more effective than a youth street protest. The president's answers would help chart America's future for years to come.

To Fulbright, the bottom line in a working democracy was honesty and ethics in government. The United States, he feared, had been losing the Vietnam War for some time, and Johnson was lying to the American people about it. The commander in chief had to be held to task for this deception, and U.S. troops needed to be withdrawn from Vietnam.

In February 1966, Fulbright went public in his opposition to the war and called for a special investigation of America's entire Vietnam policy. Privately, Johnson derided the man as "Senator Halfbright" for this decision, implying that a wartime investigation of military policy was tantamount to treason. But Fulbright organized the public hearing anyway, led by his Foreign Relations Committee, and subpoenaed most of the Johnson cabinet. Any failure to answer a congressional subpoena was a felony, punishable by two years in prison. Like many Americans at the time, Fulbright drew a distinction between Lyndon Johnson and the office of the presidency. The office continued to draw a great deal of respect, if not awe. That was about to change. In the meantime, Fulbright did not include Johnson on his subpoena list.

At the beginning of the Fulbright hearings, U.S. casualties in Vietnam were averaging 100 per week. To some Americans, Thursday was now Casualty Day, the time when the Pentagon released those weekly figures. Vietcong casualties usually numbered in the thousands, implying that the enemy should have been decimated years before. Fulbright's hearings investigated why the enemy casualty figures seemed so inflated. Central questions to the investigation included: How many more troops were going to be sent to Vietnam in 1966 or 1967? And why were they needed?

The Fulbright hearings were televised live, and all network programming ceased for the first time since the Kennedy assassination. In these years long before C-SPAN, Congress had regarded cameras as an intrusion in their daily work. The hearings offered the country a rare glimpse of that work, and millions of viewers hoped to learn the truth about Vietnam. In his opening remarks, Fulbright reviewed the rumors of atrocities, the tales of horror, and the reports of widespread opposition in South Vietnam to the very presence of American troops in the country. If all these ugly matters were true and the Johnson administration knew it was true, then the White House had much explaining to do. Did Vietnam represent America's loss of innocence, he wondered. His hearings were supposed to find the answer.

To President Johnson, the Fulbright hearings benefited only the North Vietnamese and not the American people. In an unusual venue for an official response to a senator's efforts, Johnson wrote an open letter of opposition to the *New York Times*. The hearings, Johnson argued, put the lives of American service personnel in danger across South Vietnam, for public, freewheeling discussions of U.S. strategy and military plans might lead to enemy offensives against them. Although he avoided words such as *treachery,* Johnson did denounce the hearings as "irresponsible actions" during a time of war. Implying that cabinet officials called to the hearings might not be very cooperative, Johnson asked the nation to be patient. Victory was still at hand. In support of that victory, he urged all Americans to ignore the hearings. And in the name of patriotism, he also asked the managers of individual television stations to broadcast other programs throughout Fulbright's investigation.

The row between the White House and Congress divided the country, and some TV stations, such as Milwaukee's CBS affiliate, WISN-TV, showed back-to-back reruns of the 1950s half-hour comedy *I Love Lucy* for days. Milwaukee politicians joked that the program should have been shown to the North Vietnamese and not to Americans. After hours of being subjected to this sitcom, the punch line went, the enemy would surrender within a week.

Johnson was not in a joking mood, and he tried his best to distract America's attentions from the hearings. Announcing a special Vietnam summit shortly after Fulbright's questioning began, the president left for Honolulu to meet with Premier Ky, General Westmoreland, and others. It was in Honolulu, he told the press, where success in Vietnam was being finalized. Johnson announced that more troops were being sent to Westmoreland, promised victory by Christmas 1966, and praised Ky. None of this was news, for the escalation continued, victory promises were common, and South Vietnamese leaders were always praised to the heavens. The Honolulu summit received little press coverage at all, and Johnson's diversion effort failed. Ky even interpreted Johnson's kind words to mean there had been a shift in U.S. policy. America now supported an all-out invasion of North Vietnam, he believed, and he told the world press that was the case. Ky was mistaken, and his regime would never recover from the embarrassment.

In the hearings, the American people watched a parade of White House officials under heavy questioning by the Foreign Relations Committee. Secretary of State Dean Rusk was the most vocal cabinet member at the hearings, offering personal views about the U.S. mission in Vietnam. But he volunteered no official view, had no comment on all security matters, and refused to speculate on the future. This was better than many of his White House colleagues who had absolutely nothing to say due to national security priorities. Long and carefully asked questions often won the same nonresponse. Fulbright openly complained that a "lie was a lie no matter how you looked at it," but angering White House officials had little impact either.

The hearings led to endless discussions in the press about the growing "credibility gap" over Vietnam. Some Americans wondered why the White House would not answer simple questions, accurately concluding that the war would drag out well into the 1970s. Others thought Johnson should be given a chance to win the war, but they were concerned why Rusk and others refused to answer questions even about battlefield successes. If America was winning, why hide the facts?

Fulbright's hearings raised more than enough reasonable doubt in the public mind about Vietnam, Johnson, and his relationship with Congress. It represented a certain watershed in attitude. Before the hearings and going back to 1952, a huge majority of Americans told a routine Gallup Poll that they trusted their leaders in Washington. After the hearings, the figure dropped to 50 percent and to half of that by 1974. A Vietnam-weary America longed for the truth.[6]

"DUMP JOHNSON"

In 1967, U.S. troop strength in Vietnam reached to more than 485,000 men. Some 16,000 were reported killed in action by December, and $20 billion had been budgeted for military operations there. Congress thought it would cost $6 billion, and worries about a soon-to-collapse economy were expressed openly in both parties. Antiwar rallies spread to most major cities, and even antiwar slogans became more biting. "Ho, Ho, Ho Chi Minh, the NLF is gonna win" was replaced by "Hey, hey, LBJ, how many kids did you kill today?" A poster of the docket at the Nuremberg war crimes trials in Germany after World War II, now including an angry-looking Lyndon Johnson in the back row, became a popular college dorm room necessity. And in San Francisco, the "summer of peace and love" gathering of counterculture adherents urged young people to avoid the draft, quit work or school, and never trust the federal government. The Johnson administration had little or nothing to say about the growing phenomenon of youth culture, daily protests, and rallies. Washington's silence helped the "credibility gap" grow, and it helped empower political opportunists from the sidelines.

Seeking a national audience for a 1968 run for the presidency, George Wallace spoke in favor of "dinner pail democracy," whereby hard-working, middle-aged, blue-collar workers were idolized. In Wallace's view, these people were the "real America" of patriotism, anticommunism, and family tradition. Youthful opponents of the Vietnam War, civil rights advocates everywhere, and middle-class liberals now constituted, the Alabama governor suggested, a new internal enemy of American decay and treason. Wallace's message struck a chord among those who believed that the White House had lost control of the country, had gone too far in the civil rights crusade, and had opened the door to leftist subversives through its own liberal legislation. Wallace's southern accent and racist background made it difficult for some northerners to recognize the Alabama governor as their champion, but his point of view still found national support.

To Johnson, the growing political turmoil in the country could be short-lived if only the Vietnam situation tilted in U.S. favor. And so General William Westmoreland came home. He had been to the White House many times, but Johnson wanted him to address Congress, assure the nation, and call for unity. Without question, Westmoreland cut a dashing figure on Capitol Hill. Not since General Douglas MacArthur's return from Korea in 1951 had Washington seen such fanfare for a senior military man. It was December 1967, and Westmoreland no longer suggested that the boys would be home by the next Christmas. Making such promises, he implied, had been a mistake. The boys, he now vowed, could be home in mid-1968. Enemy activity in the field, he reported, was low, and this meant the Vietcong were "on the ropes" thanks to endless U.S. bombing raids and the influx of U.S. ground troops. All was in hand, he said, and he urged the nation to rally behind their president, forget their petty differences, and move forward to victory.

Westmoreland's address might have been a stirring, memorable event in a different time and place. But Fulbright and his colleagues remained unimpressed, and much of the nation still wondered what was truly going on.

In October 1967, during what is often considered the first great protest rally against the Vietnam War, "March on the Pentagon" protesters make their point near Washington, D.C.'s Capitol mall reflecting pool. *(Frank Wolfe, Lyndon B. Johnson Library)*

Indeed, enemy activity was down, but, privately, Westmoreland's command was at odds over what it meant. During the top secret White House discussions before his congressional speech, Westmoreland had admitted that enemy supply lines from North to South Vietnam had not yet been adequately disrupted by U.S. bombing and that the South Vietnamese military was still struggling, and he urged the president to support a "scorched earth" offensive that would totally destroy enemy-held districts near Saigon and along the

Laos/Cambodian borders. A slow liberation of South Vietnam was more than possible, he concluded.

To Representative Allard Lowenstein and a small coalition of northeastern and midwestern liberal Democrats, nothing was possible in Vietnam, Johnson had lost touch with original Great Society goals, and he did not deserve the Democratic Party's nomination in 1968. Like the antiwar movement, Lowenstein's lobbying effort won the attention of the press. A president elected by a record landslide less than four years before was being denied reelection by a handful of party activists. That, of course, was news. On its own, Lowenstein's "Dump Johnson" organization had little chance of success. Instead, a combination of factors was already working against the president's political fortunes. Vietnam, urban riots, growing economic worries, youth alienation, and the Great Society itself were all matters of concern for voters by the end of 1967. These had not been issues in 1964, making Johnson more vulnerable than electable.[7]

For all effective purposes, few were worrying about the future of Lyndon Johnson. It was the future of the country that suddenly seemed so uncertain. CBS's Walter Cronkite summed up the situation well when he said in a Christmas 1967 broadcast that 1968 promised to be a "mystery year" where anything could happen. This truly proved to be the case.

CHRONICLE OF EVENTS

1966

January 2: Throughout the United States, cigarette packages are required to display health hazard warnings.

January 4: A white service station attendant, Marvin Segrest (67) is charged with the murder of Samuel Younge, Jr. (21), a black civil rights activist, in Tuskegee, Alabama.

January 10: Vernon Dahmer, a black 58-year-old civil rights leader in Hattiesburg, Mississippi, dies of burns received during a firebombing of his home.

January 11: The Justice Department files suit against five Southern states to compel full integration of their schools by fall 1966.

January 17: Robert Weaver becomes the first African American to serve as a cabinet secretary. He is appointed to head the Department of Housing and Urban Development.

January 19: While refueling off the coast of Spain, two U.S. military planes collide and drop four hydrogen bombs into the Mediterranean Sea. Only one of the bombs is recovered intact. Two of them are damaged, leaking radioactive particles onto the sea floor. The fourth and largest bomb (20-megatons) requires an extensive search, recovery, and deep burial operation.

January 22: The Democratic party of Alabama drops its motto of "White Supremacy."

January 24: President Johnson sends a record budget to Congress, asking for more than $112 billion.

January 31: Following a two-month "respite," the U.S. Air Force resumes bombing missions over North Vietnam. The bombing followed the Hanoi government's refusal to consider an American "peace offensive."

January 31: General Motors reports a record car industry profit of $2.1 billion for 1965.

February 5: In an effort to counter Soviet military hardware sales to several Middle East nations, the United States offers 200 tanks to Israel.

At the 1966 Honolulu Conference, President Johnson and Secretary of Defense McNamara meet with South Vietnamese political rivals Prime Minister Nguyen Cao Ky and Lieutenant General Nguyen Van Thieu. *(Yoichi Okamoto, Lyndon B. Johnson Library)*

February 6–8: While a Senate investigation of his Vietnam policy begins in Washington, President Johnson travels to Honolulu to meet with South Vietnamese Premier Ky and U.S. military leaders. Ky promises never to negotiate with Vietcong representatives. He also rejects any coalition government arrangement with them.

February 9: Vice president Humphrey arrives in South Vietnam promising Great Society–style programs for the Ky government.

February 14: The White House announces the engagement of the president's daughter Luci Baines to Patrick Nugent of Waukegan, Illinois.

February 23: Secretary of Defense Robert McNamara announces that it will be difficult for communist forces in Vietnam to make up for their heavy losses of 1965.

March 1: Following two weeks of heavy debate over Vietnam, Congress approves an "Emergency Fund" of nearly $5 million to assist the U.S. military throughout Southeast Asia.

March 5: In the third Japanese air disaster in a month, a 707 passenger jet crashes near Mount Fuji. Of the 124 killed, 75 are American citizens.

March 10–16: Thousands of Buddhists protest the corruption of the Ky regime in South Vietnam. Ky promises reform if he is confirmed the winner of a special election.

March 12: Thomas Bennett White, a 43-year-old white man, is charged with the attempted murder on March 11 of Donald Sims, a black U.S. Army captain, while he was talking on a public telephone in Bogalusa, Louisiana.

March 16: President Johnson signs a tax increase bill ($6 billion) to help pay for the Vietnam War.

March 16: *Gemini 8* astronauts Neil A. Armstrong and David R. Scott successfully complete an unprecedented docking operation, but they are later forced to abort their mission due to mechanical trouble.

March 24: The U.S. Supreme Court rules that a state cannot charge a "fee" (or poll tax) on its voting residents.

March 25–27: Anti–Vietnam War rallies are held in seven U.S. cities. The New York rally gathers a conservatively estimated 25,000 protesters, indicating that the antiwar movement has support outside of university campuses.

March 29: Responding to published government figures indicating an economic decline, President Johnson promises cuts in government spending and increases in corporate as well as personal income taxes "if necessary."

March 31: In a daring heist that fascinates the American press, four men rob an expensive Miami Beach hotel of $2 million in cash and valuables.

April 18: Sex researchers William Masters and Virginia Johnson publish their controversial *Human Sexual Response* findings.

May 1: After taking fire from Vietcong troops across the South Vietnamese border in Cambodia, the American First Infantry Division shells the enemy positions. This is the first U.S. military action on neutral Cambodian soil.

May 5–11: In a dramatic speech, Senator J. William Fulbright, chairman of the Senate Foreign Relations Committee, accuses the presidency of taking on imperial powers during its conduct of the Vietnam War. President Johnson defends his policies, and former presidential candidate Barry Goldwater urges that Fulbright resign due to his "attack" on a wartime president.

May 6: Senator Abraham Ribicoff, chairman of the Senate Subcommittee on Safety, reports that one out of every five automobiles made in the United States leaves the factory in a defective condition.

May 18: Secretary of Defense McNamara proposes that every young man in the United States should serve two years in the military or Peace Corps.

May 23: Twice-elected Representative Julian Bond, a leading civil rights spokesperson, is denied his seat in the Georgia legislature after making an antiwar speech.

May 30: Only 12 days following landmark surgery that gave her an artificial heart, Louise Ceraso dies in a Brooklyn hospital.

June 3: *Gemini IX-A* takes off for a three-day mission. Piloted by Eugene Cernan and commanded by Thomas Stafford, the spacecraft fails to dock with an orbiting Agena rocket due to a defective shroud that would not detach from it. Despite this complication, Cernan is able to complete a two-hour space walk (EVA, extravehicular activity).

June 5: During a 220-mile walk to encourage the registration of African-American voters, civil rights activist James Meredith is shot three times in Mississippi. Meredith survives, insisting that he had been denied federal protection throughout his march.

Astronauts Eugene Cernan (*right*) and Thomas Stafford try their best to look composed. Both men were selected to replace Elliot See and Charlie Bassett for the 1966 *Gemini IX-A* flight. See and Bassett were killed in training. *(NASA)*

June 9: Packing sustained winds of 100 miles per hour, Hurricane Alma hits the Gulf Coast. Alma destroys Crawfordsville, Florida, killing four people.

June 13: In the landmark *Miranda v. Arizona* decision, the Supreme Court requires police officers to remind all those arrested of their civil rights/civil liberties at the time of their arrest.

June 28–29: The National Organization for Women is founded, although not officially incorporated until February 1967.

June 29: Hanoi, North Vietnam, is specially targeted for the first time by the U.S. military. In one of the largest air raids of the war thus far, American jets based in Thailand or on navy carriers in the Tonkin Gulf destroy two-thirds of North Vietnam's oil supplies.

July 1: Ignoring strong American protests, President Charles de Gaulle of France orders the closing of the NATO headquarters in Paris. NATO is quickly transferred to Casteau, Belgium.

July 12: On this hot summer night, looting, firebombing, and protests begin in Chicago's impoverished West Side. Unemployment, racial tensions, poor living conditions, and the heat are all given as reasons for the rioting. Additional disturbances soon begin in Cleveland, Brooklyn, Omaha, Baltimore, San Francisco, and Jacksonville.

Searching for enthusiastic allies to back his Vietnam policies, President Johnson relaxes with the new president of the Philippines, Ferdinand Marcos, and his wife, Imelda, during the Manila Conference. A number of Southeast Asian leaders pledge their support to Johnson at this gathering to find "many flags" that oppose communist threats in South Vietnam. *(Yoichi Okamoto, Lyndon B. Johnson Library)*

July 12: The Hanoi government announces that captured American pilots will be tried and executed as war criminals. The United Nations and the Vatican lobby to change Hanoi's mind and succeed.

July 13: Eight student nurses are murdered in Chicago by Richard Speck.

July 23: President Johnson announces that the U.S. military is truly on the verge of victory in Vietnam.

August 1: Charles Whitman, a 24-year-old honors student, shoots his wife and mother at home, climbs the tower of the University of Texas–Austin, and shoots 47 others. After 90 minutes of gunfire, Whitman is killed by police.

September 6: Longtime women's rights and birth control advocate Margaret Sanger dies at age 88.

September 8: Opening to mediocre reviews and a limited audience, future cult classic *Star Trek* premieres on NBC television.

October 24–25: President Johnson meets a number of Asian/Pacific region leaders in Manila. They pledge their support for "self-determination" in Southeast Asia.

October 26: President Johnson visits the U.S. military base at Camranh Bay, South Vietnam, and decorates a number of wounded veterans.

October 30: Housewives in more than a dozen states organize boycotts against U.S. supermarket chains in an effort to bring down prices.

November 8: To President Johnson's surprise, Republicans gain three Senate seats and 47 House seats in the congressional elections.

November 17: Arthur Davis, age 26—convicted in New Haven, Connecticut, of killing six people during an August 1966 shooting spree—is sentenced to die in the electric chair.

December: The Motion Picture Association of America reports that the top three moneymaking films of 1966 are *Thunderball, Doctor Zhivago,* and *Who's Afraid of Virginia Woolf?* The top box office draws are Julie Andrews, Sean Connery, and Elizabeth Taylor.

December: The Associated Press reports that the top three single record hits of 1966 are "The Ballad of the Green Berets" by Staff Sergeant Barry Sadler, "Winchester Cathedral" by the New Vaudeville Band, and "96 Tears" by ? and the Mysterians.

December 1: More than 5,000 people rally in Berkeley, California, to protest the arrest of six students jailed for interfering with U.S. Navy recruiting on campus.

December 10: During one "friendly fire accident" in South Vietnam, 16 Marines are killed and 11 are wounded.

December 26: The Pentagon admits that civilian neighborhoods in Hanoi and other North Vietnamese cities have been "accidentally" bombed during U.S. air assaults.

1967

January: Britain's Rolling Stones appear on *The Ed Sullivan Show.* Their rendition of "Let's Spend the Night Together" stimulates a month-long debate in the press over "suggestive song lyrics."

January 3: Jack Ruby, Lee Harvey Oswald's killer, dies in a Dallas hospital of a blood clot and cancer.

January 8: The largest offensive of the Vietnam War to this date takes place in the "Iron Triangle," only 25 miles northwest of Saigon. Some 16,000 Americans and 14,000 South Vietnamese troops are involved in the fight.

January 15: The NFL champion Green Bay Packers defeat the AFL champion Kansas City Chiefs 35–10 in the first Superbowl.

January 18–26: President Ky of South Vietnam visits the Australian and New Zealand governments to

The victorious Green Bay Packers pose for their team photo of 1967. *(Green Bay Packers Photo Archives)*

thank them for their support. He is met by thousands of angry demonstrators throughout his trip.

January 27: A treaty restricting the military exploitation of outer space is signed in special ceremonies in Moscow, London, and Washington.

January 27: NASA experiences its first human tragedy when three astronauts, Virgil "Gus" Grissom, Roger Chaffee, and Edward White, die in a fire on board *Apollo 1* during an exercise on the launch pad.

January 29: Former Senate staffer Bobby Baker is found guilty on seven charges ranging from income tax evasion to stealing campaign funds.

January 31: The U.S. Commerce Department gives the U.S. auto industry four months to comply with 20 new safety standards.

February 5: The first episode of the politically controversial but popular *Smothers Brothers Comedy Hour* begins on CBS television.

February 7: A blizzard, described as one of the worst in American history, paralyzes the East Coast from Maryland to Massachusetts.

In what would become one of television's more controversial "comedy hours," the Smothers Brothers pose for a calm and sedate CBS promotional shoot. *(Courtesy of Knave Productions, Inc.)*

February 18: New Orleans district attorney Jim Garrison announces that there was a plot to kill President Kennedy. He promises arrests and convictions in the matter.

March 3: Arguing that the 19th Amendment never did enough for the cause of women's rights, Senator Eugene McCarthy (Democrat of Minnesota) introduces an Equal Rights Amendment (ERA) for women in the U.S. Senate.

March 8: Vice President Humphrey is doused in yellow paint by eight antiwar demonstrators.

March 21: The Johnson administration announces to the press that Ho Chi Minh has turned down all offers of peaceful negotiations.

March 22: Transferring from Anderson Air Base on the U.S. territory of Guam, America's B-52 bombing raids begin originating from bases in Thailand. A special U.S.-Thailand agreement was required to secure this transfer, and it saves thousands of flight miles for U.S. pilots.

April 4: Martin Luther King, Jr., denounces the disproportionate number of black troops versus white troops in Vietnam. He urges draft resistance for both blacks and whites at home, and he condemns Washington's "exporting" of violence abroad.

April 10: Black students riot at Nashville's Fisk University after hearing a "black power" speech by activist Stokely Carmichael.

April 13: In Peoria, Illinois, Richard Speck is convicted of murdering eight student nurses the previous year.

April 19: *Surveyor 3* lands on the moon to map and photograph landing sites for an upcoming manned space flight there.

April 21: Svetlana Aliluyeva, the 42-year-old daughter of the late Soviet dictator, Joseph Stalin, defects to the United States. In a press conference, she claims that those in charge of the current Soviet government once assisted her father in "crimes against humanity."

April 28: The heavyweight boxing champion of the world, Muhammad Ali, announces his refusal to serve in the U.S. Army. In quick response, the World Boxing Association strips him of his title.

May 2: Led by British philosopher Bertrand Russell, the International Tribunal on War Crimes meets in Stockholm, Sweden. They find the United States guilty of "crimes of aggression" in Vietnam.

New York Yankee baseball star Mickey Mantle hits his 500th home run in a game against the Baltimore Orioles. *(National Baseball Hall of Fame Library/Cooperstown, N.Y.)*

May 13: Directed by veterans group, labor union locals, and fraternal organizations, a demonstration of 70,000 marchers takes place in downtown New York City. It is held to voice support for the Vietnam War as well as condemn the antiwar movement.

May 14: New York Yankee Mickey Mantle hits his 500th home run against the Baltimore Orioles.

May 16: The Tennessee legislature repeals the so-called Monkey Law, which forbids the teaching of evolution in state-supported schools.

June 2: A long-awaited new album by the Beatles (*Sgt. Pepper's Lonely Hearts Club Band*) is released and becomes an instant hit.

June 8: Israeli torpedo boats attack the U.S.S. *Liberty* during the Arab-Israeli Six-Day War, killing 34 U.S. Navy personnel. The Israeli government apologizes for the "mistake." Some members of the press and U.S. government charge that it was a deliberate attack to halt *Liberty* eavesdropping operations.

June 12: The U.S. Supreme Court nullifies a Virginia law banning interracial marriages.

June 30: President Johnson extends the draft for four more years.

July 12: Race riots begin in Newark, New Jersey, resulting in 26 deaths and 1,500 injuries.

July 21: The Johnson administration reports a $9.9 billion deficit. It is the largest recorded peacetime deficit in American history.

July 23: A national black power convention in Newark, New Jersey, calls for armed rebellion against white racism and for the possible division of the United States into white and black nations.

July 23–30: A race riot in Detroit leaves 40 dead and 2,000 injured. For the first time in 24 years, federal troops are mandated to restore the civil peace. More than $300 million in property damage is reported.

July 23: Puerto Rico votes to remain a commonwealth, rejecting statehood as well as independence.

July 24: While visiting North America, French President Charles de Gaulle declares his solidarity behind the separatist movement in French-speaking Quebec by shouting on the steps of the Montreal City Hall: "Vive Québec Libre!" ("Long Live Free Quebec!") The speech is denounced by both the Canadian and American governments.

August 25: George Lincoln Rockwell, the director of the American Nazi Party, is shot and killed.

September 30: President Johnson signs the biggest defense appropriations bill in the nation's history ($70 billion).

October 2: Thurgood Marshall becomes the first black Supreme Court justice.

October 4: The month-long communist siege of Conthien, a U.S. Marine base near the North Vietnam border, ends. Some 3,000 North Vietnamese troops are reported killed.

October 6: The hippie community of San Francisco stages a public rally to oppose police harassment and poor housing policies.

October 21–22: More than 35,000 antiwar protesters rally in Washington. Nearly 650 of them are arrested while attempting to enter the Pentagon.

October 25: The newly formed Citizens Committee for Peace with Freedom in Vietnam offers its full support to President Johnson's Vietnam policy. Its membership includes many wealthy Americans as well as former Presidents Truman and Eisenhower.

November 7: General Lewis Hershey orders draft boards to put student antiwar activists who hold university/college deferments at the top of the draft lists if they interfere with the daily work of selective service offices.

November 29: Secretary of Defense McNamara announces that he will be leaving the Johnson administration to become president of the World Bank. Other than stating that America's Vietnam policy will continue to remain on course, McNamara has no further comment about his decision.

December: The Motion Picture Association of America reports that the top three box office successes of 1967 are *The Dirty Dozen, You Only Live Twice,* and *Casino Royale.* The top three box office draws are Julie Andrews, Lee Marvin, and Paul Newman.

December: The Associated Press reports that the top three single records of 1967 are "I'm a Believer" by the Monkees, "To Sir With Love" by Lulu, and "The Letter" by the Box Tops.

December 2: The pro-hippie and sexually liberated rock musical *Hair* premieres in New York, stimulating a national debate on "artistic expression."

December 12: Enemy mortar shells land only a few feet from Senator Charles Percy (Republican of Illinois) during a visit to a U.S. firebase in South Vietnam.

December 15: Congress approves an additional $1.77 billion for President Johnson's war on poverty.

December 15: During rush-hour traffic, a suspension bridge between Kanauga, Ohio, and Point Pleasant, West Virginia, collapses, killing 18 people. Another 30 are reported missing.

December 23: While visiting the Vatican, President Johnson tells Pope Paul VI that he hopes to conclude peace with the North Vietnamese in 1968.

EYEWITNESS TESTIMONY

Vietnam Issues

Slowly, but like lava pouring over a volcano, the flow is resistless—first, one concession then another, and then another, and as we adjust to each new position, we go onto the next retreat point until Fulbright and his allies pick up the new line and cut deeper into the American position.

> *White House aide Jack Valenti warning President Johnson that Senator J. William Fulbright and other congressional critics of the Vietnam War might succeed in turning U.S. opinion against his administration, in Valenti to Johnson, May 13, 1966, Office Files of the President, Box 2/Jack Valenti, Lyndon Johnson Library.*

I had the feeling that we have taken the initiative. We are beginning to really explain to the world about Vietnam, about what we can do, about the promise of this epoch in history—that we are on the move against the negation of war and communism. It was exciting. I felt as if the stalemate had had a firecracker put under it.

> *First Lady Lady Bird Johnson, noting in September 1966 that her husband's 1965 and 1966 speeches and press conferences about Vietnam are well done, in her* A White House Diary (1970), *Research Room, Lyndon Johnson Library.*

We are willing to lay on the table at any moment our schedule for withdrawal from Vietnam, if someone can also lay on the table their schedule of withdrawal—and if we can give the freedom-loving, liberty-loving people of Vietnam any assurance that

In 1966, President Johnson queries Senator Robert Kennedy about his position on Vietnam. Kennedy does not move strongly against the war until his later campaign for president. *(Yoichi Okamoto, Lyndon B. Johnson Library)*

they will not be murdered, assassinated, or killed either by infiltrators or assassins. Our Secretary of State will meet any of them whenever they need to—tomorrow, next day, or next week. I will lay our schedule on the table any day that anyone will act upon it. But we cannot say to our men that we will strip you of all of your protection and say to our allies that we will afford you no assistance without some assurance from someone else. . . . We will lay on the table our plans to withdraw if they will lay on the table their plans to cease their aggression.

President Johnson, during a September 8, 1966, press conference, responding to a charge from France's Charles de Gaulle that the United States has no interest in a Vietnam peace, in The Public Papers of President Lyndon B. Johnson, 1966, Speeches, *Lyndon Johnson Library.*

From the earliest days of this Republic, Senators have expressed themselves forcibly, eloquently—in most instances wisely. But while we always consider and evaluate and carefully look at what they suggest and take it into consideration, we don't always find that in the judgment of our more professional military leaders that this is always the wisest military judgment.

President Johnson, during an October 1966 press conference, responding to comments by Senator Strom Thurmond that the Vietnam War could be won in 90 days and remarks by Senator J. William Fulbright that U.S. troops could be home in 90 days, in The Public Papers of President Lyndon B. Johnson, 1966, *Speeches, Lyndon Johnson Library.*

I, as you know, have not proven to be the most reliable forecaster in the past, and I don't wish to run the risk of proving unreliable in the future. So I won't have any predictions of what lies ahead.

Secretary of Defense McNamara in November 1966, dodging a reporter's question about whether U.S. victory in Vietnam is possible sometime during 1967, in The Public Papers of President Lyndon B. Johnson, 1966, Speeches, *Lyndon Johnson Library.*

There are signs that the administration is getting fed up with the deceit, wrong decisions and dictatorial arrogance of Robert Strange McNamara, the man who never yet has been right about Vietnam or any other military matter. The major visible sign of

McNamara's slippage in the court of LBJ is the fact that, for the first time, military men seem free to voice the opposition to McNamara which always has been present. . . . The fact that the chiefs are now fighting him openly can only mean, it seems to me, that there is certain knowledge now that the White House is withdrawing some of that support.

Senator Barry Goldwater noting that the Vietnam War can be won, but that Secretary of Defense McNamara must resign first, quoted in his "Is McNamara Less Popular?," Atlanta Constitution, *September 7, 1967, p. 1.*

I do not believe that Hanoi is presently likely to enter into serious discussions. But I think that it is important in terms of both circumstances and public relations that we test that possibility to the hilt. I do not think we pay a heavy price in delaying hitting again a very small percentage of the targets in North Vietnam. We know that destruction of those targets this week or next can have absolutely no significance in terms of the conduct of the war. There is an outside chance that it could have some impact on the search for peace. And I would play along with that chance—which I acknowledge to be very small indeed—because the consequences are so great.

White House cabinet member Nicholas Katzenbach daring to challenge the president's Vietnam policy, putting his job on the line, and urging Johnson to take peace negotiations with the North Vietnamese seriously, in Katzenbach to Johnson, September 26, 1967, National Security File of the Papers of Walt W. Rostow, Lyndon Johnson Library.

It is time that this Administration stopped sitting back and taking it from the Vietnam critics. Every day, Senators attack us and return to the attack encouraged by our silence, while professional agitators in our own party are trying to wreck the party and others are spending huge sums to set Labor against us . . . [and] set up Martin Luther King. We have got a psychological war as well as a military war on our hands, and the Communists are winning the psychological war with our help.

President Johnson, during an October 4, 1967, cabinet meeting, pondering an offensive position against his Vietnam critics, in Box 10 of the Papers of Lyndon B. Johnson, Cabinet, Lyndon Johnson Library.

We are going to stand for limited objectives. We are going to try to keep from widening the war. We are going to try to deter aggression and to permit self-determination in South Vietnam. And when that is done, we are going to be content. We do not want bases, domination, colonization. We do not practice colonialism. We seek to do nothing except keep our commitments—try to help innocent people who want the right to live according to their own self-determination.

President Johnson, during a November 1967 lull in the Vietnam War, explaining to the press that America is on the verge of fulfilling its commitments to the Saigon regime, in The Public Papers of President Lyndon B. Johnson, Speeches, 1967, Lyndon Johnson Library.

There is nothing in the past reaction of the North Vietnamese leaders that would provide any confidence that they can be bombed to the negotiating table. . . .

The capacity of the lines of communication and of the outside sources of supply so far exceeds the minimal flow necessary to support the present level of North Vietnamese military effort in South Vietnam that the enemy operations in the South cannot, on the basis of any reports I have seen, be stopped by air bombardment—short, that is, of the virtual annihilation of North Vietnam and its people. . . .

The tragic and drawn out character of the conflict in the South makes very tempting the prospect of replying to it with some kind of new air campaign against the North. But however tempting, such an alternative seems to me completely illusory. To pursue this objective would not only be futile,

Largely a collection of longtime cold war advocates and staunch anticommunists, the "Wise Men" meet in the White House to advise President Johnson on Vietnam. *(Yoichi Okamoto, Lyndon B. Johnson Library)*

but would involve risks to our personnel and to our nation that I am unwilling to recommend.

Robert McNamara explaining his position on the August to November 1967 airwar in Vietnam to a group of concerned congressmen and reporters, quoted in McNamara, Argument Without End *(1999), p. 252.*

1. What could we do that we are not doing in South Vietnam? 2. Concerning the North, should we continue what we are doing, should we mine the ports and take out the dikes, or should we eliminate our bombing of the North altogether? 3. Should we adopt a passive policy of willingness to negotiate, should we aggressively seek negotiations, or should we bow out? 4. Should we get out of Vietnam? 5. What positive steps should the administration take to unite and better communicate with the nation?

President Johnson asking his foreign policy advisers to ponder five questions and find concrete answers before the end of the year, in McNamara, In Retrospect *(1995), p. 306.*

We believe the enemy can be forced to be "reasonable," i.e. to compromise or even capitulate, because we assume he wants to avoid pain, death, and material destruction. We assume that if these are inflicted on him with increasing severity, then at some point in the process he will want to stop the suffering. . . .

The strategy of the weak is therefore a natural choice of ideologues in Asia, for it converts Asia's capacity for endurance in suffering into an instrument for exploiting. . . . It does this, in effect, by inviting the West, which possesses unanswerable military power, to carry its strategic logic to its final conclusion, which is genocide.

Veteran diplomat and McNamara associate Townsend Hoopes reviewing the late 1967 Vietnam situation, in Hoopes, The Limits of Intervention *(1969), pp. 128–129*

Do you understand what that means, when you ask for more bombing? It means you are voting to send people, Americans and Vietnamese, to die. . . . Don't you understand that what we are doing to the Viet-namese is not very different than what Hitler did to the Jews?

In late November 1967, a shocked Sen. Robert Kennedy responding to a group of female students at Marymount College in Tarrytown, New York, who have just urged him to vote for an escalated airwar over North Vietnam, in Newfield, Robert Kennedy: A Memoir *(1969), p. 153*

Every war critic capable of producing a headline contributed, in proportion to his eminence, some comfort if not aid to the enemy.

General Maxwell Taylor accusing the antiwar movement in late November 1967 of prolonging the agony of the Vietnam War, quoted by McNamara in his "Vietnam Legacy," speech within the John F. Kennedy Library Seminar on Vietnam, May 1995.

The war in Southeast Asia cannot take the blame for the whole of our inflationary and balance of payments problems, but it is obvious that it must share a large part of them.

Robert Shaffer, the senior economist with the Bank of America during the late 1960s, testifying before Congress in December 1967 that the Vietnam War has seriously harmed U.S. economic influence in the world, quoted in Stevens, Vain Hopes, Grim Realities: The Economic Consequences of the Vietnam War *(1976), p. 231.*

Drug Culture, Film Culture, and Trends

My theory was that a good American chassis with a reliable V-8 engine moved back 28 and 1/2 inches in the frame, with a nostalgic body, could have an appeal to many more men who wanted to play at this sport. In fact, I referred to the car as a "two-way" classic, jokingly referring to my Museum cars which have, on occasion, only made it one way to a meet.

I felt it was entirely possible to convince many a housewife to put aside, for one occasion at least, the desire for a mink stole in order that the family might enjoy even going to market in a contemporary classic. At the press preview we were deluged with pho-

At Milwaukee's new Domes conservatory, a dapper Brooks Stevens poses with mink stole-clad supermodel "Yolanda" behind the just-released 1965 Excalibur Series One sports car. *(Courtesy of Alice Preston, Camelot Classic Cars, Inc.)*

tographers, overseas journalists, and American writers who for the most part said, "We don't need a script, we have been hoping for a long time that someone would do this sometime."

Designer Brooks Stevens explaining to an early 1966 convention of automotive engineers what motivated his creation of the surprisingly successful Excalibur Motor Company, in Stevens, The Excalibur Story *or* The Development of the Contemporary Classic *(1966), p. 3.*

MADNESS!! AUDITIONS! Folk and Rock Musicians-Singers for acting roles in new TV series. Running parts for four insane boys, age 17–21. Want spirited Ben Frank's types. Have courage to work. Must come down for interview.

Soliciting in January 1966 for four actor/singers to star in a new NBC television series called The Monkees, *in* Hollywood Advertiser, *January 1966, back cover.*

Maybe the Motown sound is just love and warmth. Like a family, we all work together, fight and kiss all day long. You see someone you haven't seen in an hour, and you've got to hug and kiss.

Mary Wilson of the Supremes telling Time *magazine that Detroit-based pop music is mostly about African-American family harmony, in Staff, "The Girls from Motown,"* Time, *March 4, 1966, pp. 83–84.*

Shortly past 1 a.m. a swarm of cops suddenly materialized; they bore arms and a search warrant and spoke in brusque prose of the workaday world. "You're under arrest," said one of them on entering Leary's bedroom. "Let me put my pants on," rejoined Leary, clothed only in his constitutional rights and a pajama top.

In just this way, the 45-year old high priest of LSD found his experience with the reality of the law unexpectedly expanding. Already facing a 30-year Federal prison sentence for transporting marijuana, Leary was now slapped with a new charge of possessing marijuana. So were three of the two dozen or so guests occupying various parts of the house at the time of the raid. Leary and the others waived preliminary hearings, but he flatly denied the charge—without disputing that the raiders may have found some pot somewhere on the premises. Leary put it wryly to a reporter: "You don't expect that 30 policemen could search this house for five hours without finding something, do you?"

Newsweek magazine chronicling the arrest of drug use advocate and propagandist Dr. Timothy Leary, in Staff, "On and Off," Newsweek, May 2, 1966, pp. 21–22.

If the chopped-off skirt is a fashion of protest, it is also fashion that suits an increasingly hedonistic society. There is a growing appreciation of the sensual. Not just the pure hedonistic philosophy of eat, drink and be merry, but of anything that delights the eye and the senses. People are less puritanical. The trend towards nudity can't go too far, or it becomes self-defeating. If everyone were nude, it wouldn't be interesting.

Professor of sociology Bernard Barber telling fashion writer Phyllis Lee Levin that the miniskirt is here to stay, but public nudity displays are a temporary phenomenon, in Lee, "The Short Short Story of the Skirt," Readers Digest, June 1966, pp. 112–114.

Secret Agent Maxwell Smart and his beautiful assistant, Agent 99, are searching a ship for an enemy spy. Suddenly a huge wooden mast crashes down.

"Ninety-nine, this ship is a freighter, right?"
"Right, Max."
"And freighters run on fuel oil, right?"
"Right again, Max."

"And wooden masts belong on sailboats, correct?"
"Exactly."
"And this is a wooden mast."
"Go on, Max."
"Ninety-nine. . . ."
"Yes?"
"I forgot where I started."

TV stars Don Adams and Barbara Feldon holding a typical conversation on their hit NBC sitcom Get Smart, in Smith, "Would You Believe Don Adams?," Saturday Evening Post, June 4, 1966, pp. 32–33.

I want to do something with my life. I want definitely to get out of this psychedelic state. Because I feel that every time I use LSD I lose more and more of my mind, of my sanity. I feel that if I use it again I will blow my mind completely. I mean, it is very good to have no ego, so they say. But you must have some. You have to have something. . . .

I had given up work by then, sold my agency for a few dollars to live on. When you're on LSD you just don't care about anything. I remember saying to a friend who owns an art gallery, "Why are you working? Just so that one day you can collect sick benefits, old-age benefits. Why don't you do the things you want to do?"

He looked at me, and suddenly he said, "But Iris, are you doing the things that you want to do?" And I cried, because I wasn't. It wasn't what I really wanted to do. I could have done a lot with my life.

LSD user Iris Michele telling her story to the readers of the Ladies' Home Journal, in Michele, "I Tried LSD," Ladies' Home Journal, August 1966, pp. 52–54.

Christianity will go. It will vanish and shrink. I needn't argue about that: I'm right, and I will be proved right. We're more popular than Jesus Christ right now; I don't know which will go first—rock 'n' roll or Christianity. Jesus was all right, but his disciples were thick and ordinary. It's them twisting it that ruins it for me.

Beatle John Lennon creating a summer 1966 media controversy with his comments about Christianity and popular figures to a London journalist, in Staff, "According to John," Time, August 12, 1966, p. 38.

If you ask me, the question is not whether the Beatles are more popular than Jesus but whether information is more popular than knowledge, which it is. That is one of the curses of modern man. We are all Infomaniacs, and our only god Info. Actually, I see Info as the goddess of Thin Milk; she feeds us only what can never nourish our souls and bring our thoughts to maturation.

> The New Yorker *magazine complaining in the summer of 1966 that John Lennon's comments that the Beatles are more popular than Jesus are part of a larger problem, in Staff, "Notes and Comment,"* The New Yorker, *August 27, 1966, pp. 21–22.*

At 3:30 p.m., he said: "I feel terribly strange." Tom handed him a small toy animal he had played with as an infant.

Charley cuddled the toy, kissed it, and said: "There's something very reassuring about this." . . . Charley lay with a peaceful look on his face, cuddling the toy animal.

Tom lay down outside on a deck adjoining the bedroom and his face, too, filled with peacefulness. . . .

It was a wonderful few moments for me. I felt very much at one with Charley and I knew he was living for a while as a five-year-old child. . . . The guide grows in this experience of giving. What a privilege it is to be with another person in this way! No words can describe it.

> Harper's *magazine describing the experiences of Charley, an LSD user, and his LSD "guide" Tom, in Todd, "Turned-On and Super-Sincere in California,"* Harper's, *January 1967, pp. 42–47.*

The Graduate project, originally a novel by a young writer named Charles Webb, was brought to Nichols's attention by Turman, who was struck by the story's "pertinence to the present scene." Benjamin, says the 40-year-old Turman, reflects an important element in today's youth. "Benjamin's personality reflects a wildness, yet an underlying decency," says Turman. The fact that Benjamin is wealthy is all the more attractive, he adds. "It adds pungency to the character in relation to today's affluent society."

The setting for the story is Southern California, and Nichols, a man who is not exactly bowled over by the area, plans to shoot the film on location and "show the place as it really is."

> The New York Times *examines the reasoning behind film director Mike Nichols and producer Lawrence Turman's decision to film* The Graduate, *in Bart, "Mike Nichols, Moviemaniac,"* New York Times, *January 1, 1967, pp. 1–3. URL: http://www.geocities.com/hollywood/8200/times.htm.*

There's a significantly greater communication between the music itself, the people who make it, and the people who listen to it than there was in Elvis Presley's day. One difference is that Elvis never had "acid rock" going for him. . . . It doesn't matter what the lyrics say, or who sings them. They're all the same. They say, be free—free in love, free in sex.

> Former professional model turned lead singer of the Jefferson Airplane, Grace Slick, explaining "acid rock" to Time *magazine in January 1967, in Staff, "Open Up, Tune In, Turn On,"* Time, *January 23, 1967, p. 53.*

For the strangers who were molded into Monkees, it was the classic Cinderella story told four times over. Just before Mike Nesmith answered the ad, his 1956 station wagon had been repossessed by a finance company. Mickey Dolenz was subsisting on unemployment allotments, and Peter Tork earned $50 a week washing dishes. And tiny Davy Jones, a licensed British disc jockey, seriously contemplated a return to the Newmarket turf. Within a few months after becoming The Monkees they were receiving 5,000 fan letters a day and moving their licensed merchandise as fast as James Bond's car.

> Music and film critic Richard Warren Lewis reviewing the early history of the 1967 pop rock music phenomenon the Monkees in Lewis, "When Four Nice Boys Go Ape!," Saturday Evening Post, *January 28, 1967, pp. 74–78.*

I wouldn't call it camp. Camp means something so trite and dumb that it's in. This isn't the case with posters. They are completely new, fun, kooky and cool.

> Wellesley College student Peggy Lawrence explaining to Newsweek *magazine why she and fellow students across America are hanging political posters in their apartments and dorms in March 1967, in Staff, "The Coolest Things,"* Newsweek, *March 6, 1967, p. 87.*

The Beach Boys, a California quintet that grew up singing surfer and drag-racer anthems, have lately been experimenting with more complex sounds. Their recent "Good Vibrations" is surely the most electric 3 1/2 minute-piece of music ever to sell a million copies: Spanish chord patterns, art song lyrics, castrato pitch, theremin background, baroque harmonies, tempo variations, and the "ooh-bop-bop" of Piltdown rock 'n' roll.

Music critic Richard Corliss praising the latest Beach Boys album in April 1967, in Corliss, "Pop Music: What's Been Happening," National Review, *April 4, 1967, pp. 371–374.*

When you go back to your own communities, let radio stations know that you are behind this campaign. Your support at the grass-roots level will go a very long way toward arresting the cancerous growth of that irresponsible minority in the record and music industry which unconscionable countenances subtle or down-right salacious lyrics. . . . I must take stand in favor of a rather updated version of the Boston Tea Party. Two centuries later, I suppose we might call it The Wax Party—one in which we purge all the distasteful English records that deal with sex, sin and drugs.

In May 1967, while blaming the alleged loose morals of American youth on British invasion music, "clean radio" advocate Gordon McLendon calling for a total ban of imported British tunes, in Staff, "Manners and Morals," Time, *May 26, 1967, p. 53.*

I don't believe in the midi, or sweeping New York dirt into your apartment. Thus, in most collections, though skirts are floor length for evening, they fall somewhere above the knee for daytime, and are almost always to be worn with over-the-knee boots in soft glove leather or stretch vinyl. Come winter, those boots will offer women a promise even more welcome than the thrill of feeling like a buccaneer: an end to polar kneecap.

With the exception of formal evening wear, dress designer Pauline Trigere predicting in June 1967 that the miniskirt fashion will continue through the upcoming winter of 1967–68, in Staff, "Anyone She Wants to Be," Time, *June 23, 1967, p. 75.*

Seeing the film a second time and surrounded by an audience no more or less moronic than I, but enjoying itself almost to the point of rapture, I realized that "Bonnie and Clyde" knows perfectly well what to make of its violence, and makes a cogent statement with it—that violence is not necessarily perpetrated by shambling cavemen or quivering psychopaths but may also be the casual, easy expression of only slightly aberrated citizens, of jes' folks.

I had become so surfeited and preoccupied by violence in daily life that my reaction was as excessive as the stimulus. There are indeed a few moments in which the gore goes too far, becomes stock shockery that invites standard revulsion. And yet, precisely because "Bonnie and Clyde" combines these gratuitous crudities with scene after scene of dazzling artistry, precisely because it has the power both to enthrall and appall, it is an ideal laboratory for the study of violence, a subject in which we are all matriculating these days. Violent movies are an inevitable consequence of violent life. They may also transmit the violence virus, but they do not breed it any more than the Los Angeles television stations caused Watts to riot.

Movie critic Joseph Morgenstern praising the hit summer 1967 film Bonnie and Clyde, *while also noting that its violence mirrors the real life violence of 1960s America, in Morgenstern, "The Thin Red Line,"* Newsweek, *August 28, 1967, pp. 82–83.*

With characteristic self-mockery, the Beatles are proclaiming that they have snuffed out their old selves to make room for the new Beatles incarnate. And there is some truth to it. Without having lost any of the genial anarchism with which they helped revolutionize the life style of young people in Britain, Europe and the U.S., they have moved on to a higher artistic plateau.

Rich and secure enough to go on repeating themselves—or to do nothing at all—they have exercised a compulsion for growth, change and experimentation. Messengers from beyond rock 'n roll, they are creating the most original, expressive and musically interesting sounds being heard in pop music. They are leading an evolution in which the best of current post-rock sounds are becoming something that pop music has never been before: an art form.

Time magazine praising the Beatles's decision to embrace "politically and socially relevant" music in Staff, "The Messengers," Time, September 22, 1967, p. 60.

Every narrative and criminal act, as well as the nomadic, motor-court, episodic, hand-to-mouth life of this quintet, follows from one shared fact: they are all as stupid as stupid children, but without the innocence that animates even a stupid child. Bonnie alone shows an occasional flash of wit and creativity, and is impatient with the simple recreations of her partners (such as their appreciative in camera poking of C. W.'s tattooed torso). Yet she has been led into these drearily dangerous days and nights by her fascination with Clyde's pistol, his first serious attraction for her.

Arguing that the characters of the film Bonnie and Clyde are childlike ones who approach violence in a childlike way, film critic Marion Armstrong examining the top box office draw of mid- and late 1967, in Armstrong, "Study in Infantilism," The Christian Century, October 18, 1967, p. 1,326.

Swelling the ranks of superfluity, yet in a category all its own, is the "dynamic duo" of Batman and Robin, now entering another season of crime fighting, and with an even more dynamic trio which includes the latest answer to the diabolical underworld, Batgirl. With this acquisition of the most devastating weapon of all—Woman—the masked Trinity will undoubtedly put to an end forever the threat of crime and violence. The affiliation of a co-redemptrix with the "Saviors of Gotham City" seems a clear portent of the final eschaton. The one difficulty is that because the "caped crusaders" never really engage in lethal bloodletting (only polite fisticuffs: Bam, Sock, Whamo, Zap), and because no one is ever injured or killed (only temporarily suspended, to be resurrected in subsequent episodes), the actual ushering in of the millennium may be postponed indefinitely.

Having found both religious significance and sarcasm in ABC television's surprise hit Batman, television critic and Christian commentator M. Conrad Hyers explaining the show's appeal in fall 1967, in Hyers, "Batman and the Comic Profanation of the Sacred," The Christian Century, October 18, 1967, pp. 1,322–1,323.

The test of any new trend is acceptance. Long hair passes the test. During the protest stage some three years ago, when brow-shrouding male tresses bloomed all over the classroom, they drew down a withering fire from the academic Establishment. Today most of the hirsute scholars are back at their desks, tolerated if not entirely approved. We ignore it. We do absolutely nothing against long hair even if it's down to their heels.

Noting that long hair has simply become part of college life and fashion, C. W. McDonald, the dean of men at Washington State College, telling Time magazine in the fall of 1967 that hairstyles are not a threat to academe, in Staff, "Longer Hair Is Not Necessarily Hippie," Time, October 27, 1967, p. 46.

If Dustin Hoffman's face were his fortune, he'd be committed to a life of poverty. With a schnoz that looks like a directional signal, skittish black-beady eyes and a raggedly hair-cap, he stands a slight 5-foot-6, weighs a mere 134 pounds and slouches like a puppet dangling from string. All in all, he resembles a swarthy Pinocchio.

Yet this unlikely leading man has gone from off-Broadway character actor to Hollywood star in one nimble leap. Mike Nichols, comedian-turned-director whose first film effort was the Oscar-bedecked *Who's Afraid of Virginia Woolf?*, plucked Dusty out of nowhere and made him the non-hero of this new film, *The Graduate*. The role is that of an innocent college graduate, named Ben Braddock, catapulted into a corrupting world. The script depicts him as well-fed, well-bred and handsome—a "walking surfboard," Dusty calls him. At 30, he was a decade older than the character, but Nichols gambled that Dusty's talents would triumph over his appearance. He has won his gamble.

Life magazine film critic David Zeitlin praising Dustin Hoffman at the time of the premiere of the late 1967 box office smash, The Graduate, in Zeitlin, "The Graduate," Life, November 24, 1967, pp. 111–112.

Somebody called it wearing the hair in its "happy state" and in certain circles it is known as a "freedom cap." It's an "Afro" in the argot of the Black Nationalists, and it has even been described in such unusual terms as the "nappy explosion." Name it what you will, it's all about a phenomenon that has caught on with thousands of black men. . . . However, as a contemporary term of reference to black man's hair, Natural or "Afro" has come to mean a specific set of styles as well. To be sure, it has become fashionable to wear a Natural. But is it something more profound than mere fashion? "Naturals are a significant cultural trend," says actor Ivan Dixon. "They are part of the debrainwashing of a lot of our people."

> Ebony *magazine surveying the importance of the new hairstyle for black men, in Llorens, "Natural Hair: New Symbol of Race Pride,"* Ebony, *December 1967, pp. 139–144.*

Undeniably, part of the scandal and success of *Bonnie and Clyde* stems from its creative use of what has always been a good box-office draw: violence. But what matters most about *Bonnie and Clyde* is the new freedom of its style, expressed not so much by camera trickery as by its yoking of disparate elements into a coherent artistic whole—their creation of unity from incongruity. Blending humor and horror, it draws the audience in sympathy toward its anti-heroes. It is, at the same time, a commentary on the mindless daily violence of the American '60s, and an esthetic evocation of the past. Yet it observes the '30s not as lived but as remembered, the perspective rippled by the years to show that there are mirages of time as well as space. The nostalgic Technicolor romanticism alters reality, distorting it as a straight stick under water appears to be bent.

> Time *magazine, editors discussing the popular film* Bonnie and Clyde *and its significance in a lengthy, illustrated cover story in Staff,* "The Shock of Freedom in Films," Time, *December 8, 1967, p. 67.*

Maybe I should forget Christmas—it is only another day. But I know I cannot. I am a Catholic Christian, and the memory of Christmas is in my blood. It is a special time when I can more readily steal hours from my work. But I will not steal the time to rush about in pursuit of gifts or flood the mails with cards of canned sentiments or bribe my business contacts. Christmas is a sacred time when Christ told me that I count, that I must go on living to love the friends who need my human love. Christmas reminds me of

my own beauty and bids me to tell my loved ones of theirs.

> *Leading a headline-making "anti-materialist Christmas" movement in late 1967, former priest James Kavanaugh urging Americans to abandon their pop culture interests and embrace a spiritual holiday, in Kavanaugh, "Christmas Doesn't Mean Much Any More,"* Saturday Evening Post, *December 16, 1967, pp. 10–12.*

Civil Rights Activism in Transition

The act of registering to vote does several things. It marks the beginning of political modernization by broadening the base of participation. It also does something the existentialists talk about: it gives one a sense of being. The black man who goes to register is saying to the white man, "No." He is saying: "You have said that I cannot vote. You have said that this is my place. This is where I should remain. You have contained me and I am saying 'No' to your containment." . . . But obviously this is not enough. Once the black man has knocked back centuries of fear, once he is willing to resist, he then must decide how best to use that vote. To listen to those whites who conspired for so many years to deny him the ballot would be a return to that previous subordinated condition. He must move independently. The development of this awareness is a job as tedious and laborious as inspiring people to register in the first place. In fact, many people who would aspire to the role of an organizer drop off simply because they do not have the energy, the stamina, to knock on doors day after day. That is why one finds many such people sitting in coffee shops talking and theorizing instead of organizing.

> *Black Panther Party activist Stokely Carmichael and political scientist Charles V. Hamilton recalling the voting rights challenges of 1965 and 1966, in their* Black Power—The Politics of Liberation in America *(1967), pp. 435–438.*

What really happened in the Meredith case when the state decided to resist was that they were playing out the last chapter of the Civil War. You have to understand that everyone expected that Mississippi would resist. Mississippi had long been the state which offered the most resistance since the Civil War to the idea of equality for blacks. . . . Under our system, the federal court is supreme to any state government, and the South was not agreeing to that proposition when it came to the rights for Black Americans. So our Constitution was put to the test and survived. Our country is stronger now for having had that demonstration of what the Constitution means in practical application.

Constance Baker Motley, a NAACP Legal Defense Fund attorney and lawyer for James Meredith, commenting in 1966 on the significance of the Meredith enrollment at the University of Mississippi in Meredith, Three Years in Mississippi *(1966), p. 37.*

I have said that most liberal whites react to "black power" with the question, What about me? Rather than saying: Tell me what you want me to do and I'll see if I can do it. There are more answers to the right question. One of the most disturbing things about almost all white supporters of the movement has been that they are afraid to go into their own communities—which is where the racism exists—and work to get rid of it. They want to run from Berkeley to tell us what to do in Mississippi; let them look instead at Berkeley. They admonish blacks to be nonviolent; let them preach nonviolence in the white community. They come to teach me Negro history; let them go to the suburbs and open up freedom schools for whites. Let them work to stop America's racist foreign policy; let them press this government to cease supporting the economy of South Africa.

Stokely Carmichael calling for a new era of black empowerment, activism, and self-help in 1966, quoted in Barbour, A New Black Consciousness *(1968), Research Room, Lyndon Johnson Library.*

We had seen how the police attacked the Watts community after causing the trouble in the first place. We had seen Martin Luther King come to Watts in an effort to calm the people, and we had seen his philosophy of nonviolence rejected. Black people had been taught nonviolence; it was deep in us. What good, however, was nonviolence when the police were determined to rule by force? . . . We had seen all this, and we recognized that the rising consciousness of Black people was almost at the point of explosion. . . . Out of this need sprang the Black Panther Party.

Facing heavy criticism for his refusal of U.S. military service, boxing champion Cassius Clay (Muhammad Ali) is photographed by Ira Rosenberg during early 1967. *(Ira Rosenberg, Library of Congress)*

Bobby [Seale] and I finally had no choice but to form an organization that would involve the lower-class brothers. . . .

The Black Panthers were and are always required to keep their activities within legal bounds. . . . The police, invariably shocked to meet a cadre of disciplined and armed Black men coming to the support of the community, reacted in strange and unpredictable ways. In their fright, some of them became children, cursing and insulting us. We responded in kind, calling them swine and pigs, but never cursing—this would be cause for arrest—and we took care not to be arrested with our weapons. . . .

Black Panther Party founder Huey Newton recalling 1966, in his Revolutionary Suicide *(1973), Research Room, Lyndon Johnson Library.*

But the thing that really hurt me more than anything in the world was when I came back to the States and black people considered me as a part of the establishment. Because I am an officer. Here I was, a veteran that just came back from a big conflict. And most blacks wouldn't associate with me. You see, blacks are not supposed to be officers. Blacks are supposed to be those guys that take orders, and not necessarily those that give them. If you give orders, it means you had to kiss somebody's rear end to get into that position.

One day I wore my uniform over to Howard University in Washington to help recruit officer candidates. Howard is a black school, like the one I went to in Texas, Jarvis Christian College. I thought I would feel at home. The guys poked fun at me, calling me Uncle Sam's flunky. They would say the Marine Corps sucks. The Army sucks. They would say their brother or uncle got killed, so why was I still in. They would see the Purple Heart and ask me what was I trying to prove. The women wouldn't talk to you either.

I felt bad. I felt cold. I felt like I was completely out of it.

During late 1967, a black Vietnam veteran, Wallace Terry, describing his experience "coming home," in Rotter, Light at the End of the Tunnel: A Vietnam Anthology *(1999), p. 206.*

A few minutes later, an old black man in a beat-up '58 Chevy stopped and got out of his car. He walked with a limp and leaned forward as if he couldn't stand straight. His clothes were frayed and his face deeply lined. He ran his bony fingers through his gray-black hair, then shook his head and smiled. "I don't know where you're going little girl, " he said. "But I been by here four times since early morning and you ain't got a ride yet. I can't let you spend your whole life on this road." He was only headed for the other side of Oakland, but he said he'd rather go out of his way than see me stranded. He even carried my duffel bag to the trunk. As we drove south on 101, I didn't say much other than thank you, but my disillusionment was obvious.

"People ain't all that bad, little girl," he said. "It's just some folks are crazy mixed up these days. You keep in mind that it's gotta get better, 'cause it can't get any worse."

Home from Vietnam in late 1967, nurse Lynda van Devanter, still in military uniform, remembering her frustration and disillusionment over not getting a ride sooner while hitchhiking near San Francisco, in Rotter, Light at the End of the Tunnel: A Vietnam War Anthology *(1999), p. 214.*

American Politics in Transition

"It was a great opportunity for the judge and the district attorney and the State of New York to do something," John Wyle, Celeste's grandfather, said three days after the sentencing. They had a perfect opportunity to write out a big sentence and set an example. And the only thing he got was violation of probation. It was the same old razzle-dazzle. The kids must be laughing like hell.

Look magazine charging that the justice system is too easy on the growing drug problem among America's youth, in Schaap, "Death of a Hooked Heiress," Look, *July 26, 1966, pp. 19–25.*

Success is a dirty word; it's all glittery with money and big cars. We have a lot more things than our parents did. We have the responsibility of being able to accept all this. If I can maintain my "self" throughout life, without getting stale, or dry rot by standing still, I'll be happy.

Nineteen-year-old Harriet McLeod of Montpelier, Vermont, talking about the attitudes and objectives of young antiwar activists and supporters in Sheperd, "The Look Youth Survey," Look, *September 20, 1966, pp. 44–49.*

But I found two persistent fears: One has to do with students who say they don't trust people over 30. Well, those under 30, in turn, aren't being trusted by many of those over 30. You read about the Red Guards in China, and student revolutionaries in Indonesia, India, Latin America. Can you expect many adults not to be nervous at what youth, with its volatility and its large concentrations on campuses, might do to this nation? They do not realize how different the United States is from China or Indonesia. We have here a really stable democratic society and need not fear dissent.

The second fear has to do with the intellectual. The last few years have widened the gap between the intellectual and the rest of society. There is almost no connection between intellectuals and the trade-union movement, as there was during the '30s and '40s. There is now alienation between the Federal leadership and the intellectuals over Vietnam policy, and other matters too. The intellectuals press harder for civil rights than much of the public likes. So the public wonders: Where is youth going, and where might the intellectuals want to lead it? Governor Reagan and others in Califonia politics have raised this endemic fear to almost epidemic proportions.

Clark Kerr, the president of the University of California system who was fired for his inability to quell student unrest, warning that the "generation gap" is widening, in his "The Turmoil in Higher Education," Look, *April 18, 1967, pp. 17–20.*

He's like Edward G. Robinson in the days of Little Caesar. He can strut sitting down.

Conservative writer James Jackson Kilpatrick endorsing Wallace for president, in his "What Makes Wallace Run?" National Review, *April 18, 1967, p. 400.*

This seems to be a congressional problem. I don't know how to explain it. . . . I think during this period there are going to be a great many heartaches, some frustration, and certainly dissent. I think the first part of your statement is an accurate one. I believe all of us regret that we have to do what we are doing, but I think we would regret it more if we didn't do what we are doing.

President Johnson, during a May 1967 press conference, noting that anti–Vietnam War and anti-Johnson protests would be better placed in Congress than on the streets, in The Public Papers of President Lyndon B. Johnson, 1967, Speeches, Lyndon Johnson Library.

Like the legions of Sgt. Pepper's Band, the protestors assembled from all the intersections between history and the comic books, between legend and television, the Biblical archetypes and the movies. . . . The ghosts of old battles were wheeling like clouds over Washington.

Paraphrasing his own words to the press in October 1967, novelist Norman Mailer describing the participants of an antiwar protest in Washington, D.C., in his The Armies of the Night: History as Novel, the Novel as History *(1968), Research Room, Lyndon Johnson Library.*

I would call him a first-act politician. You know it's easy to write the first act. And it's relatively easy to write the third act. Lyndon Johnson was a good third-act man. . . . But it's the second act that is toughest to write. In Congress, that's where the drudgery and hard work come.

Senator Eugene McCarthy (Democrat of Minnesota), Robert Kennedy's soon-to-be chief rival in the 1968 presidential primaries, complaining in his own careful way, in October 1967, that Kennedy is not an involved, active legislator in the Senate, quoted in Schaap, R.F.K. *(1967), p. 8.*

Many Negroes—especially among the young—are losing faith in the good will and purpose of the nation and its institutions. Frustrated hope and loss of faith breed desperation. And desperate men take to the streets. I say this not to condone such violence, but merely to state a fact—a fact which can now be seen in the streets on every television screen. We may not like this fact, but we ignore it at our peril. . . . If we allow hostility or fear to blind ourselves to this reality it will be destructive to the health of this country. . . . There is no sure way to suppress men filled with anger who feel they have nothing to lose.

Senator Robert Kennedy answering the critics in October 1967 who charge that he does not understand the problems of black youth, in his To Seek a Newer World *(1968), Research Room, John F. Kennedy Library.*

It is necessary and desirable for you to speak as the Democratic Party Leader. . . . The Democratic Party people I see from all over the country really believe (a) you do not understand them or (b) if you do, couldn't care less about them.

Lyndon Johnson's close personal friend James Rowe telling the president that the "Dump Johnson" movement is gaining strength and might soon succeed, in his memo on the "Dump Johnson" movement attached to Rowe to Johnson, October 2, 1967, Box 111 of the White House Central File, Lyndon Johnson Library.

In support of civil authority, we have the very delicate and difficult job of both upholding constitutional rights of free assembly and expression and protecting government operations and property. We cannot tolerate lawlessness; neither can we tolerate interference with the legitimate exercise of constitutional rights.

We must avoid either overreacting or under-reacting. We must behave with dignity and firmness. We must act in a way which holds to the absolute minimum the possibility of bloodshed and injury; which minimizes the need for arrest; which distinguishes to the extent feasible between those who are and are not breaking the law, and which uses minimum force consistent with the mission of protecting the employees (military and civilian), the operations, and the property of the Government.

Undersecretary of the Army David McGiffert instructing security forces on how to protect the facility as well as handle the protestors, shortly before a major antiwar demonstration in front of the Pentagon, in Announcement by Undersecretary McGiffert, October 20, 1967, Box 8 of the Papers of Warren Christopher, Lyndon Johnson Library.

You are not as strong with a majority of the country as your upswing in the polls and particularly your topping of President Johnson might suggest. . . . The press will emphasize, act out with the public the negative qualities which they have thought they disliked about you in the past: ruthlessness, self-preoccupied ambition, etc. . . . Your plunging in might be an act of conscience to some people. But it would likely also be political suicide for you. You are still not as disciplined a politician as President Kennedy. Appeal to the middle class much more! Above all, keep cool for now. Timing separates the great public men from merely the good ones.

Fred Dutton, a longtime adviser to Senator Robert Kennedy, informing the senator that challenging McCarthy, Johnson, or any Democratic national figure will not be easy, personal changes are required, and a broadened appeal is needed, in Dutton to Kennedy, November 3, 1967, Papers of Arthur M. Schlesinger, JFK Library.

6

The Perils of Power
1968

"They're sad souls who drive their Corvettes to the Revolution." According to longtime American Socialist Party activist and former Milwaukee mayor Frank P. Zeidler, this was the best description of student antiwar rioters at the volatile University of Wisconsin campus in 1968. The significance of that one power-packed sentence has been lost over the years, but Zeidler's point was well taken. In his own way, he was trying to say that the New Left–supported student protest movement was too white, too middle class, and too spoiled to make a difference. His use of symbolism (the Corvette) was obvious as well.

An icon among American sports car lovers since its appearance in 1953, the Corvette symbolized white middle-class success, luxury, and the freedom to roam with power and speed. Its production chief, former racing legend Zora Arkus-Duntov, said his fiberglass-bodied car represented America at its best:

Often considered the finest of Corvette's five production series's, the "C2"(or Sting Ray, 1963–67) represented American power and speed in the 1960s. A 1965 Small Block model is featured here. *(author's collection)*

big, aggressive, and high tech. Like America in Vietnam, the car was supposed to be invincible, and it had a record to prove it. Even Hollywood's *Route 66* television adventure drama of the early 1960s, starring instant TV stars Martin Milner and George Maharis, furthered the legend of America's attraction to speed, victory, and wanderlust. Milner and Maharis's 1960 Corvette was as much a star as themselves in this show, and together they roamed America's heartland, solving the problems of the country folk who allegedly needed their help.

To some, America had wandered into Vietnam the same way. A big, powerful machine roared into the lives of poor, struggling people and it was supposed to be for their own good. That had changed by 1968, and even the Corvette was different. In late 1967, General Motors Corvette Division changed the car's body style and drive train for only the third time in its history. With little attention to quality, fit, or finish, the car looked more outrageous than ever before and suffered from a myriad of mechanical problems.[1] It was even rejected by the road test review editors of *Car and Driver* magazine because, they complained, it was unfit to be tested. The car's brawny legend was suddenly tarnished, coinciding with the news of impending doom for the United States in Vietnam. Zeidler made his famous quote at this time, and his audience knew exactly what he was trying to say. The United States was losing the Vietnam War, its power and influence was fading, and a white middle-class 19-year-old student protester was not going to change this situation.

THE STUDENT COMPLAINT

Without question, the antiwar movement was difficult to define in 1968. In general terms, it included the antiwar presidential campaigns of both Senators Eugene McCarthy of Minnesota and Robert Kennedy of New York. It included the growing ranks of Students for a Democratic Society (SDS), the small, but highly visible Vietnam Veterans Against the War (VVAW) organization, the drop-out and get-stoned "counterculture" or "hippies," and even New York's Republican mayor, John Lindsay. From civil rights to urban renewal, America's "imperialist blundering" into Vietnam, the handsome, Kennedyesque Lindsay complained, had diverted the country's attention from important work in the big cities.

No one enjoyed a monopoly on antiwar sentiment, and the statistics of the Gallup Poll showed a nation evenly divided over keeping U.S. troops in Vietnam. But certain antiwar legends were born, and 1968 would be a year of radical protest. The Youth International Party or Yippies truly represented that new radicalism.

Founded by former New Left supporters Abbie Hoffman and Jerry Rubin, the Yippies nominated their own candidate for president. Nicknamed Pigasus, the Yippie candidate was a large swine. Although later claiming that their efforts were only designed to poke fun at democratic institutions, the Yippie promise of anarchism was taken seriously by the news media and by establishment politicians in 1968. The Yippie platform called for the legalization of psychedelic drugs and marijuana, total disarmament (including all U.S. police departments), an end to "the tyranny of capitalism," no censorship laws, and legislation that protected "free love."

Disturbed by the growing violence of student demonstrations, the swing toward anarchism with the Yippies, and less and less organization to antiwar protests, SDS leaders such as Tom Hayden worried about the direction of the movement. Women in the antiwar cause became especially annoyed, for the male-dominated protest organizations had little use for females in leadership roles. Endless debate and dissension typified the student protest movement as the 1967–68 academic year came to a close. During a summertime 1968 interview with CBS News's Mike Wallace, Hayden insisted that the 1968–69 academic year promised a "reformed and disciplined" student protest movement linked to certain AFL-CIO locals and disaffected liberal Democrats.

Like the student-led anti–de Gaulle government riots in Paris during May 1968, Hayden predicted that an alliance of peace groups, labor activists, and disgusted politicians would soon "bring down the American system." The press believed him, but Hayden had no organizational plan, no alliance was in the making, and antiwar activity remained limited during the long summer break from university classes.[2] In fact, antiwar protesters continued to react to the Vietnam War news in the usual spontaneous fashion, and the White House did its best to ignore them.

HOLLYWOOD PROTESTS AND ESCAPES

Outside of the political community, the film industry had a profound impact on American attitudes during the ending years of the Vietnam War. Much was made in the press and in conservative political circles of actress Jane Fonda's "declaration of solidarity with the North Vietnamese people." Although it took a couple of years, her "declaration" led to an unprecedented public relations tour of Hanoi and Haiphong in North Vietnam. But Hollywood's role in the movements of the day went beyond the career of Jane Fonda. Film critics, antiwar activists, and civil rights advocates tried to find "socially relevant significance" in a number of late 1960s films.

Born Michael Igor Pechkowsy, film director and ex-comedian Mike Nichols especially excited young filmgoers with *The Graduate*. Released in time for the all-important holiday season market, this late 1967 film was the number-one box office hit of 1968. Little-known Dustin Hoffman played Benjamin Braddock in the film, a sympathetic victim of a number of sexual and romantic mishaps. Hoffman's Braddock came to reject white upper-middle-class life, and, by the end of the film, he represented a late 1960s version of James Dean in *Rebel Without a Cause*. *The Graduate* hit a very responsive nerve in young audiences, and that fact resounded in the boardrooms of Hollywood film producers.

Stanley Kramer's *Guess Who's Coming to Dinner* also took on white middle-class family values. Essentially a two-hour commentary on white fear and rejection of interracial marriage, Kramer's film starred box office legends Spencer Tracy and Katharine Hepburn, as well as the new African-American superstar Sidney Poitier. The star power, plus Kramer's entertaining treatment of the differing generational opinions on black-white relations, assured another huge financial success for Hollywood. The film's central characters (the Drayton family) eventually accept the new era of racial harmony, transforming the film into a liberal appeal for reason and peace at the height of the civil rights struggle.

The quiet protest of *The Graduate* and *Guess Who's Coming to Dinner* was tilted by Arthur Penn's *Bonnie and Clyde*. Another late 1967 film that continued to rake in millions of ticket sales for the next two years, *Bonnie and Clyde* romanticized and exaggerated the sleazy life of crime led by the 1930s gangsters Clyde Barrow and Bonnie Parker. Mavericks and outcasts, Bonnie and Clyde were portrayed as 1960s-like antiestablishment heroes who turned to violence out of necessity. The film concluded with their bloody deaths, filmed in slow motion and suggesting that the only peace for the loner and radical might be a violent end. Historians, law enforcement officials, and parents complained that the film glorified a life of crime and violence, but the louder their complaints the more tickets were sold. Hollywood had found a new niche market with the protest film, but the trend was short-lived.

As the casualty figures of the Vietnam War grew and the civil rights struggle turned more violent, even young moviegoers preferred escapism to protest. Stanley Kubrick's *2001: A Space Odyssey* was the ultimate escape. This 1968 film dazzled audiences with a peek at the not-so-distant future when the Vietnam War, political assassinations, and racial violence would, they hoped, be long over. The enemy was not even human in this movie. HAL (the onboard computer of the film's spacecraft) represented a new evil. It was a machine that could think, plot, and kill. Touching on subjects ranging from man's evolution to extraterrestrial life and its possible influence on that evolution, Kubrick's film confused as well as amazed its viewers. Confusing or not, *2001* was much more preferable to yet another cinematic reminder of everyday life in the late 1960s.

The news, it seemed, was always so bad in 1968 that even noted journalists wondered if their profession had gone too far. Harrison Salisbury, one of the country's most respected print journalists, suggested that fellow reporters preferred to shock and horrify readers rather than inform them. For instance, Salisbury correctly observed that few Americans, including himself, knew anything at all about simple everyday activities in North Vietnam. He proposed a personally led investigation of North Vietnamese life and culture, and, amazingly, the North Vietnamese government agreed. So Salisbury toured North Vietnam, published his observations in record-selling copies of the *Saturday Evening Post,* and won the nation's thanks. In contrast, Jane Fonda's trip to North Vietnam was regarded as treason by some, foolishness by others, and well-intentioned activism by a handful.

On television, CBS's *The Smothers Brothers Comedy Hour* dared to satirize the Vietnam War and openly criticize the White House. Although attracting large, adoring audiences, the show's political controversy brought a great deal of grief to CBS executives. In spite of the *Comedy Hour's* renewal for the 1969 season, CBS fired Tom and Dick Smothers. The show's fans claimed that the brothers were victims of a political witch hunt, while CBS argued that the young comedians ignored corporate procedures and contractual arrangements. The Smothers versus CBS spat generated a national debate over the place of free expression on television, although the precise circumstances of the firing were never made clear.

Vietnam remained a touchy subject for the film industry, and finding financial backing for a Vietnam-related film was not easy. In contrast to the many films about World War II while that war still raged, Hollywood was slow to respond to the Vietnam story. Every night, Americans remained glued to their favorite television news programs, and the horror of Vietnam became a daily experience. Given that fact, few Hollywood producers believed that the American people would be interested in seeing a straightforward Vietnam War movie at their local theater.

An obvious exception to Hollywood's reluctance to embrace Vietnam was John Wayne's Batjac film company and its 1968 production of *The Green Berets*. A close friend of both Barry Goldwater and Ronald Reagan, Wayne enjoyed impeccable pro–Republican and pro–Vietnam War credentials. Filmed in the U.S. South, *The Green Berets* was made in tribute to Special Forces heroism in Vietnam. Employing the same ensemble cast often seen in Wayne-produced westerns, *The Green Berets* was the typical shoot–'em-up John Wayne film. This one happened to be set in Vietnam, although Wayne's character eventually admitted that "Vietnam was not a normal war." Fresh from his hit ABC televi-

While visiting the 3rd Battalion, 7th Marines in Chu Lai, South Vietnam, actor John Wayne signs the helmet of Private First Class Fonsell Wofford. *(National Archives)*

sion series *The Fugitive,* actor David Janssen was the star power next to Wayne in *The Green Berets.* Playing a Harrison Salisbury–like journalist in Vietnam, Janssen's character moved from an antiwar to pro-war position after witnessing U.S. forces in action.

The Green Berets premiere did not lead to a rash of antiwar pickets in front of America's movie theaters. SDS leaders made it clear that they did not want to "dignify" Wayne's film with special protests. Wayne insisted that his film was just good old-fashioned entertainment, but both moviegoers and film critics wondered why anyone would consider Vietnam entertaining. Hence, Wayne's trailblazing film did not lead to follow-up pro-war films or antiwar ones either. It would not be until the mid- and late 1970s that Hollywood dared to address Vietnam issues with such films as *The Deer Hunter* and *Apocalypse Now.* In the late 1960s, filmmakers and their financial backers simply assumed general public rejection.[3]

Escapism was always better on the small screen. The 1960s remained the heyday of the television era, but the news was always bad. Near the end of one of America's most tumultuous years, NBC premiered a 1968 version of 1920s vaudeville. Rowan and Martin's *Laugh-In* recycled old jokes in a hip fashion. Although it poked fun at Washington officialdom, U.S. foreign policy, and even white middle-class life, it did so in an amazingly bipartisan fashion. Cameo guest shots included Democratic and Republican party luminaries. Richard Nixon once claimed that uttering the line "sock it to me" on *Laugh-In,* and only that line, established him as the *Laugh-In* fan's "cool candidate" in contrast to his 1968 challenger, Vice President Humphrey.

The show's cast of budding young comedians, led by veteran stand-up jokesters Dan Rowan and Dick Martin, flubbed their lines and few viewers cared. NBC executives were aghast; an irreverent, chaotic comedy became the surprise mega hit of 1968. Originally slotted to replace an earlier NBC sensation that had faded, *The Man from U.N.C.L.E., Laugh-In* was expected by industry experts to be a mediocre contender in the ratings war. According to NBC's original polling, *Laugh-In* would be "somewhat interesting" to young teens alone, and that was that.

Once describing his show as "amiable anarchy," producer George Schlatter saw the madcap *Laugh-In* as the ultimate escape from the madness of 1968. Most audiences agreed, for it attracted viewers of all ages and backgrounds. The show even created overnight sensations of some of its obscure guest stars. Enjoying a certain 15 minutes of fame during *Laugh-In*'s first hit season was Herbert Khaury. Better known as Tiny Tim (alias Larry Love, alias Darry Dover, alias Emmett Swink, and alias Rollie Dell), Khaury strummed the ukulele and sang odd songs from the early years of the Great Depression. Looking more the hippie than most hippies, Khaury's high-pitched voice, overly polite manner, and sheer innocence fascinated viewers and critics alike. Was it an act or for real? Some said he represented the purity of America, a lost waif in a hostile world. Others said he was crazy. Whatever he was doing, it worked. Next to *Laugh-In* itself, Tiny Tim was America's new pop star, at least until the next sensation popped up.

In the meantime, *Laugh-In* continued to attract such long-established stars as John Wayne and Sammy Davis, Jr., to its cameo guest spots. Later serving as the inspiration for another NBC legend, *Saturday Night Live, Laugh-In* made television history for an audience that had had enough of Vietnam, political assassinations, and riots in the streets.

LIGHT AT THE END OF THE TUNNEL

For years, military historians had pointed out that a government's war weariness, frustration, and fatigue was often manifested in the desire for "decisive battle." During a long war, the side that was most disturbed by the battlefield results sought a quick resolution. A sentiment best described as "may the best man win" dominated decision making, and the resulting decision could be faulty. The French suffered this malaise in 1954, and the desire for one last battle soon became the fight for Dienbienphu. They lost. In late 1967, General William Westmoreland believed that America's last battle was at hand and that the end of the war was near. For a time, he was quite candid about these hopes.

During November 1967, U.S. intelligence reports confirmed that the North Vietnamese supply routes into South Vietnam (the Ho Chi Minh Trail) were busier than usual. Slowly, several North Vietnamese divisions were setting up positions near the U.S. base of Khe Sanh in northern Quang Tri province and the North Vietnam–South Vietnam border. During this build-up, Westmoreland's command was divided over what it meant. The war seemed to have geared down, and the resulting lack of American casualties was especially welcomed during the Thanksgiving and Christmas holidays. Publicly, Westmoreland continued to express the view that it was U.S. heavy bombing campaigns and continued commitment on the ground that explained the new quiet on the battlefield. The enemy, as he liked to say, was definitely "on the ropes," and an otherwise doubting press and public truly wished to believe him.

In the history of America's wars, from the battles of Saratoga and Yorktown in the American Revolution to Midway and Normandy in World War II, the country had met the enemy in "decisive battle" and prevailed. Khe Sanh, both President Johnson and General Westmoreland believed, might present similar opportunities and turning points. The American people were not informed about this brewing fight and their government's great optimism about it. The later ferocity of the battle would, therefore, be especially shocking to them.[4]

Politically, the potential "decisive battle" to come was good news for the Johnson team. Despite months of assault by the growing antiwar movement and the threat of an upcoming New Hampshire Democratic primary challenge by the antiwar Minnesota senator and former English professor Eugene McCarthy, the White House was convinced that 1968 could be a banner year. Johnson planned to win the Vietnam War early in the year and win another great landslide at the end of the year. The Great Society could resume its march forward, and the Democratic Party could become the unassailable political force in America well into the next century. These were grand plans and visions but not unusual for a nation down on its luck in a long, bitter war.

To Westmoreland, the North Vietnamese and the Vietcong were finally doing what he wanted them to do. A World War II–like head-to-head confrontation seemed to be in the making, the enemy was abandoning their usual guerrilla tactics in favor of an all-out assault, and America's military experience and technology would finally succeed because of it. According to Westmoreland, the North Vietnamese viewed America's Khe Sanh in the same light as

A confident General William Westmoreland briefs President Johnson and the cabinet on 1967 battlefield developments in Vietnam. *(Frank Wolfe, Lyndon B. Johnson Library)*

France's Dienbienphu. It was a base they had to assault, although, this time, the defenders would win. Offering cryptic comments to the press by Christmas 1967, Westmoreland even suggested that his men were ready for a showdown and that 1968 would be the long-desired homecoming year for U.S. forces. There was, it seemed, a bright "light at the end of the tunnel."

On the other side, Ho Chi Minh and the major planner for this coming assault, the legendary General Vo Nguyen Giap, created an intricate battle plan. A series of assaults across South Vietnam was planned for the Tet or lunar new year holidays. The holiday season coincided with stormy weather, and historically was the worst possible time for a major battle in Vietnam. Ho Chi Minh's government had promised that it would never disturb the Tet holiday season. They lied.

In the name of security, neither North Vietnamese nor Vietcong commanders were told what their objectives were until receiving their final orders, and most would be informed that their particular battle plan was the most important one of the entire assault. The battle for Khe Sanh was considered a great diversion, luring thousands of American troops from the south to take part in this alleged "decisive battle." But North Vietnam's real goal was the collapse of the Saigon regime, and that could be better accomplished if the bulk of its U.S. defenders were diverted to the north.[5.]

THE TET OFFENSIVE

The North Vietnamese assault on Khe Sanh began on January 21, 1968, and the endless shelling of U.S. Marine positions there reminded many of the opening salvo against the French in Dienbienphu. Almost immediately, the White House received reports of wild, bloody assaults on almost every town of significance in South Vietnam. At first, the reports were too shocking to accept. Then General Westmoreland interpreted the nationwide orgy of violence as a major diversionary effort. The enemy, he believed, was attempting to divert America's attentions away from the primary target, the base at Khe Sanh. It took days for Westmoreland to realize that that was exactly what the North Vietnamese wanted him to think.

The most brutal North Vietnamese attack of the Tet Offensive was on the old imperial capital of Hue in central South Vietnam. This stately, attractive city was destroyed by the North Vietnamese invaders. They took few prisoners, fighting house to house and executing innocent civilians. The civilian murders were conservatively estimated to be 3,000, and it would take American and South Vietnamese forces three weeks and 5,000 killed in action before Hue was liberated. The North Vietnamese government would always claim that the atrocities in Hue were accidents or the unfortunate consequences of urban combat. In reality, horror for the sake of horror had been part of the battle plan, and terrorizing the South Vietnamese populace into a surrender was just another tactic. More than 116,000 of Hue's 140,000 residents were left

Following the Tet Offensive, city officials in Hue, South Vietnam, supervise the identifying of bodies at a local cemetery. *(National Archives)*

homeless. This type of horror, accompanied by nationwide attacks that kept U.S. forces pinned down everywhere, were also supposed to stimulate high desertion rates and mutinies in the American ranks. In fact, most American troops saw the Tet Offensive as a fight for survival. Mass desertions or mutinies never took place. Meanwhile, American and South Vietnamese forces had also contributed to the final destruction of Hue. The Vietnam-influenced expression "it had to be destroyed in order to be saved" guided the U.S. military approach there.

Adding to all the battle plans, objectives, and horror were long-lasting myths and legends born in the misery of the Tet bloodbath. One of the more popular Tet Offensive myths was that the North Vietnamese deliberately timed the carnage to influence voters in America's first presidential primary. Giap and Ho Chi Minh supposedly expected Senator McCarthy to topple Lyndon Johnson in New Hampshire, build a bandwagon for his antiwar message, win the White House, and abandon the U.S. cause in Vietnam to Hanoi and the communist victory. However, the New Hampshire primary took place weeks after the Tet Offensive began, and it was unlikely that the North Vietnamese leadership studied the voting trends of New Hampshire residents.

Another Tet Offensive legend involved the alleged North Vietnamese plan to make sure that sympathetic South Vietnamese communists were in the first ranks of the assault. Given the wild, suicide-styled attacks in the opening days of the Tet Offensive, many of these South Vietnamese operatives would be killed. According to the legend, this South Vietnamese massacre was also the objective. Fewer troops in the field would mean less of a power base for South Vietnamese–based communists, permitting North Vietnam to win full control of all southern residents who opposed both the Saigon regime and the American presence. Consequently, whether Hanoi won or lost, this legend suggests, North Vietnam would always determine the future of the South. To early political analysts of the Tet Offensive, this interpretation seemed to make good sense. It also added to Giap and Ho's reputations as brilliant military and political strategists. But winning the war against the Americans and the Saigon regime had been the immediate and primary goal of the Hanoi regime in the Tet Offensive. Deliberately sacrificing thousands of crack troops and supporters for elusive postbattle and political reasons was never part of the grand plan. The deaths of thousands of South Vietnamese–based Vietcong would be a consequence of the carnage, not the main goal.[6]

As the battle raged, American television viewers remained transfixed. After all the effort to prop up the Saigon government, and after thousands of Americans killed, the enemy remained in control of much of the country. America's weekly casualty count, still announced every Thursday, equaled World War II–like proportions into March 1968. TV viewers even saw armed bureaucrats at the U.S. embassy in Saigon forced to shoot it out with invading Vietcong troops. Meanwhile, Associated Press photographer Eddie Adams and an NBC television news crew filmed Gen. Nguyen Ngoc Loan, head of the South Vietnamese police and troubled by personal losses in the battle for Saigon, shoot a captured Vietcong prisoner in the head. Adams's still picture of the shooting won him a Pulitzer Prize, and to many Americans that one picture came to symbolize the entire madness of the Tet Offensive.

In an extremely rare display of anger, America's most-trusted newsman, Walter Cronkite, denounced Johnson's war policy on national television, and dozens of U.S. Marines told Cronkite's CBS News that they had no idea why they were fighting in Vietnam. Years later, General Westmoreland complained that the daily television coverage of the Tet Offensive offered a "psychological victory" to the North Vietnamese, for the American people turned against the war because of it. This type of conclusion led to one more another myth. "The press lost the Vietnam War" became a common refrain for those who believed that U.S. reporters had enjoyed too much power and influence throughout the conflict.[7] Somehow, if the press had been absent from the scene, this myth implies, U.S. victory would have been possible.

U.S. military forces prevailed in the Tet Offensive, and often the historical debate over the battle's political and psychological impact misses this obvious point. To assure the victory and keep the enemy "on the ropes," Westmoreland and the Johnson administration generally agreed that 206,000 more troops were needed in Vietnam as soon as possible. This number (reservists and new draftees) were added to the 486,000 men in Vietnam at the time of the Tet Offensive. The new Vietnam buildup was supposed to be matched by international efforts as well. In other words, thousands of U.S. troops would also be sent to U.S. military bases in other potential hot spots around the world. The message would be clear. The United States might be hurting in Vietnam, but its commitment to global anticommunism remained firm.

While the conservative, normally hawkish *Wall Street Journal* editorialized that U.S. Vietnam policy was simply not working, a depressed and frustrated Robert McNamara resigned his post as secretary of defense. The call for 206,000 more troops threw the Johnson administration into emergency cabinet meetings, but it would be the new secretary of defense, Clark Clifford, who played a key decision-making role.

Although he had doubted the original decision to escalate the war, Clifford, a senior Democratic Party figure but a junior cabinet member, had been a loyal defender of the president's war policies for more than three years. Insisting on a full, comprehensive analysis before agreeing to commit huge numbers of new troops, Clifford received conflicting advice from both Defense and State Department analysts. Even Johnson's aged "Wise Men" advisers recommended immediate peace talks and no further escalation of the war. Coming to a different conclusion than Johnson expected, Clifford asked for a halt to the bombing of North Vietnam and a resulting round of peace talks with Hanoi government officials in Paris. The president agreed.[8]

Westmoreland received only 13,000 troops within the original 206,000 request, search-and-destroy missions across Vietnam were temporarily canceled, and Westmoreland himself was removed from his Vietnam post. He was named the new army chief of staff and replaced by General Creighton Abrams. All of these decisions were viewed as concessions to North Vietnam in order to help speed up the peace process in Paris once the talks began. However, the war still raged, and the North Vietnamese saw U.S. interest in fast-moving peace talks as an indication of the impending U.S. defeat. It was in their interest to wait and see who won the U.S. presidential election before committing to any peace deal, and it made sense to continue the war in earnest at the same time. While the United States dreamed of peace in 1968, North Vietnam envisioned victory.[9]

Getting "Clean for Gene"

On March 12, 1968, New Hampshire voters went to the polls. Proud of their "Live Free Or Die" Yankee independence, New Hampshire residents were well known for rejecting the status quo, "sending a message to Washington," and generally stirring things up. But Eugene McCarthy entered the primary with little support in the polls and little hope of success. He dared to challenge Lyndon Johnson only because of Vietnam, and his first denunciation of the war was a speech nervously delivered outside of Minneapolis only one year before. Aware that many Americans were weary of the endless debate over Vietnam, he often used a gentle vocabulary that kept an audience listening. Referring to himself as a "dove" instead of an "antiwar activist," or complaining about "U.S. goals in Indochina" instead of "the war in Vietnam," McCarthy chose his words carefully.

At first McCarthy came to New Hampshire noting that he only wanted to be the "moral conscience" candidate in 1968, but the Tet Offensive news suggested that he had a real shot at victory. His unusual style of avoiding political buzzwords and his strong university background excited draft-age college students. Sadly for McCarthy, most of these supporters, moved by the David versus Goliath dimensions of his challenge to Johnson, were too young to vote. In those days before the Twenty-sixth Amendment and the right to vote for those between the ages of 18 and 21, McCarthy's diehard supporters had to convince their elders to vote for him. It would be a hard sell. Nineteen-year-old university students were not the most-loved segment of the population. Long hair, attraction to radical politics or sloganism, rock music, and drug use suggested an alien culture to some older voters.

McCarthy urged his young zealots to cut their hair, wear business attire, and canvass neighborhoods in traditional fashion. "Getting Clean for Gene," he hoped, might mean the difference between success and failure. But only 10 percent of New Hampshire voters later claimed that a "Clean for Gene" canvasser had actually influenced their vote. The power of McCarthy's antiwar message in the wake of the Tet Offensive and the legal right of Republicans to cross over and vote Democratic helped the Minnesota senator's final returns on March 12.

To the media political experts, as well as to Democratic Party veterans, McCarthy was a foolish amateur at worst, a "stalking horse" at best. The latter expression meant that he was laying the foundation for others in his party with a better power base, polished message, and issues to champion besides Vietnam, such as Robert Kennedy. McCarthy's lost-lamb image, however, was manufactured. For 20 years, he had thrived in the tough political world of Minnesota, and he knew exactly what he was doing. The final tally was 48 percent Johnson and 42 percent McCarthy. The media was amazed, declaring McCarthy the "moral victor" over the president. "Landslide Lyndon" was in trouble, they said, although Johnson's supporters countered that McCarthy did indeed lose by 6 percent of the vote.

Less than one month away stood the Wisconsin primary. McCarthy's chances seemed good there, or so the conventional political wisdom of the day suggested. Minnesota shared a common border with Wisconsin, and McCarthy, like Hubert Humphrey before him, was always a welcome guest of the Wisconsin Democratic Party. Since the famous Kennedy versus Humphrey prima-ry battle there eight years earlier, Wisconsin was considered the "king maker" state. Its middle-of-the-primary-season election made or broke candidacies, creating a steamroller effect for whoever won all the way to the nominating convention in the summer. McCarthy, the press agreed, might soon be seen as the future of the Democratic Party to voters nationwide.

In a daring move, President Johnson traveled to Minneapolis shortly after the New Hampshire primary. He delivered a rousing speech denouncing McCarthy's lackluster voting record on New Frontier and Great Society issues. McCarthy, he implied, was in the wrong party, and Johnson's supporters at this farmers' convention got the message. Also promising victory in the Vietnam War, the president looked like a winner throughout this speech. In reality, he was already planning to retire from politics for good.[10]

MLK AND RFK MURDERED

From March 12 to March 31, 1968, the White House reminded the press that the president had prevailed in the New Hampshire primary. The nation,

Less than five years before his assassination, Dr. Martin Luther King, Jr., is photographed during one of his proudest and most successful moments, the March on Washington. *(National Archives)*

however, was fascinated by McCarthy's amazing come-from-behind challenge and, for a while, wondered what it all meant to an unusually quiet Senator Robert Kennedy. James Rowe, one of Johnson's most trusted political advisers and friends, believed that the president would have a tough fight ahead in the Wisconsin primary. He recommended that his friend make a dramatic Vietnam announcement on the eve of the primary, promising some sort of troop withdrawal at best or great battlefield success at the least. Whether the announcement was accurate or not, Rowe suggested, was not yet important.

Privately, Johnson grew tired of toying with the truth. The war had taken its toll on his state of mind and worsening heart condition. McCarthy troubled him, too. The press kept referring to him as the liberal "dove," but the senator's voting record had been more conservative than his 1968 antiestablishment image. To his dying day in 1973, Johnson still regarded the Democratic Party as his family. Fighting to preserve New Frontier/Great Society goals and gains was essential, he believed, to that family's fortunes in the upcoming 1970s. Although Johnson had little use for him or his tactics, he felt that Bobby Kennedy would fight to extend New Frontier/Great Society successes, and that realization was the bottom line for the president. Whether Johnson's own diehard supporters would permit a Kennedy success was another matter.

Four days after the New Hampshire primary, Kennedy announced his candidacy for the White House. McCarthy considered the Kennedy decision another example of the senator's reputation for ruthlessness, and the antiwar movement, he concluded, was now in chaos because of it. Despite Kennedy's promise of a great new Camelot, McCarthy insisted that the New York senator was not invincible. He pressed on, and the images were clear. McCarthy presented himself as the good ex-professor stabbed in the back by the Kennedy legend. Kennedy presented himself as a new man, the "Good Bobby," champion of the downtrodden, innovative civil rights legislator, and early Vietnam War policy maker who asked for the opportunity to end the war that the New Frontier had hastened. In contrast to the sometimes cryptic McCarthy, Kennedy now minced few words about his opposition to the Vietnam War. That fact, plus his New Frontier/Great Society credentials, had some reporters and pundits predicting Johnson's fall and a Kennedy win of the Democratic nomination. But could he win the presidency?

Democrats faced even more surprises when their longtime standard-bearer, Lyndon Johnson, stated on March 31, 1968, that he would not "seek or accept the nomination." According to some accounts, not even the first lady knew that her husband planned to make this nationally televised announcement. The chaotic state of the nation's largest party also troubled sympathetic civil rights activists, especially Martin Luther King, Jr. Although his own chief advisers, such as Andrew Young, recommended against it, King decided to speak out against the Vietnam War. The disproportionate number of African Americans fighting and dying in that war, made all the more visible during television coverage of the Tet Offensive, disturbed King. Viewing the Great Society White House as a friend and ally, King had had little criticism of the Johnson team outside of precise civil rights matters.

Now that Johnson was leaving politics, and the Democrats were being redefined by McCarthy and Kennedy, King's new position did not stimulate the Democratic backlash that Andrew Young and other advisers feared. King's possible leadership role within a new alliance of the Civil Rights and antiwar movements intrigued both the press and the Democrats who might benefit from the arrangement. But the alliance building would be left to others. On April 4, 1968, James Earl Ray, a white ex-convict, murdered Martin Luther King. America's champion of nonviolent protest was shot on his Memphis hotel balcony. With the nation in shock, the task of uniting civil rights activists, antiwar activists, and traditional blue-collar whites as well as African-American Democrats was now inherited by Bobby Kennedy.

Outside of the white middle-class university community that adored him, McCarthy's coalition-building skills were weak. However, he was still an important force in U.S. politics. Without Johnson in the race and Kennedy still in a rush to organize his new campaign, McCarthy won a landslide victory in the Wisconsin primary, in which Republicans, as in New Hampshire, could vote in the Wisconsin Democratic primary. Presumably, the goal of many "crossover" voters was to make sure that the weakest candidate in the other party moved ahead. McCarthy won the later Oregon primary as well. Yet, the momentum, coalition success, money, and press attention always went to Kennedy.

Sweeping a multistate primary vote on June 4, 1968, which included the huge delegate count of California, Kennedy's next stop was a dead certain win in his home state of New York. Unless Vice President Humphrey was truly determined to block the Kennedy nomination at the Democratic convention, a last-minute "Stop Kennedy" effort looked like an uphill fight to political analysts.

Although some in the press believed that Humphrey would never let his own ambitions be overtaken by yet another Kennedy, the vice president was not the passionate Johnson loyalist that many believed. Humphrey faced some difficult decisions. His differences with Johnson over Vietnam were obvious in the cabinet, but a public break with the president would make him the ultimate latecomer to the Kennedy/McCarthy antiwar cause. If Kennedy had been regarded as an "opportunist" for joining the antiwar cause late in the game, the Humphrey turnaround promised even more troubles. It would also alienate his hard-core supporters in organized labor, those who had done well in an era of endless defense contracts and Great Society projects.

Humphrey's dilemma was a challenging one, but, once again, unexpected events soon changed everything. At 12:15 A.M., June 5, 1968, Kennedy was shot and killed by Sirhan Sirhan in Los Angeles's Ambassador Hotel. Moments before the shooting, the victorious Kennedy had just thanked his California campaign workers and promised a quick road to the nomination. The dream of Camelot, part II, died with him.[11]

VIOLENCE IN THE STREETS

Nearly all of McCarthy's campaign workers and some of the late Bobby Kennedy's supporters were outraged at the idea of Humphrey, a known "hawk," being assured an easy nomination at the Democratic convention in Chicago. From the SDS to the Yippies, Chicago came to symbolize everything that was wrong with 1960s America. Major street demonstrations were planned, and Chicago's mayor, Richard J. Daley, regarded antiwar protesters as invaders of his beloved city.

Inside the convention hall, Daley turned off the microphones of non-Humphrey supporters. Outside the convention hall, the Chicago police beat, clubbed, and arrested hundreds of demonstrators in what a later investigation dubbed a "police riot." Meeting the same fate as the demonstrators, the news media was considered in collusion with the antiwar effort to disrupt the convention. CBS's Dan Rather was punched and kicked to the convention floor while attempting to cover the complaints of antiwar delegates, and outside even reporters for well-known local TV stations, such as WGN and WLS, were beaten and detained. Some television viewers admired Daley's efforts to maintain order in a chaotic situation, while others were appalled at the orgy of violence. Few remembered the key themes and points of Humphrey's nomination speech moments after it was over. The wail of police sirens and the chorus of screams could be heard throughout Humphrey's speech.

During his convention address, the vice president called for calm, praised the commitments of John Kennedy and Lyndon Johnson, and suggested a new round of domestic reform. The latter suggestion was not unexpected, given his long association with civil rights causes. Peace was possible, he said, but his comments on Vietnam were deliberately vague. Outraged antiwar delegates attempted to rally their support behind Senator George McGovern in a last-ditch effort to bring McCarthy and Kennedy delegates together. McGovern had been a World War II hero who, in the 1950s, reorganized the Democratic Party in his home state of South Dakota largely on his own. Later serving as John Kennedy's director of the Food for Peace program in South Vietnam, McGovern observed the madness of the war early on and had been one of the country's first important doubters of the U.S. mission in Southeast Asia. But the effort to nominate him came too late in the midst of political chaos. His day was yet to come.

In 1960 and 1964, American political opinion polls had given the newly nominated Democratic or Republican presidential candidates an impressive temporary boost in popularity once the convention was over. In August 1968, the Democratic Party's popularity slipped, and the convention violence was to blame. To break the slide, Humphrey needed to shock the voters.

Two months after the convention, Humphrey went with his conscience in a go-for-broke speech that outlined his new interest in Vietnam peace. Humphrey implied that he never had been a strong supporter of the war. He was right, of course, but Humphrey's behavior confused the electorate. With the election only days away, it was much too late for voters to be confused over the Democratic nominee's position. There were also other candidates to consider. Although cynics complained that the 1968 election offered the choice between Tweedledum and Tweedledee, there were, in fact, real options in this difficult contest.[12]

MIDDLE AMERICA AWAKES

During the 1960s, the generation that had been born and raised in the economic misery of the Great Depression and survived the horror of World War II had reached middle age. After years of struggle, more of them lived in the ranks of the comfortable middle class than ever before. The debate over Vietnam and civil rights threatened that comfort. Economic experts predicted a return to financial struggle in the 1970s, and young civil rights or student radicals promised a very different America from the days of Herbert Hoover or Franklin Roosevelt. Few in what would later be known as the Greatest Generation had ever questioned the wisdom of previous government policies, and to some the expression "my country right or wrong" held great meaning. To these millions, the urban race riots, student antiwar demonstrations, and endless political battles were the concerns of a very vocal minority, and the press made too much of them. The drudgery of work continued, families grew, and life went on. Who was listening to hard-working, tax-paying, flag-waving Americans? Who cared about the majority?

The cause of the forgotten majority was championed by an unlikely source. Governor George Wallace was the first national figure to hit on the disaffection of the regular guy. Sadly, in Wallace's politics, the regular guy was a racist who had had enough of hard-fought legislation for African Americans. Washington was not fighting for the white majority, Wallace contended, and a vote for him would be "sending a message" to the political community that the majority could no longer be ignored. Although a longtime Democrat, Wallace ran for president on an American Independent Party ticket. Eventually learning to pick and choose his words more carefully in order to attract a wider white middle-class and working-class audience, Wallace spoke of patriotism, "dinner pail legislation for working families," and a return to a vaguely defined set of "traditional values." His appeals continued to hit a nerve, although his Southern racist background and his struggling new third party made some Northern voters nervous.

Wallace continued to assail "pointy-headed intellectuals" (a reference to Eugene McCarthy and Robert Kennedy supporters), "Big Government" (a reference to Johnson administration efforts to pass civil rights legislation and raise taxes for inner city projects), and "experts who can't tie their shoes" (a reference to social critics, journalists, and, generally, anyone who favored new directions in both domestic and foreign policy). His running mate, General Curtis LeMay, the former head of the Strategic Air Command and nicknamed "Bombs Away" LeMay, favored nuclear strikes on North Vietnam and a "return to patriotism" at home. Wallace distanced himself from LeMay on occasion, rarely offering a straightforward answer to questions about Vietnam. Indeed, he insisted that unless Washington engaged in a World War II–like commitment to win the Vietnam War, it should "make peace." Most analysts concluded that Wallace was trying to court antiestablishment voters, including those who sought a quick U.S. military withdrawal from Vietnam. If president, he planned to direct his anticommunist energies elsewhere.

Wallace's candidacy divided Democrats and severely hurt the party's chances for success in the South. Whether the Democrats wished to admit it or not, Wallace was a serious candidate and had a strong following. Traditionally and throughout America's political history, an appealing third party challenge was short-lived. One or both of the major parties usually stole the third party's issues, although the Republicans had started life as a third party. In modern times, if challenged by the third party, the Democrats and Republicans simply adjusted their own campaigns accordingly, forever warning the voter that a vote for an amateur, outsider party was a wasted vote. In 1968, Hubert

Humphrey and the Democrats refused to believe that their Great Society accomplishments faced a serious assault by, technically, one of their own.[13] The winner of the 1968 election and a Republican, Richard Nixon, understood the Wallace appeal, took on some of his issues, called himself the "New Nixon," exploited Democratic party divisions, and built a successful coalition. Nixon's comeback was profound, and he promised a new era of peace.

THE SEARCH FOR LEADERSHIP

During the 1968 presidential campaign, none of the leading candidates foresaw the end of the protest era. Yet, at least one of them talked at length about the need for strong leadership into the uncharted land of the 1970s. In fact, that leadership, said Governor Nelson Rockefeller of New York, was the key to success in the upcoming decade. Both Republicans and Democrats, he argued in August 1968, refused to recognize the revolutionary developments of their day. The Civil Rights and antiwar movements, he said, turned away from nonviolence because too many politicians refused to recognize their desperation, commitment, and moral worth. Eugene McCarthy and the late Robert Kennedy, Rockefeller implied, had exploited these movements for their own political ends. The peace and civil rights advocates deserved leadership, he noted, not exploitation.

Rockefeller's assessment was quite daring for a longstanding member of the Republican Party—and especially daring for a presidential candidate. But "Rocky," as his friends called him, accented the "leadership issue," and he hit a responsive chord. As a liberal, Rockefeller, his critics insisted, was in the wrong party. A strong advocate of higher education for anyone who had the credentials to go to college, Rockefeller had already won the attention of the academic community. His trailblazing and innovative State University of New York (SUNY) system enjoyed high praise from the press as well. His "New Leadership" campaign for president, wedded to the promise of bringing back the can-do spirit of Kennedy's New Frontier, excited liberals, academics, and students who were tired of Democratic squabbles. Harvard University's Henry Kissinger, a former national security consultant to the John Kennedy White House, was one of those early "Rocky for President" campaigners.

Painting many Republicans and LBJ Democrats as confused reactionaries in a revolutionary age, Rockefeller insisted that the Vietnam War could be easily resolved. He favored a coalition government of pro- and anti-American forces there. He also favored even stronger White House involvement in anti-urban poverty efforts, as well as new bipartisan efforts in civil rights reform. Rockefeller presented his case in a quiet, low-key manner. From Richard Nixon to Ronald Reagan, fellow Republican rivals admitted that the New York governor brought a certain civil tone to the 1968 campaign. A civil tone was most unusual in that volatile year. Winning the White House, Rockefeller quickly discovered, required a recognition of the white middle class's growing disgust for a government that seemed to stress the concerns of African Americans and little else. These same white Americans were confused and angered over the losing war in Vietnam. They sought a return to law and order, and they feared that economic struggle might soon define the 1970s.

Thanks to his voluntary removal from the political stage in 1962, Richard Nixon, the self-proclaimed private citizen, argued that he understood the fears and concerns of America's "ignored majority" of middle-class, middle-aged, and older whites. He chose his words with great caution, avoiding the abrasive tone that defined the George Wallace campaign. In fact, most of his speeches only implied that he sympathized with the concerns of suburban whites. Instead, he said that he was the "New Nixon," the humbled loser of the 1960 national and 1962 California elections, who doubted the Democratic agenda.

No longer the anticommunist crusader who flirted with unethical politics, the former vice president insisted that he had learned from his mistakes and sought a second chance at American leadership. According to Nixon, Franklin Roosevelt's old New Deal had grown tired and fat in the hands of Lyndon Johnson. Both domestic and foreign policies were mismanaged because of it, he claimed. Reminiscent of John Kennedy but minus the eloquence, Nixon promised "new directions." This time, the effort would involve keeping the social peace at home and winning "peace with honor" in Vietnam. Nixon never detailed any precise proposals, but an electorate eager for new policies did not seem to care.

Isolating Rockefeller as a Republican version of Eugene McCarthy, Nixon proclaimed that his "Nixon's the One" campaign represented the all-important moderate center in American political life. Rockefeller lost the Republican nomination to him. The New York governor's key supporters, such as Kissinger, now drifted into Nixon's camp. Still, Nixon versus Humphrey remained a close race.

Because of the deliberately vague nature of his campaign, the press often misunderstood Nixon's intentions. An off-the-cuff discussion with a small group of reporters in fall 1968 led the media to believe that the Republican nominee had a "secret plan to end the Vietnam War." Nixon denied that that was the case and continued to do so for the next quarter century. Yet, his campaign always implied that it had the solution to America's Vietnam problem. Nixon's play on words did not help matters either. For instance, the president's claim that GOP did not stand for Grand Old Party but for Generation of Peace, suggested to many voters that a Nixon peace plan for Vietnam was truly afoot. This was never the case. Privately, Nixon had little use for the misery of Vietnam and wondered what to do about it. Once in the White House, he finally concluded that he had no interest in being the first U.S. president to lose a war. There would be no quick U.S. withdrawal.

During the campaign, the Democratic vice presidential nominee, Senator Edmund Muskie of Maine, had asked the electorate to question Nixon about the specifics of his Vietnam plans and other policies. There was nothing new about the "New Nixon," Muskie warned, and the voters should beware. Despite these attacks on Nixon's credibility, most of Muskie's speeches were more civil in tone than even Rockefeller's. He insisted that the political community must refrain from harsh, divisive rhetoric, work together, and find peaceful solutions to American problems. His call for unity and reason in U.S. politics was as vague as most of Nixon's speeches, but he was consistent and eloquent. Muskie won respect from both Democrats and Republicans for his honesty and integrity. That respect also established him as the Democratic Party's rising star and potential presidential candidate for 1972 or later.

The precise results of the 1968 election were not that comforting to the Nixon team. They won, but without a clear mandate. Nixon received 31,770,222 votes to Humphrey's 31,267,744.[14] This victory of less than 1 percent was also accompanied by the return of Democratic majorities in the Senate, House, and the nation's governorships. George Wallace might have been the spoiler in this election. His five-state win and 9.9 million votes were impressive for a third-party challenge. Meanwhile, a wounded but defiant Humphrey proclaimed that the old New Deal coalition lived on. But times were changing, and the future remained in the hands of Richard Nixon and not Humphrey.

CHRONICLE OF EVENTS

1968

January 3: The North Vietnamese government announces that peace talks could begin as soon as the United States halts all bombing raids north of the 17th parallel.

January 5: In Massachusetts, a federal grand jury indicts Dr. Benjamin Spock, a best-selling author and noted pediatrician, on charges that he and his staff had counseled young men on how to avoid the draft.

January 8: In one of the longest cold spells in U.S. history, 35 states recorded temperatures below zero.

January 9: In the last of the unmanned space flights of the 1960s, *Surveyor* 7 lands on the moon.

January 10: The Secret Service arrests three men who had built the largest counterfeiting ring in U.S. history. More than $4 million in counterfeit bills are seized at New York's Kennedy airport alone.

January 17: In his State of the Union address, President Johnson proposes a record budget of $186 billion and expanded programs to stress urban housing and employment. It would be the last balanced federal budget for nearly 30 years.

January 19: Clark Clifford replaces Robert McNamara as secretary of defense.

January 21: The siege of Khe Sanh marks the beginning of the bloody Tet Offensive in Vietnam.

January 22: Scheduled as the mid-season replacement for the once popular *Man From U.N.C.L.E., Rowan and Martin's Laugh-In* comedy/satire show premieres on NBC television.

January 23: An American intelligence-gathering ship, *Pueblo,* is seized by North Korean patrol boats. Its

Built in Kewaunee, Wisconsin, during World War II, the cargo ship *Pueblo* becomes an intelligence-gathering U.S. Navy "research ship" in the 1960s. Its capture by the North Koreans in 1968 resulted in an 11-month hostage crisis and a tense United States versus North Korea standoff. *(U.S. Naval Historical Center)*

crew of 83 is taken prisoner, and the Johnson administration claims that the ship was sailing in international waters.

January 29: A 36-hour truce held in honor of the Tet lunar new year holidays is canceled by U.S. and South Vietnamese forces. A major North Vietnamese offensive near the 17th parallel was believed to be imminent.

January 30: As part of a nationwide attack on all significant U.S. and South Vietnamese military and political targets, Vietcong troops invade the U.S. embassy compound in Saigon. The battle lasts six hours, and the invaders are killed.

February 7: The Johnson administration reports the lowest unemployment rate (3.5 percent) in 15 years. A record 73.3 million Americans were on the job, and much of the boom is credited to new defense industry contracts and Great Society programs.

February 9: After four days of racial violence, a curfew restores law and order in Orangeburg, South Carolina. The focus of the dispute involved the desegregation of a bowling alley. Three African Americans were killed and 37 were wounded.

February 19: The North Vietnamese government releases three American prisoners of war (POWs) as a "goodwill gesture" during the Tet holidays.

February 22: More than 540 American troops are reported killed during only one week of the ongoing Tet Offensive. The Pentagon admits that this is the highest U.S. casualty figure in a one-week period ever recorded in the Vietnam War.

February 23: The Johnson administration calls for a draft of 48,000 new troops for April 1968. This is the highest single draft call of the Vietnam War.

February 28: Suffering from negative press reports after he claimed that he was "brainwashed" by U.S. military officials in Saigon during a swing tour of Vietnam, Michigan governor George Romney announces that he will no longer seek the nomination of the Republican Party for president. The "brainwashed" statement was also perceived as an anti-U.S. military comment by moderates and conservatives in his party.

March 2: The Johnson administration's Advisory Commission on Civil Disorders reports that the African-American communities throughout the nation's big cities are in open rebellion against the U.S. government. In addition to revised Great Society programs, the commission calls for several new and expensive economic aid packages for the inner cities.

March 6: Disgusted with the bad news from Vietnam and the Tet Offensive, America's most-watched television newsman, Walter Cronkite, shocks the nation by stating his opposition to the Vietnam War.

March 8: The nation's longest public teachers' strike in its history (three weeks in Florida) ends with legislation to aid struggling schools in Miami.

March 10: In Operation Resolve to Win, 50,000 American and South Vietnamese troops counterattack Vietcong forces in the largest single military operation of the Vietnam War. The Vietcong Tet Offensive fails.

March 12: President Lyndon Johnson narrowly defeats Senator Eugene McCarthy of Minnesota in the New Hampshire primary. Former Vice President Richard Nixon wins a landslide in the Republican primary there.

March 16: Calling for an end to the Vietnam War, a dramatic expansion of Great Society programs, and a renewed commitment to New Frontier goals, Senator Robert Kennedy declares his candidacy for president.

March 21: New York governor Nelson Rockefeller announces that he will not run in the Republican presidential primaries but that he would accept a draft at the Republican convention.

March 22: General William Westmoreland is recalled from Vietnam and named army chief of staff.

March 31: In a surprise major address to the nation, President Johnson announces that he will not seek or accept the Democratic nomination for president. He also calls for Vietnam peace talks and suggests that the bombing of North Vietnam might soon end.

April 2: Senator Eugene McCarthy sweeps the Democratic primary in Wisconsin, and Richard Nixon wins similar landslide returns in the Republican primary there.

April 3: Stanley Kubrick's artistic science-fiction film, *2001: A Space Odyssey,* begins its run in American theaters.

April 4: The Nobel Peace Prize–winning civil rights leader Martin Luther King, Jr., is assassinated in Memphis, Tennessee.

April 6: Often compared to America's John and Robert Kennedy, Canada's Liberal Party reformer Pierre Elliott Trudeau wins the office of prime minister.

April 10: General Creighton Abrams is named the overall commander of U.S. troops in Vietnam.

April 11: Stressing the end of discrimination in U.S. housing policies and practices, the 1968 Civil Rights Act is passed by Congress.

April 19: U.S. pilots fly 160 missions over North Vietnam, a record-breaking achievement for a 24–hour period in the Vietnam War.

April 26: Vice president Hubert Humphrey declares his candidacy for the presidency.

April 28: Thousands of Japanese demonstrators march through the streets of downtown Tokyo, demanding an end to "the racist war in Vietnam" and an end to the U.S. occupation government on the island of Okinawa.

April 29: The controversial rock musical *Hair* moves from off-Broadway to Broadway in New York.

April 30: More than 720 students are arrested at Columbia University in New York following a violent demonstration against the Vietnam War.

April 30: After additional "soul-searching," Governor Nelson Rockefeller reenters the Republican primary race as a candidate in favor of "moderate reform."

May 5: In an effort to duplicate Tet Offensive horrors, the Vietcong launch a series of unsuccessful attacks in South Vietnam.

May 7: In his first confrontation with Senator Eugene McCarthy, Robert Kennedy wins the Indiana primary with 42 percent of the vote.

May 13: The Paris Peace Talks begin.

May 14: Robert Kennedy wins the Nebraska primary with 53 percent of the vote.

May 16: Unrest in Paris mounts as 20,000 workers go on strike in solidarity with thousands of protesting university students. The de Gaulle government orders hundreds of military policemen to assist local police in breaking up violent antigovernment and anti–Vietnam War demonstrations.

The Broadway cast of *Hair* is photographed during an opening scene to their soon-to-be long-running "counterculture" hit. *(Martin Swope/Time Pix)*

May 28: Eugene McCarthy scores an upset victory over Robert Kennedy in the Oregon primary.

May 30: In a pro-France, pro–"law and order" demonstration, thousands of de Gaulle supporters march through the streets of Paris. President de Gaulle welcomes the support and announces that he will never resign, and the student unrest begins to subside sooner than previously believed.

June 2: A rocket from a U.S. helicopter accidentally explodes at a South Vietnamese command post, killing the mayor of Saigon, the police chief of Saigon, and five other senior South Vietnamese officials.

June 5: A 24-year-old Jordanian, Sirhan Sirhan, shoots Robert Kennedy moments after the announcement of Kennedy's victory in the California primary.

June 10: The Cambodian government releases two captured U.S. servicemen as a "gesture" to the United States in honor of Robert Kennedy and America's grief over his assassination.

June 19: The South Vietnamese government orders a general mobilization, noting that this will preclude the need for more U.S. forces.

June 26: The Pentagon announces that the once vital base of Khe Sanh will soon be abandoned. Khe Sanh saw some of the heaviest fighting of the Vietnam War.

July 10: Famed pediatrician Dr. Benjamin Spock is sentenced to two years in prison for urging others to avoid the draft.

June 26: Senator Edward Kennedy announces that he will not consider a candidacy for vice president and has no intention to run for president either.

July 29: Pope Paul VI announces his "Humanae Vitae" encyclical, prohibiting Catholics from using artificial birth control methods or drugs.

August 6: Less than 12 hours after addressing the Republican national convention, former president Dwight Eisenhower survives a massive heart attack. It was his third heart attack since April 1968.

August 7: Former vice president Richard Nixon becomes the presidential nominee of the Republican Party.

August 25: Although outnumbered six to one, U.S. and South Vietnamese forces beat back a Vietcong assault on the U.S. Special Forces base of Duc Lap.

August 26–29: The Democratic convention platform committee endorses the continuation of the Vietnam War, including the bombing of North Vietnam.

August 28: John Gordon Mein, the U.S. ambassador to Guatemala, is machine-gunned to death by unknown assassins in the streets of Guatemala City.

August 28: On the first ballot, Vice President Hubert Humphrey wins the presidential nomination at the Democratic convention.

August 29: During the last major antiwar demonstration outside of the Democratic convention in Chicago, a combined force of National Guardsmen and Chicago policemen beat and arrest hundreds of protesters.

September 2: After four nights of violent protests, Berkeley, California, is put under a strict curfew. Thirty-seven demonstrators are arrested and one policeman seriously wounded in this effort to protest police brutality in Chicago during the Democratic convention.

September 3: The Pentagon announces the lowest draft call in several years (10,000 men).

September 7: The radical feminist Women's Liberation Party rallies in Atlantic City to protest the annual Miss America Pageant.

September 8: Black Panther leader Huey Newton is found guilty of "involuntary manslaughter" in the slaying of one white policeman but is declared innocent in the death of another.

September 12: In the first Supreme Court case of its kind, Supreme Court Justice William O. Douglas agrees with 113 army reservists who claim that they were sent to Vietnam illegally.

September 24: Television's first hour-long news magazine show, *60 Minutes,* premieres on the CBS network.

September 29: The 900th U.S. military plane is shot down by Vietcong troops in South Vietnam. This record-high number of lost aircraft prompts a major Pentagon review of air operations in Southeast Asia.

October 5: The Cox Commission investigation into university campus unrest in New York reports that student rebels have deliberately sought to disrupt university life and that university administrators prefer "authoritarian rule" to opening a dialogue with their own students.

October 7: For the first time in the history of the film industry, the Motion Picture Association of America announces a rating system for all significant, mass-marketed movies.

October 11–22: In the effort to test needed equipment and technology, *Apollo* 7 becomes NASA's first Apollo-piloted mission. Astronauts Walter Schirra, Donn Eisele, and Walter Cunningham are on board.

October 20: Jacqueline Kennedy, the former first lady and widow of the assassinated John F. Kennedy, marries Greek shipping tycoon Aristotle Socrates Onassis on his private island of Skorpios.

October 23: Believed to be planning a major campaign of terror, nine anti-Castro Cubans are arrested in New York. The group had already bombed more than a dozen U.S. businesses that, they contended, had shadowy ties to Castro.

October 24: Some 80 people are arrested at the University of California-Berkeley campus during yet another student demonstration. The students were demanding course credit for all those who attended a lecture by Black Panther activist Eldridge Cleaver.

October 24: Eleven South Vietnamese prisoners of war are released by the Vietcong, and, in turn, the Saigon regime releases 140 Vietcong prisoners. The U.S. embassy in South Vietnam hails this development as a "first great step" in Vietnamese cooperation.

November 5: New York political activist and Democrat Shirley Chisholm becomes the first African-American woman elected to the House of Representatives.

November 5: In a narrow popular vote victory, Richard Nixon defeats both Hubert Humphrey and George Wallace to becomes the 37th president of the United States.

November 9: For the first time since 1812, an earthquake shakes the U.S. Midwest. Minor damage is reported in cities stretching from Michigan's Upper Peninsula to Nashville, Tennessee.

November 12: The U.S. Supreme Court strikes down an Arkansas law that prohibits teaching evolution in statewide high school and grade school science classes.

November 15: The National Conference of Catholic Bishops defies the Vatican by noting that American Catholics will not be asked to leave the church if they use contraceptives. Nevertheless, the conference declares that the Vatican is correct in insisting that married couples should not use artificial birth controls.

November 20: After a week of numerous antiwar rallies and general unrest, a previously tranquil San Francisco State College reopens for classes.

In 1968, Shirley Chisholm, the first female African-American member of the House of Representatives, poses for her official freshman congresswoman picture. Four years later, she will make an unprecedented but unsuccessful run for the Democratic presidential nomination. *(Library of Congress)*

November 21: Following university president Roger Guiles's refusal to adhere to a list of demands by pro–Black Panther student activists, angry students begin a "campaign of destruction" at the University of Wisconsin-Oshkosh. More than 100 students are arrested.

November 21: In one of the more bizarre federal court cases of 1968, the Johnson administration charges its own housing authority employees in Little Rock, Arkansas, for maintaining pro-segregationist housing policies.

November 27: In a special announcement that shocks Wall Street, the Bureau of Labor Statistics reports that the cost of living jumped .6 percent in October. This high figure was unexpected in certain business circles and represents, according to the *Wall Street Journal,* "serious economic difficulties" ahead.

November 28: A coalition of pro-feminist activists and reformers hold their first formal convention in Chicago, Illinois.

December: The Motion Picture Association of America announces that the top three box office winners of 1968 are *The Graduate, Guess Who's Coming to Dinner,* and a restored/technologically updated version of 1939's *Gone With the Wind.* The top box office draws are Sidney Poitier, Paul Newman, and Julie Andrews.

December: The Associated Press announces that the top three single record successes of 1968 are "Hey Jude" by the Beatles, "Love Is Blue" by Paul Mauriat, and "Honey" by Bobby Goldsboro.

December 3: Tired of hearing that "Elvis is dead" in the face of the British Invasion, Elvis Presley makes a successful comeback in an hour-long television concert special.

December 4: Although having announced his retirement five months earlier, Supreme Court Chief Justice Earl Warren agrees to a request by outgoing president Lyndon Johnson to stay on the job until his court agenda is completed in June 1969.

December 6: Close to 60 percent of all of New York City's parking meter collectors are arrested for having stolen more than $5 million during a three-year period.

December 19: Six months after their boat strayed into Cambodian waters, 11 U.S. military personnel are released in the interest of "justice and humanity." The Cambodian government also reaffirms its neutrality in the Vietnam War.

December 21–27: With astronauts James Lovell, Frank Borman, and William Anders on board, *Apollo 8* successfully accomplishes the first manned orbit of the moon.

December 22: The crew of U.S.S. *Pueblo* are released following a delicately negotiated U.S.–North Korean agreement.

December 22: Gary Steven Krist is arrested for kidnaping 20-year-old Barbara Jane Mackle in Atlanta, burying her alive in a box for more than three days, and collecting $500,000 in ransom from her millionaire father. Mackle is rescued unharmed.

December 25: The U.S. embassy in Saigon reports 133 Vietcong violations of a Christmas holidays truce agreement.

December 31: For the first time since 1930, the Federal Bureau of Prisons reports that no one incarcerated in the nation's prison system was executed in 1968.

EYEWITNESS TESTIMONY

The Antiwar Protest Continues

What is different about 1968 is that people—students and teachers, housewives and professionals—have worked not just in the primary states, but in precinct caucuses and county conventions: seeking not to serve the candidate selected by the party machinery, but to exercise democratic choice. Beyond this, they have engaged hundreds of thousands, perhaps millions, of their fellow-citizens in a face-to-face discussion and debate, not just about the merits of one or another candidate, but about the substantive issues which are at the heart of the election.

Robert Kennedy on May 21, 1968, telling a group of student newspaper editors in San Francisco why the "people power" politics of 1968 will be remembered in years to come, in Robert F. Kennedy: Presidential Campaign Papers, 1968, JFK Library.

If many of the dissidents actually were in Vietnam and faced the reality of the problem, they would change.

NSC adviser Walt Rostow attempting to answer a question from President Johnson about how the White House should attempt to win back the support of angry, antiwar youth, in Rostow to Johnson, July 13, 1968, Box 233 of the White House Central File, Lyndon Johnson Library.

I had seen the two boys in the crosswalk, and I had seen the Thunderbird almost hit them. It was on Kalakaua Avenue in Honolulu, one early evening in the late spring. "Watch it," one of the boys may or may not have said. I heard him say nothing, but whatever was said or not said affected the erring driver of the Thunderbird malignantly. "Stinking hippies," he screamed, jumping from the car. "Burning your draft cards, you should've burned Germany, you should've burned Japan, stinking hippies."

"I don't know what you're talking about, Mister," one of the boys said. He was wearing a blue suit and a white shirt, and his blond hair was about as long as the average college freshman's. "I got my draft card."

Noting that "generation gap" incidents are increasing in violence, reporter Joan Didion describing a confrontation in Hawaii in late August 1968, in her "On Becoming a Cop Hater," Saturday Evening Post, August 24, 1968, p. 16.

The Yale-Princeton game was preceded by a week in which the Sons of Eli lost their cool and emblazoned the campus with signs suited to the Berkeley Free Speech Movement. Football, once on the decline in the Ivy League, brought out the frenzy of the 1960's. Yale Coach Carm Cozza said, "These kids don't go for planned rallies, but I've never seen enthusiasm like we had that one week. There was never more spirit in the Midwest. The game goes on."

Look magazine reporter Robert Blair Kaiser predicting that the violent campus-based antiwar demonstrations of September 1968 will have little impact on the new college football season, in his "College Forecast '68," Look, September 17, 1968, pp. 22–26.

They had a member of Berkeley's SDS as a speaker, and it scared me to death. I thought these people were Communists. But then I began to weigh what they were saying and what I felt, and it was the same, even if the terminology was different. . . . Six months ago I would have avoided conflict and confrontations. Now, I understand that you can't bring about change by doing nothing. Love is getting hit over the head by a cop for something you believe in. And I'm sold on the Movement because it's for change.

Simply identifying himself as "Steve," a newcomer to the SDS telling his life story to editor Ernest Dunbar in mid-October 1968, in Dunbar, "Vanguard of the Campus Revolt," Look, October 1, 1968, pp. 23–29.

We talk nitty-gritty basic radicalism, getting control of your life from the forces which are manipulating you. Dorms are a prime area to work in because the people in them are in frequent contact, will be together for a number of months and live in generally repressive circumstances. We start on the top floor of the dorm with a list of people we already know. We call meetings and talk to students about draft resistance, the nature of the university, and how you can change these things. Then we help them call meetings of people on other floors, and we exchange ideas and information on what they are doing. Soon the ferment spreads to all floors of the dorm. Our main problem is that people feel they are impotent. You have to convince them that they can change things.

That means coming back to talk with them again and again.

John Kauffman, an SDS organizer at the University of Wisconsin, telling Look *magazine senior editor Ernest Dunbar how early SDS recruitment begins, in Dunbar, "Vanguard of the Campus Revolt,"* Look, *October 1, 1968, pp. 23–29.*

This war is unjust because there are no potential results which will make up for the magnitude of death and suffering Vietnam is undergoing. . . . Only peace can offer the chance of a decent life for its people. My conscience demands that I refuse to be a part of the military forces which inflict this suffering. My conscience demands that I work to end the war.

Pvt. Steve Murtaugh explaining to reporter Christopher Wren why he deserted the U.S. Army and fled to Sweden in the fall of 1968, in Wren, "Protest in the Ranks," Look, *October 15, 1968, pp. 31–37.*

We must preserve the universities. But beware of the Fatal Friendliness. When universities serve the status quo, they must be changed. There should be continued ferment, demonstrations, education, enlightenment. Of course there are things which are not planned—forces, mechanisms. . . . The best students are Socialist but not Marxist. The don't want a Stalinist bureaucracy. They want a transvaluation of values—social protest on a high level of prosperity and comfort. The price of freedom is high! But they refuse the state of total domination by goods and comfort.

It is possible to automate to the limits of technical achievement. Then there will be either a welfare state or free society. In a free society the tasks will be tremendous—to reconstruct city and countryside and man himself.

New Left icon Herbert Marcuse stirring a group of antiwar youth during an October 1968 guest lecture in San Diego, in Gold, "Mao, Marx, et Marcuse!," Saturday Evening Post, *October 19, 1968, pp. 56–59.*

A priest who was in the crowd says he saw a boy, about 14 or 15, white, standing on the top of an automobile yelling something which was unidentifiable. Suddenly a policeman forced him down from the car and beat him to the ground by striking him three or four times with a nightstick. Other police joined in.

A well-dressed woman saw this incident and spoke angrily to a nearby police captain. As she spoke, another policeman came up from behind her and sprayed something in her face with an aerosol can. He then clubbed her to the ground. He and two other policemen then dragged her along the ground to the same paddy wagon and threw her in.

First released to the public in December 1968, the Walker Report on violence at the 1968 Democratic convention, describing a Chicago street scene, in Smith, "Corruption behind the swinging clubs," Life, *December 6, 1968, pp. 34–42.*

I suggest that a lot of today's young see the complexity of modern life not as a challenge, but as a barrier, precisely because they see no way . . . by which they can master it; and thus, instead of expending the energy needed to meet the "challenge," they rebel against the system. . . . Rebellion can be many things—and one of those things is a crutch for those who fear they can't make it. . . . By rebelling against the "system," the youth sets up an excuse for failure; by rejecting its values, he rejects in advance the anticipated negative judgment of the society that embraces those values. It's no coincidence that so much of the youthful rebellion . . . is focused on the search for simple answers, simple relationships, simple truths. Or that in its inarticulateness, this same set . . . reduces communication to little more than simple grunts or code phrases. . . . It's as though, by instinct, the herd is running from the thunder, seeking shelter: and its shelter is the simple, even the primitive.

Veteran Republican Party speechwriter Ray Price explaining to 1968 Republican candidates that the antiwar movement is led by struggling young men and women who fear failure in the complex world of the late 1960s, in his "Thoughts on Dealing With Youthful Unrest," a 1968 Memo to the Republican National Committee, White House Special Files, Box 59/Krogh, Papers of Richard M. Nixon, National Archives II, College Park, Maryland.

The young people that my daughters bring around are not like that. I just can't believe it.

President Johnson expressing his shock over campus radicalism to a friend in late 1968, in Miller, Lyndon: An Oral Biography *(1980), Research Room, Lyndon Johnson Library.*

All of a sudden, the door of one of the houses—really, it was almost like a mansion—opened and out came a young man and a girl about our age. They stopped at the top of the steps for a minute, and we looked right up at them. It was as if they were on the stage, because the streetlight was shining on them, and they were in evening clothes. The man had a tux, and the girl had a strapless gown, and she looked just beautiful. And we just stared. We stopped and just stared at them. We couldn't say anything. They were like creatures from another world. They were our age and they were going to a prom. We had thought the whole world was with us, and here were these two people living in a movie. I'll never forget that. Steve sort of shouted at them, "Don't you know there's a war on?" But they ignored us. I guess they thought we were just a couple of hippies, and probably they couldn't really see us. We were in the dark, and they were in the light.

Nearly 20 years after the fact, former antiwar activist Lorraine Sue Brill remembering the night of her first demonstration in late 1968, her New Left boyfriend Steve, and an encounter with "straights" (non-antiwar activist youth) her same age, in Morrison and Morrison, From Camelot to Kent State: The Sixties Experience in the Words of Those Who Lived It *(1987), pp. 119–120.*

The plight of South Vietnamese refugees contributed to the moral outrage of the American antiwar movement. Here a family gathers food provided by the American Red Cross. *(National Archives)*

From Rock and Laugh-In to Yippies, Hippies, and Vietnam on Film

While he is admittedly out to make a buck the same as his Dad was, he talks about it differently. First, he talks about "doing your own thing," a phrase that is virtually the Apostle's Creed of hippie belief. Then he describes the importance of doing what he is doing on his own. Finally, he gets around to mentioning the profit motive.

For many hippie entrepreneurs, commercial success brings with it a decided uneasiness—a milder version of what a corporation president might feel at setting up housekeeping in a crash pad. As James H. Newby, the luxuriantly-tressed proprietor of the Love Poster Shop in the seedy section of New Orleans' French Quarter, puts it: "Business interests me very much, it fascinates me. But I know from experience that I don't want to get too involved in it."

Business Week reminding its readers that hippies can be capitalists too, in Staff, "Hippie capitalists are making it happen," Business Week, January 27, 1968, pp. 84–85.

When you make a movie you can't have it every way. Nichols and his two screen writers—Calder Willingham and Buck Henry—open *The Graduate* with a real hero living in a real world and conclude with a parody-hero living in a parody-world. The transformation from one to the other is arbitrary. When Ben Braddock has to seize his girl violently from his enemies, he does it in a church, while swinging a gold cross overhead as a kind of ironic weapon against hypocrisy and materialism. Every time the nymphomaniac's husband comes near Ben you almost expect him to make a pass at the boy. And why not? In the context of all this pop-styled activity, one "turn" is as good as another.

Film critic Robert Kotlowitz complaining that The Graduate is a confused pop culture movie, in his "Capote's Killers, and Others," Harper's, March 1968, p. 156.

The show's producers like to say that the format follows an old trusted formula—something old and new, borrowed and blue. But *Laugh-In* has something far better than formula jokes: topical satire that is biting without being bitter.

"The President may not always be right," says one girl, "but you have to admit one thing: he's consis-

tent!" Adds another: "Boris says he won't believe it till he hears L.B.J. deny it."

Time magazine examining prime time television political satire and claiming that NBC's new Laugh-In comedy show is the natural "follow-up" to CBS's Smothers Brothers show, in Staff, "Comedians: A Put-On Is Not a Put-Down," Time, March 8, 1968, p. 65.

The Yippies aim to set up a lakefront tent village in Grant Park, where they can groove on folk songs, rock bands, "guerilla" theater, body painting and meditation. Through the park they will bear on a blue pillow their very own presidential candidate: Lyndon Pigasus Pig, a ten-week-old black and white porker now afattening at the Hog Farm, a hippie commune in Southern California. Other possibilities being considered: a lie-in at Chicago's O'Hare Field to prevent Democratic delegates from landing or, failing that, a fleet of fake cabs to pick up delegates and dump them off in Wisconsin.

Time magazine reviewing Yippie long range plans to disrupt the August 1968 Democratic convention, in Staff, "The Politics of YIP," Time, April 5, 1968, p. 61.

There are things to be said for the old days, when rock was religion, and not yet an art form. At least it was still possible to tell the worshipers from their gods.

Music critic Richard Goldstein declaring 1964 a "golden age" of rock, in his "Pop Music," Vogue, May 1968, p. 164.

It might be the evening scene in any city slum. Unkempt youths clot the stoops of dilapidated tenements, talking overboldly of drugs; drunks reel along gutters foul with garbage; young toughs from neighboring turf methodically proposition every girl who passes by, while older strangers hunt homosexual action. The night air smells of decay and anger. For all its ugly familiarity, however, this not just another ghetto. This is the scene in San Francisco's Haight-Ashbury district, once the citadel of hippiedom and symbol of flower-power love. Love has fled the Hashbury.

Time magazine reporting that crime, poverty, and misery rule America's premier hippie enclave, in Staff, "Wilting Flowers," Time, May 10, 1968, p. 31.

Tiny Tim is a gentle soul who happens to be the most bizarre entertainer this side of Barnum & Bailey's sideshow. His specialties are pop songs from early decades of the century, and his performances flicker with a genuine talent for re-creating the styles of such stars of the era as Arthur Fields, Gene Austin, Ruth Etting and Russ Columbo. But Tiny dismisses the notion that he does imitations. "The spirits of the singers whose songs I do are living within me," he insists. All this is pathetically easy to mock, yet Tiny's total absorption in his role—what one friend calls "the purity of madness"—cloaks him in an impervious aura of innocence.

> Time *magazine reviewing singer Tiny Tim and his sudden popularity after his national introduction on NBC's* Laugh-In *comedy show, in Staff, "The Purity of Madness,"* Time, *May 17, 1968, p. 66.*

There is even an encore sung by Tiny in what is probably the one voice he wishes everyone would accept as being truly his own, a voice husked by the melodic tradition and heart-string vibrato of every crooner who ever became a recording star, and yet within the husk Tiny's own brand of corn can be found clean, fresh and innocent. "This is all I ask," he sings. "Let the music play as long as there's a song to sing." The dream ends with Tiny, in his naive honesty, dedicating the album to his mother and father. He should. They are now in their 70s and Tiny, an only child in his 40s, still lives with them.

> *Pop music critic Alfred Aronowitz attempting to find some talent behind the music of Tiny Tim, in his "It's High Time Fame Came to Tiny Tim,"* Life, *June 14, 1968, p. 10.*

The most staggering leading woman in rock is Janis Joplin, who once sang folk-blues in Texas bars for the beer and the joy. . . . Janis assaults a song with her eyes, her hips, and her hair. She defies key, shrieking over one line, sputtering over the next, and clutching the knees of a final stanza, begging it not to leave. When it does leave anyway, she stands like an assertive young tree, smiling breathlessly at the audience, which has just exploded. Janis Joplin can sing the chic off any listener.

> *Music critic Richard Goldstein praising the innovative style of rock music's new 1968 sensation, Janis Joplin, in his "Janis Joplin . . . staggering,"* Vogue, *May 1968, p. 164.*

Even in repose he looks like a cross between Bob Dylan and the Wild Man of Borneo: his hair is a foot long, uncombed and stabs the air in every direction around a heavily pimpled face. He's always swathed in such things as a grimy old British military jacket, purple velvet pants and a goat hair vest, and lately he has taken to wearing a floppy hat that's banded with brass rings and filigrees.

He's Jimi Hendrix, a Seattle-born 23-year-old guitarist-singer who, since he left the U.S. for England a year and a half ago, has worked the British beat scene back up to the kind of frenzy that created Beatle-mania and made millionaires of the likes of Ringo Starr. He and his two English sidemen—drummer John (Mitch) Mitchell and bass guitarist Noel Redding—call themselves "The Jimi Hendrix Experience," and the transistorized madness they produce is a "freak out" of rhythm and blues, psychedelic and total-volume noise. But right now, "The Experience" is at the top of British and Continental record charts, and a pair of U.S. tours have popularized Hendrix so much that the question, "Is he the new black Elvis?" is being asked.

> Ebony *magazine examining the sudden popularity of "The Jimi Hendrix Experience" in Staff, "The Jimi Hendrix Experience,"* Ebony, *May 1968, p. 102.*

To Producer, Co-Director and Star John Wayne, the war is a primer-simple. There's them and there's us. Us are the Green Beret crack troops led by Wayne with a chestful of fruit salad and a no-nonsense approach to the dovish American press, personified by David Janssen. During the beating of a V.C., Reporter Janssen protests, "There's such a thing as due process." "Out here," sneers Wayne, "due process is a bullet." Built on the primitive lines of the standard Western, *Berets* even has the South Vietnamese talking like movie Sioux: "We build many camps, clobber many V.C."

> Time *magazine concluding that* The Green Berets *is "strictly for hawks," in Staff, "Far from Viet Nam and Green Berets,"* Time, *June 21, 1968, p. 84.*

In the Alamo section of *The Green Berets,* when the yellowskins are about to overrun the fort and the air cavalry is nowhere in sight, and the mortar shells are zinging in like a poison monsoon, our guys are getting zapped so bad they look like those exploded-view diagrams they have in butcher shops to show the different cuts of meat, and John Wayne as Col. Mike Kirby, glances down at one of them and says briskly, efficiently: "This man needs attention!" and you don't know whether to howl or weep or both.

Newsweek magazine arguing that The Green Berets *is an unintentionally funny film, in Staff, "Affirmative? Negative!,"* Newsweek, *July 1, 1968, p. 94.*

In short, *The Green Berets* is dead on arrival. Mr. Wayne is still fighting the same battles he waged 20 and 30 years ago. Under his command here, the topkick is still named Muldoon, poor old Kowalski is still taking the point as they move out, and in a neat package deal, Jim Hutton plays a combination of three types—WASP, scrounger and brave coward. It is perhaps a measure of this movie's irrelevancy that its makers have not even noticed that the old ethnic mix no longer applies to combat troops in Vietnam. They are still indulging in tokenism; there is only one black man in the group, although a large number are employed to impersonate Vietcong. Very odd.

Veteran movie reviewer Richard Schickel taking on the The Green Berets, *in his "Duke Talks Through His Green Beret," Life, July 19, 1968, p. 8.*

I just have to get over this period—that never in my life have I been so in love with myself. . . . I need to help articulate the feelings of the voteless young over Vietnam.

Actor Dustin Hoffman telling Look *magazine that he's ready to play a strong antiwar hero on film, in Chapman, "The Graduate Turns Bum," Look, September 17, 1968, pp. 66–72.*

In the case of Big Brother and the Holding Company, the build-up just naturally flowed—because Janis Joplin was the lead singer. Janis Joplin? If she weren't so feminine, she might have become a lady wrestler. She's pop music's only broad, and whether she's singing or talking, it's with all the soul of a Hell's Angels exhaust pipe. Like Mae West, she could be the greatest lady who ever walked the streets. Six months before she even had a record out, she was being treated as one of the biggest stars in pop music. One week after the record hit the stores, she was firing the rest of her group. Janis Joplin had decided to send Big Brother and the Holding Company back to San Francisco while she shopped around for another band.

"They don't help the words, they either fight 'em or just lay there like dead fish," she said. It was 2:30 p.m. and she was drinking screwdrivers for breakfast. "I want a bigger band with higher highs, a bigger ladder. And I want more bottom. I want more noise. When I do a rock tune, I want it to be so huge. . . ."

Music critic Alfred Aronowitz examining the quick stardom and musical challenges of Janis Joplin, in his "Singer with a Bordello Voice," Life, September 20, 1968, p. 20.

Richard Nixon? Making jokes on a TV comedy show with a bunch of weirdos? You bet, as they say, your sweet bippy. Everybody wants to make a cameo appearance on Rowan and Martin's manic Monday night affair. It is the smartest, freshest show on television. President Johnson, Igor Stravinsky and Jean-Paul Sartre have not yet appeared at the stage door, but if they do, they'll just have to get in line behind Marcel Marceau, Bing Crosby, Pat Boone, Dick Gregory and Jack Benny.

Time magazine predicting that NBC's Laugh-In *comedy show will become the most-watched series in the history of television and analyzing the phenomenon, in Staff, "Verrry Interesting . . . but Wild," Time, October 11, 1968, p. 50.*

Illusions of a different sort are created by TV. For its journalists are enmeshed in a system that looks upon news as another commodity, which sells or does not sell, attracts audiences or does not, which—like other commodities—can be shaped, reworked, and manipulated, or simply dropped. There is, however, one factor that distinguishes news from almost everything else the networks transmit: prestige.

Veteran television newsman Robert MacNeil complaining that important news stories on network news shows are subordinated to the "star power" of the news anchorman and the "telegenic nature" of the story itself, in his "The News on TV and How It is Unmade," Harper's, October 1968, p. 72.

Conspiracy? Hell, we couldn't agree on lunch.

Yippie leader Abbie Hoffman answering a reporter's question after being told in October 1968 that he has been charged with "conspiracy to disrupt" the 1968 Democratic convention, in "The Chicago Seven Trial: In Their Own Words," p. 1. Available online. URL: http://www.law.umkc.edu/faculty/projects/ftrials/Chicago7/OwnWords.html.

Walter Cronkite, anchor of the *CBS Evening News,* became one of the most trusted men of the 1960s. Cronkite is photographed during an interview while on assignment in Hue, Vietnam, in 1968. *(National Archives)*

What happened to the original flower people? Some of the hippies have gone back home; many others have moved away—to the Sierras, Vancouver, La Paz, Europe—hoping to find a better scene, but with little luck. There have been no mass movements anywhere. "I can't say I'm sorry they left," says Police Capt. Mortimer J. McInerney. "They were not a problem themselves, but their presence attracted people who preyed on them."

> Newsweek *examining the sudden end of the "hippie movement" in San Francisco and nearby communities, in* Staff, "Where Are They Now?", Newsweek, *December 2, 1968, p. 20.*

Tet Offensive Issues

I consider this area critical to us from a tactical standpoint as a launch base for Special Operations Group teams and as flank security for the strong point obstacle system; it is even more critical from a psychological viewpoint. To relinquish this area would be a major propaganda victory for the enemy. Its loss would seriously affect Vietnamese and U.S. morale. In short, withdrawal would be a tremendous step backwards.

> *General William Westmoreland arguing with General Earle Wheeler that even though U.S. forces might be outnumbered (according to the first reports of arriving North Vietnamese troops near Khe Sanh), the United States has a chance to win the Vietnam War during early 1968, in Westmoreland to Wheeler, January 12, 1968, Tet Offensive, Lyndon Johnson Library.*

We have known for some time that this offensive was planned by the enemy. Over recent weeks I have been in close touch with General Westmoreland, and over recent days in very close touch with all of our Joint

Chiefs of Staff to make sure that every single thing that General Westmoreland believed that he needed at this time was available to him, and that our Joint Chiefs believe that his strategy was sound, his men were sure, and they were amply supplied.

I am confident in the light of the information given to me that our men and the South Vietnamese will be giving a good account of themselves. As all of you know, the situation is a fluid one. We will keep the American people informed as these matters develop.

> *President Johnson, in an official statement to executive branch employees (many of whom have loved ones fighting in Vietnam), trying to ease tensions during the opening days of the Tet Offensive, in Staff Announcement by the President, January 19, 1968, Tet Offensive, Declassified Correspondence, Lyndon Johnson Library.*

Now, I am no great strategist and tactician. I know that you are not. But let us assume that the best figures we can have are from our responsible military commanders. They say 10,000 died and we lost 249 and the South Vietnamese lost 500. Now that doesn't look like a Communist victory. I can count. It looks like somebody has paid a dear price for the temporary encouragement that some of our enemies had.

We have approximately 5,900 planes and have lost 38 completely destroyed. We lost 100-odd that were damaged and have to be repaired. Maybe Secretary McNamara will fly in 150 shortly.

Now is that a great enemy victory?

> *President Johnson, on January 19, 1968, during a quickly called news conference with the White House press corps, attempting to dispel rumors that the Vietcong were winning the Tet Offensive, in The Public Papers of President Lyndon B. Johnson, 1968, Speeches, Lyndon Johnson Library.*

If this is a failure, I hope the Viet Cong never have a major success.

> *Senator George Aiken of Vermont making a press statement on February 1, 1968, in Tet Offensive, Lyndon Johnson Library.*

The analysis and recommendations are based, almost entirely, upon an assessment of U.S. public opinion

During the early hours of the Tet Offensive, fire trucks rush to a downtown Saigon neighborhood set ablaze by Vietcong attacks. *(National Archives)*

and an unspoken assumption as to the effect that should be given to it. I am in total disagreement. . . . I can think of nothing worse than the suggested program. . . . It will, indeed, produce demands in this country to withdraw—and, in fact, it must be appraised for what it is: a step in the process of withdrawal. And in my opinion, it means not domestic appeasement, but domestic repudiation (which it would deserve); a powerful tonic to Chinese Communist effectiveness in the world; and a profound retreat to the Asia dominoes.

> *Abe Fortas, one of Lyndon Johnson's best friends and advisers, complaining in February 1968 to the president that late 1967 and early 1968 antiwar opinion is polluting Vietnam decision making at the highest levels, in Tet Offensive, Lyndon Johnson Library.*

The military targets have been attacked with restraint unprecedented in modern warfare. It is not always possible to avoid damaging adjacent civilian structures, but pilots make every effort to be precise.

Richard Fryklund, the deputy assistant secretary of defense, protesting a Saturday Evening Post *article that alleges that the U.S. military has deliberately destroyed dozens of nonmilitary targets in the Tet Offensive, in Fryklund's "Targets in Vietnam,"* Saturday Evening Post, *February 10, 1968, p. 4.*

New leadership will end the war and win the peace in the Pacific. . . . There is no magic formula, no gimmick. If I had a gimmick I would tell Lyndon Johnson.

Republican candidate for president, Richard Nixon, responding to the news of the Tet Offensive in mid-February 1968 in Tet Offensive, *Lyndon Johnson Library.*

This is what I would tell any boy of draft age; this was what I told my son when it came his turn to decide just what his obligation to his country was. Much as I might agree with my Quaker friends as to the nature of wars and armies, I am more impressed by the fact that we are citizens of a great power living in a time of wars, and that maintenance of an Army is a sad necessity that has been thrust upon us. I am sorry about that, as an Army man would say. But that is the way it is. We need an Army, and someone must serve in it. . . .

I know what I am asking of him, but I also know that I am asking no more than has been asked of youth by any nation in time of war. And I know too, that if he takes his turn in serving in the ranks, the Army, in its own relentless, uncaring and impersonal way, can be of service to him by giving him an opportunity to be himself, and that he will return to civil life more sure of himself, and feeling more certain of his right to citizenship, than anyone who has not served.

Saturday Evening Post *editorialist John Keats urging the Johnson administration not to give into public pressure, generated by the horror of the Tet Offensive, to end the draft, in his "The Draft Is Good for You,"* Saturday Evening Post, *February 10, 1968, p. 8.*

We carefully reviewed his request in light of the information that had come in. We made certain adjustments and arrangements to comply with his request forthwith. That will be done.

When we reach our goal, we will be constantly reviewing the matter many times every day, at many levels. We will do whatever we think needs to be done to insure that our men have adequate forces to carry out their mission.

President Johnson, at the height of the Tet Offensive in mid-February 1968 attempting to answer the rumors in the press about a General Westmoreland request to send tens of thousands of fresh troops to Vietnam, in The Public Papers of President Lyndon B. Johnson, 1968, *Speeches, Lyndon Johnson Library.*

Mr. President, I cannot find the words to express to you the feelings that lie in my heart. Fifty-one months ago you asked me to serve in your Cabinet. No other period in my life has brought so much struggle—or so much satisfaction. The struggle would have been infinitely greater and the satisfaction immeasurably less if I had not received your full support every step of the way. . . .

One hundred years of neglect cannot be overcome overnight. But you have pushed, dragged, and cajoled the nation into basic reforms which my children and my children's children will benefit for decades to come. I know the price you have paid, both personally and politically. Every citizen of our land is in your debt.

I will not say goodbye—you know you have but to call and I will respond.

Robert McNamara resigning as secretary of defense, in McNamara to Johnson, *February 23, 1968, Box 6 of the White House Famous Names File, Lyndon Johnson Library.*

We can no longer rely on the field commander. He can want troops and want troops and want troops. He must look at the overall impact on us, including the situation here in the United States. We must look at our economic stability, our other problems in the world, our other problems at home; we must consider whether or not this thing is tieing us down so that we cannot do some of the other things we should be doing; and finally, we must consider the effects of our actions on the rest of the world—are we setting an example in Vietnam through which other nations would rather not go if they are faced with a similar threat? . . .

Now the time has come to decide where do we go from here.

The new secretary of defense, Clark Clifford, following an in-depth review of Tet Offensive matters, informing President Johnson and his foreign policy staff that new policy directions might be required, in "Notes of the President's Meeting with Senior Foreign Policy Advisors," March 4, 1968, Box 2 of the Papers of Tom Johnson, Lyndon Johnson Library.

It appears we are about to make a rather basic change in the strategy of this war: We tell the ARVN to do more fighting. We tell them we will give 20,000 men; no more. We tell them we will do no more until they do more. We tell them we will be prepared to make additional troop contributions but not unless they get with it.

A tired President Johnson calling for a policy change and telling his foreign policy staff that it is our own ally, the Army of the Republic of Vietnam (ARVN), who are keeping U.S. forces from the final victory in 1968, in "Notes of the President's Meeting with Senior Policy Advisors," March 5, 1968, Box 2 of the Papers of Tom Johnson, Lyndon Johnson Library.

There is a very significant shift in our position. When we last met we saw reason for hope. We hoped then there would be slow but steady progress. Last night and today the picture is not so hopeful particularly in the countryside. . . . We can no longer do the job we set out to do.

Veteran White House national security policy expert McGeorge Bundy recording that, for the first time, the majority of President Johnson's advisers favor a U.S. military withdrawal from Vietnam, in "Summary of Notes" (by McGeorge Bundy), March 26, 1968, Box 2 of the Papers of Tom Johnson, Lyndon Johnson Library.

We are constantly trying to strengthen the weaknesses that develop in the defense system of the Nation—the shortages that appear. Sometimes it is helicopters. Sometimes it is helicopter parts. Sometimes it is M-16 rifles. Sometimes it is ammunition. Some days it may be various fuels of certain kinds at certain spots.

Overall, I think generally there has never been a war fought as far away as this one has been fought that has been as well supplied and has had as few necessities in short supply.

But that is not to say that we don't make errors. That is not to say that we don't goof at times. We are constantly trying to find those goofs and correct them.

President Johnson admitting to the press on March 30, 1968, that the Tet Offensive taxed the strength of U.S. defense resources, mistakes were made, and problems would be corrected, in The Public Papers of President Lyndon B. Johnson, 1968, Speeches, Lyndon Johnson Library.

Tonight I want to speak to you of peace in Vietnam and Southeast Asia. . . . In these times as in times before, it is true that a house divided against itself by the spirit of faction, of party, of region, of religion, of race, is a house that cannot stand. There is division in the American house now. There is divisiveness among us all tonight. . . . But let men everywhere know, however, that a strong, a confident, and a vigilant America stands ready tonight to seek an honorable peace—and stands ready tonight to defend an honorable cause—whatever the price, whatever the burden, whatever the sacrifice that duty may require.

President Johnson, on March 31, 1968, during a speech that also announced the end of his political career, implying that an "honorable peace" is one that will not have the United States quickly pulling out of Vietnam, in The Public Papers of President Lyndon B. Johnson, 1968, Speeches, Lyndon Johnson Library.

There are a great many subjects that can be covered between the United States and Hanoi of a military nature and that's our real function. We have been there as a military shield for South Vietnam. I have not anticipated that we would get into the political settlement of South Vietnam. That is up to South Vietnam and Hanoi.

Secretary of Defense Clark Clifford arguing that the United States should not attempt to remake the government of South Vietnam while it is trying to negotiate a peace with the Hanoi regime, in "Notes on Meeting," Rostow to Johnson, November 12, 1968, Box 2 of Documents Sanitized and Declassified from Unprocessed Files, Lyndon Johnson Library.

I would like to leave office de-escalating—not esca-lating—but I do not want to make a phony gesture. I do not want to run. We have listened to dovish advisors. We have tested them. We don't want a sellout.

President Johnson making it clear, during one of his last cabinet meetings on Vietnam, in December 1968 that a U.S. military withdrawal would be a mistake, in Notes on the Tuesday Luncheon Meeting, Box 4 of the Tom Johnson Papers, Lyndon Johnson Library.

Movers and Shakers of the 1968 Campaign for President

The United States is no longer in a position to operate programs globally; it has to encourage them. It can no longer impose its preferred solution; it must seek to evoke it. In the forties and fifties, we offered remedies; in the late sixties and seventies our role will have to be to contribute to a structure that will foster the initiative of others. We are a superpower physically, but our designs can be meaningful only if they generate willing coopera-tion. We can continue to contribute to defense and positive programs, but we must seek to encourage and not stifle a sense of local responsibility. Our contribution should not be the sole or principal effort, but it should make the difference between success and failure.

Henry Kissinger writing for the "Rockefeller for President" campaign in early 1968. According to Richard Nixon, these comments won Kissinger the top spot of foreign policy adviser during the last months of Nixon's race for the White House, quoted in Nixon, U.S. Foreign Policy for the 1970s: A New Strategy for Peace *(1970), p. 167.*

A lot of people think Nixon is dull. Think he's a bore, a pain in the ass. They look at him as the kind of kid who always carried a bookbag. Who was forty-two years old the day he was born. They figure other kids got footballs for Christmas, Nixon got a briefcase and loved it. He'd always have his homework done and he'd never let you copy.

Now you put him on television, you've got a problem right away. He's a funny looking guy. He

looks like somebody hung him up in a closet overnight and he jumps out in the morning with his suit all bunched up and starts running around and saying "I want to be President." I mean this is how he strikes people.

One of Richard Nixon's media advisers in the 1968 campaign (who insisted on remaining anonymous) admitting to reporter Joe McGinnis that his boss is a "cold fish," in McGinnis, The Selling of the President, 1968 *(1969), p. 103.*

But past error is no excuse for its own perpetuation. Tragedy is a tool for the living to gain wisdom, not a guide by which to live. Now as ever, we do ourselves best justice when we measure ourselves against ancient tests, as in the Antigone of Sophocles: "All men make mistakes, but a good man yields when he knows his course is wrong, and repairs the evil. The only sin is pride."

Robert Kennedy changing his position on Vietnam, in early 1968, with words first used during a 1966 speech that outlined his evolving views on civil rights and the war on poverty, in Robert F. Kennedy: Presidential Campaign Papers 1968, JFK Library.

Beyond the urbane humor, there was a lot of work to be done. Where some campaigns open with martial trumpets and rolling drums, Eugene McCarthy's began with civility. The phone in his office rang all that afternoon, and wires of support began arriving, but no senator announced support for Gene McCarthy and of the 248 Democratic Congressmen only Don Edwards of California announced that he was in favor of the dissent. The pros were not getting involved and a Gallup Poll would presently show that 58 percent of a sample tested had never heard of the new candidate.

Saturday Evening Post *reporter Roger Kahn describing the first day of Senator Eugene McCarthy's run for the presidency, in his "The Revolt Against LBJ,"* Saturday Evening Post, *February 10, 1968, pp. 17–21.*

Sen. McCarthy proposes laws to let American draft dodgers return home scot free without punishment. . . . To honor draft dodgers and deserters will destroy the very fabric of our national devotion. This is fuzzy thinking about principles that have made our nation great. Support the loyal men who do serve this country by writing in the name of President Johnson on your ballot.

Senator Thomas McIntyre of New Hampshire urging voters in his state's 1968 Democratic primary to reject McCarthy although he never asked for draft dodger "laws," and vote for Johnson, in "Vote for the President" (a February 1968 campaign brochure), Research Room, Lyndon Johnson Library.

Suddenly there's hope among our young people. Suddenly they've come back into the mainstream of American life. And it's a different country. Suddenly the kids have thrown themselves into politics, with all their fabulous intelligence and energy. And it's a new election.

Statements in "Our Children Have Come Home" (an Elect McCarthy campaign brochure in New Hampshire), in Research Room, Lyndon Johnson Library.

Nixon and his chief aides make no bones about how they intend to defy history and win the nomination despite towering obstacles. According to the scenario, Nixon beats Gov. George Romney hands-down in New Hampshire and Wisconsin and goes on to further triumphs in the later primaries. His victories in the primaries are reflected in sharp gains in the public-opinion polls, and he goes to the convention not only as the favorite of the Republican regulars but as the people's choice as well. After that, the scenario gets a bit fuzzy. . . . Ronald Reagan is clearly more likely to profit from the bitchiness of Summer 1968 than Nelson Rockefeller or any other presently visible Republican candidate. Perhaps above all he has what Goldwater mysteriously had and Nixon mysteriously lacks—the ability to arouse genuine passion in his supporters.

Veteran political reporter Stewart Alsop predicting a Nixon or wildcard Reagan win of the Republican nomination, in his "If Nixon Stumbles," Saturday Evening Post, February 10, 1968, p. 11.

We are not trying to beat somebody with nobody. We're trying to beat nobody with somebody. Get this straight about Lyndon Johnson: If a man cheats you once, shame on him. But if he cheats you twice, shame on YOU! They say we're trying to lick Goliath

with David. Well, who the hell do they think won that one?

"Dump Johnson" movement leader Allard Lowenstein introducing Senator Eugene McCarthy at a McCarthy for President rally in Chicago, in Roger Kahn's "The Revolt Against LBJ," Saturday Evening Post, February 10, 1968, pp. 17–21.

The gulf between our people will not be bridged by those who preach violence, or by those who burn and loot. I run for President because I believe such anarchy is intolerable—and I want to do something about it. But I also run because I believe that these divisions will not be solved by demagogues—or by those who would meet legitimate grievances with the heavy hand of repression. . . . I run for President because I want to do something about violence in our streets. But I also run because I want citizens to have an equal chance for jobs and decent housing.

Senator Robert Kennedy addressing in March 1968 an all-white crowd of largely pro-Wallace supporters at the University of Alabama during the early 1968 campaign and implying that Governor George Wallace is a "demagogue" who divides the United States in Papers of Arthur M. Schlesinger, JFK Library.

Any man who offers himself for the presidency must meet three conditions of character, experience, and understanding. The President of the United States must be able to interpret and read with reasonable judgment the needs and aspirations of the people of this nation.

He must know the limitations of power and influence, particularly since there is no greater political power or influence than that entrusted by the people to their President. . . . He must guide the nation to the goals it seeks—and never impose the office upon the people.

Finally, the office of the presidency of the United States must never be a personal office. The President should not speak of "my country" but of "our country," not of "my cabinet" but of "the cabinet," not of "my Supreme Court" but of "the Supreme Court."

The role of the presidency at all times, but especially in 1968, I feel, must be one of uniting this nation, not one of adding it up in some way, not putting it together of bits and pieces, and not one even of organizing it. The need of America is not a need for organization, but a need to develop a sense of national character, with common purposes and shared ideals.

Eugene McCarthy addressing the student-packed Dane County Memorial Coliseum near the University of Wisconsin-Madison on March 25, 1968, in what later historians regard as his best speech, in Robert F. Kennedy: Presidential Campaign Papers 1968, JFK Library.

Young people have a great contribution to make. But it cannot be an exclusive contribution. It must be shared not only by white Americans, but by black Americans, seeking a new direction and a new dignity. It must be shared not only by students, or those with college educations, but also by those who did not have the opportunity to attend college. It must be shared not only by the young, but also by your parents, and those of even greater age; for though they may have fewer years remaining than youth, their desires for the future of their children and grandchildren are as deep as ours for our own.

Senator Robert Kennedy, on March 28, 1968, during a speech at the Denver City Auditorium, insisting that the youth movement goes beyond student activism, in Robert F. Kennedy: Presidential Campaign Papers 1968, JFK Library.

I don't think the question is nearly so much a matter of the individual's personality as it is his background, his training, and his philosophy. Between now and November, the American people will have adequate opportunity—more opportunity, perhaps than they want—to judge each person. Who am I, after almost 40 years in political life, in public office by virtue of the votes of the people—who am I to question their good judgment?

President Johnson, during a May 1968 news conference, refusing to comment on whether he could ever support Senator Eugene McCarthy or if he will play an active role in the remaining months of the presidential campaign, in The Public Papers of President Lyndon B. Johnson, 1968, Speeches, Lyndon Johnson Library.

It is appropriate to inject here a note both personal and public. I was involved in many of the early decisions on Vietnam, decisions which helped set us on our present path. It may be that the effort was doomed from the start, that it was never really possible to bring all the people of South Vietnam under the rule of the successive governments we supported—governments, one after another, riddled with corruption, inefficiency, and greed; governments which did not and could not successfully capture and energize the national feeling of their people. If that is the case, as it well may be, then I am willing to bear my share of the responsibility, before history and before my fellow-citizens. But past error is no excuse for its own perpetuation. Tragedy is a tool for the living to gain wisdom, not a guide by which to live.

Senator Robert Kennedy summarizing in April 1968 his march from "hawk" to "dove" on the Vietnam issue, in Robert F. Kennedy: Presidential Campaign Papers 1968, JFK Library.

Senator McCarthy is backed by the most improbable political machine in American history. It works for nothing, runs off peanut butter sandwiches and soft drinks, and spends the night in sleeping bags or empty warehouses. You can't buy a machine like this, even with the offer of money. . . . And you can't con them either, with a lot of overblown promises. They're looking for a new kind of leadership for our country and they believe that Senator McCarthy is the only one who can provide it. That's why they went out and rang every doorbell in the state of New Hampshire for him. And why they did the same in Wisconsin. And why, now, when the Senator is preparing for his biggest battles of all, they're ready to go into Oregon and California to do it all over again. . . . But unless you help, they'll never get there. They can't fight big business and personal fortunes on an empty stomach. Please don't let them down.

Statements in "McCarthy's Machine Needs Money" (a May 26, 1968, Elect McCarthy ad in the New York Times *and other newspapers) in* New York Times *(1968 record).*

The Kennedy organization was now trying to draw young people away from my campaign with offers of more pay, educational assistance, and the like. They were not very successful. I had no objection to their taking

President Lyndon Johnson (r), a "hawk," lectures Senator William Fulbright (l), a "dove," about Vietnam. *(Voichiokamoto, Lyndon B. Johnson Library)*

professional politicians, if they could get them, like Dick Goodwin, and people like Arthur Schlesinger, but young persons who had worked with me, I felt, should not have been approached.

Senator Eugene McCarthy accusing the Robert Kennedy campaign in the spring of 1968 of "dirty tricks," in his The Year of the People (1969), Research Room, Lyndon Johnson Library.

You probably wonder why I came to Crete, Nebraska. When I was trying to make up my mind whether to run for President, I discussed it with my wife and she said I should, because then I would be able to get to Nebraska. So I asked her why I should get to

Nebraska, and she said, "Because then you might have a chance to visit Crete!" All those who believe that, raise your hands!

Robert Kennedy during the 1968 Nebraska primary, joking with rural voters holding McCarthy campaign brochures that label him "ruthless" and "humorless," in Campaign Notes, Papers of Arthur M. Schlesinger, JFK Library.

I had asked my younger brother, Edward, to have some buttons made up to distribute to you today. But when he put them on the plane, they all had his picture on them. I told him it was too late for him to get into the campaign. And anyway that people would say he was ruthless.

Robert Kennedy telling a stock campaign trail joke in both the 1964 Senate and 1968 presidential campaigns, quoted in Wise, "How Bobby Plans to Win It," Saturday Evening Post, *June 1, 1968, pp. 23–27, 70.*

It's the workin' folks all over this country who are gettin' fed up and are gonna turn this country around, and a whole heap of politicians are gonna get run over when they do. . . . If one of these two national parties don't wake up and get straight, well, I can promise that you and me, we're gonna stir things up all over this country. . . . I'm not against dissent, now, but I believe anybody that stands up like this professor in New Jersey and says they long for a victory by the Viet Cong over the American imperialist troops, and anybody that goes out raising blood and money for the Viet Cong against American servicemen, they oughta be drug by the hair of their heads before a grand jury and indicted for treason, cause that's what they're guilty of.

George Wallace, during the 1968 New Hampshire primary, touching on his key issues for cheering supporters in Dartmouth, quoted in Frady's "George Wallace: The Angry Man's Candidate," Saturday Evening Post, *June 29, 1968, pp. 34–48.*

No one has a grievance in this country that gives him a right to endanger the health and life of every citizen. . . . Let the police run this country for a year or two and there wouldn't be any riots.

George Wallace, shortly after declaring his candidacy for president, explaining his summer 1968 views on "law and order," in Kazin, The Populist Persuasion: An American History *(1998), pp. 233–235.*

There are occasions on which a President must take unpopular measures. But his responsibility does not stop there. The President has a duty to decide, but the people have a right to know why. The President has a responsibility to tell them—to lay out all the facts, and to explain not only why he chose as he did but also what it means for the future. Only through an open, candid dialogue with the people can a President maintain his trust and his leadership.

Richard Nixon, for the first and last time in the 1968 campaign, outlining his vision of proper presidential leadership during a September 1968 radio address, in "Nixon's Nationwide Radio Address," New York Times, *September 20, 1968, p. 33.*

I refuse to accept the argument that there is no alternative to this war's going on and on. We must de-Americanize the conflict; we must rekindle the self-reliance of the South Vietnamese; we must urge the broadening of the popular base of their government; and we must persistently seek a just peace not on the battlefield but at the conference table.

A New Leadership must do more, however, than end this ordeal: it must learn from it. We must understand the errors of judgment that caused it—or be doomed to repeat it.

New York's governor Nelson Rockefeller discussing his race for the presidency in his "Why I Want the Job," Look, *August 20, 1968, pp. 32–34.*

As nasty as he's been I just can't quit Lyndon now. I have no doubt in the world he'd cut me up and out of the nomination if it was a matter of my spoiling his policy on the war. But that's not what holds me back. He's suffering like no other president I've seen before, and I just can't add to that.

Vice President Humphrey in the fall of 1968, shortly before his public break with Johnson over the Vietnam War, explaining to a friend, Edgar Berman, why he's remained "the president's man," in Berman, Hubert *(1979), p. 182.*

I remember one time on a plane going down to Washington. As I went through the first class section I noticed Sen. George McGovern sitting in the first seat there. He had an aide with him, and . . . had taken . . . his shoes off—there were only the two of them. Nobody else really knew he was there. By contrast, however, I saw Hubert Humphrey come out two weeks later, and he just went up and down the aisles and shook hands with every person in the place. Now you say, "that's because he loved politics." Well, he wasn't running for office at the time—he just had so many friends. I mean it was really something to see . . . how much he enjoyed going up and down the aisles.

> *Rev. Calvin Didier, the pastor of a Presbyterian church frequented by Hubert Humphrey, recalling a late 1960s plane ride with Humphrey, in Garrettson,* Hubert H. Humphrey: The Politics of Joy *(1993), p. 57.*

People who are infatuated with their ancestors are like potatoes—the best parts are underground.

> *Democratic presidential nominee Senator Hubert Humphrey, during the ending days of the 1968 campaign, answering a heckler who says that the senator's proposed policies would disgust America's Founding Fathers, noted in Humphrey,* "Perfectionism Is a Pitfall of Politics," Progressive, *December 1971, pp. 37–38.*

Nguyen Van Thieu [the head of South Vietnam] was gambling that he could get a better deal from Richard Nixon than he could from either Lyndon Johnson or Hubert Humphrey. Thieu may have had reasons for thinking that. Throughout his 1968 presidential campaign Richard Nixon implied that he had a plan to end the war, but when asked what it was, he would tap his coat pocket as if something were there and say he didn't want to interfere with the Paris talks. We appreciated his not wanting to interfere, but I am not certain his staffers held to his desires. Late in the campaign, perhaps nervous about the prospects of a settlement, some Nixon backers reportedly encouraged Thieu to hold out in the talks.

> *Twenty-two years after the fact, Secretary of State Dean Rusk recalling Richard Nixon's late 1968 "secret plan to end the war," in his* As I Saw It *(1990), p. 488.*

The legacy of violence will haunt the new Nixon administration. What happened in Chicago was in many ways even more disturbing than anybody thought. Acting upon the request of the National Commission on the Causes and Prevention of Violence, a team of investigators under the direction of Attorney Daniel Walker questioned a large cross section of those involved—police, protestors, press and other witnesses—and set down their findings in a 343-page volume. That the police were severely—and purposely—provoked is one of their conclusions. But most striking is evidence that a significant number of Chicago police units, faced with a situation calling for great discipline and restraint, simply dissolved into violent gangs and attacked protestors,

press and bystanders indiscriminately. It was, the report says, "what can only be called a police riot."

> Life *magazine, several months after the "police riot" at the 1968 Democratic convention, suggesting that the incoming Nixon administration would inherit a violent domestic confrontation over Vietnam, in Smith, "The Chicago Police Riot,"* Life, *December 6, 1968, pp. 34–38.*

My own attitude towards crisis is best expressed in the way the word "crisis" is written in the Chinese language. Two characters are combined to form the word: One brush stroke stands for "danger" and the other character stands for "opportunity."

> *President-elect Nixon describing "crisis" in the preface of the 1968 edition of his* Six Crises *(1968), p. xx.*

Race Riots

Over a period of time a disturbance may develop into an upheaval which draws in thousands or tens of thousands of participants from a Negro ghetto, exhausts the resources of the local police, severely taxes the capacities of city institutions, and involves an extraordinary wide range of lawless activities on the part of both Negroes and control authorities. After the disorder has ended, an area often looks as if it has been through a state of civil warfare. Such was the case in Detroit and Newark, 1967, and in Los Angeles, 1965. These disorders were so massive, events so much beyond the control of either civil authorities or Negro community leadership, the points of street confrontation between police and Negroes so numerous and widespread, that it is difficult to characterize the whole complex of actions over the course of a disturbance in simple terms.

> *McGill University sociologist Louis C. Goldberg examining the impact of the mid-1960s urban race riots, in his "Ghetto Riots and Others: The Faces of Civil Disorder in 1967,"* Journal of Peace Research, *Vol. 5, No. 2 (1968), pp. 116–131.*

Lining up a group of fifteen or twenty unrepresented prisoners before the bench, the judge said, "You're accused of entering without breaking, your bond is $10,000, your examination is set for August 1." Calling the next group, he continued, "You heard what I said to them, the same applies to you." This incident, witnessed by at least two observers, illustrates what might be termed the salient features of the arraignment on the warrant during the disorder: high bail, absence of counsel, failure to consider individual circumstances, failure to inform defendants of their constitutional rights, and an emphasis on expediency. Although each of these things did not necessarily occur at every arraignment or in every courtroom, each was present all too often. Secondary factors contributing to and exacerbating the elements listed included a shortage of judicial manpower coupled with a desire by the court to go it alone, a logistics problem in keeping track of and identifying prisoners, and an atmosphere pervaded by mass confusion, fear, and panic.

The editorial staff of the Michigan Law Review *accusing the Detroit court system of shoddy justice following the race riots of 1967, in their "The Administration of Justice in the Wake of the Detroit Civil Disorder of July 1967,"* Michigan Law Review, *Vol. 66, No. 7 (May 1968), pp. 1,544–1,559.*

Police brutality refers to more than the excessive use of physical force during an arrest, the manhandling of suspects in the police station and in jail, and other physical acts usually associated with the term "brutality." It means arrests, questionings, and searches of Negroes by police without apparent provocation, the use of abusive and derogatory language in addressing Negroes, such as the word "nigger," and a general attitude toward the minority groups which represents an affront to their sense of dignity. Police brutality in this sense is a reality to be reckoned with in the Negro ghetto, no matter how exaggerated some incidents turn out to be and regardless of whether political or criminal groups try to exploit the issue.

Yale University sociologist Anthony Oberschall attempting to define police brutality, in his study "The Lost Angeles Riot of August 1965," Social Problems, *vol. 15, no. 3 (winter 1968), pp. 322–341.*

7

How the "Sixties" End
1969–1970

The observation that the 1960s did not end until the early years of the 1970s goes beyond the obvious. If the 1960s were a state of mind in which Americans embraced a New Frontier, experienced a gruesome war, protested injustice, and experimented with new lifestyles, then that state of mind ended with the Vietnam War, the Watergate scandal, and the search for a quiet, fulfilling life divorced from great political causes. U.S. forces were withdrawn from Vietnam in 1973 and North Vietnam emerged the victor two years later. The Watergate scandal screamed from the headlines from 1972 through the summer of 1974, and, as early as 1973, the Gallup Poll discovered that most Americans rejected protest and reform in favor of a quiet life of self-absorption.

NIXON'S "GENERATION OF PEACE"

Nixon's theme for his inaugural address was a rehash of Rockefeller and Muskie speeches. Calling for fewer protests and more dialogue, Nixon asked Americans to "stop screaming at each other." The message was well received, but the new president's honeymoon with public opinion was short-lived. Polls with both the Harris organization and *CBS Evening News* declared Senator Edmund Muskie America's most trusted and honored leader. In the past, the U.S. electorate had always placed their president at the top of this list, and Nixon had just begun his term of office. A fragile personality, Nixon believed that the media turned public opinion against him from his first days in office. This combative relationship with the press continued throughout Nixon's years in the White House, prompting him to support drastic reforms of the Federal Communications Commission (FCC). The reforms would have required the media to submit politically sensitive material to the executive branch for review under "clear national security emergencies." The Nixon reforms enjoyed little support in Congress.

For all effective purposes, Nixon was ill at ease with the image of unifier and national dialogue leader. His vice president, Spiro Agnew, proved it. Whereas the president had little to say about national unity after his inaugural address, Vice President Agnew, a former Maryland governor, had much to

242

say about antiwar and civil rights protesters. None of it was positive. To Agnew, dubbed the "real White House spokesperson" by the press, opponents of the president's policies were "nattering nabobs of negativism." The members of Congress who opposed the White House's efforts to spend funds for the Vietnam War that were previously earmarked for domestic use were "pugnacious pups of parsimony." Agnew and his speechwriters loved alliteration, and the president's staunchest supporters loved their new vice president. Meanwhile, Nixon publicly denied that he unleashed Agnew on Congress, the media, and the antiwar/Civil Rights movements. Yet he soon admitted that his administration's policies were dedicated to that "silent majority" of Americans (white middle-class moderates and conservatives) who had never protested a thing, continued to support the Vietnam War, and trusted the judgment of their government.

Nixon's combative tone with the press and others reflected both his own personality and the frustration of a long, bitter war. As it had consumed the Johnson administration, Vietnam would occupy much of the Nixon agenda as well. Later claiming to have entered the White House with an open mind for a number of contingencies over Vietnam, Nixon continued the Johnson approach. The North Vietnamese, he concluded, were testing the will of American power and influence. A quick military withdrawal, he believed, would encourage communist offensives around the world, and America would suffer more conflicts in developing nations.[1]

Representative Gerald Ford (*R., Michigan, and to Nixon's right*) and Senator Everett Dirksen (*R., Illinois, and to Nixon's left*) escort President-elect Nixon to his inaugural speech platform. (*National Archives—Nixon Presidential Materials*)

Nixon's Vietnam assessment was bolstered by his National Security Advisor, Henry Kissinger, who favored a progressive withdrawal schedule from Vietnam, leaving behind both U.S. military hardware and a well-trained South Vietnamese military. He estimated that it would take until 1981 to see a competent South Vietnamese military in action. A persistent White House–led public relations campaign, Kissinger hoped, which stressed the irreversible nature of the U.S. withdrawal, might quiet the antiwar movement. In the name of both security and commonsense politics, the 1981 date would never be mentioned to the press.

Unmarried and always in the public eye, Kissinger dated Hollywood actresses and led a jet-setting life. Previous National Security Advisors had never enjoyed such attention in the press. Believing in "shuttle diplomacy," Kissinger spent much of his time flying to one diplomatic meeting after another. Quick to criticize his predecessors for unnecessarily amplifying cold war tensions by relying on nuclear diplomacy, Kissinger vowed to make peace with China and the Soviet Union. He advocated renewed dialogue with China first, which had not hosted a U.S. embassy since 1949. If the Soviets became suspicious that the United States and China might be building a new military relationship against them, Kissinger had no objection to a diplomatic shouting match between Moscow and Beijing over the matter. In fact, a U.S.-China military relationship was never on Kissinger's agenda, but the Soviets did not have to know that. Tension in the communist world, he reasoned, was better for U.S. interests than the traditional capitalist versus communist tension.

According to Kissinger's new global plan, a bickering Soviet Union and China would force North Vietnam to pick between them. Proud of its maverick, Vietnamese-defined communism, the Hanoi government would never choose sides. Alone, broke, and always facing the might of the U.S. military, the North Vietnamese, Kissinger believed, would eventually turn to Washington for assistance. A lasting peace would result, and America would emerge from the Vietnam War with its power and influence intact. The sticking point was how the United States withdrew from South Vietnam. It would have to be done as slowly and methodically as possible, thereby accenting the point that the United States was not in a rout from communist pressures. Nor could this mean the cold war was over. It would also make sense, Kissinger concluded, to move U.S. troops into another confrontation against communism in another developing nation. Keeping an open, friendly dialogue with Beijing and Moscow was one thing. Retreating from anticommunist obligations and principles was another. Fighting communist insurgents in small developing countries such as Angola in Africa, a very real example for Kissinger later in the mid-1970s, would continue to demonstrate America's anticommunist commitment.

Some of Kissinger's top secret plan was discerned by the press, making any change in the usual capitalist versus communist confrontation seem refreshing. Both the *Washington Post* and the *New York Times* admired Kissinger's effort to change directions and even assumed that he was trying his best to end the cold war. In reality, he was trying to win it, and his grand new plan was the 1970s twist to the old cold war tale.

The slow withdrawal from Vietnam came to be called Vietnamization, and the result, as Nixon said in his campaign, was supposed to be a "Generation of Peace" or GOP. With any luck, Nixon believed, the party that ended the Viet-

After 13 weeks of training at the South Vietnam National Training Center, young "Vietnamization" troopers march off to their new duty stations. *(National Archives)*

nam War would become the dominant party in American political life for the next generation. Like Kissinger, Nixon thought big. From 1969 to 1973, Kissinger's National Security Council represented foreign policy making in America. The State Department and its chief, Nixon's former law partner William Rogers, played a secondary role. Years later, many Americans believed that the media-savvy Kissinger had been secretary of state since the 1969 inaugural of Richard Nixon. In fact, he became secretary of state in early 1973.[2]

WOODSTOCK, USA

The realities of everyday life in America, and especially the realities of the continuing generation gap, eluded the Nixon White House. For American youth, the madness of Vietnam truly influenced their lives, and so did racial strife and an uncertain future. More and more, the struggle and concerns of young Americans were reflected in their favorite music. Any song that best depicted the moment became an instant hit and its composer an instant star.

Janis Joplin typified both the glory and heavy price of that quick rise to fame. Born in Port Arthur, Texas, in the early 1940s, Joplin was a lifelong loner, maverick, and free thinker who had experimented with drugs long before she graduated from high school. Influenced by gospel music, African-American blues, and her own nonconformist approach to life, Joplin took the rock music world by storm with her 1968 album *Cheap Thrills.* It was the first album for her and her San Francisco–based band, Big Brother and the Holding Company. She drank onstage, poked fun at mainstream singers while performing her own songs, and always looked the part of the counterculture girl who had no use for the establishment. Perfect for her time, Joplin's singles off her *Cheap Thrills* album raked in high sales for two years straight. Her October 1970 death by heroin overdose never surprised her admirers, but her self-destructive life symbolized to many the path and fate of both the counterculture and the antiwar movement.

One month before Joplin's death, Jimi Hendrix, another example of a meteoric rise to fame gone wrong, had also passed away. Like Joplin, Hendrix, considered rock's greatest guitarist, was influenced by great American blues singers. The debut album for this Seattle-born singer, *Are You Experienced?,* was cut in England in 1967. But Hendrix's unique acid rock sound soon spread to the United States. Singles such as "Foxy Lady" and "Purple Haze" excited both counterculture and noncounterculture rock fans throughout 1968 and 1969.

Like Joplin, Hendrix was a featured singer at the August 1969 Woodstock festival of rock and folk rock music. It took place in a 600-acre field near Bethel, New York. Folk rock pioneer Bob Dylan lived near there, but festival organizers failed to get him on their program. Although the local residents worked hard to prevent a "hippie invasion," they got one anyway. The thousands of rock fans who flocked to the festival were met with inclement weather, as well as by inadequate sanitary and health conditions. Many fans considered Hendrix's playing of the "Star-Spangled Banner" in his own acid rock fashion a symbolic high point of the concert. Few of the performers came to make money at Woodstock, and in fact, only a minority of the fans present in Woodstock's muddy field ever paid a fee to see the show.

Woodstock was one of Hendrix's last public appearances before his death, adding meaning and significance to that event. Years later, those who attended the concert still regarded it as an example of youth solidarity against uncaring, Vietnam War–supporting elders.[3] It also represented one of the few moments in the history of rock music in which the performers cared more about their performance than their take-home pay. But 1969 produced yet another symbol of youth rebellion and solidarity and, like Woodstock, its success came as a surprise.

Easy Rider, a low-budget film whose prospects for general distribution and moneymaking potential were always considered low, fooled the naysayers and became a classic cult hit. Punctuated by a soundtrack that rivaled the songs of Woodstock, *Easy Rider* constituted actor director Dennis Hopper's motorcycle movie protest of the status quo, the Southern hatred for change, and the need to escape the inequities of American life. Featuring sex, drugs, rock-and-roll, and even Jack Nicholson in the supporting cast, *Easy Rider* set cinematic trends for low-budget, on-location films. Because the movie's leading characters, played by actor/producer Peter Fonda and Hopper, were shot to death in the end, a message similar to *Bonnie and Clyde*'s was obvious. America might be the land of the free, but it was also the land of the violent where antiestablishment mavericks could meet an unhappy end. In real life, Hendrix and Joplin had proven a similar point in their own way.

Music trends changed quickly as America entered the 1970s. The rumors of knock-down squabbles within the Beatles were as old as the group itself. Yet this pioneer British Invasion group barely survived into the new decade, and their breakup symbolized the shifting youth culture scene. "Let It Be," a sad, interpretive song, constituted the Beatles's farewell and final message to their fans. With the lure of the activist's life already beginning to wither, some social critics observed that the end of the Beatles also meant the end of a unifying force at a critical time for America's antiestablishment youth. Whatever it meant, the Beatles had made an important difference in modern music. They would not easily be replaced.

"ROCKING AMERICA?"

In October 1969, W. Averell Harriman, a former New York governor, once one of Lyndon Johnson's Paris Peace Talks negotiators, praised the antiwar movement during a rally in New York City that included thousands. He thanked them for "rocking America" and urged them to keep up the good fight. Sometimes called the "Gentleman Democrat" by the press, Harriman, the consummate diplomat, was an unlikely figure at an antiwar gathering of young students and workers. But the antiwar movement was changing in 1969. Those, like Harriman, who once castigated the street politics of the antiwar movement, were now in the streets themselves. The rallies were larger, angrier, and more determined than ever.

In early 1968, the antiwar movement had dreamed of success by early 1969. Instead, they got Richard Nixon, Vietnamization, and Henry Kissinger's revised version of the cold war. For a time, it appeared that the antiwar cause was about to win the hearts and minds of American public opinion. The U.S. press covered the 1969 rallies more than they had in the past, and antiwar addresses, such as Harriman's, were given as much attention as a presidential press conference. Nixon's intensely loyal White House staff urged their boss to take the offensive and reclaim the upper hand in the growing public relations war. Nixon weighed this advice for months, for his image had been already tarnished.

Nixon's new "Southern Strategy," a deliberate recognition of Wallace voters and their concerns in order to keep the anti–Democratic Party backlash alive and moving across the U.S. South, truly annoyed many members of the press and the entire antiwar movement. News reports about Nixon's shady financial dealings with real estate mogul C. G. "Bebe" Rebozo and controversial business tycoon Robert Abplanalp, also reminded many of the old Nixon instead of the new one. Meanwhile, the president's decision to include the antiwar movement in speeches about the growing rate of street crime won him more derision than support.

Nixon later admitted that these were months of doubt and struggle for him. Hence, he laid low, making few comments about the antiwar movement, and his supporters wondered why. The president, said the press, misunderstood the antiwar movement, and Eric Severeid, the chief editorialist for the *CBS Evening News*, even predicted that the antiwar leaders of 1969 would be the national leaders of 1979. Nixon, said Severeid, had lost touch with the political pulse of the nation. Or had he?

White House staffers (*left to right*) H. R. Haldeman, Dwight Chapin, and John Ehrlichman meet with President Nixon. *(National Archives)*

Isolated "Days of Rage" demonstrations by antiwar extremists in a handful of big cities such as Chicago, Philadelphia, and New York saw antiwar radicals running through financial and shopping districts breaking windows and vandalizing as many "symbols of capitalist tyranny" as possible. The president's closest advisers, John Ehrlichman and H. R. "Bob" Haldeman, urged him to respond. They complained that the White House should never be cowed by a handful of extremists and their sympathizers. America was at war, they said, and legal dissent had its limits. Attorney General John Mitchell agreed. The antiwar movement had crossed the line of legitimate dissent to treason, he noted. Yet doing something about it would not be easy. The first step involved a strong public stance by the president, and Nixon finally agreed to take it. He had worked hard on his "New Nixon" image, but that strong public stance required the older, combative Nixon.

During a November 1969 speech, Nixon finally took the offensive against his critics. The intentions of the antiwar movement were not honorable, he said, and he denounced their growing attraction to violence. In contrast, he praised the flag-waving loyalties of the World War II–era generation, proclaiming that patriotism was not dead. As he had done in the 1950s, Nixon once again questioned the patriotism of those who opposed him. The antiwar activists, Nixon charged, encouraged U.S. military defeat, indirectly urged the North Vietnamese to fight on, and represented Hanoi's best behind-the-lines ally.[4]

Nixon had once been the master of divisive politics, and in one November 1969 speech he put the entire antiwar movement back on the defensive. The White House was flooded with patriotic messages, praising the president's "courageous speech." Meanwhile, antiwar leaders from Tom Hayden to Averell Harriman issued statements that they were, in fact, loyal to the country. The Days of Rage shifted to the president's supporters, as certain big city locals of the AFL-CIO organized counterdemonstrations in support of Nixon's speech and his call for a return to patriotism. The country entered the new decade of the 1970s more divided than ever on the basic question of war or peace. But there were other worries, too.

ECONOMIC WOES

To Democratic Senator Frank Church of Idaho, the Vietnam War produced more than just battlefield casualties. Reflecting the growing concerns of Wall Street, Church believed that the Vietnam War would soon be responsible for years of economic misery in the United States. A very vocal member of the Senate Foreign Relations Committee in 1969 and 1970, Church would later chair this committee and use his public spotlight to run for president in 1976. According to Church, no one in the White House was paying close attention to economic developments. His assessment was close to the mark. Henry Kissinger, for instance, had fired many of his foreign economic advisers as early as 1969. They were not essential, he believed, in the ongoing ideological struggle against communism. Unless economic issues were somehow connected to this ideological battle, they had little relevance in Kissinger's view of national security priorities.

The Vietnam War had been fought with deficit spending, and the statistics were staggering. In 1969, the Pentagon even admitted that the full monetary cost of the war might never be known, and that millions of dollars had been spent without accountability. The Nixon administration gave Church's committee conflicting data on all war costs in general, and Senator William Proxmire (Democrat of Wisconsin) on the Senate Defense Appropriations Committee found graft and corruption throughout every level of Pentagon spending. Given America's already huge foreign aid bill, its growing reliance on foreign sources for oil, new and serious competition in the consumer sector of the economy by former enemies Japan and Germany, and expensive, leftover Great Society programs, Church predicted a very rocky road for America's 1970s economy. His opinion was echoed by Robert McNamara, now the chairman of the World Bank. McNamara admitted that U.S. economic policy during his days in the Johnson administration had never been a top concern, for any policy-making difficulties were supposed to be resolved after the Vietnam victory. No one had thought the war would last into a new decade.

To George Meany, the boss of the AFL-CIO, Vietnam presented great challenges to organized labor. In fact, America's labor unions were trapped in a horrible dilemma. Since the days of Franklin Roosevelt, organized labor represented a powerful force in the American economy. Its political clout, many assumed, was responsible for the Democratic majorities in Congress and most statehouses for years. Privately, the tough, cigar-chomping Meany regarded the Vietnam War as an ugly mistake. But the war stimulated a great number of defense industry contracts, providing round-the-clock employment for companies such as Boeing, Firestone, A. O. Smith, and RCA. Many of Meany's union members had little in common with the white upper-middle-class anti-war movement, and thousands of his blue-collar colleagues had served in Vietnam. Both politically and in the name of economic self-interest, organized labor was a ready source of support for President Nixon and the Vietnam War.[5] It remained an awkward attachment.

Meany's political heart and soul was still with the Democratic Party, and he knew that the dire economic predictions from Senator Church and others were most likely correct. But taking an antiwar stance would alienate his members and might lose them their current defense-related jobs. Doing nothing, on the other hand, to head off a large-scale economic disaster, would hurt labor in the long run. Meany chose to worry about that disaster when the time came. It was a strategic mistake that made organized labor look like a sycophantic supporter of the Nixon administration and without a vision for the future. In the meantime, organized labor continued to back the president's war policies.

CARS AND THE AMERICAN DREAM

As early as 1968, the U.S. auto industry, one of labor's biggest employers, already saw the warning signs. In the interest of controlling big city air pollution, the Johnson administration had passed legislation to regulate automobile fuel emissions. The new legislation would take effect slowly, permitting U.S. auto companies to redesign and retool. But they were reluctant to do so, complaining of undue government influence in their business. These same manufacturers were also given notice to plan for cars that could run on gasoline with less lead content in order to reduce the growing number of smog alerts in cities such as Houston and Los Angeles. They were also legislated to build safer cars, including five-mile-per-hour impact bumpers, as a first step in the effort to lower traffic accident injuries. In its legislation, Congress pointed out that many of those who died in car crashes died as senselessly as U.S. troopers in Vietnam. Vietnam was difficult to resolve. Mandating safety legislation for the U.S. auto industry was supposed to be easier.

Ironically, the safety and pollution-control legislation came at a time when the American auto industry was riding a wave of "muscle car" sales successes. Stimulated by innovative car enthusiasts who were also company managers such as Pontiac's John DeLorean, most of the major U.S. auto manufacturers sold cars with so-called Big Block or high-performance engines. From Pontiac's GTO to Plymouth's Barracuda, the American driving enthusiast could purchase a car with a V-8 engine larger than 350 cubic inches (or Big Block). The purpose was pure power, and, given the lack of precise regulations, the manufacturer's horsepower claims were often higher than advertised. A 1967–69 Big Block Corvette, for instance, could make up to 435 horsepower. But the real figure was closer to 500 horsepower or beyond. Highway gas mileage for these cars was also advertised to be 10 miles per gallon, but reality suggested something much lower. To sports car buffs, these muscle machines were modern-day symbols of American freedom, independence, and brute force power. The open road, a fast car, and unlimited fuel resources to keep on rolling were all supposed to be part of the 1960s American Dream.

Taking the lead in the area of 1960s automotive excess was the tiny Excalibur Motor Company of West Allis, Wisconsin. Expensive, stylish, fast, and fuelish, the Excalibur Series One was the hip car of choice for the rich and famous. From light rock stars Sonny and Cher to TV comedian Jackie Gleason and movie box office champions Steve McQueen and Tony Curtis, the Excalibur symbolized 1960s wealth, power, and status. The creation of designer Brooks Stevens, the Excalibur had the look of an early 1930s Mercedes, but with Corvette performance and (by late 1969) modern amenities galore. Coined "the contemporary classic" and a car "for the man who thought he had everything," the Excalibur transformed Stevens's little company into the eighth-largest automobile firm in the Western Hemisphere.

From luxury motorboats to the Oscar Meyer Wienermobile to the Studebaker Golden Hawk, Stevens had been one of the country's most successful

Near his Mequon, Wisconsin homes, designer Brooks Stevens poses in his Series One Excalibur (1964–1969), the superexpensive car of choice for the rich and famous of the mid- and late 1960s. (*Courtesy of Alice Preston, Camelot Classic Cars, Inc.*)

independent designers. His Excalibur was originally built to be a 1964 Studebaker concept car for the New York auto show. Although the company folded, the car ended up the surprise hit of the New York show, and Stevens, with his two sons, David and William, decided to take a gamble and build the car themselves. The gamble worked.

Strongly identified with macho themes of male power and privilege, the Excalibur was well advertised in so-called men's magazines such as *Playboy*. Ironically, a right-hand man of the company was a woman, Alice Preston. In a field that even in the 21st century remained dominated by men, Preston played an important role in the car's engineering and racing division. The Excalibur's lure to the rich and famous faded as popular tastes and federal regulations changed in the succeeding decades, but its symbolism of 1960s excess remained intact.[6] The Excalibur company closed its doors in the 1990s.

During the mid-1960s, consumer advocate Ralph Nader put the Excalibur on his list of cars that were made with more attention to style and performance than to safety. Nader's best-selling investigation of the Chevrolet Corvair and other American cars (*Unsafe at Any Speed*) had stimulated public concern about the U.S. auto industry. Nader's muckraking efforts also stimulated a congressional investigation and resulting safety legislation. Even labor leaders worried about Nader's influence. According to Lane Kirkland of the United Auto Workers, Nader was a reckless crusader whose work would lead to the destruction of the auto industry and bad news for the economy. Spokespersons for the Big Three

A generation after its first appearance as a special 1964 1/2 model, thousands of early Ford Mustangs remain on the road. This flawlessly restored convertible was photographed at Illinois's Volo Collector Car Museum in 2002. *(author's collection)*

(General Motors, Ford, Chrysler) agreed with him, creating a unique solidarity between employee and employer. But standing tall against antipollution and safety measures was not a popular position for most Americans. News magazines such as *Life* and *Look* also investigated the auto industry in both 1968 and 1969, finding an arrogant disregard in Big Three business practice for their own consumers. During testimony before Congress, several American Motors auto workers from their Kenosha, Wisconsin, plant even admitted that they sometimes placed empty soda cans within door panels "just for fun." The resulting rattle would annoy the car's new owner no end. That was the "fun."

To antiwar activists and a growing number of liberal critics, the Big Three auto makers symbolized the arrogance of 1960s capitalism. Too big, too imperial, and out of control, the auto industry, they said, would rather self-destruct with bad business decisions than change with the times. Indeed, the Detroit-based auto manufacturers continued to make cars that were too big for many garages and narrow roads. They built huge family sedans such as the limousine-sized Chrysler Imperial or Cadillac Fleetwood, which were lucky to make eight miles per gallon on the highway. Most of these cars suffered from quality and safety problems that were unacceptable when compared to auto manufacturing techniques found in Europe or Japan. Meanwhile, each manufacturer maintained dozens of specific car lines with specific names. Only a few cars within a crowded line ever made money for those who tried to sell them. For instance, Oldsmobile's "88" made money, but its more upscale version, the "98," often did not and for several years straight. The cars within each line were usually available with a long list of engine and other options that few consumers purchased.

As the U.S. economy began to slide, the auto industry found itself with high surpluses, work slowdowns, and plant closures. For each car that did not sell, an independent car parts manufacturer, such as Dana Corporation, AC, or Champion, suffered even more. The confusion in the auto industry triggered a domino effect of misery. As Nader pointed out to Congress, "The auto industry drives the American economy." But it did not have to kill it.[7]

Without question, the American auto industry had had its bright spots in the 1960s, and most of them symbolized the booming economy at a particular moment. Ford's Lee Iacocca, director of the Mustang "pony car" project, released his attractively designed 2+2 sports car–like vehicle in mid-1964. Thousands of auto enthusiasts bought it without a test drive, and it sold an auto industry record of just fewer than 500,000 cars in a little over a year. Two years before, the second generation Corvette had been born. Beautifully designed by Larry Shinoda, who had been imprisoned in a Japanese-American internment camp during World War II, the Corvette Split Window Stingray and its convertible equivalent won both engineering and design awards around the world. Every one of these cars were quickly sold, and this year-after-year buying frenzy continued into the late 1960s.

In contrast to the Mustang, Corvette production numbers were kept well below 20,000 in order to maintain an exclusive image. But Chevrolet executives believed that hundreds of thousands might have been sold otherwise. For the U.S. auto industry, these had been the glory days, long before the country had heard of a Tet holiday, pollution controls, or an approaching energy crisis.

The Nixon administration favored a policy of limited assistance to a downsizing auto industry, but the president hedged on whether large numbers of safer, smaller, more fuel-efficient cars from abroad must be permitted into the country in order to fill both the need and the gap.[8] In the 1968 campaign, Nixon, like his Democratic opponent, Hubert Humphrey, suggested that he had little use for a generous import policy. He also said that the U.S. dollar, once an international symbol of economic success, would never be devalued during his presidency. Yet as early as 1969, he considered reversing these positions, and Henry Kissinger urged this decision.

THE SUFFERING U.S. DOLLAR

To Kissinger, the United States could no longer hide the fact that its dollar was of less value than before the Vietnam War. In the United Nations, Prime Minister Hideo Tanaka of Japan urged the United States to accept reality, help readjust the world market, and, of course, let his nation's consumer-driven economy export its automobile and electronic goods more freely to the United States. Although John Kennedy's Trade Expansion Act (TEA) had opened the U.S. door to Japanese trade, Tanaka envisioned a fuller penetration of the U.S. market, and the new auto-buying interests of the American consumer provided an obvious impetus for a change in U.S. trade policy.

Worried that the United States could lose the friendship of all of Asia while it withdrew its forces from Vietnam, Kissinger believed that U.S. foreign policy must not only maneuver one communist state against another but also "mend fences" with old allies. If the United States did not answer the Japanese lobbying effort favorably, Kissinger reasoned, the next step could be Japan's expulsion of the U.S. military bases there and a resulting U.S. security gap throughout the entire Western Pacific. Consequently, America's troubled auto industry and the weakened economy became intertwined in Kissinger's view with larger global considerations. He began to advocate what Tanaka sought, and, between 1970 and 1973, Nixon responded with a dramatically expanded TEA and a devalued U.S. dollar. The "fences" were "mended," but a panacea for the struggling U.S. economy remained nowhere in sight.

Many of Nixon's harshest economic critics were not the leftover stalwarts of the Great Society and New Frontier. The president was hit hard from the political right of his own party for his alleged acceptance of FDR and LBJ economics. After less than two years in office, Nixon even declared that he was now a believer in Keynesian economics (or deficit spending). In fact, the 1970–71 budget deficit was roughly $23 billion. Lyndon Johnson's 1968 deficit had been $21 billion, and the president's conservative supporters were shocked. Tolerating an unbalanced budget while America was at war, and when its major industries appeared to be in peril, made sense, Nixon explained. While conservative critics, such as California governor Ronald Reagan, complained that Nixon had "no principles," the president said that he reserved the right to be flexible in economic policy making.

Naturally, Nixon's longtime liberal critics had little use for his flexibility either. He imposed wage and price controls as an inflation fighter, and they failed. Meanwhile, his excitement over a December 1969 tax cut of $2.5 billion, annoyed the liberals. These continuing debates led to a political deadlock in Congress and the defeat of worthy proposals such as the Family Assistance Plan. That plan would have offered a guaranteed annual income of around $1,600 (plus food stamps) to a struggling family of four. Nixon endorsed it, although he favored work training programs for those who benefited from the plan. Additional liberal-authored riders to this legislation, calling for even more financial assistance to the poor, killed the entire measure.

By 1971, America's economic experts declared the country to be in "stagflation," a bizarre combination of 5.3 percent rate of inflation and a 6 percent unemployment rate. The 1970s would continue to be a period of economic struggle, and the excesses of the 1960s were often held to blame as much as Nixon administration policies.[9]

One of the debates over the excess issue centered on the space program. In the days of the New Frontier and the new space race with the Soviets, no one questioned John Kennedy's promise to put a man on the moon by 1970. Astronaut Neil Armstrong fulfilled that promise in July 1969 when he became the first human being to set foot on the Moon. More than 600 million viewers around the world watched the event on television, further symbolizing the technological miracle that had just taken place. Whereas this event might have stimulated a great deal of celebrating in the streets only a few years before, in summer 1969 and the succeeding months, Armstrong's walk raised some controversy and debate.

Civil rights and antiwar activists complained that the space program now represented America's misplaced priorities. Economic analysts complained about unnecessary expenses in troubled times. Others worried that America's technological rush into space would also move the arms race there, while still others worried that the country remained more committed to technology than to values, ethics, and its own people. The confident early 1960s, often symbolized by the excitement and promise of the space program, had given way to the doubt and concern of the late 1960s. Vietnam, domestic violence, and the new economic worries remained the culprits in this change of attitude. Indeed, much of this attitude translated into the need to protect the planet Earth from humanity's own destructive power. The rest of the universe would have to wait.

ENVIRONMENTALISM

Between 1969 and 1972, the amount of federal government money spent on non–Vietnam War matters nearly doubled. From the growing number of people needing food stamps to increased spending for other social programs, the new economic struggle took its toll. There was also a new agency to fund, and its role was an unprecedented one in the history of the federal government. Founded in 1970, the Environmental Protection Agency (EPA) had the power to fine or sue industries and even state or local governments that refused to comply to new antipollution laws. Although many industries and communities did refuse to comply, the EPA had limited powers and funds to take them all to task.

When Nixon entered the White House, many of the new president's moderate and conservative supporters considered the pro–environment movement a spinoff from the antiwar and Civil Rights movements. To these Nixon voters, no quarter must be given to political agitators, and the last thing the federal government needed was a new expensive agency that had the right to levy costly regulations on a business in tough economic times.

There was, however, great political capital to made off of environmentalism as well. A majority of U.S. voters favored some sort of action to save the environment. Just as many believed that it was the excesses of the 1960s that haunted the economy, many believed that those same excesses hurt America's environmental future. The rapid growth of the big city suburb was often used as the most obvious example. Former Democratic vice presidential candidate Edmund Muskie, from the environmentally pristine state of Maine, was one of the first to recognize the political gold mine of environmentalism. Along with Senator Gaylord Nelson of Wisconsin, Muskie championed EPA legislation as early as 1969. Winning high political marks for this role, in addition to the already existing nationwide respect for his gentlemanly behavior during the 1968 campaign, Muskie maintained a high profile.

Muskie's status as the Democrat to watch was confirmed following a scandal involving young Senator Edward Kennedy. In a car driven by the senator himself, a former Robert Kennedy campaign aide, Mary Jo Kopechne, was killed. That car careened off a low bridge on Chappaquiddick Island near Martha's Vineyard, Massachusetts, in summer 1969. Kopechne drowned, and Kennedy fled the scene of the accident. Although this last of the Kennedy brothers was cleared of any serious wrongdoing, many believed it was his famous last name that spared him from further legal troubles. His immediate presidential aspirations now over, Kennedy remained a cosponsor of the Muskie and Nelson environmental legislation.

There was more than political careers at stake in the environmental cause, and more than a new government agency was born because of it. Several new legislative measures were passed to rescue the United States from its march to environmental destruction, and there was already a record of success in environmental law. As early as the mid-1960s, the Water Quality Improvement Act held power companies and certain industries to task for years of unchecked water pollution. The Resource Recovery Act encouraged industry to recycle solid waste. Two Clean Air Acts passed between 1963 and 1970 created a progressive schedule of anti–air pollution requirements on industry, and Congress fought the Nixon administration over a request to fund the Super Sonic Transport (SST). The Nixon-era Congress spruced up or augmented existing environmental legislation, and, most of the time, Nixon was politically astute enough to recognize their popularity with voters.

If built, the SST promised to be America's largest, loudest, and most fuel-hungry airplane. To Muskie, Nelson, and a majority of congressmen, the battle over its funding symbolized the debate with the White House over environmentalism. President Nixon saw the plane's construction as a ready source of employment that would assist the economy and symbolize U.S. commitment to technological advance. Those who opposed it, he argued, did not understand America's economic priorities. Congress saw the plane as a leftover measure of the 1960s when bigger was always better and no one had thought about the environmental consequences. Voting against SST funding, Congress prevailed. Meanwhile, the years-long debate over SST and other environmental matters would have an impact on Nixon's views. Whether he liked it or not, environmentalism was here to stay. During the president's victorious 1972 reelection campaign, the Republican platform formally recognized the environmental legislation; however, that same platform cautioned environmentalists not to harass U.S. industry with their cause. To Nixon's most conservative supporters, the environmental movement would always be antibusiness, antidevelopment, and even anti-American.[10]

CAMBODIA AND KENT STATE

Even as early as the spring of 1969, Vietnamization was not working. The Nixon administration took great pains to announce the withdrawal of an isolated company of U.S. military personnel now and then, but total U.S. troop strength in Vietnam stood at an all-time high of 543,400 men at the end of April 1969. The problem was obvious. The U.S. military withdrawals stimulated more North Vietnamese attacks, more South Vietnamese defeats, and more territory lost to the enemy. Like Johnson, Nixon tempered his military conduct of the war with peace plans offered to Hanoi. However, the peace plans carried ridiculous prerequisites. The president's May 1969 peace plan, for instance, required North Vietnam to withdraw all its forces from South Vietnam and return all U.S. prisoners of war before any deal was concluded. The North Vietnamese government refused to discuss it.

To Nixon, there would be no improvement in the battlefield until the enemy was deprived of all safe havens or sanctuaries. The largest safe haven was the neutral country of Cambodia. Having spent $1 billion in military aid to the South Vietnamese government in 1969 (only to be repeated again in 1970), the Nixon team saw little return on the dollar. The best way to rescue Vietnamization or even win the war, Nixon concluded, required an invasion of Cambodia. Winning popular support for that invasion would be difficult. It would be a clear contradiction to the Vietnamization mission, and, most likely, also bring more Americans to the ranks of the antiwar movement.

Secretly, Nixon had ordered the bombing of the Cambodian border in 1969 but always fell short of ordering an all-out invasion. Removing the cautious leader of Cambodia, Prince Norodom Sihanouk, would be required as well, and the CIA recommended General Lon Nol as his replacement. Lon Nol had been one of the few Cambodian military figures who had opposed North Vietnamese troops hiding along the borders of his country.

In early 1970, Lon Nol led a coup against the government and then asked for South Vietnamese and U.S. military assistance. The new regime immediately faced two enemies, the North Vietnamese and Cambodia's own radical and armed communist rebels, the Khmer Rouge. Once considered on the fringes of acceptable politics in Cambodia, the Khmer Rouge now portrayed themselves as freedom fighters and heroes waging war against an illegitimate government propped up by Washington and Saigon. For years, Sihanouk had kept his country out of this bloody mess by turning a blind eye to the armies that often crossed the porous Cambodian border. His government had been similar in makeup to the non–Marxist socialist regimes of Scandinavia, and the Nixon administration's later portrayal of him as a communist sympathizer would be an exaggeration. Sihanouk had enjoyed widespread support since the end of French rule in Cambodia nearly 20 years earlier. His ouster brought thousands to the ranks of the Khmer Rouge.

President Nixon announces the "incursion" into Cambodia. The news stimulates some of the largest and violent antiwar demonstrations of the Vietnam War era. *(National Archives—Nixon Presidential Materials)*

On April 29, 1970, Nixon authorized the Cambodian incursion. The term *invasion* was deemed too strong. Politically, the incursion was supposed to reinforce the view that Vietnamization was not a U.S. retreat. Militarily, the Joint Chiefs of Staff promised a great victory, the destruction of the North Vietnamese supply line, and confusion in the enemy's ranks for months. Diplomatically, this victory and resulting North Vietnamese confusion, Nixon believed, would bolster U.S. chances to conclude a negotiated peace with Hanoi.

The president ignored the advice of his intelligence advisers before the invasion. Both the CIA and U.S. military intelligence warned against an attack on Cambodia, for there was no evidence of any great enemy headquarters there. If anything, the invasion drove the North Vietnamese and Khmer Rouge deeper into the interior of Cambodia, and it left the United States with another corrupt and disliked regime to support. By summer 1970, Nixon announced the end of U.S. military involvement, for all objectives, he said in a nationally televised address, had been achieved. This was not the case, but the alternative was to suggest that the invasion had been a mistake or that antiwar activists had succeeded in forcing the U.S. and its South Vietnamese allies out of Cambodia. A majority of Americans told the Gallup Poll that Vietnamization was never going to work, and a similar majority (71 percent) condemned the Cambodian incursion. That same number also agreed that the entire Vietnam War was a mistake, and only 31 percent said that Nixon was an adequate commander in chief. Similar sentiments were expressed in 1971 when the South Vietnamese military, strongly assisted by American air cover, invaded nearby Laos.

To the antiwar movement, the Cambodian incursion was simply a new widening of the war. The entire decade of the 1970s, they believed, now promised nothing less than endless war. The ranks of the protesters became swollen with new participants, and the resulting violence and vandalism on a number of university campuses forced university administrators to cancel the remaining weeks of classes for the spring 1970 semester. The bloodiest confrontation came at Kent State University in Ohio. Four antiwar demonstrators were killed and several others wounded after the National Guardsmen sent to maintain order there fired into a fleeing crowd. Publicly, Nixon's only comment in reference to Kent State was that "violence breeds violence."

In a sense, a new type of civil war was brewing in America, and it was not lost on the parents who observed it. Most of the student protesters were 19 or 20 years old. Most of the National Guardsmen were the same age, and many were serving in the Guard in order to avoid Vietnam service. That raised the ugly specter of antiwar young people killing antiwar young people. The tragedy of Vietnam had deepened in 1970, but the nightmare would soon be over for the United States.[11] It had just begun for Cambodia.

A TIME FOR HEALING

In Congress, the Cambodian incursion began a new round of legislative versus executive branch battles that also divided the American people. Led by Senator Church, antiwar legislators sponsored legislation to cut off funding for all Vietnam War–related expenditures. Nixon responded by threatening to transfer funds from domestic appropriations, and he accused Congress of trying to usurp the duties of the commander in chief. As always, Nixon came close to leveling treason charges but never did. Senators George McGovern (Democrat of South Dakota) and Mark Hatfield (Republican of Oregon) even proposed a special amendment that would have all U.S. forces home from Vietnam by 1972. But this legislative revolution failed in Congress. Once the emotion over Cambodia died down, a more focused, disciplined legislative reform effort began. This time, it met results.

The Twenty-sixth Amendment, or right to vote for those between the ages of 18 and 21, was championed by both the Left in Congress (represented by Senator McGovern) and the Right (represented by Senator Goldwater). To McGovern, if young antiwar activists had the right to vote, their real power would be seen in the voting returns instead of in the streets. To Goldwater, the average age of the Vietnam veteran was 19, and it was a tragedy, he said, that they did not have the right to vote during America's most controversial war. The amendment passed by a resounding majority. Meanwhile, although he first met heavy opposition from the White House, Senator Hatfield's legislation for an all-volunteer military would slowly move forward to success as well. Both the McGovern-Goldwater and Hatfield measures were described as efforts to heal America after the shock of the Cambodian incursion. The simple fact that these bills became law, combined with the steadily increasing number of U.S. troops heading home from Vietnam, led to less and not more antiwar activity.

This change took the news media by surprise. CBS News had predicted an unprecedented number of violent antiwar demonstrations for 1971. It was mistaken.

Ironically, one of the few large antiwar demonstrations of 1971 (another Moratorium Day) took place in Washington, D.C. The 1971 Moratorium Day was never one specific 24-hour period alone. The term was best used to describe the importance of the demonstration itself. A number of communities, and at different times, would host Moratorium Day protests. The Moratorium Day gatherings in Washington especially disturbed the Nixon administration. Convinced that dissent had finally, once and for all reached its limits and that it must be contained by any means necessary, the Nixon team began its slide into illegal activity. From interfering in the trial of Daniel Ellsberg, Pentagon whistle blower and antiwar activist, to authorizing a break-in at the Democratic National Committee headquarters at the new Watergate office building complex, the Nixon team went the distance to battle antiwar dissent, protect executive privilege, and prevail over all opponents.[12] It was a fateful decision for Nixon, although most of the press and later historians agreed that his forced resignation two years later truly completed the healing process that had begun shortly after the Cambodian invasion.

With Nixon went some of the darkest days of the Vietnam War era, although the war did not formally end until April 1975. Nixon's successor, former House Minority Leader Gerald Ford, summed up things nicely. In a May 1975 commencement speech, he told his alma mater of the University of Michigan that the "long nightmare of Vietnam is now over." It was time to "move forward together," he said, and his student audience, many of whom had been dedicated antiwar protesters, cheered his remarks. They were graduating into an America at peace, tired of confrontation and tired of fighting for the latest cause or concern.[13]

To some, the 1960s, and all that decade was supposed to mean, had finally transcended into something quieter, more cooperative, and maybe less violent. It may have been 1975, but it was better late than never. The journey had been an amazing one, and for those who survived it, the 1960s would remain the defining moment of their lives.

CHRONICLE OF EVENTS

1969

January 2: Senator Edward Kennedy (Democrat of Massachusetts) unseats veteran Senator Russell Long (Democrat of Louisiana) as Democratic Whip (Assistant Majority Leader of the U.S. Senate).

January 5: Henry Cabot Lodge, former U.S. ambassador to Saigon, is appointed by President-elect Nixon to head the American delegation at the Paris Peace Talks over Vietnam.

January 6: The U.S. Treasury Department reports that the national debt increased by 4 percent during 1968 ($361.2 billion).

January 10: Citing the negative impact of television news and other matters, the directors of the *Saturday Evening Post* vote to discontinue publication with their February 8, 1969, issue. The magazine was founded in 1821.

January 14: Lyndon Johnson delivers his final State of the Union address, asking his successor, Richard Nixon, to end the Vietnam War as well as continue Great Society programs.

January 16: After over two months of delay, the Paris Peace Talks negotiators meet at a round table with two rectangular tables nearby. A debate over the proper shape of the negotiation table had led to the suspension of the talks for weeks.

January 18: Lyndon Johnson signs a bill doubling the president's salary to $200,000 a year. It becomes effective on the day of Richard Nixon's inauguration.

January 20: Richard Nixon is sworn in as president.

January 27: Nine days of torrential rains in California end with the worst flooding of the century there, killing 91 people and resulting in more than $60 million in property damage.

January 29: The U.S. Treasury Department reports that the cost of living increased 4.7 percent in 1968, the biggest hike in nearly 20 years. Meanwhile, the U.S. balance of trade showed a surplus of $726 million, the lowest since the Great Depression year of 1937.

February 5: The Federal Communications Commission votes 6 to 1 to ban cigarette advertising during television and radio programs.

February 11: Attorney General John Mitchell authorizes federal agents to wiretap suspected organized crime figures.

February 13: National Guardsmen are dispatched to break up student demonstrations at both the University of Wisconsin-Madison and Duke University in North Carolina.

February 18: An Israeli airliner, carrying many U.S. citizens, is attacked by Arab terrorists while taking off from the Zurich International Airport in Switzerland. Six passengers are seriously wounded.

February 23: During the biggest assault since the Tet Offensive one year earlier, communist forces in South Vietnam shell Saigon and 124 other cities.

February 25: Several North Vietnamese suicide squads attack U.S. Marine positions near the South Vietnam/North Vietnam border. Twenty Marines die in hand-to-hand combat.

February 26: General Motors recalls a record 4.9 million cars and trucks due to faulty exhaust systems.

March 1: New Orleans businessman Clay Shaw is acquitted of "conspiring to kill President John F. Kennedy." District Attorney Jim Garrison then files perjury charges against him, but his conspiracy theory and cause wins little public support.

March 1: Immediately following a concert in Florida, Jim Morrison of the rock group the Doors is arrested on obscenity charges.

March 3: During his own trial for murder, Sirhan B. Sirhan admits that he was the assassin of Senator Robert Kennedy.

March 5: A National Airlines plane carrying 26 passengers from New York to Miami is hijacked to a Cuba by a bearded gunman who also stole $1,700 from one of those passengers. The money is returned by the Cuban government shortly after the plane lands in Havana.

March 10: James Earl Ray pleads guilty in the shooting death of Martin Luther King, Jr. Ray is sentenced to 99 years in prison.

March 13: After a 10-day journey circling the Earth, the *Apollo 9* spacecraft proves that this lunar-landing vehicle, as well as any other in the Apollo class, is ready for a mission to the moon.

March 14: A special Chicago Police Department inquiry into the violence outside the 1968 Democratic Convention, charges 41 police officers with "excessive force."

March 18: During one of the largest operations of the Vietnam War, more than 10,000 U.S. and South Vietnamese troops sweep through the plantations northwest of Saigon. This offensive was designed to safeguard the South Vietnamese capital from future enemy attack.

March 26: The 44,000 members of the International Federation of Airline Pilots threatens a general strike if the United States and other governments fail to halt the growing incidence of airplane hijackings to Cuba.

March 28: Dwight Eisenhower, the 34th president of the United States and former commander of allied forces in World War II–Europe, dies at the age of 78.

April 3: Without giving the precise number, the Pentagon announces that Vietnam War casualties have now surpassed the total number of casualties in the Korean War. That makes Vietnam the fourth-bloodiest conflict in U.S. history.

April 3: In Chicago, National Guardsmen are dispatched to quell a riot that breaks out during a memorial service for the late Dr. Martin Luther King, Jr. A curfew is imposed for the next several days.

April 10: More than 200 antiwar activists are arrested at Harvard University during a protest of the Reserve Officers Training Program (ROTC) there.

April 15–21: U.S. forces in South Korea and Japan go on full alert following the North Korean downing of a U.S. Navy electronics plane in the Sea of Japan. All 31 crewmen aboard the plane are killed. President Nixon orders a navy task force of 29 ships to the area, and rumors of an impending new war spread across Asia. The rumors are false.

April 24: Dropping more than 3,000 tons of bombs on the Cambodian border northwest of Saigon, the U.S. Air Force accomplishes its largest raid of the Vietnam War.

April 28: Nearly 100 policemen are injured and 900 student demonstrators are arrested during an anti-American protest in Tokyo. The students were demanding an end to the U.S. regime on Okinawa and other Ryukyu Islands south of the main islands of Japan. That regime remains in place for the next three years.

April 30: After a winter of record snowfall in the Midwest, the Mississippi River floods hundreds of river towns and in spite of sandbag and levee-building efforts, President Nixon declares it one of the worst natural disasters of the 20th century.

May 9: After weeks of violent student protests, which included the armed occupation of campus administration buildings, 11 fires, and the destruction of the Student Center Auditorium, Dr. Buell Gallagher, president of the City College of New York,

resigns. Joseph Copeland, a biology professor, becomes the new acting president.

May 12: Some 75 students occupy the administration offices of the Union Theological Seminary in New York. They were demanding a $500 million reparation payment by the Nixon administration to all African Americans as part of white America's apology for slavery.

May 13: Veteran civil rights activist Charles Evers defeats a white incumbent to become the first African-American mayor of Fayette, Mississippi.

May 25: John Schlesinger's *Midnight Cowboy,* a film about the seedy dark side of life in New York City, premieres to critical acclaim. The film stars Dustin Hoffman and Jon Voight.

June 13: Dan Bullock, a New Yorker who had enlisted in the U.S. Marine Corps at age 15 with false identification papers, becomes the youngest American soldier killed in Vietnam.

June 22: At their convention in Chicago, the Students for a Democratic Society admit that they are now hopelessly divided over the proper direction of the antiwar movement.

June 23: Leaving behind a legacy of unprecedented civil rights reform, Supreme Court Chief Justice Earl Warren turns over the Court to his successor, Warren Burger.

June 28: Opposition to police harassment of the gay patrons at the Stonewall Inn in New York leads to the beginning of the gay and lesbian rights movement.

July 16–24: The *Apollo 11* crew, Neil Armstrong, Michael Collins, and Edwin "Buzz" Aldrin, succeed in their mission to put a man on the Moon (Neil Armstrong) for the first time.

July 19–30: An automobile driven by Senator Edward Kennedy careens off a bridge on Chappaquiddick Island. His passenger, Mary Jo Kopechne, drowns. Kennedy pleads guilty to leaving the scene of an accident and in a television broadcast asks the voters of Massachusetts to tell him if he must resign. The senator decides to keep his seat and run for reelection in 1970.

July 21: The Pentagon announces the removal of chemical weapons from Okinawa, acknowledging for the first time that the U.S. military has chemical weapons capability and stockpiles.

July 24: Senator Eugene McCarthy, once a Democratic champion of the antiwar movement, announces his retirement from politics.

President Nixon telephones "Tranquility Base" on the Moon to speak to astronauts Neil Armstrong and Edwin "Buzz" Aldrin. *(NASA)*

August 17: The Woodstock open-air rock and folk-rock music festival near Bethel, New York, attracts more than 400,000 young people (according to some estimates), symbolizing the late 1960s youth culture to many observers and participants.

August 17–18: Hurricane Camille, the second-largest hurricane ever to hit the United States, leaves 200 dead in its wake and causes nearly $1.5 billion in damage.

September: More than one year after the Democratic convention protests and riots, the trial of YIP (Youth International Party or Yippie) leaders and other antiwar activists (nicknamed the Chicago Seven) begins. Originally known as the Chicago Eight trial, it became the Chicago Seven when one of the defendants, Bobby Seale, received a separate trial.

September 3: Ho Chi Minh, the founding father of North Vietnam and leader of that nation's war against the South Vietnamese and their American protectors, dies at the age of 79.

October 15: Despite comments from the Nixon administration that it would only give solace to the enemy, a Moratorium Day of antiwar demonstrations takes place in a number of major U.S. cities.

November 6: Black Panther leader Bobby Seale is sentenced to four years in prison for his efforts to incite violence at the 1968 Democratic convention.

November 15: Some 250,000 people (a conservative police estimate) demonstrate against the Vietnam War in Washington, D.C.

November 17: Surviving residents of the village of My Lai, South Vietnam, claim that 370 fellow villagers were murdered by U.S. troops in March 1968. The resulting investigation proves that their charges correct but divides Americans over whether or not the massacre was a war crime.

November 18: Joseph P. Kennedy, one of the country's richest men and founding father of a powerful political dynasty, dies at the age of 81.

December: The Motion Picture Association of America announces that the top three box office winners of 1969 are *The Love Bug, Funny Girl,* and *Bullitt.* The top drawing box office stars are Paul Newman, John Wayne, and Steve McQueen.

December: The Associated Press notes that the top three single records of 1969 are "I Heard It Through the Grapevine" by Marvin Gaye, "Aquarius/Let the Sunshine In" by the 5th Dimension, and "Sugar, Sugar" by the Archies.

December 6: Violence flares at the Altamont music festival, where the Rolling Stones are in concert. One spectator is killed.

December 8: Charles Manson, a self-proclaimed cult leader and mystic, is indicted with five of his followers for the brutal murder of actress Sharon Tate and seven other individuals.

December 22: Eleven people are killed when a fighter plane crashes into a hangar at Miramar Naval Air Station in San Diego.

1970

January 26: During one of the largest demonstrations in the history of the Philippines, thousands of workers and farmers attempt to take power from pro-American dictator Ferdinand Marcos. The Philippines houses the Subic Bay navy base and Clark air base, both of which were important to the United States in the nearby Vietnam War. President Nixon reaffirms U.S. support for Marcos.

February 11: President Nixon agrees to withdraw 4,200 of the 47,000 U.S. troops in Thailand, stating that he understands the precarious position of Thailand's Prime Minister Thanon Kittikachorn vis-à-vis his communist neighbors.

February 18: A federal grand jury hands down a not guilty verdict to seven antiwar leaders who helped organize the protests at the 1968 Democratic convention. According to the jury, the seven did not "incite a riot," but five of the seven are convicted of crossing a state line to be involved in a riot. The latter conviction is overturned on appeal.

February 20: Henry Kissinger arrives in Paris to begin secret peace talks with the North Vietnamese.

February 21: After an 11-day offensive, North Vietnamese troops claim full control of the strategic Plaine Des Jarres in Laos.

March 6: The Weather Underground, a pro-violence alternative to the Students for a Democratic Society (SDS), blows up an exclusive town house in downtown New York City. The town house was a Weather Underground bomb factory.

March 18: While on a European tour, Prince Norodom Sihanouk of neutral Cambodia is overthrown by General Lon Nol. Cambodia is soon renamed the Khmer Republic by Lon Nol, and a fateful relationship with the Americans begins.

April 10: Beatle Paul McCartney formally announces to the press that the rumors of a Beatles breakup are accurate.

April 11–17: Another mission to the moon (*Apollo 13*) is launched. On the third day of the mission an explosion occurs rupturing the spacecraft's oxygen, water, and power systems. Forced to make an emergency return to Earth, astronauts James Lovell, John Swigert, and Fred Haise survive the ordeal.

April 22: Complete with urban clean-ups involving thousands of schoolchildren and others, the American environmental movement succeeds with its first nationwide Earth Day, demonstrating the new movement's political clout and influence.

April 30: During a television address, President Nixon announces the Cambodian incursion and U.S. solidarity behind the Cambodian government of Lon Nol. More than 30,000 U.S. troops are involved in this effort to destroy North Vietnamese sanctuaries inside Cambodia.

May 4: Four students are killed by National Guardsmen at Ohio's Kent State University. One hundred National Guardsmen faced 500–600 student demonstrators protesting the widening of the Vietnam War into Cambodia.

May 6: In the interest of preventing more violence following the shootings at Kent State, some 100 universities and colleges cancel all remaining classes of the 1969–70 academic year.

May 11: Time magazine reports that the percentage of American women who are full-time homemakers has dropped to 48.4 percent.

May 17: Atlanta Braves baseball player Hank Aaron becomes the first player to compile both 3,000 career hits and more than 500 home runs.

June 24: In an angry rebuke of presidential executive privilege, Congress repeals the 1964 Gulf of Tonkin Resolution. President Nixon argues that this precise document is irrelevant anyway, for a wartime president can interpret the Constitutional powers of commander in chief as he sees fit.

June 30: The Cambodian incursion formally ends.

July 29: After five years of boycotts and strikes, Cesar Chavez, director of the AFL-CIO's United Farm Workers organization, wins contracts with three-quarters of California's grape-growing industry.

August 10: In a sweeping 350–15 vote, the House of Representatives approves the Equal Rights Amendment (ERA) for women.

September 18: Rock singer-guitarist Jimi Hendrix dies in London from what is officially described as "barbiturate intoxication."

October 4: Rock sensation Janis Joplin dies of what is alleged to be a heroin overdose in Hollywood, California.

November 3: Soon to be the victim of a CIA-supported coup, Salvador Allende Gossens of Chile becomes the Western Hemisphere's first freely elected Marxist president. Allende promises to nationalize most industries and open relations with a number of communist nations.

November 9: Chief Justice Warren Burger of the U.S. Supreme Court refuses to hear a case, championed by the state government of Massachusetts, that the Vietnam War is unconstitutional.

November 11: For the first time in more than five years, no U.S. soldiers are reported killed in Vietnam within a full 24-hour period.

December: The Motion Picture Association announces that *Love Story* was not only the top box office success of 1970 but, at nearly $107 million in ticket sales and climbing, one of the all-time great success stories in the history of film. The top three single records of the year are "ABC" by the Jackson 5, "Ain't No Mountain High Enough" by Diana Ross,

Rock icon Janis Joplin rests her head on a microphone during her performance at Woodstock. *(Hulton Archive/TimePix)*

and "Bridge Over Troubled Water" by Simon and Garfunkel.

December 22: Congress passes legislation preventing the Nixon administration from dispatching U.S. military advisers to Laos and Cambodia.

December 31: Thanks to Vietnamization, the Pentagon reports that the number of U.S. troops in South Vietnam has declined to 334,600 (compared to 475,200 exactly one year earlier).

EYEWITNESS TESTIMONY

Nixon, Kissinger, and the End of the 1960s

And what's the ultimate end of all this? Some of these days, you're going to get somebody elected—George Wallace or somebody like him. It's coming just as sure as the world; the only question is, how long does it take? But, you know, the old pendulum's been swinging back and forth a long time, and I don't believe it's going to take much more for the pendulum to swing back the other way. The solution won't come until we reach an agreement where both races establish a pattern they're willing to live under.

White segregationist leader Roy Harris bemoaning the upcoming inauguration of President Richard Nixon in January 1969, in Hedgepath, "The Radicals: Are They Poles Apart?" Look, January 7, 1969, pp. 34–35.

A fire rages in the hearts of black people today. Total liberty for black people or total destruction in Nixon's America. Total liberty is the absence of artificial restraint on the activities and actions of black people. Total absence of any unnecessary blocking of access to all the benefits of the economic and political and social systems. I had a phrase—we talk about an equal and proportionate share in the manipulation of the sovereignty of this country. We want to see a situation where, in every issue pertaining to the social structure as a whole, that the opinions and will of black people must be brought into consideration.

Black Panther leader Eldridge Cleaver bemoaning the upcoming inauguration of President Richard Nixon in January 1969, in Hedgepeth, "The Radicals: Are They Poles Apart?" Look, January 7, 1969, pp. 34–35.

Some blacks will develop black capitalism, while others will want cooperative enterprise. In a vast, heterogeneous society such as ours, where temperament and talent are varied, different approaches should be expected. A people emerging from under colonial rule have many avenues open to them. Black America is looking for a way to emerge constructively. We can only hope that white America

will understand this and act . . . as wisely as it is wealthy.

Black Power expert and professor of political science Charles V. Hamilton offering social policy advice to the incoming Nixon administration, in his "The Constructive Equation: Black Power + White Power = Solutions," Look, January 7, 1969, p. 81.

Communist North Vietnam and the United States are finally on the road to peace—not because either side is winning the war but because neither side can. It will be a long, hard road, for it's always easier to get into the war than to get out—gracefully. And as we travel this road in the months ahead, many Americans will wonder how three administrations managed to delude themselves and the nation so convincingly and so long. For only stubborn self-delusion can explain our refusal to see that the Vietnamese who fought hardest fought for nationalism and its living symbol, Ho Chi Minh—not for generals in Saigon; that patriotism more than communism is what made them stand up to American might; and that our soldiers in Asia looked no different to many of the long-suffering Vietnamese than the French who had been there earlier. Self-delusion has cost us dearly in blood, treasure, prestige, bitter dissent, strained alliances and neglected priorities. It has cost the North Vietnamese dearly too. But after more than 25 years of battling against strangers in their midst, they are willing to go on paying the price.

Look magazine beginning 1969 with an in-depth examination of North Vietnam and America's Vietnam War policies, quoted in Zimmermann, "Communist North Vietnam: Cocky and Patriotic," Look, January 21, 1969, pp. 19–30.

You know where the Oval Room is at? Well, on the far wall, on the left as you walk in, is an old colonial sideboard. . . . Okay? . . . Now, we always kept that key in the second little-bitty drawer from the top on the right side of the desk part. . . .

Lyndon Johnson joking with incoming President Richard Nixon over where to find the secret White House liquor cabinet, in Flagler, "Look on the Light Side," Look, January 21, 1969, p. 40.

Speaking personally, and also as the Commander of the Armed Forces, I do not want an American boy to be in Vietnam for one day longer than is necessary for our national interest. As our commanders in the field determine that the South Vietnamese are able to assume a greater portion of the responsibility for the defense of their own territory, troops will come back. However, at this time, I have no announcements to make with regard to the return of troops.

I will only say that it is high on the agenda of priorities, and that just as soon as either the training program for South Vietnamese forces and their capabilities, the progress of the Paris peace talks, or other developments make it feasible to do so, troops will be brought back.

Richard Nixon, during one of his first press conferences as president, in late January 1969, admitting that there is no "secret plan" to end the Vietnam War, in the Library of Congress's The Nixon Presidential Press Conferences *(1978), p. 11.*

The two men, at separate moments on the same day, raised their arms in victory and farewell. "I think," the new President said happily, "that 'Hail to the Chief' has a nice ring." Hours earlier, after half a life-

In 1969, members of Companies B and D, 1st Battalion, 501st Infantry Regiment, 101st Airborne Division take a break from the fighting near Tam Ky, South Vietnam. There will be no "secret plan" to bring them home. *(National Archives)*

time in government, Lyndon Johnson and his family left the capital, eager now to return to their beloved Texas hill country. If he was sad, Johnson was also unmistakably relieved. He felt, he said, "different within four seconds" after his successor had taken the oath of office.

Life magazine reporting in Staff, "The Inauguration: Rhetoric Meets Reality," Life, January 31, 1969, pp. 18–31.

In his Inaugural Address, President Nixon's boldest promise was to seek for America the honored "title of peacemaker" among the nations. He reasons that because all people want peace and their leaders fear war, "the times are on the side of peace," and we can assist the process. This is a rather new stance for Nixon, who in Ike's time was a pretty tough cold warrior and whose 1968 campaign speeches warned us against a U.S. "security gap." But he has also grown sophisticated in foreign affairs and says we have passed from "a period of confrontation" to "an era of negotiation." The new President's olive branch is up.

The surprised managing editor of Life magazine, George Hunt, noting contradictions between the new and old Nixon in January 1969, in Hunt, "Inviting an 'era of negotiation,'" Life, January 31, 1969, p. 32.

It is significant that among the 81 staff members lined up and given their oath there was only one pair of sideburns. It is also significant that the ceremony was brief, and when it was over the President left, and his men and women went back to work. Kennedy's people had made it a real party. . . .

At one of the ceremonies, a youngster surveying the East Room with its massive chandeliers and towering portraits of Martha and George Washington asked in a hushed voice, "Now where exactly is the power center?" The power center, in the person of Richard Milhous Nixon, was at that moment walking back to the Oval Office with remarkable ease and sense of pleasure, which may say a lot about the kind of President the man will be.

Presidential expert and historian Hugh Sidey commenting on Nixon's first day in office, in his "The Man with the Four-Button Phone," Life, January 31, 1969, p. 4.

Henry thinks Bill Rogers isn't very deep and Bill thinks Henry is power crazy. In a sense they are both right.

President Nixon, in a February 1969 interview with reporter William Safire, hinting that Secretary of State William Rogers and National Security Council Adviser Henry Kissinger might be rivals, quoted in Reichley, Conservatives in an Age of Change: The Nixon and Ford Administrations (1981), p. 109.

I refuse to believe that a little fourth-rate power like North Vietnam doesn't have a breaking point.

Henry Kissinger recommending in February 1969 a stepped-up B-52 bombing campaign over North Vietnam, quoted in Szulc, The Illusion of Peace: Foreign Policy in the Nixon Years (1978), p. 150.

I've always acted alone. Americans admire that enormously. Americans admire cowboys leading the caravan alone astride his horse, the cowboy entering a village or city alone on his horse. Without even a pistol, maybe, because he doesn't go in for shooting. He acts, that's all: aiming at the right spot at the right time. A Wild West tale, if you like. This romantic, surprising character suits me, because being alone has always been part of my style, or of my technique if you prefer. Independence too. Yes, that's very important to me and in me.

Henry Kissinger, during a February 1969 interview with Italian journalist Oriana Fallaci, touting his "independence" in the making of U.S. national security policy, quoted in Hersh, The Price of Power: Kissinger in the Nixon White House (1983), pp. 608–609.

The White House and Nixon are curiously matched. Nixon is a very private man who seeks protection from the harassments of political life whenever he can. Indeed, moments of quiet solitude seem as necessary as food for his nourishment. The White House, when used correctly, can be a veritable fortress—not against the great burdens of the office, but against the daily irritants and frustrations which can enervate a person as much as anything. The White House complex is almost like a medieval redoubt. There are concentric rings of security and privacy. The carpeted corridors with their husky Secret Service guards are the moats and the electronically locked doors are the drawbridges. The outside world is filtered in under absolute control. Nixon dwells in the protective layer he chooses, moving from total loneliness to the degree of exposure he wants for any particular moment, then returning to the shelter from where he came. He prepared himself for his first press conference in the serenity of the Oval Office and then—after the 456 reporters and broadcasters had been checked for security, seated in the East Room and hushed—he plunged out of this calm into the office halls, then on to the public sector of the mansion, finally into the midst of the newsmen. When it was over, he hurried back along the same route to his base.

Veteran political reporter Hugh Sidey describing the "private" Nixon during his first week as president in January 1969, in Sidey, "It was good to be home," Life, *February 7, 1969, p. 2.*

And I knew that all these problems, taken together, were chickenshit compared with what might happen if we lost Vietnam. For this time there would be Robert Kennedy out in front leading the fight against me, telling everyone that I had betrayed John Kennedy's commitment to South Vietnam. That I had let a democracy fall into the hands of the Communists. That I was a coward. An unmanly man. A man without a spine. Oh, I could see it coming alright. Every night when I fell asleep I would see myself tied to the ground in the middle of a long, open space. In the distance, I could hear the voices of thousands of people. They were all shouting at me and running toward me: "Coward! Traitor! Weakling!" They kept coming closer. They began throwing stones. At exactly that moment I would generally wake up . . . terribly shaken. But there was more. You

While some young adults tried to escape from the Vietnam War through the Beach Boys and beach blanket movies, some veterans united to protest the war. Here, more than a year before the Nixon administration, the "Veterans for Peace" lead a group of protesters at the October 1967 March on the Pentagon demonstration. *(Frank Wolfe, Lyndon B. Johnson Library)*

see, I was as sure as any man could be that once we showed how weak we were, Moscow and Peking would move in a flash to exploit our weakness. They might move independently or they might move together. But move they would. . . . And so would begin World War III. So you see, I was bound to be crucified either way I moved.

Shortly after the end of his administration, Lyndon Johnson telling historian Doris Kearns Goodwin in March 1969 that he knew the Vietnam War would destroy his presidency, in Goodwin, Lyndon Johnson and the American Dream *(1976),* Research Room, Lyndon Johnson Library.

I think that much of the responsibility rests not on the young people for not knowing what they are for, but on older people for not giving them the vision and the sense of purpose and the idealism that they should have.

In talking—and I talked with every leader about this, every one—all of us are concerned about it. All of us feel that we must find for this great Western family of ours a new sense of purpose and idealism, one that young people will understand, that they can be for.

That is not a satisfactory answer, because I am not able to describe it yet, but believe me, we are searching for it.

President Nixon, during a March 1969 news conference, stating that the "youth problem" is a matter of concern for America and all of its allies, in the Library of Congress's The Nixon Presidential Press Conferences *(1978), pp. 31–32.*

The long hard struggle in Vietnam is almost sure to be de-Americanized in the near future. There are two tasks ahead for us Americans that, as we succeed in them, will permit us to de-Americanize the effort and start bringing our men back home again with honor. These tasks depend upon American initiative and are neither simple nor easy. They are: 1) to quarantine the war within the borders of South Vietnam, and 2) to make the Vietnamese really responsible partners in seeing to it that the tremendous American material aid gets to the Vietnamese people, for whom it is intended.

There have been continuous and strenuous efforts devoted to these two tasks, but it is evident that they have been short of succeeding. The time has come for us to think and act differently.

Once the American government's top adviser on Vietnamese affairs, retired General Edward G. Lansdale writing an open letter to President Nixon on Vietnam War solutions in March 1969, in Lansdale, "Two Steps to Get Us Out of Vietnam," Look, *March 4, 1969, pp. 64–67.*

In protest against all the campus protesters the Chicago *Tribune* recently blacked out all news stories about them for one day. If the *Trib's* idea of one-day moratoriums—on news the editors are either bored or repelled by—ever catches on, here are a few other newspaper perennials we'd be happy to do without:

- Richard Burton's birthday gifts to Liz Taylor.
- Speculation on whether Ted Kennedy wants to run for President.
- Breathlessly written revelations that 1) the Alliance for Progress has failed to work and 2) New York City is either ungovernable or badly governed.
- Any more announcements from New Orleans District Attorney Jim Garrison that he has uncovered a "conspiracy" [to kill President John Kennedy].
- Interviews with movie actresses who say their first nude film scene was terribly embarrassing, wonderfully natural, or possibly both.
- All further announcements that the "final push" has begun in Nigeria's stalemated 20-month-old civil war.

And, of course, news that university authorities have agreed to the "non-negotiable" demands of student protesters.

With tongue in cheek, Life *magazine managing editor George Hunt complaining about the "non-news" items of 1969, in Hunt, "Reading we can do without,"* Life, *March 14, 1969, p. 34.*

I think the mood of the American people—that is, the people who count, the majority who are middle-aged and fairly affluent—has already become more conservative in reaction to the violence of Black Power, to the absurdity of the hippies, the anarchy of the students. Mr. Nixon, I think, is very much political-minded, and he will therefore probably respond rather sensitively to the public mood. I don't quite see him taking a lead that might be unpopular or trying to convert the American people from some attitude he thinks is wrong. He's more

Looking very much as if he is on the wrong side of the "generation gap," a formally dressed President Nixon shakes hands with the troops in the hot summer sun of 1969 South Vietnam. *(National Archives—Nixon Presidential Material)*

likely to try and discover what the American mood is and go along with it. That would be unfortunate, because the Presidency of the United States exists in order to give leadership.

In March 1969, one of the world's most respected historians, 80-year-old Arnold Toynbee, talking politics with reporter J. Robert Moskin, in Moskin, "Arnold Toynbee Talks of Peace, Power, Race in America," Look, March 18, 1969, pp. 25–27.

A settlement in Vietnam, I believe, is just the first step in creating a peaceful world order, an atmosphere in which people, wherever they may be, can give their attention to their well-being at home. I detect a new impatience, on both sides of what we have so long called "the Iron Curtain," with ideological strife. In the Communist world, the European satellites are in open rebellion against Russian dominance. In the capitals of the West, there is greater diversity of policy and opinion than at any time since World War II. The era of the superpowers may be over, and I regard this as an opportunity to be seized. If President Nixon somehow manages to write a treaty of peace for the cold war, he will earn the gratitude of countries throughout the world who are bored with doctrine but excited by the prospect of renewing their own societies. He will also keep the Republican party in office for the foreseeable future.

There's no magic formula by which Republicans can be transformed into a majority. There are difficult decisions, unpleasant struggles and hard work. Good politics is not distinguishable from good government. But I do not despair that the task can be performed and the Republican party become again—as it once was—the keeper of the destiny of our nation.

Representative Ogden Reid, a veteran New York Republican congressman, predicting that under Nixon's leadership the Republican Party can become the majority party for the rest of the century and beyond, in Reid, "Do Republicans have the courage to become the Majority Party?: It all depends on Richard Nixon," Look, May 13, 1969, pp. 76–82.

Once again, suggestions are floating around like dandelion fluff. President Nixon sent out a message in May saying he wants an all-volunteer Army, "as soon as that is feasible." Of course, he added, it won't be feasible for awhile, so he asked Congress to grant him the authority Lyndon Johnson didn't get. He endorsed a familiar random-selection system (the lottery), said the youngest men should go first, and inspired one of the few funny moments in the whole lugubrious business: San Francisco *Chronicle* columnist Arthur Hoppe's question, "Who needs an unlucky Army?". . . . So the political arguments go on, and the nation's young men watch the futility in Washington with increasing disgust. The draft is an agony nowhere near an end.

Author and Selective Service expert John Poppy arguing that the draft is a relic of the 1960s that should not be carried into the 1970s, in his "The Draft: Hazardous to Your Health?," Look, August 12, 1969, pp. 32–34.

Ideological differences between the two Communist giants are not our affair. We could not fail to be deeply concerned, however, with an escalation of this quarrel into a massive breach of international peace and security. Our national security would in the long run be prejudiced by associating ourselves with either side against the other. Each is highly sensitive about American efforts to improve relations with the other. We intend, nevertheless, to pursue a long-term course of progressively developing better relations with both. We are not going to let Communist Chinese invective deter us from seeking agreements with the Soviet Union where those are in our interest. Conversely, we are not going to let Soviet apprehensions prevent us from attempting to bring Communist China out of its angry, alienated shell.

Undersecretary of State Elliot Richardson shocking the annual meeting of the American Political Science Association with the admission that the Nixon administration plans a new relationship with both China and the Soviet Union, quoted in Richardson, "The Foreign Policy of the Nixon Administration: Its Aims and Strategy," Department of State Bulletin, September 22, 1969, p. 260.

Ralph Nader, Environmentalism, and the Economy

Nader often has been accused of arrogance and a lack of personal warmth, and some of his pronouncements make him sound like a species of vengeful deity. But he seems unconcerned about injured feelings. And one group of men—the Washington press corps—loves him most when he is least lovable.

Nader's methods are fundamentally those of an investigative reporter of the Drew Pearson type. He deals in scoops and exclusives, unpublished government documents, secret files, and unremarked conversations. His claims of FTC laxity, for example, were based chiefly on a previously undisclosed study by the Civil Service Commission, which he unearthed. His complaint that Ford Motor Company charged exorbitant mark-ups on its optional equipment was based, he says, on Ford's own computer printout. This is the sort of stuff the Washington press corps eats up.

Playing the dangerous game he does, Nader keeps his personal life stripped for action, as General

At the height of his "consumer crusader" popularity, Ralph Nader lectures to a standing-room-only crowd at the Lawrence Berkeley National Laboratory. *(Lawrence Berkeley National Laboratory)*

Motors Corporation discovered in 1965. In the wake of the publication of "Unsafe at Any Speed," GM put a private investigator on Nader's trail. All it got for its pains was much indignant public criticism—and the Highway Safety Act.

> Business Week *examining the life and tactics of consumer champion Ralph Nader, in Staff, "Crusader Widens Range of His Ire,"* Business Week, *January 25, 1969, pp. 128–130.*

The 37th President of the United States will find, as I did, that all the Presidents who have gone before him have left something of themselves behind. He will discover, as I did, that the Oval Office—while a lonely place in many ways—is filled with the presence and the thoughts of men who bore the burden of national leadership in their time.

That is the unseen Presidency. Its tradition, experience, judgment and example speak across the centuries from one President to the next, and preserving our environment has concerned them all. . . .

> *Lyndon Johnson, in a February 1969 open letter to President Richard Nixon, connecting the tradition of the presidency to the effort to save the environment, quoted in Johnson, "What It Is to Be Mr. President,"* Look, *February 4, 1969, pp. 23–25.*

Can mankind live or indeed survive with its vastly increasing powers? Human bodies are very fragile in the face of the forces of nature we now control, and human institutions are even more so. Are conventional wisdom and conventional values sufficient guides to stave off catastrophe? History lends scant grounds for hope. . . .

The founding fathers of this country dared make new and lasting institutions in the spirit of the science of their day. This generation, with its deeper understanding, should surely be able to do as well in our time.

> *I. I. Rabi, chairman of the Atomic Energy Commission and a Nobel Prize winner, arguing that Congress and the White House must concentrate all of their attentions on saving the environment, in Rabi and Dewart, "Views from Earth,"* Look, *February 4, 1969, pp. 72–78.*

Environmentalism may be a spiritual requirement. If the conception of God that revolves around God's ascendancy and man's submissiveness (or lack of it) is found inadequate, the reason is not necessarily that man has become proud and will not serve his Master. The reason may be man's discovery that, since he has not the nature of a servant, God to him is evidently not of the nature of a master. As man realizes that the very nature given him by God makes him creative and responsible, he will learn that his relationship to God must be based upon his acceptance of responsibility and his exercise of creativity.

Prominent Catholic theologian Leslie Dewart arguing that the "creative" and "responsible" person fights for the preservation of the environment, in Rabi and Dewart, "Views from Earth," Look, *February 4, 1969, pp. 72–78.*

Closer economic ties bear both cause and effect relationships to relaxation of political tension. Improvement in political relationships is a prerequisite for improved economic relationships, but, once in place, economic ties create a community of interest which in turn improves the environment for further progress on the political side.

Once set in motion, the cause-and-effect process can portend a downward spiral in political tension, a mutually beneficial economic foundation of the new relationship and tangible increases in the welfare and safety of the peoples of both countries. . . .

Our purpose is to build both countries a vested economic interest in the maintenance of an harmonious and enduring relationship. A nation's security is affected not only by its adversary's military capabilities but by the price which attends the use of those capabilities. If we can create a situation in which the use of military force would jeopardize a mutually profitable relationship, I think it can be argued that our security will have been enhanced.

Pete Peterson, the secretary of commerce, telling President Nixon in June 1969 that there is big money to be made by making peace with China and the Soviet Union, in his U.S.-Soviet Commercial Relations in a New Era *(1972), pp. 3–4.*

The "environment" has become a hot political property—so hot that two key Democratic senators are struggling for exclusive title to it. The result could be a clouded title, delays in antipollution legislation and an even slower flow of money for programs now on the books.

The two contending senators are Edmund Muskie (D.-Me.) And Henry Jackson (D-Wash.). Muskie, chairman of the air and water pollution subcommittee of the Public Works Committee, was a driving force behind the three major antipollution laws Congress has passed: the Federal Water Pollution Act, the Clean Air Act, and Solid Waste Disposal Act. Up to now, the Public Works Committee has had the environment pretty much to itself.

But this year Jackson, chairman of the Interior Committee, was the first to call hearings on the subject, and his committee was the first to bring out a bill—Jackson's "National Environmental Policy Act of 1969."

Business Week complaining that Senators Muskie and Jackson are exploiting environmental concerns to benefit their presidential aspirations and noting that the environmental cause has "lost its innocence," in Staff, "A Fight Over Who Cleans Up," Business Week, *July 12, 1969, p. 46.*

We have reached a turning in the road down which we have traveled now for some 35 years. The piling of tax money and power into the Federal establishment has mounted to the point of sharply diminishing returns. President Nixon spoke the literal truth when, in ordering consolidation of various programs in the Department of Health, Education, and Welfare, he said paralysis threatens. It is an astonishing fact that no one in Washington even knows how many Federal programs involving aid to states and cities now exist. Dr. Arthur Burns, the President's Counselor, thinks it is around six hundred. United Press International, which conducted its own study, estimates it to be at least one thousand. The tax money that never gets to the persons and places intended unquestionably runs into billions.

CBS newsman Eric Sevareid arguing that the number of costly federally funded programs might be unknown in Washington, D.C., in his "American Militarism: What Is It Doing To Us?," Look, *August 12, 1969, pp. 13–16.*

Detroit counts its successes from the Profit and Loss sheets, not technical satisfaction, and although the message about enthusiasts' cars is becoming more evident each year, the inertia of giant consumer-oriented manufacturing firms quite simply doesn't allow rapid change. Consider that since the implementation of the U.S. Safety Standards and the Clean Air Act (effectively the 1967–68 model years) Detroit's major success stories have been the Road Runner, a car made of already existing components; the Camaro, GM's answer to one of Ford's better ideas; the Javelin, ditto; and apparently, the Maverick.

> Car and Driver *magazine expressing its concerns that the U.S. auto industry will make cars in the 1970s without the consumer in mind, in Staff, "Detroit Does Its Number: A First Look at the Cars and Engines of the Next Decade,"* Car and Driver, *September 1969, p. 49.*

International politics and industrial maneuvering on the part of both American and foreign automobile manufacturers are reaching a point where a difficult diplomatic situation appears inevitable. It is no secret that many European countries resent the success American-based firms have been having in the "home" market. But, long-standing trade agreements prevent significant numbers of American-made cars to be exported to Japan, and Detroit's not happy either.

> Leon Mandel, *editor of* Car and Driver *magazine, using the late 1960s as a guide and predicting that the 1970s will be a decade of international squabbling among auto manufacturers, in his "Detroit Backlash,"* Car and Driver, *September 1969, p. 76.*

"There's no interchange between factory and dealer. I could have showed them what was wrong with the Lincoln Continental in a minute and in a lot of other ways. Although," he admits, "I don't think the Mustang would sell the way it has. What I mean is, we're the guys who have to sell the product. Or else. Yet they never draw on our experience."

> Kyle Given *reporting the belief of Ralph Williams, owner of America's most profitable Ford dealership and a southern California TV personality, that the lack of communication between the Ford Motor Co. and its dealers might destroy his business and many others, in Given's "And Now a Word from Our Sponsor,"* Car and Driver, *September 1969, p. 78.*

Now, we have attacked the source of the problem. We have cut the budget by $7 billion. We have monetary restraints. We have asked for an extension of the surtax rather than its complete elimination. And these basic policies, which go to the core of the problem, are beginning to work.

Now that the Government has set the example, I believe that labor and management would be well advised to follow the example. I am not jawboning and telling them to reform themselves, when we refuse to reform ourselves. But I do say this: that labor and management, labor that asks for exorbitant wage increases, management that raises prices too high, will be pricing themselves out of the market.

Anybody who bets on a continuing inflation will lose that bet, because our Government policies are beginning to work and we are going to stick to those policies until we cut the rise in the cost of living.

> President Nixon, *near the end of 1969, telling the press that his economic policies will end the country's economic woes, in the Library of Congress's* The Nixon Presidential Press Conferences *(1978), pp. 67–68.*

To many Americans, Nader at 35, has become something of a folk hero, a symbol of constructive protest against the status quo. When this peaceful revolutionary does battle against modern bureaucracies, he uses only the weapons available to any citizen—the law and public opinion. He has never picketed, let alone occupied, a corporate office or public agency. Yet Nader has managed to cut through all the protective layers and achieve results. He has shown that in an increasingly computerized, complex and impersonal society, one persistent man can actually do something about the forces that often seem to badger him—that he can indeed even shake and change big business, big labor and even bigger Government.

"My job is to bring issues out in the open where thy cannot be ignored," says Nader, chopping his hands, as he often does when he speaks. "There is a revolt against the aristocratic uses of technology and a demand for democratic uses. We have got to know what we are doing to ourselves. Life can be—and is being—eroded."

> Time *magazine examining Ralph Nader and his consumer advocacy cause in Staff, "Nader & Raiders: The U.S.'s Toughest Customer,"* Time, *December 12, 1969, p. 90.*

The symbol of contemporary America is no longer the Statue of Liberty, holding her lamp to beckon the poor of Europe toward the promise of a new life; it is no longer the great white dome of the U.S. Capitol, which promised them democracy, nor even the production line of Henry Ford, which promised them affluence. It is instead the new suburban shopping mall, which promises them—domestic ease.

> *Social critic Robert Hargreaves noting in late 1969 that the suburban shopping mall has become the new symbol of American life, quoted in Edelhart and Tinen,* America the Quotable *(1983), p. 193.*

The 1970s absolutely must be the years when America pays its debt to the past by reclaiming the purity of its air, its waters, and our living environment. It is literally now or never.

> *President Nixon signing the National Environmental Policy Act (NEPA) into law in 1970, quoted in Whitaker,* Striking a Balance: Environment and Natural Resources Policy in the Nixon-Ford Years *(1976), p. 91.*

Let's set up Congress to take the blame for a tax increase. They have overspent the budget on water and these other things, so we will have no choice but to change our position and ask for a necessary tax increase. Let them go home and explain that to the folks.

> *President Nixon telling his staff in April 1970 that costly appropriations for environmental issues are politically unacceptable, quoted in Ehrlichman,* Witness to Power *(1982), p. 91.*

President Nixon expresses his concern for the environment while inspecting the site of a 1969 oil spill in Santa Barbara, California. *(National Archives—Nixon Presidential Material)*

I assure you that I will not allow environmental concern to be used sometimes falsely and sometimes in a demagogic way basically to destroy the system.

President Nixon assuring the Detroit Economic Club in summer 1970 that the White House's commitment to new environmental laws has limits, quoted in Whitaker, Striking a Balance: Environment and Natural Resources Policy in the Nixon-Ford Years *(1976), p. 91.*

We have engaged in this vast environmental destruction and have not won the war nor has it protected any of our soldiers and it has done far greater damage to our ally than to the enemy. Now we have reports of weather modification activities to create rain storms and of at least three attempts to create massive fire storms to destroy vast areas. These fire storms are terribly frightening and uncontrollable in that once started they burn with explosive speeds that destroy every living thing in their wake. Tampering with the environment has a vast potential for uncontrollable and unpredictable destruction. Caution is required as neither the scientist nor the military know the long or short term ramification of these activities. We must set limits on the military lest the United States establish a precedent for others to repeat and even escalate. . . .

The grave consequences of environmental warfare are as great—if not greater—than those of internationally deplored chemical and biological warfare. It is one more dramatic example of the reckless use of modern technology to wreak environmental destruction.

Connecting his Senate leadership on environmental issues to his opposition to the Vietnam War, Senator Gaylord Nelson of Wisconsin complaining that the United States is setting a bad example on environmentalism at home and abroad, in Press Releases: Sen. Gaylord Nelson, July 21, 1972, and July 28, 1972, Box 251/Foreign Affairs-Bio. War, Papers of Sen. Gaylord Nelson, State Historical Society of Wisconsin.

Pop Culture in Transition (Again)

The Smothers Brothers took the position that we must abrogate the standards that we apply to all entertainment programs and make a special excep-

tion of them. Furthermore, they were unwilling to deliver their programs in time for us to permit the exercise of our review procedures. Under the circumstances, we do not believe that any mass medium—including *Look*—could have made any other decision about a contributor who had made it abundantly clear that he was unwilling to abide by established standards or submit material for editorial judgment.

Robert Wood, president of CBS Television, responding to charges by Look *magazine that he censored 75 percent of the scripts written for* The Smothers Brothers Comedy Hour *during 1968, quoted in Wood, "The CBS View,"* Look, *June 24, 1969, p. 29.*

Dustin Hoffman and John Wayne are two extremes of the current American folk hero. Duke Wayne has been in pictures for over 40 years, a star for 30. Through all that time he has projected an image larger and simpler than life—strong, decisive, moral and nearly always a winner. Dusty Hoffman's characters, beginning with *The Graduate* in 1967, are conspicuously short on these traditional qualities. His people are uncertain, alienated, complex and, by any familiar standard, losers. Both Duke and Dusty have huge and loyal followings, split largely by generation. But many a moviegoer, whatever his age, still finds himself cheering for both.

Life magazine studying the popular appeal of Dustin Hoffman and John Wayne, in Staff, "Dusty and the Duke," Life, *July 11, 1969, p. 36.*

Easy Rider is, in the smallest, sociological sense, a historic movie. In it, motorcycles are for the first time on screen converted from a malignant to a benign symbol, and the kids who ride them are seen not as vandals or threats to the Establishment but as innocent individuals in desperate unavailing flight from The System.

Sheer romanticism? Of course. But then the endless cycle of cycle-gang pictures to which we have been subjected in recent years is also an exaggeration, a commercialized compound of the worst figments of our most dismal imaginings about what's going on across the generation gap. At the very least, *Easy Rider* is a useful corrective. At its inconsistent best, it is an attempt to restate, in vivid, contemporary terms, certain ageless American pre-occupations.

Movie critic Richard Schickel arguing that the youth cult film Easy Rider *and its theme of "take to the open road" embraces more traditional than radical values, in his "A Lyric, Tragic Song of the Road,"* Life, *July 11, 1969, p. 10.*

Starring nobodies, directed by a weirdo. . . . In terms of contemporary mores and methods, *Easy Rider* has told its story from the far side of the generation gap. For once the aura of evil that clings to drug-and-motorcycle movies is gone. Like other films directed to—and by—youth, *Easy Rider* could have settled for catcalls and rebellion. Instead the film has refurbished the classic romantic gospel of the outcast wanderer. Walt Whitman might not have recog-

nized the bikes—but he would have understood the message.

Time magazine finding Easy Rider *a strange film but complimenting its sense of wanderlust and its no-nonsense view of American youth, in Staff, "Space Odyssey 1969,"* Time, *July 25, 1969, pp. 73–74.*

Construction plans were drawn up by the head of the engineering department of the Pratt Institute, and checked by the Army Corps of Engineers. For $18,000, telephone circuits were put in at the festival headquarters at Wallkill, a town of 18,000 not far from Woodstock. Local contractors were hired for food supplies, concrete, road building, construction, garbage pickup, and the like. The promoters estimated the event would generate more than $500,000 in business for the area.

President Nixon appeals to the "non-counter culture" during a 1969 rally of American Field Service Students. *(National Archives—Nixon Presidential Material)*

Ticket sales, backed by an advertising budget of $150,000 for radio and newspapers (including heavy promotion in the "underground" press), began moving briskly. At Wartoke Unlimited, the publicity company handling the fair, "more than a thousand people" requested press credentials, says Jane Friedman, a miniskirted young lady with a mass of corkscrew curls perched above her saucer-sized mod spectacles. Clearly the event was shaping up as something big.

Business Week reminding its readers that in stark contrast to the Woodstock Music Festival's already existing legend of spontaneity and freedom, that planning, marketing, and profiting remained an important part of the "real event," in Staff, "Rocky Road to Fame, If Not Fortune," Business Week, August 23, 1969, p. 79.

Mobs riot, cities don't, and Woodstock was the first city of the new culture. Not that it sprang from thin air. There have been signs for some time that something like this was afoot. The Be-Ins, the Love-Ins, the communal, family-like quality of the anti-Vietnam war parades, the Haight-Ashbury-East Village scenes were all early signs of pregnancy. Likewise, campus riots, the people's park, the Chicago Convention were labor pains that accompanied the birth. The Woodstock Festival was merely the final, irrevocable eruption of a life force that's been gestating for the last few years. . . .

Music is the glue that holds the young together. If radical politics, dope, sex, and magic are bricks of their new culture, music is the mortar that cements the different elements into place. Sitting in the middle of Max Yasgur's Dairy Farm cum three hundred thousand visitors was a first-class horror until a group called Canned Heat took the stage. Suddenly the waves of electricity came rolling up the slope from the distant tiny square in the center of the valley. Suddenly reefers are passing from hand to hand in a furious effort to strengthen the high. Slowly at first, then all at once, everyone is standing up and bodies are swaying.

New York writer Philip Tracy arguing that the Woodstock Music Festival symbolized the fact that "youth culture" had become an official minority group within the United States, in his "The Birth of a Culture," Commonweal, September 5, 1969, pp. 532–533.

"I continued to go to meetings. Only once did I lapse. The group had built up rapidly, and I suppose I felt I wasn't getting enough attention. I went out and got high. But I felt so bad afterward for violating the anti-drug pledge we all take that I left the project for a while month. I felt so desperately lonely, however, that I finally went back. Eventually I graduated from the group and began working as a staff trainee, a position I now hold. I wanted to see others get the kind of help I was able to get."

A teenage girl identifying herself only as "Sandy," telling Seventeen magazine that she and her friends are through with the drug scene and predicting that there will be many more like her in the 1970s, in Tunley, "Five Who Came Back from Drugs," Seventeen, January 1970, p. 136.

How does one go about telling people who weren't at the Woodstock Music and Art Fair that mud is love and rain is love and being thirsty and hungry is love as long as you are together? Picture three hundred thousand, wet and tired, listening to music on a hillside. Picture three hundred thousand separate beings each lighting a single match. Together they are a torch, maybe symbolizing the light of a new generation. A light of love and peace. Maybe symbolizing nothing. But nevertheless a torch. A light. Together. Together with three hundred thousand other muddy, damp, hungry people. And how can I tell someone who was there what it was? That would be like describing an accident to an eye witness. And how does one convey that Woodstock was together when reading is alone and writing is alone?

New York teenager Andrew Sideman, after several months of contemplating the significance of Woodstock, writing his impressions, in his "I Was There," Seventeen, January 1970, p. 87.

Bebe Rebozo and Ted Kennedy

Nixon's holiday was a far cry from the fabled touch football weekends in Hyannis Port or the Texas-size barbecues on the Pedernales. There were no children and no parties and only five staff members went along—even Mrs. Nixon stayed behind in Washington. As Vice President, Nixon was a regular visitor to Key Biscayne, where he rented a villa but spent most of his time at the home of Bebe Rebozo, a mysterious 56-year-old banker and real estate operator. Now Nixon has a compound of four houses, clustered around Rebozo's own waterfront home. His privacy is protected by police barricades, Navy frogmen and a thick hedge of hibiscus. But he still sees a lot of Rebozo, who sits in, though silently, on some of his neighbor's top-level sessions.

Life *magazine describing President Nixon's first vacation away from the White House and introducing the nation to his relationship with the shadowy Bebe Rebozo, in Silk and Pelham, "Winter White House,"* Life, *February 21, 1969, pp. 26–30.*

It seems to me, if you have the ability and the training for public service, and the opportunity, it would be a sin not to pursue it. I don't have any feelings of guilt, any of that conscience bit about noblesse oblige because I happen to be born with money. It's just that there is so much wrong in the world, so many people suffering needlessly, and, if I think I can help, it seems to me I must try.

I've heard people say, 'Oh he's a quick study,' but that simply isn't true. I've got to go at a thing four times as hard and four times as long as some other fellow. I remember at law school, I used to be up early and late, hitting the books. I had to, just to keep up with some of the other guys. It's hard work, and you keep at it, and after awhile, you begin to understand a thing and then to see a way to do something about influencing it.

Yes, it goes without saying that I don't believe in making long-range plans. We can never know what is just up ahead that might change everything. And I don't believe in the tyranny of time—that at a certain time, you must do a certain thing, take a certain step, or the opportunity will be lost forever. Some people say that 1972 is the year I must make a move for the Presidency, or 1976, or 1980. But how do I know that some young fellow—some Jay Rockefeller—won't suddenly come on the scene and make everybody forget that anybody ever considered Ted Kennedy for the Presidency? And so I just try to work in the areas and on the problems that were my brothers' concern and let the future take care of itself.

Senator Ted Kennedy, just weeks before the Chappaquiddick incident destroys his chances for the White House, telling Look *magazine that he might not be the 1972 Democratic nominee for president, in Rogers, "Ted Kennedy Talks about the Past, and his Future,"* Look, *March 4, 1969, pp. 38–46.*

I attempted to open the door and window of the car but I have no recollection of how I got out of the car. I came to the surface and repeatedly dove down to see if the passenger was still in it. I was unsuccessful in the attempt. I was exhausted and in a state of shock and I recall that I was able to get back to some friends who had a car parked in front of the cottage. I asked someone to bring me back to Edgartown. I remember walking around for a period of time and when I suddenly realized what happened, I immediately called the police.

Senator Edward Kennedy responding in June 1969 to an official inquiry into his role in the drowning death of Mary Jo Kopechne in Chappaquiddick, Massachusetts, in Simone Z., "Edward Kennedy's Chappaquiddick Accident," URL: www.gfsnet.org/msweb/sixties/ chappaquiddick.html.

Cambodia and Kent State

I do know this: Now that America is there, if we do what many of our very sincere critics think we should do, if we withdraw from Vietnam and allow the enemy to come into Vietnam and massacre the civilians there by the millions, as they would—if we do that, let me say that America is finished insofar as the peacekeeper in the Asian world is concerned. . . .

I do know when you have a situation of a crowd throwing rocks and the National Guard is called in, that there is always the chance that it will escalate into the kind of tragedy that happened at Kent State.

If there is one thing I am personally committed to, it is this: I saw the pictures of those four youngsters in the Evening Star the day after the tragedy, and I vowed then that we were going to find methods that would be more effective to deal with these problems of violence, methods that would deal with those who would use force and violence and endanger others, but, at the same time, would not take the lives of innocent people.

President Nixon, only hours after the shootings at Kent State University, responding on May 4, 1970, to reporters' questions about his views on Cambodia and the antiwar movement, in the Library of Congress's The Nixon Presidential Press Conferences *(1978), p. 103.*

One of the more bizarre incidents of the Vietnam War era occurred during the weeks of demonstrations and protests that followed the Cambodian invasion and the killings at Kent State. On May 8, more than 100,000 young protestors descended on the nation's capital. That night, President Nixon, unable to sleep and distraught over the outrage his actions in Cambodia had caused, had a driver take him to the Lincoln Memorial where some of the students who had come to Washington were camped out. It was about 4:40 a.m. when the President arrived. Earnestly trying to communicate with those young people, he rambled on about sports, global travel, racial tensions, and his own student days during the 1930s at Whittier College. The students, perhaps too sleepy or too stunned to engage the President of the United States in a dialogue about the Vietnam War, mostly listened. Within an hour, White House aides, alerted to his whereabouts, arrived and led him away.

Historian George Donelson Moss recalling a "bizarre" episode in the early morning hours of May 9, 1970 following the Kent State University shootings, in his Vietnam: An American Ordeal, *4th ed. (2002), pp. 364–365.*

Of course, we couldn't finish the year after we were ordered home. We had to finish our courses at home. Later, my father drove me back to pick up what was left of my apartment. We went into a restaurant, and they weren't very kind to us when we got something to eat. Everybody was really giving us the cold shoulder because they said we'd ruined their town. They were even giving my father the cold shoulder because he was with me. It wasn't a comfortable position to be in then, to be a student from Kent State. I was remembering my father's words to me when he drove me to college the first time the fall before. He said, "Remember, Leone, that everything you learn isn't out of books. It's life experience, too." Well, he was certainly right. I learned a lot that year, and most of it wasn't from books.

Former Kent State University student Leone Keegan remembering mid-May 1970, the first weekend after the Kent State shootings, in Morrison and Morrison, From Camelot to Kent State: The Sixties Experience in the Words of Those Who Lived It *(2001), p. 337.*

What strikes me is that those who speak "for" their generation, and extol "participatory democracy," are neither typical nor participatory nor democratic. This does not mean they are wrong (many a minority has turned out to be right); nor does it mean they are right.

Youth is impatient; its "leaders" intractable. Do they have the faintest notion of the terrible punishment any revolution imposes—even on the faithful? While the faithful dream of the brotherhood of man, their idols institute the grim, deadly processes by which they can get what they want. This is done through killings, torture, propaganda and terror.

Veteran political columnist Leo Rosten assailing the growing violence of the antiwar movement in mid-May 1970 and the resulting Kent State shooting of two weeks earlier, in Rosten, "Who Speaks for the Young?: Some Startling Facts and Fictions," Look, *May 19, 1970, p. 16.*

The students perceive that years of protest—by turns vigorous and muted—have not brought white Mississippians to respect the full human dignity of black people. It is a fact, for example, that Jackson State College remains a separate black state school. . . . Second, Jackson State students do not readily engage in protest activities because they cannot afford to, especially given their belief that the utility of such action is marginal at best. In their daily life in Mississippi, Jackson State students are too busy fighting for their physical, economic, social, and psychological lives to engage in protests. . . .

The federal government, after a rare, violent, and tragic protest demonstration at Mississippi's Jackson State College in spring 1970, examining black student attitudes there since the mid-1960s, in its The Report of the President's Commission on Campus Unrest *(1970), Appendix A.*

The tragedies of May must be answered. As college students go home this month, they face three possibilities. They can do nothing. They can draft themselves into combat revolutionaries to fight in our streets. Or they can make the Princeton University commitment to elect an anti-war Congress in November.

One month after the Kent State shootings, Look *magazine senior editor Jack Shepherd urging antiwar youth across the United States to accept Princeton University's May 1970 decision to reject revolution in favor of political change, in Shepherd, "The Princeton Commitment: A Race Against Mace,"* Look, *June 16, 1970, pp. 12–14.*

APPENDIX A
Documents

1. The Civil Rights Act of 1960, May 6, 1960
2. President John F. Kennedy's Inaugural Address, January 20, 1961
3. Executive Order 10924, establishment of the Peace Corps, March 1, 1961
4. Twenty-third Amendment to the U.S. Constitution, ratified 1961
5. President John F. Kennedy's report to the American people on the Soviet arms buildup in Cuba, October 22, 1962
6. Equal Pay Act of 1963, June 10, 1963
7. Treaty Banning Nuclear Weapon Tests in the Atmosphere, in Outer Space, and Under Water, August 5, 1963
8. The Civil Rights Act of 1964, July 2, 1964
9. The Gulf of Tonkin Resolution, August 7, 1964
10. Twenty-fourth Amendment to the U.S. Constitution, ratified 1964
11. The Voting Rights Act of 1965, August 6, 1965
12. Freedom of Information Act of 1966, July 3, 1966
13. Twenty-fifth Amendment to the U.S. Constitution, ratified 1967
14. The Age Discrimination in Employment Act of 1967, December 15, 1967
15. President Lyndon B. Johnson's Address to the nation announcing steps to limit the war in Vietnam and reporting his decision not to seek reelection, March 31, 1968
16. Robert F. Kennedy's announcement of Martin Luther King, Jr.'s assassination, April 4, 1968.
17. The Civil Rights Act of 1968, provision for open housing, April 11, 1968
18. President Richard M. Nixon's address to the nation on the Vietnam War and call to the Great Silent Majority, November 3, 1969

1. THE CIVIL RIGHTS ACT OF 1960, MAY 6, 1960

Be it enacted by the Senate and House of Representatives of the United State of America in Congress assembled, That this Act may be cited as the "Civil Rights Act of 1960."...

Title II

Flight to avoid prosecution for damaging or destroy any building or other real or personal property; and, illegal transportation, use or possession of explosives; and, threats or false information concerning attempts to damage or destroy real or personal property by fire or explosives.

SEC. 201. Chapter 49 of title 18, United States Code, is amended by adding at the end thereof a new section as follows: § 1074. Flight to avoid prosecution for damaging or destroying any building or other real or personal property

"(a) Whoever moves or travels in interstate or foreign commerce with intent either (1) to avoid prosecution, or custody, or confinement after conviction, under the laws of the place from which he flees, for willfully attempting to or damaging or destroying by fire or explosive any building, structure, facility, vehicle, dwelling house, synagogue, church, religious center or educational institution, public or private, or (2) to avoid giving testimony in any criminal proceeding relating to any such offense shall be fined not more than $5,000 or imprisoned not more than five years, or both."...

SEC. 203. Chapter 39 of title 18 of the United States Code is amended by adding at the end thereof the following new section: "§ 837. Explosives; illegal use or possession; and, threats or false information concerning attempts to damage or destroy real or personal property by fire or explosives."...

"(b) Whoever transports or aids and abets another in transporting in interstate or foreign commerce any explosive, with the knowledge or intent that it will be used to damage or destroy any building or other real or personal property for the purpose of interfering with its use for educational, religious, charitable, residential, business, or civic objectives or of intimidating any person pursuing such objectives, shall be subject to imprisonment for not more than one year, or a fine of not more than $1,000, or both; and if personal injury results shall be subject to imprisonment for not more than ten years or a fine of not more than

$10,000, or both; and if death results shall be subject to imprisonment for any term of years or for life, but the court may impose the death penalty if the jury so recommends."....

SEC. 204. The analysis of chapter 39 of title 18 is amended by adding thereto the following: "§ 837. Explosives; illegal use or possession; and threats or false information concerning attempts to damage or destroy real or personal property by fire or explosives."

Title III

FEDERAL ELECTION RECORDS

SEC. 301. Every officer of election shall retain and preserve, for a period of twenty-two months from the date of any general, special, or primary election of which candidates for the office of President, Vice President, presidential elector, Member of the Senate, Member of the House of Representatives, or Resident Commissioner from the Commonwealth of Puerto Rico are voted for, all records and papers which come into his possession relating to any application, registration, payment of poll tax, or other act requisite to voting in such election, except that, when required by law, such records and papers may be delivered to another office of election and except that, if a State or the Commonwealth of Puerto Rico designates a custodian to retain and preserve these records and papers at a specified place, then such records and papers may be deposited with such custodian, and the duty to retain and preserve any record or papers so deposited shall devolve upon such custodian. Any officer of election or custodian who willfully fails to comply with the section shall be fined not more than $1,000 or imprisoned not more than one year, or both.

SEC. 302. Any person, whether or not an officer of election or custodian, who willfully steals, destroys, conceals, mutilates, or alters any record or paper required by section 301 to be retained and preserved shall be fined not more than $1,000 or imprisoned not more than one year, or both.

SEC. 303. Any record or paper required by section 301 to be retained and preserved shall, upon demand in writing by the Attorney General or his representative directed to the person having custody, possession, or control of such record or paper, be made available for inspection, reproduction, and copying at the principal office of such custodian by the Attorney General or his representative. This demand shall contain a statement of the basis and the purpose therefore. . . .

Title IV

Extension of Powers of the Civil Rights Commission SEC. 401. Section 105 of the Civil Rights Act of 1957 (42 U.S.C. Supp. V 1975d) (71 Stat. 635) is amended by adding the following new subsection at the end thereof:

"(h) Without limiting the generality of the foregoing, each member of the Commission shall have the power and authority to administer oaths or take statements of witnesses under affirmation." . . .

Title VI

SEC. 601. That section 2004 of the Revised Statutes (42 U.S.C. 1971), as amended by section 131 of the Civil Rights Act of 1957 (71 Stat. 637), is amended as follows: . . .

"The court may appoint one or more persons who are qualified voters in the judicial district, to be known as voting referees, who shall subscribe to the oath of office required by Revised Statutes, section 1757; (5 U.S.C. 16) to serve for such period as the court shall determine, to receive such applications and to take evidence and report to the court findings as to whether or not at any election or elections (1) any such applicant is qualified under State law to vote, and (2) he has since the finding by the court heretofore specified been (a) deprived of or denied under color of law the opportunity to register to vote or otherwise to qualify to vote, or (b) found not qualified to vote by any person acting under color of law. In a proceeding before a voting referee, the applicant shall be heard ex parte at such times and places as the court shall direct. His statement under oath shall be prima facie evidence as to his age, residence, and his prior efforts to register or otherwise qualify to vote. Where proof of literacy or an understanding of other subjects is required by valid provisions of State law, the answer of the applicant, if written, shall be included in such report to the court; if oral, it shall be taken down stenographically and a transcription included in such report to the court."

"Upon receipt of such report, the court shall cause the Attorney General to transmit a copy thereof to the State attorney general and to each party to such proceeding together with an order to show cause within ten days, or such shorter time as the court may fix, why an order of the court should not be entered in accordance with such report. Upon the expiration of such period, such order shall be entered unless prior to that time there has been filed with the court and served upon all parties a statement of exceptions to such report. Exceptions as to matters of fact shall be considered only if supported by a duly verified copy of a public record or by affidavit of persons having personal knowledge of such facts or by statements or matters contained in such report; those relating to matters of law shall be supported by an appropriate memorandum of law. The issues of fact and law raised by such exceptions shall be determined by the court or, if the due and speedy administration of justice requires, they may be referred to the voting referee to determine in accordance with procedures prescribed by the court. A hearing as to an issue of fact shall be held only in the event that the proof in support of the exception disclose the existence of a genuine issue of material fact. The applicant's literacy and understanding of other subjects shall be determined solely on the basis of answers included in the report of the voting referee." . . .

"When used in the subsection, the word 'vote' includes all action necessary to make a vote effective, but not limited to, registration or other action required by State law prerequisite to voting, casting a ballot, and having such ballot counted and included by the appropriate totals of votes cast with respect to candidates for public office and propositions for which votes are received in an election; the words 'affected area' shall mean any subdivision of the State in which the laws of the State relating to voting are or have been to any extent administered by a person found in the proceedings to have violated subsection (a); and the words 'qualified under State law' shall mean qualified according to the laws, customs, or usages of the State, and shall not, in any event, imply qualifications more stringent than those used by the persons found in the proceeding to have violated subsection (a) in qualifying persons other than those of the race or color against which the pattern or practice of discrimination was found to exist."

(b) Add the following sentence at the end of subsection (c):

"Whenever, in a proceeding instituted under this subsection any official of a State or subdivision thereof is alleged to have committed any act or practice constituting a deprivation of any right or privilege secured by subsection (a), the act or practice shall also be deemed that of the State and the State may be joined as a party defendant and, if, prior to the institution of such proceeding, such official has resigned or has been relieved of his office and no successor has assumed such office, the proceeding may be instituted against the State." . . .

2. President John F. Kennedy's Inaugural Address, January 20, 1961

We observe today not a victory of party but a celebration of freedom—symbolizing an end as well as a beginning—signifying renewal as well as change. For I have sworn before you and Almighty God the same solemn oath our forebears prescribed nearly a century and three-quarters ago.

The world is very different now. For man holds in his mortal hands the power to abolish all forms of human poverty and all forms of human life. And yet the same revolutionary beliefs for which our forebears fought are still at issue around the globe—the belief that the rights of man come not from the generosity of the state but from the hand of God.

We dare not forget today that we are the heirs of that first revolution. Let the word go forth from this time and place, to friend and foe alike, that the torch has been passed to a new generation of Americans—born in this century, tempered by war, disciplined by a hard and bitter peace, proud of our ancient heritage—and unwilling to witness or permit the slow undoing of those human rights to which this nation has always been committed, and to which we are committed today at home and around the world.

Let every nation know, whether it wishes us well or ill, that we shall pay any price, bear any burden, meet any hardship, support any friend, oppose any foe to assure the survival and the success of liberty.

This much we pledge—and more.

To those old allies whose cultural and spiritual origins we share, we pledge the loyalty of faithful friends. United, there is little we cannot do in a host of co-operative ventures. Divided, there is little we can do—for we dare not meet a powerful challenge at odds and split asunder.

To those new states whom we welcome to the ranks of the free, we pledge our word that one form of colonial control shall not have passed away merely to be replaced by a far more iron tyranny. We shall not always expect to find them supporting our view. But we shall always hope to find them strongly supporting their own freedom—and to remember that, in the past, those who foolishly sought power by riding the back of the tiger ended up inside.

To those people in the huts and villages of half the globe struggling to break the bonds of mass misery, we pledge our best efforts to help them help themselves, for whatever period is required—not because the Communists may be doing it, not because we seek their votes, but because it is right. If a free society cannot help the many who are poor, it cannot save the few who are rich.

To our sister republics south of the border, we offer a special pledge—to convert our good words into good deeds—in a new alliance for progress—to assist free men and free governments in casting off the chains of poverty. But this peaceful revolution of hope cannot become the prey of hostile powers. Let all our neighbors know that we shall join with them to oppose aggression or subversion anywhere in the Americas. And let every other power know that this hemisphere intends to remain the master of its own house.

To that world assembly of sovereign states, the United Nations, our last best hope in an age where the instruments of war have far outpaced the instruments of peace, we renew our pledge of support—to prevent it from becoming merely a forum for invective—to strengthen its shield of the new and the weak—and to enlarge the area in which its writ may run.

Finally, to those nations who would make themselves our adversary, we offer not a pledge but a request: that both sides begin anew the quest for peace, before the dark powers of destruction unleashed by science engulf all humanity in planned or accidental self-destruction.

We dare not tempt them with weakness. For only when our arms are sufficient beyond doubt can we be certain beyond doubt that they will never be employed.

But neither can two great and powerful groups of nations take comfort from our present course—both sides overburdened by the cost of modern weapons, both rightly alarmed by the steady spread of the deadly atom, yet both racing to alter that uncertain balance of terror that stays the hand of mankind's final war.

So let us begin anew—remembering on both sides that civility is not a sign of weakness, and sincerity is always subject to proof. Let us never negotiate out of fear. But let us never fear to negotiate.

Let both sides explore what problems unite us instead of belaboring those problems which divide us.

Let both sides, for the first time, formulate serious and precise proposals for the inspection and control of arms—and bring the absolute power to destroy other nations under the absolute control of all nations.

Let both sides seek to invoke the wonders of science instead of its terrors. Together let us explore the stars, conquer the deserts, eradicate disease, tap the ocean depths, and encourage the arts and commerce.

Let both sides unite to heed in all corners of the earth the command of Isaiah—to "undo the heavy burdens . . . [and] let the oppressed go free."

And if a beachhead of co-operation may push back the jungle of suspicion, let both sides join in creating a new endeavor, not a new balance of power, but a new world of law, where the strong are just and the weak secure and the peace preserved.

All this will not be finished in the first one hundred days. Nor will it be finished in the first one thousand days, nor in the life of this administration, nor even perhaps in our lifetime on this planet. But let us begin.

In your hands, my fellow citizens, more than mine, will rest the final success or failure of our course. Since this country was founded, each generation of Americans has been summoned to give testimony to its national loyalty. The graves of young Americans who answered the call to service surround the globe.

Now the trumpet summons us again—not as a call to bear arms, though arms we need,—not as a call to battle, though embattled we are—but a call to bear the burden of a long twilight struggle, year in and year out, "rejoicing in hope, patient in tribulation"—a struggle against the common enemies of man: tyranny, poverty, disease, and war itself.

Can we forge against these enemies a grand and global alliance, North and South, East and West, that can assure a more fruitful life for all mankind? Will you join in that historic effort?

In the long history of the world, only a few generations have been granted the role of defending freedom in its hour of maximum danger. I do not shrink from this responsibility—I welcome it. I do not believe that any of us would exchange places with any other people or any other generation. The energy, the faith, the devotion which we bring to this endeavor will light our country and all who serve it—and the glow from that fire can truly light the world.

And so, my fellow Americans: ask not what your country can do for you—ask what you can do for your country.

My fellow citizens of the world: ask not what America will do for you, but what together we can do for the freedom of man.

Finally, whether you are citizens of America or citizens of the world, ask of us here the same high standards of strength and sacrifice which we ask of you. With a good conscience our only sure reward, with history the final judge of our deeds, let us go forth to lead the land we love, asking His blessing and His help, but knowing that here on earth God's work must truly be our own.

3. EXECUTIVE ORDER 10924, ESTABLISHMENT AND ADMINISTRATION OF THE PEACE CORPS IN THE DEPARTMENT OF STATE

By virtue of the authority vested in me by the Mutual Security Act of 1954, 68 Stat. 832, as amended (22 U.S.C. 1750 et. seq.), and as President of the United States, it is hereby ordered as follows:

Section 1. *Establishment of the Peace Corps.* The Secretary of State shall establish an agency in the Department of State which shall be known as the Peace Corps. The Peace Corps shall be headed by a Director.

Section 2. *Functions of the Peace Corps.* (a) The Peace Corps shall be responsible for the training and service abroad of men and women of the United States in new programs of assistance to nations and areas of the world, and in conjunction with or in support of existing economic assistance programs of the United States and of the United Nations and other international organizations.

(b) The Secretary of State shall delegate, or cause to be delegated to the Director of the Peace Corps, such of the functions under the Mutual Security Act of 1954, as amended, vested in the President and delegated to the Secretary, or vested in the Secretary, as the Secretary shall deem necessary for the accomplishment of the purposes of the Peace Corps.

Section 3. *Financing of the Peace Corps.* The Secretary of State shall provide for the financing of the Peace Corps with funds available to the Secretary for the performance of functions under the Mutual Security Act of 1954, as amended.

Section 4. *Relation to the Executive Order No. 10893.* This order shall not be deemed to supersede or derogate from any provision of Executive Order No. 10893 of November 8, 1960, as amended, and any delegation made by or pursuant to this order shall, unless otherwise specifically provided therein, be deemed to be in addition to any delegation made by or pursuant to that order.

JOHN F. KENNEDY
THE WHITE HOUSE.
March 1, 1961

4. Twenty-third Amendment to the U.S. Constitution, Ratified 1961

Presidential Electors for District of Columbia (1961)

Section 1. The District constituting the seat of Government of the United States shall appoint in such manner as the Congress may direct:

A number of electors of President and Vice President equal to the whole number of Senators and Representatives in Congress to which the District would be entitled if it were a State, but in no event more than the least populous state; they shall be in addition to those appointed by the States, but they shall be considered, for the purposes of the election of President and Vice President, to be electors appointed by a State; and they shall meet in the District and perform such duties as provided by the twelfth article of amendment.

Section 2. The Congress shall have power to enforce this article by appropriate legislation.

5. President John F. Kennedy's Report to the American People on the Soviet Arms Buildup in Cuba, October 22, 1962

Good evening my fellow citizens:

This Government, as promised, has maintained the closest surveillance of the Soviet Military buildup on the island of Cuba. Within the past week, unmistakable evidence has established the fact that a series of offensive missile sites is now in preparation on that imprisoned island. The purpose of these bases can be none other than to provide a nuclear strike capability against the Western Hemisphere.

Upon receiving the first preliminary hard information of this nature last Tuesday morning at 9 a.m., I directed that our surveillance be stepped up. And having now confirmed and completed our evaluation of the evidence and our decision on a course of action, this Government feels obliged to report this new crisis to you in fullest detail.

The characteristics of these new missile sites indicate two distinct types of installations. Several of them include medium range ballistic missiles capable of carrying a nuclear warhead for a distance of more than 1,000 nautical miles. Each of these missiles, in short, is capable of striking Washington, D.C., the Panama Canal, Cape Canaveral, Mexico City, or any other city in the southeastern part of the United States, in Central America, or in the Caribbean area.

Additional sites not yet completed appear to be designed for intermediate range ballistic missiles—capable of traveling more than twice as far—and thus capable of striking most of the major cities in the Western Hemisphere, ranging as far north as Hudson Bay, Canada, and as far south as Lima, Peru. In addition, jet bombers, capable of carrying nuclear weapons, are now being uncrated and assembled in Cuba, while the necessary air bases are being prepared.

This urgent transformation of Cuba into an important strategic base—by the presence of these large, long range, and clearly offensive weapons of sudden mass destruction—constitutes an explicit threat to the peace and security of all the Americas, in flagrant and deliberate defiance of the Rio Pact of 1947, the traditions of this Nation and hemisphere, the joint resolution of the 87th Congress, the Charter of the United Nations, and my own public warnings to the Soviets on September 4 and 13. This action also contradicts the repeated assurances of Soviet spokesmen, both publicly and privately delivered, that the arms buildup in Cuba would retain its original defensive character, and that the Soviet Union had no need or desire to station strategic missiles on the territory of any other nation.

The size of this undertaking makes clear that it has been planned for some months. Yet only last month, after I had made clear the distinction between any introduction of ground-to-ground missiles and the existence of defensive antiaircraft missiles, the Soviet Government publicly stated on September 11, and I quote, "the armaments and military equipment sent to Cuba are designed exclusively for defensive purposes," that, and I quote the Soviet Government, "there is no need for the Soviet Government to shift its weapons . . . for a retaliatory blow to any other country, for instance Cuba," and that, and I quote their government, "the Soviet Union has so powerful rockets to carry these nuclear warheads that there is no need to search for sites for them beyond the boundaries of the Soviet Union." That statement was false.

Only last Thursday, as evidence of this rapid offensive buildup was already in my hand, Soviet Foreign Minister Gromyko told me in my office that he was instructed to make it clear once again, as he said his government had already done, that Soviet assistance to Cuba, and I quote, "pursued solely the purpose of contributing to the defense capabilities of Cuba," that, and I quote him, "training by Soviet specialists of Cuban nationals in handling defensive armaments was by no means offensive, and if it were otherwise," Mr. Gromyko went on, "the Soviet Government would never become involved in rendering such assistance." That statement also was false.

Neither the United States of America nor the world community of nations can tolerate deliberate deception and offensive threats on the part of any nation, large or small. We no longer live in a world where only the actual firing of weapons represents a sufficient challenge to a nation's security to constitute maximum peril. Nuclear weapons are so destructive and ballistic missiles are so swift, that any substantially increased possibility of their use or any sudden change in their deployment may well be regarded as a definite threat to peace.

For many years both the Soviet Union and the United States, recognizing this fact, have deployed strategic nuclear weapons with great care, never upsetting the precarious status quo which insured that these weapons would not be used in the absence of some vital challenge. Our own strategic missiles have never been transferred to the territory of any other nation under a cloak of secrecy and deception; and our history—unlike that of the Soviets since the end of World War II—demonstrates that we have no desire to dominate or conquer any other nation or impose our system upon its people. Nevertheless, American citizens have become adjusted to living daily on the Bull's-eye of Soviet missiles located inside the U.S.S.R. or in submarines.

In that sense, missiles in Cuba add to an already clear and present danger—although it should be noted the nations of Latin America have never previously been subjected to a potential nuclear threat.

But this secret, swift, and extraordinary buildup of Communist missiles—in an area well known to have a special and historical relationship to the United States and the nations of the Western Hemisphere, in violation of Soviet assurances, and in defiance of American and hemispheric policy—this sudden, clandestine decision to station strategic weapons for the first time outside of Soviet soil—is a deliberately provocative and unjustified change in the status quo which cannot be accepted by this country, if our courage and our commitments are ever to be trusted again by either friend or foe.

The 1930's taught us a clear lesson: aggressive conduct, if allowed to go unchecked and unchallenged ultimately leads to war. This nation is opposed to war. We are also true to our word. Our unswerving objective, therefore, must be to prevent the use of these missiles against this or any other country, and to secure their withdrawal or elimination from the Western Hemisphere.

Our policy has been one of patience and restraint, as befits a peaceful and powerful nation, which leads a worldwide alliance. We have been determined not to be diverted from our central concerns by mere irritants and fanatics. But now further action is required—and it is under way; and these actions may only be the beginning. We will not prematurely or unnecessarily risk the costs of worldwide nuclear war in which even the fruits of victory would be ashes in our mouth—but neither will we shrink from that risk at any time it must be faced.

Acting, therefore, in the defense of our own security and of the entire Western Hemisphere, and under the authority entrusted to me by the Constitution as endorsed by the resolution of the Congress, I have directed that the following initial steps be taken immediately:

First: To halt this offensive buildup, a strict quarantine on all offensive military equipment under shipment to Cuba is being initiated. All ships of any kind bound for Cuba from whatever nation or port will, if found to contain cargoes of offensive weapons, be turned back. This quarantine will be extended, if needed, to other types of cargo and carriers. We are not at this time, however, denying the necessities of life as the Soviets attempted to do in their Berlin blockade of 1948.

Second: I have directed the continued and increased close surveillance of Cuba and its military buildup. The foreign ministers of the OAS, in their communique of October 6, rejected secrecy in such matters in this hemisphere. Should these offensive military preparations continue, thus increasing the threat to the hemisphere, further action will be justified. I have directed the Armed Forces to prepare for any eventualities; and I trust that in the interest of both the Cuban people and the Soviet technicians at the sites, the hazards to all concerned in continuing this threat will be recognized.

Third: It shall be the policy of this Nation to regard any nuclear missile launched from Cuba against any nation in the Western Hemisphere as an attack by the Soviet Union on the United States, requiring a full retaliatory response upon the Soviet Union.

Fourth: As a necessary military precaution, I have reinforced our base at Guantanamo, evacuated today the dependents of our personnel there, and ordered additional military units to be on a standby alert basis.

Fifth: We are calling tonight for an immediate meeting of the Organ of Consultation under the Organization of American States, to consider this threat to hemispheric security and to invoke articles 6 and 8 of the Rio Treaty in support of all necessary action. The United Nations Charter allows for regional security arrangements—and the nations of this hemisphere decided long ago against the military presence of outside powers. Our other allies around the world have also been alerted.

Sixth: Under the Charter of the United Nations, we are asking tonight that an emergency meeting of the Security Council be convoked without delay to take action against this latest Soviet threat to world peace. Our resolution will call for the prompt dismantling and withdrawal of all offensive weapons in Cuba, under the supervision of U.N. observers, before the quarantine can be lifted.

Seventh and finally: I call upon Chairman Khrushchev to halt and eliminate this clandestine, reckless and provocative threat to world peace and to stable relations between our two nations. I call upon him further to abandon this course of world domination, and to join in an historic effort to end the perilous arms race and to transform the history of man. He has an opportunity now to move the world back from the abyss of destruction—by returning to his government's own words that it had no need to station missiles outside its own territory, and withdrawing these weapons from Cuba—by refraining from any action which will widen or deepen the present crisis—and then by participating in a search for peaceful and permanent solutions.

This Nation is prepared to present its case against the Soviet threat to peace, and our own proposals for a peaceful world, at any time and in any forum—in the OAS, in the United Nations, or in any other meeting that could be useful—without limiting our freedom of action. We have in the past made strenuous efforts to limit the spread of nuclear weapons. We have proposed the elimination of all arms and military bases in a fair and effective disarmament treaty. We are prepared to discuss new proposals for the removal of tensions on both sides—including the possibility of a genuinely independent Cuba, free to determine its own destiny. We have no wish to war with the Soviet Union—for we are a peaceful people who desire to live in peace with all other peoples.

But it is difficult to settle or even discuss these problems in an atmosphere of intimidation. That is why this latest Soviet threat—or any other threat which is made either independently or in response to our actions this week—must and will be met with determination. Any hostile move anywhere in the world against the safety and freedom of peoples to whom we are committed—including in particular the brave people of West Berlin—will be met by whatever action is needed.

Finally, I want to say a few words to the captive people of Cuba, to whom this speech is being directly carried by special radio facilities. I speak to you as a friend, as one who knows of your deep attachment to your fatherland, as one who shares your aspirations for liberty and justice for all. And I have watched and the American people have watched with deep sorrow how your nationalist revolution was betrayed—and how your fatherland fell under foreign domination. Now your leaders are no longer Cuban leaders inspired by Cuban ideals. They are puppets and agents of an international conspiracy which has turned Cuba against your friends and neighbors in the Americas—and turned it into the first Latin American country to become a target for nuclear war—the first Latin American country to have these weapons on its soil.

These new weapons are not in your interest. They contribute nothing to your peace and well-being. They can only undermine it. But this country has no wish to cause you to suffer or to impose any system upon you. We know that your lives and land are being used as pawns by those who deny your freedom.

Many times in the past, the Cuban people have risen to throw out tyrants who destroyed their liberty. And I have no doubt that most Cubans today look forward to the time when they will be truly free—free from foreign domination, free to choose their own leaders, free to select their own system, free to own their own land, free to speak and write and worship without fear or degradation. And then shall Cuba be welcomed back to the society of free nations and to the associations of this hemisphere.

My fellow citizens: let no one doubt that this is a difficult and dangerous effort on which we have set out. No one can see precisely what course it will take or what costs or casualties will be incurred. Many months of sacrifice and self-discipline lie ahead—months in which our patience and our will will be tested—months in which many threats and denunciations will keep us aware of our dangers. But the greatest danger of all would be to do nothing.

The path we have chosen for the present is full of hazards, as all paths are—but it is the one most consistent with our character and courage as a nation and our commitments around the world. The cost of freedom is always high—and Americans have always paid it. And one path we shall never choose, and that is the path of surrender or submission.

Our goal is not the victory of might, but the vindication of right—not peace at the expense of freedom, but both peace and freedom, here in this hemisphere, and, we hope, around the world. God willing, that goal will be achieved.

Thank you and good night.

6. Equal Pay Act of 1963, June 10, 1963

To prohibit discrimination on account of sex in the payment of wages by employers engaged in commerce or in the production of goods for commerce.

Be it enacted by the Senate and House of Representatives of the United States of America in Congress assembled, That this Act may be cited as the "Equal Pay Act of 1963."

Declaration of Purpose

SEC. 2. (a) The Congress hereby finds that the existence in industries engaged in commerce or in the production of goods for commerce of wage differentials based on sex—

(1) depresses wages and living standards for employees necessary for their health and efficiency;
(2) prevents the maximum utilization of the available labor resources;
(3) tends to cause labor disputes, thereby burdening, affecting and obstructing commerce;
(4) burdens commerce and the free flow of goods in commerce; and
(5) constitutes an unfair method of competition.

(b) It is hereby declared to be the policy of this Act, through exercise by Congress of its power to regulate commerce among the several States and with foreign nations, to correct the conditions above referred to in such industries.

SEC. 3. Section 6 of the Fair Labor Standards Act of 1938, as amended (29 U.S.C. et seq.), is amended by adding thereto a new subsection (d) as follows: Discrimination prohibited. 52 Stat. 1062; 63 Stat. 912.

(d) (1) No employer having employees subject to any provisions of this section shall discriminate, within any establishment in which such employees are employed, between employees on the basis of sex by paying wages to employees in such establishment at a rate less than the rate at which he pays wages to employees of the opposite sex in such establishment for effort, and responsibility, and which are performed under similar working conditions, except where such payment is made pursuant to (i) a seniority system; (ii) a merit system; (iii) a system which measures earnings by quantity or quality of production; or (iv) a differential based on any other factor other than sex: Provided, That an employer who is paying a wage rate differential in violation of this subsection shall not, in order to comply with the provisions of this subsection, reduce the wage rate of any employee. 29 U.S.C. 206.

(2) No labor organization, or its agents, representing employees of an employer having employees subject to any provisions of this section shall cause or attempt to cause such an employer to discriminate against an employee in violation of paragraph (1) of this subsection.

(3) For purposes of administration and enforcement, any amounts owing to any employee which have been withheld in violation of this subsection shall be deemed to be unpaid minimum wages or unpaid overtime compensation under this Act.

(4) As used in the subsection, the term "labor organization" means any organization of any kind, or any agency or employee representation committee or plan, in which employees participate and which exists for the purpose, in whole or in part, of dealing with employers concerning grievances, labor disputes, wages, rate of pay, hours of employment or conditions of work.

7. Treaty Banning Nuclear Weapon Tests in the Atmosphere, In Outer Space, and Under Water

Signed at Moscow August 5, 1963
Ratification advised by U.S. Senate September 24, 1963
Ratified by U.S. President October 7, 1963
U.S. ratification deposited at Washington, London, and Moscow October 10, 1963
Proclaimed by U.S. President October 10, 1963
Entered into force October 10, 1963

The Governments of the United States of America, the United Kingdom of Great Britain and Northern Ireland, and the Union of Soviet Socialist Republics, hereinafter referred to as the "Original Parties,"

Proclaiming as their principal aim the speediest possible achievement of an agreement on general and complete disarmament under strict international con-trol in accordance with the objectives of the United Nations which would put an end to the armaments race and eliminate the incentive to the production and testing of all kinds of weapons, including nuclear weapons,

Seeking to achieve the discontinuance of all test explosions of nuclear weapons for all time, determined to continue negotiations to this end, and desiring to put an end to the contamination of man's environment by radioactive substances,

Have agreed as follows:

Article I

1. Each of the Parties to this Treaty undertakes to prohibit, to prevent, and not to carry out any nuclear weapon test explosion, or any other nuclear explosion, at any place under its jurisdiction or control:

(a) in the atmosphere; beyond its limits, including outer space; or under water, including territorial waters or high seas; or

(b) in any other environment if such explosion causes radioactive debris to be present outside the territorial limits of the State under whose jurisdiction or control such explosion is conducted. It is understood in this connection that the provisions of this subparagraph are without prejudice to the conclusion of a Treaty resulting in the permanent banning of all nuclear test explosions, including all such explosions underground, the conclusion of which, as the Parties have stated in the Preamble to this Treaty, they seek to achieve.

2. Each of the Parties to this Treaty undertakes furthermore to refrain from causing, encouraging, or in any way participating in, the carrying out of any nuclear weapon test explosion, or any other nuclear explosion, anywhere which would take place in any of the environments described, or have the effect referred to, in paragraph 1 of this Article.

Article II

1. Any Party may propose amendments to this Treaty. The text of any proposed amendment shall be submitted to the Depositary Governments which shall circulate it to all Parties to this Treaty. Thereafter, if requested to do so by one-third or more of the Parties, the Depositary Governments shall convene a conference, to which they shall invite all the Parties, to consider such amendment.

2. Any amendment to this Treaty must be approved by a majority of the votes of all the Parties to this Treaty, including the votes of all of the Original Parties. The amendment shall enter into force for all Parties upon the deposit of instruments of ratification by a majority of all the Parties, including the instruments of ratification of all of the Original Parties.

Article III

1. This Treaty shall be open to all States for signature. Any State which does not sign this Treaty before its entry into force in accordance with paragraph 3 of this Article may accede to it at any time.

2. This Treaty shall be subject to ratification by signatory States. Instruments of ratification and instruments of accession shall be deposited with the Governments of the Original Parties—the United States of America, the United Kingdom of Great Britain and Northern Ireland, and the Union of Soviet Socialist Republics—which are hereby designated the Depositary Governments.

3. This Treaty shall enter into force after its ratification by all the Original Parties and the deposit of their instruments of ratification.

4. For States whose instruments of ratification or accession are deposited subsequent to the entry into force of this Treaty, it shall enter into force on the date of the deposit of their instruments of ratification or accession.

5. The Depositary Governments shall promptly inform all signatory and acceding States of the date of each signature, the date of deposit of each instrument of ratification of and accession to this Treaty, the date of its entry into force, and the date of receipt of any requests for conferences or other notices.

6. This Treaty shall be registered by the Depositary Governments pursuant to Article 102 of the Charter of the United Nations.

Article IV

This Treaty shall be of unlimited duration.

Each Party shall in exercising its national sovereignty have the right to withdraw from the Treaty if it decides that extraordinary events, related to the subject matter of this Treaty, have jeopardized the supreme interests of its country. It shall give notice of such withdrawal to all other Parties to the Treaty three months in advance.

Article V

This Treaty, of which the English and Russian texts are equally authentic, shall be deposited in the archives of the Depositary Governments. Duty certified copies of this Treaty shall be transmitted by the Depositary Governments to the Governments of the signatory and acceding States.

IN WITNESS WHEREOF the undersigned, duly authorized, have signed this Treaty.

DONE in triplicate at the city of Moscow the fifth day of August, one thousand nine hundred and sixty-three.

For the Government of the United States of America
DEAN RUSK

For the Government of the United Kingdom of Great Britain and Northern Ireland
SIR DOUGLAS HOME

For the Government of the Union of Soviet Socialist Republics
A. GROMYKO

8. THE CIVIL RIGHTS ACT OF 1964, JULY 2, 1964

Title I – Voting Rights

SEC. 101(2). No person acting under color of law shall—

(a) in determining whether any individual is qualified under State law or laws to vote in any Federal election, apply any standard, practice, or procedure different from the standards, practices, or procedures applied under such law or laws to other individuals within the same county, parish, or similar political subdivision who have been found by State officials to be qualified to vote; . . .

(c) employ any literacy test as a qualification for voting in any Federal election unless (i) such test is administered to each individual wholly in writing; and (ii) a certified copy of the test and of the answers given by the individual is furnished to him within twenty-five days of the submission of his request made within the period of time during which records and papers are required to be retained and preserved pursuant to Title III of the Civil Rights Act of 1960 . . .

Title II - Injunctive Relief Against Discrimination in Places of Public Accommodation

SEC. 201. (a) All persons shall be entitled to the full and equal enjoyment of the goods, services, facilities, privileges, advantages, and accommodations of any place of public accommodation, as defined in this section, without discrimination or segregation on the grounds of race, color, religions, or national origin.

(b) Each of the following establishments which serves the public is a place of public accommodation within the meaning of this title if its operations affect commerce, or if discrimination or segregation by it is supported by State action:

(1) any inn, motel, or other establishment which provides lodging to transient guests, other than an establishment located within a building which contains not more than five rooms for rent or hire and which is actually occupied by the proprietor of such establishment as his residence;

(2) any restaurant, cafeteria, lunch room, lunch counter, soda fountain, or other facility principally engaged in selling food for consumption on the premises . . .

(3) any motion picture house, theater, concert hall, or sports arena, stadium or other place of exhibition or entertainment . . .

(d) Discrimination or segregation by an establishment is supported by State action within the meaning of this title if such discrimination or segregation (1) is carried on under color of any law, statute, ordinance, or regulation; or (2) is carried on under color of any custom or usage required or enforced by officials of that State or political subdivision thereof . . .

SEC. 202. All persons shall be entitled to be free, at any establishment or place, from discrimination or segregation of any kind on the grounds of race, color, religion, or national origin, if such discrimination or segregation is or purports to be required by any law, statute, ordinance, regulation, rule, or order of a State or any agency or political subdivision thereof . . .

SEC. 206. (a) Whenever the Attorney General has reasonable cause to believe that any person or group of persons is engaged in a pattern or practice of resistance to the full enjoyment of any of the rights secured by this title, the Attorney General may bring a civil action in the appropriate district court of the United States by filing with it a complaint . . . requesting such preventive relief, including an application for a permanent or temporary injunction, restraining order or other order against the person or persons responsible for such pattern or practice, as he deems necessary to insure the full enjoyment of the rights herein described.

Title VI - Nondiscrimination in Federally Assisted Programs

SEC. 601. No person in the United States shall, on the ground of race, color, or national origin, be excluded from participation in, be denied the benefits of, or be subjected to discrimination under any program or activity receiving Federal financial assistance.

9. THE GULF OF TONKIN RESOLUTION, AUGUST 7, 1964

(Adopted August 7, 1964. Signed by President Johnson August 10, 1964.)

Whereas naval units of the Communist regime in Vietnam, in violation of the principles of the Charter of the United Nations and of international law, have deliberately and repeatedly attacked United States naval vessels lawfully present in international waters, and have thereby created a serious threat to international peace; and

Whereas these attacks are part of a deliberate and systematic campaign of aggression that the Communist regime in North Vietnam has been waging against its neighbors and the nations joined with them in the collective defense of their freedom; and

Whereas the United States is assisting the peoples of Southeast Asia to protect their freedom and has no territorial, military or political ambitions in that area, but desires only that these peoples should be left in peace to work out their own destinies in their own way: Now, therefore, be it

Resolved by the Senate and House of Representatives of the United States of America in Congress assembled, That the Congress approves and supports the determination of the President, as Commander in Chief, to take all necessary measures to repel any armed attack against the forces of the United States and to prevent further aggression.

Sec. 2. The United States regards as vital to its national interest and to world peace the maintenance of international peace and security in Southeast Asia. Consonant with the Constitution of the United States and Charter of the United Nations in accordance with its obligations under the Southeast Asia Collective Defense Treaty, the United States is, therefore, prepared, as the President determines, to take all necessary steps, including the use of armed force, to assist any member or protocol state of the Southeast Asia Collective Defense Treaty requesting assistance in defense of its freedom.

Sec. 3. This resolution shall expire when the President shall determine that the peace and security of the area is reasonably assured by international conditions created by action of the United Nations or otherwise, except that it may be terminated earlier by concurrent resolution of the Congress.

10. Twenty-fourth Amendment to the U.S. Constitution, Ratified 1964

Poll Tax Banned in National Elections (1964)

Section 1. The right of citizens of the United States to vote in any primary or other election for President or Vice President, for electors for President or Vice President, or for Senator or Representative in Congress, shall not be denied or abridged by the United States or any state by reason of failure to pay any poll tax or other tax.

Section 2. The Congress shall have power to enforce this article by appropriate legislation.

11. The Voting Rights Act of 1965, August 6, 1965

SEC. 2. No voting qualification or prerequisite to voting, or standard, practice, or procedure shall be imposed or applied by any State or political subdivision to deny or abridge the right of any citizen of the United States to vote on account of race or color.

SEC. 3. (a) Whenever the Attorney General institutes a proceeding under any statute to enforce the guarantees of the fifteenth amendment in any State or political subdivision the court shall authorize the appointment of Federal examiners by the United States Civil Service Commission in accordance with

section 6 to serve for such period of time and for such political subdivisions as the court shall determine is appropriate to enforce the guarantees of the fifteenth amendment (1) as part of any interlocutory order if the court determines that the appointment of such examiners is necessary to enforce such guarantees or (2) as part of any final judgment if the court finds that violations of the fifteenth amendment justifying equitable relief have occurred in such State or subdivision: *Provided,* That the court need not authorize the appointment of examiners if any incidents of denial or abridgement of the right to vote on account of race or color (1) have been few in number and have been promptly and effectively corrected by State or local action, (2) the continuing effect of such incidents has been eliminated, and (3) there is no reasonable probability of their recurrence in the future.

SEC. 4. (a) To assure that the right of citizens of the United States to vote is not denied or abridged on account of race or color, no citizen shall be denied the right to vote in any Federal, State, or local election because of his failure to comply with any test or device in any State with respect to which the determinations have been made under subsection (b) or in any political subdivision with respect to which such determinations have been made as a separate unit, unless the United States District Court for the District of Columbia in an action for a declaratory judgment brought by such State or subdivision against the United States has determined that no such test or device has been used during the five years preceding the filing of the action for the purpose or with the effect of denying or abridging the right to vote on account of race or color: *Provided,* That no such declaratory judgment shall issue with respect to any plaintiff for a period of five years after the entry of a final judgment of any court of the United States, other than the denial of a declaratory judgment under this section, whether entered prior to or after the enactment of this Act, determining that denials or abridgments of the right to vote on account of race or color through the use of such tests or devices have occurred anywhere in the territory of such plaintiff. (2) No person who demonstrates that he has successfully completed the sixth primary grade in a public school in, or a private school accredited by, any State or territory, the District of Columbia, or the

Commonwealth of Puerto Rico in which the predominant classroom language was other than English, shall be denied the right to vote in any Federal, State, or local election because of his inability to read, write, understand, or interpret any matter in the English Language, except that in States in which State law provides that a different level of education is presumptive of literacy, he shall demonstrate that he has successfully completed an equivalent level of education in a public school in, or private school accredited by, any State or territory, the District of Columbia, or the Commonwealth of Puerto Rico in which the predominant classroom language was other then English.

SEC. 5. Whenever a State or political subdivision with respect to which the prohibitions set forth in section 4(a) are in effect shall enact or seek to administer any voting qualification or prerequisite to voting, or standard, practice, or procedure with respect to voting different from that in force or effect on November 1, 1964, such State or subdivision may institute an action in the United States District Court for the District of Columbia for a declaratory judgment that such qualification, prerequisite, standard, practice, or procedure does not have the purpose and will not have the effect of denying or abridging the right to vote on account of race or color, and unless and until the court enters such judgment no person shall be denied the right to vote for failure to comply with such qualification, prerequisite, standard, practice, or procedure . . .

SEC. 9. (a) Any challenge to a listing on an eligibility list prepared by an examiner shall be heard and determined by a hearing officer appointed by and responsible to the Civil Service Commission and under such rules as the Commission shall by regulation prescribe.

SEC. 10. (a) The Congress finds that the requirement of the payment of a poll tax as precondition to voting (i) precludes persons of limited means from voting or imposes unreasonable financial hardship upon such persons as a precondition to their exercise of the franchise, (ii) does not bear a reasonable relationship to any legitimate State interest in the conduct of elections, and (iii) in some areas has the purpose or effect of denying persons the right to vote because of race or color. Upon the basis of these findings, Congress

declares that the constitutional right of citizens to vote is denied or abridged in some areas by the requirement of the payment of a poll tax as a precondition to voting.

SEC. 11. (a) No person acting under color of law shall fail or refuse to permit any person to vote who is entitled to vote under any provision of this Act or is otherwise qualified to vote, or willfully fail or refuse to tabulate, count, and report such person's vote.

(b) No person, whether acting under color of law or otherwise, shall intimidate, threaten, or coerce, or attempt to intimidate, threaten or coerce any person for voting or attempting to vote, or intimidate, threaten, or coerce, or attempt to intimidate, threaten, or coerce any person for urging or aiding any person to vote or attempt to vote, or intimidate, threaten, or coerce any person for exercising any powers or duties under section 3(a), 6, 8, 9, 10, or 12(e). . . .

SEC. 14. (a) All cases of criminal contempt arising under the provisions of this Act shall be governed by section 151 of the Civil rights Act of 1957 (42 U.S.C. 1995).

(b) No court other than the District Court for the District of Columbia or a court of appeals in any proceeding under section 9 shall have jurisdiction to issue any declaratory judgment pursuant to section 4 or section 5 or any restraining order or temporary or permanent injunction against the execution or enforcement of any provision of the Act or any action of any Federal officer or employee pursuant hereto.

(c)(1) The terms "vote" or "voting" shall include all action necessary to make a vote effective in any primary, special, or general election, including, but not limited to, registration, listing pursuant to this Act or other action required by law prerequisite to voting, casting a ballot, and having such ballot counted properly and included in the appropriate totals of votes cast with respect to candidates for public or party office and propositions for which votes are received in an election. . . .

SEC. 16. The Attorney General and the Secretary of Defense, jointly, shall make a full and complete study to determine whether, under the laws or practices of any State or States, there are preconditions to voting, which might tend to result in discrimination against citizens serving in the Armed Forces of the United

States seeking to vote. Such officials shall, jointly, make a report to Congress not later than June 30, 1966, containing the results of such study, together with a list of any States in which such preconditions exist, and shall include in such report such recommendations for legislation as they deem advisable to prevent discrimination in voting against citizens serving in the Armed Forces of the United States.

12. FREEDOM OF INFORMATION ACT OF 1966, JULY 3, 1966

AN ACT

To amend section 3 of the Administrative Procedure Act, chapter 324, of the Act of June 11, 1946 (60 Stat. 238), to clarify and protect the right of the public to information, and for other purposes.

Be it enacted by the Senate and House of Representatives of the United States of America in Congress assembled, That section 3, chapter 324, of the Act of June 11, 1946 (60 Stat. 238), is amended to read as follows:

"SEC. 3. Every agency shall make available to the public the following information:

"(a) Publication in the Federal Register.—Every agency shall separately state and currently publish in the Federal Register for the guidance of the public (A) descriptions of its central and field organization and the established places at which, the officers from whom, and the methods whereby, the public may secure information, make submittals or requests, or obtain decisions; (B) statements of the general course and method by which its functions are channeled and determined, including the nature and requirements of all formal and informal procedures available; (C) rules of procedure, descriptions of forms available or the places at which forms may be obtained, and instructions as to the scope and contents of all papers, reports, or examinations; (D) substantive rules of general applicability adopted as authorized by law, and statements of general policy or interpretations of general applicability formulated and adopted by the agency; and (F) every amendment, revision, or repeal of the foregoing. Except to the extent that a person has actual and timely notice of the terms thereof, no person shall in any manner be required to resort to, or be adversely affected by any matter required to be published in the Federal Register and not so published. For purposes of this subsection, matter which

is reasonably available to the class of persons affected thereby shall be deemed published in the Federal Register when incorporated by reference therein with the approval of the Director of the Federal Register.

"(b) Agency Opinions and Orders.—Every agency shall, in accordance with published rules, make available for public inspection and copying (A) all final opinions (including concurring and dissenting opinions) and all orders made in the adjudication of cases, (B) those statements of policy and interpretations which have been adopted by the agency and are not published in the Federal Register, and (C) administrative staff manuals and instructions to staff that affect any member of the public, unless such materials are promptly published and copies offered for sale. To the extent required to prevent a clearly unwarranted invasion of personal privacy, an agency may delete identifying details when it makes available or publishes an opinion, statement of policy, interpretation, or staff manual or instruction: *Provided,* That in every case the justification for the deletion must be fully explained in writing. Every agency also shall maintain and make available for public inspection and copying a current index providing identifying information for the public as to any matter which is issued, adopted, or promulgated after the effective date of this Act and which is required by this subsection to be made available or published. No final order, opinion, statement of policy, interpretation, or staff manual or instruction that affects any member of the public may be relied upon, used or cited as precedent by an agency against any private party unless it has been indexed and either made available or published as provided by this subsection or unless that private party shall have actual and timely notice of the terms thereof.

"(c) Agency Records.—Except with respect to the records made available pursuant to subsections (a) and (b), every agency shall, upon request for identifiable records made in accordance with published rules stating the time, place, fees to the extent authorized by statute and procedure to be followed, make such records promptly available to any person. Upon complaint, the district court of the United States in the district in which the complainant resides, or has his principal place of business, or in which the agency records are situated shall have jurisdiction to enjoin the agency from the withholding of agency records and to order the production of any agency records improperly withheld from the complainant. In such cases the court shall determine the matter de novo and the burden shall be upon the agency to sustain its action. In the event of noncompliance with the court's order, the district court may punish the responsible officers for contempt. Except as to those causes which the court deems of greater importance, proceedings before the district court as authorized by this subsection shall take precedence on the docket over all other causes and shall be assigned for hearing and trial at the earliest practicable date and expedited in every way.

"(d) Agency Proceedings.—Every agency having more than one member shall keep a record of the final votes of each member in every agency proceeding and such record shall be available for public inspection.

"(e) Exemptions.—The provisions of this section shall not be applicable to matters that are (1) specifically required by Executive order to be kept secret in the interest of the national defense or foreign policy; (2) related solely to the internal personnel rules and practices of any agency; (3) specifically exempted from disclosure by statute; (4) trade secrets and commercial or financial information obtained from any person and privileged or confidential; (5) interagency or intra-agency memorandums or letters which would not be available by law to a private party in litigation with the agency; (6) personnel and medical files and similar files the disclosure of which would constitute a clearly unwarranted invasion of personal privacy; (7) investigatory files compiled for law enforcement purposes except to the extent available by law to a private party; (8) contained or related to examination, operating, or condition reports prepared by, on behalf of, or for the use of any agency responsible for the regulation or supervision of financial institutions; and (9) geological and geophysical information and data (including maps) concerning wells.

"(f) Limitation of Exemptions.—Nothing in this section authorizes withholding of information or limiting the availability of records to the public except as specifically stated in this section, nor shall this section be authority to withhold information from Congress.

"(g) Private Party.—As used in this section, 'private party' means any party other than an agency.

"(h) Effective Date.—This amendment shall become effective one year following the date of the enactment of this Act."
Approved July 4, 1966.

13. Twenty-fifth Amendment to the U.S. Constitution, Ratified 1967

Presidential Disability And Succession (1967)

Section 1. In case of the removal of the President from office or his death or resignation, the Vice President shall become President.

Section 2. Whenever there is a vacancy in the office of the Vice President, the President shall nominate a Vice President who shall take office upon confirmation by a majority vote of both houses of Congress.

Section 3. Whenever the President transmits to the President pro tempore of the Senate and the Speaker of the House of Representatives his written declaration that he is unable to discharge the powers and duties of his office, and until he transmits to them a written declaration to the contrary, such powers and duties shall be discharged by the Vice President as Acting President.

Section 4. Whenever the Vice President and a majority of either the principal officers of the executive departments or of such other body as Congress may by law provide, transmit to the President pro tempore of the Senate and the Speaker of the House of Representatives their written declaration that the President is unable to discharge the powers and duties of his office, the Vice President shall immediately assume the powers and duties of the office as Acting President.

Thereafter, when the President transmits to the President pro tempore of the Senate and the Speaker of the House of Representatives his written declaration that no inability exists, he shall resume the powers and duties of his office unless the Vice President and a majority of either the principal officers of the executive department or of such other body as Congress may by law provide, transmit within four days to the President pro tempore of the Senate and the Speaker of the House of Representatives their written declaration that the President is unable to discharge the powers and duties of his office. Thereupon Congress shall decide the issue, assembling within 48 hours for that purpose if not in session. If the Congress, within 21 days after receipt of the later written declaration, or, if Congress is not in session, within 21 days after Congress is required to assemble, determines by two-thirds vote of both houses that the President is unable to discharge the powers and duties of his office, the Vice President shall continue to discharge the same as Acting President; otherwise, the President shall resume the powers and duties of his office.

14. THE AGE DISCRIMINATION IN EMPLOYMENT ACT OF 1967, DECEMBER 15, 1967

An Act to prohibit age discrimination in employment.

Be it enacted by the Senate and House of Representatives of the United State of America in Congress assembled, that this Act may be cited as the "Age Discrimination in Employment Act of 1967."

Statement of Findings and Purpose

SEC. 621. (Section 2) (a) The Congress hereby finds and declares that—

(1) in the face of rising productivity and affluence, older workers find themselves disadvantaged in their efforts to retain employment, and especially to regain employment when displaced from jobs;

(2) the setting of arbitrary age limits regardless of potential for job performance has become a common practice, and certain otherwise desirable practices may work to the disadvantage of older persons;

(3) the incidence of unemployment, especially long term unemployment with resultant deterioration of skill, morale, and employer acceptability is, relative to the younger ages, high among older workers; their numbers are great and growing; and their employment problems grave;

(4) the existence in industries affecting commerce, of arbitrary discrimination in employment because of age, burdens commerce and the free flow of goods in commerce.

(b) It is therefore the purpose of this chapter to promote employment of older persons based on their ability rather than age; to prohibit arbitrary age discrimination in employment; to help employers and workers find ways to meeting problems arising from the impact of age on employment . . .

SEC. 623 (Section 4) (a) It shall be unlawful for an employer—

(1) to fail or refuse to hire or to discharge any individual or otherwise discriminate against any individual with respect to his compensation, terms, conditions, or privileges of employment, because of such individual's age;

(2) to limit, segregate, or classify his employees in any way which would deprive or tend to deprive any individual of employment opportunities or otherwise adversely affect his status as an employee, because of such individual's age; or

(3) to reduce the wage rate of any employee in order to comply with this chapter.

(b) It shall be unlawful for an employment agency to fail or refuse to refer for employment, or otherwise to discriminate against any individual because of such individual's age, or to classify or refer for employment any individual on the basis of such individual's age.

(c) It shall be unlawful for a labor organization—

(1) to exclude or to expel from its membership, or otherwise to discriminate against, any individual because of his age;

(2) to limit, segregate, or classify its membership, or to classify or fail or refuse to refer for employment any individual, in any way which would deprive or tend to deprive any individual of employment opportunities, or would limit such employment opportunities or otherwise adversely affect his status as an employee or as an applicant for employment, because of such individual's age . . .

(d) It shall be unlawful for an employer to discriminate against any of his employees or applicants for employment, for an employment agency to discriminate against any individual, or for a labor organization to discriminate against any member thereof or applicant for membership, because such individual, member or applicant for membership has opposed any practice made unlawful by this section, or because such individual, member or applicant for membership has made a charge, testified, assisted, or participated in any manner in an investigation, proceeding, or litigation under this chapter.

(e) It shall be unlawful for an employer, labor organization, or employment agency to print or publish, or cause to be printed or published, any notice or advertisement relating to employment by such an employer or membership in or any classification or referral for employment by such a labor organization, or relating to any classification or referral for employment by such an employment agency, indicating any preference, limitation, specification, or discrimination, based on age . . .

15. PRESIDENT LYNDON B. JOHNSON'S ADDRESS TO THE NATION ANNOUNCING STEPS TO LIMIT THE WAR IN VIETNAM AND REPORTING HIS DECISION NOT TO SEEK REELECTION, MARCH 31, 1968

Good evening, my fellow Americans:

Tonight I want to speak to you of peace in Vietnam and Southeast Asia.

No other question so preoccupies our people. No other dream so absorbs the 250 million human beings who live in that part of the world. No other goal motivates American policy in Southeast Asia.

For years, representatives of our Government and others have traveled the world—seeking to find a basis for peace talks.

Since last September, they have carried the offer that I made public at San Antonio. That offer was this:

That the United States would stop its bombardment of North Vietnam when that would lead promptly to productive discussions—and that we would assume that North Vietnam would not take military advantage of our restraint.

Hanoi denounced this offer, both privately and publicly. Even while the search for peace was going on, North Vietnam rushed their preparations for a savage assault on the people, the government, and the allies of South Vietnam.

Their attack—during the Tet holidays—failed to achieve its principal objectives.

It did not collapse the elected government of South Vietnam or shatter its army—as the Communists had hoped.

It did not produce a "general uprising" among the people of the cities as they had predicted.

The Communists were unable to maintain control of any of the more than 30 cities that they attacked. And they took very heavy casualties.

But they did compel the South Vietnamese and their allies to move certain forces from the countryside into the cities.

They caused widespread disruption and suffering. Their attacks, and the battles that followed, made refugees of half a million human beings.

The Communists may renew their attack any day.

They are, it appears, trying to make 1968 the year of decision in South Vietnam—the year that brings, if not final victory or defeat, at least a turning point in the struggle.

This much is clear:

If they do mount another round of heavy attacks, they will not succeed in destroying the fighting power of South Vietnam and its allies.

But tragically, this is also clear: Many men—on both sides of the struggle—will be lost. A nation that has already suffered 20 years of warfare will suffer once again. Armies on both sides will take new casualties. And the war will go on.

There is no need for this to be so.

There is no need to delay the talks that could bring an end to this long and this bloody war.

Tonight, I renew the offer I made last August—to stop the bombardment of North Vietnam. We ask that talks begin promptly, that they be serious talks on the substance of peace. We assume that during those talks Hanoi will not take advantage of our restraint.

We are prepared to move immediately toward peace through negotiations.

So, tonight, in the hope that this action will lead to early talks, I am taking the first step to deescalate the conflict. We are reducing—substantially reducing—the present level of hostilities.

And we are doing so unilaterally, and at once.

Tonight, I have ordered our aircraft and our naval vessels to make no attacks on North Vietnam, except in the area north of the demilitarized zone where the continuing enemy buildup directly threatens allied forward positions and where the movements of their troops and supplies are clearly related to that threat.

The area in which we are stopping our attacks includes almost 90 percent of North Vietnam's population, and most of its territory. Thus there will be no attacks around the principal populated areas, or in the food-producing areas of North Vietnam.

Even this very limited bombing of the North could come to an early end—if our restraint is matched by restraint in Hanoi. But I cannot in good conscience stop all bombing so long as to do so would immediately and directly endanger the lives of our men and our allies. Whether a complete bombing halt becomes possible in the future will be determined by events.

Our purpose in this action is to bring about a reduction in the level of violence that now exists.

It is to save the lives of brave men—and to save the lives of innocent women and children. It is to permit the contending forces to move closer to a political settlement.

And tonight, I call upon the United Kingdom and I call upon the Soviet Union—as cochairmen of the Geneva Conferences, and as permanent members of the United Nations Security Council—to do all they can to move from the unilateral act of deescalation that I have just announced toward genuine peace in Southeast Asia.

Now, as in the past, the United States is ready to send its representatives to any forum, at any time, to discuss the means of bringing this ugly war to an end.

I am designating one of our most distinguished Americans, Ambassador Averell Harriman, as my personal representative for such talks. In addition, I have asked Ambassador Llewellyn Thompson, who returned from Moscow for consultation, to be available to join Ambassador Harriman at Geneva or any other suitable place—just as soon as Hanoi agrees to a conference.

I call upon President Ho Chi Minh to respond positively, and favorably, to this new step toward peace.

But if peace does not come now through negotiations, it will come when Hanoi understands that our common resolve is unshakable, and our common strength is invincible.

Tonight, we and the other allied nations are contributing 600,000 fighting men to assist 700,000 South Vietnamese troops in defending their little country.

Our presence there has always rested on this basic belief: The main burden of preserving their freedom must be carried out by them—by the South Vietnamese themselves.

We and our allies can only help to provide a shield behind which the people of South Vietnam can survive and can grow and develop. On their efforts—on their determination and resourcefulness—the outcome will ultimately depend.

That small, beleaguered nation has suffered terrible punishment for more than 20 years.

I pay tribute once again tonight to the great courage and endurance of its people. South Vietnam supports armed forces tonight of almost 700,000 men—and I call your attention to the fact that this is the equivalent of more than 10 million in our own population. Its people maintain their firm determination to be free of domination by the North.

There has been substantial progress, I think, in building a durable government during these last 3 years. The South Vietnam of 1965 could not have survived the enemy's Tet offensive of 1968. The elected government of South Vietnam survived that attack—and is rapidly repairing the devastation that it wrought.

The South Vietnamese know that further efforts are going to be required:

—to expand their own armed forces,

—to move back into the countryside as quickly as possible,

—to increase their taxes,

—to select the very best men that they have for civil and military responsibility,

—to achieve a new unity within their constitutional government, and

—to include in the national effort all those groups who wish to preserve South Vietnam's control over its own destiny.

Last week President Thieu ordered the mobilization of 135,000 additional South Vietnamese. He plans to reach—as soon as possible—a total military strength of more than 800,000 men.

To achieve this, the Government of South Vietnam started the drafting of 19-year-olds on March 1st. On May 1st, the Government will begin the drafting of 18-year-olds.

Last month, 10,000 men volunteered for military service—that was two and a half times the number of volunteers during the same month last year. Since the middle of January, more than 48,000 South Vietnamese have joined the armed forces—and nearly half of them volunteered to do so.

All men in the South Vietnamese armed forces have had their tours of duty extended for the duration of the war, and reserves are now being called up for immediate active duty.

President Thieu told his people last week:

"We must make greater efforts and accept more sacrifices because, as I have said many times, this is our country. The existence of our nation is at stake, and this is mainly a Vietnamese responsibility."

He warned his people that a major national effort is required to root out corruption and incompetence at all levels of government.

We applaud this evidence of determination on the part of South Vietnam. Our first priority will be to support their effort.

We shall accelerate the reequipment of South Vietnam's armed forces—in order to meet the enemy's increased firepower. This will enable them progressively to undertake a larger share of combat operations against the Communist invaders.

On many occasions I have told the American people that we would send to Vietnam those forces that are required to accomplish our mission there. So, with that as our guide, we have previously authorized a force level of approximately 525,000.

Some weeks ago—to help meet the enemy's new offensive—we sent to Vietnam about 11,000 additional Marine and airborne troops. They were deployed by air in 48 hours, on an emergency basis. But the artillery, tank, aircraft, medical, and other units that were needed to work with and to support these infantry troops in combat could not then accompany them by air on that short notice.

In order that these forces may reach maximum combat effectiveness, the Joint Chiefs of Staff have recommended to me that we should prepare to send—during the next 5 months—support troops totaling approximately 13,500 men.

A portion of these men will be made available from our active forces. The balance will come from reserve component units which will be called up for service.

The actions that we have taken since the beginning of the year:

—to reequip the South Vietnamese forces,

—to meet our responsibilities in Korea, as well as our responsibilities in Vietnam,

—to meet price increases and the cost of activating and deploying reserve forces,

—to replace helicopters and provide the other military supplies we need, all of these actions are going to require additional expenditures.

The tentative estimate of those additional expenditures is $2.5 billion in this fiscal year, and $2.6 billion in the next fiscal year.

These projected increases in expenditures for our national security will bring into sharper focus the Nation's need for immediate action: action to protect the prosperity of the American people and to protect the strength and the stability of our American dollar.

On many occasions I have pointed out that, without a tax bill or decreased expenditures, next year's deficit would again be around $20 billion. I have emphasized the need to set strict priorities in our spending. I have stressed that failure to act and to act promptly and decisively would raise very strong doubts throughout the world about America's willingness to keep its financial house in order.

Yet Congress has not acted. And tonight we face the sharpest financial threat in the postwar era—a threat to the dollar's role as the keystone of international trade and finance in the world.

Last week, at the monetary conference in Stockholm, the major industrial countries decided to take a big step toward creating a new international monetary asset that will strengthen the international monetary system. I am very proud of the very able work done by Secretary Fowler and Chairman Martin of the Federal Reserve Board.

But to make this system work the United States just must bring its balance of payments to—or very close to—equilibrium. We must have a responsible fiscal policy in this country. The passage of a tax bill now, together with expenditure control that the Congress may desire and dictate, is absolutely necessary to protect this Nation's security, to continue our prosperity, and to meet the needs of our people.

What is at stake is 7 years of unparalleled prosperity. In those 7 years, the real income of the average American, after taxes, rose by almost 30 percent—a gain as large as that of the entire preceding 19 years.

So the steps that we must take to convince the world are exactly the steps we must take to sustain our own economic strength here at home. In the past 8 months, prices and interest rates have risen because of our inaction.

We must, therefore, now do everything we can to move from debate to action—from talking to voting. There is, I believe—I hope there is—in both Houses of the Congress—a growing sense of urgency that this situation just must be acted upon and must be corrected.

My budget in January was, we thought, a tight one. It fully reflected our evaluation of most of the demanding needs of this Nation.

But in these budgetary matters, the President does not decide alone. The Congress has the power and the duty to determine appropriations and taxes.

The Congress is now considering our proposals and they are considering reductions in the budget that we submitted.

As part of a program of fiscal restraint that includes the tax surcharge, I shall approve appropriate reductions in the January budget when and if Congress so decides that that should be done.

One thing is unmistakably clear, however: Our deficit just must be reduced. Failure to act could bring on conditions that would strike hardest at those people that all of us are trying so hard to help.

These times call for prudence in this land of plenty. I believe that we have the character to provide it, and tonight I plead with the Congress and with the people to act promptly to serve the national interest, and thereby serve all of our people.

Now let me give you my estimate of the chances for peace:

—the peace that will one day stop the bloodshed in South Vietnam,

—that will permit all the Vietnamese people to rebuild and develop their land,

—that will permit us to turn more fully to our own tasks here at home.

I cannot promise that the initiative that I have announced tonight will be completely successful in achieving peace any more than the 30 others that we have undertaken and agreed to in recent years.

But it is our fervent hope that North Vietnam, after years of fighting that have left the issue unresolved, will now cease its efforts to achieve a military victory and will join us in moving toward the peace table.

And there may come a time when South Vietnamese—on both sides—are able to work out a way to settle their own differences by free political choice rather than by war.

As Hanoi considers its course, it should be in no doubt of our intentions. It must not miscalculate the pressures within our democracy in this election year.

We have no intention of widening this war.

But the United States will never accept a fake solution to this long and arduous struggle and call it peace.

No one can foretell the precise terms of an eventual settlement.

Our objective in South Vietnam has never been the annihilation of the enemy. It has been to bring about a recognition in Hanoi that its objective—taking over the South by force—could not be achieved.

We think that peace can be based on the Geneva Accords of 1954—under political conditions that permit the South Vietnamese—all the South Vietnamese—to chart their course free of any outside domination or interference, from us or from anyone else.

So tonight I reaffirm the pledge that we made at Manila—that we are prepared to withdraw our forces from South Vietnam as the other side withdraws its forces to the north, stops the infiltration, and the level of violence thus subsides.

Our goal of peace and self-determination in Vietnam is directly related to the future of all of Southeast Asia—where much has happened to inspire confidence during the past 10 years. We have done all that we knew how to do to contribute and to help build that confidence.

A number of its nations have shown what can be accomplished under conditions of security. Since 1966, Indonesia, the fifth largest nation in all the world, with a population of more than 100 million people, has had a government that is dedicated to peace with its neighbors and improved conditions for its own people. Political and economic cooperation between nations has grown rapidly.

I think every American can take a great deal of pride in the role that we have played in bringing this about in Southeast Asia. We can rightly judge—as responsible Southeast Asians themselves do—that the progress of the past 3 years would have been far less likely—if not completely impossible—if America's sons and others had not made their stand in Vietnam.

At Johns Hopkins University, about 3 years ago, I announced that the United States would take part in the great work of developing Southeast Asia, including the Mekong Valley, for all the people of that region. Our determination to help build a better land—a better land for men on both sides of the present conflict—has not diminished in the least. Indeed, the ravages of war, I think, have made it more urgent than ever.

So, I repeat on behalf of the United States again tonight what I said at Johns Hopkins—that North Vietnam could take its place in this common effort just as soon as peace comes.

Over time, a wider framework of peace and security in Southeast Asia may become possible. The new cooperation of the nations of the area could be a foundation-stone. Certainly friendship with the nations of such a Southeast Asia is what the United States seeks—and that is all that the United States seeks.

One day, my fellow citizens, there will be peace in Southeast Asia.

It will come because the people of Southeast Asia want it—those whose armies are at war tonight, and those who, though threatened, have thus far been spared.

Peace will come because Asians were willing to work for it—and to sacrifice for it—and to die by the thousands for it.

But let it never forgotten: Peace will come also because America sent her sons to help secure it.

It has not been easy—far from it. During the past 4½ years, it has been my fate and my responsibility to be Commander in Chief. I have lived—daily and nightly—with the cost of this war. I know the pain that it has inflicted. I know, perhaps better than anyone, the misgivings that it has aroused.

Throughout this entire, long period, I have been sustained by a single principle: that what we are doing now, in Vietnam, is vital not only to the security of Southeast Asia, but it is vital to the security of every American.

Surely we have treaties which we must respect. Surely we have commitments that we are going to keep. Resolutions of the Congress testify to the need to resist aggression in the world and in Southeast Asia.

But the heart of our involvement in South Vietnam—under three different presidents, three separate administrations—has always been America's own security.

And the larger purpose of our involvement has always been to help the nations of Southeast Asia become independent and stand alone, self-sustaining, as members of a great world community—at peace with themselves, and at peace with all others.

With such an Asia, our country—and the world—will be far more secure than it is tonight.

I believe that a peaceful Asia is far nearer to reality because of what America has done in Vietnam. I believe that the men who endure the dangers of battle—fighting there for us tonight—are helping the entire world avoid far greater conflicts, far wider wars, far more destruction, than this one.

The peace that will bring them home someday will come. Tonight I have offered the first in what I hope will be a series of mutual moves toward peace.

I pray that it will not be rejected by the leaders of North Vietnam. I pray that they will accept it as a means by which the sacrifices of their own people may be ended. And I ask your help and your support, my fellow citizens, for this effort to reach across the battlefield toward an early peace.

Finally, my fellow Americans, let me say this:

Of those to whom much is given, much is asked. I cannot say and no man could say that no more will be asked of us.

Yet, I believe that now, no less than when the decade began, this generation of Americans is willing to "pay any price, bear any burden, meet any hardship, support any friend, oppose any foe to assure the survival and the success of liberty."

Since those words were spoken by John F. Kennedy, the people of America have kept that compact with mankind's noblest cause.

And we shall continue to keep it.

Yet, I believe that we must always be mindful of this one thing, whatever the trials and the tests ahead. The ultimate strength of our country and our cause will lie not in powerful weapons or infinite resources or boundless wealth, but will lie in the unity of our people.

This I believe very deeply.

Throughout my entire public career I have followed the personal philosophy that I am a free man, an American, a public servant, and a member of my party, in that order always and only.

For 37 years in the service of our Nation, first as a Congressman, as a Senator, and as Vice President, and now as your President, I have put the unity of the people first. I have put it ahead of any divisive partisanship.

And in these times as in times before, it is true that a house divided against itself by the spirit of faction, of party, of region, of religion, of race, is a house that cannot stand.

There is division in the American house now. There is divisiveness among us all tonight. And holding the trust that is mine, as President of all the people, I cannot disregard the peril to the progress of the American people and the hope and the prospect of peace for all peoples.

So, I would ask all Americans, whatever their personal interests or concern, to guard against divisiveness and all its ugly consequences.

Fifty-two months and 10 days ago, in a moment of tragedy and trauma, the duties of this office fell upon me. I asked then for your help and God's, that we might continue America on its course, binding up our wounds, healing our history, moving forward in new unity, to clear the American agenda and to keep the American commitment for all of our people.

United we have kept that commitment. United we have enlarged that commitment.

Through all time to come, I think America will be a stronger nation, a more just society, and a land of greater opportunity and fulfillment because of what we have all done together in these years of unparalleled achievement.

Our reward will come in the life of freedom, peace, and hope that our children will enjoy through ages ahead.

What we won when all of our people united just must not now be lost in suspicion, distrust, selfishness, and politics among any of our people.

Believing this as I do, I have concluded that I should not permit the Presidency to become involved in the partisan divisions that are developing in this political year.

With America's sons in the fields far away, with America's future under challenge right here at home, with our hopes and the world's hopes for peace in the balance every day, I do not believe that I should devote an hour or a day of my time to any personal partisan causes or to any duties other than the awesome duties of this office—the Presidency of your country.

Accordingly, I shall not seek, and I will not accept, the nomination of my party for another term as your President.

But let men everywhere know, however, that a strong, a confident, and a vigilant America stands ready tonight to seek an honorable peace—and stands ready tonight to defend an honored cause—whatever the price, whatever the burden, whatever the sacrifice that duty may require.

Thank you for listening.

Good night and God bless all of you.

NOTE: The President spoke at 9 p.m. in his office at the White House. The address was broadcast nationally.

16. ROBERT F. KENNEDY'S ANNOUNCEMENT OF MARTIN LUTHER KING, JR.'S ASSASSINATION, APRIL 4, 1968

Indianapolis, Indiana
April 4, 1968

I have bad news for you, for all of our fellow citizens, and people who love peace all over the world, and that is that Martin Luther King was shot and killed tonight.

Martin Luther King dedicated his life to love and to justice for his fellow human beings, and he died because of that effort.

In this difficult day, in this difficult time for the United States, it is perhaps well to ask what kind of a nation we are and what direction we want to move in. For those of you who are black—considering the evidence there evidently is that there were white people who were responsible—you can be filled with bitterness, with hatred, and a desire for revenge. We can move in that direction as a country, in great polarization—black people amongst black, white people amongst white, filled with hatred toward one another.

Or we can make an effort, as Martin Luther King did, to understand and to comprehend, and to replace that violence, that stain of bloodshed that has spread across our land, with an effort to understand with compassion and love.

For those of you who are black and are tempted to be filled with hatred and distrust at the injustice of such an act, against all white people, I can only say that I feel in my own heart the same kind of feeling. I had a member of my family killed, but he was killed by a white man. But we have to make an effort in the United States, we have to make an effort to understand, to go beyond these rather difficult times.

My favorite poet was Aeschylus. He wrote: "In our sleep, pain, which cannot forget, falls drop by drop upon the heart until, in our own despair, against our will, comes wisdom through the awful grace of God."

What we need in the United States is not division; what we need in the United States is not hatred; what we need in the United States is not violence or lawlessness, but love and wisdom, and compassion toward one another, and a feeling of justice towards those who still suffer within our country, whether they be white or they be black.

So I shall ask you tonight to return home, to say a prayer for the family of Martin Luther King, that's true, but more importantly to say a prayer for our own country, which all of us love—a prayer for understanding and that compassion of which I spoke.

We can do well in this country. We will have difficult times. We've had difficult times in the past. We will have difficult times in the future. It is not the end of violence; it is not the end of lawlessness; it is not the end of disorder.

But the vast majority of white people and the vast majority of black people in this country want to live together, want to improve the quality of our life, and want justice for all human beings who abide in our land.

Let us dedicate ourselves to what the Greeks wrote so many years ago: to tame the savageness of man and to make gentle the life of this world.

Let us dedicate ourselves to that, and say a prayer for our country and for our people.

17. The Civil Rights Act of 1968, Provision for Open Housing, April 11, 1968

Discrimination in the Sale or Rental of Housing

SEC. 804. As made applicable by section 803 and except as exempted by sections 803(b) and 807, it shall be unlawful—

(a) To refuse to sell or rent after the making of a bona fide offer, or to refuse to negotiate for the sale or rental of, or otherwise made unavailable or deny, a dwelling to any person because of race, color, religion, or national origin.

(b) To discriminate against any person in the terms, conditions, or privileges of sale or rental of a dwelling, or in the provision of services or facilities in connection therewith, because of race, color, religion, or national origin.

(c) To make, print, or publish or cause to be made, printed, or published any notice, statement, or advertisement, with respect to the sale or rental of a dwelling that indicates any preference, limitation, or discrimination based on race, color, religion, or national origin, or an intention to make any such preference, limitation, or discrimination.

(d) To represent to any person because of race, color, religion, or national origin that any dwelling is not available for inspection, sale or rental when such dwelling is in fact so available.

(e) For profit, to induce or attempt to induce any person to sell or rent any dwelling by representations regarding the entry or prospective entry into the neighborhood of a person or persons of a particular race, color, religion, or national origin.

18. President Richard M. Nixon's Address to the Nation on the Vietnam War and Call to the Great Silent Majority, November 3, 1969

Good evening, my fellow Americans:

Tonight I want to talk to you on a subject of deep concern to all Americans and to many people in all parts of the world—the war in Vietnam.

I believe that one of the reasons for the deep division about Vietnam is that many Americans have lost confidence in what their Government has told them about our policy. The American people cannot and should not be asked to support a policy which involves the overriding issues of war and peace unless they know the truth about that policy.

Tonight, therefore, I would like to answer some of the questions that I know are on the minds of many of you listening to me.

How and why did America get involved in Vietnam in the first place?

How has this administration changed the policy of the previous administration?

What has really happened in the negotiations in Paris and on the battlefront in Vietnam?

What choices do we have if we are to end the war?

What are the prospects for peace?

Now, let me begin by describing the situation I found when I was inaugurated on January 20.

—The war had been going on for 4 years.

—31,000 Americans had been killed in action.

—The training program for the South Vietnamese was behind schedule.

—540,000 Americans were in Vietnam with no plans to reduce the number.

—No progress had been made at the negotiations in Paris and the United States had not put forth a comprehensive peace proposal.

—The war was causing deep division at home and criticism from many of our friends as well as our enemies abroad.

In view of these circumstances there were some who urged that I end the war at once by ordering the immediate withdrawal of all American forces.

From a political standpoint this would have been a popular and easy course to follow. After all, we became involved in the war while my predecessor was in office. I could blame the defeat which would be the result of my action on him and come out as the Peacemaker. Some put it to me quite bluntly: This was the only way to avoid allowing Johnson's war to become Nixon's war.

But I had a greater obligation than to think only of the years of my administration and of the next election. I had to think of the effect of my decision on the next generation and on the future of peace and freedom in America and in the world.

Let us all understand that the question before us is not whether some Americans are for peace and some Americans are against peace. The question at issue is not whether Johnson's war becomes Nixon's war.

The great question is: How can we win America's peace?

Well, let us turn now to the fundamental issue. Why and how did the United States become involved in Vietnam in the first place?

Fifteen years ago North Vietnam, with the logistical support of Communist China and the Soviet Union, launched a campaign to impose a Communist government on South Vietnam by instigating and supporting a revolution.

In response to the request of the Government of South Vietnam, President Eisenhower sent economic aid and military equipment to assist the people of South Vietnam in their efforts to prevent a Communist takeover. Seven years ago, President Kennedy sent 16,000 military personnel to Vietnam as combat advisers. Four years ago, President Johnson sent American combat forces to South Vietnam.

Now, many believe that President Johnson's decision to send American combat forces to South Vietnam was wrong. And many others—I among them—have been strongly critical of the way the war has been conducted.

But the question facing us today is: Now that we are in the war, what is the best way to end it?

In January I could only conclude that the precipitate withdrawal of American forces from Vietnam would be a disaster not only for South Vietnam but for the United States and for the cause of peace.

For the South Vietnamese, our precipitate withdrawal would inevitably allow the Communists to repeat the massacres which followed their takeover in the North 15 years before.

—They then murdered more than 50,000 people and hundreds of thousands more died in slave labor camps.

—We saw a prelude of what would happen in South Vietnam when the Communists entered the city of Hue last year. During their brief rule there, there was a bloody reign of terror in which 3,000 civilians were clubbed, shot to death, and buried in mass graves.

—With the sudden collapse of our support, these atrocities of Hue would become the nightmare of the entire nation—and particularly for the million and a half Catholic refugees who fled to South Vietnam when the Communists took over in the North. For the United States, this first defeat in our Nation's history would result in a collapse of confidence in American leadership, not only in Asia but throughout the world.

Three American Presidents have recognized the great stakes involved in Vietnam and understood what had to be done.

In 1963, President Kennedy, with his characteristic eloquence and clarity, said: ". . . we want to see a stable government there, carrying on a struggle to maintain its national independence.

"We believe strongly in that. We are not going to withdraw from that effort. In my opinion, for us to withdraw from that effort would mean a collapse not only of South Viet-Nam, but Southeast Asia. So we are going to stay there."

President Eisenhower and President Johnson expressed the same conclusion during their terms of office.

For the future of peace, precipitate withdrawal would thus be a disaster of immense magnitude.

—A nation cannot remain great if it betrays its allies and lets down its friends.

—Our defeat and humiliation in South Vietnam without question would promote recklessness in the councils of those great powers who have not yet abandoned their goals of world conquest.

—This would spark violence wherever our commitments help maintain the peace—in the Middle East, in Berlin, eventually even in the Western Hemisphere.

Ultimately, this would cost more lives.

It would not bring peace; it would bring more war.

For these reasons, I rejected the recommendation that I should end the war by immediately withdrawing all of our forces. I chose instead to change American policy on both the negotiating front and battlefront.

In order to end a war fought on many fronts, I initiated a pursuit for peace on many fronts.

In a television speech on May 14, in a speech before the United Nations, and on a number of other occasions I set forth our peace proposals in great detail.

—We have offered the complete withdrawal of all outside forces within 1 year.

—We have proposed a cease-fire under international supervision.

—We have offered free elections under international supervision with the Communists participating in the organization and conduct of the elections as an organized political force. And the Saigon Government has pledged to accept the result of the elections.

We have not put forth our proposals on a take-it-or-leave-it basis. We have indicated that we are willing to discuss the proposals that have been put forth by the other side. We have declared that anything is negotiable except the right of the people of South Vietnam to determine their own future. At the Paris peace conference, Ambassador Lodge has demonstrated our flexibility and good faith in 40 public meetings.

Hanoi has refused even to discuss our proposals. They demand our unconditional acceptance of their terms, which are that we withdraw all American forces immediately and unconditionally and that we overthrow the Government of South Vietnam as we leave.

We have not limited our peace initiatives to public forums and public statements. I recognized, in January, that a long and bitter war like this usually cannot be settled in a public forum. That is why in addition to the public statements and negotiations I have explored every possible private avenue that might lead to a settlement.

Tonight I am taking the unprecedented step of disclosing to you some of our other initiatives for peace—initiatives we undertook privately and secretly because we thought we thereby might open a door which publicly would be closed.

I did not wait for my inauguration to begin my quest for peace.

—Soon after my election, through an individual who is directly in contact on a personal basis with the leaders of North Vietnam, I made two private offers for a rapid, comprehensive settlement. Hanoi's replies called in effect for our surrender before negotiations.

—Since the Soviet Union furnishes most of the military equipment for North Vietnam, Secretary of State Rogers, my Assistant for National Security Affairs, Dr. Kissinger, Ambassador Lodge, and I, personally, have met on a number of occasions with representatives of the Soviet Government to enlist their assistance in getting meaningful negotiations started. In addition, we have had extended discussions directed toward that same end with representatives of other governments which have diplomatic relations with North Vietnam. None of these initiatives have to date produced results.

—In mid-July, I became convinced that it was necessary to make a major move to break the deadlock in the Paris talks. I spoke directly in this office, where I am now sitting, with an individual who had known Ho Chi Minh [President, Democratic Republic of Vietnam] on a personal basis for 25 years. Through him I sent a letter to Ho Chi Minh.

I did this outside of the usual diplomatic channels with the hope that with the necessity of making statements for propaganda removed, there might be constructive progress toward bringing the war to an end. Let me read from that letter to you now.

"Dear Mr. President:
"I realize that it is difficult to communicate meaningfully across the gulf of four years of war. But precisely because of this gulf, I wanted to take this opportunity to reaffirm in all solemnity my desire to work for a just peace. I deeply believe that the war in Vietnam has gone on too long and delay in bringing it to an end can benefit no one—least of all the people of Vietnam. . . .
"The time has come to move forward at the conference table toward an early resolution of this tragic war. You will find us forthcoming and open-minded in a common effort to

bring the blessings of peace to the brave people of Vietnam. Let history record that at this critical juncture, both sides turned their face toward peace rather than toward conflict and war."

I received Ho Chi Minh's reply on August 30, 3 days before his death. It simply reiterated the public position North Vietnam had taken at Paris and flatly rejected my initiative.

The full text of both letters is being released to the press.

—In addition to the public meetings that I have referred to, Ambassador Lodge has met with Vietnam's chief negotiator in Paris in 11 private sessions.—We have taken other significant initiatives which must remain secret to keep open some channels of communication which may still prove to be productive.

But the effect of all the public, private, and secret negotiations which have been undertaken since the bombing halt a year ago and since this administration came into office on January 20, can be summed up in one sentence: No progress whatever has been made except agreement on the shape of the bargaining table.

Well now, who is at fault?

It has become clear that the obstacle in negotiating an end to the war is not the President of the United States. It is not the South Vietnamese Government.

The obstacle is the other side's absolute refusal to show the least willingness to join us in seeking a just peace. And it will not do so while it is convinced that all it has to do is to wait for our next concession, and our next concession after that one, until it gets everything it wants.

There can now be no longer any question that progress in negotiation depends only on Hanoi's deciding to negotiate, to negotiate seriously.

I realize that this report on our efforts on the diplomatic front is discouraging to the American people, but the American people are entitled to know the truth—the bad news as well as the good news where the lives of our young men are involved.

Now let me turn, however, to a more encouraging report on another front.

At the the time we launched our search for peace I recognized we might not succeed in bringing an end to the war through negotiation. I, therefore, put into effect another plan to bring peace—a plan which will bring the war to an end regardless of what happens on the negotiating front.

It is in line with a major shift in U.S. foreign policy which I described in my press conference at Guam on July 25. Let me briefly explain what has been described as the Nixon Doctrine—a policy which not only will help end the war in Vietnam, but which is an essential element of our program to prevent future Vietnams.

We Americans are a do-it-yourself people. We are an impatient people. Instead of teaching someone else to do a job, we like to do it ourselves. And this trait has been carried over into our foreign policy.

In Korea and again in Vietnam, the United States furnished most of the money, most of the arms, and most of the men to help the people of those countries defend their freedom against Communist aggression.

Before any American troops were committed to Vietnam, a leader of another Asian country expressed this opinion to me when I was traveling in Asia as a private citizen. He said: "When you are trying to assist another nation defend its freedom, U.S. policy should be to help them fight the war but not to fight the war for them."

Well, in accordance with this wise counsel, I laid down in Guam three principles as guidelines for future American policy toward Asia:

—First, the United States will keep all of its treaty commitments.

—Second, we shall provide a shield if a nuclear power threatens the freedom of a nation allied with us or of a nation whose survival we consider vital to our security.

—Third, in cases involving other types of aggression, we shall furnish military and economic assistance when requested in accordance with our treaty commitments. But we shall look to the nation directly threatened to assume the primary responsibility of providing the manpower for its defense.

After I announced this policy, I found that the leaders of the Philippines, Thailand, Vietnam, South Korea, and other nations which might be threatened by Communist aggression, welcomed this new direction in American foreign policy.

The defense of freedom is everybody's business—not just America's business. And it is particularly the responsibility of the people whose freedom is threatened. In the previous administration, we Americanized the war in Vietnam. In this administration, we are Vietnamizing the search for peace.

The policy of the previous administration not only resulted in our assuming the primary responsibility for fighting the war, but even more significantly did not adequately stress the goal of strengthening the South Vietnamese so that they could defend themselves when we left.

The Vietnamization plan was launched following Secretary Laird's visit to Vietnam in March. Under the plan, I ordered first a substantial increase in the training and equipment of South Vietnamese forces.

In July, on my visit to Vietnam, I changed General Abrams' orders so that they were consistent with the objectives of our new policies. Under the new orders, the primary mission of our troops is to enable the South Vietnamese forces to assume the full responsibility for the security of South Vietnam.

Our air operations have been reduced by over 20 percent.

And now we have begun to see the results of this long overdue change in American policy in Vietnam.

—After 5 years of Americans going into Vietnam, we are finally bringing American men home. By December 15, over 60,000 men will have been withdrawn from South Vietnam—including 20 percent of all of our combat forces.

—The South Vietnamese have continued to gain in strength. As a result they have been able to take over combat responsibilities from our American troops.

Two other significant developments have occurred since this administration took office.

—Enemy infiltration, infiltration which is essential if they are to launch a major attack, over the last 3 months is less than 20 percent of what it was over the same period last year.

—Most important—United States casualties have declined during the last 2 months to the lowest point in 3 years.

Let me now turn to our program for the future.

We have adopted a plan which we have worked out in cooperation with the South Vietnamese for the complete withdrawal of all U.S. combat ground forces, and their replacement by South Vietnamese forces on an orderly scheduled timetable. This withdrawal will be made from strength and not from weakness. As South Vietnamese forces become stronger, the rate of American withdrawal can become greater.

I have not and do not intend to announce the timetable for our program. And there are obvious reasons for this decision which I am sure you will understand. As I have indicated on several occasions, the rate of withdrawal will depend on developments on three fronts.

One of these is the progress which can be or might be made in the Paris talks. An announcement of a fixed timetable for our withdrawal would completely remove any incentive for the enemy to negotiate an agreement. They would simply wait until our forces had withdrawn and then move in.

The other two factors on which we will base our withdrawal decisions are the level of enemy activity and the progress of the training programs of the South Vietnamese forces. And I am glad to be able to report tonight progress on both of these fronts has been greater than we anticipated when we started the program in June for withdrawal. As a result, our timetable for withdrawal is more optimistic now than when we made our first estimates in June. Now, this clearly demonstrates why it is not wise to be frozen in on a fixed timetable.

We must retain the flexibility to base each withdrawal decision on the situation as it is at that time rather than on estimates that are no longer valid.

Along with this optimistic estimate, I must—in all candor—leave one note of caution.

If the level of enemy activity significantly increases we might have to adjust our timetable accordingly.

However, I want the record to be completely clear on one point.

At the time of the bombing halt just a year ago, there was some confusion as to whether there was an understanding on the part of the enemy that if we stopped the bombing of North Vietnam they would stop the shelling of cities in South Vietnam. I want to be sure that there is no misunderstanding on the part of the enemy with regard to our withdrawal Program.

We have noted the reduced level of infiltration, the reduction of our casualties, and are basing our withdrawal decisions partially on those factors.

If the level of infiltration or our casualties increase while we are trying to scale down the fighting, it will be the result of a conscious decision by the enemy.

Hanoi could make no greater mistake than to assume that an increase in violence will be to its advantage. If I conclude that increased enemy action jeopardizes our remaining forces in Vietnam, I shall not hesitate to take strong and effective measures to deal with that situation.

This is not a threat. This is a statement of policy, which as Commander in Chief of our Armed Forces, I am making in meeting my responsibility for the protection of American fighting men wherever they may be.

My fellow Americans, I am sure you can recognize from what I have said that we really only have two choices open to us if we want to end this war.

—I can order an immediate, precipitate withdrawal of all Americans from Vietnam without regard to the effects of that action.

—Or we can persist in our search for a just peace through a negotiated settlement if possible, or through continued implementation of our plan for Vietnamization if necessary—a plan in which we will withdraw all of our forces from Vietnam on a schedule in accordance with our program, as the South Vietnamese become strong enough to defend their own freedom.

I have chosen this second course.

It is not the easy way.

It is the right way.

It is a plan which will end the war and serve the cause of peace—not just in Vietnam but in the Pacific and in the world.

In speaking of the consequences of a precipitate withdrawal, I mentioned that our allies would lose confidence in America.

Far more dangerous, we would lose confidence in ourselves. Oh, the immediate reaction would be a sense of relief that our men were coming home. But as we saw the consequences of what we had done, inevitable remorse and divisive recrimination would scar our spirit as a people.

We have faced other crisis in our history and have become stronger by rejecting the easy way out and taking the right way in meeting our challenges. Our greatness as a nation has been our capacity to do what had to be done when we knew our course was right.

I recognize that some of my fellow citizens disagree with the plan for peace I have chosen. Honest and patriotic Americans have reached different conclusions as to how peace should be achieved.

In San Francisco a few weeks ago, I saw demonstrators carrying signs reading: "Lose in Vietnam, bring the boys home."

Well, one of the strengths of our free society is that any American has a right to reach that conclusion and to advocate that point of view. But as President of the United States, I would be untrue to my oath of office if I allowed the policy of this Nation to be dictated by the minority who hold that point of view and who try to impose it on the Nation by mounting demonstrations in the street.

For almost 200 years, the policy of this Nation has been made under our Constitution by those leaders in the Congress and the White House elected by all of the people. If a vocal minority, however fervent its cause, prevails over reason and the will of the majority, this Nation has no future as a free society.

And now I would like to address a word, if I may, to the young people of this Nation who are particularly concerned, and I understand why they are concerned, about this war.

I respect your idealism.

I share your concern for peace.

I want peace as much as you do.

There are powerful personal reasons I want to end this war. This week I will have to sign 83 letters to mothers, fathers, wives, and loved ones of men who have given their lives for America in Vietnam. It is very little satisfaction to me that this is only one-third as many letters as I signed the first week in office. There is nothing I want more than to see the day come when I do not have to write any of those letters.

—I want to end the war to save the lives of those brave young men in Vietnam.

—But I want to end it in a way which will increase the chance that their younger brothers and their sons will not have to fight in some future Vietnam someplace in the world.

—And I want to end the war for another reason. I want to end it so that the energy and dedication of you, our young people, now too often directed into bitter hatred against those responsible for the war, can be turned to the great challenges of peace, a better life for all Americans, a better life for all people on this earth.

I have chosen a plan for peace. I believe it will succeed.

If it does succeed, what the critics say now won't matter. If it does not succeed, anything I say then won't matter.

I know it may not be fashionable to speak of patriotism or national destiny these days. But I feel it is appropriate to do so on this occasion.

Two hundred years ago this Nation was weak and poor. But even then, America was the hope of millions in the world. Today we have become the strongest and richest nation in the world. And the wheel of destiny has turned so that any hope the world has for the survival of peace and freedom will be determined by whether the American people have the moral stamina and the courage to meet the challenge of free world leadership.

Let historians not record that when America was the most powerful nation in the world we passed on the other side of the road and allowed the last hopes for peace and freedom of millions of people to be suffocated by the forces of totalitarianism.

And so tonight—to you, the great silent majority of my fellow Americans—I ask for your support.

I pledged in my campaign for the Presidency to end the war in a way that we could win the peace. I have initiated a plan of action which will enable me to keep that pledge.

The more support I can have from the American people, the sooner that pledge can be redeemed; for the more divided we are at home, the less likely, the enemy is to negotiate at Paris.

Let us be united for peace. Let us also be united against defeat. Because let us understand: North Vietnam cannot defeat or humiliate the United States. Only Americans can do that.

Fifty years ago, in this room and at this very desk, President Woodrow Wilson spoke words which caught the imagination of a war-weary world. He said: "This is the war to end war." His dream for peace after World War I was shattered on the hard realities of great power politics and Woodrow Wilson died a broken man.

Tonight I do not tell you that the war in Vietnam is the war to end wars. But I do say this: I have initiated a plan which will end this war in a way that will bring us closer to that great goal to which Woodrow Wilson and every American President in our history has been dedicated—the goal of a just and lasting peace.

As President I hold the responsibility for choosing the best path to that goal and then leading the Nation along it.

I pledge to you tonight that I shall meet this responsibility with all of the strength and wisdom I can command in accordance with your hopes, mindful of your concerns, sustained by your prayers.

Thank you and good night.

APPENDIX B
Biographies of Major Personalities

Abernathy, Ralph (1926–1990) *civil rights leader*
Born in poverty in rural Alabama, Abernathy became a Baptist minister during the late 1940s and also received a graduate degree from Atlanta University. Throughout the 1950s, he served as pastor for the First Baptist Church of Montgomery, Alabama. Preaching a gospel of racial tolerance, Abernathy championed a new era of African-American civil rights. He first received national recognition for his support of fellow Montgomery resident Rosa Parks and her mid-1950s protest of the segregated public bus company there. Organizing a city-wide boycott on her behalf, Abernathy (with the full support of Martin Luther King, Jr.,) put his church at the center of the civil rights struggle. Although that church was attacked by angry white racists, Abernathy insisted on no counterattack. He favored a nonviolence agenda similar to his Alabama colleague, Martin Luther King, Jr. Abernathy had little interest in leading the civil rights cause himself but was happy to cofound the Southern Christian Leadership Conference (SCLC) with King in 1957. Content with the role of "lieutenant" in this King-led effort, Abernathy became King's most trusted adviser during the 1960s. Following the King assassination in 1968, Abernathy was suddenly the nation's most visible nonviolent advocate of civil rights reform. Nevertheless, he resigned from the SCLC in 1977. He then ran unsuccessfully for a Georgia congressional seat, established the Foundation for Economic Enterprises Development during the 1980s, and died after a long illness in the spring of 1990.

Abzug, Bella (1920–1998) *antiwar leader, feminist congresswoman*
The daughter of struggling Eastern European refugees, Abzug spent much of her life in New York City. Her first political experiences were associated with her role as Hunter College student government president in the 1930s where she organized student protests against the Hitler regime in Germany. A 1945 graduate of the Columbia University Law School, Abzug's law career stressed civil rights–related cases. In 1961, she helped organize the Women's Strike for Peace demonstrations against America's nuclear policies, and, in 1963, she became an early leader of the first anti–Vietnam War protests. Abzug won a great deal of press attention for her effort to bring women's rights advocates, peace activists, the poor, and labor leaders together into one antiwar coalition. She met little success in this endeavor, but it won her a strong political base to run for Congress. Elected to the House of Representatives in 1970, Abzug quickly became a media sensation thanks to her outrageous hats, angry speechs, and tireless advocacy of liberal causes. Abandoning Congess for the speaker's circuit in 1977, Abzug died of heart failure in 1998.

Agnew, Spiro (1918–1996) *governor of Maryland, vice president*
A World War II veteran and graduate of the Johns Hopkins University Law School, Agnew entered Maryland politics in the mid-1950s. Although his political philosophy was more at home with the Democratic Party, Agnew found greater career opportunities with the Republicans. Elected governor in 1966, Agnew won a quick reputation as a "hawk" on Vietnam War issues. He also positioned himself as a champion of white middle-class values in the face of changing times. Selected as the Republican vice presidential nominee in 1968, Agnew was supposed to draw support from the American Independent Party candidate for president, George Wallace. Richard Nixon denied that Agnew was tapped for that reason, but, once in office, Vice President Agnew would continue to appeal to Wallace voters. He became a very

visible critic of both antiwar and civil rights leaders. Famous for his colorful use of alliteration during his public denunciations of liberals, Agnew was a sought-after speaker by the U.S. political right. To Agnew, those journalists and others who did not believe in a Vietnam War victory were "nattering nabobs of negativism." Meanwhile, the antiwar movement, he said, was led by "pugilistic pups" who jousted with treason. During October 1973, in a legal clash unrelated to the Watergate affair, Agnew received a $10,000 fine and three years probation for his role in a Maryland bribery scandal. His resulting resignation from office foreshadowed Nixon's fate less than one year later.

Ali, Muhammad (Cassius Marcellus Clay)
(1942–   ) *boxing hero*

Born Cassius Marcellus Clay in Louisville, Kentucky, Ali grew up in a racially divided neighborhood. He claims that he became interested in boxing at the age of 12 when he was forced to fight the thieves who had stolen his bicycle. After winning two National Golden Gloves championships as well as two National Amateur Athletic Union awards, Ali represented the United States in the light-heavyweight boxing division at the 1960 Olympic Games. He won the gold medal in that division as well as great attention from the world press. Considered an innovative tactician when he fought, Ali became famous for his carefully planned and landed punches and amazingly fast footwork. A good promoter, Ali insisted that boxing must be considered a mainstream sport and not a violent act. At the age of 18, he was already a professional boxer and, four years later in 1964, he defeated the highly touted Sonny Liston for the title of heavyweight champion of the world. Ali became even more famous for his outrageous behavior with the press. Predicting the round when his opponent would lose the fight, Ali also read his own tongue-in-cheek poetry about upcoming matches. Converting to the Nation of Islam in 1964, the champ formally changed his name to Ali and promised to battle all forms of racism. He also denounced the Vietnam War. An unsympathetic press criticized his alleged politicalization of sports. Although Ali successfully defended his crown in 1967, the title was taken from him by boxing officials due to his decision, based on the teachings of the Nation of Islam, to reject his induction into the U.S. military. An unanimous Supreme Court deci-

sion in Ali's favor permitted his return to boxing in 1971 and his eventual regaining of the heavy-weight title. He retired from boxing in 1981, dedicating himself to social causes at home and abroad. Parkinson's disease slowed but failed to halt his efforts.

Allen, Woody (Allen Stuart Konigsberg)
(1935–   ) *actor, director*

Born Allen Stuart Konigsberg in Brooklyn, New York, Woody Allen was a professional joke writer before the age of 15. A graduate of the NBC Television Network's Writer Development Program at the age of 20, Allen wrote jokes for a number of television shows in the late 1950s. By 1960, his colleagues persuaded him to tell his own jokes in stand-up comedy acts throughout Hollywood. Allen gave it a try, also creating a unique character in his comedy club acts. On the stage, Allen usually portrayed himself as a troubled soul who could never live up to his own lofty ambitions. Claiming to be always in need of psychological help, and forever influenced by his strict Jewish background and weak physical condition, the thin, diminutive Allen poked fun at men who could never live up to Hollywood's image of the rough-and-tough male hero. In the early 1960s, Allen's act struck a chord in an America tired of Madison Avenue imagery and phony role models. He wrote two popular Broadway plays in the mid-1960s (*Don't Drink the Water* and *Play It Again, Sam*) but dedicated the last months of the decade to his own films. *Take the Money and Run* (1969) was a fairly low-budget film, poking fun at America's growing crime rate as well as Hollywood's view of criminal antiheroes. It established Allen as a decent filmmaker. He won an Academy Award in 1977 for the film *Annie Hall,* but his star was tarnished following press accusations of an immoral private life.

Arkus-Duntov, Zora (1909–1996) *race driver, automotive engineer*

Born to Russian parents in Brussels, Belgium, Arkus-Duntov raced motorcycles as a teenager in Europe but switched to race cars following a series of life-threatening accidents. Graduating with a degree in mechanical engineering (specializing in automobile engine development and supercharging) at Berlin's Institute of Charlottenburg in 1934, Arkus-Duntov became the chief consultant to the Mercedes Grand Prix racing team and published trailblazing articles on four-wheel-drive design and sports car steering dynamics. After a stint with England's Allard Motor Company, Arkus-Duntov was hired by the General Motors Chevrolet Division to improve and rescue its Corvette sports car project. Using his own designs for fuel injection and cam technology, Arkus-Duntov transformed the lackluster Corvette into a world-class sports car. Sales escalated, numerous racing titles were won, and the car, partially through Arkus-Duntov's own promotion efforts, became an American icon by the early 1960s. With award-winning designer Larry Shinoda at his side, Arkus-Duntov saw his second-generation Corvette Stingray (1963–67) win further accolades for its technological advances, trend-setting design, and speed-setting records. In 1968, the first year of Arkus-Duntov's third-generation Corvette (1968–82), thousands of new "shark-style" Corvettes were sold sight unseen, further enhancing the car's reputation as the ultimate American sports car. Arkus-Duntov retired in 1975 but continued to consult for General Motors and others. He died of cancer-induced kidney failure in Grosse Pointe, Michigan, in April 1996.

Ashe, Arthur (1943–1993) *tennis player*

The son of the city parks administrator for Richmond, Virginia, Ashe grew up playing tennis in his father's park system. Before the age of 11, Ashe was already on the tournament circuit playing in summer programs funded by the American Tennis Association. In his teens, Ashe was considered the country's top high school tennis player, winning a fully paid scholarship in 1961 to attend the University of California–Los Angeles. Ashe's career continued to skyrocket. During 1968, his triumph at the U.S. Open made Ashe America's most recognizable tennis champ. He used his fame to champion the concerns of fellow African-American athletes. Ashe had been denied the right to play in a variety of tennis clubs because of whites-only stipulations, and in 1969 he was unable to play in an important international tournament in South Africa due to the latter's apartheid policies. Ashe became a spokesperson for the antiapartheid movement because of it. With the exception of the 1975 Wimbledon tennis match, Ashe's victories in the 1970s were never as spectacular as the decade before. Retiring in the 1980s, Ashe contracted AIDS due to a tainted blood transfusion during surgery. He died in early 1993.

Baez, Joan (1941–   ) *singer, political activist*

Born in New York City, Baez grew up in Palo Alto, California. Proud of her Hispanic roots and commitment to nonviolence, Baez was taunted and discriminated against throughout most of her school years. A guitarist since age 12, she began to study folk music in Boston during the late 1950s. Her first folk concerts in the Midwest and New England led to recording contracts in 1959, but she preferred to cut her first record in her own way. In 1960, that first album, simply titled *Joan Baez,* included a number of folk songs praising Hispanic Americans and her own family. It would be one of a dozen albums cut during the 1960s. By the mid-1960s, her albums included political protest songs as well. It won her the attention of other singer/activists, such as Bob Dylan, and she agreed to sing at the major civil rights and antiwar demonstrations of the day. Refusing to pay any taxes that might be spent on the Vietnam War, Baez won the ire of many mainstream politicians and conservatives. Her records were not sold on U.S. military installations, and traditional concert halls in Washington, D.C., and elsewhere rarely invited her to sing. In 1968, she married antiwar activist David Harris, and one year later she capped her 1960s career with a rousing performance at the Woodstock Music Festival. Baez continued her fight for various social and peace-making causes into the 21st century.

Baldwin, James (1924–1987) *novelist, civil rights activist*

Once dedicated to God and the religious life, Baldwin abandoned plans to be a clergyman upon discovery of his gift for writing. Working at a variety of odd jobs in New York and New Jersey, Baldwin met successful writer and later mentor Richard Wright in the mid-1940s. Wright sponsored Baldwin's application for a writer's fellowship and urged him to write his first novel, *In My Father's House.* Baldwin could not find a publisher for the book, and he turned his energies to another project. *Go Tell It on the Mountain* was written in France and published in the early 1950s. Although Baldwin remained an American citizen, St. Paul Vence, a writer and artist's enclave in the south of France, became his adopted home. As an African-American homosexual, Baldwin understood the problems of discrimination quite well, and his writing in the early 1960s, such as *Nobody Knows My Name,* included passionate appeals to end legalized racism in the U.S.

South and elsewhere. Both John and Robert Kennedy claimed to be enthusiastic fans of Baldwin's work, although Baldwin was never convinced that the Kennedys were truly on the side of all African Americans. Nevertheless, the Kennedy assassinations shocked him, and the up-and-down struggles of the Civil Rights movement soured him. Baldwin remained in France, writing plays, essays, and novels. Haunted by the lack of success, in his view, of the Civil Rights movement, Baldwin attempted suicide on more than one occasion. He died in November 1987.

Beach Boys, The (1961–) *singing group*
Stimulated by their songwriter father, Murry Wilson, Dennis, Brian, and Carl Wilson formed a band in 1961. The elder Wilson held grand ambitions for his sons, urging them to find their own unique sound. Allegedly, Wilson was physically abusive to them if they failed to practice hard and long enough. Along with family friend Al Jardine and first cousin Mike Love, the Wilson boys called their new band Kenny and the Cadets, soon changed it to Carl and the Passions, then the Pendletons, and, finally, the Beach Boys. When he was not practicing his music in the Wilson family home of Hawthorne, California, Dennis Wilson was surfing. He had to convince fellow band members that his pastime could also be turned into an interesting song. The result was "Surfin'," a hit in the southern California area alone in late 1961. At first, national radio stations had little interest in what appeared to be a narrowly focused and local group. Nevertheless, the Beach Boys' unusual combination of wild guitar and tight vocal harmonies created the unique sound that their father had long sought. The Wilsons won their first record contract in early 1962, and their songs about surfing, fast American-made muscle cars, and California girls won a national audience. Quick fame and fortune took their toll on the band. Illegal drug use and alcoholism led to Brian Wilson's exit from the group, and squabbles erupted over further efforts in musical experimentation. Yet, their music soon became intimately linked to the so-called quiet and innocent America before the escalation of the Vietnam War. In later years, a number of bands claimed that their inspiration came from the Beach Boys. Dennis Wilson drowned in 1983, and Carl Wilson died of cancer 15 years later. Yet, a reconstituted Beach Boys continues to perform into the 21st century.

Beatles, The (1960–1970) *singing group*
Originally consisting of John Lennon, Paul McCartney, George Harrison, Stuart Sutcliffe, and Pete Best, the Beatles rock group was a product of Liverpool, England, working-class and lower-middle-class life. Before the band's claim to fame, Sutcliffe left the group for an artist's life, and Ringo Starr replaced Best in 1962. Already a sensation in England thanks to their unusual pop rock sound and haircuts, the Beatles' first hit in America was "I Want to Hold Your Hand" in 1964. The song represented what the American press soon labeled the "British invasion," a reference to the successful importing of British pop culture (music, films, and fashion) to America in the mid-1960s. Appearing on CBS's *The Ed Sullivan Show* in February 1964, the Beatles excited American teenagers eager for something new in rock-and-roll. Their parents were left wondering why the Beatles excited their children, although music critics reminded them that previous musical icons in previous decades (Frank Sinatra in the 1940s or Elvis Presley in the 1950s) had their fair share of screaming fans as well. The Beatles' music evolved from cute romantic ditties in the mid-1960s to social protest and concern in the late 1960s. Wealthy beyond their dreams in a short period of time, the Beatles turned to Eastern mysticism and philosophy for solace and inspiration. They also bickered among themselves over who held the upper hand in the band's future direction. In turn, America's antiwar movement welcomed some of the Beatles' songs as peace anthems, and the breakup of the group at the beginning of the new decade of the 1970s was greeted with shock and disbelief by adoring fans across the United States. John Lennon was shot in 1980. George Harrison died of cancer in 2001.

Berrigan, Daniel (1921–) *Catholic priest, peace activist*
Born in tiny Two Harbors, Minnesota, Daniel Berrigan was ordained a Catholic priest in 1952. Fascinated by the worker-priest movement while studying in France, Berrigan concluded that American priests had a moral obligation to speak out against the injustices of the cold war. His first venue of protest was poetry, winning him the Lamont Poetry Award in 1957. Following a stint as assistant editor of *Jesuit Missions* magazine in New York, Berrigan became the associate director of the United Religious Work organization

in 1966. It was from that post that he began to organize protest marches and demonstrations against the Vietnam War. Together with Professor Howard Zinn, a New Left academic spokesperson, the two visited North Vietnam and denounced American policy in Southeast Asia. Along with his younger brother, Philip, the elder Berrigan won national attention on behalf of draft resistance. But their attempt to destroy draft registration files in Catonsville, Maryland, made the Berrigans wanted men. Sentenced to three years in prison for the 1968 Catonsville protest alone, Berrigan fled authorities but was captured several months later. Upon his release from prison, Berrigan took up new causes, such as nuclear disarmament, and remained active in a number of protest movements into the 21st century.

Berrigan, Philip (1923–2002) *Catholic priest, political activist*

The younger brother of peace activist Daniel Berrigan, Philip Berrigan embraced a number of causes outside the anti–Vietnam War and antinuclear movements. A Catholic priest, Philip Berrigan graduated from Holy Cross College in 1950. He immediately joined Martin Luther King, Jr.'s Civil Rights movement and founded the Catholic Peace Fellowship to support it. By the mid-1960s, he came to the aid of his peace activist brother, Daniel. Together, they sought a national spotlight for the cause of draft resistance to what both considered the "racist war" in Vietnam. Arrested in 1968 with his brother for using homemade nepalm to destroy draft records in Catonsville, Maryland, Philip Berrigan urged his supporters to "fire bomb" other draft centers as well. Soon implicated in a bizarre plot to kidnap National Security Council adviser Henry Kissinger, Philip Berrigan was sometimes seen by authorities as the more dangerous of the two Berrigan brothers. After the Vietnam War, Philip, like his older brother, Daniel, drifted into other protest movements and causes. He died in 2002.

Bond, Julian (Horace Julian Bond) (1940–) *civil rights activist, Georgia legislator*

The son of the chancellor of Lincoln University, Horace Julian Bond was born into a distinguished and comfortable African-American family. Also the product of schools run by the Society of Friends (or Quakers), Bond won an early respect for peace, morality, and social change. In 1960, along with Lonnie King, Bond organized an Atlanta University student movement dedicated to the end of racism. It was at a pro–civil rights demonstration organized by Bond that Martin Luther King, Jr., was arrested and jailed on the eve of the 1960 election. John Kennedy's follow-up phone call to King led thousands of African Americans to vote for Kennedy in one of history's closest presidential elections. Bond was also one of the founders of the Student Nonviolent Coordinating Committee (SNCC) and won more than 80 percent of the vote when he first ran for the Georgia House of Representatives in 1965. Handsome, articulate, and headline-making, Bond was nominated for vice president at the 1968 Democratic convention. The nomination failed, and his strong anti–Vietnam War position also alienated him from many fellow Democrats in Georgia. Although he preferred a low national profile in later years, Bond continued to inspire young Georgians to make a difference in politics.

Brown, H. Rap (Hubert Geroid Brown, Jamil Abdullah Al-Amin) (1943–) *black militant*

Born Hubert Geroid Brown in Louisiana, Brown earned the nickname "Rap" because of his skill in communicating with poor blacks while he attended a school run by white churchmen. Later attending Southern University in Baton Rouge, Brown left his studies to work with Stokely Carmichael and the Student Nonviolent Coordinating Committee (SNCC). To Brown, the nonviolence message was counterproductive, for he believed that whites understood only force. His call for a violent revolution, if necessary, to achieve black power won the attention of the press. During 1967, he replaced Carmichael as the SNCC director. Carrying a gun to press conferences, Brown soon symbolized the growing violence of the civil rights cause. Insisting that African Americans should follow his example and wage a race war against white America, Brown also won the attention of law enforcement agencies. Jailed for his 1971 attempted armed robbery of a New York bar, Brown converted to Islam and changed his name to Jamil Abdullah Al-Amin. Following his release from prison, Al-Amin attempted to live a quiet, religious life in Georgia, but he eventually returned to crime. In March 2002, he was found guilty of murdering a sheriff's deputy and was sentenced to life in prison.

Brown, James (1933–   ) *soul singer*
Born in poverty in rural South Carolina, Brown learned to sing and dance at the age of four. Arrested at the age of 16 for stealing cars, Brown served three years in prison. Having formed a gospel group while in jail, Brown pursued a singing career immediately after his parole. His new group, the Flames, combined gospel and rhythm-and-blues music that attracted the attention of King Records in the mid-1950s. Although the Flames had two popular recordings in the late 1950s, neither made them much money. Wearing outrageous costumes and presenting an exhausting, energetic stage act, Brown sang in a variety of nightclubs. By the early 1960s, he was nicknamed the "hardest-working man in show business." He liked the label, and his 1962 performance at Harlem's Apollo theater was a sellout. Hits from his Apollo performance later topped the rhythm-and-blues charts, and his "Papa's Got a Brand New Bag" (1965) as well as other songs were crossover successes on the pop and rock charts. As a radio superstar, Brown endorsed a multitude of 1960s causes, ranging from educational reform to civil rights. Although his endorsement of Hubert Humphrey for president in 1968 won him the wrath of black Muslims, it had little impact on his career. He was voted America's top male vocalist of the late 1960s by the music industry. Quickly squandering his fortune, hounded by the Internal Revenue Service, and further financially drained by a divisive divorce, Brown disappeared from the public eye for years. His career resurfaced in the mid-1980s with a new hit ("Living in America") and a special guest appearance on TV's popular *Miami Vice* (1986).

Brown, Jim (1936–   ) *football star*
Although born and raised in Georgia, Brown spent most of his life in New York. A high school star in football, track, and even basketball, Brown won a scholarship to attend Syracuse University. Winning the title of All-American there in both football and lacrosse, Brown was drafted by the Cleveland Browns football team in the early 1960s. By the end of the 1963 football season, Brown had broken all records for yardage gained by one player in any given season. Declared football player of the year in both 1963 and 1965, Brown became a prominent promoter of African-American businesses in Ohio and New York. Meanwhile, his retirement from football led to supporting actor roles in 1960s films ranging from *Rio Conchos* with Stuart Whitman to *The Dirty Dozen* with Lee Marvin. Soon left in semiretirement from his fast-moving Hollywood career, Brown dedicated himself to community activist work.

Buckley, William F. (1925–   ) *conservative spokesperson*
Born to great wealth, Buckley became a conservative activist and skilled debater while serving as the editor of the Yale University student newspaper. After graduation, he joined the Central Intelligence Agency and later worked for *American Mercury* magazine. In 1955, he founded his own conservative journal, *National Review.* Attempting to redefine American conservatism for the new decade of the 1960s, Buckley and his *National Review* associates were staunch anticommunists, but he considered Republicans such as Dwight Eisenhower and Richard Nixon too moderate to be considered conservatives. Buckley also had little use for right-wing activists such as the John Birch Society and the racist Ku Klux Klan. Instead, he favored a conservative philosophy that rejected both government-led social policies and Washington's role in the national economy. *National Review* became the voice of a growing conservative movement that rejected Kennedy's New Frontier and Lyndon Johnson's Great Society. Endorsing Barry Goldwater for president, Buckley was helped rather than harmed by the Arizona senator's defeat. Labeling Goldwater's failed campaign a "lost opportunity" for the United States, Buckley won significant press attention for his conservative alternatives to the political status quo. He won even more recognition for his lively ABC television debate with liberal critic and cynic Gore Vidal during the 1968 election. Later on, Buckley's *Firing Line* talk show on PBS television further popularized his message, providing an ideological foundation for the 1980 success of Ronald Reagan's presidential campaign.

Burger, Warren (1907–1995) *Supreme Court chief justice*
Born and raised in Minnesota, Burger taught law at William Mitchell College in the 1940s and early 1950s. A longtime Republican Party activist, Burger was an early supporter of the 1952 Eisenhower campaign for president. Burger's campaign efforts won him a number of positions in the resulting Eisenhower administration, including assistant attorney general. During the 1960s, Burger served as a circuit

judge in Washington, D.C. He favored more powers for the police, less civil rights protection for defendants, and opposed insanity pleas by defense lawyers for their clients. He was an especially strong critic of the 1966 Miranda decision that stressed the civil rights/liberties of the arrested. Yet, his conservative record was balanced by his efforts to halt discrimination against African-American journalists in the South and his insistence that the prison system stress rehabilitation over punishment. In 1969, Richard Nixon appointed him to serve as chief justice of the Supreme Court. Expected to be a conservative who would reject the judicial reforms championed by his predecessor, Earl Warren, Burger instead maintained a centrist position. He retired in 1986 and died in Washington, D.C., nine years later.

Carmichael, Stokely (1941–1995) *black militant*

Hailing from the island of Trinidad in the Caribbean, Carmichael and his family moved to New York in the late 1940s. As a high school student, Carmichael befriended white socialists and communists, spending his summers protesting racism in the U.S. South. Later attending Howard University, Carmichael took control of the Nonviolent Action Group, a subsidiary of the Student Nonviolent Coordinating Committee (SNCC). From the Freedom Rides to Martin Luther King's Selma March, Carmichael participated in all the major civil rights actions of the early and mid-1960s. Nevertheless, in 1966, he announced his disgust and frustration with the lack of civil rights progress, reiterating a number of longstanding leftist complaints about American life and society. Carmichael also took command of SNCC in 1966, announcing a new direct action agenda for the group. His visits to a number of West African governments won him even greater respect in the African-American community, and he soon assumed the leadership of the Black Panther Party. Given the ideological arguments between the SNCC and the Black Panthers over the proper path to civil rights success, SNCC expelled Carmichael in 1968. He also left the Black Panthers shortly afterward, married an African singer, and moved to Conakry, Guinea, where he died in 1995.

Castro, Fidel (Fidel Castro Ruz) (1926–   )
Cuban revolutionary and dictator

A strong believer in the political visions of both Cuban nationalist José Martí and leftist icon Karl Marx, Fidel Castro Ruz was brought up in the comforts of a wealthy landowning family. The 1952 coup led by Cuban army general Fulgencio Batista and the corruption and economic mismanagement of his resulting government convinced young intellectuals such as Castro that a violent revolution was necessary. Castro and his supporters attempted to spark a revolt as early as 1953, but its failure prompted a cautious period of planning and organizing. By January 1, 1959, the Batista government was overthrown, only Castro's communists were declared the legal political party of Cuba, non-Cuban owned land was seized, and U.S.-Cuban relations quickly soured. Hastily labeled a pro-Soviet ally only 90 miles from Miami, Cuba was seen as a major diplomatic embarrassment by the Kennedy administration. The resulting Bay of Pigs invasion of April 1961 was meant to overthrow Castro by fellow Cubans, but the attack failed. This pushed Castro closer to the Soviets, who gambled with world peace by offering the Cuban leader a joint Cuban-Soviet defense of medium-range nuclear missiles. The U.S. vs. Soviet crisis that followed was resolved in October 1962 by a combination of clever diplomatic maneuvers and a U.S. Navy "quarantine," but Castro remained a source of embarrassment to America's hemispheric clout and influence for years to come.

Cleaver, Eldridge (Leroy Eldridge Cleaver) (1935–1998) *Black Panther leader*

Although born Leroy Eldridge Cleaver in tiny Wabbaseka, Arkansas, Cleaver grew up as a ghetto youth in California. He spent the early 1960s in jail for assault and attempted rape, flirted with Islam, and then developed his own ideas on black nationalism and pride. Those ideas and observations were published in 1968 as *Soul on Ice*. This book became an important piece of literature in the Black Power movement and a best-seller that intrigued anyone interested in the twists and turns of the civil rights cause. Cleaver took charge of publicizing Black Panther goals and objectives, becoming the party's most visible member in the press. Advocating an armed response to police harassment of Black Panther community events, Cleaver's interests in violence split the party. Wanted by police for his role in a 1968 gun battle with them, Cleaver left the country for a new life in Algeria. He returned home seven years later and was sentenced to a year in prison. Once a free man, he denounced his radical past, championed a born-again Christian agenda, and supported a once diehard opponent, California's Ronald Reagan, for president of the United States. He died in 1998.

Cronkite, Walter (1916–) *CBS News anchor*

A Texas-based newspaper reporter who later covered World War II battles for the United Press, Cronkite bolted print press for broadcast journalism in the late 1940s. While serving as Washington, D.C., bureau chief for a coalition of Midwest radio news stations, Cronkite became interested in the news-covering potential of the newly founded television networks. He joined CBS in 1950, helping the fledgling television network develop its news-gathering apparatus. Although it took 12 years, he was finally rewarded for his efforts when the network named him the television anchor of their nightly 15-minute news program. In less than a year, Cronkite had expanded it to 30 minutes. His personal coverage of important events, such as the John Kennedy assassination, made him one of America's most recognized media personalities. Lauded for his objective, no-nonsense reporting, Cronkite was called "America's most trusted man" by the mid-1960s. Given the high-ratings success of the *CBS Evening News,* many Americans said that they "watched Walter Cronkite" when in fact they meant to say that they watched television news. Although Cronkite urged Americans to continue reading their newspapers, more and more of them turned to his program as the only source of daily news. His rare display of emotion during the Vietnam Tet Offensive of early 1968 led many Americans to reconsider their support for Lyndon Johnson's war policies. Cronkite retired from CBS in 1981 but continued to host special news and public affairs programs.

Dirksen, Everett McKinley (1896–1969)
U.S. Senate minority leader

A graduate of the University of Minnesota, Everett McKinley Dirksen became one of the Midwest's most decorated army heroes of World War I. Representing his hometown of Pekin, Illinois, Dirksen was one of the few freshmen Republicans elected to Congress during the Democratic sweep of 1932. A staunch conservative whose congressional district represented one of the North's strongest bastion's of Ku Klux Klan support, Dirksen won a close, upset victory for the U.S. Senate in 1950. A fine orator with a distinctively deep and raspy voice, Dirksen was a sought-after speaker by conservative groups across the country. Rising to the role of Senate minority leader in 1959, Dirksen moderated all but his anticommunist views. He once noted that if Vietnamese communism was not defeated, the United States would soon be fighting hordes of Asian communists in "the streets of San Francisco." On civil rights, he proved to be an unexpectedly strong ally of Lyndon Johnson's reform efforts, winning him the respect of liberals and moderates across the country. Dirksen made good use of television and his own speaking skills to persuade fellow Republicans to support Democratic-led civil rights reforms. During 1969, following what was supposed to have been "routine lung surgery," Dirksen died in Washington, D.C.

Dylan, Bob (Robert A. Zimmerman) (1941–) *folk rock music pioneer*

Born Robert A. Zimmerman, Dylan spent his formative years in tiny Hibbing, Minnesota. Although originally influenced by the country western songs that were popular in northern Minnesota, Dylan became interested in rock-and-roll after viewing the James Dean film *Rebel Without a Cause.* Dean's quiet loner/rebel character in the film became the young Dylan's role model. In high school, he formed his first band, the Golden Chords, playing blues music. But Dylan switched to folk music when he entered the University of Minnesota in 1959. Folk artist and part-time revolutionary Woody Guthrie became his new hero, and he traveled to New York to meet him. Dylan made his living there singing Guthrie-like folk songs and was discovered by Columbia Records in 1961. His first album, *Bob Dylan,* was largely dedicated to Guthrie, and Dylan's "rough cut" style excited folk music fans. His second album the following year blended folk, blues, and protest music. His "Blowin' in the Wind" helped define this new sound, later becoming something of the national anthem to antiwar protesters and counterculture advocates. Other folk/protest music singers, such as Joan Baez and Peter, Paul and Mary, turned his songs into their own radio hits, and Dylan's music continued to win large audiences. In 1964, "The Times They Are a-Changin'" helped enunciate many of the feelings of angry, impatient youth in the 1960s, soon representing the importance of musical expression within the decade's protest movements. A motorcycle accident in 1966 kept Dylan in recovery and away from the stage for nearly two years. He returned to his original country western interests in 1969 when he performed with country western star Johnny Cash. Dylan continued to perform in the following decades. He flirted with Christian music in the early 1980s and even hard rock in the mid-1980s, but his image as a 1960s protest singer would never leave him. The late 1960s/early 1970s radical Weather Underground or Weathermen antiwar group even took their name from the lyrics of one of Dylan's tunes.

Evers, Medgar (1925–1963) *nonviolent civil rights leader*

Born in Decatur, Mississippi, Medgar Evers was a young teen when he witnessed the lynching of a family friend for allegedly harassing a white woman. That event led Evers to a life of civil rights activism. While working for the National Association for the Advancement of Colored People (NAACP) in Mississippi, Evers investigated the lynching of African Americans as well as court rulings against African Americans made by all-white juries. Although he advocated a nonviolent path to civil rights reform, Evers faced numerous death threats because of his legal work. In 1962, he became the recognized leader of civil rights activism in Jackson, Mississippi, organizing boycotts of white businesses and helping African Americans register to vote. His efforts led to the successful integration of the school system there as well. On June 12, 1963, Evers was shot to death in the front yard of his own home. The killing symbolized the growing racial violence of the day, placing great press and legal attention on Evers's cause in Mississippi. Evers's killer was a white supremacist leader, Byron de la Beckwith, who was released from jail twice due to mistrials spearheaded by all-white juries. De la Beckwith was finally found guilty of the Evers murder 31 years after the crime was committed.

Fleming, Peggy Gale (1948–) *Olympic skating champion*

Even as a fifth grader, Peggy Gale Fleming demonstrated a gift for competitive skating. Before the age of 12, she had won her first skating title in her home state of Ohio, but tragedy kept her from national success for several years. In 1961, Fleming's entire skating team, including her coach, were killed in a plane crash. (She

was not on the plane.) Under the watchful eye of legendary skating trainer Carlo Fassi, Fleming won her first national titles. Only in her early teens, Fleming was the youngest female skating champion in U.S. history. In 1968, she entered the Olympic Games in France with an invincible reputation. Her innovative double-axel, spread eagle combinations wowed the judges, and her Gold Medal success was seen as an encouragement to young American women to "go for the gold" in whatever they do. Fleming retired from the competitive skating circuit immediately following the 1968 Olympics, although she appeared on several television skating specials in the 1970s. She continued skating in various professional events into the 1990s.

Fonda, Jane (1937–) *film actress, activist*

As the daughter of popular film star and liberal Democrat Henry Fonda, Jane Fonda was a Vassar College dropout who tried to make a living at both painting and writing before turning to her father's profession. First appearing with her father in summer stock theater in the late 1950s, Fonda's embarrassing performances prompted her to study acting at the Actor's Studio in New York. In 1960, she played a rape victim in her first Broadway role, and in her first film role (also in 1960), she played a teenage temptress. For years, none of her performances won critical acclaim, but that changed in 1965 with her role in the satirical western *Cat Ballou*. Following her marriage to French film director Roger Vadim, Fonda starred in cheaply made erotic films in France before landing the lead in Vadim's internationally released *Barbarella* (1968). This bizarre space fantasy had Fonda playing, once again, a temptress, but, this time, her film was a box office hit. While in Paris, she became fascinated with the growing youth protest and antiwar movements there. Following her divorce from Vadim, she returned to the United States and became one of the country's high-profile spokespersons for a variety of antiestablishment causes. In 1970, she donated much of her film career earnings to the Black Panthers, antiwar groups, and the American Indian Movement (AIM). Upon her marriage to Students for a Democratic Society (SDS) founder Tom Hayden, Fonda traveled to Hanoi and spoke out against "American war crimes" in Vietnam. This 1972 trip was considered outrageous and even treasonous by some American moderates and conservatives, but she abandoned the activist's life in the 1980s and 1990s.

Friedan, Betty (Bettye A. Goldstein) (1921–)
feminist leader

Born and raised in Peoria, Illinois, Bettye N. Goldstein graduated from Smith College with a degree in psychology. Her writing skills were honed while working as editor of the Smith student paper, and she worked briefly as a reporter in New York. Marrying Carl Friedan in 1947, she abandoned her career goals in favor of housewife chores and motherhood. Grossly unhappy with her new life, she asked other women (mostly fellow Smith graduates) if they also rejected the male-defined role of the housewife. Their answers, combined with an in-depth research effort of six years in the making, resulted in her 1963 book *The Feminine Mystique*. The book represented the feminist complaint against a male-dominated society. It also served as a springboard for the biggest resurgence in women's rights activism since the days of the Nineteenth Amendment more than 40 years earlier. Quickly recognized as the leading spokesperson for women's rights issues, Friedan helped found the National Organization for Women (NOW) in 1966 and the National Abortion Rights League three years later. Her well-organized national demonstration in favor of women's issues (The Women's Strike for Equality) in 1970 helped publicize the growing strength of the feminist cause. Friedan continued her activist role in succeeding years, adding the problems of the elderly to her list of concerns as well.

Ginsberg, Allen (1926–1997) *poet, counterculture advocate*

The homosexual son of a professional poet and communist activist, Allen Ginsberg always saw himself as a rebel, loner, and antiestablishment figure. Fascinated by literature that expressed how he felt, Ginsberg, while still a young Columbia University student, surrounded himself with poets and literary activists who shared the same disgust with the status quo. Nicknamed the "Beat Generation," Ginsberg and his colleagues already had a national audience before the 1960s. During the early 1960s, Ginsberg began to study Eastern religions, traveled to India, grew his hair long, and returned to the United States with what would soon be regarded as the trademark look of the counterculture adherent. An early antiwar activist and spokesman, Ginsberg even praised the use of psychedelic drugs. Although his speeches in favor of the counterculture life of "tune out and turn on"

could gather thousands, Ginsberg still regarded himself as a poet and not a leftist political figure. His writing talent and contributions finally won him a slew of literary awards in the 1970s and 1980s. Ginsberg died in 1997.

Goldwater, Barry (1909–1998) *conservative leader, 1964 Republican nominee for president*

The son of a department store chain owner in Arizona, Goldwater used his inheritance to finance his first Republican campaigns and boost the tiny Arizona Republican party as well. Elected to the Senate in 1952, Goldwater led the conservative fight against Democratic-stimulated fiscal policies. Also in charge of the Senate's Republican Campaign Committee, Goldwater helped finance a number of conservative races across the country. By 1960, the *Washington Post* already called him "Mr. Conservative," and Richard Nixon's defeat to John Kennedy put even grander focus on Goldwater's efforts to unify conservative forces in his party. His 1962 best-seller, *Conscience of a Conservative*, defined 1960s conservatism as anticommunist, pro-individual, and anti–"Big Government." It served as the ideological foundation for his 1964 race for the presidency, and his loyal conservative supporters gave him state-by-state primary victories in that race. Although his general appeal was weak in the face of successful New Frontier and Great Society programs, Goldwater won the Republican nomination. Poor campaigning decisions and the inability to moderate his views further harmed his conservative challenge. Although he won less than 39 percent of the vote, Goldwater was soon seen as an honest, no-nonsense conservative whose message had been misunderstood. Becoming a legend and icon to conservative politicos ranging from Ronald Reagan to Pat Buchanan, Goldwater and his lost 1964 campaign became a rallying cry for the Conservative Revolution of the 1970s and 1980s. Goldwater died in 1998.

Gregory, Dick (1932–) *comedian, civil rights and antiwar activist*

Born and raised in the African-American ghetto of St. Louis, Gregory became one of Missouri's greatest track stars. He attended Southern Illinois University briefly, served in the U.S. Army in the mid-1950s, but drifted into menial jobs for years. Since he had an amazing knack for turning issues of racial tension into humorous escapades, his fellow workers urged him to audition for stand-up comedian jobs in nightclubs. He became a club scene favorite, as well as the first comedian who dared to poke fun at both white racists and civil rights leaders at the same time. His act was soon discovered by TV executives, and his career took off in the early 1960s. Martin Luther King, Jr., complimented Gregory for his ability to laugh at racial strife, inviting him to play a leadership role in his civil rights marches. In the mid-1960s, Gregory helped organize most the major civil rights demonstrations of the day and soon turned to anti–Vietnam War activism as well. His fasts of 40 and then 45 days in protest of the war won him great national attention. He ran as a "peace candidate" for mayor of Chicago, and, in 1968, he became the presidential candidate of the university campus-led Peace and Freedom Party. The author of several books on political activism, Gregory formally abandoned stand-up comedy in 1970. He continued to lecture at college campuses but became a successful natural health foods promoter and businessman in the 1980s.

Hayden, Tom (1940–) *Students for a Democratic Society founder, California politician*

Brought up in an activist household, Hayden developed an obvious respect for the challenges of political change at an early age. As a university student fascinated with reform movements ranging from Catholic humanism to traditional Marxism and even Jeffersonianism, Hayden provided the ideological impetus for the Students for a Democratic Society (SDS). Defined by their 1962 Port Huron Statement, Hayden and his SDS colleagues believed that a new democracy was required in America. Within it, each citizen would be required to assist in the betterment of their community, fight racism and poverty, reject the cold war, and challenge the business elite. Inspired by some of the speeches of John Kennedy as well as the writings of Henry Thoreau and Jean-Paul Sartre, Hayden helped establish the American New Left. His SDS dominated university student governments during the height of the antiwar demonstrations, but it suffered from endless ideological debates over the place of violence in social and political change. Hayden found these debates impossible to resolve, and he soured on his own creation as early as 1969. He later married activist actress Jane Fonda and then drifted into Democratic politics. Becoming one of the longest-sit-ting state senators in the history of the California legislature, Hayden also turned to historical writing, completing a book on Irish immigration.

Hendrix, Jimi (John Allen Hendrix, James Marshall Hendrix) (1942–1970) *rock guitarist, songwriter*

Born in Seattle as John Allen Hendrix, Jimi Hendrix was renamed James Marshall Hendrix three years later. He learned to play guitar at the age of 12 and was inspired by the talent and onstage antics of blues artists such as Muddy Waters and Aaron Walker. Following service in the U.S. Army, Hendrix took a number of backup guitarist jobs for some of the leading African-American singers of the day (including Wilson Pickett and Little Richard). Moving to Britain in 1966, Hendrix formed his own band, the Jimi Hendrix Experience. Releasing three albums between 1967 and 1969, Hendrix identified with the U.S. counterculture more than most musicians at the time. He was increasingly fascinated by psychedelic drugs and eager to sing about experiences with them. Soon his unique guitar sound and voice was labeled "acid rock." He received great criticism for his interpretation of the "Star-Spangled Banner" at the 1969 Woodstock festival, but to his admirers it capped his reputation as an antiestablishment icon. Declared dead of "barbiturate intoxication" in September 1970, Hendrix had just formed a new group (The Band of Gypsies) and allegedly planned to attend the Juilliard School of Music.

Hoover, J. Edgar (1895–1972) *Federal Bureau of Investigation director*

The son of Swiss immigrants, Hoover spent nearly all of his life in Washington, D.C. In 1917, he became part of the U.S. Justice Department's new effort to boost its World War I surveillance operation. That operation was soon called the Federal Bureau of Investigation (FBI), and by 1924 Hoover was in charge of it. Although Hoover's tasks were supposed to stress the pursuit of those who commit federal crimes, he never forgot his days as a young surveillance operative. A political conservative who worried that America's reform movements were, in fact, run by communist sympathizers, Hoover launched electronic and traditional surveillance operations against 1960s civil rights leaders, antiwar activists, liberal Democrats, or anyone he deemed a "subversive influence." In

1969, he wiretapped more than a dozen journalists believed to be in possession of Vietnam War–related secrets. The discovery of these taps resulted in a national debate over the power and privilege of the reclusive FBI director and his definition of "subversive" activities. Although the integrity of the FBI was seriously hurt by this debate, Hoover refused to step down or reform the FBI. His death in May 1972 led to years of redefining and modernizing FBI operations.

Hughes, Howard (1905–1976) tycoon, aviator

A shy, quiet man, Hughes inherited his father's multi-million-dollar tool company at the age of 20. While investing this money wisely, Hughes became one of the country's top aviators and plane designers. His other interests ranged from producing Hollywood films to politics, but aviation remained close to this billionaire's heart. During his weeks of recovery upon crashing his own XF-11 experimental aircraft, Hughes became addicted to morphine. This addiction led to other drug abuse problems as well, influencing his decision to remain far away from the public eye. By 1965, he was considered America's richest man. Recluse or not, Hughes continued to build an unassailable empire. His Hughes Aircraft Corporation was one of the more successful companies of the 1960s. Meanwhile, his Hughes Research Laboratory built the first laser in 1963, and his Hughes Electronics firm supplied the world's best communications equipment to the NASA moon flights. By the late 1960s, Hughes's behavior became more and more bizarre. Suffering from a variety of phobias, he left his long-time Las Vegas home for the Bahamas in 1970. He died six years later.

Humphrey, Hubert (1911–1978) Minnesota politician, vice president, the 1968 Democratic presidential nominee

Born in tiny Wallace, South Dakota, Humphrey owed his liberal political philosophy to prairie populism, his pharmacist father's admiration of Woodrow Wilson, and the influence of the Great Depression. While studying at Louisiana State University, Humphrey was shocked by the poverty and struggle of the African Americans he met there. He returned home to Minnesota dedicated to ending racism, uplifting the downtrodden, and furthering the cause of Wilsonian-like reform. As the first Democrat elected from Min-

nesota to the U.S. Senate, Humphrey insisted that his agenda was not a lofty one. His exuberant speaking style, photographic memory, optimism, and good humor won him the nickname the "Happy Warrior." But his challenge to John Kennedy for the White House failed in 1960. One of Humphrey's political mentors, Lyndon Johnson, selected him for vice president in 1964. Although his liberal reformist credentials remained intact, Humphrey's continued support for the Vietnam War during the heyday of the antiwar protests alienated him from the liberal wing of the Democratic Party. Privately, this shocked and frustrated him, but he responded much too slowly to his critics. Humphrey broke with Johnson on the war in the last days of his 1968 presidential race against Richard Nixon. He lost in one of the closest presidential contests in U.S. history. Humphrey went on to challenge Senator George McGovern for the Democratic presidential nomination four years later but lost again. Despite ill health, Humphrey was elected to a fifth term in the Senate but died shortly afterward in 1978.

Iacocca, Lee (Lido Anthony Iacocca) (1924–) automotive executive

Born Lido Anthony Iacocca in Allentown, Pennsylvania, Iacocca graduated from Princeton University with a degree in mechanical engineering. Working his way up the Ford corporate ladder from engineering trainee to sales manager, Iacocca won the attention of Robert McNamara, Ford's young general manager in the late 1950s. Hired to restore decent sales and produce exciting new products for the then struggling Ford Motor Company, McNamara surrounded himself with innovative designers and sales experts. When McNamara accepted the role of defense secretary in the Kennedy administration, Iacocca succeeded him as Ford general manager. During the mid-1960s, Iacocca's sporty Ford Mustang broke all post–World War II automobile sales records in the United States, creating the "pony car" craze soon adopted by competitors General Motors and Chrysler. Iacocca's follow-up Mercury Cougar and Lincoln Mark III also broke 1960s sales records and won Ford a slew of automobile achievement awards. But Iacocca's relationship with the Ford family soured in the 1970s, leading to his 1978 dismissal. Quickly hired by Chrysler to rescue their collapsing company, Iacocca's fuel-efficient "K Car" accomplished that rescue within two years. His corporate innovations were the subjects of 1980s best-sellers, and both political parties urged him to accept senior government posts. Some Democrats even asked him to run for president. He rejected these invitations, preferring to remain, he insisted, a "car guy."

Jackson, Jesse (1941–) *civil rights advocate*
Born in Greenville, South Carolina, Jackson won a football scholarship to attend the University of Illinois. Due to racist guidelines that forbade African Americans from playing quarterback for that football team, Jackson dropped out. Instead, he played quarterback for the football team at North Carolina Agricultural and Technical State College. It was there that he discovered his talent for civil rights work, and he became the college's student government president. Jackson joined Martin Luther King's Southern Christian Leadership Conference (SCLC) shortly afterward. On behalf of the SCLC, he organized the nonviolent school desegregation movement in Chicago. Admired for his organizational skills, King selected Jackson to head Operation Breadbasket in Illinois and elsewhere. Designed to accent black pride and bring struggling African Americans into economic self-sufficiency, Operation Breadbasket was a success under Jackson's leadership. Using the upbeat motto "I Am Somebody," Jackson's probusiness efforts offered a different focus to the civil rights cause. Following King's assassination in 1968, Jackson hoped to be named King's successor at the SCLC. Largely because he was only in his 20s at the time, Jackson was passed over in favor of Ralph Abernathy. In the 1970s, Operation Breadbasket expanded to become Operation PUSH (People United to Save Humanity). The so-called Rainbow Coalition (the different races and ethnic groups who supported PUSH) served as the foundation for Jackson's 1984 and 1988 efforts to win the Democratic nomination for president.

Johnson, Lyndon Baines (1908–1973) *36th president of the United States*
Born on a farm in south Texas, Lyndon Johnson worked as a schoolteacher in an impoverished district during his youth. That experience, combined with the economic struggles of rural Texas, forever influenced his political philosophy of generous government and reform. First elected to Congress in 1937, Johnson considered Franklin Roosevelt his "political papa." A strong believer in government activism on behalf of the have-nots, Johnson also enjoyed the wheeling-dealing nature of congressional lawmaking. Elected to the Senate in 1948, he became the majority leader only five years later. Running for president in 1960, Johnson was shocked to come in second behind John Kennedy at the Democratic convention. But Kennedy needed Johnson's political skills in the general election, and Johnson agreed to serve in the vice presidential slot. Although he disagreed with Kennedy's overly cautious approach in dealing with Congress, Johnson remained loyal to the president's New Frontier agenda. That agenda was transformed into Johnson's own Great Society program following the Kennedy assassination, winning great legislative success for Kennedy's lingering measures in civil rights, health care, and other matters. Johnson's military escalation of the Vietnam War diverted his attentions from his ambitious domestic plans. The growing revulsion in his own party against the war led to Johnson's March 1968 decision for an early retirement. Following his presidency, Johnson returned to the teaching profession (serving at the University of South Texas) and died only hours before President Nixon announced the final U.S. military withdrawal from South Vietnam. He died in 1973.

Joplin, Janis (Janis Lyn Joplin) (1943–1970) *rock singer*
Janis Lyn Joplin was born into a Republican and Christian fundamentalist family in south Texas. Although considered a gifted student with a promising academic future, Joplin was a maverick and loner who had already experimented with drugs before she left high school. Attracted to blues singing and the counterculture lifestyle, Joplin joined the San Francisco–based rock group Big Brother and the Holding Company in 1966. By 1968, their first album, *Cheap Thrills,* was a surprise success. Joplin's onstage performances also brought her quick fame. She talked to her audiences, boosting that a white girl could sing African-American blues music. She often brought a bottle of hard liquor with her to the stage as well and punctuated her blues-rock songs with shrill screams. In 1970, she formed a new group, Full-Tilt Boogie, but died of a heroin overdose shortly after recording another album. Her unique brand of music and self-destructive lifestyle has fascinated rock fans for years.

Kennedy, Edward Moore (Ted Kennedy)
(1932–   ) *Massachusetts senator*

The fourth son of multimillionaire and former ambassador Joseph P. Kennedy, Edward Moore Kennedy graduated from Harvard University in 1956. It was his second attempt to graduate. Kennedy had been expelled from the school five years earlier. By 1960, while working in his brother John's presidential campaign, Kennedy had opened his own law firm in Massachusetts. In November 1962, Kennedy (nicknamed "Ted") won a landslide election to the U.S. Senate in spite of heavy criticism in the New England press over his lack of political experience. In contrast to John and Robert Kennedy, Ted Kennedy enjoyed his congressional work and built a strong reputation as a liberal legislator. Following the assassinations of his older brothers, Kennedy faced great political pressures. Most Democratic activists, and much of the press, assumed that he was the early front-runner for the 1972 presidential nomination. After the 1969 drowning death of former Robert Kennedy campaign worker Mary Jo Kopechne in a car driven by Ted Kennedy, his presidential aspirations were destroyed for years. His 1980 primary challenge to President Jimmy Carter divided the Democratic Party and only served to assist the successful Republican campaign of Ronald Reagan. Although the country's political mood continued to move to the right, Kennedy remained a hard-working liberal senator, who helped pass groundbreaking legislation in immigration/refugee law and health care reform.

Kennedy, Jacqueline (Jacqueline L. Bouvier, Jacqueline Kennedy Onassis) (1929–1994)
first lady

Born into a wealthy Franco-American family in New York, Jacqueline L. Bouvier was a socialite and photojournalist when she married Senator John Kennedy in 1953. Proud of her French background, Mrs. Kennedy had studied at the Sorbonne in Paris. Her husband was almost 13 years older, and she had little use for national politics. Once in the White House, the first lady was praised in the press for her beauty, grace, and lavish social gatherings. Her daily dress set fashion trends across the United States, and her 1962 televised tour of the White House was the first of its kind. A strong patron of the arts, Mrs. Kennedy invited classical musicians to the White House as well. Although her marriage suffered thanks to her husband's infidelities, she

had two children. Throughout the early 1960s, Americans remained fascinated by their charismatic first family. Mrs. Kennedy was heavily responsible for the royalist or Camelot image accorded to the New Frontier. Her discipline and control during the funeral for her assassinated husband further impressed the country, but her 1968 marriage to Greek tycoon Aristotle Onassis surprised her admirers. Kennedy later worked as an editor for Doubleday publishing and died of cancer in May 1994.

Kennedy, John Fitzgerald (1917–1963) *35th president of the United States*

The second son of multimillionaire and former ambassador Joseph P. Kennedy, John Fitzgerald Kennedy was a World War II–Pacific naval hero and Harvard graduate with a gift for political rhetoric. Representing a working-class district of Boston for six years before winning election to the U.S. Senate in 1953, Kennedy published the Pulitzer Prize–winning *Profiles in Courage* in the mid-1950s and ran unsuccessfully for the vice presidential nomination at the 1956 Democratic convention. The positive visibility gained from his 1956 spotlight served as a springboard for his 1960 race for the presidency. Defeating some of the luminaries of his party, Kennedy promised great change. He was one of the first presidential candidates to use television as a political tool, and his speaking skills and good looks played as much a role in his victory over Vice President Richard Nixon as his call for "new directions" in domestic and foreign policy making. Once in the White House, Kennedy moved slowly on civil rights reform, but he was plagued by a series of foreign policy crises over Berlin, Soviet missiles in Cuba, and communist inroads in Southeast Asia. His November 1963 assassination shocked the nation, elevated his 1,000 days in office to legendary proportions, and led many to believe that he was the victim of an elaborate conspiracy.

Kennedy, Robert Francis (1925–1968) *attorney general of the United States, New York senator, 1968 presidential candidate*

The third son of multimillionaire and former ambassador Joseph P. Kennedy, Robert Francis Kennedy was a 1951 University of Virginia Law School graduate who spent much of the 1950s with the U.S. Justice Department or as a lawyer to the Senate Investigations Committee. His 1959 book, *The Enemy Within,* exposed the role of organized crime in the labor movement and other organizations. Following his stint as director of John Kennedy's successful presidential campaign, Robert Kennedy served as attorney general. Although dedicated to the enforcement of civil rights law, Robert Kennedy also served as an adviser to his older brother on most significant matters of policy. At odds with John Kennedy's successor, President Lyndon Johnson, over a variety of issues, Robert Kennedy left his post in favor of a successful 1964 race for a New York Senate seat. Becoming increasingly liberal as the months went by, Kennedy ran for president in 1968 as a staunch opponent to the Vietnam War. After a slow start and significant opposition from early antiwar candidate Senator Eugene McCarthy, Kennedy appeared destined for the Democratic nomination following a slew of primary victories. He was assassinated on June 5, 1968, at Los Angeles's Ambassador Hotel.

Khrushchev, Nikita S. (1894–1971) *Soviet premier*
Born into an illiterate peasant family near the Ukrainian border, Khrushchev began working in a factory before his teens. At age 18, he was already a labor organizer and strike leader but did not join the Bolshevik Party until the Russian civil war. Becoming a young protégé of Joseph Stalin in the Ukraine, Khrushchev worked his way up through the Soviet bureaucracy. Following Stalin's death in 1953, Khrushchev competed in the power scramble to replace him and won. Although he owed his career to the oppressive Stalinist regime, he denounced that oppression in the late 1950s. Insisting that the cold war confrontation with the United States had gone far enough, Khrushchev said that the row with the United States had distracted Soviet policy makers from taking care of their own people. He promised "peaceful coexistence" with the Americans and humane policies at home. But the resulting anti-Soviet movements in Eastern Europe were crushed under his orders. Misjudging the competence of President Kennedy, Khrushchev triggered World War III–threatening crises over the future of Germany and Cuba. In the United States, his "We Will Bury You" against the capitalist West symbolized the continuing tyranny of communism. But Khrushchev returned to his original "peaceful coexistence" mission when he signed the 1963 Nuclear Test Ban Treaty with John Kennedy. That

treaty outraged old-line Stalinist and staunchly anti-American members of Khrushchev's own government, leading to the crusty premier's ousting from power in 1964. He died seven years later.

King, Martin Luther, Jr. (1929–1968) *Civil Rights movement leader*
A 1948 sociology graduate from Morehouse College and a 1955 graduate in divinity studies from Boston University, Martin Luther King, Jr., won numerous awards for his speaking skills throughout his student life. The son and grandson of Baptist ministers, King was destined to follow in their footsteps. During the mid-1950s, he became the pastor of Dexter Avenue Baptist Church in Montgomery, Alabama, and led that city's first boycott against segregated businesses. A cofounder of the nonviolent Southern Christian Leadership Conference (SCLC) in 1957, King became America's most recognized civil rights spokesman. From Albany, Georgia, to Birmingham, Alabama, King supported nonviolent actions against legalized racism in the early 1960s. Both morally and legally supported by the Kennedy and Johnson administrations, King's efforts became linked to Democratic Party–sponsored civil rights reforms. His 1963 March on Washington represented the height of his oratorical skill and demonstrated the power of his appeal to African Americans everywhere. Once reluctant to speak out against the Vietnam War because of his political attachments to Washington policy makers, King joined the antiwar cause against the wishes of some of his advisers. Although King's civil rights leadership was challenged by young black radicals who favored a violent path to change, he remained the central force in the fight against racism. His April 1968 assassination in Memphis left the Civil Rights movement in a power vacuum from which it never fully recovered.

Kissinger, Henry (1923–   ) *academic, National Security Council Advisor, secretary of state*
The son of German refugees from the Hitler regime, Kissinger received both his Ph.D. and his first teaching job from Harvard University. An admirer of historical figures known for their diplomatic skill and maneuvering, such as Austria's Prince Metternich or Germany's Otto von Bismarck, Kissinger believed that U.S. foreign policy needed to be less rigid and more flexible. A foreign policy consultant to the Kennedy and Johnson administrations, as well as to the 1968 Rockefeller for

President campaign, Kissinger joined the Nixon administration as its National Security Council adviser in early 1969. In favor of peace deals with America's nuclear war-threatening opponents (the Soviet Union and China), but continuing the anticommunist mission in developing nations, Kissinger changed the rules of cold war confrontation. His clever, unique diplomacy excited the press, and many Americans assumed he was the secretary of state because of it. But he did not become secretary of state until 1973 when U.S. forces withdrew from South Vietnam. He remained in that position until 1977, later published books about his White House days, and became a foreign affairs consultant to a number of television networks.

Leary, Timothy (1920–1996) *Harvard researcher, drug use advocate*

Expelled from a number of schools (including West Point), Leary was a maverick and loner who advocated new approaches in the field of psychology. Appointed to lead Harvard University's Psychedelic Research Project in 1959, Leary studied the influence of LSD and other potent drugs within a group therapy format. Counterculture icon Allen Ginsberg was one of several well-known figures to take part in Leary's experiments. In the mid-1960s, Leary's conversion to Hinduism led him to declare that psychedelic drug use was both a helpful and religious experience for all who accepted his approach to therapy. The resulting controversy over his news conferences on this issue led to Leary's removal from the Harvard faculty. But he continued to preach his cause of clinical psychology reform from a new research lab in New York. His championing of drug use won a public endorsement by the Beatles, but Leary annoyed parents, law officials, and politicians no end. Forever in trouble with the police for drug possession, Leary fled to the Middle East in the early 1970s, was extradited from Afghanistan in the mid-1970s, but was paroled shortly afterward. In the 1980s, he entered the budding and lucrative field of computer software research, and he died in Beverly Hills of prostate cancer in May 1996.

Lombardi, Vince (1913–1970) *football coach*

Born in Brooklyn to Italian Catholic immigrants, Lombardi played football for New York's Fordham University and coached high school football for several years. He also coached at West Point, where he learned a healthy respect for military discipline and precision. His first professional coaching job was with the New York Giants in the mid-1950s, but he became general manager and coach of the Green Bay Packers in 1959. A struggling, losing team, the Packers were rebuilt thanks to Lombardi's accent on physical and mental conditioning. Under his leadership, the Packers became the most victorious team in 1960s professional football, winning five NFL championships in seven years and the first two Superbowls of 1967 and 1968. Famous for his inspirational quips, Lombardi insisted that winning was "everything" and that "moral victories are for losers." Following a brief retirement, he returned to coaching in 1969, leading the Washington Redskins through their best season in many years. He died of cancer in September 1970.

McCarthy, Eugene (1916–   ) *1968 antiwar candidate for president, Minnesota senator*

Born in Watkins, Minnesota, Eugene McCarthy taught English at both the high school and university levels for a decade. Elected to the House of Representatives in 1948 as a Democratic-Farmer-Labor Party candidate, McCarthy maintained a staunchly independent voting record. His maverick reputation only assisted in his election to the Senate in 1958. Rather conservative on the domestic social issues of the day but opposed to America's anticommunist crusade, McCarthy became an early critic of the Vietnam War. Running for president on a 1968 antiwar platform, McCarthy challenged Lyndon Johnson's reelection. His respectable showing in the New Hampshire primary played a significant role in Johnson's decision to retire from politics. Hoping that young antiwar campaigners would serve as his springboard to the presidency, McCarthy ran an unusual presidential primary campaign. He was opposed by fellow Democrats Robert Kennedy and Hubert Humphrey. Although he failed to win the nomination, McCarthy's bold stand against the war and the Johnson wing of his party won him the admiration of antiestablishment youth. McCarthy left the Senate in 1970, ran a largely ignored independent campaign for president in 1976, and worked in the publishing field for many years.

McGovern, George (1922–   ) *1972 Democratic presidential nominee, South Dakota senator, antiwar leader*

Born into a poor but strict Methodist family, George McGovern graduated from Illinois's Northwestern

University with a Ph.D. in history. Winner of the Distinguished Flying Cross, McGovern was one of South Dakota's most decorated World War II heroes. He taught history at Dakota Wesleyan University throughout the early 1950s and, following his rebuilding of the South Dakota Democratic Party, was elected to the House of Representatives in 1956. While serving as President Kennedy's director of the Food for Peace program in Vietnam, McGovern soured on the U.S. mission there. Elected to the Senate in 1962, McGovern soon became an outspoken critic of U.S. policy throughout Southeast Asia. A coalition of former Robert Kennedy and Eugene McCarthy supporters nominated him for president at the 1968 Democratic Party convention. He lost to Hubert Humphrey but quickly positioned himself as a Democratic liberal leader. Challenged by more moderate voices in his party, including Humphrey and Edmund Muskie, McGovern at first was given little chance to win the 1972 nomination. But his consistent antiwar message, combined with proposed reforms in social policy, galvanized the liberal wing of his party. He won the nomination handily but lost the general election in a sweeping landslide to President Nixon. McGovern abandoned the political life following his 1980 defeat for a fourth Senate term. He reemerged years later on the speaker's circuit as an opponent to Operation Enduring Freedom and President George W. Bush's policies in the Middle East.

McLuhan, Marshall (1911–1980) *media expert*
Born in Edmonton, Alberta, McLuhan, a Canadian citizen, had a profound impact on how Americans viewed the growing impact of television in the 1960s. Interested in the interweaving of technology and literature since the 1940s, McLuhan founded *Explorations,* a journal dedicated to studying the role of what he called "mass media" in modern life and culture. By the early 1960s, he was the recognized authority on the subject, and he wrote four well-received books. *The Medium Is the Message* (1967) helped define his views. Predicting that television and the computer would soon replace books and print press as the primary source of information, McLuhan saw the 1960s as the beginning of a new era. His vision and ideas prompted a great deal of debate and discussion, but the excitement over his work faded quickly in the 1970s. McLuhan had enjoyed the limelight, but the lack of press attention for his work had

an unfortunate impact on his state of mind and physical health. He died of a stroke in December 1980.

McNamara, Robert (1916–) *Ford Motor Company executive, secretary of defense, World Bank president*
A gifted student of economics and business administration, Robert McNamara became a business professor at Harvard University at the age of 24. Immediately after his service in the Army Air Corps during World War II, McNamara rose through the ranks of the Ford Motor Company. He had been director of the company for less than a year when John Kennedy asked him to serve as secretary of defense. At the age of 44, McNamara typified the brilliant work hard/play hard cabinet member of the Kennedy administration. Expected to revamp the Defense Department and control its spending habits at the same time, McNamara approached his difficult task with a Kennedyesque can-do commitment. His navy quarantine proposal helped resolve the Cuban Missile Crisis of 1962, and his commitment to a strong military response in South Vietnam influenced Presidents Kennedy and Johnson's Southeast Asian policies. Nevertheless, by 1967 McNamara urged a negotiated settlement for Vietnam. He resigned from his post in early 1968 due to disagreements with President Johnson over Tet Offensive developments. Accepting the directorship of the World Bank, McNamara refused to talk to the press about Vietnam for many years. He retired in the 1980s, later writing two books stressing his Vietnam experiences. The books rekindled a late 1990s debate in academe and the press over Vietnam decision making.

Malcolm X (Malcolm Little, El-Hajj Malik El-Shabazz) (1925–1965) *Nation of Islam spokesperson, black separatist*
Born Malcolm Little in Omaha, Nebraska, Malcolm changed his last name to "X" while serving time in prison for burglary. The "X" symbolized the dehumanization of slavery. It was in prison that Malcolm converted to the Nation of Islam. In the early 1960s, Malcolm's organizational savvy and gift for oratory was responsible for the growing popularity of the black Muslims in African-American neighborhoods. Malcolm and the Nation of Islam stressed the liberation of African Americans from a continued cycle of white oppression. Martin Luther King, Jr.'s nonvio-

lence approach was rejected, and by 1963 Malcolm was considered the most important African-American leader next to King himself. Following arguments with Nation of Islam leader Elijah Muhammad, Malcolm bolted the group, visited Islamic holy places in the Middle East, and returned to the United States with a more tolerant and cooperative view toward whites and black King supporters. He changed his name to El-Hajj Malik El-Shabazz. Forming the organization of Afro-American Unity in 1964, Malcolm sought international support for his new views on patient change. In 1965, Malcolm was assassinated in New York. His supporters blamed their Nation of Islam rival for the murder, but no evidence was discovered to back up the charge.

Mantle, Mickey (1931–1995) *baseball player*
Quick, intense, and able to hit powerful home runs, Mantle became a New York Yankee at the age of 20. He also became the American League's home run king during his ninth season with the team. In 1961, President Kennedy dubbed him "America's best baseball player since Babe Ruth," and most fans agreed. During his frenetic 1960s career alone, Mantle played more than 2,400 games (a record). In public, Mantle warmed to the press and children, adding to his heroic status in the nation. In private, Mantle was tormented by on-the-job injuries and suffered from liver problems aggravated by years of alcoholism. Mantle retired in 1968, but the hero worship continued even beyond his August 1995 death.

Maris, Roger (1934–1985) *baseball player*
Born in the same small town as rock legend Bob Dylan (Hibbing, Minnesota), Maris was a gifted athlete who was invited to play football for the University of Oklahoma. Maris decided against both football and the university life. Instead, he joined the Cleveland Indians baseball team at the age of 19. Later, after a brief stint with the Kansas City Athletics, Maris was traded to the New York Yankees and began a home run hitting streak that continued for two years straight. In 1961, he even challenged Babe Ruth's one season record of 60 home runs, and he finally broke it in October of that year. Nevertheless, baseball experts and Babe Ruth fans pointed out that Maris's 61 home runs were hit in a 162-game season while Ruth's 60 came in a 154-game season. This did not diminish the Maris hero worship at the time. Maris never matched

his golden year of 1961 again, although he broke other records in 1962. He died of cancer in December 1985.

Max, Peter (1937–) *artist*
Although born in Germany, Max grew up in a variety of countries. This early globe-trotting experience influenced his painting, along with his fascination with Eastern religions. Max considered himself a modern realist painter, whereby everything from American cartoon strips to ancient Chinese drawings combined to define his personal style. That style first appeared in 1967 with his psychedelic posters of 1960s life. The Beatles loved his "cosmic world of art," selecting him to illustrate the cover of their *Yellow Submarine* album. Some American conservatives, namely Senator Everett Dirksen, considered Max a subversive influence who glorified psychedelic drug use through his art. But Max's mass-produced poster art was more of the capitalist success story than anything else, offering a view of the 1960s with a wild splash of color. As early as the 1970s, Max's art was forever linked to a flower child's portrait of a bygone era. In later years, Max painted on behalf of environmental activists and even the U.S. postal service.

Meredith, James (1933–) *civil rights advocate*
Born into a struggling African-American farming family from Mississippi, Meredith—like many young post–World War II African-American males—joined the military to escape poverty and build a new life. Meredith spent nine years with the U.S. Air Force before returning home to begin his university studies. His school of choice, however, the University of Mississippi, was a whites-only institution. His efforts to register there in 1962 sparked a race riot, forcing the Kennedy administration to take action on their many pro-civil rights promises. Meanwhile, Mississippi's governor, Ross Barnett, took a staunchly racist stance against Meredith, which lost him the support of moderate and even some conservative Mississippi voters. This experience prompted another segregationist governor, George Wallace of Alabama, to act more cautiously in his own race battles with the White House. President Kennedy ordered more than 23,000 troops to protect Meredith's enrollment, and Meredith won a heroic reputation in African-American communities for his refusal to attend school elsewhere. Meredith was a complex personality, and years

after his 1963 graduation, some questioned his motives during the violent confrontations at the University of Mississippi. In the 1980s, Meredith became the legislative assistant for domestic affairs to Republican conservative icon Senator Jesse Helms of North Carolina.

The Monkees (1965–1969) *television rock stars*
Hoping to cash in on the success of the Beatles's 1964 film, *A Hard Day's Night,* NBC cast an irreverent and hip half-hour situation comedy that showcased a Beatles-like rock band. Called the Monkees, actors David Jones, Mickey Dolenz, Peter Tork, and Michael Nesmith constituted this TV band. At first they had more acting than musical experience, and music fans who admired the maverick, antiestablishment character of 1960s rock bands criticized "corporate America's creation" of the Monkees. Heavy criticism or not, the television show was still a hit (1966–68), and so were songs like "Daydream Believer" and "Last Train to Clarksville." Led by Nesmith, the group found and accented their musical talent, continuing to surprise the critics and top the charts with new hits. By 1968, their audience proved quite fickle. Rock was changing, becoming influenced by the horrors of Vietnam and other headlines. The Monkees' television show was canceled and the band broke up in late 1969. In any event, numerous rock stars in later years claimed that the Monkees influenced their work. Like the Beach Boys, the group came to represent a certain innocent time in the evolution of American rock music.

Monroe, Marilyn (Norma Jeane Mortenson, Norma Jean Mortenson) (1926–1962) *actress, sex symbol*
Born Norma Jeane Mortenson in southern California, Monroe was a teenage model when she first auditioned for a Hollywood contract shortly after World War II. Thanks to her blond bombshell appearances in low-budget films, as well as by cheesecake and nude photos taken of her during her teenage modeling years, the young actress's career moved quickly to starring roles. Also appearing nude in the premier issue of *Playboy* magazine in 1953, Monroe was soon considered the sex queen of the decade. Starring roles in such films as *Gentleman Prefer Blondes* and *How to Marry a Millionaire* assured this status. Much of her career, however, depended upon

the fortunes of her contractor, Twentieth-Century Fox. This studio remained on the edge of bankruptcy in the early 1960s and fired Monroe thanks to her high absentee record during the making of a new film, *Something's Got to Give.* Monroe's blond bombshell character was also losing its luster to early 1960s audiences. Meanwhile, her private life was troubled by bad marriages and an increasing dependency on drugs. Her April 1962 singing of "Happy Birthday" at a New York party for President Kennedy even stimulated rumors of a Kennedy-Monroe affair. Monroe died in August 1962, and the official cause of death was declared an overdose of sleeping pills. Sensational studies were soon published, insisting that Monroe was the victim of elaborate conspiracies, while other writers remained fascinated by her tragic life. To some, Monroe would always represent the transition from the innocent 1950s to the hard-nosed reality of the 1960s.

Muskie, Edmund S. (1914–1996) *U.S. senator, 1968 Democratic vice presidential nominee, 1972 Democratic presidential candidate, secretary of state*
A lawyer from Rumford, Maine, Muskie served in both the Atlantic and the Pacific during World War II. Despite his heroic U.S. navy war record, Muskie lost his first race to become the mayor of Waterville, Maine. This unfortunate experience helped him hone his political skills, and he eventually served as governor and as a member of the House of Representatives. In 1958, he won his first Senate seat by a landslide. A passionate supporter of the New Frontier and Great Society, Muskie was considered a "workhorse liberal" in the Senate, but he distinguished himself from other liberals by his interest in environmental protection. His public hearings on water and air pollution brought great visibility to the issue in the mid-1960s and laid the foundation for the nation's first environmental legislation. His no-nonsense demeanor and reputation for honesty also won him the vice presidential nomination for the Democrats in 1968. Following the narrow defeat of the Humphrey-Muskie ticket to the Nixon campaign, Muskie emerged as a front runner for the 1972 Democratic nomination. As president, he promised careful reassessments of both domestic and foreign policies, but he lost the 1972 nomination to the antiwar candidacy of Senator George McGovern. In later years, Muskie spearheaded the foreign policy legisla-

tion of the Jimmy Carter administration in the Senate and, in 1980, won the job of secretary of state because of it. Muskie joined the pro-environment law firm of Chadwick and Parke in the 1980s, and he died in March 1996.

Nader, Ralph (1934–) *automobile safety advocate, environmentalist*
A graduate of the Harvard University School of Law, Nader began the 1960s teaching history courses for his alma mater. His investigation into the impact of automobile design on fatal accidents, published as *Unsafe at Any Speed* in 1965, won him quick national attention. The book accused a number of automobile manufacturers of deliberately designing cars that could kill people. He used the rear-engine Corvair, a product of General Motors (GM), as a strong example, and GM took offense at being singled out. Their harassment of Nader's further investigations hurt GM's public image. The Corvair, once considered America's answer to Germany's rear-engine Porsche, was canceled due to the lack of sales—only four years after *Unsafe at Any Speed* was published. Nader's success also led to the passing of the National Traffic and Motor Vehicle Safety Act, as well as other safety acts during 1968 and 1969. Beloved by safety-conscious consumers and environmentalists, Nader became more involved in national politics. Stressing environmental reform, Nader was an independent candidate for president in 1996 and 2000.

Nixon, Richard Milhous (1913–1994) *37th president of the United States*
Born and raised in Whittier, California, Nixon received his law degree from Duke University and served in the U.S. Navy during World War II. He won his first congressional seat just weeks after leaving the navy in 1946. From his early campaigns in the 1940s to his resignation from the presidency in 1974, Nixon dodged accusations of corruption and unethical behavior. He had won early national recognition because of his staunch anticommunism and investigations into the loyalties of executive branch officials. Serving as vice president throughout Dwight Eisenhower's two terms in office, Nixon traveled extensively and was admired for his foreign policy expertise. Failing to win both the U.S. presidency in 1960 and the California governorship in 1962, Nixon became a trade lawyer representing

Japanese companies hoping to break into U.S. markets. He used this time to study and prepare for his own political comeback. In 1968, he campaigned for president as the "New Nixon," who had learned from his many previous mistakes. His resulting presidential administration was dominated by the daunting task of ending the Vietnam War and realigning America's foreign policy in light of that military defeat. Intolerant of dissent and prepared to do anything on behalf of his 1972 reelection, Nixon covered up the Watergate break-in and might have authorized it as well. His August 1974 resignation and a special pardon authorized by President Gerald Ford spared him from further legal investigations. In succeeding years, former supporters and some historians attempted to resurrect Nixon's reputation as a competent foreign policy maker. Nevertheless, Nixon's long career remains a controversial one.

Oswald, Lee Harvey (1939–1963) *assassin*
Born in New Orleans, Oswald suffered from psychological traumas throughout his youth, struggled in school, and went through psychotherapy. Joining the U.S. Marines after entering a special program to complete the ninth grade, Oswald quickly asked for a special discharge in order to care for his impoverished and sick mother. Oswald headed to the Soviet Union instead, spent three years there, but was denied citizenship rights. Upon his return to the United States, Oswald worked for a pro-Castro group in New Orleans but later drifted to Dallas. On November 22, 1963, he was apprehended in downtown Dallas as the leading suspect in the assassination of President John Kennedy. Killed by nightclub owner Jack Ruby 48 hours after his arrest, Oswald was later declared the lone gunman by a special assassination investigation headed by Supreme Court Chief Justice Earl Warren. This swift investigation, combined with Oswald's mysterious past and conflicting eyewitness testimony at the scene of the crime, led to a myriad of assassination theories throughout the 1960s and beyond. A Gallup Poll of November 1968 indicated that a sizable majority of Americans, five years after the Kennedy killing, believed that Oswald did not act alone.

Powell, Adam Clayton, Jr. (1908–1972) *Harlem congressman, civil rights spokesman*
The son of a New York Baptist preacher, Powell became a civil rights advocate at a young age. Hold-

ing a master's degree from Columbia University, Powell followed in his father's footsteps and became a Baptist minister and pastor. From the pulpit, Powell championed the cause of civil rights reform before World War II. In 1944, Powell became the first African American in Congress to represent an East Coast district, and by 1961 he was the first African American to chair a congressional committee (Education and Labor). Criticized for his extravagant lifestyle, and while legislating landmark civil rights reform at the same time, Powell had a long list of enemies in both the white and African-American communities. Impeached and removed from his Harlem congressional seat in 1967 due to alleged fiscal improprieties, Powell fought hard to reestablish his good name. Winning a landslide election in 1968, Powell returned to Congress. The Supreme Court also declared his 1967 impeachment an illegal act. In ill health when he returned to Congress, Powell faded from the national limelight. He died in April 1972.

Presley, Elvis (1935–1977) *rock-and-roll pioneer*
Born into an impoverished family in Tupelo, Mississippi, Presley won singing/guitar talent contests when he was in his early teens. By the mid-1950s, his combination of country western, blues, and personal expression had already established him as a music sensation. His "Heartbreak Hotel" became a number-one hit in 1956, and, within a year, the press considered him a symbol of youth rebellion. By the 1960s, Presley was also a film star who shied away from the live concerts that had once made him famous. But his records continued to break all sales predictions, even though he moved away from rebellion and embraced a more generic, easy-listening style. Overshadowed by the British invasion of new rock groups of the mid-1960s, Presley made a dramatic comeback in a 1968 television special. Looking very much like the rebel of 10 years before, Presley recaptured the music world's attention once again. His 1969 hit "In the Ghetto" (written by Mac Davis) demonstrated that he had a social conscience as well, although he was criticized for being a latecomer to activist music. Using 1960s terminology, Presley said that his music would continue to evolve for he always did his "own thing." Presley's August 1977 death shocked his fans, although his drug abuse, obesity, and erratic behavior were widely reported in the press in the early and mid-1970s.

Quant, Mary (1934–) *clothing designer*
Born into a large family in Wales, Quant wore hand-me-down clothes as a child and early teen. Unhappy wearing old clothes, the young Quant resewed them to meet her own tastes. Those tastes developed further while she studied art in London, and in the mid-1950s she opened a small shop in the Chelsea section of London and sold unusual clothing. The store suffered financially, and Quant attempted to lure new customers with her own designs. Called the "Chelsea Girl" or "Mod" look, Quant's designs stressed the miniskirt. Usually worn by a thin woman dressed in high boots and a wide belt, the miniskirt often came with stripes and bright colors. One of her models, Leslie Hornsby, "Twiggy," became England and America's most popular model of the 1960s thanks to the Quant designs. Quant's clothes entered the U.S. retail business in the mid-1960s when J.C. Penney, a Milwaukee-based department store giant, decided to concentrate on the youth market. By 1966, Quant's miniskirt enjoyed record dress sales in the United States, sometimes symbolizing the sexual revolution of the decade. Quant's success was part of the British invasion of the 1960s, and she continued to work out of her Chelsea location into the 1990s.

Rockefeller, Nelson A. (1908–1979) *New York governor, 1968 Republican presidential candidate, vice president*
An heir to the Standard Oil fortune of John D. Rockefeller, Nelson Rockefeller was one of the 20th century's richest men. A graduate of Dartmouth College, Rockefeller worked in his family's business for a decade before turning to public service. Franklin Roosevelt appointed him assistant secretary of state for Latin America affairs, and he appeared to be destined to a life in the diplomatic corps. Instead, he kept his options open, becoming an adviser in both financial and foreign affairs to Presidents Truman and Eisenhower. Switching his attentions to social affairs in 1953, Rockefeller helped organize and direct the new Health, Education, and Welfare bureaucracy in Washington, D.C., and in 1958 he won the New York governorship on a liberal, social reform platform. It was an unusual platform for his increasingly conservative Republican Party. As governor, he supervised the effort to overhaul the state welfare system and passed the country's first pro-environment legislation. He especially endeared himself to academics nationwide

with his creation of the State University of New York (SUNY), a system dedicated to nontraditional students and with locations across the state. Running for president in 1968, Rockefeller attempted to position himself between the Right and the Left of both of the major parties but failed to win the Republican nomination. He later served as vice president under President Gerald Ford and then retired from politics in favor of full-time devotion to the arts. He died in January 1979.

Rusk, Dean (1909–1994) *secretary of state for Presidents Kennedy and Johnson*
Born and raised in rural Georgia, Rusk was a Rhodes Scholar who spent much of his working life in the State Department. As assistant secretary of state, Rusk observed the 1946 Fontainebleau Conference, where the French committed themselves to the reestablishment of their colonial empire in Southeast Asia. An early expert on Vietnam policy, Rusk believed that the United States had a moral obligation to assist noncommunist governments there. Tapped for his experience to be secretary of state by President Kennedy, Rusk felt out of place with the tight, inner circle of Harvard intellectuals in Kennedy's cabinet. Nevertheless, he helped resolve crises from Berlin to Cuba, and he recommended more and not less military involvement for the United States in Laos and Vietnam. His commitment to a strong military posture in Southeast Asia won great respect and recognition from President Johnson, but by early 1968 Rusk supported a negotiated peace in Vietnam. Despised by many academics for his pro–Vietnam War background, Rusk struggled to find an academic appointment following his tenure as secretary of state. He found a job at the law school of the University of Georgia in 1970 and retired 14 years later. He died shortly after publishing *As I Saw It,* a revealing memoir of his policy-making days.

Steinem, Gloria (1934–) *feminist leader, journalist*
An honors graduate from Smith College, Steinem was especially influenced by her humanist studies in India. A talented journalist who wrote both witty and serious articles about sexism and other challenges facing women in the workplace, Steinem won a quick reputation in the early 1960s as a trailblazing feminist writer. By 1968, her columns for *The New Yorker* and other magazines included endorsements for the anti-

war movement and civil rights causes. She proved to be an eloquent and sought-after lecturer on feminist issues, winning her a number of television interview spots and national attention. Honored at the 1972 Democratic convention as the true spokesperson for the modern women's movement, Steinem announced the creation of *Ms.,* a magazine solely dedicated to feminist concerns. Steinem went on to serve as director of a special commission established by President Jimmy Carter and dedicated to the rights of women. She then wrote her only best-seller, *Outrageous Acts and Everyday Rebellions,* in 1982. Although less active on the lecturing and television circuit than in the 1960s, Steinem continued to champion feminist causes into the 1990s.

Stevens, Brooks (1911–1995) *designer, Excalibur Motor Company founder*
The son of a wealthy Wisconsin-based industrialist, Stevens was a survivor of an early 20th-century polio epidemic. While recovering from the disease, he learned to draw and later studied design at Cornell University. Following graduation, he opened his own design studio in Milwaukee. His clients ranged from Harley-Davidson motorcycles to the Miller Brewery, and in 1958 he even designed the Wienermobile for the Oscar Meyer Company. But Stevens's love was automobiles, and by the early 1960s his automotive designs were sought by most of the leading car manufacturers of the United States, Germany, and Italy. In the early 1960s, he agreed to take over the design operation of the struggling Studebaker company of South Bend, Indiana. With the exception of Studebaker's Avanti car line, Stevens's influence was obvious in all Studebaker products. In 1964, Stevens proposed something wild and different to perk up Studebaker sales and national interest. Hence, a car that resembled an updated version of a 30-year-old Mercedes race car was delivered to the New York auto show as an example of the new Studebakers to come. Nevertheless, it was a little too wild and different for Studebaker, and Stevens, encouraged by his two sons William and David, founded a new company to build and sell the New York concept car. Called the Excalibur, the car soon became the "car of the stars" (Tony Curtis, Sonny and Cher, and other Hollywood luminaries), an example of 1960s wealth, status, and power. As luxurious as a Rolls-Royce and as fast as a Corvette, the Excalibur represented the height of U.S.

automotive technology and excess in the 1960s. The car's popularity waned during the oil crises of the late 1970s and because of changing status symbols. Stevens died in 1995.

Tiny Tim (Herbert Khaury) (1922–1996) *singer*
Born Herbert Khaury in New York, Tiny Tim was a falsetto-voiced singer who also played the ukulele. Inspired by obscure singer/ukulele groups of the 1920s and 1930s, Tiny Tim wore a mix and match of clothes from that period while performing. He also altered his deep voice to mimic the high-pitched and squeaky recordings of his favorite music. However, his odd act and music interests remained out of step with 1950s nightclub acts. Although well over six feet, Khaury called himself Tiny Tim, for he lived a spartan life similar to the Charles Dickens characters that he also admired. By the mid-1960s, Tiny Tim wore his hair extremely long, and his act had won a following of counterculture activists in New York's Greenwich Village. The producers of NBC's irreverent *Laugh-In* comedy hour discovered Tiny Tim singing in a coffee shop and invited him to sing his version of the early 1930s hit "Tiptoe Through the Tulips" on national television. Tiny Tim's bizarre performance created an odd fascination, making him a symbol of counterculture escapism to some and a circuslike figure to others. His recording of "Tiptoe Through the Tulips" became one of 1968's top hits, and his marriage on NBC's *Tonight Show* to a young counterculture fan, Victoria "Miss Vicky" Budinger, broke late-night TV records in 1969. Tiny Tim's fame was short-lived, however, and his career was forever linked to the counterculture experience of the late 1960s. He died in poverty in 1996.

Wallace, George C. (1919–1998) *Alabama governor, 1964, 1968, 1972, and 1976 presidential candidate*
The son of struggling south Alabama farmers, Wallace received a law degree from the University of Alabama while winning boxing titles across the state. A World War II veteran and even a district judge, Wallace followed in the footsteps of his political mentor, Governor "Big Jim" Folsom. Running for governor himself in 1958, Wallace emulated Folsom's New Deal–like approach to important issues. His political opposition accused him of being too liberal and too tolerant of Martin Luther King's civil rights successes in

Alabama. Wallace lost the 1958 election. Vowing never to be labeled liberal or pro–African American again, Wallace took a strong segregationist position that also criticized Washington's interference in Alabama affairs. His outspoken manner led to success in the next election for governor, and his nationally televised efforts to block the integration of the University of Alabama won him the support of those who believed that social change was moving too fast. Running for president in a handful of Democratic primaries in 1964, Wallace realized that his anti-Washington, anti-civil rights position had nationwide support. On his own American Independent Party ticket in 1968, he ran a much more vigorous campaign than he did in 1964. His efforts divided the Democratic Party and helped elect Republican Richard Nixon. During the next four years, Wallace moderated his rhetoric even further, but he did not abandon the anti–civil rights, anti–big government cause. An attempted assassination during the Maryland Democratic primary of 1972 left him paralyzed. Wallace's toned-down version of his 1960s presidential campaigns had been winning him wide support in 1972, but it was unlikely that the pro–civil rights Democratic Party would have granted him the nomination even if he had won a majority of primaries. In later years, Wallace had a change of heart on race-related issues, appointed African Americans to key positions in Alabama state government, and apologized to African-American leaders for his past behavior. Left in a great deal of pain from the attempted assassination, Wallace led a difficult life up to his 1998 death in Montgomery, Alabama.

Warhol, Andy (Andrew Warhola) (1928–1987) *artist*
Born Andrew Warhola in Pennsylvania, Andy Warhol was profoundly influenced by the economic struggles of the 1930s. Graduating from the Carnegie Institute of Technology with a degree in commercial art, Warhol worked as a commercial artist throughout much of the 1950s. In a bold change of career, Warhol became a freelance artist in the early 1960s. Focusing his work on such recognizable objects as a soup can presented in bright colors, Warhol's realistic, brightly illustrated, and no-nonsense work was labeled "pop art." Welcomed by some observers as the artist who provided the "look" of the 1960s but rejected by others for the same reason, Warhol was considered a controversial pioneer of artistic self-expression. His

colorful depictions of simple household items were a hit with Americans who had never appreciated art before. Meanwhile, he turned his attentions to film-making, promoting rock bands, and magazine publishing. He was almost killed in a shooting in June 1968, but he continued to influence the art world until his death in February 1987.

Warren, Earl (1891–1974) *Supreme Court chief justice*
A California progressive who was comfortable in both the Republican and Democratic Parties, Warren served as the 1940s governor of California. He was the Republican Party's pick for vice president in 1948 and made an ill-fated run for the presidency four years later. His work on behalf of the Eisenhower for President campaign at the 1952 Republican Party convention later led Eisenhower to appoint Warren chief justice of the Supreme Court. Dismissed by critics as a lackluster political appointee, Warren shocked his detractors by becoming one of Washington's leading voices on behalf of civil rights reform. According to Martin Luther King, Jr., Warren's landmark 1954 decision in favor of integration (*Brown v. Board of Education of Topeka*) formally established the modern Civil Rights movement. In the 1960s, Warren enjoyed majority support from the bench for sweeping reforms in civil rights and liberties, although congressional critics contemplated his impeachment due to

this alleged leadership of a "personal crusade." His investigation into the Kennedy assassination stimulated more confusion than answers to many observers. Using the law as a vehicle for social change, he insisted, always remained his top priority. Warren died at the height of the Watergate crisis in July 1974.

Young, Andrew Jackson (1932–) *civil rights leader, Democratic Party politician*
Born and raised in Louisiana, Young held a divinity degree from Hartford Theological Seminary and remained in the religious profession throughout much of the 1950s. Helping to organize the Citizenship Education Program in 1961, Young trained teachers to be civil rights activists in various locations across the South. Becoming more involved with Martin Luther King, Jr.'s, Southern Christian Leadership Conference (SCLC), Young participated in the major civil rights leadership protests of the 1960s. Demonstrating an early gift for negotiation and diplomacy, Young helped bring battling civil rights demonstrators and Southern city officials together on several occasions, and because of it, King made Young his executive assistant. Young continued in his mediation/diplomatic role after the King assassination in 1968 but entered Georgia politics two years later. Serving two terms in the U.S. Congress, Young later became President Jimmy Carter's United Nations ambassador and served as mayor of Atlanta in the 1980s.

APPENDIX C
Maps and Graphs

1. U.S. and USSR Nuclear Tests, 1945–1970
2. U.S. and USSR Nuclear Stockpile, 1945–1970
3. United States and Cuba, 1961–1962
4. Vietnam War, 1964–1975
5. U.S. Presidential Election: Electoral Vote, 1960
6. U.S. Presidential Election: Electoral Vote, 1964
7. U.S. Presidential Election: Electoral Vote, 1968

U.S. AND USSR NUCLEAR TESTS, 1945–1970

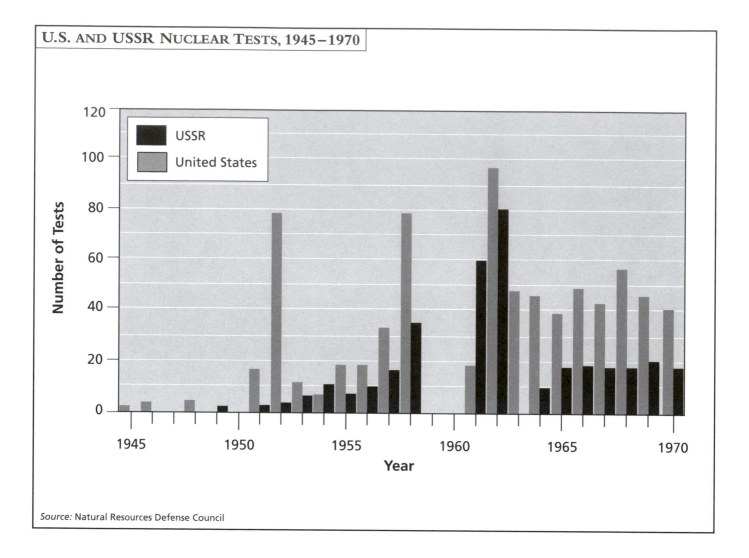

Source: Natural Resources Defense Council

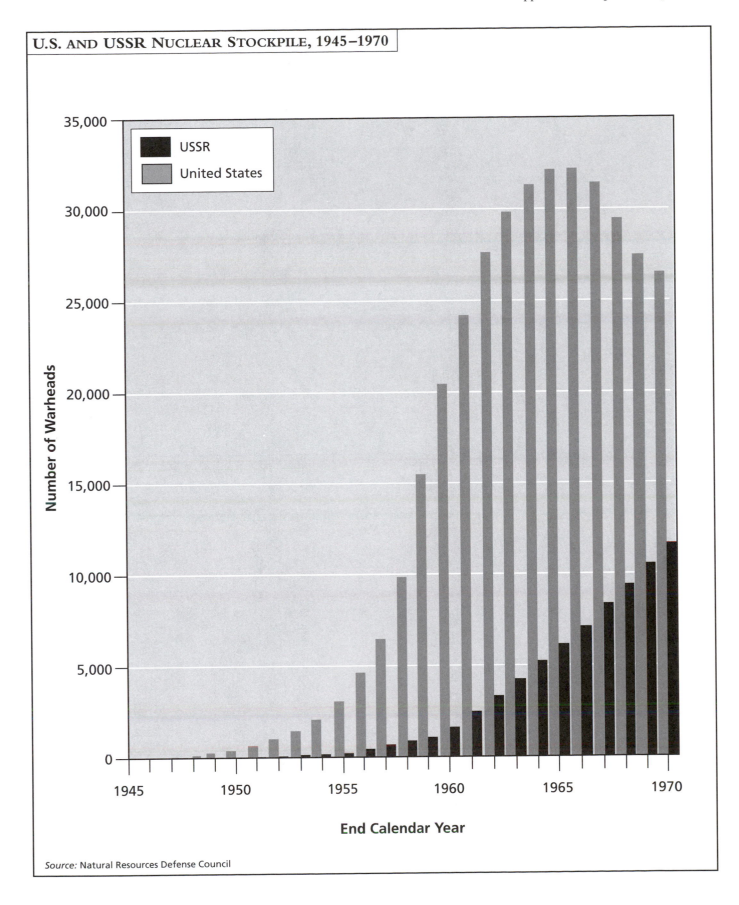

U.S. AND USSR NUCLEAR STOCKPILE, 1945–1970

Number of Warheads

End Calendar Year

Source: Natural Resources Defense Council

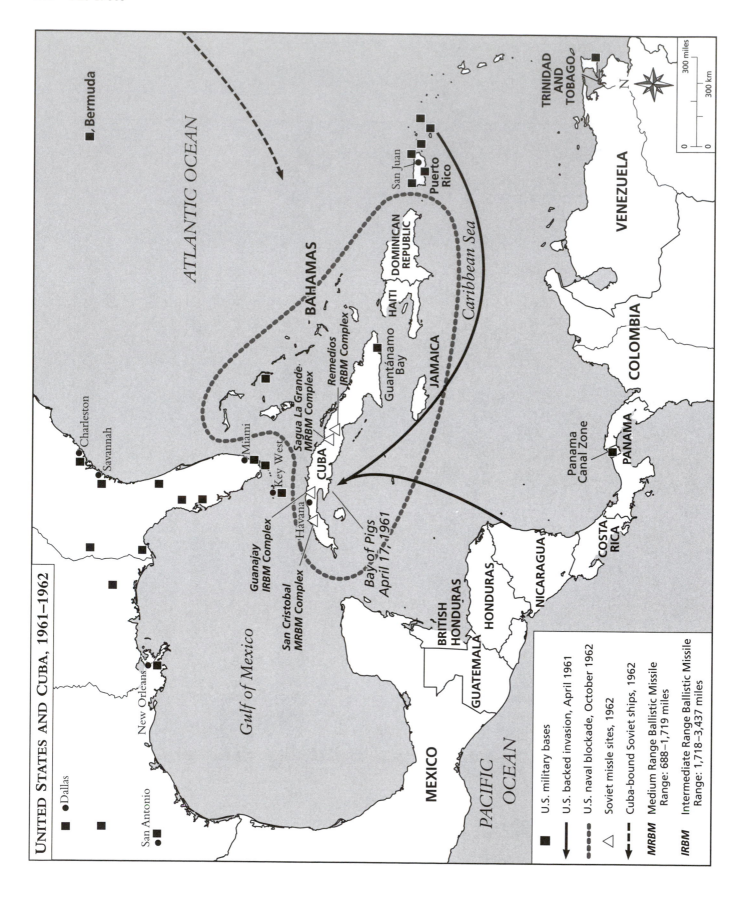

UNITED STATES AND CUBA, 1961–1962

Legend:
- U.S. military bases
- U.S. backed invasion, April 1961
- U.S. naval blockade, October 1962
- Soviet missile sites, 1962
- Cuba-bound Soviet ships, 1962
- **MRBM** Medium Range Ballistic Missile Range: 688–1,719 miles
- **IRBM** Intermediate Range Ballistic Missile Range: 1,718–3,437 miles

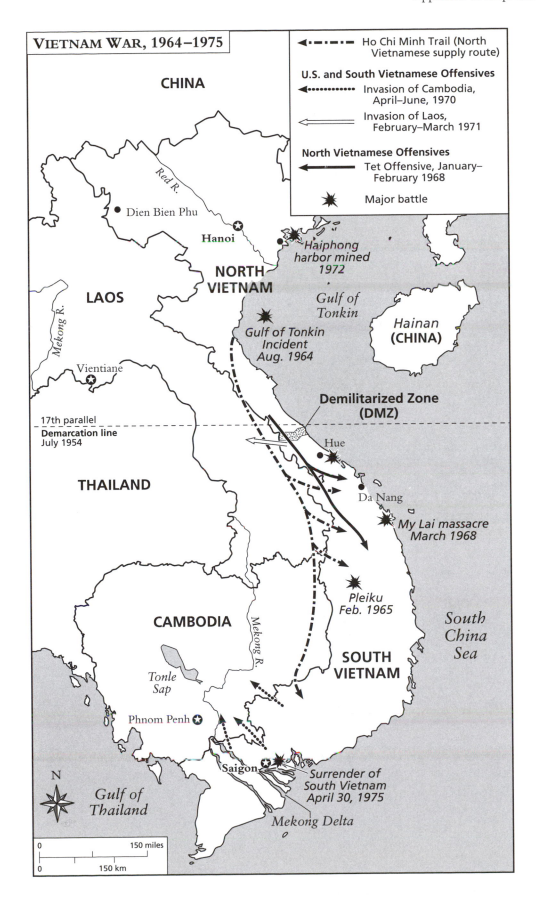

VIETNAM WAR, 1964–1975

Ho Chi Minh Trail (North Vietnamese supply route)

U.S. and South Vietnamese Offensives
Invasion of Cambodia, April–June, 1970
Invasion of Laos, February–March 1971

North Vietnamese Offensives
Tet Offensive, January–February 1968
Major battle

CHINA

Red R.

Dien Bien Phu

Hanoi

NORTH VIETNAM

Haiphong harbor mined 1972

Gulf of Tonkin

Hainan (CHINA)

LAOS

Mekong R.

Vientiane

Gulf of Tonkin Incident Aug. 1964

17th parallel
Demarcation line July 1954

Demilitarized Zone (DMZ)

Hue

THAILAND

Da Nang

My Lai massacre March 1968

Pleiku Feb. 1965

CAMBODIA

Mekong R.

Tonle Sap

SOUTH VIETNAM

South China Sea

Phnom Penh

Saigon

Surrender of South Vietnam April 30, 1975

N

Gulf of Thailand

Mekong Delta

0   150 miles
0   150 km

U.S. PRESIDENTIAL ELECTION: ELECTORAL VOTE, 1960

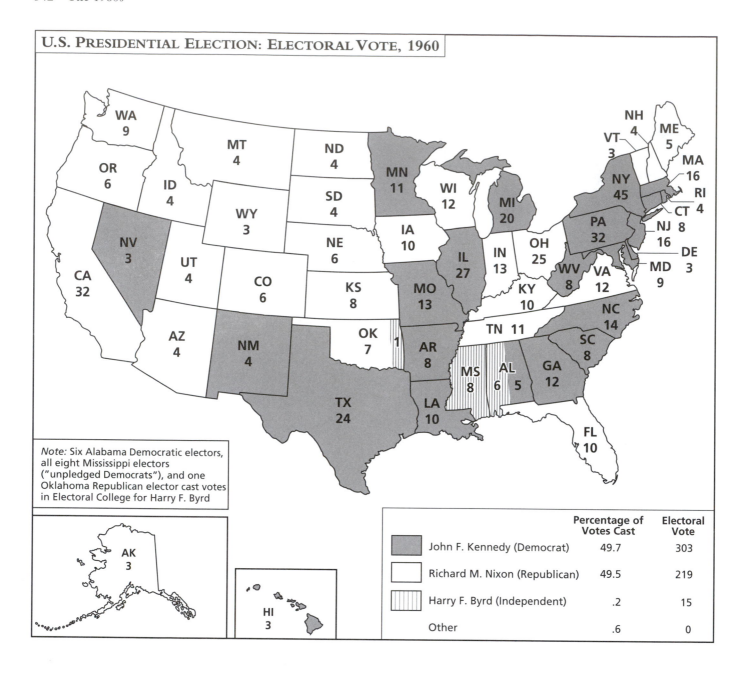

WA 9 · OR 6 · MT 4 · ID 4 · ND 4 · SD 4 · WY 3 · MN 11 · WI 12 · MI 20 · NH 4 · VT 3 · ME 5 · MA 16 · NY 45 · RI 4 · CT 4 · PA 32 · NJ 16 · IA 10 · NE 6 · IL 27 · IN 13 · OH 25 · WV 8 · VA 12 · DE 3 · MD 9 · CA 32 · NV 3 · UT 4 · CO 6 · KS 8 · MO 13 · KY 10 · NC 14 · AZ 4 · NM 4 · OK 7 1 · AR 8 · TN 11 · SC 8 · GA 12 · MS 8 · AL 6 5 · TX 24 · LA 10 · FL 10 · AK 3 · HI 3

Note: Six Alabama Democratic electors, all eight Mississippi electors ("unpledged Democrats"), and one Oklahoma Republican elector cast votes in Electoral College for Harry F. Byrd

	Percentage of Votes Cast	Electoral Vote
John F. Kennedy (Democrat)	49.7	303
Richard M. Nixon (Republican)	49.5	219
Harry F. Byrd (Independent)	.2	15
Other	.6	0

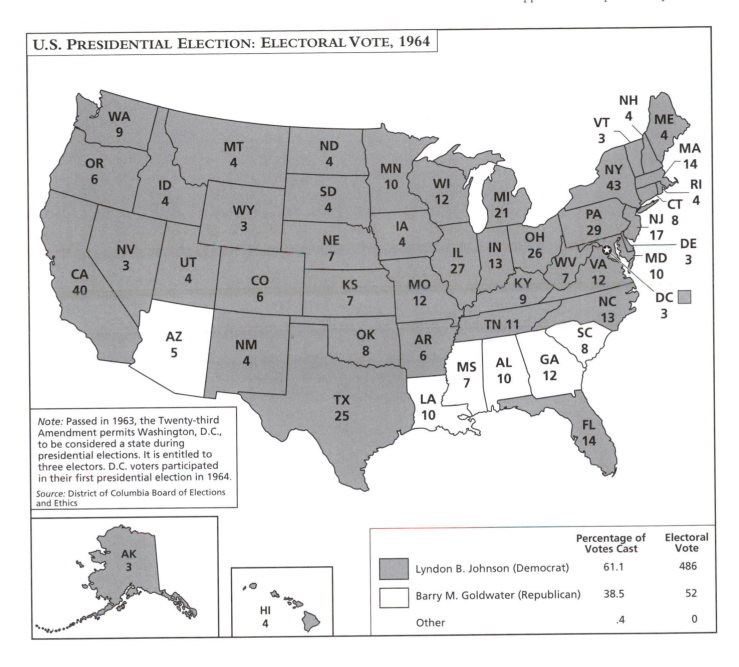

U.S. PRESIDENTIAL ELECTION: ELECTORAL VOTE, 1964

WA 9
OR 6
MT 4
ND 4
MN 10
WI 12
MI 21
NY 43
NH 4
VT 3
ME 4
MA 14
RI 4
CT 8
NJ 17
PA 29
ID 4
SD 4
IA 4
OH 26
WV 7
VA 12
DE 3
MD 10
DC 3
NV 3
WY 3
NE 7
IL 27
IN 13
KY 9
NC 13
CA 40
UT 4
CO 6
KS 7
MO 12
TN 11
SC 8
AZ 5
NM 4
OK 8
AR 6
MS 7
AL 10
GA 12
TX 25
LA 10
FL 14

Note: Passed in 1963, the Twenty-third Amendment permits Washington, D.C., to be considered a state during presidential elections. It is entitled to three electors. D.C. voters participated in their first presidential election in 1964.

Source: District of Columbia Board of Elections and Ethics

AK 3

HI 4

	Percentage of Votes Cast	Electoral Vote
Lyndon B. Johnson (Democrat)	61.1	486
Barry M. Goldwater (Republican)	38.5	52
Other	.4	0

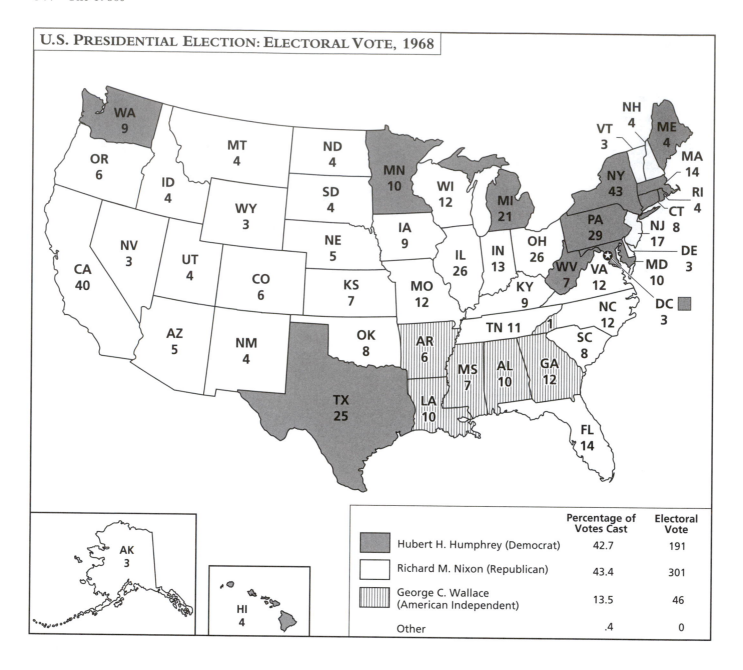

U.S. PRESIDENTIAL ELECTION: ELECTORAL VOTE, 1968

WA 9

OR 6

MT 4

ND 4

MN 10

WI 12

MI 21

NH 4

VT 3

ME 4

NY 43

MA 14

RI 4

CT 8

PA 29

NJ 17

DE 3

ID 4

SD 4

IA 9

OH 26

WV 7

MD 10

DC 3

NV 3

UT 4

WY 3

NE 5

IL 26

IN 13

KY 9

VA 12

CA 40

CO 6

KS 7

MO 12

TN 11

NC 12

AZ 5

NM 4

OK 8

AR 6

MS 7

AL 10

GA 12

SC 8

1

TX 25

LA 10

FL 14

AK 3

HI 4

	Percentage of Votes Cast	Electoral Vote
Hubert H. Humphrey (Democrat)	42.7	191
Richard M. Nixon (Republican)	43.4	301
George C. Wallace (American Independent)	13.5	46
Other	.4	0

NOTES

INTRODUCTION

1. Robert A. Divine, "The Education of John F. Kennedy," in *Makers of American Diplomacy,* eds. Frank Merli and Theodore Wilson (New York: Scribners, 1974), pp. 317–343.

2. Doris Kearns Goodwin, *The Fitzgeralds and the Kennedys* (New York: Simon & Schuster, 1987), pp. 769–774.

3. Cynthia E. Harrison, "A 'New Frontier' for Women: The Public Policy of the Kennedy Administration," *Journal of American History* 67 (December 1980): 630–635.

4. Stephen Brier, ed., *Who Built America? Working People and the Nation's Economy, Politics, Culture, and Society,* vol. 2 (New York: Worth Publishers, 2000), pp. 622–623. See also William H. Chafe, *The Unfinished Journey—America Since World War II* (New York: Oxford Unversity Press, 1999), pp. 143–144

5. Thomas Cronin, "On the American Presidency: A Conversation with James MacGregor Burns," *Presidential Studies Quarterly* 16 (Summer 1986): 528–542.

1. TO THE NEW FRONTIER: JANUARY 1960–DECEMBER 1961

1. Theodore C. Sorensen, "JFK—His Vision, Then and Now," *U.S. News and World Report,* October 24, 1988, p. 33.

2. Dean Rusk, "Reflections on Foreign Policy," in *The Kennedy Presidency,* ed. Kenneth W. Thompson (Lanham, Md.: University Press of America, 1985), pp. 190–201.

3. William Lederer and Eugene Burdick, *The Ugly American* (New York: Norton, 1960), pp. 166, 233. See also Joseph Buttinger, "Fact and Fiction on Foreign Aid: A Critique of 'The Ugly American,'" *Dissent, A Quarterly of Socialist Opinion* 6 (Summer 1959): 319–320.

4. Arthur M. Schlesinger, Jr., *Robert Kennedy and His Times* (New York: Ballantine, 1978), pp. 206–238. See also Lawrence O'Brien, *No Final Victories* (New York: Doubleday, 1974), p. 2.

5. Theodore H. White, *The Making of the President, 1960* (New York: Atheneum, 1967), p. 337.

6. H. W. Brands, Jr., *Cold Warriors: Eisenhower's Generation and American Foreign Policy* (New York: Columbia University Press, 1988), p. 211.

7. Richard M. Nixon, *The Memoirs of Richard Nixon* (New York: Grosset & Dunlap, 1978), pp. 215–218.

8. J. Richard Snyder, ed., *John F. Kennedy: Person, Policy, Presidency* (Wilmington, Del.: Scholarly Resources Press, 1988), pp. 11–24.

9. Walt W. Rostow, *The Diffusion of Power* (New York: Macmillan, 1972), p. 296.

10. Timothy Maga, *John F. Kennedy and New Frontier Diplomacy, 1961–1963* (Malabar, Fla.: Krieger, 1994), pp. 125–139.

11. Allen J. Matusow, *The Unraveling of America: A History of Liberalism in the 1960s* (New York: Harper, 1984), p. 31.

12. Jane Stern and Michael Stern, *Sixties People* (New York: Knopf, 1990), pp. 3, 5, 88–89, 91, 92–93, 95.

13. Thomas G. Paterson, "Fixation with Cuba," in Thomas G. Paterson, ed., *Kennedy's Quest for Victory: American Foreign Policy, 1961–1963* (New York: Oxford University Press, 1989), pp. 123–155. See also Peter Wyden, *Bay of Pigs: The Untold Story* (New York: Simon & Schuster, 1979), p. 310.

14. Georg Schild, "The Berlin Crisis," in *Kennedy: The New Frontier Revisited,* ed. Mark J. White (New York: New York University Press, 1998), pp. 91–131.

15. Matusow, pp. 89, 138–140, 400.

16. Chafe, pp. 111–136.

2. LOST IN THE COLD WAR: JANUARY 1962–SEPTEMBER 1962

1. Philip T. Hartung, "The Lawrence Legend," *Commonweal*, January 18, 1963, pp. 439–440. See also Douglas Little, "From Even-Handed to Empy-Handed: Seeking Order in the Middle East," in Thomas Paterson, ed. *Kennedy's Quest for Victory* (New York: Oxford University Press, 1989), pp. 156–177.

2. Jane E. Stromseth, *The Origins of Flexible Response: NATO's Debate over Strategy in the 1960s* (New York: St. Martin's Press, 1988), pp. 26–31, 35–41. See also Lawrence Freedman, *The Evolution of Nuclear Strategy* (New York: St. Martin's Press, 1981), pp. 232–233, 287.

3. I. M. Destler, *Managing an Alliance: The Politics of U.S.-Japanese Relations* (Washington, D.C.: Institute for International Economics, 1976), pp. 89–124.

4. NSC Meeting (Japan Relations), January 22, 1963, and Defense Department Report, "International Security Affairs—Japan, 1962–63," March 25, 1963, Boxes 4-6/President's Views, Papers of Roger Hilsman and Box 294/Basic National Security Policy, John F. Kennedy Library, Boston, Massachusetts.

5. McGeorge Bundy, *Danger and Survival: Choices about the Bomb in the First Fifty Years* (New York: Vantage Books, 1990), pp. 371–378.

6. Carl M. Brauer, *John F. Kennedy and the Second Reconstruction* (New York: Columbia University Press, 1977), pp. 315–321. See also Jim Heath, *John F. Kennedy and the Business Community* (Chicago: University of Chicago Press, 1969), pp. 125–127; Victor Navasky, *Kennedy Justice* (New York: Atheneum, 1971), pp. 97–135, 185, 244, 445; and Taylor Branch, *Parting the Waters: America in the King Years, 1954–1963* (New York: Simon & Schuster, 1988), pp. 918–922.

7. Chris Strodder, *Swingin' Chicks of the '60s* (San Rafael, Calif.: Cedco Publishing Company, 2000), pp. 84–85.

8. Jane Stern and Michael Stern, *Sixties People* (New York: Knopf, 1990), pp. 104–107.

9. David Denoon, "Indonesia: Transition to Stability?" *Current History* 61 (December 1971): 332–338. See also National Security Memorandum No. 179: U.S. Policy Toward Indonesia, August 16, 1962, POF/Box 119, John F. Kennedy Library, Boston, Massachusetts.

10. Frank Costigliola, "The Failed Design: Kennedy, DeGaulle, and the Struggle for Europe," *Diplomatic History* 8 (Summer 1984): 227–251. See also Robert O. Paxton and Nicholas Wahl, eds., *DeGaulle and the United States: A Centennial Reappraisal* (Oxford, U.K.: Berg, 1994), pp. 169–94.

11. Williamj J. Duiker, *U.S. Containment Policy and the Conflict in Indochina* (Stanford, Calif.: Stanford University Press, 1994), pp. 249–308. See also Larry Berman, *Planning a Tragedy: The Americanization of the War in Vietnam* (New York: Norton, 1982), pp. 145–153.; George Donelson Moss, *Vietnam: An American Ordeal,* 4th ed. Upper Saddle River, N.J.: Prentice Hall, 2002) pp. 120–121

12. Dean Rusk, *As I Saw It* (New York: Norton, 1990), pp. 441–442. See also Blema Steinberg, *Shame and Humiliation: Presidential Decision Making on Vietnam* (Pittsburgh: University of Pittsburgh Press, 1996), pp. 78–79; Paul Kattenburg, *The Vietnam Trauma in American Foreign Policy, 1945–75* (New Brunswick, N.J.: Transaction Publishers, 1980), pp. 134–135; and Clark Clifford, *Counsel to the President: A Memoir* (New York: Random House, 1991), pp. 342–344.

13. "Observations on Proposal for a New Pacific Community," internal State Department memorandum and report, November 2, 1961, NSF/Box 345, John F. Kennedy Library, Boston, Massachusetts. See also Timothy Maga, *John F. Kennedy and the New Pacific Community, 1961–1963* (London: Macmillan, 1990), pp. 1–13.

14. Raymond D'Angelo, *The American Civil Rights Movement: Readings and Interpretations* (New York: McGraw-Hill/Dushkin, 2001), pp. 307–314. See also Harvard Sitkoff, *The Struggle for Black Equality, 1954–1980* (New York: Hill & Wang, 1981): 105–156.

3. LESSONS OF THE CUBAN MISSILE CRISIS: OCTOBER 1962–DECEMBER 1963

1. James G. Hershberg, "Before the Missiles of October: Did Kennedy Plan a Military Strike Against Cuba?" *Diplomatic History* 14 (Spring 1990): pp. 163–198.

2. Mark J. White, *The Cuban Missile Crisis* (New York: New York University Press, 1996), pp. 89–114. See also Elie Abel, *The Missile Crisis* (Philadelphia: J. B. Lippincott, 1966), pp. 1–75.

3. Nikita S. Khrushchev, *Khrushchev Remembers* (Boston: Little, Brown, 1970), pp. 492–493.

4. Donald Schulz, "Kennedy and the Cuban Connection," *Foreign Policy* 26 (Spring 1977): 57–139.

5. Jane Stern and Michael Stern, *Sixties People* (New York: Knopf, 1990), pp. 43–52, 202–204.

6. Thomas Paterson and William J. Brophy, "October Missiles and November Elections: The Cuban Missile Crisis and American Politics, 1962," *Journal of American History* 73 (June 1986): 87–119.

7. Richard M. Nixon, *The Memoirs of Richard Nixon* (New York: Grosset & Dunlap, 1978), pp. 237–245.

8. Ibid., pp. 245–247.

9. Arthur M. Schlesinger, Jr., *Robert Kennedy and His Times* (New York: Ballantine, 1978), pp. 421–439; Theodore Sorenson, *Kennedy* (New York-Bantam, 1966), pp. 441–527.

10. Donald C. Hafner, "Bureaucratic Politics and 'Those Frigging Missiles,'" *Orbis* 21 (Summer 1977): 307–333. See also Glenn T. Seaborg, *Kennedy, Khrushchev and the Test Ban* (Berkeley: University of California Press, 1981), p. 259.

11. Raymond D'Angelo, *The American Civil Rights Movement* (New York: McGraw-Hill/Dushkin, 2001), pp. 310–31. See also, pp. 549–569.

12. Jack M. Bloom, *Class, Race, and the Civil Rights Movement* (Bloomington: Indiana University Press, 1987), pp. 186–213. See also Raymond S. Franklin, *Shadows of Race and Class* (Minneapolis: University of Minnesota Press, 1991), pp. 1–21.

13. Paul Harper and Joann P. Krieg, eds., *John F. Kennedy: The Promise Revisited* (Westport, Conn.: Greenwood Press, 1988), pp. 207–24. See also Mark M. Amen, "Recurring Influences on Economic Policy: Kennedy and Reagan Compared," in Paul Johnson and William Thompson, eds., *Rhythms in Politics and Economic* (New York: Praeger, 1985), pp. 181–209.

14. Patricia Zelman, *Women, Work, and National Policy: The Kennedy-Johnson Years* (Ann Arbor: University of Michigan Research Press, 1982), pp. 26–38. See also Harper and Krieg, pp. 237–260.

15. Kitty Kelley, "The Dark Side of Camelot," *People Weekly* 29 February 29, 1988, pp. 106–114. See also Peter Collier, and David Horowitz, *The Kennedys: An American Drama* (New York: Warner Books, 1984), pp. 395–404, 422–423, 428–429.

16. John H. Davis, *The Kennedys: Dynasty and Disaster, 1848–1984* (New York: McGraw-Hill, 1984), pp. 362–381. See also William H. Chafe, *The Unfinished Journey* (New York: Oxford University Press, 1999), pp. 218–219, 228–229; Arthur M. Schlesinger, Jr., *Robert Kennedy and His Times* (New York: Ballantine, 1978), pp. 662–665.

4. "ALL THE WAY WITH LBJ:" 1964–1965

1. Bruce Miroff, *Icons of Democracy: American Leaders as Heroes, Aristocrats, Dissenters, and Democrats* (New York: Basic Books, 1993), pp. 301–306.

2. H. W. Brands, *The Wages of Globalism: Lyndon Johnson and the Limits of American Power* (New York: Oxford University Press, 1995), pp. 3–29.

3. McGeorge Bundy, "The Presidency and the Peace," *Foreign Affairs* 42 (April 1964): 353–365. See also Richard Goodwin, "Reflections," *The New Yorker* 44, January 4, 1969, pp. 38–58.

4. Paul S. Boyer, *Promises to Keep: The United States Since World War II* (Lexington, Mass.: D. C. Heath, 1995), pp. 220–223.

5. Theodore H. White, *The Making of the President, 1964* (New York: Atheneum, 1965), pp. 132–133. See also Barry Goldwater, *Where I Stand* (New York: McGraw-Hill, 1964), p. 67.

6. Harry S. Ashmore, *Hearts and Minds: The Anatomy of Racism from Roosevelt to Reagan* (New York: McGraw-Hill, 1982), pp. 411–413.

7. Robert S. McNamara, *In Retrospect: The Tragedy and Lessons of Vietnam* (New York: Random House, 1995), pp. 127–143. See also Boyer, pp. 306–307.

8. James S. Olson and Randy Roberts, *Where the Domino Fell: America and Vietnam, 1945–1995,* 2d ed. (New York: St. Martin's Press, 1996), pp. 105–128.

9. Loren Baritz, *Backfire: A History of How American Culture Led Us into Vietnam and Made Us Fight the Way We Did* (New York: William Morrow, 1985), pp. 299–378. See also Tom Wells, *The War Within: America's Battle Over Vietnam* (New York: Henry Holt, 1996), pp. 13–33; CBS News, *Vietnam: Chronicle of a War* (Beverly Hills, Calif: Fox Video, 1981), VHS tape.

10. Jane Stern and Michael Stern, *Sixties People* (New York: Knopf, 1990), pp. 123–145. See also Boyer, p. 298.

11. CBS News, *Vietnam: Chronicle of a War.*

12. Ibid.

13. George W. Ball, *The Past Has Another Pattern: Memoirs* (New York: Norton, 1982), pp. 399–506.

14. McNamara, pp. 186–187.

15. Brands, pp. 240–242. See also Bruce Schulman, *Lyndon B. Johnson and American Liberalism: A Brief Biography with Documents* (Boston: Bedford Books, 1995), pp. 133–138

16. David Kaiser, *American Tragedy: Kennedy, Johnson and the Origins of the Vietnam War* (Cambridge, Mass.: Harvard University Press, 2000), pp. 412–483. See also Moss, pp. 185–199, 205–213.

17. Schlesinger, pp. 710–756.

5. BEACH BOYS AMERICA: 1966–1967

1. Yuen Foong Khong, *Analogies at War* (Princeton, N.J.: Princeton University Press, 1992), pp. 174–205. See also Lloyd C. Gardner, *Pay Any Price: Lyndon Johnson and the Wars for Vietnam* (Chicago: Ivan R. Dee, 1995), pp. 151–176.

2. Robert Griffith and Paula Baker, eds., *Major Problems in American History Since 1945, Documents and Essays,* 2nd ed. (Boston: Houghton Mifflin, 2001), pp. 323–365. See also Melvin Small, "The Impact of the Antiwar Movement on Lyndon Johnson, 1965–1968," *Peace and Change* 10 (Spring 1984): 1–22; Moss, pp. 260–262.

3. H. W. Brands, *The Wages of Globalism* (New York: Oxford University Press, 1995), pp. 15, 22, 29, 32, 50–61, 131, 171, 176, 235–236, 241, 256–262.

4. Jane Stern and Michael Stern, *Sixties People* (New York: Knopf, 1990), pp. 80–87, 155.

5. Allen J. Matusow, *The Unraveling of America* (New York: Harper, 1984), pp. 243–271. See also Schulman, pp. 114–123.

6. Ibid., pp. 380–85. See also Oscar Patterson III, "An Analysis of Television Coverage of the Vietnam War," *Journal of Broadcasting* 28 (Fall 1984): 397–404; and Sidney Verba, "Public Opinion and the War in Vietnam," *American Political Science Review* 61 (June 1967): 317–333.

7. James S. Olson and Randy Roberts, *Where the Domino Fell* (New York: St. Martin's Press, 1996), pp. 150–152, 174–175, 201–202.

6. THE PERILS OF POWER: 1968

1. Jay Koblenz, *Corvette, America's Sports Car* (Skokie, Ill.: Publications International, 1984), pp. 92–138.

2. James Miller, "Democracy Is in the Streets:" *From Port Huron to the Siege of Chicago* (New York: Simon & Schuster, 1987), pp. 1–130.

3. James S. Olson and Randy Roberts, *Where the Domino Fell* (New York: St. Martin's Press, 1996), pp. 207–209.

4. Robert Pisor, *The End of the Line: The Siege of Khe Sanh* (New York: Norton, 1982), pp. 120–183.

5. Ibid., pp. 184–202.

6. Robert S. McNamara, James G. Blight, and Robert K. Brigham, *Argument Without End: In Search of Answers to the Vietnam Tragedy* (New York: Public Affairs, 1999), pp. 295–299, 362–368.

7. John E. Mueller, "The Search for the 'Breaking Point' in Vietnam: The Statistics of a Deadly Quarrel," *International Studies Quarterly* 4 (December 1980): 497–519. See also Moss, pp. 305–309.

8. Clark Clifford, "A Vietnam Reappraisal," *Foreign Affairs* 47 (July 1969): 601–622.

9. Mitchell K. Hall, *The Vietnam War* (New York: Longman, 2000), pp. 47–56.

10. Leslie Gelb, "The Essential Domino: American Politics and Vietnam," *Foreign Affairs* 50 (April 1972): 459–472. See also William H. Chafe, *The Unfinished Journey* (New York: Oxford University Press, 1999) pp. 344–346.

11. Jack Newfield, *Robert Kennedy: A Memoir* (New York: E. P. Dutton, 1969), pp. 229–335.

12. Maurice Isserman and Michael Kazin, *America Divided: The Civil War of the 1960s* (New York: Oxford University Press, 2000), pp. 230–240. See also Chafer, pp. 373–375.

13. Mary C. Brennan, *Turning Right in the Sixties* (Chapel Hill: University of North Carolina Press, 1995), pp. 101–103. See also Jeffrey P. Kimball, "The Stab-in-the-Back Legend and the Vietnam War," *Armed Forces and Society* 14 (Spring 1988): 433–458; and Paul S. Boyer, *Promises to Keep* (Lexington, Mass.: D. C. Heath, 1995), pp. 338–342.

14. Chafe, pp. 373–82. See also Richard Nixon, *The Memoirs of Richard Nixon* (New York: Grosset and Dunlap, 1978), pp. 298–335.

7. HOW THE "SIXTIES" END: 1969–1970

1. Gloria Emerson, *Winners and Losers: Battles, Retreats, Gains, Losses, and Ruins from a Long War* (New York: Random House, 1974), pp. 125–132. See also James William Gibson, *The Perfect War: The War We Couldn't Lose and How We Did* (New York: Grove/Atlantic, 1986), pp. 11–78.

2. Henry A. Kissinger, *White House Years* (Boston: Little, Brown, 1979), pp. 239–354.

3. Maurice Isserman and Michael Kazin, *America Divided* (New York: Oxford University Press, 2000), pp. 147–164, 297, 305.

4. Nixon, pp. 350–51, 356, 388–389, 398–404, 412–14.

5. Ibid., pp. 424–28, 438, 451. See also Stephen Brier, ed., *Who Built America?* vol. 2 (New York: Worth, 2000), pp. 670–671.

6. Jonathan A. Stein and Daniel Simkin, "Excalibur: Subtle Like A Broad Sword," *Automobile Quarterly* 38 (December 1998): 7–17. See also Brooks Stevens, *The Excalibur Story, or the Development of the Contemporary Classic* (Detroit: Society of Automotive Engineers, 1966), pp. 1–8.

7. "Crusader Widens Range of His Ire," *Business Week,* January 25, 1969, pp. 128–130. See also "Nader and Raiders: The U.S.'s Toughest Customer," *Time,* December 12, 1969, pp. 89–98.

8. Lee Iacocca, *Iacocca: An Autobiography* (New York: Bantam, 1986), pp. 91–116.

9. Nixon, pp. 426–428. See also Melvin Small, *The Presidency of Richard Nixon* (Lawrence-University Press of Kansas, 1999) pp. 203–214.

10. Ibid., pp. 196–200. See also Robert Gottlieb, *Forcing the Spring: The Transformation of the American Environmental Movement* (Washington, D.C.: Island Press, 1993), pp. 177–84.

11. William Shawcross, *Sideshow: Kissinger, Nixon and the Destruction of Cambodia* (New York: Simon & Schuster, 1979), pp. 19–35. See also Moss, pp. 357–369.

12. Ibid., pp. 373–78. See also Nixon, pp. 508–515.

13. Mitchell K. Hall, *The Vietnam War* (New York: Longman, 2000), pp. 73–87; Olson and Roberts, pp. 237–261.

BIBLIOGRAPHY

BOOKS

Abel, Elie. *The Missile Crisis.* New York: Bantam, 1966.

Ambrose, Stephen E. *Eisenhower: The President.* Vol. 2. New York: Simon & Schuster, 1984.

Ambrose, Stephen, and Douglas Brinkley, eds. *Witness to America.* New York: HarperCollins, 1999.

Amen, Mark M., "Recurring Influences on Economic Policy: Kennedy and Reagan Compared," in Paul Johnson and William Thompson, eds. *Rhythms in Politics and Economics.* New York: Praeger, 1985.

Ashmore, Harry S. *Hearts and Minds: The Anatomy of Racism from Roosevelt to Reagan.* New York: McGraw-Hill, 1982.

The Associated Press. *The World in 1965: History As We Lived It.* New York: The Associated Press, 1966.

Attwood, William. *The Twighlight Struggle: Tales of the Cold War.* New York: Harper, 1987.

Ball, George W. *The Past Has Another Pattern: Memoirs.* New York: Norton, 1982.

Barbour, Floyd. *A New Black Consciousness.* Boston: Porter-Sargent, 1968.

Baritz, Loren. *Backfire: A History of How American Culture Led Us into Vietnam and Made Us Fight the Way We Did.* New York: William Morrow, 1985.

Bartlett's Familiar Quotations. Boston: Little, Brown, 1980.

Berman, Edgar. *Hubert.* New York: G. P. Putnam's Sons, 1979.

Berman, Larry. *Planning a Tragedy: The Americanization of the War in Vietnam.* New York: Norton, 1982.

Blight, James G., Bruce J. Allyn, and David Welch, eds. *Cuba on the Brink: Castro, the Missile Crisis, and the Soviet Collapse.* New York: Pantheon Books, 1993.

Bloom, Alexander, ed. *Long Time Gone: Sixties America Then & Now.* New York: Oxford University Press, 2001.

Bloom, Jack M. *Class, Race, and the Civil Rights Movement.* Bloomington: Indiana University Press, 1987.

Boyer, Paul. *Promises to Keep: The United States Since World War II.* Lexington, Mass.: D. C. Heath, 1995.

Branch, Taylor. *Parting the Waters: America in the King Years, 1954–1963.* New York: Simon & Schuster, 1988.

Brands, H. W., Jr. *Cold Warriors: Eisenhower's Generation and American Foreign Policy.* New York: Columbia University Press, 1988.

———. *The Wages of Globalism: Lyndon Johnson and the Limits of American Power.* New York: Oxford University Press, 1995.

Brauer, Carl M. *John F. Kennedy and the Second Reconstruction.* New York: Columbia University Press, 1977.

Breitman, George, ed. *Malcolm X: By Any Means Necessary: Speeches, Interviews and a Letter by Malcolm X.* New York: Pathfinder Press, 1970.

Brennan, Mary C. *Turning Right in the Sixties.* Chapel Hill: University of North Carolina Press, 1995.

Brier, Stephen, ed. *Who Built America? Working People and the Nation's Economy, Politics, Culture, and Society.* Vol. 2. New York: Worth Publishers, 2000.

Carabillo, Toni, Judith Meuli, and June Bundy Csida. *Feminist Chronicles, 1953–1993.* Los Angeles: Women's Graphics, 1993.

Carmichael, Stokely, and Charles V. Hamilton. *Black Power: The Politics of Liberation in America.* New York: Vantage Books, 1967.

Carter, Dan T. *The Politics of Rage: George Wallace, the Origins of the New Conservatism, and the Transformation of American Politics.* Baton Rouge: Louisiana State University Press, 1995.

Chafe, William H. *The Unfinished Journey: America Since World War II.* New York: Oxford University Press, 1999.

Charlton, Michael, and Anthony Moncrieff. *Many Reasons Why: The American Involvement in Vietnam.* New York: Hill & Wang, 1978.

Chicago Auto Dealer Association. *Program of the 55th Annual Chicago Auto Show.* Chicago: Chicago Auto Dealer Association, 1963.

Clifford, Clark. *Counsel to the President: A Memoir.* New York: Random House, 1991.

Cohen, Dan. *Undefeated.* Minneapolis, Minn.: Lerner Publications, 1978.

Colbert, David. *Eyewitness to America.* New York: Pantheon Books, 1997.

Collier, Peter, and David Horowitz. *The Kennedys: An American Drama.* New York: Warner Books, 1984.

D'Angelo, Raymond. *The American Civil Rights Movement: Readings and Interpretations.* New York: McGraw-Hill/Dushkin, 2001.

Davis, Gareth. *From Opportunity to Entitlement.* Lawrence: University Press of Kansas, 1996.

Davis, John H. *The Kennedys: Dynasty and Disaster, 1848–1984.* New York: McGraw-Hill, 1984.

Department of Defense. *United States–Vietnam Relations, 1945–1967, Book 3.* Boston: Beacon Press, 1971.

Desmond, Kevin. *A Timetable of Inventions and Discoveries: From Pre-History to the Present Day.* New York: M. Evans, 1986.

Destler, I. M. *Managing an Alliance: The Politics of U.S.-Japanese Relations.* Washington, D.C.: Institute for International Economics, 1976.

Diven, Frances Fox, and Richard Cloward. *Poor Peoples Movements: Why They Succeed, Why They Fail.* New York: Random House, 1977.

Dubofsky, Melvyn, and Athan Theoharis. *Imperial Democracy: The United States Since 1945.* Englewood Cliffs, N.J.: Prentice Hall, 1988.

Duiker, William J. *U.S. Containment Policy and the Conflict in Indochina.* Stanford, Calif.: Stanford University Press, 1994.

Edelhart, Mike, and James Tinen. *America the Quotable.* New York: Facts On File, 1983.

Ehrlichman, John. *Witness to Power.* New York: Simon & Schuster, 1982.

Elliot, Jeffrey, and Mervyn Dymally. *Fidel Castro: Nothing Can Stop the Course of History.* Havana: Editora Política, 1985.

Emerson, Gloria. *Winners and Losers: Battles, Retreats, Gains, Losses, and Ruins from a Long War.* New York: Random House, 1974.

Fairclough, Adam. *Martin Luther King, Jr.* Athens: University of Georgia Press, 1990.

Firestone, Bernard J., and Robert C. Vogt, eds. *Lyndon Baines Johnson and the Uses of Power.* New York: Greenwood Press, 1988.

Ford, Harold P. *CIA and the Vietnam Policymakers: Three Episodes 1962–1968.* Washington, D.C.: CIA, 1998.

Franklin, Raymond S. *Shadows of Race and Class.* Minneapolis: University of Minnesota Press, 1991.

Freedman, Lawrence. *The Evolution of Nuclear Strategy.* New York: St. Martin's Press, 1981.

Fursenko, Alexander, and Timothy Naftali. *"One Hell of a Gamble": Khrushchev, Castro, and Kennedy, 1958–1964.* New York: Norton, 1997.

Gardner, Lloyd C. *Pay Any Price: Lyndon Johnson and the Wars for Vietnam.* Chicago: Ivan R. Dee, 1995.

Garrettson, Charles Lloyd. *Hubert H. Humphrey: The Politics of Joy.* New Brunswick, N.J.: Transaction Publishers, 1993.

Garthoff, Raymond L. *Reflections on the Cuban Missile Crisis.* Washington, D.C.: Brookings Institute, 1989.

de Gaulle, Charles. *Memoirs of Hope: Renewal and Endeavor.* New York: Simon & Schuster, 1971.

Gibson, James William. *The Perfect War: The War We Couldn't Lose and How We Did.* New York: Grove/Atlantic, 1986.

Gillon, Steven M., and Diane Kunz. *America During the Cold War.* Fort Worth, Tex.: Harcourt, Brace, 1993.

Gitlin, Todd. *The Sixties: Years of Hope, Days of Rage.* New York: Bantam Books, 1987.

Goldman, Eric F. *The Tragedy of Lyndon Johnson.* New York: Knopf, 1969.

Goldwater, Barry. *Where I Stand.* New York: McGraw-Hill, 1964.

Goodwin, Doris Kearns. *Lyndon Johnson and the American Dream*. New York: Harper & Row, 1976.

———. *The Fitzgeralds and the Kennedys*. New York: Simon & Schuster, 1987.

Gottlieb, Robert. *Forcing the Spring: The Transformation of the American Environmental Movement*. Washington, D.C.: Island Press, 1993.

Grant, Joanne. *"Political Mama," Ella Baker: Freedom Bound*. New York: John Wiley, 1998.

Greenhaw, Wayne. *Watch Out for George Wallace*. Englewood Cliffs, N.J.: Prentice Hall, 1976.

Griffith, Robert, and Paula Baker, eds. *Major Problems in American History Since 1945*. Boston: Houghton Mifflin, 2001.

Grissom, Virgil "Gus." *Gemini: A Personal Account of Man's Venture into Space*. New York: Macmillan, 1968.

Gurr, Ted Robert, and Hugh Davis Graham, eds. *The History of Violence in America*. New York: Bantam Books, 1969.

Guthman, Edwin O., and Jeffrey Shulman, eds. *Robert Kennedy in His Own Words: The Unpublished Recollections of the Kennedy Years*. Toronto: Bantam Books, 1988.

Haley, Alex. *The Autobiography of Malcolm X*. New York: Grove Press, 1965.

Hall, Mitchell K. *The Vietnam War*. New York: Longman, 2000.

Hampton, Henry, and Steve Fayer. *Voices of Freedom: An Oral History of the Civil Rights Movement from the 1950s Through the 1980s*. New York: Bantam, 1990.

Harper, Paul, and Joann P. Krieg, eds. *John F. Kennedy: The Promise Revisited*. Westport, Conn.: Greenwood Press, 1988.

Harris, Jay S., ed. *TV Guide: The First 25 Years*. New York: Simon & Schuster, 1978.

Havel, James T. *U.S. Presidential Candidates and Elections. A Biographical and Historical Guide*. Vol. 2: *The Elections, 1789–1992*. New York: Simon & Schuster Macmillan, 1996.

Hayden, Tom. *Reunion: A Memoir*. New York: Random House, 1988.

Heath, Jim. *John F. Kennedy and the Business Community.* Chicago: University of Chicago Press, 1969.

Hersh, Seymour M. *The Price of Power: Kissinger in the Nixon White House.* New York: Summit, 1983.

Hoopes, Townsend. *The Limits of Intervention.* New York: Longman, 1969.

Humphrey, Hubert H. *The Cause Is Mankind: A Liberal Program for Modern America.* New York: Praeger, 1964.

Iacocca, Lee. *Iacocca: An Autobiography.* New York: Bantam, 1986.

Isserman, Maurice, and Michael Kazin. *America Divided: The Civil War of the 1960s.* New York: Oxford University Press, 2000.

Johnson, Lady Bird. *A White House Diary.* New York: Holt, Rinehart & Winston, 1970.

Johnson, Lyndon Baines. *The Vantage Point: Perspectives of the Presidency.* New York: Holt, Rinehart & Winston, 1971.

Jones, Bill. *The Wallace Story.* Northport, Ala.: American Southern Publishing, 1966.

Jordan, Barbara, and Elspeth D. Rostow, eds. *The Great Society: A Twenty Year Critique.* Austin, Tex.: Lyndon Baines Johnson Library and Lyndon Baines Johnson School of Public Affairs, 1986.

Kaiser, David. *American Tragedy: Kennedy, Johnson, and the Origins of the Vietnam War.* Cambridge, Mass.: Belknap Press of Harvard University Press, 2000.

Kattenburg, Paul. *The Vietnam Trauma in American Foreign Policy, 1945–75.* New Brunswick, N.J.: Transaction Publishers, 1980.

Kazin, Michael. *The Populist Persuasion: An American History.* Ithaca, N.Y.: Cornell University Press, 1998.

Kennedy, Robert F. *To Seek a Newer World.* New York: Bantam, 1968.

Khong, Yuen Foong. *Analogies at War.* Princeton, N.J.: Princeton University Press, 1992.

Khrushchev, Nikita S. *Khrushchev Remembers.* Boston: Little, Brown, 1970.

Kissinger, Henry A. *White House Years.* Boston: Little, Brown, 1979.

Kluger, Richard. *Simple Justice.* New York: Random House, 1977.

Koblenz, Jay. *Corvette, America's Sports Car.* Skokie, Ill.: Publications International, 1984.

Kuralt, Charles. *On the Road with Charles Kuralt.* New York: G. P. Putnam's Sons, 1985.

Lande, Nathaniel. *Dispatches from the Front: News Accounts of American Wars, 1776–1991.* New York: Henry Holt, 1995.

Lane, Mark. *Rush to Judgment: A Critique of the Warren Commission's Inquiry into the Murders of President John F. Kennedy, Officer J. D. Tippit, and Lee Harvey Oswald.* New York: Holt, Rinehart & Winston, 1966.

Lederer, William, and Eugene Burdick. *The Ugly American.* New York: Norton, 1960.

Library of Congress. *The Johnson Presidential Press Conferences.* Vols. 1 and 2. New York: Earl M. Coleman Enterprises, 1978.

————. *The Nixon Presidential Press Conferences.* Washington, D.C.: Library of Congress, 1978.

Livingston, Jon, Joe Moore, and Felicia Oldfather. *The Japan Reader: Postwar Japan, 1945 to the Present.* New York: Pantheon Books, 1973.

Maga, Timothy. *The Complete Idiot's Guide to the Vietnam War.* New York: Macmillan, 2000.

————. *John F. Kennedy and New Frontier Diplomacy, 1961–1963.* Malabar, Fla.: Krieger, 1994.

Mailer, Norman. *The Armies of the Night: History as a Novel, the Novel as History.* New York: New American Library, 1968.

Margolis, Jon. *The Last Innocent Year: America in 1964, The Beginning of the "Sixties."* New York: Morrow, 1999.

Mates, Leo. *Nonalignment Theory and Current Policy.* Dobbs Ferry, N.Y.: Oceana Publications, 1972.

Matusow, Allen J. *The Unraveling of America: A History of Liberalism in the 1960s.* New York: Harper, 1984.

May, Elaine Tyler. *Homeward Bound: American Families in the Cold War Era.* New York: Basic Books, 1988.

May, Ernest R., and Philip D. Zelikow. *The Kennedy Tapes: Inside the White House During the Cuban Missile Crisis.* Cambridge, Mass.: Belknap Press, 1997.

McAdams, Douglas. *Political Process and the Development of Black Insurgency, 1930–1970.* Chicago: University of Chicago Press, 1982.

McAuliffe, Mary S., ed. *CIA Documents on the Cuban Missile Crisis, 1962.* Washington, D.C.: CIA, 1992.

McCarthy, Eugene S. *The Year of the People.* New York: Doubleday, 1969.

McGinniss, Joe. *The Selling of the President, 1968.* New York: Pocket Books, 1969.

McNamara, Robert S. *In Retrospect: The Tragedy and Lessons of Vietnam.* New York: Random House, 1995.

McNamara, Robert S., James G. Blight, and Robert K. Brigham. *Argument Without End: In Search of Answers to the Vietnam Tragedy.* New York: Public Affairs, 1999.

McPherson, Harry. *A Political Education: A Washington Memoir.* Boston: Houghton Mifflin, 1988.

Meredith, James. *Three Years in Mississippi.* Bloomington: Indiana University Press, 1966.

Merli, Frank, and Theodore Wilson, eds. *Makers of American Diplomacy.* New York: Scribners, 1974.

Miller, James. *"Democracy Is in the Streets:" From Port Huron to the Siege of Chicago.* New York: Simon & Schuster, 1987.

Miller, Merle. *Lyndon: An Oral Biography.* New York: Putnam's, 1980.

Miroff, Bruce. *Icons of Democracy: American Leaders as Heroes, Aristocrats, Dissenters and Democrats.* New York: Basic Books, 1993.

Montgomery, Ruth. *Hail to the Chiefs: My Life and Times with Six Presidents.* New York: Coward-McCann, 1970.

Moore, Robin. *The Green Berets.* New York: Moore-Hill Publishing, 1965.

Morgan, Charles. *A Time to Speak.* New York: Harper, 1964.

Morrison, Joan, and Robert K. Morrison. *From Camelot to Kent State: The Sixties Experience in the Words of Those Who Lived It.* New York: Oxford University Press, 1987.

Moss, George Donelson. *Vietnam: An American Ordeal.* Upper Saddle River, N.J.: Prentice Hall, 2002.

Navasky, Victor. *Kennedy Justice.* New York: Atheneum, 1971.

Neal, Valerie, Cathleen S. Lewis, and Frank H. Winter. *Spaceflight, a Smithsonian Guide.* New York: Macmillan, 1995.

Newfield, Jack. *Robert Kennedy: A Memoir.* New York: E. P. Dutton, 1969.

Newton, Huey P. *Revolutionary Suicide.* New York: Harcourt Brace Jovanovich, 1973.

Nite, Norm N. *Rock on Almanac, The First Four Decades of Rock 'n' Roll: A Chronology.* New York: Harper & Row, 1989.

Nixon, Richard M. *The Memoirs of Richard Nixon.* New York: Grosset & Dunlap, 1978.

———. *Six Crises.* New York: Pyramid Books, 1968.

———. *U.S. Foreign Policy for the 1970s: A New Strategy for Peace.* Washington, D.C.: GPO, 1970.

O'Brien, Lawrence. *No Final Victories.* New York: Doubleday, 1974.

Olson, James, and Randy Roberts. *Where the Domino Fell: America and Vietnam, 1945–1995.* New York: St. Martin's Press, 1996.

O'Toole, George. *The Assassination Tapes: An Electronic Probe into the Murder of John F. Kennedy and the Dallas Coverup.* New York: Penthouse Press, 1975.

Paar, Jack. *P. S. Jack Paar.* New York: Doubleday, 1983.

Parker, Thomas, and Douglas Nelson. *Day by Day: The Sixties.* Vol. 1: *1960–1964.* New York: Facts On File, 1983.

Paterson, Thomas G., ed. *Kennedy's Quest for Victory: American Foreign Policy, 1961–1963.* New York: Oxford University Press, 1989.

Paxton, Robert O., and Nicholas Wahl, eds., *De Gaulle and the United States: A Centennial Reappraisal.* Oxford, U.K.: Berg, 1994.

Penkovskiy, Oleg. *The Penkovskiy Papers.* New York: Doubleday, 1965.

Peterson, Peter G. *U.S.-Soviet Commercial Relations in a New Era.* Washington, D.C.: U.S. Department of Commerce, 1972.

Pisor, Robert. *The End of the Line: The Siege of Khe Sanh.* New York: Norton, 1982.

Potter, Andrew J., ed. *Light at the End of the Tunnel: A Vietnam War Anthology.* Wilmington, Del.: SR Books, 1999.

Powledge, Fred. *The Civil Rights Movement and the People Who Made It.* Boston: Little, Brown, 1991.

Presidential Elections, 1789–1996. Washington, D.C.: Congressional Quarterly, 1997.

Reagan, Ronald. *A Time for Choosing: The Speeches of Ronald Reagan, 1961–1982.* Washington, D.C.: Regnery Publishing, 1983.

Reichley, A. James. *Conservatives in an Age of Change: The Nixon and Ford Administrations.* Washington, D.C.: Brookings Institute, 1981.

Ross, Douglas, ed. *Robert F. Kennedy: Apostle of Change.* New York: Trident Press, 1968.

Rostow, Walt W. *The Diffusion of Power.* New York: Macmillan, 1972.

Rotter, Andew J., ed. *Light at the End of the Tunnel: A Vietnam War Anthology.* Wilmington, Del.: Scholarly Resources, 1999.

Rusk, Dean. *As I Saw It.* New York: Norton, 1990.

Scammon, Richard M., ed. *America Votes 4: 1960, a Handbook of Contemporary American Election Statistics.* Pittsburgh, Pa.: University of Pittsburgh Press, 1962.

———. *America Votes 8: 1968, a Handbook of Contemporary American Election Statistics.* Washington, D.C.: Congressional Quarterly, Inc., 1970.

Schaap, Dick. *R.F.K.* New York: Signet, 1967.

Schachtman, Tom. *Decade of Shocks: Dallas to Watergate, 1963–1974.* New York: Poseidon Press, 1983.

Schlesinger, Arthur M., Jr. *The Cycles of American History.* Boston: Houghton Mifflin, 1986.

———. *Robert Kennedy and His Times.* New York: Ballantine Books, 1978.

Seaborg, Glenn T. *Kennedy, Khrushchev and the Test Ban.* Berkeley: University of California Press, 1981.

Segel, Thomas D. *Men in Space.* Boulder, Colo.: Paladin Press, 1975.

Sein, Jean. *American Journey: The Times of Robert Kennedy.* New York: Harcourt Brace Jovanovich, 1970.

Sellars, Cleveland. *The River of No Return: The Autobiography of a Black Militant and the Life and Death of SNCC.* New York: Morrow, 1973.

Shadegg, Stephen. *What Happened to Goldwater? The Inside Story of the 1964 Republican Campaign.* New York: Holt, Rinehart & Winston, 1965.

Shawcross, William. *Sideshow: Kissinger, Nixon and the Destruction of Cambodia.* New York: Simon & Schuster, 1979.

Sheehan, Neil, ed. *The Pentagon Papers, As Published by the* New York Times; *Based on Investigative Reporting by Neil Sheehan.* New York: Bantam, 1971.

Shelton, William. *American Space Exploration: The First Decade.* Boston: Little, Brown, 1967.

Sitkoff, Harvard. *The Struggle for Black Equality, 1954–1980.* New York: Hill & Wang, 1981.

Small, Melvin. *The Presidency of Richard Nixon.* Lawrence: University Press of Kansas, 1999.

Small, Melvin, and William D. Hoover, eds. *Give Peace a Chance: Exploring the Vietnam Antiwar Movement.* Syracuse, N.Y.: Syracuse University Press, 1992.

Snyder, J. Richard, ed. *John F. Kennedy: Person, Policy, Presidency.* Wilmington, Del.: Scholarly Resources Press, 1988.

Sorensen, Theodore C. *Kennedy.* New York: Bantam, 1966.

———. *The Kennedy Legacy.* New York: Macmillan, 1969.

Steinberg, Blema. *Shame and Humiliation: Presidential Decision Making on Vietnam.* Pittsburgh, Pa.: University of Pittsburgh Press, 1996.

Stern, Jane, and Michael Stern. *Sixties People.* New York: Knopf, 1990.

Stevens, Brooks. *The Excalibur Story, or the Development of the Contemporary Classic.* Detroit: Society of Automotive Engineers, 1966.

Stevens, Robert Warren. *Vain Hopes, Grim Realities: The Economic Consequences of the Vietnam War.* New York: Viewpoints, 1976.

Strodder, Chris. *Swingin' Chicks of the '60s.* San Rafael, Calif.: Cedco Publishing Company, 2000.

Stromseth, Jane E. *The Origins of Flexible Response: NATO's Debate over Strategy in the 1960s.* New York: St. Martin's Press, 1988.

Sugrue, Thomas J. *The Origins of the Urban Crisis.* Princeton, N.J.: Princeton University Press, 1998.

Szulc, Tad. *The Illusion of Peace: Foreign Policy in the Nixon Years.* New York: Viking, 1978.

Taylor, Maxwell, D. *Swords and Plowshares.* New York: Norton, 1972.

Terkel, Studs. *Working.* New York: Pantheon, 1972.

Thompson, Kenneth W., ed. *The Kennedy Presidency.* Lanham, Md.: University Press of America, 1985.

————. *The Nixon Presidency.* Lanham, Md.: University Press of America, 1987.

Tucker, Spencer C., ed. *Encyclopedia of the Vietnam War: A Political, Social, and Military History.* Santa Barbara, Calif.: ABC-CLIO, 1998.

Turner, W. W. *Hoover's FBI.* New York: Dell, 1971.

U.S. Congress. *Executive Sessions of the Senate Foreign Relations Committee, vol. 15, 1963.* Washington, D.C.: GPO, 1987.

U.S. Department of State. *Documents on Germany, 1944–1985.* Washington, D.C.: GPO, 1986.

————. *Foreign Relations of the United States: Berlin Crisis, 1961–1962.* Washington, D.C.: GPO, 1993.

————. *Foreign Relations of the United States: Cuban Missile Crisis and Aftermath, 1961–1963.* Washington, D.C.: GPO, 1996.

U.S. Senate. Foreign Relations Committee. *Executive Sessions of the Senate Foreign Relations Committee, vol. 14, 87th Congress, 2nd session, 1962.* Washington, D.C.: GPO, 1986.

————. *Joint Hearing on Southeast Asia Resolution before the Senate Foreign Relations and Armed Services Committees, 88th Congress, 2nd Session, August 6, 1964.* Washington, D.C.: GPO, 1966.

————. Select Committee to Study Governmental Operations with Respect to Intelligence Activities. *Final Report.* Washington, D.C.: GPO, November 1975.

U.S. Government. *Public Papers of the Presidents of the United States: John F. Kennedy, 1961*. Washington, D.C.: GPO, 1962.

————. *Public Papers of the Presidents of the United States: John F. Kennedy, 1962*. Washington, D.C.: GPO, 1963.

————. *Public Papers of the Presidents of the United States: John F. Kennedy, 1963*. Washington, D.C.: GPO, 1964.

————. *Public Papers of the Presidents of the United States: Lyndon B. Johnson, 1963*. Washington, D.C.: GPO, 1964.

————. *Public Papers of the Presidents of the United States: Lyndon B. Johnson, 1964*. Washington, D.C.: GPO, 1965.

————. *Public Papers of the Presidents of the United States: Lyndon B. Johnson, 1965*. Washington, D.C.: GPO, 1966.

————. *Report of the President's Commission on the Assassination of President John F. Kennedy*. Washington, D.C.: GPO, 1964.

————. *Report of the President's Commission on Campus Unrest*. Washington, D.C.: GPO, 1970.

Wallace, Terry. *Bloods: An Oral History of the Vietnam War*. New York: Random House, 1984.

Walters, Pat, and Reese Cleghorn. *Climbing Jacob's Ladder: The Arrival of Negroes in Southern Politics*. New York: Harcourt, Brace and World, 1967.

Walton, Hanes, Jr. *Black Politics and Black Political Behavior*. Westport, Conn.: Praeger, 1994.

Ward, Brian, and Tony Badger, eds. *The Making of Martin Luther King and the Civil Rights Movement*. New York: New York University Press, 1996.

Wells, Tom. *The War Within: America's Battle over Vietnam*. New York: Henry Holt, 1994.

Westmoreland, William. *A Soldier Reports*. New York: Dell, 1976.

Wetteran, Bruce. *The New York Public Library Book of Chronologies*. New York: Prentice-Hall/Stonesong Press, 1990.

Wexler, Sanford. *An Eyewitness History of the Civil Rights Movement*. New York: Checkmark Books, 1993.

————. *The Vietnam War, An Eyewitness History*. New York: Facts On File, 1992.

Whitaker, John C. *Striking a Balance: Environment and Natural Resources Policy in the Nixon-Ford Years.* Washington, D.C.: American Enterprise Institute, 1976.

White, Mark J. *The Cuban Missile Crisis.* New York: Macmillan, 1996.

White, Mark J., ed. *Kennedy: The New Frontier Revisited.* New York: New York University Press, 1998.

White, Theodore H. *The Making of the President, 1960.* New York: Atheneum, 1967.

———. *The Making of the President, 1964.* New York: Atheneum, 1965.

Wicker, Tom. *One of Us: Richard Nixon and the American Dream.* New York: Random House, 1991.

Wofford, Harris. *Of Kennedys and Kings: Making Sense of the Sixties.* New York: Farrar, Straus, Giroux, 1980.

Wyden, Peter. *Bay of Pigs: The Untold Story.* New York: Simon & Schuster, 1979.

Zelman, Patricia. *Women, Work, and National Policy: The Kennedy-Johnson Years.* Ann Arbor: University of Michigan Research Press, 1982.

ARCHIVAL DOCUMENTS

Assassination File. Research Room. John F. Kennedy Library.

Attwood, William. Papers. John F. Kennedy Library.

Bundy, William. Papers. Lyndon B. Johnson Library.

Bush, Gerald. Peace Corps Papers. John F. Kennedy Library.

Campaign Files. Vice Presidential Collection. Richard M. Nixon Birthplace, Library, and Museum (Yorba Linda, California).

Council of Economic Advisors (CEA) Administrative History Correspondence. Lyndon B. Johnson Library.

Documents Sanitized and Declassified from Unprocessed Files. Lyndon B. Johnson Library.

Food for Peace Official History. Arthur M. Schlesinger, Jr., Papers. John F. Kennedy Library.

Guam Files. John F. Kennedy Library.

Hilsman, Roger. Papers. John F. Kennedy Library.

Johnson, Lyndon B. Cabinet Papers. Lyndon B. Johnson Library.

Johnson, Lyndon B. Public Papers (1963–1969). Lyndon B. Johnson Library.

Johnson, Tom. Papers. Lyndon B. Johnson Library.

Kennedy, John F. Public Papers (1961–1963). John F. Kennedy Library.

Kennedy, John F. Selected Speeches. Research Room. John F. Kennedy Library.

Kennedy, John F. Senate Files. John F. Kennedy Library.

The Kennedy–Nixon Debate Transcript. Research Room. John F. Kennedy Library.

Kennedy, Robert F. Oral History Project. John F. Kennedy Library.

Kennedy, Robert F. Presidential Campaign Papers 1968. John F. Kennedy Library.

Marshall, Burke. Papers. John F. Kennedy Library.

McNamara, Robert. "Vietnam Legacy." Speech to the John F. Kennedy Library Seminar on Vietnam, May 1995.

Meeting Notes File. Lyndon B. Johnson Library.

National Security File (NSF)—Cuba. John F. Kennedy Library.

National Security File (NSF). John F. Kennedy Library.

National Security File (NSF). Lyndon B. Johnson Library.

National Security Memorandum No. 179: U.S. Policy Toward Indonesia, August 16, 1962, POF/Box 119. John F. Kennedy Library.

Notes and Excerpts. Presidential Biographers. Research Room. John F. Kennedy Library.

Notes and Excerpts. Presidential Biographers. Research Room. Lyndon B. Johnson Library.

Office Files of the President. Lyndon B. Johnson Library.

President's Appointment File. Lyndon B. Johnson Library.

President's Official File (POF). John F. Kennedy Library.

Reagan, Ronald. Public Papers. Pre-Presidential Collection. Reading Room. Ronald Reagan Library.

Rostow, Walt W. Papers. Lyndon B. Johnson Library.

Sanjuan, Pedro. Papers. John F. Kennedy Library.

Schlesinger, Arthur M., Jr. Papers. John F. Kennedy Library.

Sorensen, Theodore C. Papers. John F. Kennedy Library.

State Department memorandum and report, "Observations on Proposal for a New Pacific Community," November 2, 1961, NSF/Box 345, John F. Kennedy Library.

Tet Offensive. Lyndon B. Johnson Library.

Transcript of the Lyndon B. Johnson Library School of Public Affairs Conference (1986). Lyndon B. Johnson Library.

U.S. Government. Report of the President's Commission on the Assassination of President John F. Kennedy (1964). Reading Room. John F. Kennedy Library.

White House Central File. John F. Kennedy Library.

White House Central File. Lyndon B. Johnson Library.

White House Famous Names File. Lyndon B. Johnson Library.

White House Special File. Papers of Richard M. Nixon. National Archives II (College Park, Maryland).

Wofford, Harris Llewellyn. Papers. John F. Kennedy Library.

PERIODICALS

"According to John." *Time,* August 12, 1966, p. 38.

"The Administration of Justice in the Wake of the Detroit Civil Disorder of July 1967." *Michigan Law Review* 66, no. 7 (May 1968): 1,544–1,559.

"The Adventurous Ones." *Vogue,* August 1, 1963, pp. 74–75.

"Affirmative? Negative!" *Newsweek,* July 1, 1968, p. 94.

Alsop, Stewart. "If Nixon Stumbles." *Saturday Evening Post,* February 10, 1968, p. 11.

"Anyone She Wants to Be." *Time,* June 23, 1967, p. 75.

Armbrister, Trevor. "The GI's Best Friend." *Saturday Evening Post,* March 12, 1966, pp. 93–95.

Armstrong, Marion. "Study in Infantilism." *The Christian Century,* October 18, 1967, p. 1,326.

Aronowitz, Alfred. "It's High Time Fame Came to Tiny Tim" *Life,* June 14, 1968, p. 10.

———. "Singer with a Bordello Voice." *Life,* September 20, 1968, p. 20.

———. "Three's Company: Peter, Paul and Mary," *Saturday Evening Post,* May 30, 1964, p. 30.

———. "Yeah! Yeah! Yeah!" *Saturday Evening Post,* March 21, 1964, pp. 30–35.

Beers, Jack. "Front Page Photo Tells Grim Story." *Dallas Morning News,* November 25, 1963, p. I:1.

"Book-O-Mat." *Library Journal,* December 1, 1962, p. 1.

Brossard, Chandler. "A Cry from Harlem." *Look,* December 15, 1965, pp. 125–129.

Bundy, McGeorge. "The Presidency and the Peace." *Foreign Affairs* 42 (April 1964): 353–365.

Buttinger, Joseph. "Fact and Fiction on Foreign Aid: A Critique of 'The Ugly American.'" *Dissent, a Quarterly of Socialist Opinion* 6 (Summer 1959): 319–320.

"Can You Top This?" *Newsweek,* July 6, 1964, pp. 72–73.

Cannon, James, and Charles Roberts. "Interview with the President." *Newsweek,* August 7, 1963, pp. 20–21.

Carter, George. "Similarity to Death Gun Tightens Murder Case." *Dallas Times Herald,* November 24, 1963, p. 1.

"Castro and U.S. Policy Toward Cuba, 1960." *United Nations Review* (November 1960): 46–47.

Chapman, Robert. "The Graduate Turns Bum." *Look,* September 17, 1968, 66–72.

Checker, Chubby, and Geoffrey Holder. "To Twist or Not to Twist." *Ebony,* February 1962, pp. 106–110.

Clifford, Clark. "A Vietnam Reappraisal." *Foreign Affairs* 47 (July 1969): 601–622.

"Comedians: A Put-On Is Not a Put-Down." *Time,* March 8, 1968, p. 65.

"The Coolest Things." *Newsweek,* March 6, 1967, p. 87.

Corliss, Richard. "Pop Music: What's Been Happening." *National Review,* April 4, 1967, pp. 371–374.

Costigliola, Frank. "The Failed Design: Kennedy, de Gaulle, and the Struggle for Europe." *Diplomatic History* 8 (Summer 1984): 227–251.

Cronin, Thomas. "On the American Presidency: A Conversation with James MacGregor Burns." *Presidential Studies Quarterly* 16 (Summer 1986): 528–542.

"Crusader Widens Range of His Ire." *Business Week,* January 25, 1969, pp. 128–130.

Denoon, David. "Indonesia: Transition to Stability?" *Current History* 61 (December 1971): 332–338.

"Detroit Does Its Number: A First Look at the Cars and Engines of the Next Decade." *Car and Driver,* September 1969, pp. 49–51, 79.

Didion, Joan. "On Becoming a Cop Hater." *Saturday Evening Post,* August 24, 1968, p. 16.

Dunbar, Ernest. "Vanguard of the Campus Revolt." *Look,* October 1, 1968, pp. 23–29.

"Dusty and the Duke." *Life,* July 11, 1969, pp. 36–45.

"End of the Beginning." *Time,* March 21, 1960, pp. 13–14.

"Far from Viet Nam and Green Berets." *Time,* June 21, 1968, p. 84.

Feith, Herbert. "Soviet Aid to Indonesia." *Nation,* November 3, 1962, p. 11.

Flagler, J. M. "Look on the Light Sight." *Look,* January 21, 1969, p. 40.

Frady, Marshall. "George Wallace: The Angry Man's Candidate." *Saturday Evening Post,* June 29, 1968, pp. 34–48.

"From 'No' to 'Yes.'" *Newsweek,* April 13, 1964, pp. 93–94.

Fryklund, Richard. "Targets in Vietnam." *Saturday Evening Post,* February 10, 1968, p. 4.

Gelb, Leslie. "The Essential Domino: American Politics and Vietnam." *Foreign Affairs* 50 (April 1972): 459–72.

"Girls of Motown." *Time,* March 4, 1966, pp. 83–84.

Given, Kyle. "And Now a Word from Our Sponsor." *Car and Driver,* September 1969, pp. 70–73, 77–79.

"Going to Great Lengths." *Newsweek,* October 8, 1965, p. 81.

Gold, Herbert. "Mao, Marx, et Marcuse!" *Saturday Evening Post,* October 19, 1968, pp. 56–59.

Goldberg, Louis C. "Ghetto Riots and Others: The Faces of Civil Disorder in 1967." *Journal of Peace Research* 5, no. 2 (1968):116–131.

Goldstein, Richard. "Janis Joplin . . . Staggering." *Vogue,* May 1968, p. 164.

———. "Pop Music." *Vogue,* May 1968, p. 164.

Goldwater, Barry. "Is McNamara Less Popular?" *Atlanta Constitution,* September 7, 1967, p. 1.

———. "Statement of Principles." *New York Herald-Tribune,* May 18, 1964, p. 1.

Goodwin, Richard. "Reflections." *New Yorker,* January 4, 1969, pp. 38–58.

"The Government Still Lives." *Time,* November 29, 1963, pp. 21–32.

Grossman, Michael Baruch, and Francis E. Rourke. "The Media and the Presidency: An Exchange Analysis." *Political Science Quarterly* 91 (1976): 455–457.

Hafner, Donald C. "Bureaucratic Politics and 'Those Frigging Missiles.'" *Orbis* 21 (Summer 1977): 307–333.

Halberstam, David. "The Face of the Enemy in Vietnam." *Harper's Magazine,* February 1965, p. 10.

Hamilton, Charles V. "The Constructive Equation: Black Power + White Power = Solutions." *Look,* January 7, 1969, p. 81.

Harrison, Cynthia E. "A 'New Frontier' for Women: The Public Policy of the Kennedy Administration." *Journal of American History* 67 (December 1980): 630–635.

Hartung, Philip T. "The Lawrence Legend." *Commonweal,* January 18, 1963, pp. 439–440.

Hedgepeth, William. "The Radicals: Are They Poles Apart?" *Look,* January 7, 1969, pp. 34–35.

Hershberg, James G. "Before the Missiles of October: Did Kennedy Plan a Military Strike Against Cuba?" *Diplomatic History* 14 (Spring 1990): 163–198.

Hill, Gladwin. "Pillow-Fight Underwater." *New York Times,* May 18, 1964, p. 1.

"Hippie Capitalists Are Making It Happen." *Business Week,* January 27, 1968, pp. 84–94.

Hollywood Advertiser. January 1966, back cover.

Humphrey, Hubert. "Perfectionism Is a Pitfall of Politics." *Progressive* (December 1971): 37–38.

Hunt, George. "Inviting an 'Era of Negotiation.'" *Life,* January 31, 1969, p. 32.

———. "Reading We Can Do Without." *Life,* March 14, 1969, p. 34.

Hyers, M. Conrad. "Batman and the Comic Profanation of the Sacred." *The Christian Century,* October 18, 1967, pp. 1,322–1,323.

"The Inauguration: Rhetoric Meets Reality." *Life,* January 31, 1969, pp. 18–31.

"Indonesia's Armoury." *Far Eastern Economic Review* (November 1, 1962): 283.

"I Spy: Comedian Bill Cosby Is First Negro Co-star in TV Network Series." *Ebony,* September 1965, pp. 65–71.

"Jaguar advertisement." *Road and Track,* December 1964, p. 18.

Jennings, C. Robert. "There'll Always Be an Elvis." *Saturday Evening Post,* September 11, 1965, pp. 76–79.

"The Jimi Hendrix Experience." *Ebony,* May 1968, pp. 102–106.

Johnson, Lyndon. "What It Is to Be Mr. President." *Look,* February 4, 1969, pp. 23–25.

"Just Playin' Folks." *Saturday Evening Post,* May 30, 1964, p. 25.

Kahn, Roger. "The Revolt Against LBJ." *Saturday Evening Post,* February 10, 1968, pp. 17–21.

Kaiser, Robert Blair. "College Forecast, '68." *Look,* September 17, 1968, pp. 22–26.

Karnow, Stanley. "Bill Cosby: Variety Is the Life of Spies." *Saturday Evening Post,* September 25, 1965, pp. 86–88.

Kavanaugh, James. "Christmas Doesn't Mean Much Any More." *Saturday Evening Post,* December 16, 1967, pp. 10–12.

Keats, John. "The Draft Is Good For You." *Saturday Evening Post,* February 10, 1968, p. 8.

Kelley, Kitty. "The Dark Side of Camelot." *People Weekly,* February 29, 1988, pp. 106–114.

"Kennedy Proposes Legislation." *New York Times,* October 7, 1964, p. 37.

Kerr, Clark. "The Turmoil in Higher Education." *Look,* April 18, 1967, pp. 17–20.

Kimball, Jeffrey P. "The Stab-in-the-Back Legend and the Vietnam War." *Armed Forces and Society* 14 (Spring 1988): pp. 433–458.

Kotlowitz, Robert. "Capote's Killers, and Others." *Harper's Magazine,* March 1968, pp. 155–156.

Lansdale, Edward G. "Two Steps to Get Us Out of Vietnam." *Look,* March 4, 1969, pp. 64–67.

Lawrenson, Helen. "Androgyne, You're a Funny Valentine." *Esquire,* March 1963, pp. 80–83.

Levin, Phyllis L. "The Short Short Story of the Skirt." *Readers Digest,* June 1966, pp. 112–114.

Lewis, Richard Warren. "When Four Nice Boys Go Ape!" *Saturday Evening Post,* January 28, 1967, pp. 74–78.

Llorens, David. "Natural Hair: New Symbol of Race Pride." *Ebony,* December 1967, pp. 139–144.

"Longer Hair Is Not Necessarily Hippie." *Time,* October 27, 1967, p. 46.

MacNeil, Robert. "The News on TV and How It Is Unmade." *Harper's Magazine,* October 1968, pp. 72–80.

Mandel, Leon. "Detroit Backlash." *Car and Driver,* September 1969, p. 76.

"Manners and Morals." *Time,* May 26, 1967, p. 53.

Manning, Rip. "Jackie Leaves Ring with Her Husband." *San Diego Evening Tribune,* November 23, 1963, p. A4.

Martin, Robert P. "Jungle War from Inside: An Eyewitness Report." *U.S. News & World Report,* October 30, 1961, p. 10.

Matthias, Willard. "How Three Estimates Went Wrong." *Studies in Intelligence* 12 (Winter 1968): 27.

"The Messengers." *Time,* September 22, 1967, pp. 60–68.

Michele, Iris. "I Tried LSD." *Ladies' Home Journal,* August 1966, pp. 52–54.

Mohr, Charles. "Times Talk." *New York Times,* March 10, 1964, p. 1.

Morgenstern, Joseph. "The Thin Red Line." *Newsweek,* August 28, 1967, pp. 82–83.

Moskin, J. Robert. "Arnold Toynbee Talks of Peace, Power, Race in America." *Look,* March 18, 1969, pp. 25–27.

Mueller, John E. "The Search for the 'Breaking Point' in Vietnam: The Statistics of a Deadly Quarrel." *International Studies Quarterly* 4 (December 1980): 497–519.

"Nader's Raiders: the U.S.'s Toughest Customer." *Time,* December 12, 1969, pp. 89–98.

Nixon, Richard M. "Nixon's Nationwide Radio Address." *New York Times,* September 20, 1968, p. 33.

"Notes and Comment." *New Yorker,* August 27, 1966, pp. 21–22.

Oberschall, Anthony. "The Los Angeles Riot of August 1965." *Social Problems* 15, no. 3 (Winter 1968): 322–341.

"On and Off." *Newsweek,* May 2, 1966, pp. 21–22.

"Open Up, Tune In, Turn On." *Time,* January 23, 1967, p. 53.

Packard, Vance. "Building the Beatle Image." *Saturday Evening Post,* March 21, 1964, p. 36.

Paterson, Thomas, and William J. Brophy. "October Missiles and November Elections: The Cuban Missile Crisis and American Politics, 1962." *Journal of American History* 73 (June 1986): 87–119.

Patterson, Oscar, III. "An Analysis of Television Coverage of the Vietnam War." *Journal of Broadcasting* 28 (Fall 1984): 397–404.

"The Politics of YIP." *Time,* April 5, 1968, p. 61.

Poppy, John. "The Draft: Hazardous to Your Health?" *Look,* August 12, 1969, pp. 32–34.

"The Purity of Madness." *Time,* May 17, 1968, p. 68.

Quinn, Mike. "Governor Connally Resting Well." *Dallas Morning News,* November 23, 1963, p. I: 1.

Rabi, I. I., and Leslie Dewart. "Views from Earth." *Look,* February 4, 1969, pp. 72–78.

Raffeto, Francis. "Act of Maniac." *Dallas Morning News,* November 23, 1963, p. I: 15.

Reid, Ogden. "Do Republicans Have the Courage to Become the Majority Party? It All Depends on Richard Nixon." *Look,* May 13, 1969, pp. 76–82.

Reston, James. "Goldwater." *New York Times,* June 2, 1964, p. 1.

Richardson, Elliot L. "The Foreign Policy of the Nixon Administration: Its Aims and Strategy." *Department of State Bulletin,* September 22, 1969: 260.

Rockefeller, Nelson. "Why I Want the Job." *Look,* August 20, 1968, pp. 32–34.

"Rocky Road to Fame, If Not Fortune." *Business Week,* August 23, 1969, pp. 78–80.

Rogers, Warren. "Ted Kennedy Talks About the Past, and His Future." *Look,* March 5, 1969, pp. 38–46.

Rollin, Betty. "A New Beat: Topical Folk Singers, Their Songs." *Vogue,* September 1, 1964, pp. 60, 82–83, 130.

Rosten, Leo. "How to Hate in One Easy Lesson." *Look,* December 15, 1965, p. 26.

———. "Who Speaks for the Young?: Some Startling Facts and Fictions." *Look,* May 19, 1970, p. 16.

Schaap, Dick. "Death of a Hooked Heiress." *Look,* July 26, 1966, pp. 19–25.

Schickel, Richard. "A Lyric, Tragic Song of the Road." *Life,* July 11, 1969, p. 10.

———. "Duke Talks Through His Green Beret." *Life,* July 19, 1968, p. 8.

Schulz, Donald. "Kennedy and the Cuban Connection." *Foreign Policy* 26 (Spring 1977): 57–139.

Sevareid, Eric. "American Militarism: What Is It Doing to Us?" *Look,* August 12, 1969, pp. 13–16.

Shepherd, Jack. "The Look Youth Survey." *Look,* September 20, 1966, pp. 44–49.

———. "The Princeton Commitment: A Race Against Mace." *Look,* June 16, 1970, pp. 12–14.

"The Shock of Freedom in Films." *Time,* December 8, 1967, pp. 66–76.

Sideman, Andrew. "I Was There." *Seventeen,* January 1970, pp. 87, 126.

Sidey, Hugh. "It Was Good to Be Home." *Life,* February 7, 1969, p. 2.

———. "The Man with the Four-Button Phone." *Life,* January 31, 1969, p. 4.

Silk, George, and Lynn Pelham. "Winter White House." *Life,* February 21, 1969, pp. 26–30.

Small, Melvin. "The Impact of the Antiwar Movement on Lyndon Johnson, 1965–1968." *Peace and Change* 10 (Spring 1984): 1–22.

Smith, Gene. "Would You Believe Don Adams?" *Saturday Evening Post,* June 4, 1966, pp. 32–33.

Smith, Sandy. "The Chicago Police Riot—Corruption Behind the Swinging Clubs." *Life,* December 6, 1968, pp. 34–42.

Sorenson, Theodore C. "JFK—His Vision, Then and Now." *U.S. News & World Report,* October 24, 1988, p. 33.

"Space Odyssey 1969." *Time,* July 25, 1969, pp. 73–74.

"The Spy." *Newsweek,* December 14, 1964, p. 51.

Stein, Jonathan A., and Daniel Simkin. "Excalibur: Subtle Like a Broad Sword." *Automobile Quarterly* 38 (December 1998): 7–17.

Todd, Richard. "Turned-On and Super-Sincere in California." *Harper's Magazine,* January 1967, pp. 42–47.

Tracy, Philip. "The Birth of a Culture." *Commonweal,* September 5, 1969, pp. 532–533.

Tunley, Roul. "Five Who Came Back from Drugs." *Seventeen,* January 1970, pp. 92–93, 136.

"Twist Wiggles into Big Time." *Business Week,* December 2, 1961, pp. 44–46.

U.S. Department of State. *Bulletin* 51, no. 1313 (August 24, 1964): 268.

———. *Bulletin* 52, no. 1343 (March 22, 1965): 404–427.

Verba, Sidney. "Public Opinion and the War in Vietnam." *American Political Science Review* 61 (June 1967): 317–333.

"Verrry Interesting . . . but Wild." *Time,* October 11, 1968, pp. 50–55.

"Vietnam's Wider War." *New York Times,* April 6, 1965, p. A38.

Weisman, Bernard. "Welcome Mr. Kennedy." *Dallas Morning News,* November 22, 1963, p. I: 14.

"Where Are They Now?" *Newsweek,* December 2, 1968, p. 20.

Whitworth, William, and Tom Wolfe. "How Does One Go about Meeting a Beatle: The Beatles Arrive." *New York Herald Tribune,* February 7, 1964, p. 1.

"Wilting Flowers." *Time,* May 10, 1968, p. 31.

Wise, David. "How Bobby Plans to Win It." *Saturday Evening Post,* June 1, 1968, pp. 23–27, 70.

Wood, Robert. "The CBS View." *Look,* June 24, 1969, p. 29.

Wren, Christopher. "Protest in the Ranks." *Look,* October 15, 1968, pp. 31–37.

Wright, Jim. "Corvette Sting Ray." *Motor Trend,* May 1963, pp. 18–23.

Zeitlin, David. "The Graduate." *Life,* November 24, 1967, pp. 111–112.

Zimmermann, Gereon. "Communist North Vietnam: Cocky and Patriotic." *Look,* January 21, 1969, pp. 19–30.

INTERNET SITES

Adamskii, Viktor. "Dear Mr. Krushchev." *Bulletin of the Atomic Scientists.* Available online. URL: http://www.thebulletin.org/issues/1995/nd95/nd95.adamskii.html. Downloaded May 29, 2001.

Barnes, Dave "Digger." "1960s British Pop Culture: Where Is Liverpool, Anyway?" Sixties Pop Culture. Available online. URL: http://home.clara.net/digger/sixties/info3.htm. Downloaded February 15, 2002.

Bart, Peter. "Mike Nichols, Moviemaniac." *New York Times.* Available online. URL: http://www.geocities.com/Hollywood/8200/times.htm. Downloaded February 12, 2002.

"The Beach Boys." Wilson and Alroy's Record Reviews. Available online. URL: http://www.warr.org/brian.html. Downloaded February 18, 2002.

Bodroghkozy, Aniko. "The Smothers Brothers Comedy Hour." The Museum of Broadcast Communication. Available online. URL: http://www.museum.tv/archives/etv/S/htmlS/smothersbrot/smothersbrot.htm. Downloaded February 2, 2002.

"The Chicago Seven Trial: In Their Own Words." University of Missouri, Kansas City Famous Trials. Available online. URL: www.law.umkc.edu/faculty/projects/ftrials/Chicago7/chicago7.html. Downloaded February 4, 2002.

"Chubby Checker Biography." Chubby Checker website. Available online. URL: http://www.chubbychecker.com/Bio.htm. Downloaded March 9, 2002.

"Chubby Checker." The Rock 'n' Roll Vault. Available online. URL: http://www.rocknrollvault.com/timeline/chubbychecker.htm. Downloaded February 26, 2002.

"The Cuban Missile Crisis, 1962/Chronology." National Security Digital Archives. Available online. URL: http://www.gwu.edu/~nsarchiv/nsa/ cuba_mis_cri/cmcchron3.html. Downloaded May 29, 2001.

"The Crisis: USSR/Cuba." Central Intelligence Agency Memorandum, October 27, 1962. National Security Archives. Available online. URL: http://www.gwu.edu/~nsarchiv/nsa/cuba_mis_cri/09-01.gif and www.gwu.edu/~nsarchiv/nsa/cuba_mis_cri/09-03.gif. Downloaded June 22, 2001.

Denvir, John. "The Lawyer Gets the Girl—and Creates the Future." University of San Francisco. Available online. URL: http://www.usfca.edu/pj/ articles/liberty.htm. Posted January 14, 2000.

Freek, Jim. "No Exit: Al Jardine Interview." *BAM Magazine*. December 18, 1998, p. 1–3. Angel Fire website. Available online. URL: http://angelfire.com/ la/Beachboysbritain/alint.html. Downloaded February 18, 2002.

Greenberg, David. "Fishy Outcome: The Legend of Nixon's 1960 Loss." Free Republic Conservative News Forum. Available online. URL: http:// www.freerepublic.com/forum/a3a245dbe741c.htm. Downloaded May 16, 2001.

Gutmann, Stephanie. "Half a Century of Student Protest." College Resources for Students and Facility. *The New York Times*. Available online. URL: http://college4nytimes.com/guests/articles/2001/11/11/883611/xml. Downloaded February 19, 2002.

Haslam, Dave. "What the Twist Did for the Peppermint Lounge." *London Review of Books*. Available online. URL: http://www.lrb.co.uk/v22/n01/ has12201.htm. Posted January 6, 2000.

Ingram, Billy. "Route 66." TV Party. Available online. URL: http://www. tvparty.com/route1.html. Downloaded February 25, 2002.

"Jack Nicklaus: Major Championship Performances." Jack Nicklaus website. Available online. URL: http://www.nicklaus.com/nicklaus_facts/ majors.php. Downloaded August 19, 2002.

Kennedy, Jacqueline. "Jackie's Letter to the Kremlin after the Assassination, December 1, 1963. Clint Bradford's John F. Kennedy website. Available online. URL: http://www.jfk-info.com/rus-jackie.htm. Downloaded August 4, 2002.

Kennedy, John F. "Inaugural Address, Friday, January 20, 1961." John Fitzgerald Kennedy Library and Museum. Available online. URL: www.jfklibrary.org/j012061.htm. Downloaded August 17, 2002.

"Marilyn Monroe Biography." MarilynMonroe.com. Available online. URL: http://www.marilynmonroe.com/bio.html. Downloaded February 25, 2002.

"Mickey Mantle." National Baseball Hall of Fame. Available online. URL: http://www.baseballhalloffame.org/hofers_and_honorees/hofer_bios/mantle_mickey.htm. Downloaded March 14, 2002.

Morris, Gary. "Beyond the Beach: AIP's Beach Party Movies." *Bright Lights Film Journal*. Available online. URL: http://www.brightlightsfilm.com/21/21_beach.html. Downloaded February 18, 2002.

"National Security Action Memorandum No. 72—Civil Defense Progress." 8/20/61. National Archives. Available online. URL: http://nara.gov/cgi-bin/starfinder/16820/images.txt. Downloaded February 18, 2002.

"New York Yankees and the National Baseball Hall of Fame." National Baseball Hall of Fame. Available online. URL: http://www.baseballhalloffame.org/teams/AL/yankees.htm.

"President Dwight D. Eisenhower's Farewell Address, January 17, 1961." Copperas website. Available online. URL: http://www.copperas.com/jfk/ikefw.htm. Downloaded August 2, 2002.

"Robert F. Kennedy Memorial." Arlington Cemetery. Available online. URL:http://www.arlingtoncemetery.org/visitor_information/Robert_F_Kennedy.html. Downloaded August 9, 2002.

"Robert F. Kennedy Obituary." *New York Times,* June 6, 1968. Arlington Cemetery. Available online. URL: http://www.arlingtoncemetery.com/rfk.htm. Downloaded August 9, 2002.

"Rock and Roll Timeline." The Rock 'n' Roll Vault. Available online. URL: http://www.rocknrollvault.com/timeline.htm. Downloaded February 26, 2002.

"Roger Maris Record." North Dakota's Roger Maris website. Available online. URL: http://www.ndrogermaris.com/maris_record.html. Downloaded March 14, 2002.

"Speech of Senator John F. Kennedy, Boston Garden, Boston, Mass., November 7, 1960." JKF Link website. Available online. URL: http://jfklink.com/speeches/jfk/nov60/jfk071160_boston02.html. Downloaded August 2, 2002.

"The Student Nonviolent Coordinating Committee Papers, 1959–1972 (SNCC)." University Microfilms Institute Research Collections. Available online. URL: http://pgdweb.umi.com/hp/Support/Research/Files/187.html. Downloaded February 28, 2002.

Warren, Bill. "Dr. No." Audiorevolution.com. Available online. URL: http://www.audiorevolution.com/dvd/revs/drno.html. Downloaded February 15, 2002.

———. "From Russia with Love." Audiorevolution.com. Available online. URL: http://www.audiorevolution.com/dvd/revs/fromrussia.html. Downloaded on February 15, 2002.

Weil, Martin. "Basketball Legend Chamberlain Dies at 62." *Washington Post.* Available online. URL: http://www.washingtonpost.com/wp-srv/sports/nba/daily/oct99/13/chamberlain13.htm. Downloaded August 18, 2002.

Yesterdayland. "Beach Party (series)." Available online. URL: http://www.yesterdayland.com/popopedia/shows/movies/mv1623.php. Downloaded on February 18, 2002.

Z, Simone. "Edward Kennedy's Chappaquiddick Accident." Germantown Friends School. Available online. URL: http://www.gfsnet.org/msweb/sixties/chappaquiddick.html. Downloaded August 14, 2002.

OTHER RESOURCES

Vietnam: Chronicle of a War. Beverly Hills, Calif.: Fox Video, 1981. VHS tape.

INDEX

Page numbers in **boldface** indicate biographical entries. Page numbers in *italics* indicate an illustration. Page numbers followed by *g* indicate glossary entries. Page numbers followed by *m* indicate maps.

A

Aaron, Hank 264
Abel, Rudolf 57
Abernathy, Ralph **313**
Abplanalp, Robert 247
Abrams, Creighton 209, 220
Abzug, Bella **313**
Academy Awards 21, 59
Acheson, Dean 134
acid rock 191, 246
Ackley, Gardner 152
Adams, Don 167, 190
Adams, Eddie 208
Adamskii, Vicktor 97
Admiral Corporation 18
Advisory Commission on Civil Disorders 220
A-11 aircraft 138
affirmative action 171
AFL-CIO 249
Africa, civil rights movement and 7
African Americans xvi. *See also* civil rights; *specific persons*
Afro (hairstyle) 193–194
draft 163
election of 1960 21
families 169–170
Guess Who's Coming to Dinner 201–202
Moynihan Report 169–170
reparations 262
urban migration xvii
Vietnam soldiers 120, 163
Vietnam veterans 196
Vietnam war opposition 182, 183
view of suburbs xv
Afro (hairstyle) 193–194
The Age Discrimination in Employment Act of 1967 (December 15, 1967) 298–299

"age of the common man" xv
Agnew, Spiro 242–243, **313–314**
Aiken, George 232
AIP (American-International Pictures) 166
Air Force, U.S. 141, 262
airline crashes 178
airline highjacking 261
airline strikes 262
Alabama. *See also* Birmingham, Alabama
Democratic Party 177
Freedom Riders 23
Montgomery protests 23
James J. Reeb 141
Selma protests 141
Selma-to-Montgomery march 142
University of Alabama 17, 94
voter registration drives in Selma 141
George Wallace 16–18
Al-Amin, Jamil Abdullah. *See* Brown, H. Rap
Alaska xix
Albany, Georgia (Albany Movement) 24, 53–54, 60
Aldrin, Edwin "Buzz" 262, *263*
Algeria 46, 57, 62
Ali, Muhammad (Cassius Clay) 138, 182, *195*, **314**
Aliluyeva, Svetlana 182
Allen, Woody **314**
Allende, Salvador 265
Alliance for Progress 23, 72
all-volunteer military 258
Allyn, Bruce J. 99
Alsop, Stewart 236
Altamont music festival 264
Ambrose, Stephen 31
America During the Cold War (Steven M. Gillon and Diane Kunz) 28

American Bandstand 10
The American Civil Rights Movement: Readings and Interpretations (Raymond D'Angelo) 37, 145
"American Dream" xv
American Independent Party 215
American-International Pictures (AIP) 166
American Nazi Party 184
American Space Exploration: The First Decade (William Shelton) 32
American values, movies and 76
America the Quotable (Mike Edelhart and James Tinen) 276
Anchorage, Alaska 139
Anders, William 224
Anderson, William 24, 53–54
anti-Americanism 11, 12, 45–46, 138
anticommunism
Bay of Pigs 11
and Berlin Wall 14
Cuban Missile Crisis 73
defense of Europe 15
Dominican Republic intervention 142
"Great Society" and 117
and Japan trade 22
Lyndon Johnson 114, 120
John Kennedy xvi, 2, 5, 6–7
Laos 48
NPC 51–53, 69
post-Berlin strategy 15–16
antiwar movement 162–163, 171–173, 196–198. *See also* campus unrest
Agnew's rhetoric 243
auto industry, view of 253

Berkeley-Oakland march 142–143
Berkeley recruitment protests 181
Cambodian incursion 257–259
Columbia University 221
in Congress 259–260
Democratic National Convention (1968) 213–214
disparate elements in 1968 200–201, 225–227
divisions in SDS 262
draft card burning 143
"Dump Johnson" movement 174–176, 197, 236
election of 1968 200
end of student deferment 163
Hubert Humphrey 182
International Tribunal on War Crimes 182
Kent State 259, 280–281
Martin Luther King and 182, 212–213
march by war supporters 183
Eugene McCarthy 210
middle-class youth and 199–200
Moratorium Day (1970) 263
Norman Morrison 143
New Left 200–201, 225–227
Nixon era 247–249, 259–260
organized labor 249–250
protest music 167
protest rallies 178
Nelson Rockefeller's view of 216
The Smothers Brothers Comedy Hour 202
and space program 255
Tokyo demonstrations 221, 262

antiwar movement *(continued)*
    TV coverage of war 209
    Washington, D.C. 184, 263
    Yippies 200
Apollo 1 fire 182
Apollo 7 mission 223
Apollo 9 mission 261
Apollo 11 mission 262
Apollo 13 mission 264
Appalachia 81
Are You Experienced? (Jimi
    Hendrix) 246
*Argument Without End: In Search
    of Answers to the Vietnam
    Tragedy* (Robert S.
    McNamara, James G. Blight,
    and Robert K. Brigham) 188
Arkansas 223
Arkus-Duntov, Zora 199,
    314–315
Armbrister, Trevor 106
arms control pact 82, 83
Armstrong, Marion 193
Armstrong, Neil 255, 262, *263*
Army of the Republic of
    Vietnam (ARVN) 49
Aronowitz, Alfred 156, 229, 230
ARVN (Army of the Republic
    of Vietnam) 49
Ashe, Arthur **315**
Asian/Pacific region. *See* New
    Pacific Community (NPC)
The Associated Press 143, 157,
    158, 181, 184, 224, 264
Astrodome 142
astronauts. *See* space program;
    specific astronauts
Athlete of the Year (Sandy
    Koufax) 138
Atlanta, Georgia 224
Atlanta Braves 264
atrocities 207, 263–264
Attwood, William 33, 65, 69,
    100
Australia 52–53, 131, 142
Austria Winter Olympics (1964)
    138
auto emissions legislation 250,
    253
automobile industry 157, 177,
    178, 182, 250–254, 261,
    274–276
automobiles
    Chevrolet Corvair 252
    Chevrolet Corvette 23

Chrysler Imperial 253
Corvette Sting Ray 23, 103,
    104, *199,* 199–200, 250,
    253
Excalibur 188–189, *189, 251,*
    251–252
Ford Mustang 156, *252,* 253
Jaguar XK-E 157
automobile safety legislation
    250, 253
auto parts industry 253
auto workers 253
Avalon, Frankie 166, *166*

B
baby boom ix, xv
Baez, Joan 21, *59,* 157, 167, **315**
Baker, Bobby 182
Baker, Ella 26, 145
Balaguer, Joaquín 164
balanced budget, John Kennedy's
    insistence on 43
Baldwin, James **315–316**
Ball, George 51, 130, 133–134,
    152
Barber, Bernard 190
Barbour, Floyd 195
Barnes, Dave "Digger" 105
Barnett, Ross 16, 142
Barrow, Clyde 202
baseball 183, 264
baseball commissioner 143
Batian Pinto, Luis 92
Batista, Fulgencio 11
Batman (TV show) 193
Bay of Pigs 11–13, 23, 33, 93
Beach Blanket Bingo (film) 166,
    166
The Beach Boys 102–103,
    164–166, *165,* 192, **316**
Beach Party movies 166
The Beatles *140,* **316**
    Beach Boys as competition
        164, 165
    "Beatlemania" 155–156
    breakup of 247, 264
    creative growth 192–193
    Ed Sullivan Show appearance
        128, 138
    first American tour 138
    "more popular than Jesus"
        controversy 190
    Queen Elizabeth bestows
        M.B.E. 158
    Sgt. Pepper 164, 183
    Stu Sutcliffe's death 59–60
    top singles of 1964 141

Bedford–Stuyvesant riots 140
Beers, Jack 109
Belafonte, Harry 56
Ben Bella, Mohammed 62
Ben-Hur 21, 22
Bennett, W. Tapley 153, 163
Berkeley, California 181, 222
Berkeley-Oakland antiwar march
    142–143
Berlin crisis 13–16, 23, 34
Berlin Wall 14–15, 23, 94
Berman, Edgar 239
Berrigan, Daniel **316–317**
Berrigan, Philip **317**
"Better Deal" 117
The Beverly Hillbillies 102
Bien Hoa 141
Big Three Automakers 253
Billboard magazine 10
Birmingham, Alabama
    church bombing 95
    civil rights 84–85
    Arthur Hanes on race relations
        106, 107
    Martin Luther King and 17,
        54–56, 84, 85, 94
    "Letter from Birmingham Jail"
        84, 85
    Burke Marshall negotiations
        94
    Wallace's reaction to protests
        106
    Andrew Young on protests 70
birth control 22, 222, 223
black market, in Vietnam 130
Black Muslims. *See* Nation of
    Islam
black nationalism 138
blackout of 1965 143
Black Panthers 223
black power 182, 183, 195
*Black Power: The Politics of
    Liberation in America* (Stokely
    Carmichael and Charles V.
    Hamilton) 194
Blight, James G. 99
blizzard 182
blockade 75, 92
Blue Hawaii 76
B-movies 166
Bob Dylan (LP) 58
Bogalusa, Louisiana 178
Bond, James. *See* James Bond
    movies
Bond, Julian 178, **317**

Bonnie and Clyde (film)
    192–194, 202
Borman, Frank 224
Boros, Julius 94
Bosch, Juan 163, 164
Bowles, Chester 33
boxing 62, 138
boycotts, supermarket 180
Boyer, Paul 26
Bradlee, Benjamin 125
"brainwashing" 220
Branch, Taylor 37
Brando, Marlon 11
Brezhnev, Leonid 134, 140
bridge collapse 184
Brill, Lorraine Sue 227
Brinkley, Douglas 31
"British Invasion" (pop culture)
    105, 128–129, 155–158, 192
Brossard, Chandler 148
Brown, H. Rap **317**
Brown, James **318**
Brown, Jim **318**
Brown, Pat 78–79
Bruce, Lenny 57
brutality. *See* police brutality
Buckley, William F. **318**
Buddhism 94, 178
budget deficit 183, 254
*Bulletin, Vol. 51, No. 1313, August
    24, 1964* (U.S. Department of
    State) 149
Bullock, Dan 262
Bundy, McGeorge 98, 150, 234
Bundy, William 153
Burdick, Eugene 2–3
Bureau of Labor Statistics 223
Burger, Warren 262, 265,
    318–319
business leaders, Lyndon Johnson
    and 119
Business Week 31, 228, 273, 274,
    279

C
Cadillac Fleetwood 253
California 78–80, 164, 213
Cambodia 222, 224, 257–259,
    264, 265
"Camelot" 7–9, 91, 118,
    135–136
Camp Holloway attack 124
campus unrest 225–227
    City College of New York
        (CCNY) 262

Cox Commission 222
Harvard University 262
Kent State University 259,
    264, 280–281
San Francisco State College
    223
Union Theological Seminary
    262
University of
    California–Berkeley 223
University of
    Wisconsin–Oshkosh 223
Camranh Bay, South Vietnam
    180
Canada 60, 184, 220
cancer, cigarettes and 138
"Can't Help Falling in Love"
    (Elvis Presley) 76
Capehart, Homer 72
capitalism 52, 117, 130
capital punishment 181
Car and Driver 200, 275
Caribbean 60, 61
Carmichael, Stokely 182, 194,
    195, 319
cars. See automobile industry
Castro, Fidel 319
  anti-Castro terrorists 223
  attempted assassination of 12,
    13
  Bay of Pigs 11–13
  Cuban Missile Crisis 76, 92
  denunciation of United States
    26
  exodus of antigovernment
    Cubans 142
  Guantánamo naval base 138
  Hero of the Soviet Union
    Award 94
  influence on Latin America
    11, 23
  and nuclear war threat 72
  and Soviet Union 12, 57, 61
  on U.S. view of Cuba 69
Castro Ruz, Juana 140
Catholic Church. See Roman
    Catholicism
The Cause Is Mankind: A Liberal
    Program for Modern America
    (Hubert H. Humphrey) 148
CBS Evening News
  antiwar activity predictions
    260
  election of 1960 21
  poll on trusted politicians 242

on television's future 18
  Vietnam War 125
CBS television network 182,
    202, 222
CCNY (City College of New
    York) 262
Census Bureau 21
Central American Common
    Market 94
Central Intelligence Agency
    (CIA)
  Bay of Pigs 11, 12
  Cuban invasion 61
  and Laos 47, 48
  planned invasion of Cuba 11
  Sukarno assassination attempt
    45
Ceraso, Louise 178
Cernan, Eugene 178, 179
Chafe, William H. 26
Chaffee, Roger 135, 182
Chamberlain, Wilt 58
Chaney, James 139
change, Kennedy era xiv–xv, 4,
    5, 43–44
Chapin, Dwight 248
Chappaquiddick scandal 256,
    262, 280
Charles, Ray 93
Charlie Company 126
Charlton, Michael 152
Chavez, Cesar 265
Cheap Thrills (Big Brother and
    the Holding Company) 246
Checker, Chubby 10, 11, 31,
    63–64, 93
Chehab, Fuad 24
chemical weapons 262
Chevrolet Corvair 252
Chiang Kai-shek 93
Chicago
  "Days of Rage" demonstrations
    248
  Democratic National
    Convention (1968)
    213–214, 222, 226, 228
  riots 140, 179, 262
Chicago Auto Dealer Association
    103
Chicago Police Department 261
Chicago Seven Trial 263, 264
Chile 265
China 2, 93, 134, 141, 142, 243
China-India border war 92
Chisholm, Shirley 223, 223

Christmas, materialism and 194
Christmas Island nuclear tests 60
Christmas Truce (Vietnam) 143
Chrysler Imperial 253
Church, Frank 249, 258
CIA. See Central Intelligence
    Agency
CIA and the Vietnam Policymakers:
    Three Episodes 1962–1968
    (Harold P. Ford) 68
cigarettes 138, 177, 261
Citizens Committee for Peace
    with Freedom in Vietnam
    184
City College of New York
    (CCNY) 262
civil liberties 179, 297–298
The Civil Rights Act of 1960
    284–286
The Civil Rights Act of 1964
    117, 118, 140, 293–294
The Civil Rights Act of
    1966/1967 170
The Civil Rights Act of 1968
    221, 306
civil rights/Civil Rights
    movement. See also voting
    rights
  Age Discrimination in
    Employment Act 298–299
  Agnew's rhetoric 243
  Albany Movement 24, 53–54,
    60
  and antiwar movement
    212–213
  Birmingham, Alabama 17,
    54–56, 70, 84–85, 94, 95,
    106, 107
  black power 195
  Civil Rights Act of 1964 117
  and cold war 7, 17, 53–56,
    69–70
  conservative backlash 215
  Vernon Dahmer 177
  Medgar Evers 94
  Freedom Riders 23
  impatience with Johnson's
    progress 119
  interracial marriages 183
  Jimmie Lee Jackson 141
  Lyndon Johnson and 114,
    116–117, 119–120,
    144–145
  Martin Luther King and xix
  John Kennedy and Congress 8

John Kennedy's commitment
    to 1, 44
  John Kennedy's policies 53
  Robert Kennedy and 137
  Ku Klux Klan 62, 144
  Malcolm X 85–87
  March on Washington (1963)
    87, 94
  James Meredith 16, 37, 62, 64,
    142, 178, 194–195,
    330–331
  Moscow protests 96
  murder of activists in
    Mississippi 139
  Nashville, Tennessee, sit-ins 21
  as national moral issue 17
  post–Voting Rights Act era
    169–171, 194–196
  James J. Reeb 141
  reform legislation 138
  Nelson Rockefeller's view of
    216
  Selma, Alabama 141
  Selma-to-Montgomery march
    142
  and space program 255
  Special Protocol Service 7
  Tuskegee High School 95
  University of Alabama 94
  and Vietnam War 120
  voting rights 119, 148
  George Wallace 16–18, 215
  "war on poverty" 116,
    144–145
  and women's movement 88
  Samuel Younge, Jr. 177
Civil War xv
Clark air base, Philippines 264
Clay, Cassius. See Ali,
    Muhammad
Clean Air Act 256
"Clean for Gene" campaigners
    210
Cleaver, Eldridge 223, 266,
    319–320
Clifford, Clark 209, 219, 234
Colbert, David 32
cold war xvi, 38–70
  Algeria 62
  antiwar movement 247
  Bay of Pigs 11–13, 23, 33, 93
  Berlin crisis 13–16
  and Civil Rights movement 7,
    17, 53–56, 69–70
  election of 1960 2, 4

cold war (continued)
　and foreign aid 3, 23
　Charles de Gaulle 45–47, 67
　Barry Goldwater and 118
　"hot line" 95
　Japan 40
　Kissinger's Vietnam plans 243
　John Kennedy and 5–7
　New Pacific Community
　　51–53, 69
　nuclear weapons 39–40
　Sukarno 45–46, 66–67
　U-2 spy plane incident 22, 57
　Vietnam, John Kennedy and
　　. 49–51, 67–69
　Western Europe 38–41
Collins, Michael 262
color television 18–19
Columbia University antiwar
　protests 221
Columbia University School of
　Journalism 125
Commerce Department 87, 182
Common Market. See European
　Common Market
communism xvi, 11, 48. See also
　cold war
Communist Party–Indonesia 46
Communist Party—USA 162
communists, South Vietnamese
　208
communist sympathizers 17, 88
Congress, U.S.
　antiwar sentiment/legislation
　　258
　Civil Rights Act of 1968 221
　deadlock on Nixon proposals
　　254–255
　election of 1962 78–80
　election of 1966 180
　environmental legislation 256
　Fulbright hearings on Vietnam
　　171–173
　Lyndon Johnson's civil rights
　　legislation 113–117
　Lyndon Johnson's
　　persuasiveness as president
　　114, 115
　John Kennedy assassination
　　reinvestigation 91
　John Kennedy's deadlock with
　　8, 41–44
　John Kennedy's years in xviii
　and Nixon communication
　　reforms 242

Super Sonic Transport (SST)
　plane 256
Tonkin Gulf Resolution, repeal
　of 265
unemployment benefits (1961)
　23
Vietnam legislation 265
Vietnam War, waning support
　for 160–161
Vietnam War powers for
　Lyndon Johnson 122
"war on poverty"
　appropriations 184
William Westmoreland's address
　174
"Women's Strike for Peace"
　investigations 88
Connally, John 89
Connor, Theophilus Eugene
　"Bull" 17, 54–56, 55, 84,
　106
Connery, Sean 77
Conrad, Charles, Jr. 142
conscription. See draft
conservative Americans. See
　"Middle America"; "silent
　majority"
conservatives 114, 116, 174,
　256–257
Conservatives in an Age of Change:
　The Nixon and Ford
　Administrations (James A.
　Reichley) 268
conspiracy theorists, John
　Kennedy assassination
　89–91, 113, 182, 261
Constitution of the United
　States
　Twenty-third Amendment 288
　Twenty-fourth Amendment
　　295
　Twenty-fifth Amendment
　　299–300
　Twenty-sixth Amendment 258
consumer goods, in Vietnam
　129–130
Conthien, Vietnam, siege 184
contraceptive pill 22, 222, 223
conventional forces 15, 39
Conversations with Stalin (Milovan
　Dijlas) 59
Cooper, L. Gordon 142
Copeland, Joseph 262
Corliss, Richard 192
corruption 130, 131, 249

Corvair (Chevrolet) 252
Corvette Sting Ray 23, 103,
　104, 199, 199–200, 250, 253
Cosby, Bill 142, 157–159, 167,
　168, 168
cost of living 223, 261
counterculture ix–x. See also
　campus unrest; folk music;
　rock and roll/popular music
　Altamont music festival 264
　antiwar movement 162, 174,
　　200
　hippies 184, 200, 228, 231
　movies 246
　music 245–247
　Woodstock music festival 246,
　　263
counterfeiting 219
Court, John 157
Cox Commission 222
Crawfordsville, Florida 179
"credibility gap" 173, 174
"crimes against humanity" 182
Cronkite, Walter 231, 320
　American concerns, mid-'60s
　　160
　Christmas 1967 broadcast 176
　denunciation of Johnson war
　　policy 209, 220
　on Lyndon Johnson 5
　Vietnam reporting 126
"crossover" voters 210, 213
C. Turner Joy, USS 122, 140
Cuba. See also Bay of Pigs;
　Castro, Fidel
　aid from United States 93
　airline highjacking 261
　anti-Castro terrorists 223
　blockade of 92
　Juana Castro Ruz's defection
　　140
　exodus of antigovernment
　　citizens 142
　Guantánamo naval base 138
　Guatemalan protests 58
　invasion plans 72, 92
　map (1961–1962) 340m
　preparations for U.S. invasion
　　of 60, 62
　Soviet military in 72
　Soviet weapons 57, 60–61
　weapons from USSR 71–72
Cuban Missile Crisis 60, 61,
　71–76, 92, 93, 97–102
　effect on Nuclear Test Ban
　　Treaty 81–82

election of 1962 78
Kennedy's report 288–291
and Nixon's California
　gubernatorial bid 79
Cuba on the Brink: Castro, the
　Missile Crisis, and the Soviet
　Collapse (James G. Blight,
　Bruce J. Allyn, and David
　Welch, eds.) 99
Culp, Robert 167, 168, 168
Cultural Revolution 142
Cunningham, Walter 223
Curry, Jesse 108

D
Dahmer, Vernon 177
Daley, Richard J. 214
Dallas, Texas 89, 107–109
dance crazes 10, 10–11, 31,
　63–64
D'Angelo, Raymond 37, 145
Davis, Arthur 181
Davis, James 24
Davis, Sammy, Jr. 204
Day, Doris 92–93
"Days of Rage" demonstrations
　248
Dean, James 201
death penalty 224
debates 4, 21, 22, 28
"decade of change" 1
"decisive battle" 205, 206
Decker, George 22
Dee, Joey, and the Starlighters 11
defense contract corruption
　68–69, 249
defense industries 250
defense policy, U.S., women's
　opposition to 88
defense spending 43, 184
deficits, government 120
deficit spending 254
de Gaulle, See Gaulle, Charles de
Dellinger, Arthur 69
DeLorean, John 250
Democratic National
　Convention (1964) 119, 135
Democratic National
　Convention (1968) 213–214,
　222, 226, 228, 261, 263, 264
Democratic Party
　Alabama 177
　Civil Rights/antiwar
　　movement alliance 213
　congressional majority 119

"dump Johnson" movement 197
  effect of Wallace candidacy on 215
  election of 1956 xx
  election of 1960 21
  election of 1962 78
  election of 1968 176, 205
  fair housing backlash 170
  House of Representatives 119
  John Kennedy and xix
  labor unions 250
  Eugene McCarthy and 210
  National Convention (1960) 22
  primaries (1968) 212
  Roosevelt as standard-bearer xiii
  southern backlash against 247
  urban riots 170
  Vietnam War, waning support for 161
  Vietnam withdrawal as political suicide 134
  George Wallace and 118–119
demonstrations. See antiwar movement; campus unrest; civil rights/Civil Rights movement
Dennison, Robert 92
Denvir, John 105
desegregation 220. See also civil rights/Civil Rights movement
Detroit, Michigan, race riots 184, 240–241
Dewart, Leslie 274
The Dick Clark Show 10
Didier, Calvin 240
Didion, Joan 225
Diefenbaker, John 60
Diem, Ngo Dinh 65
  ambitions for Vietnam 50, 51
  assassination of 120
  Buddhist protests 94
  coup attempt against 57
  Averell Harriman testimony 57
  recognition of rule 50
  regime overthrown 95
  request for military advisers 23
  Strategic Hamlet program 94
  Vietnam fact-finding mission 49
Dijlas, Milovan 59

Dillon, C. Douglas 81
Dinerstein, Herbert 26
diplomacy 7, 74–75
Dirksen, Everett 117, 148, 161–162, 243, 320
divisive politics 249
Dobrynin, Anatoly 61, 75
Dr. No 77
dollar, devaluation of 254
Dominican Republic 136, 142, 153–155, 154, 163–164
domino effect 48
"doomsday" strategy 39
The Doors 261
Douglas, William O. 222
draft
  for antiwar activists 184
  evasion 219, 222
  extension (1967) 183
  increase, for Vietnam War 142, 220
  Martin Luther King's opposition to 182
  reduction (1968) 222
  student deferment 163
draft card burning 143
drugs, illicit 22, 200, 245, 246
Duc Lap, Vietnam 222
Duke University 261
Dulles, John Foster 39
"Dump Johnson" movement 174–176, 197, 236
Dunbar, Ernest 225
Dutton, Fred 198
Dylan, Bob 59, 320–321
  appeal of 157
  career begins 22
  first album released 58
  prediction of social change 23
  and protest music 167
  second album released 45
  and Woodstock 246
Dymally, Mervyn 69

E
Earth Day 264
earthquakes 139, 223
Easy Rider 246
Ebony magazine 64, 159, 194, 229
Eckert, William 143
economic conservatism, John Kennedy's embrace of 2, 42–43
economic disparity 87

Economic Opportunity Act 116
economic warfare 12, 51–53, 69
economy, U.S.
  automobile industry 250–254, 274–276
  cost of living 223, 261
  devaluation of dollar 254
  disparity of wealth 87–88
  early Nixon years 249–250, 254–255
  effect of Vietnam War on 249–250
  improvement in early 1964 81
  inflation 223, 254, 261
  Johnson's confidence in, 1964-1965 123–124
  and space program 255
  Super Sonic Transport (SST) plane 256
  unemployment rate (1968) 220
Edelhart, Mike 276
The Ed Sullivan Show 128, 138, 181
education spending 43
EEOC (Equal Employment Opportunity Commission) 171
Ehrlichmann, John 248, 248, 276
Eichmann, Adolf 24
Eisele, Donn 223
Eisenhower, Dwight D.
  and anticommunist Vietnamese regimes 121
  and Cuba 11, 12
  on Cuban Missile Crisis 78
  death of 262
  election of 1956 xix, xix–xx
  election of 1960 3–4
  farewell address 25–26
  on Barry Goldwater 146
  governing style, vs. '60s activism xiv
  on Laos 48
  on leadership 26
  planned invasion of Cuba 11
  Sukarno assassination attempt 45
  Vietnamese elections 50
elderly Americans 23
election of 1928 2
election of 1956 xix–xx
election of 1960 1–5, 20–22, 342m

"Getting the country moving again" xiii
  Kennedy-Nixon debates 4, 22, 28
  John Kennedy and xvii, xx, 1–5, 3
  Nixon and xx, 3–5
  West Virginia primary 20–21
  Wisconsin primary 21, 27
election of 1962 48, 78–80
election of 1964 88–89, 118–119, 135–136, 141, 145–148, 343m
election of 1966 180
election of 1968 210–218, 235–240, 344m
  antiwar movement 200
  California primary 213
  Democratic National Convention 213–214, 222, 226
  Democratic Party 176, 205
  "Dump Johnson" movement 174–176, 197, 236
  Great Society 176, 205
  Hubert Humphrey 221–223
  import policies 254
  Indiana primary 221
  Lyndon Johnson 176, 212, 237
  Johnson's decision not to seek reelection 300–305
  Johnson's Vietnam hopes 205
  Edward M. Kennedy 222
  Robert F. Kennedy 210, 212, 220–222, 235–239
  law and order 216
  Eugene McCarthy 200, 205, 210–213, 220–222, 235–238
  "Middle America" 214–216
  Edmund Muskie 216
  Nebraska primary 221, 238
  New Hampshire primary 208, 210–212, 220, 235–236, 239
  Richard Nixon 216–217, 220, 222, 223, 233, 235, 236, 239, 240
  North Vietnam and peace negotiations 209
  Oregon primary 213, 222
  "Pigasus" 200
  Republican Party 216–218
  results 216
  Nelson Rockefeller 216, 220, 221

election of 1968 (continued)
George Romney 220
James Rowe 212
Tet Offensive 208
third parties 215–216
total votes cast 216
Vietnam War 176
voting age 210
George Wallace 174, 215–216, 223, 236, 239
Wisconsin primary 210–213, 220
Yippie platform 200
election of 1972, environmentalism and 256–257
Elliot, Jeffrey 69
Ellsberg, Daniel 260
embargo, Cuba 57
Emerson, Ralph Waldo xiii
employment rate (1964–1965) 120
Engel v. Vitale 60
entertainment industry 18–19. See also movies; rock and roll/popular music; television
environmentalism 255–257, 264, 273–274, 276, 277
environmental legislation 256
Environmental Protection Agency (EPA) 255–256
Equal Employment Opportunity Commission (EEOC) 171
Equal Pay Act of 1963 (June 10, 1963) 94, 291–292
Equal Rights Amendment (ERA) 182, 265
escalation (of Vietnam War) 122, 133–135, 148–153, 209
escapism 202, 204
"the Establishment" xvi
Europe, defense against USSR 15
Europe, Western 15, 38–41
European Common Market 61–62
Evers, Charles 262
Evers, Medgar 94, 321
evolution, teaching of 183, 223
Excalibur sports car 188–189, 189, 251, 251–252
The Excalibur Story, or the Development of the Contemporary Classic (Brooks Stevens) 189

Executive Committee of the National Security Council (ExComm) 92
Executive Order 10924, Establishment and Administration of the Peace Corps in the Department of State 287–288
executive privilege 122, 171
Executive Sessions of the Senate Foreign Relations Committee, vol. 15, 1963 (U.S. Congress) 35, 63, 67
exports, Japanese 53
"Extremism in the defense of liberty is no vice" 118
Eyewitness to America (David Colbert) 32

F
fair housing legislation 170–171
fallout shelters 14, 35
families, African-American 169–170
Family Assistance Plan 255
family farms, collapse of 21
Farmer, James 1
Farnham, Marynia xvii
fashion 103, 104, 128–129, 159, 190, 192–194
Fayette, Mississippi 262
federal budget 177, 219
Federal Bureau of Prisons 224
Federal Communications Commission (FCC) 242, 261
federal spending 143, 255
Feldon, Barbara 190
Female Athlete of the Year (Mickey Wright) 138
The Feminine Mystique (Betty Friedan) 94
feminism xvii, 128
Fidel Castro: Nothing Can Stop the Course of History (Jeffrey Elliot and Mervyn Dymally) 69
Fifth Republic 45, 46
figure skating 138
films. See movies
firebombings 177
"first strike" 73
"The 5 O'Clock Follies" 128
Fleming, Ian 77
Fleming, Peggy Gale 138, 321
"flexible response" 39
floods 261, 262

Florida public school strike 220
folk music
Joan Baez 21, 59, 157, 167, 315
Bob Dylan 22, 23, 45, 58, 59, 157, 167, 246, 320–321
Phil Ochs 104–105
Peter, Paul, and Mary 156–157
Pete Seeger 21
Fonda, Jane 202, 321
Fonda, Peter 246
food, surplus 22
Food and Drug Administration 22
Food for Peace 22, 214
football 181
Ford, Gerald 89, 243, 260
Ford, Harold P. 68
Ford, John 76
Ford Mustang 156, 252, 253
Foreign Affairs Committee (House of Representatives) 160
foreign aid, as cold war weapon 3, 23
Foreign Relations Committee 172, 173
Fortas, Abe 232
Foster, William 63
The Four Seasons 93
France. See also Gaulle, Charles de
Dienbienphu 205
embassy in China 138
Geneva disarmament conference 58
NATO headquarters closing 179
nuclear policy independence 93
Paris strikes (1968) 221, 222
Vietnam 50, 133
Free at Last? The Civil Rights Movement and the People Who Made It (Fred Powledge) 107
Freedom of Information Act of 1966 (July 3, 1966) 297–298
Freedom Riders 23, 60
The Freewheelin' Bob Dylan (Bob Dylan) 45
Friedan, Betty 87, 88, 94, 322
Friendly, Fred 125
"friendly fire" 181
Friendship 7 spacecraft 57, 58

From Camelot to Kent State: The Sixties Experience in the Words of Those Who Lived It (Joan Morrison and Robert K. Morrison) 227, 281
From Russia with Love 77
Fryklund, Richard 233
Fulbright, J. William 238
Cuban Missile Crisis 92
Cuba/Panama speech 138–139
Lyndon Johnson's Vietnam war powers 124
Vietnam hearings 171–173, 178, 186
Westmoreland's address to Congress 174
Fulbright, William J. 149, 153
Funicello, Annette 166, 166
Fursenko, Alexander 63

G
Gallagher, Buell 262
Gallup Poll
American values xv, 242
Cambodian incursion 258
movies 18
Nixon approval 259
trust in government 173
Vietnam War 130, 173, 200, 258–259
women's rights xvii
World War III 71
Gardner, Lloyd C. 150
Garner, James 23
Garrettson, Charles Lloyd 240
Garrison, Jim 182, 261
Garvey, Marcus 86
gasoline, unleaded 250
Gaulle, Charles de
on change in European defense policy 15
cold war relations with United States 45–47, 67
embassy in China 138
French colonialism 57
NATO headquarters closing 179
on nonalignment 67
nuclear policy independence 93
Quebec separatist movement 184
Gavin, James 133

gay/lesbian rights movement 262

Gemini: A Personal Account of Man's Venture into Space (Virgil "Gus" Grissom) 32

Gemini 3 spacecraft 141

Gemini 4 spacecraft 142

Gemini IX-A spacecraft 178

General Motors 177, 261

generation gap ix, 163

"Generation of Peace" 243, 244

Geneva Accords 50

Geneva Conference on Asia 49–50

Geneva disarmament conference 58

Georgia 24, 53–54, 60

Germany 13–16, 47

Get Smart 167, 169, 190

"Getting the country moving again" xiii

Giap, Vo Nguyen 28, 206, 208

Gillon, Steven M. 28

Ginsberg, Allen **322**

Given, Kyle 275

Glenn, John 32, 57, *58*

Goldberg, Louis C. 240

Goldman, Eric F. 67

Goldstein, Richard 228, 229

Goldwater, Barry 146, 186, **322**
and Berlin crisis 14–15
election of 1964 118–119, 141, 145–147
Fulbright hearings 178
Great Society backlash 170
voting age change support 258
John Wayne and 203

golf 60, 94, 138

Golman, Eric 67

Goodman, Andrew 139

Goodwin, Doris Kearns 133, 270

The Graduate 191, 193, 201, 228

Grand Design 39, 40

granny dresses 159

Grant, Cary 93

Grant, Joanne 26

grassroots campaigning 3

Great Britain 57, 61–62, 82

Great Depression xv

Great Society 115–117
African-American families 169–170
and business 119
conservative backlash 170

election of 1968 176, 205
Lyndon Johnson's outline for 141
Robert Kennedy and 136, 137
underfunding of 120
and Vietnam War 123, 131–133

Green Bay Packers 181, *181*

The Green Berets (film) 203, 204, 229–230

Greene, Graham 49

Greenhaw, Wayne 148

Greensboro, North Carolina 22

Gregory, Dick **322–323**

Gribkov, Anatoly I. 99

Grissom, Virgil "Gus" 32, *135*, 141, 182

Gromyko, Andrei 62

Gruening, Ernest 122–123

Guantánamo naval base, Cuba 138

Guatemala 58, 222

Guess Who's Coming to Dinner (film) 201–202

Guiles, Roger 223

Gulf of Tonkin Resolution (August 7, 1964) 293–294

"guns and butter" 123–125

The Guns of August (Barbara Tuchman) 8, 94

H

Haight-Ashbury district 228

Hail to the Chiefs: My Life and Times with Six Presidents (Ruth Montgomery) 33, 66

Haiphong, North Vietnam 143

Hair (Broadway musical) 184, 221, *221*

Haise, Fred 264

Halberstam, David 68

Haldeman, H. R. 248, *248*

Hall, Gus 162

Hamilton, Charles V. 194, 266

Hanes, Arthur 107

Hanoi, North Vietnam 179

Harbour, William 36

Hargreaves, Robert 276

Harkins, Paul 57

Harlem riots 140

Harper's Magazine 68, 191

Harriman, Averell 57, 67, 102, 247, 249

Harrington, Michael xvii, 81

Harris, Jay S. 30–31

Harris, Roy 266

Harrison, George 155

Harris Poll 242

Harvard University xviii, 262

Haslam, Dave 32

Hatfield, Mark 258

Hattiesburg, Mississippi 177

Hawaii xix

Hayden, Tom 60, 162, 201, 249, **323**

health care reform 119, 138

health insurance 23

heart, artificial 178

"hearts and minds," battle for 7, 247

Heller, Walter 65

Hendrix, Jimi 229, 246, 265, **323**

Hepburn, Katharine 201

Hero of the Soviet Union Award 94

Herrick, John J. *121*

Hersh, Seymour M. 268

Hershey, Lewis 163, 184

Highway Beautification Act 142, 143

hijacking, airline 261, 262

Hill, Gladwin 146

hippies 184, 200, 228, 231. *See also* counterculture

Ho Chi Minh *50*
antiwar movement, U.S. 162
death of 263
Dominican intervention as message to 163–164
Gulf of Tonkin incident 122
Tom Hayden's view of 162
on Laos 48
negotiations with 125, 130, 143
1965 lull in Vietnam War 130
recognition of rule 50
strategy 134
Tet Offensive 206, 208

Ho Chi Minh Trail 205

Hoffa, Jimmy 110

Hoffman, Abbie 200, 230

Hoffman, Dustin 201, 230, 262

Holder, Geoffrey 64

Hollywood. *See* movies

Holocaust 24

"Holy Trinity" 1

Hong Kong 60

Honolulu, Hawaii, summit 173

Hoopes, Townsend 188

Hoover, Herbert 2

Hoover, J. Edgar 29, 78, **323–324**

Hoover's FBI (W. W. Turner) 29

Hope, Bob 105–106

Hopper, Dennis 246

Hornby, Leslie. *See* Twiggy

"hot line" 95

House of Representatives 138, 141, 160–161, 180, 223

House Rules Committee 41, 44

House Un-American Affairs Committee 88

housing 170–171, 221, 223, 306

Housing and Urban Development Department 177

How to Stuff a Wild Bikini 166

Hubert (Edgar Berman) 239

Hubert H. Humphrey: The Politics of Joy (Charles Lloyd Garrettson) 240

Hudson, Rock 93

Hue, South Vietnam 207–208

Hughes, Howard **324**

Human Sexual Response (Masters and Johnson) 178

Humphrey, Hubert *111,* **324**
antiwar demonstrations against 182
on business support 119
Democratic National Convention (1960) 22
Democratic National Convention (1968) 213–214
election of 1960 1, 20, 21, 213–214
election of 1968 216, 221, 223
import policies 254
Kennedy debates 21
presidential nomination (1968) 222
Vietnam stance (1968) 213
Vietnam visit 178
Vietnam War, waning support for 162
Voting Rights Act 169
and Wallace candidacy 215–216

Humphrey, Hubert H. 144, 148, 239, 240

Hunt, George 268, 270

Huntley-Brinkley Report 126

Huong, Tran Van 131

Hurricane Alma 179
Hurricane Camille 263
hydrogen bomb 177
Hyers, Conrad M. 193

I

Iacocca, Lee 156, 253, **324–325**
Iacocca: An Autobiography (Lee Iacocca) 156
"I Have a Dream" speech (Martin Luther King, Jr.) 87, 94, *95*
Ikeda, Hayato 22, 40, 52, 53
The Illusion of Peace: Foreign Policy in the Nixon Years (Tad Szulc) 268
I Love Lucy 173
"imperial presidency" 178
import policies 254
inaugural address, John Kennedy 5, 22, 286–287
India 24, 92
Indiana primary election (1968) 221
Indonesia 61, 141. *See also* Sukarno, Achmed
inflation 223, 254, 261
infrastructure bills 120
In Retrospect: The Tragedy and Lessons of Vietnam (Robert S. McNamara) 68–69, 188
integration. *See* civil rights
International Federation of Airline Pilots 262
International Tribunal on War Crimes 182
interracial marriage 183, 201–202
investigative journalism 126, 127
"Iron Triangle" 181
I Spy 142, 157–159, 167–169, *168*
Israel 139, 177, 183

J

Jackson, Andrew xv
Jackson, Henry "Scoop" 2
Jackson, Jesse **325**
Jackson, Jimmie Lee 141
Jackson, Robert 26
Jaguar Motor Company 157
Jaguar XK-E 157
Jamaica 61
James Bond movies 76–78, 156
Jansen, David 204

Japan
  air disasters 178
  cold war relations with United States 40
  and New Pacific Community (NPC) 52, 53
  Tokyo antiwar demonstrations 221, 262
  Tokyo population 60
  Tokyo Summer Olympics (1964) 141
  trade with U.S. 22
  and U.S. import policies 254
The Japan Reader: Postwar Japan, 1945 to the Present 25
Jardine, Al 164, *165*
Javits, Jacob 72
J. C. Penney 128
Jefferson, Thomas xv
Jefferson Airplane 191
Jennings, Robert C. 105, 158
JFK (movie) 89
Joan Baez (LP) 167
John Birch Society 79
John F. Kennedy and the New Pacific Community, 1961–1963 (Timothy Maga) 66
John XXIII (pope) 92, 94
Johnson, Lady Bird 136, 143, 146, 185
Johnson, Luci Baines 178
Johnson, Lyndon Baines *109*, 113–143, *115, 132, 139, 161, 177, 180, 187, 206, 238*, **325**
  on 1965 lull in Vietnam War 130
  address on limiting Vietnam War 300–305
  antiwar movement 152, 171–172, 197
  assumption of presidency 89, 95, 110
  auto emissions legislation 250
  bombing of North Vietnam 141
  budget deficits, Nixon's vs. 254
  on campus radicalism 226
  civil rights 17, 119–120, 144–145, 148
  Cuban policies 138
  James Davis and 24
  decision not to seek reelection 212, 220, 304–305

Democratic National Convention (1960) 22
Dominican Republic 142, 153, 155
draft numbers doubled 142
"Dump Johnson" movement 174–176, 197, 236
early legislation as president 113–115
economy (1964–1965) 123–125
election of 1960 2, 20
election of 1964 89, 118–119, 141, 146, 147
election of 1968 176, 212, 237
executive privilege 149
federal budget (1968) 219
final State of the Union address 261
Barry Goldwater and 118–119
Great Society programs 115–117, 141
"guns and butter" 123–125
Highway Beautification Act 142
Honolulu summit 173, 178
Indonesia 141
as John Kennedy's running mate 22
Robert Kennedy's Senate campaign 136
on legacy of presidency 273
Manila conference 180
Eugene McCarthy's challenge 210
Medicare 142
New-Deal style activism xiv
New Hampshire primary (1968) 211, 220
New York Times letter on Fulbright hearings 172–173
and NPC 53
Nuclear Test Ban Treaty 82
post-Tet escalation of troops 209
record federal budget 177
Roosevelt's influence xiii
Selma-to-Montgomery march 142
South Vietnam tour (1961) 23
Soviet-American relations 138
State of the Union address (1968) 219
Tet Offensive 205, 231–235

Tonkin Gulf Resolution 120–123, 140
Vatican visit 184
as vice president 5, 8–9, 44
Vietnam, peace in 150
Vietnam critics 186
Vietnam mission limits 187
Vietnam negotiations 125, 130
Vietnam strategy questions 188
Vietnam War 120–135, 174–176, 269, 270
and voting rights 119
Voting Rights Act 142, 169
war on poverty 81, 144
White House liquor cabinet 266
Johnson, Paul 142
Joint Chiefs of Staff 57, 73, 258
Joint Hearing on the Southeast Asia Resolution before the Senate Foreign Relations and Armed Services Committees, 88th congress, 2nd Session, August 6, 1964. (U.S. Senate) 149
Joplin, Janis 229, 230, 245–246, 265, *265*, **325**
journalism
  antiwar demonstrations 171
  demise of *Saturday Evening Post* 261
  Democratic National Convention (1968) 214
  effect on antiwar sentiment 209
  Great Society/Vietnam backlash 170
  investigative 126, 127
  Nixon's relationship with 242
  reaction to events of 1968 202
  Tet Offensive 208
  Vietnam War 125–128, 130, 131
Jupiter missiles 59, 60
Justice Department 85, 177

K

Kahn, Roger 235
Kaiser, Robert Blair 225
Kansas City Chiefs 181
Karnow, Stanley 158
Katzenbach, Nicholas 186
Kauffman, John 226
Kavanaugh, James 194
Kazin, Michael 239

Keating, Kenneth 136
Keats, John 233
Keegan, Leone 281
Kennan, George 63, 81
Kennedy (Theodore C. Sorensen) 111
Kennedy, Arthur 38
Kennedy, Edward M. *107,* **326**
 Chappaquiddick scandal 256, 262, 280
 as Democratic Whip 261
 election of 1968 222
 environmental legislation 256
 on his upbringing xviii
 Robert Kennedy and 136
Kennedy, Jacqueline *34, 42,* **326**
 Dallas visit 89
 French diplomatic visit 47
 on John Kennedy as potential vice president 27
 Onassis marriage 223
 the twist 10
 White House 8, 57
Kennedy, John Fitzgerald xvii–xx, 1–9, *6, 9, 13, 71, 74, 90, 96, 107,* **326**. *See also* "Camelot"; Cuban Missile Crisis
 Albany Movement 54
 Alliance for Progress 33, 34
 anticommunist Vietnamese regimes 121
 assassination of xvii, 88–91, 95, 107–110
 Bay of Pigs 11–13, 23, 33, 93
 Berlin crisis 34
 Berlin Wall 94
 Birmingham protests 56
 campaign goals 1
 Central American Common Market 94
 Civil Defense 36
 Civil Rights movement 53–56, 69–70
 civil rights reform 1, 8, 16
 cold war victory promise xvi
 Commerce Department 1963 report 87
 Congress, relationship with 41–44
 on Cuba 63
 Cuban invasion 57, 62
 on deficit 63
 economic conservatism 42–43
 economy, late 1963 87

education bill 43
 election of 1956 xix–xx
 election of 1960 xx, 1–5, 20–22, 88
 election of 1964 plans 88–89
 European conventional forces 41
 on "first strike" 57
 French colonialism 57
 and French diplomatic visit 47
 and de Gaulle 46–47
 Tom Hayden's view of 162
 Humphrey debates 21
 inaugural address 5, 22, 29, 286–287
 on Indonesia 66
 on Japanese-American relations 36
 and Martin Luther King xix
 and Robert Kennedy's Senate campaign 136
 Ku Klux Klan denunciation 62
 Laos 48, 60, 67
 lifestyle of 5
 Moon landing promise xvi
 New-Deal style activism xiv
 and New Pacific Community (NPC) 51–53
 news conferences 8
 Nixon debates 4, 22, 28
 Nuclear Test Ban Treaty 81–84, 292–293
 on Philippines 66
 racism, promise to end xvi
 Roosevelt's influence xiii
 as seminal 1960s leader ix
 in Senate xviii–xix
 Social Security legislation 23
 space program 255
 steel industry crisis 60
 stump speech 27–28
 and Sukarno 45–46
 transportation bill 43–44
 Tuskegee High School 95
 and TV xvii
 and U.S. import policies 254
 Vietnam policies 49–51, 67–69
 "war against poverty" 80–81
 Warren Commission report 89, 90, 140
 on Wisconsin primary 27
Kennedy, Joseph P. xviii, 264

Kennedy, Robert Francis *71, 107,* **326–327**
 on activism in 1968 225
 assassination of 213, 222
 as attorney general 8, 29
 Birmingham, Alabama protests 85, 106
 on black youth 197
 California primary (1968) 213
 civil rights 144
 on civil rights reform 37
 conference with black leaders 87
 on congressional battles 65, 66
 Cuban invasion 57, 61
 Cuban Missile Crisis 61, 75, 92
 election of 1960 xx, 3
 election of 1964 141
 election of 1968 198, 210, 212, 220, 222, 235–239
 and J. Edgar Hoover 29
 on Indochina 69
 and Lyndon Johnson 9, 44, 116
 Martin Luther King's assassination 213, 305–306
 murder trial 261
 Nebraska primary 238
 post–Cuban Missile Crisis era 80
 on poverty 145
 presidential candidacy announcement 212, 220
 primaries (1968) 213
 Nelson Rockefeller's view of 216
 as Senator 135–137
 and Sukarno 46
 Vietnam position 188, 235, 237
 on voting rights 69–70
 "war against poverty" 81
Kennedy: The New Frontier Revisited (Mark J. White, ed.) 34
Kennedy-Humphrey debates 21
Kennedy-Nixon debates 4, 22, 28
Kennedy's Quest for Victory: American Foreign Policy, 1961-1963 (Thomas G. Paterson, ed.) 29, 30
Kent State 259, 264, 280–281
Kerr, Clark 197

Keynesian economics 254
Khanh, Nguyen 138
Khaury, Herbert. *See* Tiny Tim
Khe Sahn 205–207, 219, 222. *See also* Tet Offensive
Khmer Republic 264
Khmer Rouge 257, 258
Khrushchev, Nikita S. *13,* **327**
 Berlin crisis 13–14
 on Cadillac tail fins 30
 and Cuba 12
 Cuban Missile Crisis 59–61, 75–76, 78, 92–94
 fall from power 140–141
 Geneva disarmament conference 58
 and Gulf of Tonkin incident 122
 on Indonesia 66
 on Laos 48
 Nuclear Test Ban Treaty 83
 Soviet-American relations 138
kidnapping 224
Kilpatrick, James Jackson 197
King, Martin Luther, Jr. xv, xix, *95, 211,* **327**
 Albany Movement 24, 60
 antiwar movement 182, 183, 212–213
 assassination of 171, 213, 220, 305–306
 Birmingham, Alabama 17, 54–56, 84, 85, 94
 centralized leadership 145
 Civil Rights movement xix, 53–56, 69–70
 and Bull Connor 54–56
 draft resistance 182
 economics of racism 87
 FBI surveillance 70
 "I Have a Dream" speech 87, 94, *95*
 and John Kennedy 22, 53–56
 "Letter from Birmingham Jail" 84, 85
 and Malcolm X 87
 March on Washington (1963) 87, 94
 murder trial 261
 Nobel Peace Prize 141
 Selma, Alabama 141
 Selma-to-Montgomery march 142
 sermon (1961) 28

King, Martin Luther, Jr.
  (continued)
  Vietnam war opposition 182,
    183, 212–213
  Voting Rights Act 169
  Watts riots 195
Kirkland, Lane 252
Kissinger, Henry **327–328**
  antiwar movement 247
  firing of foreign economic
    advisors 249
  and Japanese exports 254
  leadership style 268
  Nixon candidacy (1968) 216
  Paris Peace Talks 264
  Rockefeller campaign 216,
    235
  Vietnam policies 243
Kittikachorn, Thanon 264
Klein, Herbert 79
Kluger, Richard 26–27
Knox, William 92
Kopechne, Mary Jo 256, 262,
  280
Korea, North 219–220, 224, 262
Korea, South 131, 139
Kosygin, Aleksei 134, 140
Kotlowitz, Robert 228
Koufax, Sandy 138
Kramer, Stanley 201
Kremlin 95
Krist, Gary Steven 224
Kubrick, Stanley 202, 220
Ku Klux Klan 62
Kunz, Diane 28
Kuralt, Charles 126–128, 151
Ky, Nguyen Cao 130–131, 142,
  173, *177,* 178, 181–182

L
labor unions 249–250
Lane, Mark 89
Lansdale, Edward G. 270
Laos 23, 47–49, 60, 67, 264
*The Last Innocent Year: America in
  1964, The Beginning of the
  "Sixties"* (Jon Margolis) 149
Latin America 11, 23, 58
Laugh-In (TV show) 204, 219,
  228, 230
law and order 170, 216
Lawrence, Peggy 191
Lawrence, T. E. 38, 39
Lawrence of Arabia 38–39
Lawrenson, Helen 104

leadership xvi
Leary, Timothy 22, 190, **328**
Lebanon 24
Lederer, William 2–3
Lefcourt, Peter *30*
the Left (political) 114, 258. *See
  also* New Left
LeMay, Curtis 215
Lemnitzer, Lyman 22, 68
Lennon, John 158, 190, 191
Leonard, Sheldon 167
"Let It Be" (The Beatles) 247
"Let's Spend the Night
  Together" (the Rolling
  Stones) 181
"Let's Twist Again" (Chubby
  Checker) 11
"Letter from Birmingham Jail"
  (Martin Luther King, Jr.) 84,
  85
Levittowns xv
Lewis, John 53
Lewis, Richard Warren 191
liberalism 2, 133, 216, 254
Liberty, USS 183
Liberty Bell 141
Library Journal 102
Library of Congress 267, 270,
  275, 280
Life magazine xx, 240, 253, 268,
  277, 280
"light at the end of the tunnel"
  206
*Light at the End of the Tunnel: A
  Vietnam War Anthology*
  (Andrew J. Rotter, ed.) 196
The Limits of Intervention
  (Townsend Hoopes) 188
Lincoln, Abraham xv
Lindsay, John 200
Lin Piao 142
Lippman, Walter 22
Liston, Sonny 62, 138
Livingston, Jon 25
Loan, Nguyen Ngoc 208
lobbyists 81
Lodge, Henry Cabot, Jr. 4, 94,
  261
Lombardi, Vince **328**
Long, Russell 261
Lon Nol 257, 264
Look magazine 196, 253, 266
Los Angeles 142, 213
Love, Mike 164, *165*
Lovell, James 224, 264

Lowenstein, Allard 170, 176, 236
LSD 22, 190, 191
Lubell, Samuel 106
Lucey, Patrick 21
lunar landing 255, 262
Lundahl, Art 97
Lundberg, Ferdinand xvii
Lyndon: An Oral Biography (Merle
  Miller) 226
*Lyndon Johnson and the American
  Dream* (Doris Kearns
  Goodwin) 270

M
Mackle, Barbara Jane 224
Macmillan, Harold 48, 61–63
MacNeil, Robert 230
Maddox, USS *121,* 121–122,
  140
Maga, Timothy 66
Maharis, George 200
Mailer, Norman 45
Malcolm X *86,* 87, 88, 138, 141,
  329–330
Malraux, André 91
Mandel, Leon 275
The Man from U.N.C.L.E. 140,
  167, 169, 204
Mankiewicz, Joseph 49
Mann, Tom 153
Mansfield, Mike 152, 153
Manson, Charles 264
Mantle, Mickey 183, *183,* 330
The Man Who Shot Liberty Valence
  76, 105
"Many Flags" campaign 131
*Many Reasons Why: The American
  Involvement in Vietnam*
  (Michael Charlton and
  Anthony Moncrieff) 152
March on the Pentagon *175,*
  184, 198, *269*
March on Washington (1963)
  77, 87, 94
Marcos, Ferdinand 143, *180,*
  264
Marcos, Imelda *180*
Marcula 75
Marcuse, Herbert 162, 226
Margolis, Jon 149
marijuana 190
Mariner spacecraft 61
Marines, U.S. 124, 209
Maris, Roger 23, *23,* **330**
marriages, interracial 183

Marshall, Burke 56, 94, 144
Marshall, Thurgood 184
Martha's Vineyard 256
Martin, Ann 29
Martin, Dick 204
Martin, Robert P. 36
Marvin, Lee 76
Marxism 265
"massive retaliation" 39, 72, 82,
  83
mass murder 182
Masters and Johnson 178
Mates, Leo 67
Max, Peter **330**
McCarthy, Eugene **328**
  election of 1968 200, 205,
    210–213, 220, 222, 235–238
  ERA 182
  financing of primaries 237
  Robert Kennedy's campaign
    197, 237–238
  New Hampshire primary 210,
    212, 220, 235–236
  Oregon primary 222
  reaction to Robert Kennedy's
    presidential ambitions 212
  retirement of 262
  Nelson Rockefeller's view of
    216
  Wisconsin primary 210–213,
    220
McCartney, Paul 156, 165, 264
McCone, John 61, 68, 133
McDivitt, James 142
McDonald, C. W. 193
McGiffert, David 198
McGinnis, Joe 235
McGovern, George 25, 214,
  258, **328–329**
McIntyre, Thomas 236
McLendon, Gordon 192
McLeod, Harriet 196
McLuhan, Marshall **329**
McManus, George 57
McNamara, Robert *151, 177,*
  329
  on 1970s economic forecasts
    249
  Berlin crisis, reaction to 15
  on cold war allies 40
  Cuba, military action against
    92
  Cuban Missile Crisis 61, 98
  on defense contract corruption
    68–69

on Eisenhower 68
Lyndon Johnson administration 116
John Kennedy's secretary of defense 6
mandatory service 178
Nuclear Test Ban Treaty 81–83
resignation as Secretary of Defense 184, 209, 219, 233
on Soviet negotiations 35
Vietnam, assistance to 57
Vietnam, potential military collapse 124
Vietnam bombing missions 134
Vietnam escalation 130, 133
Vietnam outlook 125, 186, 188
Vietnam's effect on U.S. economy 124
Meany, George 249–250
Medicare 142
medium range ballistic missiles (MRBMs) 92
Meet the Press 20
Mein, John Gordon 222
Memoirs of Hope: Renewal and Endeavor (Charles de Gaulle) 67
The Memoirs of Richard Nixon (Richard M. Nixon) 29, 33, 64
Memphis, Tennessee 213, 220
Men in Space (Thomas D. Segel) 32
Menon, Krishna 24
Menzies, Robert 52–53, 142
Mercury space program 23
Meredith, James 16, 37, 62, 64, 142, 178, 194–195, **330–331**
Miami Beach, Florida, hotel robbery 178
Michele, Iris 190
Michigan Law Review 241
"Middle America" 214–216. See also "silent majority"
middle class xvii, 116
Middle East 24, 177
midiskirt 192
Midnight Cowboy (film) 262
military advisers 49
Military Assistance Command, Vietnam (MACV) 57, 59, 67
military reservists case 222
milk, powdered 130

Miller, David 143
Miller, Merle 226
Mills, Wilbur 153
Milner, Martin 200
Milwaukee Journal 21
minimum wage 23, 42
miniskirt 128–129, 190, 192
minorities xvi–xvii
Miranda v. Arizona 179
Mirmar Naval Air Station crash 264
Miss America Pageant 222
missile gap 2
Mississippi
    Vernon Dahmer 177
    Democratic National Convention (1964) 119
    floods 262
    James Meredith 16, 37, 62, 64, 142, 178, 194–195, **330–331**
    murder of civil rights activists 139
    Oxford riots 16, 62
    University of Mississippi integration 16, 37, 62, 64, 142, 194–195
Mitchell, John 248, 261
Miyazawa, Kiichi 22, 25, 53
moderate Americans. See "Middle America"; "silent majority"
Modern Woman: The Lost Sex (Ferdinand Lundberg and Marynia Farnham) xvii
Mohr, Charles 146
Moncrieff, Anthony 152
The Monkees 189, 191, **331**
"Monkey Law" 183
Monroe, Marilyn 44–45, 61, **331**
Montgomery, Ruth 33, 66
Moon exploration, unmanned 141, 182, 219, 224
Moon landing, manned 255, 262
Moore, Joe 25
moral leadership xvi
"morally bankrupt" xv
Moratorium Day (1970) 263
Moratorium Day (1971) 260
Morgan, Charles 106
Morgenstern, Joseph 192
Morrison, Jim 261
Morrison, Joan 227, 281
Morrison, Norman 143

Morrison, Robert K. 227, 281
Morse, Wayne 122–123, 149
Morton, Bruce 130
Moss, George Donelson 281
Motion Picture Association of America 24, 76, 222
Motley, Constance Baker 195
Motown 189
movies 18, 22, 24, 105, 166, 167
    Academy Awards 21, 59
    Beach Blanket Bingo 166, 166
    Ben-Hur 21, 22
    Blue Hawaii 76
    Bonnie and Clyde 192–194, 202
    counterculture 246
    Dr. No 77
    Easy Rider 246
    The Graduate 191, 193, 201, 228
    The Green Berets 203, 204, 229–230
    Guess Who's Coming to Dinner 201–202
    How to Stuff a Wild Bikini 166
    Lawrence of Arabia 38–39
    The Man Who Shot Liberty Valence 76, 105
    Midnight Cowboy 262
    The Quiet American 49
    Rebel Without a Cause 201
    From Russia with Love 77
    top box office successes (1960) 22
    top box office successes (1961) 24
    top box office successes (1962) 92, 93
    top box office successes (1963) 95
    top box office successes (1964) 141
    top box office successes (1965) 143
    top box office successes (1966) 181
    top box office successes (1967) 184
    top box office successes (1968) 224
    top box office successes (1969) 264
    top box office successes (1970) 265
    2001: A Space Odyssey 202, 220
    Vietnam War and 203, 204

movie theaters 19
Moynihan, Daniel Patrick 169–170
muckraking 252–253
murders 182
Murphy, Audie 49
Murrow, Edward R. 31, 126
Murtaugh, Steve 226
"muscle cars" 250–251
music. See folk music; rock and roll/popular music
Muskie, Edmund S. 216, 242, 256, **331–332**
Mutual Assured Destruction (MAD) 40–41
"my country right or wrong" 215
My Lai massacre 263–264

N
Nader, Ralph 252–253, 273, 273, 275, **332**
Naftali, Timothy 63
NASA 57, 182. See also space program
Nashville, Tennessee sit-ins 21
The Nation 66
National Conference of Catholic Bishops 223
national debt 261
National Guard
    Birmingham church bombing 95
    Cuban Missile Crisis 73
    Kent State University 258, 264
    King memorial service, Chicago 262
    Selma-to-Montgomery march 142
    student demonstrations 261
    Tuskegee High School 95
National Liberation Front (NLF). See Vietcong
National Organization for Women (NOW) 179
National Security Advisor 243
National Security Council (NSC) 48, 61, 152, 162, 245
National Security Memorandum No. 181 61
National Technical Means (NTM) 83
Nation of Islam 85, 86, 141
Native Americans xvi

NATO. *See* North Atlantic Treaty Organization
Navy, U.S. 75, 122, 149, 262
Nazi Party, American 184
Nazi war crimes prosecutions 24
NBC 126, 142, 169, 180, 204, 208
Nebraska primary election (1968) 221, 238
Nehru, Jawaharlal 65
Nelson, Gaylord 78, 123–124, 256, 277
"new American Revolution" xv
Newark, New Jersey, race riots 183
A New Black Consciousness (Floyd Barbour) 195
New Deal
  Goldwater's opposition to 118
  influence on Lyndon Johnson xiii, 114
  influence on John Kennedy xiii, 6
  legacy under Lyndon Johnson 216
  message as conveyed by Stevenson xx
  model for 1960s government activism xiii, xiv
  political/social upheaval xv
"New Economics" 43
Newfield, Jack 98, 188
New Frontier xiii, 5–7
  election of 1962 78
  Great Society, continuity with 115–116
  Lyndon Johnson's expansion of programs 113–114
  John Kennedy's speeches 43–44
  Robert Kennedy's Senate campaign 136
  New Pacific Community (NPC) 51, 53
  Social Security legislation 23
  "war against poverty" 81
New Guinea 46, 61
New Hampshire
  primary election (1960) 21
  primary election (1968) 208, 210–212, 220, 235–236, 239
New Haven, Connecticut 181
New Jersey riots 140
New Left
  antiwar movement 162, 200–201, 225–227

birth of 120
ideology 162
Port Huron Statement 60
post–Voting Rights Act era 170
Newman, Paul 136
"New Nixon" 216
New Orleans 60
New Pacific Community (NPC) 51–53, 69
Newport Folk Festival 21
news conferences 8, 138
newspapers, competition from television 125–126
Newsweek 72, 156–159, 190, 191, 230, 231
Newton, Huey P. 195, 222
New York City 178, 223, 224, 248
The New Yorker 191
The New York Times 110, 191, 237
  Johnson letter on Fulbright hearings 172–173
  Kissinger's Vietnam plans 243
  Robert Kennedy as Senator 136, 137
  Soviet military in Cuba 72
  the twist 11
New York Yankees 183
New Zealand 131
Ngo Quang Duc 94
Nhu, Ngo Dinh 95
Nichols, Mike 191, 201
Nicholson, Jack 246
Nicklaus, Jack 60
1960s, end of 242
Nixon, Richard M. *243, 248, 258, 263, 271, 276, 278,* **332**
  on American youth 270
  antiwar movement 247–249
  Bay of Pigs 33
  budget deficits, Johnson's vs. 254
  California governor's race 64, 78–80
  Cambodian incursion 264
  early days of presidency 242–245, 266–272
  on economic policies 275
  and economy 254–255
  election of 1960 xx, 3–5, 21–22
  election of 1962 78–80

election of 1968 216–217, 222, 223, 233, 235, 236, 239, 240
  election to presidency 223
  environmental legislation 255–257, 276, 277
  import policies 254
  inauguration 242, 261
  Kennedy debates 4, 22, 28
  Kent State University 258, 280
  Robert Kennedy's Senate campaign 136
  on last day as vice president 28–29
  Laugh-In appearance 204, 230
  media advisers' view of 235
  Moratorium Day 260, 263
  New Hampshire primary (1968) 220
  organized labor support 250
  Philippines 264
  presidency, early days 268–269
  presidential nomination (1968) 222
  on *Profiles in Courage* 4
  response to antiwar legislation 258
  "secret plan to end the Vietnam War" 216, 240
  "Southern Strategy" 247
  TEA expansion 254
  on Tet Offensive 233
  Tonkin Gulf Resolution, repeal of 265
  on *The Ugly American* 3, 4
  Vietnam War address 306–312
  Vietnam War progress 266–267
  Wallace candidacy 216
The Nixon Presidential Press Conferences (Library of Congress) 267, 270, 275, 280
"Nixon's the One" 216
Nobel Prize 8, 141
nonaligned nations 62. *See also* France; Indonesia
Nonalignment Theory and Current Policy (Leo Mates) 67
Norodom Sihanouk (Cambodian prince) 257, 264
North Atlantic Treaty Organization (NATO) 15, 46, 179
NPC. *See* New Pacific Community

NSC. *See* National Security Council
NTM (National Technical Means) 83
nuclear disarmament 58, 141
nuclear stockpiles 339*g*
Nuclear Test Ban Treaty 57, 81–84, 94, 292–293
nuclear tests, China 141
nuclear tests, U.S. 60, 338*g*
nuclear tests, USSR 338*g*
nuclear war, threat of xvi, 14, 73, 76, 81–82
nuclear weapons 15, 23, 39–40, 47, 215
Nugent, Patrick 178

O
OAS. *See* Organization of American States
Oberschall, Anthony 241
Ochs, Phil 104–105
OEO (Office of Economic Opportunity) 138
Office of Economic Opportunity (OEO) 138
Of Kennedys and Kings: Making Sense of the Sixties (Harris Wofford) 65
Ogier, Herbert L. *121*
oil 45
Okinawa 262
Oldfather, Felicia 25
Oldsmobile 253
Olson, James 28
Olympic Games 22, 138, 141
Onassis, Aristotle 223
Onassis, Jacqueline Kennedy. *See* Kennedy, Jacqueline
"One Hell of a Gamble": Khrushchev, Castro, and Kennedy, 1958–1964 (Alexander Fursenko and Timothy Naftali) 63
On the Road with Charles Kuralt (Charles Kuralt) 151
Open Housing Act of 1968 171, 306
Operation MONGOOSE 12–13, 57, 58, 61
Operation Resolve to Win 220
Operation ROLLING THUNDER 124, 130
Operation WHIP LASH 60

Orangeburg, South Carolina, race riots 220
Oregon primary election (1968) 213, 222
Organization of American States (OAS) 57, 142, 164
Oswald, Lee Harvey 89, 95, 113, 140, **332**
The Other America (Michael Harrington) xvii
O'Toole, Peter 38
Oxford, Mississippi 16, 62

P
Paar, Jack 25, 64
Packard, Vance 156
Palestine Liberation Organization (PLO) 139
Palestine National Congress 139
Palmer, Arnold 60, 94
Panama 138
paperback books 102
Paris Peace Talks 209, 221, 261, 264
Paris strikes (1968) 221, 222
Park Chung Hee 131, 139
Parker, Bonnie 202
Parkland Hospital, Dallas 89
Partial Test Ban Treaty 83
Paterson, Thomas G. 29, 30
Pathet Lao 48, 60
Patterson, Floyd 62
Paul VI (pope) 142, 184, 222
Pay Any Price: Lyndon Johnson and the Wars for Vietnam (Lloyd C. Gardner) 150
Peace Corps 3, 23, *30*, 65, 178, 287–288
"peaceful coexistence" 13, 83–84
peace negotiations, Vietnam 209, 219, 257, 258. *See also* Paris Peace Talks
"peace with honor" 216
Penn, Arthur 202
The Pentagon Papers, As Published by the New York Times; *Based on Investigative Reporting by Neil Sheehan* (Neil Sheehan, ed.) 152
Peppermint Lounge 11
Percy, Charles 184
Peter, Paul, and Mary 156–157
Peterson, Pete 274
Pet Sounds (Beach Boys) 164

Pham Van Dong 125
Philadelphia 10, 140, 248
Philippines 143, 264
"Pigasus" (Yippie presidential candidate) 200, 228
"the pill." *See* contraceptive pill
Plaine Des Jarres, Laos 264
Playboy magazine xvii, 252
Pleiku, Vietnam 141
PLO (Palestine Liberation Organization) 139
Poitier, Sidney 201
police brutality 54, 55, 57, 241
"police riot" 214
"Political Mama," Ella Baker: Freedom Bound (Joanne Grant) 26
poll tax, elimination of 138
pollution, water 23
Pontiac Motors 250
Pope, Alan 45, 46
Poppy, John 272
popular culture xiii, 18–19, 76–78, 102–106, 155–159, 164–167, 188–194. *See also* counterculture; fashion; folk music; movies; rock and roll/popular music; television
"British Invasion" 128–129, 155–158
and election of 1960 2
movies 18, 166
reaction to events of late 1960s 201–205, 228–231
and social change 23, 44–45
"the twist" *10,* 10–11, 31, 63–64
population, global 60
The Populist Persuasion: An American History (Michael Kazin) 239
Port Huron Statement 60
Postal Service 142
poverty xvi, 85. *See also* "war on poverty"
powdered milk 130
Powell, Adam Clayton, Jr. 43, **332–333**
Powell, Wesley 21
power, political xv
power failure (1965) 143
Powers, Francis Gary 22, 57, 58
Powledge, Fred 107
POWs. *See* prisoners of war
presidential salary 261

President John F. Kennedy's Inaugural Address (January 20, 1961) 286–287
President John F. Kennedy's Report to the American People on the Soviet Arms Buildup in Cuba (October 22, 1962) 288–291
President Lyndon B. Johnson's Address to the Nation Announcing Steps to Limit the War in Vietnam and Reporting His Decision Not to Seek Reelection (March 31, 1968) 300–305
President Richard M. Nixon's Address to the Nation on the Vietnam War and Call to the Great Silent Majority (November 3, 1969) 306–312
President's Commission on the Status of Women 24, 88
Presley, Elvis 77, **333**
American values xv
in Beatles era 128, 158
hits in 1960 22
isolation of 105
movies 76
television special (1968) 224
press, the. *See* journalism
Preston, Alice 252
Price, Ray 226
The Price of Power: Kissinger in the Nixon White House (Seymour M. Hersh) 268
Prichett, Laurie G. 54
primary elections
California (1968) 213
Indiana (1968) 221
Nebraska (1968) 221, 238
New Hampshire (1968) 208, 210–212, 220, 235–236, 239
Oregon (1968) 213, 222
West Virginia (1960) 20–21
Wisconsin (1960) 21, 27
Wisconsin (1968) 210–213, 220
prisoners of war (POWs) 220, 222, 223, 257
Profiles in Courage (John F. Kennedy) 4
Program of the 55th Annual Chicago Auto Show (Chicago Auto Dealer Association) 103

Promises to Keep: The United States Since World War II (Paul Boyer) 26
protest music 167. *See also* Baez, Joan; Dylan, Bob
Proxmire, William 249
P.S. Jack Paar (Jack Paar) 25, 64
psychedelia. *See* acid rock; LSD
public opinion polls 4, 22, 214, 242. *See also* Gallup Poll
Public Papers of the Presidents of the United States: Lyndon B. Johnson, 1964 (U.S. government) 149
Public Papers of the Presidents of the United States: Lyndon B. Johnson, 1965 (U.S. government) 148, 155
public transportation 43
Pueblo, USS *219,* 219–220, 224
Puerto Rico 184
Pulitzer Prize
Eddie Adams photo 208
Profiles in Courage (John F. Kennedy) 4
Tet Offensive photo 208
Barbara Tuchman 94

Q
Quakers 143
Quant, Mary 104, 128–129, **333**
quarantine (blockade) 75, 76, 92
Quebec separatist movement 184
The Quiet American (film) 49
Quinhon, Vietnam 141

R
Rabi, I. I. 273
race riots
Advisory Commission on Civil Disorders 220
Bedford-Stuyvesant 140
Chicago 179
Democratic Party view 170
Detroit, Michigan 184, 240–241
Fisk University, Nashville 182
Harlem 140
Moynihan's view on 169
Newark, New Jersey 183
Orangeburg, South Carolina 220
Oxford, Mississippi 16
Watts (Los Angeles) 142, 195

racism xv
radiation sickness 73
radical extremists 141
radical protest 200, 215
Ranger 9 spacecraft 141
Rather, Dan 214
Ray, James Earl 213, 261
Reagan, Ronald 118, 145, 203, 236, 254
Reagon, Cordell 54
Rebel Without a Cause (film) 201
Rebozo, C. G. "Bebe" 247
recalls, automobile 261
recession (1960) 4
Red Army 41
Redgrave, Michael 49
Reeb, James J. 141
Reichley, James A. 268
Reid, Ogden 272
Reischauer, Edwin 40, 125
religion 5, 20, 73
reparations 262
Report on the President's Commission on Campus Unrest (U.S. government) 281
Republican Convention (1964) 118
Republican Convention (1968) 222
Republican Party
  election of 1964 119
  election of 1966 180
  fair housing backlash 170
  Barry Goldwater 118
  Lyndon Johnson's civil rights legislation 117
  Vietnam war, support for 161–162
  John Wayne and 203
Reserve Officers Training Corps (ROTC) 262
Resource Recovery Act 256
Reston, James 72, 146
Revolutionary Suicide (Huey P. Newton) 195
Reynolds, Miller 29–30
Ribicoff, Abraham 178
Richardson, Elliot 272
the Right (political) 114, 118, 254, 258
Rike, Aubrey 108
riots 214, 222, 226. *See also* campus unrest; race riots
robberies 178

Robert F. Kennedy's Announcement of Martin Luther King, Jr.'s Assassination (April 4, 1968) 305–306
Robert Kennedy: A Memoir (Jack Newfield) 98, 188
Roberts, Randy 28
rock and roll/popular music 24, 93, 228. *See also* The Beatles; Presley, Elvis
  Altamont music festival 264
  The Beach Boys 102–103, 164–166, *165*, 192, **316**
  counterculture and 245–247
  Jimi Hendrix 229, 246, 265, **323**
  Janis Joplin 229, 230, 245–246, 265, *265*, **325**
  Rolling Stones 181, 264
  Tiny Tim (Herbert Khaury) 204
  top-selling records (1960) 22
  top-selling records (1961) 24
  top-selling records (1962) 93
  top-selling records (1963) 95, 96
  top-selling records (1964) 141
  top-selling records (1965) 143
  top-selling records (1966) 181
  top-selling records (1967) 184
  top-selling records (1968) 224
  top-selling records (1969) 264
  top-selling records (1970) 265
  "the twist" *10*, 10–11, 31, 63–64
  Woodstock music festival 246, 263
Rockefeller, Nelson A. 216, 220, 221, 239, **333–334**
Rockwell, George Lincoln 184
Rogers, William 245
Rolling Stones 181, 264
Rollins, Betty 105, 157
Roman Catholicism
  birth control controversy 222, 223
  election of 1960 2, 20, 21
  Pope John XXIII 92, 94
  Kennedy family and xviii
  John Kennedy and 20, 43
  Pope Paul VI 142, 184, 222
Romney, George 220
Roosevelt, Eleanor 20, *20*, 22, 24

Roosevelt, Franklin D. xiii, *xiv*, xviii, 114, 118, 171, 216
Roper, Elmo 21
Roper, Hugh Trevor 126
Rosten, Leo 148, 281
Rostow, Walt
  on cold war allies 40
  Cuban Missile Crisis 61
  Nuclear Test Ban Treaty 82, 83
  on Sukarno 46
  Vietnam costs 124
  on Vietnam dissidents 225
  Vietnam fact-finding mission 49, 51
  Vietnam War military technology 133
ROTC (Reserve Officers Training Corps) 262
Rotter, Andrew J. 196
Route 66 (TV show) 200
Rowan, Dan 204
Rowan and Martin's Laugh-In. See Laugh-In
Rowe, James 197, 212
Rubin, Jerry 200
Ruby, Jack 89, 181
Rudolph, Wilma 24
Rules Committee. *See* House Rules Committee
Rush to Judgment (Mark Lane) 89
Rusk, Dean **334**
  Bay of Pigs 33
  Berlin crisis 34–35
  Cuba 57
  Cuban Missile Crisis 61, 98, 100, 101
  Dominican Republic 155
  foreign aid to Asian/Pacific region 51–52
  Fulbright hearings 173
  on function of Secretary of State 35
  on Indonesia 66–67
  Lyndon Johnson administration 116
  as John Kennedy's secretary of state 8
  Nixon's "secret plan to end the war" 240
  "war against poverty" 81
  on World War III 41
Russell, Bertrand 182
Russell, Richard 92

S
safety, automobile 250
salary, presidential 261
Salisbury, Harrison 202
San Francisco 184, 228
San Francisco State College 223
Sanger, Margaret 180
Sanjuan, Pedro 7, 36–37
Sgt. Pepper's Lonely Hearts Club Band (Beatles) 164, 183
Sartre, Jean-Paul 162
satellites 61
Sato, Eisaku 69, 131
Saturday Evening Post 156, 202, 261
Schickel, Richard 230, 278
Schirra, Walter 223
Schlatter, George 204
Schlesinger, Arthur 64, 125–126
Schlitz Beer 129–130
school prayer 60
Schwerner, Michael 139
"scorched earth" policy 175–176
SDS. *See* Students for a Democratic Society
Seale, Bobby 263
Secret Army Organization 57
"secret plan to end the Vietnam War" 216
Seeger, Pete 21
Segel, Thomas D. 32
segregation. *See* civil rights
Segrest, Marvin 177
Seldes, Gilbert 102
"self-determination" 180
self-immolation 94, 143
The Selling of the President, 1968 (Joe McGinnis) 235
Selma-to-Montgomery march 142
Senate, U.S.
  Bobby Baker scandal 182
  Cuban aggression resolution 62
  election of 1966 180
  ERA 182
  Lyndon Johnson's civil rights legislation 116–117
  John Kennedy's years in xviii–xix, 261
  Robert Kennedy in 135–137
separatist movement, Quebec 184
Serling, Rod xv

Sevareid, Eric 247, 274
Seventeen magazine 279
sexuality, female xvii
"sexual revolution" 128
Shadegg, Stephen 147
Shaffer, Robert 188
Shaw, Clay 261
Sheehan, Neil 152
Shell, Joe 79
Shelton, William 32
Shepard, Alan 23, 27
Shepard, Jack 281
Sherrod, Charles 54
Shinoda, Larry 253
Shires, Tom 108
Shockley, Henry A. 68
Shriver, R. Sargent 29
"shuttle diplomacy" 243
Sideman, Andrew 279
Sidey, Hugh 268, 269
Sihanouk, Prince. *See* Norodom
    Sihanouk
"silent majority" 243, 312
Sims, Donald 178
Sirhan, Sirhan B. 213, 222,
    261
Six Crises (Richard Nixon) 79
Six-Day War 183
60 Minutes 222
Slick, Grace 191
Smith, Al 2
Smith, Howard K. 119
smog 250
*The Smothers Brothers Comedy
    Hour* 182, *182,* 202
sniper attacks 180
social programs 255
"soft on communism" 72, 83
"soft on crime" 170
A Soldier Reports (William
    Westmoreland) 152
Solomon, Anthony 18
Sommerville, Brian 155
Sorensen, Theodore 64, 101,
    111, 138
Southeast Asia. *See* Cambodia;
    Laos; Thailand; Vietnam
"Southern Strategy" 247
Southern United States. *See also*
    Alabama; Georgia; Mississippi
    Barry Goldwater and 118
    integration orders 177
    George Wallace 16–18,
    118–119
    "war against poverty" 81

Souphanouvong Phouma (Lao
    prince) 48
Souvanna Phouma (Lao prince)
    47–48, 60
Soviet Union. *See also* cold
    war
    America's distrust of xvi
    Cuba 12, 57, 60–61, 71–72
    Cuban Missile Crisis 92
    Kissinger and 243
    John Kennedy's "no first strike"
        policy 57
    military sales in Middle East
        177
    Moscow civil rights protests
        96
    as nuclear target 39
    Nuclear Test Ban Treaty 57,
        82, 83
    Olympics (Austria Winter
        Games, 1964) 138
    Olympics (Rome Summer
        Games, 1960) 22
    Olympics (Tokyo Summer
        Games, 1964) 141
    Lee Harvey Oswald 89
    Vietnam policy 134
space, military exploitation treaty
    182
space program. *See also specific
    astronauts, e.g.:* Shepard, Alan
    Apollo, Project 182, 223, 224,
        261, 262, 264
    Apollo 1 fire 182
    Friendship 7 57, *58*
    Gemini 141, 142, 178
    Lyndon Johnson 138
    John Kennedy 23, 43
    Mariner 61
    Mercury 23
    Nixon 255
    Ranger 9 141
    Surveyor 182, 219
"space race" 138
space walk 142, 178
special interests 81
Special Protocol Service 7
Speck, Richard 182
sphere of influence 51
Spock, Benjamin 219, 222
SST (Super Sonic Transport)
    256
Stafford, Thomas 178, *179*
"stagflation" 255
Starr, Ringo 158

"Star Spangled Banner" (Jimi
    Hendrix version) 246
Star Trek 169
State of the Union Address
    (1965) 141
State University of New York
    (SUNY) 216
Statue of Liberty 141
steel industry crisis 60
Steinem, Gloria **334**
Stern, Jane 104
Stevens, Brooks 188–189, *189,
    251,* 251–252, **334–335**
Stevens, David and William
    252
Stevens, Robert Warren 188
Stevenson, Adlai xix–xx, 2, 20,
    20, 22, 75, 101
Stewart, James 76
Stockholm, Sweden 182
Stone, Oliver 89
Stonewall protests 262
Strategic Hamlet program 59,
    94
strikes
    airline pilots 262
    public schools 220
*Striking a Balance: Environment
    and Natural Resources Policy in
    the Nixon-Ford Years* (John C.
    Whitaker) 276, 277
Studebaker 252
Students for a Democratic
    Society (SDS)
    antiwar movement 162–163,
        200, 201
    and change 225
    Chicago convention 262
    The Green Berets, reaction to
        204
    Port Huron Statement 60
    Weather Underground 264
student unrest. *See* campus unrest
Subic Bay naval base, Philippines
    264
suburbs xv, xvii, 170, 256
suicide squads 261
Sukarno, Achmed 45–46, 66–67
Sullivan, Ed. *See The Ed Sullivan
    Show*
"summer of peace and love" 174
Summer Olympics (Rome,
    1960) 22
Summer Olympics (Tokyo, 1964)
    141

Super Sonic Transport (SST)
    256
Supreme Court, U.S.
    Engel v. Vitale 60
    interracial marriage 183
    mail interception ruling
        142
    Thurgood Marshall 184
    military reservists case 222
    Miranda v. Arizona 179
    Vietnam War case 265
    Warren retirement 262
Surveyor 3 spacecraft 182
Surveyor 7 spacecraft 219
Sutcliffe, Stuart 59–60
Suu, Phan Khac 131
Swigert, John 264
Symington, Stuart 1, 20, 21
Szulc, Tad 268

T
Taiwan 138
Tanaka, Hideo 254
Tate, Sharon 264
tax cuts 81, 114, 116, 254
Taylor, Elizabeth 11
Taylor, Maxwell 49, 51, 58, 61,
    130, 150, 188
TEA. *See* Trade Expansion Act
technology, Vietnam War and
    133
television
    American Bandstand 10
    Batman 193
    children 30–31
    debates 4, 21, 22
    Democratic National
        Convention (1968) 214
    The Dick Clark Show 10
    The Ed Sullivan Show 128, 138,
        181
    election of 1960 4
    Fulbright hearings 172–173
    I Love Lucy 173
    I Spy 142, 157–159, 167–169,
        168
    Lyndon Johnson news
        conference 138
    journalism 230
    Kennedy-Nixon debates 4, 22,
        28
    John Kennedy and xvii
    John Kennedy's news
        conferences 8
    Laugh-In 204, 219, 228, 230

television (continued)
The Man from U.N.C.L.E.
 140, 167, 169, 204
Meet the Press 20
Nixon's California
 gubernatorial bid 79
and politics 31
Elvis Presley special (1968)
 224
Route 66 200
sales of TV sets 18–19
60 Minutes 222
Smothers Brothers Comedy Hour
 182
*The Smothers Brothers Comedy
 Hour* 202
Star Trek 180
Tet Offensive 208, 209
Vietnam War 125–128, 209
Telstar satellite 61
Tennessee 183
terrorism 57, 223, 261
Terry, Wallace 196
Tet Offensive 205–208, 210,
 219–220, 231–235
Texas 113–114
Texas Democratic Party 89
Texas Tower sniper attacks
 180
Thailand 182, 264
Thieu, Nguyen Van 177
third parties 215–216
Thor nuclear missile test 60
Thresher, USS 94, *94*
Ticonderoga, USS 122, *123*
Time magazine 27, 193, 194,
 228–230, 264, 275, 278
A Time to Speak (Charles
 Morgan) 106
Tinen, James 276
Tiny Tim (Herbert Khaury)
 204, 229, **335**
Tokyo, Japan 60, 221, 262
Tonkin Gulf Resolution
 120–123, 124, 140, 265
tornadoes 142
To Seek a Newer World (Robert F.
 Kennedy) 197
Toynbee, Albert 272
Tracy, Philip 279
Tracy, Spencer 201
trade, international 254
Trade Expansion Act (TEA) 22,
 42, 254
trade surplus 261

The Tragedy of Lyndon Johnson
 (Eric F. Goldman) 67
transportation bill 43–44
Treasury Department, U.S. 261
Treaty Banning Nuclear Weapon
 Tests in the Atmosphere, In
 Outer Space, and Under
 Water (Partial Test Ban Treaty
 or Nuclear Test Ban Treaty)
 83, 292–293
Trigere, Pauline 192
Trindad and Tobago 61
Trudeau, Pierre 220
Truman, Harry S. 2, 20, 39
trust, in political leadership xvi
Tuchman, Barbara 8, 94, 136
Turkey 59, 60
Turner, W. W. 29
Tuskegee High School,
 integration of 95
TV Guide: The First 25 Years (Jay
 S. Harris, ed.) 30–31
Twenty-third Amendment to the
 U.S. Constitution (ratified
 1961) 288
Twenty-fourth Amendment to
 the U.S. Constitution (ratified
 1964) 138, 295
Twenty-fifth Amendment to the
 U.S. Constitution (ratified
 1967) 299–300
Twenty-sixth Amendment to the
 U.S. Constitution (ratified
 1971) 258
Twiggy 129
Twiggy contest *129*
*The Twilight Struggle: Tales of the
 Cold War* (William Attwood)
 33, 65
The Twilight Zone xv
twist, the (dance) *10,* 10–11, 31,
 63–64
2001: A Space Odyssey 202, 220

U

"ugly American" 38, 51
The Ugly American (William
 Lederer and Eugene Burdick)
 2–3
unemployment rate (1968)
 220
*The Unfinished Journey: America
 Since World War II* (William H.
 Chafe) 26
unilateralism, U.S. 131

Union Theological Seminary
 262
United Auto Workers 252
United Farm Workers 265
"united front" 134
United Mine Workers 21
United Nations
 aid to Asian/Pacific region 51
 Cuban Missile Crisis 75, 76
 Goldwater's opposition to 118
 import policies 254
 North Vietnamese stance on
  captured pilots 180
 Pope Paul VI 142
 West Irian 61
United Nations Disarmament
 Commission 82
United Nations Review 26
United States and Cuba, 1961–
 1962 340m
*United States–Vietnam Relations,
 1945–1967* (Department of
 Defense) 67, 68
University of Alabama 17, 94
University of California–
 Berkeley 223
University of Mississippi 16, 37,
 62, 64, 142, 194–195
University of Wisconsin–
 Madison 261
University of Wisconsin–
 Oshkosh 223
Unsafe at Any Speed (Ralph
 Nader) 252
*U.S. Foreign Policy for the 1970s: A
 New Strategy for Peace*
 (Richard M. Nixon) 235
U.S. News and World Report 36
U.S. Open 60
U.S. Steel 60
U-2 reconnaissance photos 61,
 92
U-2 spy plane incident 4, 22, 57

V

*Vain Hopes, Grim Realities: The
 Economic Consequences of the
 Vietnam War* (Robert Warren
 Stevens) 188
Valenti, Jack 185
*The Vantage Point: Perspectives of
 the Presidency* (Lyndon Baines
 Johnson) 112
Vatican II 92, 180
V-8 engine 250

Vidal, Gore xv, 136
Vienna meeting (John
 Kennedy/Khrushchev) 14
Vietcong
 direct combat with 142
 establishment of NLF 22
 Laos 264
 POWs 223
 suicide squads 261
 Tet Offensive 205, 206
 U.S. consumer goods 130
 U.S. helicopters downed 93
Vietnam: An American Ordeal
 (George Donelson Moss)
 281
Vietnamization 244, 247,
 257–258, 265
Vietnam Veterans Against the War
 (VVAW) 200
Vietnam War *127, 140, 207,
 221, 227, 231, 245, 267,
 341m*
 Creighton Abrams assumes
  U.S. command 209, 220
 African-American soldiers
  120, 163, 196
 Agnew's rhetoric 243
 aircraft losses 222
 American business and
  129–130
 American youth culture
  245–247
 antiwar movement. *See* antiwar
  movement; campus unrest
 arrival of U.S. combat troops
  141
 arrival of U.S. helicopter
  companies 24
 George Ball's view on
  escalation 51
 Bien Hoa 141
 bombing raids on North 134,
  135, 141, 177, 179, 181,
  221, 262
 Cambodia 224, 257–259
 Camp Holloway attack 124
 captured U.S. pilots as war
  criminals 180
 casualties 172, 174, 181, 207,
  208, 262
 Chevrolet Corvette as
  metaphor for 199–200
 Christmas Truce 143, 224
 congressional support, loss of
  160–161

constitutionality of 265
Conthien siege 184
coup attempt 57
"credibility gap" 173
James Davis 24
"decisive battle" 205
George Decker 22
Dienbienphu 205
domestic debate 160–163,
    171–176, 185–188
Dominican Republic
    intervention and 163–164
economic effects 249–250
election of 1964 and 118
election of 1968 and 176
"Emergency Fund" 178
erosion of trust in U.S. political
    leadership xvi
escalation 133–135, 148–153
Jane Fonda's trip to North
    Vietnam 202
"friendly fire" 181
Fulbright hearings 171–173
The Green Berets (film) 203,
    204, 229–230
Haiphong bombing 143
Hanoi bombing 179
Averell Harriman testimony
    57
Honolulu summit 173, 178
Humphrey candidacy (1968)
    213
Humphrey visit 178
International Tribunal on War
    Crimes 182
"Iron Triangle" offensive 181
Lyndon Johnson and 23,
    120–135
Khanh's coup 138
Kissinger plans 243
John Kennedy's commitment
    to xvi
John Kennedy's policies
    49–51, 67–69
John Kennedy's visit to xix
Robert Kennedy's stance as
    Senator 136
Ky's assumption of power
    130–131, 142
Laos as potential arsenal for
    Vietcong 48
Laotian cease-fire 23
Curtis Lemay's stance 215
lull in war (1965) 130
lull in war (1967) 205

MACV 57, 59
march by war supporters 183
George Meany and 250
military advisers 23
Gaylord Nelson's opposition to
    78
Ngo Quang Duc 94
Nixon's address to nation
    306–312
Nixon's continuation of
    Johnson policies 243
Nixon's "secret plan" 216
NLF 22
Operation ROLLING
    THUNDER 124, 130
organized labor support 250
Paris Peace Talks 209, 221,
    261, 264
peace negotiations 125, 130,
    209, 219, 257, 258, 266
Pleiku and Quinhon attacks
    141
POW release 223
POWs 220
The Quiet American (film) 49
Republican support for
    161–162
Nelson Rockefeller's plan 216
rocket explosion at command
    post 222
Saigon attack 261
Saigon defense 261–262
Harrison Salisbury report on
    North Vietnam 202
The Smothers Brothers Comedy
    Hour 202
Strategic Hamlet program 59,
    94
television's impact 125–128
Tet Offensive 205–208,
    219–220, 231–235
Thailand 264
Tonkin Gulf Resolution
    120–123, 140, 293–294
U.S. air bases in Thailand 182
U.S. helicopters downed 93
U.S. troop strength (1963) 96
U.S. troop strength (1969) 257
veterans 196
Vietcong. See Vietcong
Vietnamization 243, 244, 247,
    257–258, 265
John Wayne and 203
William Westmoreland. See
    Westmoreland, William

withdrawal, effect of 257
withdrawal as political suicide
    for Lyndon Johnson 134
withdrawal under Nixon 243,
    244
Vogue magazine 104
Voight, Jon 262
volunteerism (youth services) 3
voter fraud in election of 1960 5
voter registration drives 62, 178
voting age 210, 259
voting rights 148
    Civil Rights Act of 1964
        293–294
    Democratic National
        Convention (1964) 119
    Robert Kennedy's strategy
        69–70
    Selma-to-Montgomery march
        142
    Twenty-fourth Amendment
        138, 295
    The Voting Rights Act of 1965
        (August 6, 1965) 142,
        169–171, 194, 295–297
VVAW (Vietnam Veterans
    Against the War) 200

W
wage and price controls 254
wages, women's vs. men's xvi
The Walker Report 226
Wallace, George **335**
    Birmingham protests 106
    election of 1964 118–119
    election of 1968 174, 197,
        215–216, 223, 236, 239
    on Lyndon Johnson's civil
        rights achievements 148
    law and order 170, 239
    Middle America's reaction to
        215
    political influence during
        Kennedy years 16–18
    Selma-to-Montgomery march
        142
    Tuskegee High School 95
    University of Alabama 94
Wallace, Mike 201
The Wall Street Journal 209, 223
Warhol, Andy **335–336**
"war on poverty" 80–81, 87,
    116, 138, 144–145, 184
Warren, Earl 89, 224, 262, **336**
Warren Commission 89, 90, 140

Washington, D.C. 184, 288
Washington Monument 141
The Washington Post 72, 243
Watch Out for George Wallace
    (Wayne Greenhaw) 148
Watergate break-in 260
Water Quality Improvement Act
    256
Watson, Albert 141
Watts riots 142, 195
Wayne, John 76, 203, 204,
    229–230
wealth, disparity of 87–88
Weather Underground 264
Weaver, Robert 177
Weisman, Bernard 108
Welch, Carrie 108
Welch, David 99
West Irian 46, 61
Westmoreland, William 151,
    206
    congressional address 174
    consumer goods in Vietnam
        130
    direct combat with Vietcong
        142
    escalation 133
    Honolulu summit 173
    North Vietnam bombing
        missions 135
    post-Tet escalation of troops
        209
    private doubts on progress of
        war 175–176
    removal from Vietnam
        command 209, 220
    Tet Offensive 205–207, 209,
        231
    on Vietnam withdrawl/victory
        151–152
West Virginia primary election
    (1960) 20, 21
What Happened to Goldwater? The
    Inside Story of the 1964
    Republican Campaign (Stephen
    Shadegg) 147
Where the Domino Fell: America
    and Vietnam, 1945–1995
    (James Olson and Randy
    Roberts) 28
Whitaker, John C. 276, 277
White, Edward 135, 142, 182
White, Mark J. 34
White, Theodore xv
White, Thomas Bennett 178

"white flight" xv, xvii, 170
White House 8, 22, 95
white power 16
"White Supremacy" 177
Whitman, Charles 180
Whitworth, William 155
Williams, John Bell 141
Wilson, Brian 164, 165, *165*
Wilson, Carl 164, *165*
Wilson, Dennis 164, *165*
Wilson, Mary 189
Wilson, Murry 164
Winter Olympics (1964) 138
wiretaps 261
Wisconsin primary election 21, 27, 210–213, 220
Wise, Robert 59
Witness to America (Stephen Ambrose and Douglas Brinkley, eds.) 31
Witness to Power (John Ehrlichmann) 276

Wofford, Fonsell *203*
Wofford, Harris 36, 37, 65, 70
Wolfe, Tom 155
Woman Athlete of the Year (Wilma Rudolph) 24
Women's Liberation Party 222
"Women Strike for Peace" 88, *103*
women/women's rights
  antiwar movement (1968) 201
  Chicago convention 224
  employment xvi
  Equal Pay Act of 1963 94, 291–292
  The Feminine Mystique (Betty Friedan) 94
  Betty Friedan 88, 94
  Gallup Poll xvii
  Miss America Pageant protest 222
  President's Commission on the Status of Women 24, 88

Margaret Sanger 180
wages xvi
Women's Liberation Party 222
"Women's Strike for Peace" 88
workforce 264
Wood, Robert 277
Woodstock music festival 246, 263
workplace rights 171
World Bank 184
World Boxing Association 182
The World in 1965: History As We Lived It (The Associated Press) 158
World War II xviii
World War III, threat of
  Cuban Missile Crisis 75, 92
  Gallup Poll 71
  Barry Goldwater and 118
  Gulf of Tonkin incident 122
  Vietnam 120, 131, 134
Wright, Jim 104

Wright, Mickey 138
Wyoming 22

Y
Yarmouth Castle disaster 143
Ydigoras Fuente, Miguel 58
Yippies 200, 228, 230, 263
Yothers, Jean 32
Young, Andrew Jackson 70, 182, 183, **336**
Young, John W. 141
Younge, Samuel, Jr. 177
Youth International Party. *See* Yippies
youth volunteerism 3
Yugoslavia 59

Z
Zablocki, Clement 160–161
Zeidler, Frank P. 199, 200
Zeitlin, David 193
Zorin, V. I. 75